THE IDEA OF AMERICA

THE IDEA OF AMERICA

Reflections on the Birth of the United States

GORDON S. WOOD

THE PENGUIN PRESS | New York | 2011

THE PENGUIN PRESS
Published by the Penguin Group
Penguin Group (USA) Inc., 375 Hudson Street, New York, New York 10014, U.S.A. • Penguin
Group (Canada), 90 Eglinton Avenue East, Suite 700, Toronto, Ontario, Canada M4P 2Y3 (a division of
Pearson Penguin Canada Inc.) • Penguin Books Ltd, 80 Strand, London WC2R 0RL, England •
Penguin Ireland, 25 St. Stephen's Green, Dublin 2, Ireland (a division of Penguin Books Ltd) • Penguin
Books Australia Ltd, 250 Camberwell Road, Camberwell, Victoria 3124, Australia (a division of Pearson
Australia Group Pty Ltd) • Penguin Books India Pvt Ltd, 11 Community Centre, Panchsheel Park,
New Delhi – 110 017, India • Penguin Group (NZ), 67 Apollo Drive, Rosedale, Auckland 0632,
New Zealand (a division of Pearson New Zealand Ltd) • Penguin Books (South Africa) (Pty) Ltd,
24 Sturdee Avenue, Rosebank, Johannesburg 2196, South Africa

Penguin Books Ltd, Registered Offices: 80 Strand, London WC2R 0RL, England

First published in 2011 by The Penguin Press, a member of Penguin Group (USA) Inc.

Page 387 constitutes an extension of this copyright page.

LIBRARY OF CONGRESS CATALOGING-IN-PUBLICATION DATA
Wood, Gordon S.
The idea of America : reflections on the birth of the United States / Gordon S. Wood.
p. cm.
Includes bibliographical references and index.
ISBN 978-1-59420-290-2
1. United States—History—Revolution, 1775–1783—Influence. 2. United States—Politics and government—
1775–1783. 3. United States—Politics and government—1783–1809. 4. United States. Constitution.
5. Democracy—United States. 6. Republicanism—United States. I. Title.
E302.1.W77 2011
973.3—dc22   2010045829

Printed in the United States of America
1   3   5   7   9   10   8   6   4   2

Designed by Marysarah Quinn

*To my friends and colleagues
at Brown University*

CONTENTS

THE IDEA OF AMERICA

INTRODUCTION

WELL OVER A HALF CENTURY ago Isaiah Berlin published a little book entitled *The Hedgehog and the Fox: An Essay on Tolstoy's View of History*. He borrowed his title from a line among the fragments of the Greek poet Archilochus which says, "The fox knows many things, but the hedgehog knows one big thing." Berlin interpreted the words broadly and found in them one of the deepest differences that divide writers and thinkers and perhaps even human beings in general. On one side of this chasm, wrote Berlin, were the foxes, "who pursue many ends, often unrelated and even contradictory, connected, if at all, only in some de facto way, for psychological or physiological cause, related by no moral or aesthetic principle." On the other side were the hedgehogs, "who relate everything to a single central vision, one system less or more coherent or articulate, in terms of which they understand, think and feel—a single, universal, organizing principle in terms of which alone all that they are and say has significance."

So in this scheme of things Berlin labels Dante as a hedgehog and Shakespeare as a fox. "Plato, Lucretius, Pascal, Hegel, Dostoevsky, Nietzsche, Ibsen, Proust are, in varying degrees, hedgehogs; Herodotus, Aristotle, Montaigne, Erasmus, Molière, Goethe, Pushkin, Balzac, Joyce are foxes."[1]

Although Berlin was interested mainly in placing great writers into one or another of these two categories, one might do the same with more mundane historians. There are historians who work on many different subjects, jumping from topic to topic as their various interests lead them. I have a remarkable colleague who began with a study of Congress in the 1930s, and followed that by an analysis of the impact of the New Deal on the states. Then, after he had written an impressive biography of an important politician of the 1940s and early 1950s, he wrote an extraordinary book on America's struggle with poverty in the twentieth century. This work was followed by a fascinating history of cancer in modern American culture, which in turn was succeeded by an examination of an important Supreme Court decision of the 1950s. At the same time, this colleague was writing a huge narrative account of twentieth-century America and a prize-winning book on the decades in America following World War II. Even now he is on to brand-new subjects in modern America.

This colleague of mine is a fox and a superb one. He knows many things and is interested in many things. He even once said to me as he was casting about for a new subject to write about that if I had any ideas for him to please let him know.

By contrast, as a historian I fear I am a simple hedgehog. Throughout my career I have been most interested in the American Revolution and the political, social, and cultural changes that it engendered. Of course, I have taught university lecture courses that ranged from Columbus to the Jacksonian era and have led seminars on various topics. But nearly all of my publications have dealt with the American Revolution and its consequences. In addition to several books on the Revolution and its leaders, I have published a number of articles on the Revolutionary era, some of which are collected in this book.

My preoccupation with the Revolution comes from my belief that it is the most important event in American history, bar none. Not only did the Revolution legally create the United States, but it infused into our culture all of our highest aspirations and noblest values. Our beliefs in liberty, equality, constitutionalism, and the well-being of ordinary people came out of the Revolutionary era. So too did our idea that we Americans are a special people with a special destiny to lead the world toward liberty and democracy. The Revolution, in short, gave birth to whatever sense of nationhood and national purpose we Americans have had.

Establishing their nationhood was not easy for the Revolutionaries, as my essay on "The American Enlightenment" in this volume attempts to show. Americans knew that they were not yet a nation, at least not a nation in the European sense of the term. Since the identity of the United States as a nation remains unusually fluid and elusive, we Americans have had to look back repeatedly to the Revolution and the Founding (as we call it) in order to know who we are. We go back to the Revolution and the values and institutions that came out of it in order to refresh and reaffirm our nationhood. That for me is why the Revolutionary era remains so significant.

ALTHOUGH I HAVE BEEN WORKING on the Revolutionary era for my entire career, I don't now conceive of it in the same way as I did a half century ago. Like most other graduate students in the country in the early 1960s, I was trained to think of early American history as the period from the initial settlements in the seventeenth century to the establishment of the Constitution in 1787–1788. Specializing in the several decades following 1789 meant that one was not a colonial-Revolutionary historian but an early national historian. One specialized either in the colonial-Revolutionary period or in the early decades of the national period, but not in both. If colonial-Revolutionary historians did happen to spill over into the 1790s, they tended to see those years as the culmination of what had gone on before—the eighteenth century and the Revolution.

Early national historians who began their teaching and research on the 1790s not only rarely looked back to the colonial or Revolutionary periods but generally tended to look ahead to the Civil War or to the urbanization and industrialization that essentially occurred after the 1820s. So they often treated the period between 1789 and the 1820s as a prelude to what was really important to them in the nineteenth century. Consequently, graduate students in the 1960s who wished to study the early decades of the nation's history were apt to fall between two specializations of the historical profession. Colonial-Revolutionary historians knew the period only as an epilogue; early national historians knew it only as a prologue. Neither group saw it in its own right.

Thus I began my teaching in the 1960s thinking of myself as exclusively a colonial-Revolutionary historian. I taught a two-semester course, with one semester dealing with the colonial period up to 1760 and a second dealing with the Revolutionary period from 1760 to 1788. But since my university had no history course covering the period from 1789 to the age of Jackson, I began to feel obliged to offer such a course. The experience in the 1970s of organizing a course on this period was eye-opening and ultimately very rewarding.

When I first began exploring the period, I was surprised by the nature of the historical scholarship on these decades following the creation of the Constitution. It didn't seem to treat the period as seriously as I had expected; indeed, as historian James H. Broussard, who founded the Society for the History of the Early American Republic (SHEAR) in the late 1970s and almost single-handedly revived interest in the period, once pointed out, it was "often treated almost as a backwater of historical scholarship."[2] There were, of course, many good books and articles, especially biographies of the great men and the not-so-great men of the Revolutionary era. Mammoth editing projects promising to publish virtually everything written to and by each of the major Founders had been launched and were well along. Some works of scholarship—for example, a study of racial attitudes of early white Americans and an analysis of the Massachusetts Federalists—were truly outstanding, but they remained isolated and unconnected to any overall interpretation of the period.[3] Despite publications like these, the early decades of America's history seemed to lack what Broussard called an "organizing theme." All kinds of labels and books flew about, but, as Broussard lamented, the problem was "how to group them together in a meaningful whole."[4]

In the early 1960s the origins of political parties had attracted some scholarly interest, but they did little to invigorate the period. Political scientists and political sociologists like William Nisbet Chambers and Seymour Martin Lipset were not really interested in the history of the 1790s per se but instead in the conditions out of which political structures and political parties were created. They wanted to form generalizations about politics that were applicable to their present. Thus the United States became the "first new nation" and the conflict between the Federalists and the Jeffersonian Republicans became the "first party system"—object lessons for the newly developing and ex-colonial nations of the 1950s and 1960s.[5] Consequently, these political scientists were not always sensitive to the differentness of the past, and in their works they often left readers with a very unhistorical and anachronistic view of America's political parties in the 1790s.

All in all, the lack of any comprehensive synthesis of the period seemed to have given the decades of early national history a reputation for dreariness and insignificance. It seemed to be the most boring part of American history to study and teach.[6]

This was baffling to me. After all, the decades between 1789 and the 1820s seemed to have an immediate and palpable importance for all Americans. Not only was the period dominated by some of the greatest and most heroic figures in American history (Washington, Hamilton, Adams, Madison, Jefferson, and Marshall), but during these decades Americans established their political institutions—the presidency, the Congress, the Supreme Court—and created both political parties and modern democratic politics. Indeed, so much of political significance occurred in this period of the early Republic that the historians' neglect of it was puzzling.

After much pondering, I concluded that historians themselves had created the problem. The so-called consensus interpretation of American history that dominated what has been called the "golden age" of historical writing in the 1950s and early 1960s was responsible for the diminished respect accorded the period of the early Republic.[7] In fact, those historians who had written in the aftermath of World War II had effectively destroyed the dominant synthesis of the period created in the first half of the twentieth century and had not put anything else in its place.

During the first half of the twentieth century the Progressive generation of historians—those professional historians whose assumptions about reality came out of the Progressive era at the beginning of the twentieth century—not only had an overarching scheme for understanding the early Republic, but also had a special fascination for this period. Although the Progressive historians offered a framework for understanding all of American history, it was the period of the early Republic— from the Revolution to the age of Jackson—that particularly interested them. All the giants among them—Carl Becker, Charles Beard, Arthur Schlesinger Sr., Vernon Parrington—tackled problems in this period and felt most at home in this period. Even Frederick Jackson Turner thought his "frontier thesis" had a special applicability to the half century following the Revolution. The early Republic seemed to be the natural arena for demonstrating the truth of the Progressive historians' interpretation of American history.[8]

These historians tended to see American history as full of conflicts, especially conflicts between a populist majority, usually agrarian, and a narrow aristocratic or business minority. According to these historians, the Revolution and the early Republic were essentially characterized by the seesawing struggle between these two groups. The aristocratic and merchant interests of the 1760s lost control of the resistance movement to more popular and radical elements who moved America into revolution. By the 1780s, however, the conservative and mercantile interests had reasserted themselves to the point where they were able to write the new federal Constitution of 1787. Charles Beard's provocative book *An Economic Interpretation of the Constitution* (1913) became the linchpin of this Progressive interpretation. These historians saw the 1790s as a continuation of the struggle between the commercial interests led by Alexander Hamilton and the popular agrarian and artisanal forces led by Thomas Jefferson.

With Jefferson's election in 1800, the popular agrarian majorities finally came into their own. The next two or three decades saw the relentless emergence of the "common man" in American history. The last remnants of the colonial ancien régime were cast aside or destroyed. The churches were disestablished, the suffrage gates were opened, and the clamoring populace rushed to the polls and overthrew the commercial aristocracy, at least outside the South. The entire struggle climaxed with the election of Andrew Jackson, marking the completion of the unfinished business of the Revolution.

It was a powerful interpretative framework. It accommodated a wide variety of facts, and it was simple enough to be applied by hosts of student disciples. No wonder that some of the best and most durable monographs on the period, particularly the histories of states, have been written by followers of the Progressive historians. All had similar titles and themes, and all described political developments in terms of "from aristocracy to democracy."[9]

This Progressive paradigm dominated historical writing about America's past during the first half of the twentieth century. But in the years following World War II, this interpretative framework was assaulted from a hundred different directions and dismantled by a thousand different monographs. Book after book, article after article in the 1950s and 1960s ate away at every aspect of the Progressive explanation of America's past. In this rich and flourishing period of American history writing, often labeled the era of "consensus" history, the Progressive interpretation that had featured social conflicts in America's past was replaced by one that emphasized the similarity and like-mindedness of all Americans. This destruction of the Progressive interpretation affected all aspects and all eras of American history, but it affected the period of the early Republic the most.

The 1950s and 1960s assault on the Progressive understanding of the early Republic took the form of denying the extent of change that had taken place in the period. Colonial America, it appeared from a number of consensus studies, was not an ancien régime after all. Since roughly 60 percent of adult white males in the colonial period could legally vote, the high suffrage barriers that the Progressive historians had posited turned out to be not so high after all. The churches in the eighteenth century were already weak and did not much need disestablishment. The aristocracy that existed was hardly an aristocracy by European standards and scarcely required elimination. All in all, colonial Americans did not have much to revolt against; their revolution seemed to be essentially a mental shift, an intellectual adjustment to what had already taken place over the previous century or more. The Americans were born free and equal and thus, as Tocqueville had written, did not have to become so. The American Revolution therefore became a peculiarly conservative affair, an endorsement and realization, not a transformation, of the society.[10]

As early American historians were reinterpreting the colonial period, other historians were reevaluating the Jacksonian era. Not only did it now appear that the Jacksonians had less unfinished business to deal with than historians used to think, but Jacksonian society seemed less egalitarian and less democratic than earlier historians had believed. The distribution of wealth in the 1820s and 1830s was more unequal than it had been earlier in the century; indeed, some studies showed that the distribution of wealth after the Revolution was more unequal than in the colonial period. Some historians even suggested that the age of Jackson ought to be called "the era of the uncommon man."[11]

Thus it seemed that no democratic Jacksonian revolution had occurred after all. It was hard to see much difference between the Democratic and Whig parties. As historians Richard Hofstadter and Bray Hammond emphasized, both parties were composed of men on the make; certainly they did not stand for coherent social classes in conflict.[12] Nearly everyone in the North, at least, seemed to belong to the middle class. America was liberal and individualistic to its toes, and, according to Louis Hartz, whose 1955 book *The Liberal Tradition in America* epitomized the so-called consensus interpretation of the post–World War II decades, it had been so from the very beginning of its history.[13]

These attacks on the Progressive paradigm affected all periods of America's past, but they especially ravaged the period between the

Revolution and the age of Jackson, for the Progressive interpretation really had its heart and soul in these decades of the early Republic. If the Progressive interpretation was true anywhere, the Progressive historians believed, it was true there in the early Republic. This, after all, was the time when the conservative European-like aristocratic forces were supposed to have been finally shattered, when American democracy was first established, and when modern American liberalism was born.

But if this were not truly the case, if Revolutionary Americans were in fact already free and equal and did not have to experience a democratic revolution, then what significance could this period of the early Republic have? According to the findings of the consensus historians of the 1950s and 1960s, the period was not formative after all. The Progressive historians had been wrong about it; and with the collapse of their interpretative framework, the period of the early Republic on which they had rested so much of their case sank into insignificance.

By the time I began putting my course on the early Republic together in the 1970s, there were some tentative efforts to reinvigorate the period and to see it whole. Some historians tried to apply the social science concept of "modernization" to the period. But, as often happens, historians began using the concept just as it was going out of fashion among social scientists. Thus the effort died aborning, and much of the scholarship of the period remained diffuse and unconnected, without compelling significance.[14]

One of the problems faced in the 1970s by historians who were trying to deal with the period of the early Republic was the overriding dominance of politics and the presence of so many heroic political figures, such as Washington, Hamilton, and Jefferson. By writing so many biographies of these great men and thus describing the early Republic mainly in terms of the actions of great individual political leaders, historians tended to fragment our understanding of the period. Moreover, political events and political institutions in general tended to overwhelm the period and prevent historians who wished to write about other things from having much breathing room. With the establishment of America's political institutions, a major rebellion, crises of various sorts, crucial elections, the beginnings of judicial review, the use of economic sanctions as an alternative to war, and a war itself, the period is full of what might be called headline events. Indeed, there is probably no period of American history that has more of these headline events concerning politics and diplomacy than the early Republic.[15]

Unfortunately, the new generation of historians coming of age in the late 1960s and early 1970s did not want to write about great headline political events. The social and cultural history they were interested in tended to deal with impersonal long-term developments. Such new history might involve changing demographic patterns over several generations or shifting attitudes toward childhood or death. The early Republic was probably the period of American history least receptive to treatment by these new social and cultural historians. Its extraordinary number of major political and diplomatic happenings tended to inhibit social and cultural studies that sought to sweep through decades and ignore prominent individuals and national elections in favor of statistical aggregates and long-term mentalities. Unlike the colonial period, when there were no presidents and congressional elections and very few headline events, the early Republic seemed to be an unattractive place for the new social and cultural history.

Yet in the end it was the new social and cultural historians themselves who helped revive interest in the early Republic. It was they who first began conceiving of the Revolutionary era in the most comprehensive manner and began knitting together the two periods that hitherto had been separated from one another: the colonial-Revolutionary era and the early Republic. In the late 1970s and the 1980s they wrote increasing numbers of broad social and cultural histories that ranged in time from the middle or last quarter of the eighteenth century to the early decades of the nineteenth century. These included impressive works on women and the family, the emerging professions, the decline of apprenticeship, the rise of statistics, the creation of common schools, the spread of alcohol drinking, the transformation of artisans, the emergence of capitalism, the change in urban mobs, the experience of the native Indians, the development of slavery and antislavery, and the emergence of the postal system. New studies of law were less interested in the decisions of the Marshall Court and more concerned with the long-term relationship between law and society. Indeed, even the most seemingly insignificant subjects—log construction in Ohio from 1750 to 1840, for example—were worthy of histories as long as they covered a long enough period of time.[16]

Not only did these social and cultural historians, together with the formation of SHEAR and the *Journal of the Early Republic*, help turn the early Republic into one of the most exciting and vibrant fields of American history writing, but they created new ways of dating developments—such as from 1750 to 1820, or 1780 to 1840—that ignored or transcended the traditional periodization that had used prominent political events to separate one era from another.[17] Within these new and broader perspectives, the Revolution, when it was mentioned at all, became merely a political event expressive of wide-ranging social and cultural changes that took longer than a decade to work out. I came to believe that this new periodization marked a radical and rewarding change in American historiography.

It certainly had a powerful effect on my understanding of early America, and I began to think of the Revolution in new ways—not as a political event that could be confined to the period between 1763 and 1787 but one with great social and cultural significance that ran from at least the middle of the eighteenth century to the early decades of the nineteenth.

When I began studying and teaching both the colonial era and the early Republic up to the Jacksonian era, I was increasingly struck by how different the two periods were from one another politically, socially, and culturally. I became convinced that more had changed between 1760 and 1820 than the "consensus" historians of the 1950s had allowed. I began to suspect that the old Progressive historians had been more right than not in their interpretation of the Revolution and its consequences. Colonial society appeared to me much more of an ancien régime than the "consensus" historians had thought. It was certainly not quite the ancien régime that the Progressives had described—of rigid classes, legally restricted voting, and rich, exploitative merchants—but it was not the liberal, egalitarian, democratic society of Tocqueville's America either.

Colonial society seemed to me to be hierarchical and patriarchal, a society generally organized vertically, not horizontally, and tied together by kinship and patron-client relations. Some of this traditional, hierarchical, small-scale eighteenth-century world survived the Revolution, but not much, at least not in the North. Many of the new social and cultural studies of the 1970s and 1980s, especially those having to do with economic developments, tended to stress the fundamental differences between the old aristocratic pre-Revolutionary society and the new bumptious popular commercial society that emerged in the nineteenth century. Studies of mid-eighteenth-century farm families in New England suggested their almost medieval-like practices and outlooks; they were portrayed as patriarchal communities concerned with patrimony and kin and resembling nothing like the brash capitalistic world of the early Republic. America, it seemed, was not born liberal after all, but became so in the decades following the Revolution.[18]

With this new understanding in hand, I tried to express these changes that had taken place between the mid-eighteenth century and the early decades of the nineteenth century. In effect, I hoped to create a more refined, more complicated, and more nuanced version of the old Progressive interpretation of the Revolution and the early Republic. I sought to recover the social conflict that had taken place—not quite the conflict the Progressive historians had emphasized, but a social conflict nonetheless. My theme became essentially the same as the Progressive historians' theme: the change from aristocracy to democracy.

By seeking to write a more subtle version of the Progressive historians' interpretation of the Revolution and early Republic, I hoped to improve upon that interpretation in two important respects. First, I wanted to emphasize the importance of ideas in the historical process—something the Progressive historians, in their preoccupation with economic and other underlying interests, had tended to belittle. And second, I wanted to avoid the partiality that plagued their histories, a partiality that was prompted by the need to find antecedents for the divisions of their own time.

As I point out in the opening essay, "Rhetoric and Reality in the American Revolution," the Progressive historians generally had considered ideas to be manipulated entities, rationalizations or propaganda, mere epiphenomenal coverings for the underlying and determinative social reality. I thought they were wrong to conceive of ideas in this way. Without denying the importance of the underlying social reality, I wanted in my own work to write history that gave a proper place to the significance of ideas and to escape from the polarities that have plagued the historical profession. As historian Daniel T. Rodgers has reminded us, many of the debates historians have with one another have long been "reflexively dualistic: ideas versus behavior; rhetoric versus 'the concrete realities of life'; propaganda and mystification on the one hand, the real stuff on the other."[19] I wanted to avoid these false dichotomies and see events like the Revolution or the making of the Constitution from both sides, both the intellectual and the social—in other words, to see events whole.

Although I have most often written about ideas, I have never assumed that ideas were the driving force explaining social change. As I tried to make clear in my "Rhetoric and Reality" essay of 1966, I have never believed that any event as momentous as the Revolution could be explained solely by the ideas of the participants. Ideas are important, but they ought never be set in opposition to economic interests as "causes" of human action. In fact, I do not believe that ideas "cause" human behavior. I am with David Hume in holding that passions, not reason, are the ruling element in all human action. T. H. Breen, in a recent book on the Revolution, has rightly emphasized this point. Of course, he writes, the American Revolutionaries had ideas. "But these were ideas driven by immediate passions; they were amplified through fear, fury, and resentment."[20]

There are always forces larger than reason driving events, and I have indicated as much many times in my writings. I had a section on "Whig

Resentment" in my first book, *The Creation of the American Republic, 1776–1787,* and in my subsequent work I have always emphasized the underlying importance of structural forces—demographic, economic, and social changes—in accounting for the various expressions of ideas, including the periodic eruptions of religious enthusiasm.

In much of my work I have concentrated on ideas simply because I find them more interesting to write about than economic behavior and not because I believe they are a more important cause of events. As I suggested in my essay "Interests and Disinterestedness in the Making of the Constitution," for example, economic interests of various sorts may have been crucially important in creating the Constitution.

Explaining human behavior is complicated, and the notion of "cause" is not very helpful. In fact, as I try to indicate in my essay entitled "Conspiracy and the Paranoid Style," I think it is difficult, if not impossible, to apply the physical notion of "cause" to human action. Ideas do not "cause" people to act. Even if they did, historians would never be able to prove it; all they could do is multiply their citations of the documents in which ideas were expressed and stress their conviction that the historical participants were really sincere when they said they acted out of principles of republicanism or the public good. But hard-nosed realists like the twentieth-century historians Charles Beard and Sir Lewis Namier will simply smile knowingly at the naivety of those who would make ideas the cause of behavior and inform them of how little they know about the "real" world of human experience. Indeed, all that we have learned about the psychology and sociology of human behavior during the past century suggests that the realists are right and that the simple-minded notion that people's professed beliefs—"no taxation without representation" or "devotion to our country"—are the motives for their behavior will never be persuasive. The tough-minded realists will always tell us otherwise, will tell us, in Namier's words, that "what matters most is the underlying emotions, the music, to which ideas are a mere libretto, often of a very inferior quality."[21]

Such realists or materialists—that is, the Progressive historians—may be right that ideas do not "cause" behavior, but it does not follow that ideas are unimportant and have little or no effect on behavior, or that they can be treated as just one "factor" that now and then comes into play in human experience. Otherwise we would not spend so much time and energy arguing about ideas. I think it is possible to concede the realist or materialist position—that passions and interests lie behind all our behavior—without deprecating the role of ideas. Even if ideas are not the underlying motives for our actions, they are constant accompaniments of our actions. There is no behavior without ideas, without language. Ideas and language give meaning to our actions, and there is almost nothing that we humans do to which we do not attribute meaning. These meanings constitute our ideas, our beliefs, our ideology, and collectively our culture. As we have learned from both "the linguistic turn" and "the cultural turn" over the past several decades, our minds are essential to the ordering of our experience.

Elite and popular thinking are of a piece in this ordering of our experience. One of the great contributions that the so-called cultural turn has made to recent historiography has been to bring high intellectual life, the so-called classic texts, down to the level of the general culture. It turns out that when we thoroughly contextualize the thinking or the texts of the likes of Locke, Montesquieu, or James Madison, we find that they were expressing ideas that grew out of and had great resonance in the culture of their time and place. Others were saying similar things but not as elegantly, not as pointedly, not as persuasively as they were. If they were not products of their society and culture and speaking directly to that society and culture, they, like Giambattista Vico earlier in the eighteenth century, would have been ignored, not listened to. Elite thinkers, in other words, are only refined extensions of other more popular thinkers in the culture, and, like ordinary thinkers, they have to be understood in relation to the context—the cultural and social circumstances—of their time.

Culture and society are not really separate entities. Because human behavior is of a piece with the meanings or ideas we give to it, our ideas do not exist apart from social circumstances or some more real world of economic behavior. Hence it is foolish to try to divide up historical explanations for events such as the Revolution or the making of the Constitution into "ideological" or "economic" schools. Ideas are essential to our experience. They are the means by which we perceive, understand, rationalize, judge, and manipulate our actions. The meanings that we give to our actions form the structure of our social world. Ideas or meanings make social behavior not just comprehensible but possible. We really cannot act unless we make our actions meaningful, unless we can find words that justify, legitimate, or explain our actions.

Of course, we are not free at any moment to give whatever meaning we wish to our behavior. This is where the Progressive historians went wrong. Ideas are not the easily manipulated entities they thought they were; ideas are not mere propaganda. We cannot simply create new words or a new language to justify and explain our actions. The words we use, the meanings we give to our behavior, are public ones, and they are defined and limited by the conventions and the available normative language of the culture of the time. Since democracy, for example, is highly valued in our society, we often try to label some controversial action we wish to engage in as "democratic." But if we are unable to convince most people of our attributed meaning, then those who oppose our action or behavior as undemocratic win the intellectual debate, and we are inhibited in behaving in an undemocratic manner.

It is in this sense that culture—the collection of meanings available to us—both limits and creates behavior. It does so by forcing us to describe our actions in its terms. The definitions and meanings that we seek to give to our behavior cannot be bizarre or arbitrary; they have to be to some extent acceptable to the culture, to be part of the culture. Our actions thus are meaningful only publicly, only with respect to an inherited system of conventions and values. What is "liberal" or "tyrannical," "democratic" or "aristocratic," is determined by this cultural structure of meanings.

Our intellectual life is made up of struggles over getting people to accept different meanings of our experiences—in effect, trying to change the culture. The stakes are always high because actions that we cannot make meaningful—cannot conceive of, rationalize, legitimate, or persuade other people to accept—we in some sense cannot undertake. What is permissible culturally affects what is permissible socially or politically, so that although ideas may not be the motives for behavior (underlying interests and passions are the real motives), ideas do affect and limit behavior. They are not mere superstructure or epiphenomena.[22]

Indeed, once a new idea is expressed and becomes reasonably acceptable to many people, it can spawn new and sometimes unexpected behavior. When Alexander Hamilton, in *The Federalist* No. 78, suggested that judges were as much agents of the people as were the members of the state legislatures (a point developed in this collection of essays), he was only trying to find a novel justification for the judicial review of legislation. But others soon picked up Hamilton's suggestion and began running with it. Before long some polemicists were arguing that if the judges were in fact a kind of representative of the people, then maybe the people ought to elect them. And sure enough this began to happen in the Jacksonian era; today, as I indicate in my essay on American constitutionalism, some thirty-nine states elect their judges in one way or another. This was a development that Hamilton could never have imagined and would have been appalled by, yet he helped to produce it. In our efforts to make new behavior meaningful, we create all sorts of unanticipated consequences.

This is certainly what happened with the arguments of the Federalists in 1787–1788. They were faced with the difficult task of justifying their new and strong national government in the face of both deeply rooted American fears of far-removed central power and the traditional theory that held that republics had to be small in size and homogeneous in character. Their opponents in the debate, the Anti-Federalists (the very name foisted on them suggests the polemical effectiveness of the Federalists), thought that the Constitution was an aristocratic and undemocratic document designed to limit certain popular pressures on government. They had considerable evidence to support their position; they had, in other words, many inherited meanings drawn from past Whig experience in the British Empire that made distant centralized power dangerous, and they made a persuasive case that the Constitution was a consolidated and an elitist threat to popular liberty.

If the Federalists were to combat these arguments and convince people that the new expanded federal government was thoroughly republican and not a threat to liberty, they would have to find new meanings for old words and somehow not repudiate the Americans' long-existing Whig experience with power and liberty. In the debates over ratification of the Constitution, they were extraordinarily successful in exploiting the old idea of separation of powers in new ways and in giving a novel twist to the conventional meaning of sovereignty by locating it in the people. Yet by using the popular and democratic rhetoric that had emerged in the polemics of the previous decade to justify the aristocratic and expanded republic created by the Constitution, the Federalists created consequences they never intended. Their concessions to popular sovereignty and their many new democratic ideas were now on the table to be taken up and used by others in new ways. The Anti-Federalists may have lost the battle over the Constitution, but during the subsequent generation they essentially won the war over the character of the new nation.

When confronted with this 1787–1788 debate over the "aristocratic" and "democratic" nature of the Constitution, historians are not supposed to decide which was more "correct" or more "true." The historians' task, rather, is to explain the reasons for these contrasting meanings and why each side should have attempted to give to the Constitution the meanings it did. There was not in 1787–1788 one "correct" or "true" meaning of the Constitution. The Constitution meant whatever the Federalists or the Anti-Federalists could convince the country to accept. That is why the debate over the Constitution was so important.

I wish we could avoid the polarization of interpretations—setting those that are "ideological" against those that are "economic"—that seems to afflict the historical profession and instead try to explain events of the past in their entirety, from the top down as well as from the bottom up. Of course, the past is so complicated that there will always be disagreement over historians' varying perceptions of it. Despite the fact that we collectively know much more now about the origins of the Revolution and the writing of the Constitution than Charles Beard and the other Progressive historians ever did, no single historian can know everything; thus the debates over our various historical explanations for the Founding or any other great event in our past will never cease.

IN ADDITION TO EMPHASIZING the importance of ideas in past behavior, I wanted my revisionist interpretation of the Progressive approach to the Revolution and the early Republic to avoid what I took to be the partisanship and one-sidedness of their interpretation. The partiality of the Progressive historians came out of their experience at the beginning of the twentieth century. Disgusted with the way the big corporations and the robber barons were exploiting the farmers and working people of their own time, they were naturally biased against Alexander Hamilton and the Federalists, whom they assumed were the progenitors of this despicable business world. They thus made Jefferson their hero; he was the one who led all the ordinary working people of the Democratic-Republican Party against those whom the popular historian of the 1920s Claude G. Bowers called "the rich, the powerful, and their retainers" in whose "drawing room were heard the sentiments of Chambers of Commerce—in glorification of materialism."[23] Unfortunately, too much of our history writing tends to take sides in this gross manner, crudely reading back into the past the issues of the present.

We have a somewhat different present now from that of a century ago. Class struggles against the rich and powerful still preoccupy many scholars, but in many cases their anticapitalist concerns have been supplanted by issues of race and gender. This in turn has transformed many historians' perspectives on the early Republic. They still see a contest between Federalists and Republicans, but their bias has shifted. Because Jefferson and the other Southern leaders of the Republican Party were slaveholders, many present-day scholars have switched sides in accord with the political and cultural needs of our own time. Much as most historians continue to dislike businessmen and the commercial classes, they dislike slaveholders and racists more.

Since most of the Federalists were Northerners and opposed to slavery, their status has dramatically risen in the eyes of present-day scholars.[24] In today's society, where many scholars see an illiberal and narrow-minded populism running rampant, the elitism of the Federalists doesn't seem all that bad. The Federalists might have been aristocrats, but, as some recent historians contend, at least they "were significantly more receptive than the Jeffersonians to the inclusion of women in the political process." Indeed, the Federalists' "conservative elitism" appears to present a "kinder face" on issues of gender and race than the Jeffersonian Democratic-Republicans do. "Federalists encouraged the migration of women to the West, believing that the presence of families there would counter the wildness of the frontiersmen. They called for fair treatment of Indians and tried to prohibit the spread of slavery into the region. The defeat of the Federalist vision by the new democratic order," these historians conclude, "spelled a diminished status for women, Indians, and Africans." Perhaps most damaging for the reputation of the Jeffersonian Republicans in our own time was their promotion of minimal government, which some scholars believe was motivated mainly by the need to protect slavery. By contrast, the Federalists were "committed to the idea that government was necessary to protect the weak."[25]

So it has gone, each generation of historians finding in the era of the Revolution and early Republic whatever fits its particular political and cultural needs. This is perhaps understandable but nonetheless lamentable. Because the present is so strong and can easily overwhelm and distort interpretations of the past, we historians have to constantly guard against it. Of course, historians live in the present, and they cannot and should not ignore it in their forays into the past; historians are not antiquarians who wallow in the past for its own sake. Indeed, historical reconstruction is only possible because historians have different perspectives from those of the past about whom they write. The present is important in stimulating historical inquiry and the questions historians ask of the past. "There is always," writes the eminent historian Bernard Bailyn, "a need to extract from the past some kind of bearing on contemporary problems, some message, commentary, or instruction to the writer's age, and to see reflected in the past familiar aspects of the present." But without "critical control," says Bailyn, this need "generates an obvious kind of presentism, which at worst becomes indoctrination by historical example."[26]

In many recent studies of the era of the Revolution and the early Republic, this "critical control" has not always been what it should have been. Our present preoccupation with race and gender has sometimes tended to misrepresent the period in much the same way that Charles Beard's Progressive generation misrepresented the period with their preoccupation with the common people against the business interests. One would think that the exaggerations of Progressive historiography (which most historians now recognize as such) would make present-day historians wary of making the same mistake—of reading their present so heavy-handedly into their interpretations of the past. It is one thing for the present to provoke questions about the past; it is quite another when it shapes and controls what historians find there.[27]

I don't believe that historians should take sides with the contestants of the past, whether Anti-Federalists versus Federalists or Republicans versus Federalists. The responsibility of the historian, it seems to me, is not to decide who in the past was right or who was wrong but to explain why the different contestants thought and behaved as they did.

Once we transcend this sort of partisan view of the past, once we realize that people in the past did not know their future any more than we know ours, and once we try to understand their behavior in their terms and not ours, then we will acquire a much more detached historical perspective. We can then come to appreciate more fully, for example, just how many illusions the generation of Founders lived with. Many of them hated political parties and tried to avoid them, and yet parties arose. Many of them thought their society in time would become more like Europe's, and yet it did not, at least not during the first half of the nineteenth century. Many also believed that slavery would sooner or later die a natural death—that it would simply wither away. They could not have been more wrong. Many of them also thought that the West could be settled in an orderly fashion, in a manner that could protect Indian culture and keep the native peoples west of the Appalachians from disappearing as they believed they had in New England.

They had many illusions about the future, as I suggest in my essay "Illusions of Power in the Awkward Era of Federalism." As late as 1822 Thomas Jefferson thought that "there is not a *young man* now living in the United States who will not die a Unitarian."[28] A Unitarian! What could he have been thinking? And this at a time when the evangelical Methodists and Baptists were growing by leaps and bounds.

If Jefferson, as smart and as well-read as he was, had illusions about the future, there is not much hope for the rest of us avoiding illusions about our future. But that is precisely the point of studying history. Before we become arrogant and condescending toward these people in the past, we should realize that we too live with illusions, only we don't know what they are. Perhaps every generation lives with illusions, different ones for each generation. And that is how history moves from one generation to another, exploding the previous generation's illusions and conjuring up its own.

If we approach the past in this way, we become more aware of just how much people then were victims as well as drivers of the historical process. We come to realize that those in the past were restricted by forces that they did not understand nor were even aware of—forces such as demographic movements, economic developments, or large-scale cultural patterns. The drama, indeed the tragedy, of history comes from our understanding of the tension that existed between the conscious wills and intentions of the participants in the past and the underlying conditions that constrained their actions and shaped their future. If the study of history teaches anything, it teaches us the limitations of life. It ought to produce prudence and humility.

PART I

THE *American Revolution*

CHAPTER ONE

RHETORIC *and* REALITY
in the AMERICAN REVOLUTION

F ANY CATCHPHRASE IS TO characterize the work being done on the American Revolution by this generation of historians, it will probably be "the American Revolution considered as an intellectual movement."[1] For we now seem to be fully involved in a phase of writing about the Revolution in which the thought of the Revolutionaries, rather than their social and economic interests, has become the major focus of research and analysis. This recent emphasis on ideas is not, of course, new, and indeed right from the beginning it has characterized almost all our attempts to understand the Revolution. The ideas of a period which Samuel Eliot Morison and Harold Laski once described as, next to the English revolutionary decades of the seventeenth century, the most fruitful era in the history of Western political thought could never be completely ignored in any phase of our history writing.[2]

It has not been simply the inherent importance of the Revolutionary ideas, those "great principles of freedom,"[3] that has continually attracted the attention of historians. It has been rather the unusual nature of the Revolution and the constant need to explain what on the face of it seems inexplicable that has compelled almost all interpreters of the Revolution, including the participants themselves, to stress its predominantly intellectual character and hence its uniqueness among Western revolutions. Within the context of Revolutionary historiography, the one great effort to disparage the significance of ideas in the Revolution—an effort which dominated our history writing in the first half of the twentieth century—becomes something of an anomaly, a temporary aberration into a deterministic social and economic explanation from which we have been retreating for the past two decades. Since roughly the end of World War II we have witnessed a resumed and increasingly heightened insistence on the primary significance of conscious beliefs, and particularly of constitutional principles, in explaining what once again has become the unique character of the American Revolution. In the hands of idealist-minded historians, the thought and principles of the Americans have consequently come to repossess that explanative force which the previous generation of materialist-minded historians had tried to locate in the social structure.

Indeed, our renewed insistence on the importance of ideas in explaining the Revolution has now attained a level of fullness and sophistication never before achieved, with the consequence that the economic and social approach of the previous generation of behaviorist historians has never seemed more anomalous and irrelevant than it does at present. Yet paradoxically it may be that this preoccupation with the explanatory power of the Revolutionary ideas has become so intensive and so refined, assumed such a character, that the apparently discredited social and economic approach of an earlier generation has at the same time never seemed more attractive and relevant. In other words, we may be approaching a crucial juncture in our writing about the Revolution where idealism and behaviorism meet.

IT WAS THE REVOLUTIONARIES THEMSELVES who first described the peculiar character of what they had been involved in. The Revolution, as those who took stock at the end of three decades of revolutionary activity noted, was not "one of those events which strikes the public eye in the subversions of laws which have usually attended the revolutions of governments." Because it did not seem to have been a typical revolution, the sources of its force and its momentum appeared strangely unaccountable. "In other revolutions, the sword has been drawn by the arm of offended freedom, under an oppression that threatened the vital powers of society."[4] But this seemed hardly true of the American Revolution. There was none of the legendary tyranny that had so often driven desperate peoples into revolution. The Americans were not an oppressed people; they had no crushing imperial shackles to throw off. In fact, the Americans knew they were probably freer and less burdened with cumbersome feudal and monarchical restraints than any part of mankind in the eighteenth century. To its victims, the Tories, the Revolution was truly incomprehensible. Never in history, said Daniel Leonard, had there been so much rebellion with so "little real cause." It was, wrote Peter Oliver, "the most wanton and unnatural rebellion that ever existed."[5] The Americans' response was out of all proportion to the stimuli. The objective social reality scarcely seemed capable of explaining a revolution.

Yet no American doubted that there had been a revolution. How then was it to be justified and explained? If the American Revolution, lacking "those mad, tumultuous actions which disgraced many of the great revolutions of antiquity," was not a typical revolution, what kind of revolution was it? If the origin of the American Revolution lay not in the usual passions and interests of men, wherein did it lay? Those Americans who looked back at what they had been through could only marvel at the rationality and moderation, "supported by the energies of well weighed choice," involved in their separation from Britain, a revolution remarkably "without violence or convulsion."[6] It seemed to be peculiarly an affair of the mind. Even two such dissimilar sorts of Whigs as Thomas Paine and John Adams both came to see the Revolution they had done so much to bring about as especially involved with ideas, resulting from "a mental examination," a change in "the minds and hearts of the people."[7] The Americans were fortunate in being born at a time when the principles of government and freedom were better known than at any time in history. The Americans had learned "how to define the rights of nature—how to search into, to distinguish, and to comprehend, the principles of physical, moral, religious, and civil liberty," how, in short, to discover and resist the forces of tyranny before they could be applied. Never before in history had a people achieved "a revolution by reasoning" alone.[8]

The Americans, "born the heirs of freedom,"[9] revolted not to create but to maintain their freedom. American society had developed differently from that of the Old World. From the time of the first settlements in the seventeenth century, wrote Samuel Williams in 1794, "every thing tended to produce, and to establish the spirit of freedom." While the speculative philosophers of Europe were laboriously searching their minds in an effort to decide the first principles of liberty, the Americans had come to experience vividly that liberty in their everyday lives. The American Revolution, said Williams, joined together these enlightened ideas with America's experience. The Revolution was thus essentially intellectual and declaratory: it "explained the business to the world, and served to confirm what nature and society had before produced." "All was the result of reason. . . ."[10] The Revolution had taken place not in a succession of eruptions that had crumbled the existing social structure, but in a succession of new thoughts and new ideas that had vindicated that social structure.

The same logic that drove the participants to view the Revolution as peculiarly intellectual also compelled Moses Coit Tyler, writing at the end of the nineteenth century, to describe the American Revolution as "preeminently a revolution caused by ideas, and pivoted on ideas." That ideas played a part in all revolutions Tyler readily admitted. But in most revolutions, like that of the French, ideas had been perceived and acted upon only when the social reality had caught up with them, only when the ideas had been given meaning and force by long-experienced "real evils." The American Revolution, said Tyler, had been different: it was directed "not against tyranny inflicted, but only against tyranny anticipated." The Americans revolted not out of actual suffering but out of reasoned principle. "Hence, more than with most other epochs of revolutionary strife, our epoch of revolutionary strife was a strife of ideas:

a long warfare of political logic; a succession of annual campaigns in which the marshalling of arguments not only preceded the marshalling of armies, but often exceeded them in impression upon the final result."[11]

IT IS IN THIS HISTORIOGRAPHICAL context developed by the end of the nineteenth century, this constant and at times extravagant emphasis on the idealism of the Revolution, that the true radical quality of the Progressive generation's interpretation of the Revolution becomes so vividly apparent. For the work of these Progressive historians was grounded in a social and economic explanation of the Revolutionary era that explicitly rejected the causal importance of ideas. These historians could scarcely have avoided the general intellectual climate of the first part of the twentieth century, which regarded ideas as suspect. By absorbing the diffused thinking of Marx and Freud and the assumptions of behaviorist psychology, men had come to conceive of ideas as ideologies or rationalizations, as masks obscuring the underlying interests and drives that actually determined social behavior. For too long, it seemed, philosophers had reified thought, detaching ideas from the material conditions that produced them and investing them with an independent will that was somehow alone responsible for the determination of events.[12] As Charles Beard pointed out in his introduction to the 1935 edition of *An Economic Interpretation of the Constitution*, previous historians of the Constitution had assumed that ideas were "entities, particularities, or forces, apparently independent of all earthly considerations coming under the head of 'economic.'" It was Beard's aim, as it was the aim of many of his contemporaries, to bring into historical consideration "those realistic features of economic conflict, stress, and strain" which previous interpreters of the Revolution had largely ignored.[13] The product of this aim was a generation or more of historical writing about the Revolutionary period (of which Beard's was but the most famous expression) that sought to explain the Revolution and the formation of the Constitution in terms of socioeconomic relationships and interests rather than in terms of ideas.[14]

Curiously, the consequence of this reversal of historical approaches was not the destruction of the old-fashioned conception of the nature of ideas. As Marx had said, he intended only to put Hegel's head in its rightful place; he had no desire to cut it off. Ideas as rationalization, as ideology, remained—still distinct entities set in opposition to interests, now, however, lacking any deep causal significance, becoming merely a covering superstructure for the underlying and determinative social reality. Ideas therefore could still be the subject of historical investigation as long as one kept them in their proper place, interesting no doubt in their own right but not actually counting for much in the movement of events.

Even someone as interested in ideas as Carl Becker never seriously considered them to be in any way determinants of what happened. Ideas fascinated Becker, but it was as superstructure that he enjoyed examining them, their consistency, their logic, their clarity, the way men formed and played with them. In his *Declaration of Independence: A Study in the History of Political Ideas*, the political theory of the Americans takes on an unreal and even fatuous quality. It was as if ideas were merely refined tools to be used by the colonists in the most adroit manner possible. The entire Declaration of Independence, said Becker, was calculated for effect, designed primarily "to convince a candid world that the colonies had a moral and legal right to separate from Great Britain." The severe indictment of the king did not spring from unfathomable passions but was contrived, conjured up, to justify a rebellion whose sources lay elsewhere. Men to Becker were never the victims of their thought, but always the masters of it. Ideas were a kind of legal brief. "Thus step by step, from 1764 to 1776, the colonists modified their theory to suit their needs."[15] The assumptions behind Becker's 1909 behaviorist work on New York politics in the Revolution and his 1922 study of the political ideas in the Declaration of Independence were more alike than they at first might appear.

Bringing to their studies of the Revolution similar assumptions about the nature of ideas, some of Becker's contemporaries went on to expose starkly the implications of those assumptions. When the entire body of Revolutionary thinking was examined, these historians could not avoid being struck by its generally bombastic and overwrought quality. The ideas expressed seemed so inflated, such obvious exaggerations of reality, that they could scarcely be taken seriously. The Tories were all "wretched hirelings, and execrable parricides"; George III, the "tyrant of the earth," a "monster in human form"; the British soldiers, "a mercenary, licentious rabble of banditti," intending to "tear the bowels and vitals of their brave but peaceable fellow subjects, and *to wash the ground with a profusion of innocent blood.*"[16] Such extravagant language, it seemed, could be nothing but calculated deception, at best an obvious distortion of fact, designed to incite and mold a revolutionary fervor. "The stigmatizing of British policy as 'tyranny,' 'oppression' and 'slavery,'" wrote Arthur M. Schlesinger, the dean of the Progressive historians, "had little or no objective reality, at least prior to the Intolerable Acts, but ceaseless repetition of the charge kept emotions at fever pitch."[17]

Indeed, so grandiose, so overdrawn, it seemed, were the ideas that the historians were necessarily led to ask not whether such ideas were valid but why men should have expressed them. It was not the content of such ideas but the function that was really interesting. The Revolutionary rhetoric, the profusion of sermons, pamphlets, and articles in the patriotic cause, could best be examined as propaganda, that is, as a concerted and self-conscious effort by agitators to manipulate and shape public opinion. Because of the Progressive historians' view of the Revolution as the movement of class minorities bent on promoting particular social and economic interests, the conception of propaganda was crucial to their explanation of what seemed to be a revolutionary consensus. Through the use of ideas in provoking hatred and influencing opinion and creating at least "an appearance of unity," the influence of a minority of agitators was out of all proportion to their number. The Revolution thus became a display of extraordinary skillfulness in the manipulation of public opinion. In fact, wrote Schlesinger, "no disaffected element in history has ever risen more splendidly to the occasion."[18]

Ideas thus became, as it were, parcels of thought to be distributed and used where they would do the most good. This propaganda was not, of course, necessarily false, but it was always capable of manipulation. "Whether the suggestions are to be true or false, whether the activities are to be open or concealed," wrote Philip Davidson, "are matters for the propagandist to decide." Apparently ideas could be turned on or off at will, and men controlled their rhetoric in a way they could not control their interests. Whatever the importance of propaganda, its connection with social reality was tenuous. Since ideas were so self-consciously manageable, the Whigs were not actually expressing anything meaningful about themselves but were rather feigning and exaggerating for effect. What the Americans said could not be taken at face value but must be considered as a rhetorical disguise for some hidden interest. The expression of even the classic and well-defined natural rights philosophy became, in Davidson's view, "the propagandist's rationalization of his desire to protect his vested interests."[19]

With this conception of ideas as weapons shrewdly used by designing propagandists, it was inevitable that the thought of the Revolutionaries should have been denigrated. The Revolutionaries became by implication hypocritical demagogues, "adroitly tailoring their arguments to changing conditions." Their political thinking appeared to possess neither consistency nor significance. "At best," said Schlesinger in an early summary of his interpretation, "an exposition of the political theories of the antiparliamentary party is an account of their retreat from one strategic position to another." So the Whigs moved, it was strongly suggested, easily if not frivolously from a defense of charter rights to the rights of Englishmen, and finally to the rights of man, as each position was exposed and became untenable. In short, concluded Schlesinger, the Revolution could never be understood if it were regarded "as a great forensic controversy over abstract governmental rights."[20]

IT IS ESSENTIALLY ON THIS point of intellectual consistency that Edmund S. Morgan has fastened for the past decade and a half in an attempt to bring down the entire interpretive framework of the socioeconomic argument. If it could be shown that the thinking of the Revolutionaries was not inconsistent after all, that the Whigs did not actually skip from one constitutional notion to the next, then the imputation of Whig frivolity and hypocrisy would lose its force. This was a central intention of Morgan's study of the political thought surrounding the Stamp Act. As Morgan himself has noted and others have repeated, "In the last analysis the significance of the Stamp Act crisis lies in the emergence, not of leaders and methods and organizations, but of well-defined constitutional principles." As early as 1765 the Whigs "laid down the line on which Americans stood until they cut their connections with England. Consistently from 1765 to 1776 they denied the authority of Parliament to tax them externally or internally; consistently they affirmed their willingness to submit to whatever legislation Parliament should enact for the supervision of the empire as a whole."[21] In other words, from the beginning they consistently denied Parliament's right to tax them, but at the same time they consistently affirmed Parliament's right to regulate their trade. This consistency thus becomes, as one scholar's survey of the current interpretation puts it, "an indication of American devotion to principle."[22]

It seemed clear once again after Morgan's study that the Americans were more sincerely attached to constitutional principles than the behaviorist historians had supposed, and that their ideas could not be viewed as simply manipulated propaganda. Consequently the cogency of the Progressive historians' interpretation was weakened if not unhinged. And as the evidence against viewing the Revolution as rooted in internal class conflict continued to mount from various directions, it appeared more and more comprehensible to accept the old-fashioned notion that the Revolution was after all the consequence of "a great forensic controversy over abstract governmental rights." There was, it seemed, no deprived and depressed populace yearning for a participation in politics that had long been denied; no coherent merchant class victimizing a mass of insolvent debtors; no seething discontent with the British mercantile system; no privileged aristocracy, protected by law, anxiously and insecurely holding power against a clamoring democracy. There was, in short, no internal class upheaval in the Revolution.[23]

If the Revolution was not to become virtually incomprehensible, it must have been the result of what the American Whigs always contended it was—a dispute between Mother Country and colonies over constitutional liberties. By concentrating on the immediate events of the decade leading up to independence, the historians of the 1950s have necessarily fled from the economic and social determinism of the Progressive historians. And by emphasizing the consistency and devotion with which Americans held their constitutional beliefs, they have once again focused on what seems to be the extraordinary intellectuality of the American Revolution and hence its uniqueness among Western revolutions. This interpretation, which, as Jack P. Greene notes, "may appropriately be styled neo-whig," has turned the Revolution into a rationally conservative movement, involving mainly a constitutional defense of existing political liberties against the abrupt and unexpected provocations of the British government after 1760. "The issue then, according to the neo-whigs, was no more and no less than separation from Britain and the preservation of American liberty." The Revolution has therefore become "more political, legalistic, and constitutional than social or economic." Indeed, some of the neo-Whig historians have implied not just that social and economic conditions were less important in bringing on the Revolution than we once thought, but rather that the social situation in the colonies had little or nothing to do with causing the Revolution. The Whig statements of principle iterated in numerous declarations appear to be the only causal residue after all the supposedly deeper social and economic causes have been washed away. As one scholar who has recently investigated and carefully dismissed the potential social and economic issues in pre-Revolutionary Virginia has concluded, "What remains as the fundamental issue in the coming of the Revolution, then, is nothing more than the contest over constitutional rights."[24]

In a different way, Bernard Bailyn in a recent article has clarified and reinforced this revived idealistic interpretation of the Revolution. The accumulative influence of much of the latest historical writing on the character of eighteenth-century American society has led Bailyn to the same insight expressed by Samuel Williams in 1794. What made the Revolution truly revolutionary was not the wholesale disruption of social groups and political institutions, for compared to other revolutions such disruption was slight; rather it was the fundamental alteration in the Americans' structure of values, the way they looked at themselves and their institutions. Bailyn has seized on this basic intellectual shift as a means of explaining the apparent contradiction between the seriousness with which the Americans took their Revolutionary ideas and the absence of radical social and institutional change. The Revolution, argues Bailyn, was not so much the transformation as the realization of American society.

The Americans had been gradually and unwittingly preparing themselves for such a mental revolution since they first came to the New World in the seventeenth century. The substantive changes in American society had taken place in the course of the previous century, slowly, often imperceptibly, as a series of small piecemeal deviations from what was regarded by most Englishmen as the accepted orthodoxy in society, state, and religion. What the Revolution marked, so to speak, was the point when the Americans suddenly blinked and saw their society, its changes, its differences, in a new perspective. Their deviation from European standards, their lack of an established church and a titled aristocracy, their apparent rusticity and general equality now became desirable, even necessary, elements in the maintenance of their society and politics. The comprehending and justifying, the endowing with high moral purpose, of these confusing and disturbing social and political divergences, Bailyn concludes, was the American Revolution.[25]

Bailyn's more recent investigation of the rich pamphlet literature of the decades before independence has filled out and refined his idealist interpretation, confirming him in his "rather old-fashioned view that the American Revolution was above all else an ideological-constitutional struggle and not primarily a controversy between social groups undertaken to force changes in the organization of society." While Bailyn's book-length introduction to the first of a multivolumed edition of Revolutionary pamphlets makes no effort to stress the conservative character of the Revolution and indeed emphasizes (in contrast to the earlier article) its radicalism and the dynamic and transforming rather than the rationalizing and declarative quality of Whig thought, it nevertheless represents the culmination of the idealist approach to the history of the Revolution. For "above all else," argues Bailyn, it was the Americans' worldview, the peculiar bundle of notions and beliefs they put together during the imperial debate, "that in the end propelled them into Revolution." Through his study of the Whig pamphlets Bailyn became convinced "that the fear of a comprehensive conspiracy against liberty throughout the English-speaking world—a conspiracy believed to have been nourished in corruption, and of which, it was felt, oppression in America was only the most immediately visible part—lay at the heart of the Revolutionary movement." No one of the various acts and measures of the British government after 1763 could by itself have provoked the extreme and violent response of the American Whigs. But when linked together they formed in the minds of the Americans, imbued with a particular historical understanding of what constituted tyranny, an extensive and frightening program designed to enslave the New World. The Revolution becomes comprehensible only when the mental framework, the Whig worldview into which the Americans fitted the events of the 1760s and 1770s, is known. "It is the development of this view to the point of overwhelming persuasiveness to the majority of American leaders and the meaning this view gave to the events of the time, and not simply an accumulation of grievances," writes Bailyn, "that explains the origins of the American Revolution."[26]

It now seems evident from Bailyn's analysis that it was the Americans' peculiar conception of reality more than anything else that convinced them that tyranny was afoot and that they must fight if their liberty was to survive. By an empathic understanding of a wide range of American thinking Bailyn has been able to offer us a most persuasive argument for the importance of ideas in bringing on the Revolution. Not since Tyler has the intellectual character of the Revolution received such emphasis and never before has it been set out so cogently and completely. It would seem that the idealist explanation of the Revolution has nowhere else to go.[27]

.   .   .

LABELING THE RECENT historical interpretations of the Revolution as "neo-Whig" is indeed appropriate, for, as Page Smith has pointed out, "After a century and a half of progress in historical scholarship, in research techniques, in tools and methods, we have found our way to the interpretation held, substantially, by those historians who themselves participated in, or lived through the era of, the Revolution." By describing the Revolution as a conservative, principled defense of American freedom against the provocations of the English government, the neo-Whig historians have come full circle to the position of the Revolutionaries themselves and to the interpretation of the first generation of historians.[28] Indeed, as a consequence of this historical atavism, praise for the contemporary or early historians has become increasingly common.

But to say that "the Whig interpretation of the American Revolution may not be as dead as some historians would have us believe" is perhaps less to commend the work of David Ramsay and George Bancroft than to indict the approach of recent historians.[29] However necessary and rewarding the neo-Whig histories have been, they present us with only a partial perspective on the Revolution. The neo-Whig interpretation is intrinsically polemical; however subtly presented, it aims to justify the Revolution. It therefore cannot accommodate a totally different, an opposing, perspective, a Tory view of the Revolution. It is for this reason that the recent publication of Peter Oliver's "Origin and Progress of the American Rebellion" is of major significance, for it offers us—"by attacking the hallowed traditions of the revolution, challenging the motives of the founding fathers, and depicting revolution as passion, plotting, and violence"—an explanation of what happened quite different from what we have been recently accustomed to.[30] Oliver's vivid portrait of the Revolutionaries, with his accent on their vicious emotions and interests, seriously disturbs the present Whiggish interpretation of the Revolution. It is not that Oliver's description of, say, John Adams as madly ambitious and consumingly resentful is any more correct than Adams's own description of himself as a virtuous and patriotic defender of liberty against tyranny. Both interpretations of Adams are in a sense right, but neither can comprehend the other because each is preoccupied with seemingly contradictory sets of motives. Indeed, it is really these two interpretations that have divided historians of the Revolution ever since.

Any intellectually satisfying explanation of the Revolution must encompass the Tory perspective as well as the Whig, for if we are compelled to take sides and choose between opposing motives—unconscious or avowed, passion or principle, greed or liberty—we will be endlessly caught up in the polemics of the participants themselves. We must, in other words, eventually dissolve the distinction between conscious and unconscious motives, between the Revolutionaries' stated intentions and their supposedly hidden needs and desires, a dissolution that involves somehow relating beliefs and ideas to the social world in which they operate. If we are to understand the causes of the Revolution, we must therefore ultimately transcend this problem of motivation. But this we can never do as long as we attempt to explain the Revolution mainly in terms of the intentions of the participants. It is not that men's motives are unimportant; they indeed make events, including revolutions. But the purposes of men, especially in a revolution, are so numerous, so varied, and so contradictory that their complex interaction produces results that no one intended or could even foresee. It is this interaction and these results that recent historians are referring to when they speak so disparagingly of those "underlying determinants" and "impersonal and inexorable forces" bringing on the Revolution. Historical explanation which does not account for these "forces," which, in other words, relies simply on understanding the conscious intentions of the actors, will thus be limited. This preoccupation with men's purposes was what restricted the perspectives of the contemporaneous Whig and Tory interpretations, and it is still the weakness of the neo-Whig histories, and indeed of any interpretation which attempts to explain the events of the Revolution by discovering the calculations from which individuals supposed themselves to have acted.

No explanation of the American Revolution in terms of the intentions and designs of particular individuals could have been more crudely put than that offered by the Revolutionaries themselves. American Whigs, like men of the eighteenth century generally, were fascinated with what seemed to the age to be the newly appreciated problem of human motivation and causation in the affairs of the world. In the decade before independence, the Americans sought endlessly to discover the supposed calculations and purposes of individuals or groups that lay behind the otherwise incomprehensible rush of events. More than anything else, perhaps, it was this obsession with motives that led to the prevalence in the eighteenth century of beliefs in conspiracies to account for the confusing happenings in which men found themselves caught up. Bailyn has suggested that this common fear of conspiracy was "deeply rooted in the political awareness of eighteenth-century Britons, involved in the very structure of their political life"; it "reflected so clearly the realities of life in an age in which monarchical autocracy flourished, [and] in which the stability and freedom of England's 'mixed' constitution was a recent and remarkable achievement."[31]

Yet it might also be argued that the tendency to see conspiracy behind what happened reflected as well the very enlightenment of the age. To attribute events to the designs and purposes of human agents seemed after all to be an enlightened advance over older beliefs in blind chance, providence, or God's interventions. It was rational and scientific, a product of both the popularization of politics and the secularization of knowledge. It was obvious to Americans that the series of events in the years after 1763, those "unheard of intolerable calamities, spring not of the dust, come not causeless." "Ought not the PEOPLE therefore," asked John Dickinson, "to watch? to observe facts? to search into causes? to investigate designs?"[32] And these causes and designs could be traced to individuals in high places, to ministers, to royal governors, and their lackeys. The belief in conspiracy grew naturally out of the enlightened need to find the human purposes behind the multitude of phenomena, to find the causes for what happened in the social world just as the natural scientist was discovering the causes for what happened in the physical world.[33] It was a necessary consequence of the search for connections and patterns in events. The various acts of the British government, the Americans knew, should not be "regarded according to the simple force of each, but as parts of a system of oppression."[34] The Whigs' intense search for the human purposes behind events was in fact an example of the beginnings of modern history.

In attempting to rebut those interpretations disparaging the colonists' cause, the present neo-Whig historians have been drawn into writing as partisans of the Revolutionaries. And they have thus found themselves entangled in the same kind of explanation used by the original antagonists, an explanation, despite obvious refinements, still involved with the discovery of motives and its corollary, the assessing of a personal sort of responsibility for what happened. While most of the neo-Whig historians have not gone so far as to see conspiracy in British actions (although some have come close),[35] they have tended to point up the blundering and stupidity of British officials in contrast to "the breadth of vision" that moved the Americans. If George III was in a position of central responsibility in the British government, as English historians have recently said, then, according to Edmund S. Morgan, "he must bear most of the praise or blame for the series of measures that alienated and lost the colonies, and it is hard to see how there can be much praise." By seeking "to define issues, fix responsibilities," and thereby to shift the "burden of proof" onto those who say the Americans were narrow and selfish and the empire was basically just and beneficent, the neo-Whigs have attempted to redress what they felt was an unfair neo-Tory bias of previous explanations of the Revolution;[36] they have not, however, challenged the terms of the argument. They are still obsessed with why men said they acted and with who was right and who was wrong. Viewing the history of the Revolution in this judicatory manner has therefore restricted the issues over which historians have disagreed to those of motivation and responsibility, the very issues with which the participants themselves were concerned.

The neo-Whig "conviction that the colonists' attachment to principle was genuine"[37] has undoubtedly been refreshing, and indeed necessary, given the Tory slant of earlier twentieth-century interpretations. It now seems clearer that the Progressive historians, with their naive and crude reflex conception of human behavior, had too long treated the ideas of the Revolution superficially if not superciliously. Psychologists and sociologists are now willing to grant a more determining role to beliefs, particularly in revolutionary situations. It is now accepted that men act not simply in response to some kind of objective reality but to the meaning they give to that reality. Since men's beliefs are as much a part of the given stimuli as the objective environment, the beliefs must be understood and taken seriously if men's behavior is to be fully explained. The American Revolutionary ideas were more than cooked-up pieces of thought served by an aggressive and interested minority to a gullible and unsuspecting populace. The concept of propaganda permitted the Progressive historians to account for the presence of ideas, but it prevented them from recognizing ideas as an important determinant of the Americans' behavior. The weight attributed to ideas and constitutional principles by the neo-Whig historians was thus an essential corrective to the propagandist studies.

Yet in its laudable effort to resurrect the importance of ideas in historical explanation, much of the writing of the neo-Whigs has tended to return to the simple nineteenth-century intellectualist assumption that history is the consequence of a rational calculation of ends and means, that what happened was what was consciously desired and planned. By supposing "that individual actions and immediate issues are more important than underlying determinants in explaining particular events," by emphasizing conscious and articulated motives, the neo-Whig historians have selected and presented that evidence which is most directly and clearly expressive of the intentions of the Whigs—that is, the most well-defined, the most constitutional, the most reasonable of the Whig beliefs, those found in their public documents, their several declarations of grievances and causes. It is not surprising that for the neo-Whigs the history of the American Revolution should be more than anything else "the history of the Americans' search for principles."[38] Not only, then, did nothing in the Americans' economic and social structure really determine their behavior, but the colonists in fact acted from the most rational and calculated of motives: they fought, as they said they would, simply to defend their ancient liberties against British provocation.

By implying that certain declared rational purposes are by themselves an adequate explanation for the Americans' revolt—in other words, that the Revolution was really nothing more than a contest over constitutional principles—the neo-Whig historians have not only threatened to deny what we have learned of human psychology in the twentieth century, but they have also in fact failed to exploit fully the terms of their own idealist approach by not taking into account all of what the Americans believed and said. Whatever the deficiencies and misunderstandings of the role of ideas in human behavior present in the propagandist studies of the 1930s, these studies did for the first time attempt to deal with the entirety and complexity of American Revolutionary thought—to explain not only all the well-reasoned notions of law and liberty that were so familiar but, more important, all the irrational and hysterical beliefs that had been so long neglected. Indeed, it was the patent absurdity and implausibility of much of what the Americans said that lent credence and persuasiveness to their mistrustful approach to the ideas. Once this exaggerated and fanatical rhetoric was uncovered by the Progressive historians, it should not have subsequently been ignored—no matter how much it may have impugned the reasonableness of the American response. No widely expressed ideas can be dismissed out of hand by the historian.

In his recent analysis of Revolutionary thinking, Bernard Bailyn has avoided the neo-Whig tendency to distort the historical reconstruction of the American mind. By comprehending "the assumptions, beliefs, and ideas that lay behind the manifest events of the time," Bailyn has attempted to get inside the Whigs' mind, and to experience vicariously all of what they thought and felt, both their rational constitutional beliefs and their hysterical and emotional ideas as well. The inflammatory phrases—"slavery," "corruption," "conspiracy"—that most historians had either ignored or readily dismissed as propaganda took on a new significance for Bailyn. He came "to suspect that they meant something very real to both the writers and their readers: that there were real fears, real anxieties, a sense of real danger behind these phrases, and not merely the desire to influence by rhetoric and propaganda the inert minds of an otherwise passive populace."[39] No part of American thinking, Bailyn suggests—not the widespread belief in a ministerial conspiracy, not the hostile and vicious indictments of individuals, not the fear of corruption and the hope for regeneration, not any of the violent seemingly absurd distortions and falsifications of what we now believe to be true, in short, none of the frenzied rhetoric—can be safely ignored by the historian seeking to understand the causes of the Revolution.

Bailyn's study, however, represents something other than a more complete and uncorrupted version of the common idealist interpretations of the Revolution. By viewing from the "interior" the Revolutionary pamphlets, which were "to an unusual degree, *explanatory*," revealing "not merely positions taken but the reasons why positions were taken," Bailyn like any idealist historian has sought to discover the motives the participants themselves gave for their actions, to reenact their thinking at crucial moments, and thereby to recapture some of the "unpredictable reality" of the Revolution.[40] But for Bailyn the very unpredictability of the reality he has disclosed has undermined the idealist obsession with explaining why, in the participants' own estimation, they acted as they did. Ideas emerge as more than explanatory devices, as more than indicators of motives. They become as well objects for analysis in and for themselves, historical events in their own right to be treated as other historical events are treated. Although Bailyn has examined the Revolutionary ideas subjectively from the inside, he has also analyzed them objectively from the outside. Thus, in addition to a contemporary Whig perspective, he presents us with a retrospective view of the ideas—their complexity, their development, and their consequences—that the actual participants did not have. In effect his essay represents what has been called "a Namierism of the history of ideas,"[41] a structural analysis of thought that suggests a conclusion about the movement of history not very different from Sir Lewis Namier's, where history becomes something "started in ridiculous beginnings, while small men did things both infinitely smaller and infinitely greater than they knew."[42]

In his *England in the Age of the American Revolution*, Namier attacked the Whig tendency to overrate "the importance of the conscious will and purpose in individuals." Above all he urged us "to ascertain and recognize the deeper irrelevancies and incoherence of human actions, which are not so much directed by reason, as invested by it *ex post facto* with the appearances of logic and rationality," to discover the unpredictable reality, where men's motives and intentions were lost in the accumulation and momentum of interacting events. The whole force of Namier's approach tended to squeeze the intellectual content out of what men did. Ideas setting forth principles and purposes for action, said Namier, did not count for much in the movement of history.[43]

In his study of the Revolutionary ideas, Bailyn has come to an opposite conclusion: ideas counted for a great deal, not only being responsible for the Revolution but also for transforming the character of American society. Yet in his hands ideas lose that static quality they have commonly had for the Whig historians, the simple statements of intention that so exasperated Namier. For Bailyn the ideas of the Revolutionaries take on an elusive and unmanageable quality, a dynamic self-intensifying character that transcended the intentions and desires of any of the historical participants. By emphasizing how the thought of the colonists was "strangely reshaped, turned in unfamiliar directions," by describing how the Americans "indeliberately, half-knowingly" groped toward "conclusions they could not themselves clearly perceive," by demonstrating how new beliefs and hence new actions were the responses not to desire but to the logic of developing situations, Bailyn has wrested the explanation of the Revolution out of the realm of motivation in which the neo-Whig historians had confined it.

With this kind of approach to ideas, the degree of consistency and devotion to principles become less important, and indeed the major issues of motivation and responsibility over which historians have disagreed become largely irrelevant. Action becomes not the product of rational and conscious calculation but of dimly perceived and rapidly changing thoughts and situations, "where the familiar meaning of ideas and words faded away into confusion, and leaders felt themselves peering into a haze, seeking to bring shifting conceptions somehow into focus." Men become more the victims than the manipulators of their ideas, as their thought unfolds in ways few anticipated, "rapid, irreversible, and irresistible," creating new problems, new considerations, new ideas, which have their own unforeseen implications. In this kind of atmosphere the Revolution, not at first desired by the Americans, takes on something of an inevitable character, moving through a process of escalation into levels few had intended or perceived. It no longer makes sense to assign motives or responsibility to particular individuals for the totality of what happened. Men were involved in a complicated web of phenomena, ideas, and situations from which in retrospect escape seems impossible.[44]

By seeking to uncover the motives of the Americans expressed in the Revolutionary pamphlets, Bailyn has ended by demonstrating the autonomy of ideas as phenomena, where the ideas operate, as it were, over the heads of the participants, taking them in directions no one could have foreseen. His discussion of Revolutionary thought thus represents a move back to a deterministic approach to the Revolution, a determinism, however, which is different from that which the neo-Whig historians have so recently and self-consciously abandoned. Yet while the suggested determinism is thoroughly idealist—indeed, never before has the force of ideas in bringing on the Revolution been so emphatically put—its implications are not. By helping to purge our writing about the Revolution of its concentration on constitutional principles and its stifling judicial-like preoccupation with motivation and responsibility, the study serves to open the way for new questions and new appraisals. In fact, it is out of the very completeness of his idealist interpretation, out of his exposition of the extraordinary nature—the very dynamism and emotionalism—of the Americans' thought that we have the evidence for an entirely different, a behaviorist, perspective on the causes of the American Revolution. Bailyn's book-length introduction to his edition of Revolutionary pamphlets is therefore not only a point of fulfillment for the idealist approach to the Revolution, it is also a point of departure for a new look at the social sources of the Revolution.

IT SEEMS CLEAR that historians of eighteenth-century America and the Revolution cannot ignore the force of ideas in history to the extent that Namier and his students have done in their investigations of eighteenth-century English politics. This is not to say, however, that the Namier approach to English politics has been crucially limiting and distorting. Rather it may suggest that the Namier denigration of ideas and principles is inapplicable for American politics because the American social situation in which ideas operated was very different from that of eighteenth-century England. It may be that ideas are less meaningful to a people in a socially stable situation. Only when ideas have become stereotyped reflexes do evasion and hypocrisy and the Namier mistrust of what men believe become significant. Only in a relatively settled society does ideology become a kind of habit, a bundle of widely shared and instinctive conventions, offering ready-made explanations for men who are not being compelled to ask any serious questions. Conversely, it is perhaps only in a relatively unsettled, disordered society, where the questions come faster than men's answers, that ideas become truly vital and creative.[45]

Paradoxically it may be the very vitality of the Americans' ideas, then, that suggests the need to examine the circumstances in which they flourished. Since ideas and beliefs are ways of perceiving and explaining the world, the nature of the ideas expressed is determined as much by the character of the world being confronted as by the internal development of inherited and borrowed conceptions. Out of the multitude of inherited and transmitted ideas available in the eighteenth century, Americans selected and emphasized those which seemed to make meaningful what was happening to them. In the colonists' use of classical literature, for example, "their detailed knowledge and engaged interest covered only one era and one small group of writers": Plutarch, Livy, Cicero, Sallust, and

Tacitus—those who "had hated and feared the trends of their own time, and in their writing had contrasted the present with a better past, which they endowed with qualities absent from their own, corrupt era."[46] There was always, in Max Weber's term, some sort of elective affinity between the Americans' interests and their beliefs, and without that affinity their ideas would not have possessed the peculiar character and persuasiveness they did. Only the most revolutionary social needs and circumstances could have sustained such revolutionary ideas.[47]

When the ideas of the Americans are examined comprehensively, when all of the Whig rhetoric, irrational as well as rational, is taken into account, one cannot but be struck by the predominant characteristics of fear and frenzy, the exaggerations and the enthusiasm, the general sense of social corruption and disorder out of which would be born a new world of benevolence and harmony where Americans would become the "eminent examples of every divine and social virtue."[48] As Bailyn and the propaganda studies have amply shown, there is simply too much fanatical and millennial thinking even by the best minds that must be explained before we can characterize the Americans' ideas as peculiarly rational and legalistic and thus view the Revolution as merely a conservative defense of constitutional liberties. To isolate refined and nicely reasoned arguments from the writings of John Adams and Jefferson is not only to disregard the more inflamed expressions of the rest of the Whigs but also to overlook the enthusiastic extravagance—the paranoiac obsession with a diabolical crown conspiracy and the dream of a restored Saxon era—in the thinking of Adams and Jefferson themselves.

The ideas of the Americans seem, in fact, to form what can only be called a revolutionary syndrome. If we were to confine ourselves to examining the Revolutionary rhetoric alone, apart from what happened politically or socially, it would be virtually impossible to distinguish the American Revolution from any other revolution in modern Western history. In the kinds of ideas expressed, the American Revolution is remarkably similar to the seventeenth-century Puritan Revolution and to the eighteenth-century French Revolution: the same general disgust with a chaotic and corrupt world, the same anxious and angry bombast, the same excited fears of conspiracies by depraved men, the same utopian hopes for the construction of a new and virtuous order.[49] It was not that this syndrome of ideas was simply transmitted from one generation or from one people to another. It was rather perhaps that similar, though hardly identical, social situations called forth within the limitations of inherited and available conceptions similar modes of expression. Although we need to know much more about the sociology of revolutions and collective movements, it does seem possible that particular patterns of thought, particular forms of expression, correspond to certain basic social experiences. There may be, in other words, typical modes of expression, typical kinds of beliefs and values, characterizing a revolutionary situation, at least within roughly similar Western societies. Indeed, the types of ideas manifested may be the best way of identifying a collective movement as a revolution. As one student of revolutions writes, "It is on the basis of a knowledge of men's beliefs that we can distinguish their behavior from riot, rebellion or insanity."[50]

It is thus the very nature of the Americans' rhetoric—its obsession with corruption and disorder, its hostile and conspiratorial outlook, and its millennial vision of a regenerated society—that reveals, as nothing else apparently can, the American Revolution as a true revolution with its sources lying deep in the social structure. For this kind of frenzied rhetoric could spring only from the most severe sorts of social strain. The grandiose and feverish language of the Americans was indeed the natural, even the inevitable, expression of a people caught up in a revolutionary situation, deeply alienated from the existing sources of authority and vehemently involved in a basic reconstruction of their political and social order. The hysteria of the Americans' thinking was but a measure of the intensity of their revolutionary passions. Undoubtedly the growing American alienation from British authority contributed greatly to this revolutionary situation. Yet the very weakness of the British imperial system and the accumulating ferocity of American antagonism to it suggests that other sources of social strain were being fed into the revolutionary movement. It may be that the Progressive historians, in their preoccupation with internal social problems, were more right than we have recently been willing to grant. It would be repeating their mistake, however, to expect this internal social strain necessarily to take the form of coherent class conflict or overt social disruption. The sources of revolutionary social stress may have been much more subtle but no less severe.

Of all of the colonies in the mid-eighteenth century, Virginia seems the most settled, the most lacking in obvious social tensions. Therefore, as it has been recently argued, since conspicuous social issues were nonexistent, the only plausible remaining explanation for the Virginians' energetic and almost unanimous commitment to the Revolution must have been their devotion to constitutional principles.[51] Yet it may be that we have been looking for the wrong kinds of social issues, for organized conflicts, for conscious divisions, within the society. It seems clear that Virginia's difficulties were not the consequence of any obvious sectional or class antagonism, Tidewater versus Piedmont, aristocratic planters versus yeoman farmers. There was apparently no discontent with the political system that went deep into the social structure. But there does seem to have been something of a social crisis within the ruling group itself, which intensely aggravated the Virginians' antagonism to the imperial system. Contrary to the impression of confidence and stability that the Virginia planters have historically acquired, they seemed to have been in very uneasy circumstances in the years before the Revolution. The signs of the eventual nineteenth-century decline of the Virginia gentry were, in other words, already felt if not readily apparent.

The planters' ability to command the acquiescence of the people seems extraordinary compared to the unstable politics of the other colonies. But in the years before independence there were signs of increasing anxiety among the gentry over their representative role. The ambiguities in the relationship between the burgesses and their constituents erupted into open debate in the 1750s. And men began voicing more and more concern over the mounting costs of elections and growing corruption in the soliciting of votes, especially by "those who have neither natural nor acquired parts to recommend them."[52] By the late sixties and early seventies the newspapers were filled with warnings against electoral influence, bribery, and vote seeking. The freeholders were stridently urged to "strike at the Root of this growing Evil; be influenced by Merit alone," and avoid electing "obscure and inferior persons."[53] It was as if ignoble ambition and demagoguery, one bitter pamphlet remarked, were a "Daemon lately come among us to disturb the peace and harmony, which had so long subsisted in this place."[54] In this context, Robert Munford's famous play *The Candidates*, written in 1770, does not so much confirm the planters' confidence as it betrays their uneasiness with electoral developments in the colony, "when coxcombs and jockies can impose themselves upon it for men of learning." Although disinterested virtue eventually wins out, Munford's satire reveals the kinds of threats the established planters faced from ambitious knaves and blockheads who were turning representatives into slaves of the people.[55]

By the eve of the Revolution, the planters were voicing a growing sense of impending ruin, whose sources seemed in the minds of many to be linked more and more with the corrupting British connection and the Scottish factors but for others frighteningly rooted in "our Pride, our Luxury, and Idleness."[56] The public and private writings of Virginians became obsessed with "corruption," "virtue," and "luxury." The increasing defections from the Church of England, even among ministers and vestrymen, and the remarkable growth of dissent in the years before the Revolution, "so much complained of in many parts of the colony," further suggests some sort of social stress. The strange religious conversions of Robert Carter may represent only the most dramatic example of what was taking place less frenziedly elsewhere among the gentry.[57] By the middle of the eighteenth century it was evident that many of the planters were living on the edge of bankruptcy, seriously overextended and spending beyond their means in an almost frantic effort to fulfill the aristocratic image they had created of themselves.[58] Perhaps the importance of the Robinson affair in the 1760s lies not in any constitutional changes that resulted but in the shattering effect the disclosures had on that virtuous image.[59] Some of the planters expressed openly their fears for the future, seeing the products of their lives being destroyed in the reckless gambling and drinking of their heirs, who, as Landon Carter put it, "play away and play it all away."[60]

The Revolution in Virginia, "produced by the wantonness of the Gentleman," as one planter suggested,[61] undoubtedly gained much of its force from this social crisis within the gentry. Certainly more was expected from the Revolution than simply a break from British imperialism, and it was not any crude avoidance of British debts.[62] The Revolutionary reforms, like the abolition of entail and primogeniture, may have signified something other than mere symbolic legal adjustments to an existing reality. In addition to being an attempt to make the older Tidewater plantations more economically competitive with lands farther west, the reforms may have represented a real effort to redirect what was believed to be a dangerous tendency in social and family development within the ruling gentry. The Virginians were not after all aristocrats who could afford having their entailed families' estates in the hands of weak or ineffectual eldest sons. Entail, as the preamble to the 1776 act abolishing it stated, had often done "injury to the morals of youth by rendering them independent of, and disobedient to, their parents."[63] There was too much likelihood, as the Nelson family sadly demonstrated, that a single wayward generation would virtually wipe out what had been so painstakingly built.[64] George Mason bespoke the anxieties of many Virginians when he warned the Philadelphia Convention in 1787 that "our own Children will in a short time be among the general mass."[65]

Precisely how the strains within Virginia society contributed to the creation of a revolutionary situation and in what way the planters expected independence and republicanism to alleviate their problems, of course, need to be fully explored. It seems clear, however, from the very nature of the ideas expressed that the sources of the Revolution in Virginia were much more subtle and complicated than a simple antagonism to the British government. Constitutional principles alone do not explain the Virginians' almost unanimous determination to revolt. And if the

Revolution in the seemingly stable colony of Virginia possessed internal social roots, it is to be expected that the other colonies were experiencing their own forms of social strain that in a like manner sought mitigation through revolution and republicanism.

It is through the Whigs' ideas, then, that we may be led back to take up where the Progressive historians left off in their investigation of the internal social sources of the Revolution. By working through the ideas— by reading them imaginatively and relating them to the objective social world they both reflected and confronted—we may be able to eliminate the unrewarding distinction between conscious and unconscious motives, and eventually thereby to combine a Whig with a Tory (an idealist with a behaviorist) interpretation. For the ideas, the rhetoric, of the Americans was never obscuring but remarkably revealing of their deepest interests and passions. What they expressed may not have been for the most part factually true, but it was always psychologically true. In this sense their rhetoric was never detached from the social and political reality; and indeed it becomes the best entry into an understanding of that reality. Their repeated overstatements of reality, their incessant talk of "tyranny" when there seems to have been no real oppression, their obsession with "virtue," "luxury," and "corruption," their devotion to "liberty" and "equality"—all these notions were neither manipulated propaganda nor borrowed empty abstractions, but ideas with real personal and social significance for those who used them. Propaganda could never move men to revolution. No popular leader, as John Adams put it, has ever been able "to persuade a large people, for any length of time together, to think themselves wronged, injured, and oppressed unless they really were, and saw and felt it to be so."[66] The ideas had relevance; the sense of oppression and injury, although often displaced onto the imperial system, was nonetheless real. It was indeed the meaningfulness of the connection between what the Americans said and what they felt that gave the ideas their propulsive force and their overwhelming persuasiveness.

It is precisely the remarkable revolutionary character of the Americans' ideas now being revealed by historians that best indicates that something profoundly unsettling was going on in the society, that raises the question, as it did for the Progressive historians, why the Americans should have expressed such thoughts. With their crude conception of propaganda, the Progressive historians at least attempted to grapple with the problem. Since we cannot regard the ideas of the Revolutionaries as simply propaganda, the question still remains to be answered. "When 'ideas' in full cry drive past," wrote Arthur F. Bentley in his classic behavioral study *The Process of Government*, "the thing to do with them is to accept them as an indication that something is happening; and then search carefully to find out what it really is they stand for, what the factors of the social life are that are expressing themselves through the ideas."[67] Precisely because they sought to understand both the Revolutionary ideas and American society, the behaviorist historians of the Progressive generation, for all of their crude conceptualizations, their obsession with "class" and hidden economic interests, and their treatment of ideas as propaganda, have still offered us an explanation of the Revolutionary era so powerful and so comprehensive that no purely intellectual interpretation will ever replace it.

AFTERWORD TO CHAPTER I

If the tendency of subsequent scholarship is any indication, this 1966 article—my first publication in early American history—seems to have had very little influence on the historical profession. Much of the scholarship on the Revolution during the several decades following its publication ignored the "reality" of American society and instead concentrated very heavily on the "rhetoric" of the Revolution, which was by and large equated with something called "republicanism." I suppose my book *The Creation of the American Republic, 1776–1787* (1969) contributed its share to the so-called republican synthesis that emerged in the 1970s and 1980s to become something of a monster that threatened to devour us all. My article, however, was supposed to tame the monster before it was unleashed.

When I wrote the "Rhetoric and Reality" piece, I had already essentially completed my *Creation of the American Republic*, even though the book was published several years later. In that book I never intended to argue that the Revolution was fundamentally an "ideological" movement, or that the Revolution could be explained solely in "ideological" terms. Indeed, as I have pointed out in the introduction to this collection, I have never thought that one could explain anything fully by referring only to the beliefs of people. In writing the article I was well aware of the powerful implications of Bernard Bailyn's introduction to his *Pamphlets of the American Revolution*, which had just been published in 1965 and which would eventually become *The Ideological Origins of the American Revolution* (1967). As shatteringly important as I knew Bailyn's work to be, I nevertheless thought it tried to explain the Revolution too much in terms of the professed beliefs of the participants. Thus I wrote the "Rhetoric and Reality" article as a corrective to the idealist tendency I saw in the neo-Whig historical literature of the 1950s and early 1960s that I believed had climaxed with Bailyn's stunning work. Without denying in any way the significance of ideas (after all, I had just completed a book on the political thought of the Revolution), I simply tried to urge historians not to get too carried away with exclusively intellectual explanations of the Revolution. If we were ultimately to see the Revolution whole—from both the top and from the bottom—then, I suggested, we had to examine its social sources as well.

The problem with such a suggestion was that it too easily reinforced the traditional assumptions of neo-Progressive social history, which, as I indicated in my introduction, tended to create polarities of ideas versus behavior, rhetoric versus reality. Despite my perverse and misguided title, I wrote my article as a protest against just such dualities, against such sharp separations of ideas from social circumstances. I wanted to acknowledge the importance of both ideas and underlying psychological and social determinants in shaping human behavior and yet avoid returning to the crude neo-Progressive polarities of the past made famous by such historians as Charles Beard. In parts of my *Creation of the American Republic*, I tried to do just that, which is probably why so many historians could not decide what school of historical interpretation that book put me in.

Although cultural history of one sort or another has seized the day during the past generation (even the Marxists now write only cultural history), several historians have explicitly attempted to explore the linkages between culture and society that I suggested existed in the relatively stable colony of Virginia. Rhys Isaac, in his *Transformation of Virginia*, T. H. Breen in his *Tobacco Culture*, Richard R. Beeman in his study of Lunenburg County, and Jack P. Greene in several articles have all sought to relate social developments in Virginia to the ideology of the Revolution.[1]

Although these works are very different, they are imaginative examples of what might be done. History that recognizes the importance of both culture and society and both consciousness and underlying social and material circumstances is ultimately the kind of history we need to write.

CHAPTER TWO

The LEGACY of ROME
in the AMERICAN REVOLUTION

HE LATE EIGHTEENTH CENTURY in the Atlantic world has been called "the age of the democratic revolution." It might better be called "the age of the republican revolution." For it was republicanism and republican principles, not democracy, that brought down the ancient monarchies.[1]

It was an astonishing moment in Western history, and we are living with its effects still. Monarchies that had existed for centuries were suddenly overthrown and replaced by new republican governments. Since republican governments have become so natural and normal for most of the world in the early twenty-first century, it is hard to recover the surprisingly novel and radical character of those eighteenth-century republican revolutions. In the eighteenth century, monarchy was still the standard for most people, and, as events in our own time demonstrate, there was always something to be said for large and diverse countries being ruled from the top by a single authority. Monarchy had history on its side; the kings of Europe had spent centuries consolidating their authority over unruly nobles and disparate peoples. The Bible endorsed kingship. Had not the ancient Israelites proclaimed that "we will have a king over us; that we . . . may be like all the nations"?[2]

Since most people in the Atlantic world and elsewhere had lived with kings for all of their recorded histories, why in the late eighteenth century should these kings have been so suddenly overthrown by republican revolutions? Why, as John Adams wondered in 1776, should "[i]dolatry to Monarchs, and servility to Aristocratical Pride [be] so totally eradicated from so many minds in so short a Time"?[3] If change were inevitable, why should republicanism have been chosen as the alternative to the ancien régimes? There were political and constitutional changes short of establishing republics that could have been tried. Hereditary lines could have been shifted; new kings could have been set upon the thrones. After all, the English in their Glorious Revolution in 1688–1689 and in their constitutional adjustment in 1714 had not abolished monarchy; they merely had found new heirs to the crown and placed some new limits on their king. Besides, during the seventeenth century the English had already tried a brief experiment in republicanism, and it had ended in disaster and dictatorship. Why would anyone want to try such an experiment again? The tiny self-proclaimed republics that did exist in eighteenth-century Europe—the Swiss cantons, the Italian city-states, and the Dutch provinces—were in various stages of confusion and decay and were very unlikely models for the large and populous countries of the Western world. Why would any state—either the sprawling provinces of British North America or the conglomeration that constituted the ancien régime of France—want to emulate them?

Amidst this monarchy-dominated culture, however, there was one republican model that did seem worth emulating—one republic that had achieved in glory and fame all that any people anywhere could ever hope for. And that republic was ancient Rome. While the eighteenth century was not much interested in the past, antiquity was the exception; no modern era has ever invested so much in the classical past. And although all the ancient republics—Athens, Sparta, Thebes—were familiar to educated people in the eighteenth century (their names had "grown trite by repetition," said one American), none was more familiar than that of Rome. People could not hear enough about it. "It was impossible," said

Montesquieu, "to be tired of as agreeable a subject as ancient Rome." There was nothing startling about Edward Gibbon's choice of subject for his great history. "Rome," he wrote in his *Autobiography*, "is familiar to the schoolboy and the statesman." To be educated in the eighteenth century was to know about Rome; Latin, as John Locke had said, was still regarded as "absolutely necessary to a gentleman."[4]

If any one cultural source lay behind the republican revolutions of the eighteenth century, it was ancient Rome—republican Rome—and the values that flowed from its history. It was ancient Rome's legacy that helped to make the late eighteenth century's apparently sudden transition to republicanism possible. If the eighteenth-century Enlightenment was, as Peter Gay has called it, "the rise of modern paganism," then classical republicanism was its creed.[5] To be enlightened was to be interested in antiquity, and to be interested in antiquity was to be interested in republicanism. Certainly classical antiquity could offer meaningful messages for monarchy too, but there is no doubt that the thrust of what the ancient world, and particularly Rome, had to say to the eighteenth century was latently and at times manifestly republican.

If the Enlightenment was to discover the sources of a flourishing society and human happiness, it was important to learn what lay behind the ascendency of republican Rome and its eventual decline and fall. The French and American revolutionaries' view of the ancient past was therefore very selective, focusing on the moral and social basis of politics and on social degeneracy and corruption. Since the eighteenth century believed that "similar causes will forever operate like effects in the political, moral, and physical world," the history of antiquity inevitably became a kind of laboratory in which autopsies of the dead republics, especially Rome, would lead to a science of political sickness and health—"political pathology," one American called it—matching the medical science of the natural world.[6]

It was the writings of the golden age of Latin literature that fascinated the eighteenth-century Enlightenment, preoccupied as it was with cyclical history and the decline and fall of the Roman republic. These

Roman writings of the Enlightenment spanned the two centuries from the breakdown of the republic in the middle of the first century B.C. to the reign of Marcus Aurelius in the middle of the second century A.D. Together with the Greek Plutarch, the Roman authors of this literature—Cicero, Sallust, Livy, Virgil, Tacitus—set forth republican ideals and values about politics and society that have had a powerful and lasting effect on Western culture. Writing at a time when the greatest days of the Roman republic were crumbling or were already gone, these Latin writers contrasted the growing corruption, luxury, and disorder they saw about them with an imagined earlier republican world of ordered simplicity and Arcadian virtue and sought to explain why the republic had withered and decayed.[7]

These classical ideals and values were revived and refurbished by the Italian Renaissance—becoming what has been variously called "civic humanism" or "classical republicanism"—and were carried into early modern Europe and made available in the seventeenth and eighteenth centuries to wider and deeper strata of the population, which rarely possessed an original or unglossed antiquity; they often saw a refracted image of the vanished republic, saw the classical past and classical values as Machiavelli and the Renaissance had passed them on. While some in the English-speaking world did own and read the ancient authors in Latin, most generally preferred translations, popularizations, and secondary surveys such as Thomas Gordon's *Sallust* and *Tacitus*, Basil Kennett's *Roman Antiquities*, Walter Moyle's dabblings in antiquity, Charles Rollin's popular histories, Thomas Blackwell's *Memoirs of the Court of Augustus*, Oliver Goldsmith's history of Rome, and Edward Wortley Montagu's *Reflections on the Rise and Fall of the Antient Republicks*. By the eighteenth century, monarchical culture in Europe and particularly in Great Britain was thoroughly infused with these republican writings and their classical values and to that extent at least was already republicanized.[8]

The source of monarchy's destruction and replacement by republicanism in the late eighteenth century was already present several generations earlier. Consequently, monarchy was not supplanted by republicanism all at once—not in 1776 with the Declaration of Independence, not in 1789 with the calling of the Estates General, not even in 1792–1793 with the National Convention's proclamation of the republic and the execution of Louis XVI. The change came before these events, and slowly. Classical republican values ate away at monarchy—corroding it, gradually, steadily—for much of the eighteenth century. Republicanism seeped everywhere in the eighteenth-century Atlantic world, eroding monarchical society from within, wearing away all the traditional supports of kingship, ultimately desacralizing monarchy in France and America to the point where, as David Hume observed, "the mere name of king commands little respect; and to talk of a king as God's vice-regent upon earth, or to give him any of these magnificent titles which formerly dazzled mankind, would but excite laughter in everyone."[9]

Of course, the French and English subscribed to these classical republican values with varying degrees of intensity, and the term "republican" remained pejorative, something to hang on the head of an opponent in order to damage his credibility, if not his loyalty to the crown. Nevertheless, what is remarkable is the extent to which the thinking of the educated eighteenth-century French and English on both sides of the Atlantic was republicanized in substance, if not in name. It is true that many thinkers, such as Montesquieu, Mably, and Rousseau, despite their admiration for ancient Rome, conceded that a country like France was too large to become a republic. But some, like Mme. Roland, actually confessed that reading Plutarch "had disposed me to become a republican; he had aroused in me that force and pride which give republicanism its character, and he had inspired in me a veritable enthusiasm for the public virtues and for liberty."[10] Although most others were reluctant to admit to being republican, some responded as did the editor of the *South Carolina Gazette*, Peter Timothy, in 1749 when he was denounced as a republican for publishing *Cato's Letters*: he was not a "Republican . . . ," Timothy said, "unless Virtue and Truth be Republican."[11]

These classical ideals, this vision of what James Thomson in his Whig poem "Liberty" called "old virtuous Rome," thus became the best means by which the disgruntled French and dissatisfied Britons on both sides of the Atlantic could voice their objections to the luxury, selfishness, and corruption of the monarchical world in which they lived.[12] Although the intellectuals and critics who invoked republican principles and classical values were opposed to the practices and values of the dominant monarchical world, few of them actually intended to foment revolution and overthrow monarchy. They sought to reform and revitalize their society and to enlighten and improve monarchical rule, not cut off the heads of kings. These critics and many others—including good, loyal colonial subjects of His Britannic Majesty—used republicanism of classical antiquity merely as a counterculture to monarchy. Though rarely cited specifically by name, classical republicanism represented all those beliefs and values that confronted and criticized the abuses of the eighteenth-century monarchical world.

Monarchical and republican values therefore existed side by side in the culture, and many good monarchists, including many good English Tories, adopted what were in substance if not in name republican ideals and principles without realizing the long-run political implications of what they were doing. Although they seldom mentioned the term, educated people of varying political persuasions celebrated classical republicanism for its spirit, its morality, its freedom, its sense of friendship and duty, and its georgic vision of the good society. Classical republicanism as a set of values, an explanation of history, and a form of life was much too pervasive, comprehensive, and involved with being liberal and enlightened to be seen as subversive or as antimonarchical.

Instead of being some thin eddy that ran only on the edges of British or European culture, this classical republicanism thus became an important current in its own right that blended and mingled with the monarchical mainstream and influenced its color, tone, and direction. Eighteenth-century republicanism did not so much displace monarchy as transform it. At times it became virtually indistinguishable from monarchy. Certainly it came to stand for something other than a set of political institutions based on popular election. In fact, republicanism was not to be reduced to a mere form of government at all; instead it was what Franco Venturi has called "a form of life," classical ideals and values that were entirely compatible with monarchical institutions. Republicanism "was separated from the historical forms it had taken in the past, and became increasingly an ideal which could exist in a monarchy."[13]

This republicanism rooted in the Latin writings of ancient Rome was thus never a besieged underground ideology, confined to cellar meetings and marginal intellectuals. On the contrary: kings themselves participated in the cult of antiquity. While reading a passage from Livy's Roman history to the artist Benjamin West, George III suggested to West that he paint *The Departure of Regulus* (1767) as an example of self-sacrificial patriotism. The archbishop of York likewise requested a classical painting from West, drawing on a passage from Tacitus. There were no more enthusiastic promoters of classical republicanism than many members of the English and French nobility, who were presumably closest to monarchy and whose privileges depended upon it. All those French nobles who in 1785 flocked to the Paris salon to ooh and aah over Jacques-Louis David's severe classical painting *The Oath of the Horatii* had no idea they were contributing to the weakening of monarchy and their own demise. Likewise, all those aristocratic sponsors of the 1730 edition of James Thomson's Virgilian-derived georgic poem "The Seasons"—including the queen, ten dukes, thirty-one earls and countesses, and a larger number of the lesser peerage and their sons and daughters—little sensed that their celebration of agricultural simplicity and rural virtue was contributing to the erosion of the monarchical values that made their dominance possible. When even hereditary aristocrats, "disclaiming as it were [their] birthright, and putting [themselves] upon the foot of a Roman," could subscribe enthusiastically to the view voiced by Conyers Middleton in his *Life of Cicero* (1741) that "no man, howsoever born, could arrive at any dignity, who did not win it by his personal merit," then we know something of the power of these republican sentiments in the culture. "Radical chic" was not an invention of the twentieth century.[14]

No culture in the Western world was more republicanized than that of

England and its North American colonies. The literature of the first half of the eighteenth century in the English-speaking world—both belles lettres and political polemics—was a literature of social criticism, and this social criticism was steeped in classical republican values. Most English writers of the period—whether Tory satirists like Pope and Swift or radical Whig publicists like John Trenchard and Thomas Gordon—expressed a deep and bitter hostility to the great social, economic, and political changes taking place in England during the decades following the Glorious Revolution of 1688. The rise of banks, trading companies, and stock markets, plus the emergence of new moneyed men, the increasing public debt, and the corruption of politics all threatened traditional values and led opposition poets and polemicists alike to set classical models and morality against the spreading luxury and commercialization. They knew from the experience of ancient Rome that the same energy that produced a country's rise eventually caused an excess of wealth and luxury that in turn led to its inevitable fall.[15]

Classical republican Rome, like some South Sea tribes for twentieth-century anthropologists, became the means by which the enlightened eighteenth-century English could distance themselves from their own society and criticize it. Gibbon admired Juvenal because the Roman satirist refused to surrender his republican ideals in the face of monarchical realities. He had, said Gibbon, "the soul of a republican" and was "the sworn enemy of tyranny." Thus Dr. Johnson found that the best way to condemn the corruption of eighteenth-century London was to imitate Juvenal's third satire on Nero's Rome.[16]

So pervasive, so dominant was this literature of social criticism that it is difficult to find anything substantial that stood against it. All the great eighteenth-century British writers spoke in republican tones. The long administration of Sir Robert Walpole (1722–1742) eventually united in intellectual opposition all of what William Pulteney called "the gay, the polite and witty Part of the World"; and that opposition, whether from the Tory John Gay in *The Beggar's Opera* or the Whig James Thomson in his poem "Liberty," inevitably drew on classical republican values to voice its love of freedom and its antagonism to corruption. Hume in 1742 thought that more than half of what had been written during the previous twenty years had been devoted to satirizing the machinations of Walpole, the figure who seemed most responsible for what ailed Britain. One administration defender in 1731 concluded that, simply for the sake of getting at Walpole, "the whole nation hath been abused, Corruption and Degeneracy universally charged." All the country-opposition citations to Roman writers were moral strictures against a polluted court, and as such they were often unwitting celebrations of republican values. Consequently, it is virtually impossible to separate the country-opposition tradition, which included radical Whigs and estranged Tories, from this republican heritage of antiquity, so intertwined were they.

Although some Englishmen in the late seventeenth century had found in the age of Augustus a model of restored stability where the arts were allowed to flourish, most after 1688—even aristocrats close to the court—criticized Augustus and looked to the Roman republic for values and inspiration. Cicero and Cato, not Augustus, were the Romans to be admired. To Voltaire, Augustus was "*ce poltron qui osa exiler Ovide*" ("this coward who dared to exile Ovid"). For Jefferson, Augustus was always that "parricide scoundrel." Augustus, Montesquieu said, had led the Romans "gently into slavery," and most Englishmen agreed. Augustus became a code word for tyrant, and as such he was attacked by nearly everyone except royal absolutists. The Tories, thinking of George I, called Augustus a despot, but the court Whigs and all defenders of the Hanoverian settlement, thinking of the Stuarts, did likewise.

From 1688 on, the need for the government to defend the Whig settlement and to attack the Stuart pretensions to the crown meant that a quasirepublican, antiroyalist bias was necessarily built into the official center of English culture. During Walpole's era, both court and country writers alike condemned Augustus as an imperial dictator, the murderer of Cicero, and the destroyer of the republic. If Virgil and Horace were tainted by their too-close association with, in Gibbon's words, "the crafty tyrant," then it had to be argued, as Thomas Blackwell and Thomas Sheridan did, that these great Augustan poets were really republican in spirit, that their talent had actually been formed under the republican era that preceded Augustus's monarchical takeover.

From Addison to Dr. Johnson, English intellectuals expressed their admiration for Tacitus's anti-Augustan, prorepublican view of Roman history. Tacitus remained for Jefferson "the first writer in the world without a single exception." Thomas Gordon originally dedicated his edition of *Tacitus* to Walpole, his patron, but the work so fully expressed a republican antagonism toward Augustus ("the best of his Government was but the sunshine of Tyranny") that it was celebrated by English commonwealthmen as well. David Hume thought that even the Tories had been so long obliged to talk "in the republican stile" that they had at length "embraced the sentiments as well as the language of their adversaries."[17]

These appeals to antiquity made anything other than a classical conception of leadership difficult to justify. All political leaders were measured by the ancient republicans:

> You then whose Judgment the right Course wou'd steer,
> Know well each ANCIENT's proper Character,
> His Fable, Subject, Scope in ev'ry Page,
> Religion, Country, Genius, of his Age.[18]

SO ALEXANDER POPE TOLD HIS countrymen, and nearly every gentleman agreed. It was almost always classical standards—Catonic and Ciceronian standards—that British opposition writers invoked to judge the ragged world of eighteenth-century politics. They all placed the character of classical republicanism—integrity, virtue, and disinterestedness—at the center of public life.[19]

Although these classical republican ideals were set within a monarchical framework, they nonetheless established the foundations not only for liberal arts education and for political debate in the English-speaking world but also for what a good society ought to be. The writings of classical antiquity thus provided more than scholarly embellishment and window dressing for educated Britons on both sides of the Atlantic; they were in fact the principal source of their public morality and values. All political morality was classical morality; people could not read enough about Cato and Cicero. Every lawyer aspired to be another Cicero, and Cato—well, there was no ancient hero like him. Addison's play *Cato* was one of the most popular in the English-speaking world; Thomas Gray even declared it to be a better model for English tragedy than anything by Shakespeare.[20] In America the play went through at least eight editions before 1800. George Washington saw it over and over and incorporated its lines into his correspondence; he learned from it what it was to be a stoical classical hero and an uncorrupt public leader.

The classical past helped to form much of eighteenth-century political theory in the English-speaking world—from the ideal of balanced government to the conception of virtuous citizenship. According to the antique republican tradition, man was by nature a political being, a citizen who achieved his greatest moral fulfillment by participating in a self-governing republic. Public or political liberty—or what we now call positive liberty—meant participation in government. And this political liberty in turn provided the means by which the personal liberty and private rights of the individual—what we today call negative liberty—were protected. In this classical republican tradition, our modern distinction between positive and negative liberties was not yet clearly perceived, and the two forms of liberty were still often seen as one.[21]

Of course, the English did not need ancient Rome to tell them about liberty—at least, not about negative liberty. An acute sense of their liberties and rights, expressed and reinforced by their common law, had been a central part of their culture from time immemorial—from before the Norman conquest and, some said, from before the Roman invasion. Yet however little the classical republican conception of liberty may have affected English law and culture on the home island, it did have important effects on some of the North American colonists. To the extent that colonial Americans' thinking about liberty was affected by the classical past and made positive and republicanized, so was liberty made compatible with the maintenance of slavery. The ancient Romans, after all, had seen no inconsistency between their love of liberty and their practice of slavery; indeed, the labor of their slaves was what made possible their liberty—that is, their independence and their participation in government. All of this made the slaveholding Southern planters of America extraordinarily receptive to classical republicanism.

This kind of positive liberty was realized when the citizens were virtuous—that is, willing to sacrifice their private interests for the sake of the community, including serving in public office without pecuniary rewards. This virtue could be found only in a republic of equal, active, and independent citizens. To be completely virtuous citizens, men—never women, because it was assumed they were never independent—had to be free from dependence, and from the petty interests of the marketplace. Any loss of independence and virtue was corruption.

The virtue that classical republicanism encouraged was public virtue. Private virtues such as prudence, frugality, and industry were important but, said Hume, they only made men "serviceable to themselves, and enable them to promote their own interest"; they were not "such as make them perform their part in society." Public virtue was the sacrifice of private desires and interests for the public interest. It was devotion to the commonweal. All men of genius and leisure, all gentlemen, had an obligation to serve the state. "Let not your love of philosophical amusements have more than its due weight with you," Benjamin Franklin admonished the New York royal official Cadwallader Colden in 1750. Public service was far more important than science. In fact, said Franklin, even "the finest" of Newton's "Discoveries" could not have excused his neglect of serving the commonwealth if the public had needed him.[22]

The power of the ancient Roman republic had flowed from the freedom of its citizens to govern themselves. But as Rome's fate showed, republics required a high degree of civic virtue and disinterestedness among their citizens, and thus they were very fragile polities, extremely liable to corruption. Republics demanded far more morally from their citizens than monarchies did of their subjects. In monarchies each man's desire to do what was right in his own eyes could be restrained by fear or force, by patronage or honor. In republics, however, each man somehow had to be persuaded to sacrifice his personal desires, his luxuries, for the sake of the public good. Monarchies could tolerate great degrees of self-interestedness, private gratification, and corruption among their subjects. After all, they were based on dependence and subservience and had all sorts of adhesives and connections besides virtue to hold their societies together. Monarchies relied on blood, family, kinship, patronage, and—ultimately—fear, as one loyalist clergyman in western Massachusetts tried to make clear to several of his neighbors who were thinking of taking up arms against their king in 1775. Do not do it, the cleric warned. "The king can send a company of horse through the country and take off every head; and in less than six weeks you will be glad to labor a week for sheep's head and pluck."[23] But republics could never resort to such force. In their purest form they had no adhesives, no bonds holding themselves together, except their citizens' voluntary patriotism and willingness to obey public authority. Without virtue and self-sacrifice, republics would fall apart.

One did not have to be a professed republican or a radical Whig, however, to believe in virtue and the other classical values that accompanied it. Virtue, along with the concept of honor, lay at the heart of all prescriptions for political leadership in the eighteenth-century English-speaking world.

If virtue was based on liberty and independence, then it followed that only autonomous individuals free from any ties of interest and paid by no master were qualified to be citizens. Jefferson and many other republican idealists hoped that all ordinary yeoman farmers who owned their own land and who depended for their subsistence only "on their own soil and industry" and not "on the casualties and caprice of customers" would be independent and free enough of pecuniary temptations and market-place interests to be virtuous.[24]

Others, however, questioned the capacity of most ordinary people to rise above self-interest, particularly those who were dependent on "the casualties and caprice of customers." No doubt Cicero and other ancients believed that everyone was born to seek what was morally right, and that this heritage reinforced the moral sense philosophy of the eighteenth century that formed a basis for the eventual emergence of democracy. Indeed, Jefferson's famous aphorism about a ploughman knowing right from wrong better than a professor can be traced through Trenchard and Gordon's "Cato" back to Cicero.[25] Yet Cicero and classical republicanism scarcely celebrated the democratic mass of ordinary people. The classical republican heritage assumed that common people and others involved in the marketplace would be usually overwhelmed by their interests and would thus be incapable of disinterestedness. Of course, these common people were not to be the leaders of the society. Although republicanism, compared to monarchy, rested on a magnanimous view of common people, it retained a traditional classical patrician bias in regard to office-holding. Many good Whigs and republicans believed that important public offices, including even membership of grand juries, ought to be filled only with "the better sort because they are less liable to temptations, less fearful of the frowns of power, may reasonably be supposed of more improved capacities than those of an inferior station." As ancients from Aristotle to Cicero had pointed out, people who had occupations, who needed to engage in the market, who worked with their hands, who were without a liberal education could scarcely possess the enlightenment and disinterestedness to stand above the haggling of the marketplace and act as impartial umpires.[26]

Classical republicanism was naturally suspicious of the marketplace, of commerce and business. Of course, commerce as the handmaiden of agriculture was considered benign and in the eighteenth century was even applauded as a source of peace and prosperity among nations. Still, classical republicanism was mistrustful of merchants as political leaders. Despite the fact that they moved agricultural goods abroad and brought great wealth into the country, merchants were thought to put their own interests ahead of those of their country and thus seemed incapable of disinterestedness.

Since merchants and mechanics and others who worked for a living were generally unqualified for disinterested public office, the responsibility rested on those leisured gentry whose income came to them, as Adam Smith and Francis Hutcheson said, without much exertion.[27]

If public service were to be truly disinterested, the officeholder ought to serve without salary—in accord with what Jefferson called "the Roman principle." "In a virtuous government," he said, ". . . public offices are, what they should be, burthens to those appointed to them, which it would be wrong to decline, though foreseen to bring with them intense labor, and great private loss." Public employment contributes "neither to advantage nor happiness. It is but honorable exile from one's family and affairs." For these reasons Washington refused a salary as commander in chief and attempted to refuse his salary as president. And for these same reasons Benjamin Franklin at the Philadelphia Convention proposed that all members of the executive branch of the new federal government receive no fees or salaries.[28]

Leaders were not to be modern professional politicians but ideally aristocratic farmers who temporarily assumed the burdens of office out of patriotic obligation. In ancient Rome, wrote James Wilson, magistrates and army officers were always gentlemen farmers, always willing to step down "from the elevation of office" and, like Washington in 1783, resume "with contentment and with pleasure, the peaceful labours of a rural and independent life." These Horatian and Virgilian notions of agriculture as a sacred activity were central to eighteenth-century English culture; Addison described Virgil's *Georgics* as "the most complete, elaborate, and finished piece of all antiquity." Many gentlemen on both sides of the Atlantic sought to establish country houses where they could escape from the trials and tribulations of the world. The wealthy Virginia planter Landon Carter named his plantation Sabine Hall after Horace's rural retreat "Sabine vale" located in the hills behind Rome.[29]

But classical agrarianism was not seen simply as Horatian retirement. It was celebrated as well for being a Virgilian source of virtue and social health. Indeed, the georgic vision of moral and social happiness flowing from the simple life of field and plow was shared equally by Southern planters and New England Federalists. Jefferson's praise of the yeoman farmer and the georgic writings of Connecticut poets such as Timothy Dwight and David Humphreys are virtually unintelligible except within this classical republican tradition.[30] How else but in the context of this classical heritage can we make sense of John Dickinson's pose in 1767 as a "Pennsylvania Farmer"? Dickinson was in fact a wealthy Philadelphia lawyer very much involved in city business, yet at the outset he had to assure his readers of his disinterestedness by informing them that he was a farmer "contented" and "undisturbed by worldly hopes or fears," living not off participation in the market but off "a little money at interest."[31] How else can we explain the fervor with which New England Revolutionary War officers in the 1780s set out to establish landed estates in the wilds of the newly acquired territory of Ohio in emulation of those military veterans described by Gibbon who settled in the provinces conquered by Rome? Well into the early decades of the new American Republic's history, establishing a seat in the country and experimenting georgic style with new agricultural products remained a consuming passion, especially among the New England gentry.[32]

The American Revolutionaries exploited all of these classical ideas in their creation of the United States. Many of them saw the new country as a rebirth of the ancient Roman republic. They established mixed constitutions in emulation of ancient Rome and re-created the Roman conception of citizenship open to everyone in the world. For Alexander Hamilton, Rome had been "the nurse of freedom." For John Adams, it had "formed the noblest people and the greatest power that has ever existed."[33] The Revolutionaries hoped to realize what England, according to its critics, had been unable to realize—the antique republican values of the good society, free of contention, selfishness, and luxury. The American leaders went to extraordinary lengths to fulfill classical ideals and to create suitable classical settings and personae. On the banks of a tiny tributary of the Potomac (called Goose Creek and renamed the Tiber) they laid out grandiose plans for a spacious and magnificent classical capital for their new Rome. Like David Humphreys, they believed the Revolution represented a recovery of antique virtue:

> What Rome, once virtuous, saw, this gives us now—
> Heroes and statesmen, awful from the plough.[34]

Joseph Warren actually wore a toga while delivering the Boston Massacre oration in 1775. Joseph Hawley, in a supreme act of Catonian denial, resolved never to accept any promotion, office, or emolument under any government. Patrick Henry's "Give me liberty or give me death" echoed the cry of Cato in Addison's play: "Gods, can a Roman senate long debate / Which of the two to choose, slavery or death!" Likewise, Nathan Hale's dying words, "I only regret that I have but one life to give for my country," resembled Cato's "What a pity is it / That we can die but once to serve our country." John Adams, like Brissot de Warville, idolized Cicero and yearned to have his own Ciceronian moment in which talent alone would count as it had in Roman times. Samuel Adams's virtue was legendary, and he became known as "one of Plutarch's men." And George Washington became the perfect Cincinnatus, the Roman patriot who returned to his farm after his victories in war.[35]

It was a neoclassical age and it was a neoclassical revolution the Americans undertook. They hoped to make their new republic a worthy place—a Columbia, the poets called it—where, in the words of Ezra Stiles, the enlightened president of Yale, "all the arts may be transported from Europe and Asia and flourish . . . with an augmented lustre." Of course, the Americans realized, as Benjamin Rush said, that the arts "flourish chiefly in wealthy and luxurious countries" and were symptoms of social decay. To the end of his life, John Adams, despite his sensuous attraction to the arts, remained convinced, as he told his wife in 1778 in a letter from France, "that the more elegance, the less virtue, in all times and countries." Buildings, paintings, sculpture, music, gardens, and furniture—however rich, magnificent, and splendid—were simply "bagatelles introduced by time and luxury in change for the great qualities and hardy, manly virtues of the human heart."[36] If Americans were to exceed Europe in dignity, grandeur, and taste, they would somehow have to create a republican art that avoided the vices of overrefinement and luxury.

The solution lay in the taut rationality of republican classicism. Classicism allowed artistic expression without fostering corruption and social decay; it froze time and defied change. Classicism offered a set of values that emphasized, as the commissioners who were charged with supervising the construction of public buildings in Washington, D.C., put it in 1793, "a grandeur of conception, a Republican simplicity, and that true elegance of proportion, which correspond to a tempered freedom excluding Frivolity, the food of little minds."[37] Such a neoclassical art was not an original art in any modern sense, but it was never intended to be. The Americans' aim in their literature, painting, and architecture of the 1780s and 1790s was to give a new and fresh republican spirit to old forms, to isolate and exhibit in their art the eternal and universal principles of reason and nature that the ancients had expressed long ago. Poets in the wilds of the New York frontier thus saw nothing incongruous in invoking comparisons with Virgil or Horace. And Joel Barlow could believe that his epic of America, *The Columbiad*, precisely because of its high moral and republican message, could exceed in grandeur even Homer's *Iliad*.

Jefferson was completely taken with neoclassicism. Although in the 1780s he momentarily accepted the Benjamin West–inspired fashionableness of having Houdon's statue of Washington done in contemporary dress, several decades later his true feelings came out: he was more than happy that Canova's statue of Washington was done in a Roman toga. "Every person of taste in Europe" preferred the Roman costume, he said. "Our boots and regimentals have a very puny effect." Jefferson was contemptuous and even ashamed of the "gothic" Georgian architecture of his native Virginia, and he sought in Monticello to build a house that would do justice to those Palladian villas that harked back to Roman antiquity. In the 1780s he badgered his Virginia colleagues into erecting as the new state capitol in Richmond a magnificent copy of the Maison Carrée, a Roman temple in Nîmes from the first century A.D., because he wanted an

American public building that would be a model for the people's "study and imitation" and "an object and proof of national good taste." The Maison Carrée was a building, he said, that "has pleased universally for near 2,000 years." Almost single-handedly he became responsible for making America's public buildings resemble Roman temples.[38]

The cultural relics of these revolutionary classical dreams are with America still: in the names of cities and towns like Rome, Syracuse, and Troy; in the designation of political institutions like senates and capitols; in the profusion of unread georgic poems like Timothy Dwight's "Greenfield Hill"; in the political symbols like the goddess Liberty, the numerous Latin mottos, and the Great Seal of the United States with its Roman eagle, its phrases *novus ordo seclorum* and *annuit coeptis* from Virgil's *Georgics* and *Eclogues*, and its Roman numerals, MDCCLXXVI, for greater dignity; and of course in the endless proliferation of Roman temples. But the spirit that inspired these things—the meaning these institutions, artifacts, and symbols had for the revolutionaries—has been lost, and it was being lost even as they were being created.

The American leaders may have begun their Revolution trying to recover an idealized and vanished Roman republic, but they soon realized that they had unleashed forces that were carrying them and their society much further than they had anticipated. Instead of becoming a new and grand incarnation of ancient Rome, a land of virtuous and contented farmers, America within decades of the Declaration of Independence had become a sprawling, materialistic, and licentious popular democracy unlike any state that had ever existed. Buying and selling were celebrated as never before, and the antique meaning of virtue was transformed. Ordinary people who knew no Latin and had few qualms about disinterestedness began asserting themselves with new vigor in the economy and in politics. Far from sacrificing their private desires for the good of the whole, Americans of the early Republic came to see that the individual's pursuit of wealth or happiness (the two were now interchangeable) was not only inevitable but justifiable as the only proper basis for a free state.

In the rapid transformation to democracy in the decades following the Revolution, ancient Rome lost much of its meaning for Americans. The transformation began early, often initially taking the form of attacks on the relevance of learning Latin or Greek in school. These democratic assaults on republican values, like the earlier ones on monarchical values, were undertaken by people who had little idea of the ultimate consequences of their actions. Benjamin Rush, for example, had contended that the study of Greek and Latin was "improper in a peculiar manner in the United States" because it tended to confine education to only a few, when in fact republicanism required everyone to be educated. Within a few years, however, Rush became alarmed that too many ordinary people were going to college and lowering the standards of civilization. But it was too late to stop the spread of this bumptious and bustling democracy.[39]

By the 1820s American society had left the georgic dreams of quiet farms and settled husbandmen far behind. Classical Rome was now thought to be too stolid and imitative to express the restlessness and vulgar originality of this new democratic America. Ancient Greece, said Edward Everett, was a better model. Ancient Greece, Homer's Greece, was tumultuous, wild, and free, said Everett, "free to licentiousness, free to madness."[40] For most Americans the great legacy of ancient Rome was gone.

AFTERWORD TO CHAPTER 2

This piece was presented as a lecture several times, including at a conference held in Rome in October 2008 sponsored by the Robert H. Smith International Center for Jefferson Studies at Monticello. In the course of reading and listening to the other papers at that conference, I concluded that some of our historical debates over the influence of the classics on the Founders were misplaced.

No doubt the classical world was an important part of the political memory of the Founders. We might even say that the relationship between the Founders and the classical past was similar to our present relationship to the Founders. Just as we use the Founders, such as Jefferson and Washington, to get our bearings and reaffirm our beliefs and reinvigorate our institutions, so too did the Founders use antiquity, especially republican antiquity, to help shape their values and justify their institutions. It was a memory bank that they drew on to make sense of their experience. Today this classical memory bank—those sets of ancient meanings—no longer exists for most Americans.

My distinguished mentor Bernard Bailyn once wrote that the classics played a minor role in the thought of the Founders. Antiquity, he said, was mere "window dressing" to the ideas of the Revolutionaries. It was "illustrative, not determinative" of their thought—not determinative, he says, in the way their radical Whig ideology was. The classics "contributed a vivid vocabulary but not the logic or grammar of thought, a universally respected personification but not the source of political and social beliefs. They heightened the colonists' sensitivity to ideas and attitudes otherwise derived."[1]

One of many discussions at the Rome conference focused on Bailyn's provocative remarks. The question I raised is the following: are the ideas of one era ever *determinative* of the thought of another? I don't think so. I don't believe ideas of an earlier period ever *determine* the ideas of a later period. What really *determines* thought are the events of the participants' present, their immediate interests and emotional needs, their present experience. Reality presses in upon us, and we look to bodies of ideas, or sets of meanings, to make sense of that reality, to explain, justify, or condemn it. For the Revolutionaries the classical past offered a body of meanings that they could draw upon to make meaningful their behavior and their goals. They didn't absorb it intact but drew upon it willy-nilly to fit their particular needs.

That's the way we still use ideas. Who reads a book and absorbs the whole thing? Rather, we select those parts that seem relevant or meaningful to us. We pick and choose the ideas from those available to us that seem most appropriate and that make our experience and circumstances most meaningful. But it is our experience that is determinative. Madison did not get his ideas for reforming the federal government in the 1780s from reading the trunks of books that Jefferson sent him from Paris. As I try to indicate in my "Interests and Disinterestedness" essay, his ideas were shaped by his experience in several sessions of the Virginia Assembly, and he used what ideas he could find, from David Hume as much as anyone, to justify and explain what he wanted to do in limiting the excesses of democracy in the state legislatures. His effort to use antiquity in order to justify the need for an upper house or senate, as described by historian Caroline Winterer at the conference, is another such example.

Moreover, as I suggest in the introduction to this volume, if we are using ideas to persuade someone of something, we have to select those ideas that will be most persuasive to whatever audience we are addressing. Of course, we can't just make up ideas out of whole cloth or concoct any old notion to make things meaningful. We have to draw upon those ideas, those sets of meanings, that are publicly available to us. For the Revolutionaries, the classical past offered a rich set of meanings to draw upon.

We borrow what we need from the ideas of the past, and in the process we inevitably distort those past ideas. Of course, the Founders' use of classicism was different from the classicism of antiquity, just as our use of the ideas of the Founding bears little resemblance to the thinking of the eighteenth century. But I would say that this sort of distortion went on with the ideas of the radical Whigs as well. In other words, ideas by themselves are never determinative of thought. Eighteenth-century Americans selected and used what they found relevant and appropriate in the ideas of Locke, Trenchard and Gordon, or James Burgh and in the process fit what they read into their circumstances. This is inevitably how ideas are used, and since our experience of reality is constantly changing, and we always have to make it meaningful, it is not surprising that our intellectual life is always dynamic and changing. Our intellectual quarrels are over what meanings we will give to our experience, to fulfill our present-day needs.

Yet by questioning whether the ideas of antiquity were determinative of the Founders' thinking, I do not mean to suggest that the classical past was unimportant to them. Even if ideas of an earlier era are not determinative of later thinking, it does not follow that these earlier ideas were simply ornamentation and had little influence. I believe that the classical past was much more than illustrative of the Founders' thoughts. Earlier ideas can, as I tried to indicate in the essay, influence and affect behavior.

CONSPIRACY *and the* PARANOID STYLE: CAUSALITY *and* DECEIT *in the* EIGHTEENTH CENTURY

*W*ERE THE AMERICAN REVOLUTIONARIES MENTALLY disturbed? Was the Revolution itself a consequence of anxieties buried deep in the psyches of its leaders? Bizarre and preposterous questions, it would seem, and scarcely the sorts of questions one expects to be asked about the Founding Fathers. Yet these are precisely the questions some historians are now suggesting we ought to be asking about the Revolution.

The Revolution seems to have become very much a psychological phenomenon. Recent writings on the subject are filled with psychological terms, and popular interpretations such as the "search for identity" on the part of insecure provincials are grounded in psychological conceptions.[1] With the growing interest in family history and child rearing, historians are making strenuous although contradictory efforts to explore the "interrelationship of private and public experience."[2] The upbringing of the colonists is being linked to their rejection of their "mother" country and "fatherly" king, and the familial relationship between Britain and the colonies is being wrung dry of every bit of psychological significance it may contain.[3] One by one the Founding Fathers are psychoanalyzed and their unconscious fears and drives brought to the surface.[4] The restraints of the British authorities, it now appears, threatened the colonists' "ego capacities" and aroused "large-scale personal anxiety, guilt, shame, and feelings of inadequacy that could only be overcome by a *manly* resistance to those restraints." Indeed, the colonists' widespread "fear of effeminacy," it has been suggested, may be "a source for some of the inner anxieties of many Americans" and "a useful clue to the psychological roots of the paranoid vision of the political world that dominated the politics of the period."[5] All of this psychologizing has been carried to the point where it is no longer strange or unreasonable to refer to the Revolution as "a cathartic event, . . . a psychological release" for a multitude of pent-up feelings and anxieties. It has even become possible to call the Revolution "a delusion explicable by the principles of psychology."[6]

No doubt much of this application of psychology to the Revolution can be explained by its influence on historical writing generally. Not only is psychohistory bidding to become a legitimate field, but psychological terms and theories have so insinuated themselves into our culture that we historians are often unaware that we are using them. Still, the recent impact of psychology on Revolutionary history writing is peculiarly intensive and cannot be accounted for simply by its effect on the discipline of history as a whole. What seems crucially important in explaining the extraordinary reliance on psychology in recent Revolutionary historiography is the coincidental publication in 1965 of two significant books— Bernard Bailyn's introduction to his *Pamphlets of the American Revolution* (subsequently enlarged and republished in 1967 as *The Ideological Origins of the American Revolution*) and Richard Hofstadter's *The Paranoid Style in American Politics*.[7] Neither of these works was influenced by the other, and each separately has strongly affected our understanding of American history. But when read together and interrelated in the thinking of historians, these books have taken on an unusual force in helping to shape our current interest in the Revolution as a psychological event.

Bailyn's interpretation of the origins of the Revolution is familiar enough. He argued that a pattern of ideas and attitudes bearing on the realities of colonial politics was "built into the very structure of political culture in eighteenth-century Britain and America" and provided "the sufficient background for understanding why there was a Revolution." A long-existing and integrated intellectual tradition drawn from various English sources, wrote Bailyn, prepared Americans for a particular interpretation of the welter of events that occurred in the 1760s and 1770s. "They saw about them, with increasing clarity, not merely mistaken, or even evil, policies violating the principles upon which freedom rested, but what appeared to be evidence of nothing less than a deliberate assault launched surreptitiously by plotters against liberty both in England and in America." It was the overwhelming evidence of a "design"—a conspiracy—"that was signaled to the colonists after 1763, and it was this above all else that in the end propelled them into Revolution."[8]

Bailyn's interpretation has had a powerful effect on our understanding of the Revolution, and every student of the Revolution has had to come to terms with it in one way or another. No one now can deny the prevalence of conspiratorial fears among the Revolutionaries. Indeed, historians largely take such fears for granted and have become preoccupied with explaining why the Revolutionaries should have had them. This need to make sense of these conspiratorial beliefs seems, more than anything else, to lie behind the extraordinary use of psychology in recent writing about the Revolution. While recognizing that there may be rational explanations for fears of conspiracy, most historians cannot help assuming that such fears are mainly rooted in nonrational sources. This assumption grew out of the experience of American politics, particularly McCarthyism, in the years following World War II—an assumption expressed in numerous sociological studies of those years and most strikingly in Hofstadter's conception of a "paranoid style."[9]

Hofstadter's book on the "paranoid style," which he found pervasive in American politics, demonstrated that the Revolutionary leaders were not unique in their fears of a conspiracy hatched by hidden diabolical forces. They were only one of many generations of Americans who have thought in terms of conspiracies throughout our history. Hofstadter became aware of Bailyn's interpretation when it was too late to integrate it into his argument, and thus he began his study of the "paranoid style" with the Bavarian Illuminati scare of the 1790s. He traced the style through the anti-Masonic, nativist, and Populist fears of the nineteenth century and concluded with an analysis of the beliefs in a communist conspiracy in the 1950s. By leaving the Revolution out of his story and by assuming that the "paranoid style" was "the preferred style only of *minority* movements" and marginal elements in American society, Hofstadter avoided the troubling implications of describing the Revolutionaries as paranoid personalities.[10]

Hofstadter said his use of "paranoid style" was not intended to suggest any medical or clinical significance; he meant only to use the term metaphorically to describe "a way of seeing the world and of expressing oneself." Medically, as he pointed out, paranoia is defined as a chronic mental disorder characterized by systematized delusions of persecution. However overly suspicious and apocalyptical in expression American paranoid spokesmen may have been, said Hofstadter, they could not be described as "certifiable lunatics." Yet—and it was a very big, drawn-out yet—this style was not quite normal; it was, Hofstadter wrote, "a distorted style" and thus "a possible signal that may alert us to a distorted judgment." It indicated that some kind of "political pathology" was at work; it was a recurrent mode of expression in American public life "which has frequently been linked with movements of suspicious discontent." Although believers in conspiracy may not have been crazy, they were persons, Hofstadter suggested, who had perverse and fanciful views of reality and were thus fit subjects for the application of some sort of "depth psychology."[11]

Other historians, sharing Hofstadter's assumption that politics was often "a projective arena for feelings and impulses that are only marginally related to the manifest issues," also sought to relate Americans' recurring fears of conspiracy to some underlying social or psychological process.[12] Some thought "that fear of conspiracy characterizes periods when traditional social and moral values are undergoing change" and therefore focused on the unusual fluidity of American society. People who were unsure of their identity and status, socially disrupted or alienated in some way, were, it seemed, especially susceptible to conspiratorial interpretations of events. Possibly, suggested David Brion Davis, who has most meticulously uncovered the conspiratorial fears of nineteenth-century Americans, various groups, from Anti-Masons to opponents of the Slave Power, found in the paranoid style a common means of expressing their different torments and troubles. Obviously, historians were careful to note, the great numbers of people who relied on such imagery of subversion—from Abraham Lincoln to Justice Robert H. Jackson—could not be dismissed as "charlatans, crackpots, and the disaffected." Davis in particular warned against any facile assumption "that the fear of subversion is always generated by internal, psychological needs." Despite such qualifications and cautions, however, the implications of these historical accounts of the paranoid style were clear: Americans seemed prone to fears of subversion, and these fears were symptomatic of severe social and psychological strains.[13]

Once America's paranoid style was revealed to be so prevalent, its connection with the ideology of the Revolution became inevitable. Not only was Bailyn's account of the colonists' fears of conspiracy widely reprinted, but historians now suggested that the Revolution had set "the basic pattern" of the paranoid style. "Is it possible," asked Davis, "that the circumstances of the Revolution conditioned Americans to think of resistance to a dark subversive force as the essential ingredient of their national identity?"[14] With the paranoid style associated with the ideology of the Revolution in this way, historians were quick to find traces of it everywhere in their sources. Although Bailyn had stressed in his *Ideological Origins* the rational basis of the colonists' fears, the term "paranoia" soon proliferated in historical writings on the Revolution. "The insurgent whig ideology," it now seemed clear, "had a frenzied, even paranoid cast to it," and leaders like John Adams and Thomas Jefferson were even accused of suffering from some form of paranoia.[15] The mounting evidence could lead to only one conclusion: "The era of the American Revolution was a period of political paranoia" in which "visions of conspiracy were endemic."[16]

In many cases these references to paranoia were clearly metaphorical. But given the current interest in psychohistory, it is not surprising that other references to paranoia have taken on an authentically psychological character, presuming a close connection between paranoid thinking and particular psychic sensibilities. Some historians, while acknowledging that the American Whigs' belief in a ministerial design against their liberties may have had some rational and conscious sources, have emphasized that "the fear of conspiracy also had roots buried deeply in the innermost recesses of the psyches of numerous Americans." Certain types of colonists unconsciously experienced tensions and anxieties over their personal autonomy and sexual identities "that may very well have shaped their public fears and fostered their sense of conspiracies endangering them."[17]

Other writers, taking Bailyn's argument as a "point of departure," have attempted a stark and quite literal "psychological interpretation of the coming of the Revolution," even going so far as to suggest that the Revolutionary leaders were clinically paranoiac—that is, that they were suffering from actual delusions of persecution and were unable to assess reality in a rational fashion. Far from being profoundly reasonable men, they were "prone to emotional instability, predisposed to psychological problems, vulnerable to them under the goad of an appropriate precipitant," like the Stamp Act, which left "in its wake the paranoid delusions that Britain was conspiring to enslave Americans."[18]

HOW MUCH FURTHER can we go? It is difficult to imagine that more psychological significance can be extracted from the conspiratorial beliefs of the Revolutionaries. Maybe it is time to pause in our psychological explorations, step back, and get a quite different, wider perspective on this mode of thinking—not to explain the Revolution but to explain why eighteenth-century Americans should have thought as they did. In other words, we need to reach through and beyond the Revolution to the larger culture of the English-speaking or, indeed, the entire Atlantic world of the eighteenth century. We may find that it was quite possible for all manner of people—not just British country-opposition groups and suspicious colonists, but "reasonable people," indeed the most enlightened minds of the day—to believe in malevolent conspiracies.[19]

There are explanations for the eighteenth century's conspiratorial beliefs that are rooted not in any modern notions of psychic strain or even in the peculiar suspicions of the radical Whigs and country-opposition tradition, but rather in the general presuppositions and conventions—in the underlying metaphysics—of eighteenth-century culture. Indeed, such conspiratorial beliefs grew so much out of the common ways in which enlightened thinkers conceived of events that they can scarcely be used to explain any particular happening of the period, including the Revolution. Such beliefs may accurately describe the American Revolutionaries' mode of thinking in the 1760s and 1770s, but they cannot account for the Revolution, and they cannot be used as evidence that the Revolutionaries were suffering from some emotional instability peculiar to themselves. For the one thing about conspiratorial interpretations of events that must impress all students of early modern Western history is their ubiquitousness: they can be found everywhere in the thought of people on both sides of the Atlantic.

More than any other period of English history, the century or so following the Restoration was the great era of conspiratorial fears and imagined intrigues. The Augustan Age, said Daniel Defoe, was "an Age of Plot and Deceit, of Contradiction and Paradox." Pretense and hypocrisy were everywhere, and nothing seemed as it really was. Politics, especially in the decades from the Restoration to the Hanoverian accession, appeared to be little more than one intrigue and deception after another. It had to be a "horrid plot," said Scrub in George Farquhar's *The Beaux' Stratagem* of 1707. "First, it must be a plot because there's a woman in't. Secondly, it must be a plot because there's a priest in't. Thirdly, it must be a plot because there's French gold in't. And fourthly, it must be a plot because I don't know what to make on't." With so many like Scrub wanting to know but with so little revealed, inferences of hidden designs and conspiracies flourished. So prevalent seemed the plotting that Jonathan

Swift in his inimitable fashion suggested that only the most ingenious scatological devices could uncover the many conspirators. Everywhere people sensed designs within designs, cabals within cabals; there were court conspiracies, backstairs conspiracies, ministerial conspiracies, factional conspiracies, aristocratic conspiracies, and by the last half of the eighteenth century even conspiracies of gigantic secret societies that cut across national boundaries and spanned the Atlantic. Revolutionary Americans may have been an especially jealous and suspicious people, but they were not unique in their fears of dark, malevolent plots and plotters.[20]

In the Anglo-American world at the time of the Revolutionary crisis there was scarcely a major figure who did not tend to explain political events in these terms. The American Whigs were not unique; opponents of the Revolution—American Tories and members of the British administration alike—were convinced that they themselves were victims of subversives who cloaked what George III called their "desperate conspiracy" in "vague expressions of attachment to the parent state and the strongest protestations of loyalty . . . whilst they were preparing for a general revolt." Others besides the deeply involved participants in the Revolutionary crisis saw the world in these same terms. John Wesley did. So, too, did sophisticated thinkers like Horace Walpole and Edmund Burke rely on hidden schemes to account for otherwise inexplicable events. Such conspiratorial thinking, moreover, was not confined to the English-speaking world. Some of the most grandiose and elaborate plots of the century were imagined by the French of various social ranks. Like the American Revolution, the French Revolution was born in an atmosphere of conspiratorial fears. There were plots by the ministers, by the queen, by the aristocracy, by the clergy; everywhere there were secret managers behind the scenes pulling the strings of the great events of the Revolution. The entire Revolution was even seen by some as the planned consequence of a huge Masonic conspiracy. The paranoid style, it seems, was a mode of expression common to the age.[21]

If all manner of people in the eighteenth century resorted readily to conspiratorial modes of explanation and habitually saw plots by dissembling men behind patterns of events, can the paranoid style carry the peculiarly American significance attributed to it? Can it have been, as we are told, the particular means by which certain kinds of disturbed people, especially unsettled Americans, released their hidden fears into the public arena? Yet if the prevalent eighteenth-century disposition to think in conspiratorial terms was not simply a symptom of American emotional instability, what then was it?

To understand how "reasonable people" could believe in the prevalence of plots, we should begin by taking their view of events at face value and examine what it rationally implied. It was obviously a form of causal explanation, a "tendency of many causes to one event," said Samuel Johnson. To us this is a crude and peculiar sort of causal explanation because it rests entirely on individual intentions or motives. It is, as Hofstadter pointed out, a "rationalistic" and "personal" explanation: "decisive events are not taken as part of the stream of history, but as the consequences of someone's will." To those who think in conspiratorial terms, things do not "just happen"; they are "brought about, step by step, by will and intention."[22] Concatenations of events are the products not, as we sophisticated historians might say, of "social forces" or "the stream of history" but of the concerted designs of individuals.

The paranoid style, in other words, is a mode of causal attribution based on particular assumptions about the nature of social reality and the necessity of moral responsibility in human affairs. It presumes a world of autonomous, freely acting individuals who are capable of directly and deliberately bringing about events through their decisions and actions, and who thereby can be held morally responsible for what happens. We are the heirs of this conception of cause, and its assumptions still permeate our culture, although, as our system of criminal punishment shows, in increasingly archaic and contradictory ways. Most of the eighteenth-century world of thought remains our world, so much so, indeed, that we have trouble perceiving how different we really are. We may still talk about causes and effects, but, as Hofstadter's invocation of "the stream of history" suggests, we often do so in ways the eighteenth century would not have understood. If we are to make sense of that period's predilection for conspiratorial thinking, we must suspend our modern understanding about how events ought to be explained and open ourselves to that different world.

There had, of course, been many conspiratorial interpretations of political affairs before the eighteenth century. Such interpretations rested on modes of apprehending reality that went back to classical antiquity. For centuries men had relied on "the spirit of classic ethical psychology, upon an *analyse du coeur humain*, not upon discovery or premonitions of historical forces," in explaining public events.[23] There was nothing new in seeing intrigue, deceit, and cabals in politics. From Sallust's description of Cataline through Machiavelli's lengthy discussion in his *Discourses*, conspiracy was a common feature of political theory. But classical and Renaissance accounts of plots differed from most of the conspiratorial interpretations of the eighteenth century. They usually described actions by which ambitious politicans gained control of governments: conspiracy was taken for granted as a normal means by which rulers were deposed. Machiavelli detailed dozens of such plots. Indeed, he wrote, "many more princes have lost their lives and their positions through them than through open war."[24] Such conspiracies occurred within the small ruling circles of a few great men—in limited political worlds where everyone knew everyone else. The classical and Renaissance discussions of conspiracies have a matter-of-fact quality. They were not imagined or guessed at; they happened. Cataline actually plotted to take over Rome; Brutus and Cassius really did conspire against Caesar.

During the early modern era, conspiracy continued to be a common term of politics. Seventeenth-century England was filled with talk and fears of conspiracies of all kinds. There were French plots, Irish plots, Popish plots, Whig plots, Tory plots, Jacobite plots; there was even the "Meal Tub Plot." Yet by this period many of the conspiracies had become very different from those depicted in earlier centuries of Western history. To be sure, some of them, like the Gunpowder Plot of 1605 to blow up Parliament or the "Rye House Plot" of 1683 to seize the king, were of the traditional sort described by Machiavelli, designed to subvert the existing government. But other references to conspiracy took a new and different form. The term was still pejorative and charged with suspicion, but now it became used more vaguely and broadly to refer to any combination of persons, including even members of the government itself, united for a presumed common end. The word acquired a more general and indeterminate meaning in political discourse. Its usage suggested confusion rather than certainty. Conspiracies like those of Charles II's Cabal became less matters of fact and more matters of inference. Accounts of plots by court or government were no longer descriptions of actual events but interpretations of otherwise puzzling concatenations of events. By the eighteenth century conspiracy was not simply a means of explaining how rulers were deposed; it had become a common means of explaining how rulers and others directing political events really operated. It was a term used not so much by those intimate with the sources of political events as by those removed from the events and, like Farquhar's Scrub, bewildered by them.

Unlike the schemes of antiquity and the Renaissance, which flowed from the simplicity and limitedness of politics, the conspiratorial interpretations of the Augustan Age flowed from the expansion and increasing complexity of the political world. Unprecedented demographic and economic developments in early modern Europe were massively altering the nature of society and politics. There were more people more distanced from one another and from the apparent centers of political decision making. The conceptual worlds of many individuals were being broadened and transformed. The more people became strangers to one another and the less they knew of one another's hearts, the more suspicious and mistrustful they became, ready as never before in Western history to see deceit and deception at work. Relationships between superiors and subordinates, rulers and ruled, formerly taken for granted, now became disturbingly problematical, and people became uncertain of who was who and who was doing what. Growing proportions of the population were more politically conscious and more concerned with what seemed to be the abused power and privileges of ruling elites. Impassioned efforts were made everywhere to arouse "the vigilance of the public eye" against those few men "who cannot exist without a scheme in their heads," those "turbulent, scheming, maliciously cunning, plotters of mischief." The warnings against rulers grew more anxious and fearful, the expressions of suspicion more frenzied and strident, because assumptions about how public affairs operated became more and more separated from reality. It was easy for a fifteenth-century nobleman, describing political events, to say that "it will be sufficient to speak of the high-ranking people, for it is through them that God's power and justice are made known."[25] But by the eighteenth century this tracing of all events back to the ambitions and actions of only the high-ranking leaders was being stretched to the breaking point. Society was composed not simply of great men and their retainers but of numerous groups, interests, and "classes" whose actions could not be easily deciphered. Human affairs were more complicated, more interdependent, and more impersonal than they had ever been in Western history.

Yet at this very moment when the world was outrunning man's capacity to explain it in personal terms, in terms of the passions and schemes of individuals, the most enlightened of the age were priding themselves on their ability to do just that. The widespread resort to conspiratorial interpretations grew out of this contradiction.

CONSPIRATORIAL INTERPRETATIONS—attributing events to the concerted designs of willful individuals—became a major means by which educated men in the early modern period ordered and gave meaning to their political world. Far from being symptomatic of irrationality, this conspiratorial mode of explanation represented an enlightened stage in Western man's long struggle to comprehend his social reality. It flowed from the scientific promise of the Enlightenment and represented an effort, perhaps in retrospect a last desperate effort, to hold men personally and morally responsible for their actions.

Personalistic explanations had, of course, long been characteristic of premodern European society and are still characteristic of primitive peoples. Premodern men lacked our modern repertory of explanations and could not rely on those impersonal forces such as industrialization, modernization, or the "stream of history" that we so blithely invoke to account for complicated combinations of events. They were unable, as we say, to "rise to the conception of movements."[26] For that different, distant world the question asked of an event was not "How did it happen?" but "Who did it?"

Yet despite this stress on persons rather than processes, premodern men always realized that much of what happened was beyond human agency and understanding. Even those classical and Renaissance writers who stressed that events were due to "the wisdoms and follies, the virtues and vices of individuals who made decisions" built their histories and tragic dramas around the extent to which such heroic individuals could prevail against unknown fortune. Ultimately the world seemed uncontrollable and unpredictable, ruled by mysterious forces of fate or chance, shadowed in inscrutability.[27]

At the opening of the modern era, Protestant reformers invoked divine providence and the omnipotence of God in order to stamp out the traditional popular reliance on luck and magic and to renew a sense of design and moral purpose in the world. Life, they held, was not a lottery but the working out of God's purpose and judgments, or "special providences." Men were morally responsible for events; even natural catastrophes like earthquakes and floods were seen as divine punishments for human misbehavior.[28] Still, it remained evident that life was uncertain and precarious and that God moved in very mysterious ways. As the Puritan Increase Mather observed as late as 1684, "Things many times come to pass contrary to humane probabilities and the rational Conjectures and expectations of men." Nature itself was not always consistent, for things sometimes acted "otherwise than according to their natures and proper inclinations." Humans might glimpse those parts of God's design that he chose to reveal, but ultimately they could never "be able fully to understand by what Rules the Holy and Wise God ordereth all events Prosperous and adverse which come to pass in the world." If there was comfort in knowing that what seemed chaotic, fortuitous, or accidental was in reality directed by God, it nonetheless remained true that the "ways of Providence are unsearchable."[29]

At the very time that Mather was writing, however, God was preparing to "let Newton be": the treatise that was to be enlarged into the first book of the *Principia* was completed in 1684. Of course, the scientific revolution of the seventeenth century—or, more accurately, the new Western consciousness of which that revolution was the most important expression—did not make all immediately light. Yet many people now had less fear of chaos and contingency and greater confidence in their ability to understand events, so much so that sophisticates like George Savile, marquis of Halifax, could even warn against "that common error of applying God's judgments upon particular occasions." The world lost some of its mystery and became more manipulatable. Although the new science tended to remove man from the center of the physical universe at the same time it brought him to the center of human affairs in ways that even classical and Renaissance thinkers had scarcely conceived of. It promised him the capacity to predict and control not only nature but his own society, and it proceeded to make him directly and consciously responsible for the course of human events. Ultimately the implications of this momentous shift created the cultural matrix out of which eighteenth-century conspiratorial interpretations developed.[30]

The new science assumed a world of mechanistic cause and effect in which what happens does so only because something else happened before. Philosophers since Aristotle had talked of causes but never before in terms of such machine-like regularity, of such chains of consequences. "When the world became a machine," writes Jacob Bronowski, "[cause] became the god within the machine." Mechanistic causality became the paradigm in which the enlightened analysis of all behavior and events now had to take place. Cause was something that produced an effect; every effect had a cause; the cause and its effect were integrally related. Such thinking created a new world of laws, measurements, predictions, and constancies or regularities of behavior—all dependent on the same causes producing the same effects. "The knowledge of particular phenomena may gratify a barren curiosity," Samuel Stanhope Smith told a generation of Princeton students, "but they are of little real use, except, as they tend to establish some general law, which will enable the accurate observer to predict similar effects in all time to come, in similar circumstances, and to depend upon the result. Such general laws alone deserve the name of science."[31]

The change in consciousness came slowly, confusedly, and reluctantly. Few were immediately willing to abandon belief in the directing providence of God. Newton himself endeavored to preserve God's autonomy. "A God without dominion, providence, and final causes," he said, "is nothing but Fate and Nature." In fact, the Christian belief that nature was ordered by God's will was an essential presupposition of early modern science. Yet despite the continued stress by Newton's followers on God's control over the workings of nature, many eighteenth-century philosophers gradually came to picture the deity as a clockmaker, and some even went so far as to deny that God had anything at all to do with the physical movement of the universe. The logic of the new science implied a world that ran itself.[32]

To posit the independence of the natural world was exciting enough; to conceive of a human world without God's judgments and providences was simply breathtaking: it was in fact what centrally defined the Enlightenment. The work of John Locke and other philosophers opened reflective minds to the startling supposition that society, though no doubt ordained in principle by God, was man's own creation—formed and sustained, and thus alterable, by human beings acting autonomously and purposefully. It came to seem that if men could understand the natural order that God had made, then perhaps they could eventually understand the social order that they themselves had made. From the successes of natural science, or what the eighteenth century termed natural philosophy, grew the conviction that moral laws—the chains of cause and effect in human behavior—could be discovered that would match those of the physical world. Thus was generated eighteenth-century moral philosophy—the search for the uniformities and regularities of man's behavior that has proliferated into the various social sciences of our own time.[33]

Finding the laws of behavior became the consuming passion of the Enlightenment. In such a liberal and learned world there could no longer be any place for miracles or the random happenings of chance. Chance, it was now said, was "only a name to cover our ignorance of the cause of any event." God may have remained the primary cause of things, but in the minds of the enlightened he had left men to work out the causes and effects of their lives free from his special interventions. All that happened in society was to be reduced to the strictly human level of men's motivations and goals. "Humanity," said William Warburton in 1727, "is the only cause of human vicissitudes." The source of man's calamities, wrote Constantin François de Chasseboeuf, comte de Volney, in 1791, lay not in "the distant heavens . . . it resides in man himself, he carries it with him in the inward recesses of his own heart."[34] Such beliefs worked their way through every variety of intellectual endeavor in the age. They produced not only a new genre of literature—the novel with its authorial control and design—but also a new kind of man-centered causal history, one based on the same assumptions as the age's conspiratorial interpretations.[35]

English history since the Revolution of 1688, as Henry St. John, Viscount Bolingbroke, saw it from the vantage point of the 1730s, was "not the effect of ignorance, mistakes, or what we call chance, but of design and scheme in those who had the sway at that time." This could be proved by seeing "events that stand recorded in history . . . as they followed one another, or as they produced one another, causes or effects, immediate or remote." "History supplies the defects of our own experience" and demonstrates that there are really no such things as accidents; "it shows us causes as in fact they were laid, with their immediate effects: and it enables us to guess at future events." "History," said Edward Gibbon simply, "is the science of causes and effects."[36]

Extending this concept from the realm of natural phenomena into the moral world of human affairs was not an easy matter. Natural philosophers like Newton had sought to stave off the numbing necessitarianism implied in a starkly mechanistic conception of cause and effect by positing various God-inspired "active principles" as the causal agents of motion, gravity, heat, and the like. Even those later eighteenth-century scientists who saw nature as self-contained and requiring no divine intervention whatsoever still presumed various energizing powers in matter itself.[37] The need for some sort of active principle in human affairs was felt even more acutely, for the new mechanistic philosophy posed a threat to what Arthur O. Lovejoy has called the "intense ethical inwardness" of Western Christendom. The belief "that whatever moves and acts does so mechanically and necessarily" was ultimately incompatible with personalistic thinking and cast doubt on man's moral responsibility for his actions.[38] If human affairs were really the consequence of one thing repeatedly and predictably following upon another, the social world would become as determined as the physical world seemed to be. Theologians like Jonathan Edwards welcomed this logic and subtly used the new cause-and-effect philosophy to justify God's sovereignty. But other moral philosophers had no desire to create a secular version of divine providence or to destroy the voluntarism of either God or man, and thus sought to find a place for free will in the operations of the machine. They did so not by repudiating the paradigm of cause and effect but by trying to identify causes in human affairs with the motives, mind, or will of individuals. Just as natural scientists like Cadwallader Colden, believing that in a mechanistic physical world "there must be some power or force, or principle of Action," groped toward a modern concept of energy, so too did moral philosophers seek to discover the powers or principles of action that lay behind the sequences of human affairs—in effect, looking within the minds and hearts of men for the moral counterpart of Colden's physical energy.[39]

Such efforts to reconcile the search for laws of human behavior with the commitment to moral capability lay behind the numerous controversies over free will that bedeviled the eighteenth century. To be enlightened, it seemed, was to try one's hand at writing an essay on what David Hume called "the most contentious question of metaphysics"—the question of

liberty and necessity. Despite all the bitter polemics between the libertarians and the necessitarians, however, both sides were caught up in the
new thinking about causality. Both assumed, as Hume pointed out, that
"the conjunction between motives and voluntary actions is as regular and
uniform, as that between the cause and effect in any part of nature." Men's
motives or will thus became the starting point in the sequential chain of
causes and effects in human affairs. All human actions and events could
now be seen scientifically as the products of men's intentions. If they were
not, if men "are not necessarily determined by motives," then, said the
Scottish moralist Thomas Reid, "all their actions must be capricious."[40]
Only by identifying causes with motives was any sort of human science
and predictability possible, and only then could morality be preserved in
the new, mechanistic causal world.

Since it was "granted on all hands, that moral good and evil lie in the
state of mind, or prevailing internal disposition of the agent," searching out the causes of social events meant discovering in these agents the
motives, the "voluntary choice and design," that led them to act—the
energizing principle, the inner springs of their behavior. "Every moral
event must have an answerable cause. . . . Every such event must then have
a *moral* cause."[41] Moral deeds implied moral doers; when things happen
in society, individuals with particular intentions, often called "designs,"
must be at the bottom of them. All social processes could be reduced to
specific individual passions and interests. "Ambition and avarice," wrote
the Revolutionary historian Mercy Otis Warren, "are *the leading springs*
which generally actuate the restless mind. From these *primary sources of
corruption* have arisen all the rapine and confusion, the depredation and
ruin, that have spread distress over the face of the earth from the days
of Nimrod to Cesar, and from Cesar to an arbitrary prince of the house
of Brunswick." This widespread belief that explanations of social phenomena must be sought in the moral nature of man himself ultimately
reduced all eighteenth-century moral philosophy—its history and its
social analysis—to what would come to be called psychology.[42]

Once men's designs were identified as the causes of human events, the new paradigm of causality worked to intensify and give a scientific gloss to the classic concern with the human heart and the ethical inwardness of Christian culture. Indeed, never before or since in Western history has man been held so directly and morally responsible for the events of his world. Because the new idea of causality presumed a homogeneous identity, an "indissoluble connection," between causes and effects, it became difficult to think of social effects, however remote in time, that were not morally linked to particular causes—that is, to particular human designs. There could be no more in the effects than existed in the causes. "Outward actions being determined by the will," they partook "of the nature of moral good or evil only with reference to their cause, viz. internal volition."[43]

It could now be taken for granted that the cause and the effect were so intimately related that they necessarily shared the same moral qualities. Whatever the particular moral character of the cause—that is, the motive or inclination of the actor—"the effect appears to be of the same kind."[44] Good intentions and beliefs would therefore result in good actions; evil motives caused evil actions. Of course, mistakes might happen, and occasionally actions "proceeded not from design." But continued or regular moral actions could follow only from similar moral intentions. Only by assuming this close relationship between causes and effects—"this *inference* from motives to voluntary actions; from characters to conduct," said Hume—was the eighteenth-century science of human behavior made possible.[45]

This presumed moral identity between cause and effect, between motive and deed, accounts for the excited reaction of moralists to Bernard Mandeville's satiric paradox of "private vices, publick benefits." Mandeville was unusual for his time in grasping the complexity of public events and the ways in which political effects could outrun and differ from their causes. "We ought," he wrote, "to forebear judging rashly of ministers and their actions, especially when we are unacquainted with every circumstance of an affair. Measures may be rightly concerted, and such casualties intervene, as may make the best design miscarry. . . . Humane understanding is too shallow to foresee the result of what is subject to many variations."[46] Such skepticism could not be easily tolerated by that enlightened and moral age. Mandeville and all those who would ignore private intentions in favor of public results threatened to unhinge both man's moral responsibility for his actions and the homogeneous relation that presumably existed between cause and effect. To break the necessary moral connection between cause and effect, to make evil the author of good and vice versa, would be, it was said, "to confound all differences of character, to destroy all distinction between right and wrong, and to make the most malicious and the most benevolent being of precisely the same temper and disposition."[47]

Mandeville clearly perceived that much of human activity had become an "incomprehensible Chain of Causes." But he, like others of his time, had no better way of describing the multitude of complicated and criss-crossing causal chains he saw than to invoke the traditional Protestant concept of "providence."[48] For those who would be enlightened and scientific, this resort to the mysterious hand of God was no explanation of human affairs at all but rather a step backward into darkness. Things happened, as John Adams noted, by human volition, either "by Accident or Design."[49] Some confusing event or effect might be passed off as an accident—the result of somebody's mistaken intention—but a series of events that seemed to form a pattern could be no accident. Having only the alternative of "providence" as an impersonal abstraction to describe systematic linkages of human actions, the most enlightened of the age could only conclude that regular patterns of behavior were the conse-quences of concerted human intentions—that is, the result of a number of people coming together to promote a collective design or conspiracy. The human mind, it seemed to Jonathan Edwards, had a natural disposition, "when it sees a thing begin to be," not only "to conclude certainly, that there is a *Cause* of it," but also, "if it sees a thing to be in a very orderly, regular and exact manner to conclude that some Design regulated and disposed it." Although Edwards was arguing here for God's "exact reg-ulation of a very great multitude of particulars," a similar leap from a particular cause to a general design was made by eighteenth-century the-orists who sought to account for the regularity of human actions by the coincident purposes not of God but of human beings.[50]

Many enlightened thinkers of the eighteenth century could therefore no more accept the seeming chaos and contingency of events than could the Puritans. Like the Puritans, they presumed the existence of an order-ing power lying beneath the apparently confused surface of events—not God's concealed will, of course, but natural causes embodied in the hid-den intentions and wills of men. Those who saw only random chance in events simply did not know enough about these hidden human wills. Just as devout Puritans believed that nothing occurred without God's providence, so the liberal-minded believed that nothing occurred without some person willing it. Earlier, men had sought to decipher the concealed or partially revealed will of God; now they sought to understand the con-cealed or partially exposed wills of human beings. That, in a nutshell, was what being enlightened was all about.

IT WAS PRECISELY these assumptions that lay behind American Whig conspiratorial thinking, indeed all conspiratorial thinking, in the eigh-teenth century. To be sure, there was a long-existing Christian tradi-tion that stressed, in the words of Revelation 12:9, the wiles of "that old serpent, called the Devil, and Satan, which deceiveth the whole world." This creature, whether called the dragon, the beast, or Satan, was easily pictured by devout Christians and readers of John Milton as "the chief directing agent in all the dark plots of tyranny, persecution and oppression." There is no denying the importance of this religious tradition in preparing American Protestants to detect a British ministeral plot that was "as black and dark as the powder-treason plot." People who read their Bibles and heeded the fervid millennial sermons of their ministers were conditioned to believe that the forces of evil were like the frogs that issued from the mouth of the satanic dragon, "slyly creeping into all the holes and corners of the land, and using their enchanting art and bewitching policy, to lead aside, the simple and unwary, from the truth, to prepare them for the shackles of slavery and bondage." Sermons of the period were filled with references to the "hidden intent," the "pernicious scheme," and the "intrigues and dark plots"—references that owed more to the apocalyptic beliefs of the clergy than to the Whig tradition of political jealousy and suspicion.[51] Nor can it be denied that the heated ideological atmosphere in America in the early 1770s intensified the colonists' readiness to suspect British intentions and to see deep dark plots at work. Yet ultimately it was neither the atmosphere of Whiggish suspicion and mistrust nor the Christian tradition of a deceitful Satan that was fundamental to the age's susceptibility to conspiratorial interpretations; for people who were neither radical Whigs nor devout Protestants nonetheless believed naturally in conspiracies. What was fundamental is that American secular thought—in fact, all enlightened thought of the eighteenth century—was structured in such a way that conspiratorial explanations of complex events became normal, necessary, and rational.

The rush of momentous events in the years leading to the Revolution demanded explanation, for, as the colonists told themselves, "these unheard of intolerable calamities spring not of the dust, come not causeless." Some Americans, of course, still relied on traditional religious presuppositions and warned of the necessity to "remain ignorant of the intentions of Providence, until the series of events explain them," so "vastly large, complicate and intricate" was God's design. Others, mostly Tories, doubted whether there was a design at all, whether in fact the actions of the British government added up to anything systematic. Most of the British acts, wrote the New York loyalist Peter Van Schaack as late as 1776, "seem to have sprung out of particular occasions, and are unconnected with each other." But most American patriots in the 1760s and 1770s gradually convinced themselves that the British actions were indeed linked in what Jefferson called "a deliberate, systematical plan of reducing us to slavery" and that this plan could be explained in terms not of the intentions of providence but of the intentions of British officials.[52]

Thus the central question for Americans from 1765 on was always:

what were the members of the British government up to? John Dickinson rested the entire argument of his famous *Letters from a Farmer in Pennsylvania* on the colonists' ability "to discover the intentions of those who rule over us." The colonists in effect turned their decade-long debate with the mother country into an elaborate exercise in the deciphering of British motives. To know what response to make to British acts, wrote James Iredell in 1776, "it was necessary previously to consider what might be supposed the sentiments and views of the administration of Great Britain, the fatal original authors of all these dire extremities." Had George Grenville, in promoting the Stamp Act of 1765, for example, "acted from *principle* and not from any *bad motive*"?[53]

This was the crux of the matter, not only for the American Revolutionaries but for all eighteenth-century thinkers: how were the real intentions of individuals—what John Adams referred to time and again as "the Secret Springs, Motives and Principles of human Actions"—to be discovered? Certainly the motives of most humble men, the "people," the multitude, were easily known from their expressions. Such simple, ordinary folk were "men of feeling": they wore their hearts on their sleeves and in their ignorance openly revealed their passionate, often violent, natures from which sprang the motives for their actions.[54] But the motives of others—the learned few, the gentlemanly elite, those who directed political affairs—were not so easily discovered. Some of these extraordinary men were, of course, "men of principle," acting benevolently out of disinterested judgment and with rational self-control; they revealed "sincerity" and "manly candor" in their actions. But others were men not of principle but of "policy," or concealed intentions, who exploited their reason and learning shrewdly and artfully to bring about selfish and wicked ends. Samuel Richardson's character Lovelace was an outwardly charming and respected gentleman, but he had "the plottingest heart in the universe." Such cultivated but evil-minded men could pretend they were something they were not and disguise their inner motives. They could smile and smile and yet be villains. "It is very hard under all these masks," wrote Defoe, "to see the true countenance of any man."[55]

Masquerades and hidden designs formed the grammar and vocabulary for much of the thought of the age. From Molière to Lord Chesterfield, intellectuals debated the advantages and disadvantages of politeness, frankness, and hiding one's true feelings in order to get along in the world. "Nothing in Courts is exactly as it appears to be," wrote Chesterfield. "Courts are unquestionably the seats of politeness and good-breeding; were they not so, they would be the seats of slaughter and desolation. Those who now smile upon and embrace, would affront and stab each other if manners did not interpose: but ambition and avarice, the two prevailing passions at Courts, found dissimulation more effectual than violence; and dissimulation introduced that habit of politeness which distinguishes the courtier from the country gentleman." Yet what was prudence and sociability to some became deceit and flattery to others. Perhaps never in Western history have the issues of hypocrisy and sincerity been more centrally engaged.[56] John Adams filled his diary and other writings with lengthy analyses of "Dissimulation," which he called "the first Maxim of worldly Wisdom," and anxiously tried to work out the extent to which a public figure could legitimately conceal his motives. The patronage politics of the age put a premium on circumspection, discretion, and the suppressing of one's real feelings in the interest of cultivating the friendship of patrons. This in turn encouraged an opposition politics dedicated to the unmasking of hypocrisy.

By the middle of the eighteenth century, if not earlier, this concern with the deceit and dissembling of sophisticated elites had turned "courtier" into a generic term of abuse and was leading some to suggest that common people, "men of feeling," despite their ignorance, brutality, and simplicity, might be better trusted in political affairs than men of learning. Such simple folk at least could be counted on to express their inner passions and motives spontaneously and honestly. "Ninety-nine parts out of one hundred of mankind, are ever inclined to live at peace, and cultivate a good understanding with each other." Only members of "the remaining small part"—those whose "considerable abilities" were "joined to an intriguing disposition"—were "the real authors, advisers, and perpetrators of wars, treasons, and those other violences, which have, in all ages, more or less disgraced the annals of man." It was "necessary," wrote historian Mercy Otis Warren, "to guard at every point, against the intrigues of artful or ambitious men," since such men were involved in a "game of deception . . . played over and over." Everywhere there seemed to be a frightening gap between public appearances and the inner motives of rulers.[57]

Because no one could ever actually penetrate into the inner hearts of men, true motives had to be discovered indirectly, had to be deduced from actions. That is, the causes had to be inferred from the effects. Since the scientific paradigm of causality presumed a homogenous connection, a moral likeness, between causes and effects, such deductions and inferences, however elaborate, were not only plausible but necessary. "The actions of men," wrote the novelist Henry Fielding in a concise essay on this Augustan theme of the separation of appearance and reality, "are the surest evidence of their character." The intentions of sophisticated and cunning men, especially those in public life, could be known neither by their countenances nor by their statements, for these were but masks. Although an "honest man," wrote a South Carolina polemicist in 1769, was supposed "to let his language express the real sentiments of his soul," words could no longer be trusted. Only men's outward actions could reveal their inner dispositions and expose deceit and dissembling. The "dark counsels" of the "Cabal" of Charles II's reign, wrote Hume in his *History of England*, "were not thoroughly known but by the event." "By their fruits so shall ye know them" was the common refrain of religious and secular thinkers alike.[58]

Americans in the 1760s and 1770s were far removed from the sources of what was happening—John Adams, for example, knew something was afoot "by somebody or other in Great-Britain"—and thus they necessarily fell back on this common inferential method of determining designs. "As in nature we best judge of causes by their effects, so," declared the Massachusetts minister Samuel Cooke in his Election Sermon of 1770, "rulers hereby will receive the surest information of the fitness of their laws and the exactness of their execution." For Americans, the execution of those laws provided the only way to discover whether Grenville and other ministers acted from principle or from bad motives. The intentions of the British officials, wrote Dickinson, were not to be judged by their declarations of good will; only "conduct . . . would in time sufficiently explain itself."[59] The British government's claim to have the interests of the colonies at heart, while its actions seemed clearly harmful to those interests, only confirmed its duplicity in colonial eyes. Indeed, it was this sort of discrepancy between the professed motives of an actor and the contrary effects of his actions that lay behind the eighteenth century's preoccupation with deception.

THE IDEA OF DECEPTION BECAME the means by which the Augustan Age closed the gaps that often seemed to exist between causes and effects, between men's proclaimed intentions and their contrary actions. Since cause and effect were inherently, mechanistically related, both possessing the same moral nature, any persistent discrepancy between the two presented a serious problem of explanation. Whenever effects seemed different from their ostensible causes, philosophers were certain, as Hume repeatedly pointed out, that "the contrariety of events" did "not proceed from any contingency in the cause but from the secret operation of contrary causes."[60] If bad effects continually resulted from the professedly benevolent intentions of an actor, then something was wrong. Some sort of deceit or dissimulation was to be suspected; the actor had to be concealing his real motives. It was, as Samuel Stanhope Smith said, the "arts of disguise" that made human actions complicated.[61]

This problem of deception was a source of continuing fascination in eighteenth-century Anglo-American culture. The Augustans, of course, did not invent the notion of deception, but because of their identification of cause and effect with human intentions and actions, and because of their assumption of man-made designs lying beneath the surface of seemingly contingent events, they made much more of it than other ages have. Given the influence of Locke's sensationalist epistomology, people were always in danger of mistaking false appearances for reality, words for things. Radical Whigs constantly warned of the ease by which the human mind was misled. If people were dependent for their knowledge on the information provided by their senses, then they had to be especially careful of what they saw and heard. Like jugglers fooling people by "sleight of Hand," artful political leaders knew how "to dally and play" upon the people's "Foibles" by using "fine Figures and beautiful Sounds" to "disguise and vanish Sense." What men often saw and heard was not reality. Beneath the surface of experience there existed, they had been told, a wonderful but invisible world of forces—gravity, electricity, magnetism, and fluids and gases of various sorts—that produced, said Joseph Priestley, "an almost infinite variety of visible effects."[62]

No wonder then that men were tempted to think that they were "formed to deceive and be deceived," that "Mankind are in Masquerade, and Falsehood assumes the Air of Reality." In a rapidly changing world of sense impressions, nothing seemed as it really was, and hypocrisy was a charge on everyone's lips. Men presumed, as did Robert Munford's hero in *The Patriots*, that "secrecy is generally the veil of iniquity" from which followed the "confident" conclusion of "some evil design." Sincerity, which Archbishop John Tillotson defined as making "our outward actions exactly agreeable to our inward purposes and intentions," became an ever more important ideal.[63] There even developed a politics of sincerity, with which republicanism became associated. With all social relationships in a free state presumably dependent on mutual trust, it is not surprising that the courts of eighteenth-century Massachusetts treated instances of cheating and deception far more severely than overt acts of violence.[64] The differences between appearance and reality, disguise and sincerity, were the stock themes of eighteenth-century literature and drama. The artful manipulation of innocent virtue was the traditional device by which most comic situations in novels and plays were created.

Satire, the kind of literature celebrated by the age—indeed, the eighteenth century was the greatest era of satire in Western history—presumed the prevalence of deception. It posited a distinction between appearance and reality—that the world we see is not the world that really exists—and rested on the discrepancy between what people profess to be and what they really are.[65] Satire was made for an enlightened age; it took for granted that individuals are autonomous rational beings fully responsible for the good and evil they bring about. Its object was always to expose to shame and ridicule any behavior contrary to what men of reason had a right to expect, to strip away the virtuous appearances that vice used to clothe itself. Since everyone professed to be pursuing truth and virtue, how was it, asked John Adams in one of his many discourses on this problem, that human affairs so often resulted "in direct opposition to both"? Only deception, including self-deception, could explain the discrepancy. "From what other source can such fierce disputations arise concerning the two things [truth and virtue] which seem the most consonant to the entire frame of human nature?"[66]

The conspiratorial interpretations of the age were a generalized application to the world of politics of the pervasive duplicity assumed to exist in all human affairs.[67] Only by positing secret plots and hidden machinations by governments was it possible, it seemed, to close the bewildering gaps between what rulers professed and what they brought forth. It was true, wrote Hume in his history of Charles II's court, that at first beliefs in conspiracies and cabals seemed preposterous and that often no concrete evidence could be found for them. "But the utter impossibility of accounting, by any other hypothesis, for those strange measures embraced by the court, as well as for the numerous circumstances which accompanied them obliges us to acknowledge, though there remains no direct evidence of it, that a formal plan was laid for changing the religion and subverting the constitution of England, and that the king and the ministry were in reality conspirators against the people."[68]

The same notion of deception lay behind Edmund Burke's celebrated "Thoughts on the Cause of the Present Discontents" (1770), which more than any other single piece of writing in the pre-Revolutionary period pinpointed the nature of the deceit at work in the early years of George

III's reign. There were, said Burke, no discernible causes that would explain the present discontents of the British nation—no great party agitations, no famine, no war, no foreign threat, no oppression. The effects, the national discontents, were out of all proportion to the apparent causes. They could be accounted for only by hidden causes—the existence of a "double cabinet," thought Burke, operating behind the scenes of George III's government against the will of the people. If enlightened thinkers like Hume and Burke could use such logic, it is not surprising that others relied on it as well.[69] As political consequences in an increasingly complicated world appeared more and more contrary to the avowed aims of rulers, only deception on a large scale seemed capable of resolving the mysterious discrepancies.

No wonder, then, that mistrust and jealousy grew, for, as the South Carolina merchant Henry Laurens noted in 1765, a "malicious Villain acting behind the Curtain . . . could be reached only by suspicion." Such suspicion could ripen into certainty through events. Words lost all capacity to reveal motives; only actions could reveal the secret designs of those in power. "What was their view in the beginning or [how] far it was Intended to be carried Must be Collected from facts that Afterwards have happened."[70] The more glaring the disparity between these facts and the professed good intentions of their perpetrators, the more shrill became the accusations of hidden designs and dark plots. Some might continue to suggest that "the ways of Heaven are inscrutable; and frequently, the most unlooked-for events have arisen from seemingly the most inadequate causes," and of course others continued to believe that motives and actions did not always coincide, trusting with Dr. Johnson in the old English proverb that "Hell is paved with good intentions."[71] But for those who knew how cause and effect really worked, deception and conspiracy were more morally coherent and intellectually satisfying explanations of the apparent difference between professions and deeds. When effects "cannot be accounted for by any visible cause," it was rational to conclude that "there must be, therefore, some men behind the curtain" who were secretly bringing them about.[72] This commonplace image of figures operating "behind the curtain" was the consequence of a political world that was expanding and changing faster than its available rational modes of explanation could handle.

SUCH WERE THE PRESUPPOSITIONS and circumstances that explain the propensity of Anglo-Americans and others in the eighteenth century to resort to conspiratorial interpretations of events. The belief in plots was not a symptom of disturbed minds but a rational attempt to explain human phenomena in terms of human intentions and to maintain moral coherence in the affairs of men. This mode of thinking was neither pathological nor uniquely American. Certainly, the American Revolution cannot serve as an adequate context for comprehending the obsession with conspiratorial beliefs. Perhaps we can perceive better their larger place in Western history by examining, however briefly, the newer modes of causal explanation that gradually came to replace them.

Well before the close of the eighteenth century, even while conspiratorial interpretations were flourishing under the aegis of enlightened science, alternative ways of explaining events were taking form, prompted by dynamic social changes that were stretching and contorting any simple linkage between human intentions and actions, causes and effects. The expanding, interdependent economic order obviously relied on the activity of thousands upon thousands of insignificant producers and traders whose various and conflicting motives could hardly be deciphered, let alone judged. The growing number of persons and interests participating in politics made causal evaluations ever more difficult. Causes seemed farther and farther removed from their consequences, sometimes disappearing altogether into a distant murkiness. As a result, the inferences of plots and deceptions used to close the widening gap between events and the presumed designs of particular individuals became even more elaborate and contrived. Many were still sure that every social effect, every political event, had to have a purposive human agent as a cause. But men now distinguished more frequently between "remote" and "proximate" causes and between "immediate" and "permanent" effects. Although many continued to assume that the relationship between causes and their effects was intrinsic and morally homogeneous, some moralists noted bewilderingly and sometimes cynically how personal vices like self-love and self-interest could have contrary, indeed beneficial, consequences for society. Men everywhere wrestled with the demands the changing social reality was placing on their thought. Some suggested that self-love might even be a virtue; others complained of "a kind of *mandevillian* chymistry" that converted avarice into benevolence; still others questioned the presumed identity between private motives and public consequences.[73]

Little of this was followed out in any systematic way in the Anglo-American world until the appearance in the latter half of the eighteenth century of that remarkable group of Scottish intellectuals who worked out, in an extraordinary series of writings, a new understanding of the relationship between individuals and events. These Scottish "social scientists" did not and could not by themselves create a new way of conceiving of human affairs, but their writings were an especially clear crystallization of the changes gradually taking place in Western consciousness during the last third of the eighteenth century. Adam Ferguson, Adam Smith, and John Millar sought to undermine what Duncan Forbes has called "a dominant characteristic of the historical thought of the age"— the "tendency to explain events in terms of conscious action by individuals." These Scottish moral philosophers had come to realize more clearly than most eighteenth-century thinkers that men pursuing their own particular aims were led by an "invisible hand" into promoting an end that was no part of their intentions. Traditional historians, complained Ferguson in his *History of Civil Society*, had seen all events as the "effect of design. An author and a work, like cause and effect, are perpetually coupled together." But reality was not so simple. Men, "in striving to remove inconveniencies, or to gain apparent and contiguous advantages, arrive at ends which even their imagination could not anticipate, . . . and nations stumble upon establishments, which are indeed the result of human action, but not the execution of any human design."[74]

Such momentous insights would in time help to transform all social
and historical thinking in the Western world. But it took more than
the writings of philosophers—it took the experiencing of tumultuous
events—to shake most European intellectuals out of their accustomed
ways of thinking. The French Revolution, more than any other single
event, changed the consciousness of Europe. The Revolution was simply
too convulsive and too sprawling, involving the participation of too many
masses of people, to be easily confined within conventional personalistic and rationalistic modes of explanation. For the most sensitive European intellectuals, the Revolution became the cataclysm that shattered
once and for all the traditional moral affinity between cause and effect,
motives and behavior. That the actions of liberal, enlightened, and well-
intentioned men could produce such horror, terror, and chaos, that so
much promise could result in so much tragedy, became, said Shelley, "the
master theme of the epoch in which we live." What the French Revolution
revealed, wrote Wordsworth, speaking for a generation of disillusioned
intellectuals, was "this awful truth" that "sin and crime are apt to start
from their very opposite qualities."[75] Many European thinkers continued,
of course, to describe what happened as the deliberate consequence of
the desires and ambitions of individuals. But the scale and complexity of
the Revolution now required conspiratorial interpretations of an unprecedented sort. No small group of particular plotters could account for its
tumult and mass movements; only elaborately organized secret societies,
like the Illuminati or the Freemasons, involving thousands of individuals
linked by sinister designs, could be behind the Europe-wide upheaval.[76]

Although such conspiratorial interpretations of the Revolution were
everywhere, the best minds—Hegel's in particular—now knew that the
jumble of events that made up the Revolution were so complex and overwhelming that they could no longer be explained simply as the products of personal intention. For these thinkers, history could no longer be
a combination of individual events managed by particular persons, but
had to become a complicated flow or process, a "stream," that swept men
along.

. . .

THE STORY OF THIS VAST TRANSFORMATION in the way men explain events is central to the history of modern Western thought. Indeed, so huge and complicated is it that our easy generalizations are apt to miss its confused and agonized significance for individuals and to neglect the piecemeal ways in which it was worked out in the minds of people—not great philosophers like Hegel or Adam Smith, but more ordinary people, workaday clergymen, writers, and politicians caught up in the problems and polemics of the moment.

Certainly late eighteenth-century Americans did not experience this transformation in consciousness as rapidly and to the same extent as Europeans, but it is evident that some were coming to realize that the social and moral order was not as intelligible as it once had been. Few active minds were able to resist the pressures a new complicated commercial reality was placing on familiar assumptions about human nature and morality. Even the cynical and worldly New York merchant-politician, Gouverneur Morris, found himself ensnared in an apparent conflict between motives and consequences and, in an unfinished essay, groped to make sense of the problematical nature of late eighteenth-century experience.

Morris began his essay on "Political Enquiries," as nearly all eighteenth-century writers did, with happiness and declared his agreement with the conventional belief that virtue and the avoidance of evil were the keys to realizing it: "To inculcate Obedience to the moral Law is therefore the best Means of promoting human Happiness." But immediately problems arose. Which should government encourage more, public or private virtue? "Can there be any Difference between them? In other Words," asked Morris, in a question that directly confronted Mandeville's paradox, "can the same Thing be right and wrong?" Could selfishness, for example, result in public benefits? If so, how should self-interest be judged? "If an Action be in its own Nature wrong," said Morris in a summary of the traditional moral view, "we can never justify it from a Relation to the public Interest." It had to be judged "by the Motive of the Actor." But then, "who can know his Motive?" Was motive the criterion of judgment after all? "From what Principle of the human Heart," wondered Morris, "is public Virtue derived?"[77]

Despite such scattered musings and questionings, most Americans found it as difficult as Morris to escape from the presuppositions of a traditional moral order. Only by assuming that the beliefs or motives of individuals caused events could those individuals be held morally accountable for what happened. These assumptions had underlain the Revolutionaries' charge of a British conspiracy, and they underlay every succeeding American notion of conspiracy. By the last decade of the eighteenth century, however, the polemics surrounding these continuing charges of conspiracy were unsettling older views and forcing new explorations into the problems of causation in human affairs.

The climax in America of the late eighteenth century's frenzy of plots and counterplots came in 1798 with the most serious crisis the young nation had yet faced. This crisis brought the country close to civil war and led, in New England at least, to Federalist accusations that the Republican Party was in league with an international Jacobinical conspiracy dominated by the Order of the Bavarian Illuminati. This Illuminati conspiracy, the Federalists charged, had not only brought about the French Revolution but was now threatening to subvert America's new government. In elaborating for their fellow Americans the nature of this plot, impassioned Federalists, especially those in the standing order of New England clergy, were compelled to expose the premises of their ideas about causality in an unprecedented manner.[78]

Federalist spokesmen in 1798 argued that Americans ought to be suspicious of the Illuminati and other similar organizations that claimed to have benevolent purposes. Had not the perpetrators of the French Revolution likewise professed a "fraternal intention" and made "splendid and passionate harangues on universal freedom and equality"? But everyone knew what "evil effects" they had produced. Such men were designing hypocrites, "void of sincerity" and not to be trusted.[79] Yet such suspicion and mistrust, such fears of duplicity, could just as easily be turned against any leaders, as the Federalists knew only too well. Throughout the 1790s the Republicans had accused them of just this sort of deception, of fomenting beneath their high-sounding professions of devotion to the new republic secret designs for monarchizing American society and government. In self-defense, therefore, the Federalists were pressed in the debates of the late 1790s into exploring the ways in which people could distinguish between hypocrisy and sincerity in their leaders. The public needed to be convinced that Federalist leaders were men whose words and motives could be trusted. The Federalists thus set out to show why people should confide their government only into the hands of honest, respectable, and well-bred gentlemen like themselves, who in contrast to the upstart and irreligious Republicans had the worth, religiosity, and status deserving of political authority.

The Federalists were thoroughly eighteenth-century minded (which is why they resorted to satire much more readily than did their Republican opponents). They assumed the existence of a rational moral order and a society of deliberately acting individuals who controlled the course and shape of events. They were sure that men's beliefs or motives mattered in determining actions and that such causes and effects were intrinsically related. "As the volitions and consequent actions of men are mainly governed by their prevailing belief," David Tappan, Hollis Professor of Divinity at Harvard, declared in 1798, "so he who steadily believes and obeys truth is a virtuous man; while he who chooses and obeys falsehood is a vitious character." Clinging to this traditional assumption that events were the direct consequence of individuals' intentions and opinions, which they summed up as "character," the Federalists could only conclude that the character of individuals, particularly of leaders, shaped the general character of society. Society in fact was only the individual writ large. "If each man conducts himself aright, the community cannot be conducted wrong," said Timothy Dwight, president of Yale. "If private life be unblamable, the public state must be commendable and happy." This being so, it followed that the established Federalist gentry, who even the Republicans admitted were honest and respectable men of character, were the best leaders for the society and could do it no harm. Good private motives, in other words, could have only good public consequences.[80]

Confronted with these self-serving arguments, Jeffersonian Republicans and others who opposed the privileged position of the Federalist gentry were eventually led to question and defy the Federalists' basic assumption: that men's intentions and beliefs—their private "character"—were necessarily and directly translated into public consequences. No one struggled more persistently with this issue than the fiery Connecticut Jeffersonian Abraham Bishop. Although Bishop eventually accused the Federalists of fomenting their own Illuminati conspiracy, he also tried in a series of speeches to work out an explanation for the perplexing discrepancy between causes and effects in human affairs. His thought was remarkable for both its boldness and originality.

Bishop at times fell back on the conventional notion of deception. "The great, the wise, rich and mighty men of the world" were always trying to delude those beneath them "with charming outsides, engaging manners, powerful address and inexhaustible argument." But Bishop admitted that such an explanation was not fully satisfactory. He knew that many of the Federalist leaders possessed "integrity in *private* life." Yet at the same time this private integrity had "no manner of connection with *political* character." How then to account for the difference between this respectable private character and its obnoxious public effects? Perhaps, Bishop suggested, honest and reputable men behaved differently in groups and organizations. "Thus committees of societies, selectmen and legislators will do certain things, officially, which would ruin them as individuals." It was hard to know how things happened; all we can know, said Bishop, is that men who exhibited no wicked passions at home or among their neighbors did so as politicians, as "evinced by correspondent actions."[81]

Perhaps, suggested Bishop, with an audacity rare among eighteenth-century Americans, personal character and intentions do not really count at all in explaining events. Since men always profess decent motives for their actions, he argued, we can never judge them by their motives. People seem to be caught up in a "system," and it is the "system," and not particular individuals, that we must combat and condemn. To account for the country's revolt against Great Britain, said Bishop, Americans in the 1770s had blamed the greater part of the respectable men in the British nation. "Did we by this intend to charge each of these men with a personal disposition to oppress, plunder and destroy us? Surely not!—But we charged to the system, which they supported, all these dispositions, and dreadful facts proved our charges to be well-founded."[82]

These kinds of thoughts were too new and too frightening in their moral implications to be easily followed up.[83] But at least one American saw very clearly what belief in conspiracies, like that of the Bavarian Illuminati, meant for men's understanding of events. In 1799, in a brilliant review of one of the many Federalist Fourth of July orations that laid out the diabolical designs of the Illuminati, the novelist and editor Charles Brockden Brown went right to the heart of the misconception that was at work.

Those who believe in such conspiracies, Brown wrote, have no idea how things really happen. They have no sense that "men are liable to error, and though they may intend good, may commit enormous mistakes in the choice of means." While enlightened philosophes, for example,

> imagine themselves labouring for the happiness of mankind, loosening the bonds of superstition, breaking the fetters of commerce, out-rooting the prejudice of birth, by which father transmits to son absolute power over the property, liberty and lives of millions, they may, in reality, be merely pulling down the props which uphold human society, and annihilate not merely the chains of false religion, but the foundations of morality—not merely the fetters of commerce, and federal usurpations upon property, but commerce and property themselves. The apology which may be made for such is, that though their activity be pernicious, their purposes are pure.

But those who believe in the Illuminati conspiracy deny liberal reform-ers "the benefits of this construction." They assume that all the disastrous consequences were produced by certain individuals and were "*foreseen and intended.*" To avoid such simple-minded conspiratorial beliefs, wrote Brown, we must be "conscious of the uncertainty of history" and recog-nize that "actions and motives cannot be truly described," for they are not always integrally related.[84]

Brown returned again and again to this theme of what has been called "the unanticipated consequences of purposive action."[85] Indeed, his signifi-cance as a writer comes not from his creation of the American romance or the American gothic tale, but from his relentless attempts to probe Words-worth's "awful truth," to examine the moral implications of evil caused by well-intentioned and benevolent persons. Unlike the oppressive didactic fic-tion of his American contemporaries, Brown's novels are intellectual explo-rations into causality, deception, and the moral complexity of life. In his fiction, not only do moral obligations such as sincerity and benevolence often contradict one another, but virtuous motives time and again lead to contrary consequences. Despite all the tedious analyses of motives his characters go through, none of them is able to avoid unfortunate results.[86] Each, like Wieland, finds he has "rashly set in motion a machine over whose progress [he] had no control." "How little cognizance have men over the actions and motives of each other!" Brown's character Edgar Huntly exclaims. "How total is our blindness with regard to our own performances!" Motives and intentions, Brown suggested, could no longer be crucial in judging moral responsibility, since "the causes that fashion men into instruments of happiness or misery, are numerous, complex, and operate upon a wide surface. . . . Every man is encompassed by numerous claims, and is the sub-ject of intricate relations. . . . Human affairs are infinitely complicated."[87]

These American explorations into the relationship between aims and consequences were only small and modest examples of what was taking place generally in Western thought during the late eighteenth century. Others elsewhere were also becoming more and more conscious of the complicatedness of human affairs. The growing awareness of the difficulty of delving into the human heart and the increasing unwillingness to esteem men simply for their aristocratic character were forcing moralists, sometimes imperceptibly, to shift the basis of judgment of human action from the motives and personal qualifications of the actors to the public consequences of their acts. The common practice of deducing motives from their effects in actions only furthered this transition and blurred what was happening. What counted now was less the beliefs and intentions, or the "character," of the actor and more the consequences of his actions, or his contributions to human happiness. And any man, however much he lacked "character," however ordinary and insignificant he may have been, could make such contributions.

In just such shifts from motives to consequences was a democratic consciousness strengthened and what came to be called utilitarianism created. Naturally, for most people there remained no discrepancy between benevolent aims and good effects, and the familiar belief that private virtue was the obvious source of human happiness continued strong. But for Jeremy Bentham and other stark utilitarians, there could no longer be any such thing as good or bad motives: "If they are good or bad, it is only on account of their effects, good on account of their tendency to produce pleasure, or avert pain: bad, on account of their tendency to produce pain, or avert pleasure."[88]

Many Americans were reluctant to separate motives from consequences, causes from effects, in this unequivocal utilitarian manner. But by the early nineteenth century there were some, usually those most eager to disparage "aristocratic" heroic individuals and to magnify the popular "masses," who increasingly emphasized what Bishop had clumsily called the "system" of society. Now it was described as the "natural order" or the "aggregate result" of events formed out of the diverse and clashing motives of countless insignificant individuals. Men no doubt caused this "aggregate result," but they did so in large numbers and unthinkingly by following their particular natural inclinations. This concept of the

social process eventually became identified with what Jacksonian Democrats called the "voluntary" or "democratic" principle—the principle that
was able by itself "to work out the best possible general result or order
and happiness from the chaos of characters, ideas, motives and interests:
human society." Despite this separation of individuals' intentions from
the consequences of their actions, the consequences nonetheless seemed
to form a process or pattern that could be trusted. Perhaps, it was suggested, there was some kind of moral force in each person—sympathy
or a moral feeling of some sort—that held the innumerable discordant
individuals in a society together and, like gravity in the physical world,
created a natural harmony of interests.[89]

Although this concept of the social process transcending the desires of
particular individuals presaged a new social order, it was in some respects
merely a throwback to a premodern Protestant understanding of divine
sovereignty. Many Americans, even nonevangelicals like George Washington, had always been able to "trace the finger of Providence through
those dark and mysterious events."[90] Now this traditional notion of
providence took on a new importance and even among secular-minded
thinkers became identified with "progress" and with the natural principles of society created by multiplicities of people following their natural desires free from artificial restraints, particularly those imposed by
laws and government. Providence no longer meant, as it often had in the
past, the special interpositions of God in the events of the world but was
now increasingly identified almost wholly with the natural pattern these
events seemed to form.[91] With such a conception, the virtuous or vicious
character of individual beliefs and intentions in the movement of events
no longer seemed to matter. Even the "pursuit of gold" could have beneficial results, for "by some interesting filiation, 'there's a Divinity, that
shapes our ends.' "[92]

Although these ideas of a collective social process were strongly
voiced by some Jacksonian Democrats and permeated some of the history writing of the romantic era, they were never able to dominate
nineteenth-century American popular thinking.[93] Many Americans were

too sure of the integral and homogeneous relationship between cause and effect, and too preoccupied with the moral purposes of men, to embrace fully and unequivocally any notion that stressed the impersonal and collective nature of the workings of society. Despite all the talk of usefulness and happiness as the consequence of behavior, most Americans in the early nineteenth century could scarcely conceive of a moral order that was not based on intentions. America as a republic, Timothy Dwight said, was necessarily "a government by motives, addressed to the understanding and affections of rational subjects, and operating on their minds, as inducements to voluntary obedience."[94] Many agreed with John Taylor that "it is unnatural that evil moral qualities, should produce good moral effects"; it was "a violation of the relation between cause and effect" and a denial of "the certainty with which moral inferences flow from moral causes." Traditionalists and moralists of all sorts clung determinedly to what Alexis de Tocqueville called the "aristocratic" assumption that society was still composed of autonomous individuals capable of deliberately causing good or evil events and therefore of being held morally accountable for them.[95]

In an oration of 1825 commemorating the fiftieth anniversary of the battle of Concord, Edward Everett paused to ponder the dilemma faced by anyone seeking to explain how things happened. It was difficult, Everett noted, to separate out of the processes of history "what is to be ascribed to the cooperation of a train of incidents and characters, following in long succession upon each other; and what is to be referred to the vast influence of single important events." Thoroughly captivated by the paradigm of mechanistic causality, Everett could readily perceive in the history of the American Revolution "a series of causes and effects, running back into the history of the dark ages in Europe." Yet at the same time he knew that on that particular day, April 19, 1775, in Concord, "the agency of individual events and men" was crucial in bringing on the Revolution. There seemed to be two distinct viewpoints—one a long-term distant perspective that traced a "chain of events, which lengthens, onward by blind fatality," involving innumerable participants; the other, a close-up perspective that focused on the heroic individuals and actions of the day itself, against which "every thing else seems lost in the comparison." Like many other Americans, Everett was reluctant to envelop the glorious and willful exploits of America's individual patriots in the deterministic processes of history. Despite their underlying sense that history was an orderly chain of causes and effects, most of America's early national historians continued to stress the contingency and openness of events and the moral responsibility of individual actors.[96]

As nineteenth-century society became more interdependent and complicated, however, sensitive and reflective observers increasingly saw the efficient causes of events becoming detached from particular self-acting individuals and receding from view. "Small but growing numbers of people," writes historian Thomas L. Haskell in the most perceptive account we have of this development, "found it implausible or unproductive to attribute genuine causal power to those elements of society with which they were intimately and concretely familiar."[97] As these ideas evolved, laying the basis for the emergence of modern social science, attributing events to the conscious design of particular individuals became more and more simplistic. Conspiratorial interpretations of events still thrived, but now they seemed increasingly primitive and quaint.

By our own time, dominated as it is by professional social science, conspiratorial interpretations have become so out of place that, as we have seen, they can be accounted for only as mental aberrations, as a paranoid style symptomatic of psychological disturbance. In our postindustrial, scientifically saturated society, those who continue to attribute combinations of events to deliberate human design may well be peculiar sorts of persons—marginal people, perhaps, removed from the centers of power, unable to grasp the conceptions of complicated causal linkages offered by sophisticated social scientists, and unwilling to abandon the desire to make simple and clear moral judgments of events. But people with such conspiratorial beliefs have not always been either marginal or irrational. Living in this complicated modern world, where the very notion of causality is in doubt, should not prevent us from seeing that at another time and in another culture most enlightened people accounted for events in just this particular way.

AFTERWORD TO CHAPTER 3

This article was stimulated first by the simultaneous appearance in 1965 of Richard Hofstadter's *The Paranoid Style in American Politics and Other Essays*; the introduction to Bernard Bailyn's *Pamphlets of the American Revolution*, which became *The Ideological Origins of the American Revolution* two years later; and then by the publication in 1976 of James H. Hutson's article "The American Revolution: The Triumph of a Delusion."

These works forced me to puzzle over the significance of conspiratorial thinking. I knew that Hofstadter's notion that such thinking was a distorted style that suggested some sort of political pathology at work was simply not applicable to the Founding Fathers. Whatever they were, the Revolutionary leaders were not fanciful or pathological thinkers; nor were they delusional, as Hutson suggested. Moreover, as Bailyn demonstrated, conspiratorial thinking was very prevalent in the eighteenth century. The Founders were not the only figures in the eighteenth century who thought in conspiratorial terms. The British leaders, including someone as sophisticated as Edmund Burke, did as well. I consequently became preoccupied with working out the questions of why so many people in the eighteenth century explained events in conspiratorial terms and why most sophisticated thinkers by the beginning of the nineteenth century had stopped doing so. My answer to these questions became the article here republished.

PART II

THE *Making* OF THE *Constitution* AND *American Democracy*

CHAPTER FOUR

INTERESTS *and* DISINTERESTEDNESS
in the MAKING *of the* CONSTITUTION

*D*URING OUR BICENTENNIAL CELEBRATIONS of the Constitution, we will gather many times to honor the makers of that Constitution, the Federalists of 1787–1788. We have certainly done so many times in the past. We have repeatedly pictured the Founders, as we call them, as men of vision—bold, original, open-minded, enlightened men who deliberately created what William Gladstone once called "the most wonderful work ever struck off at a given time by the hand and purpose of man."[1] We have described them as men who knew where the future lay and went for it. Even those like Charles Beard who have denigrated their motives have seen the Founders as masters of events, realistic pragmatists who knew human nature when they saw it, farsighted, economically advanced, modern men in step with the movement of history.

In contrast, we have usually viewed the opponents of the Constitution, the Anti-Federalists, as very tame and timid, narrow-minded and parochial men of no imagination and little faith, caught up in the ideological rigidities of the past—inflexible, suspicious men unable to look ahead and see where the United States was going. The Anti-Federalists seem forever doomed to be losers, bypassed by history and eternally disgraced by their opposition to the greatest constitutional achievement in our nation's history.

But maybe we have got it all wrong. Maybe the Federalists were not men of the future after all. Maybe it was the Anti-Federalists who really saw best and farthest. Is it possible that all those original, bold, and far-sighted Federalists had their eyes not on what was coming, but on what was passing? Perhaps the roles of the participants in the contest over the Constitution in 1787–1788 ought to be reversed. If either side in the conflict over the Constitution stood for modernity, perhaps it was the Anti-Federalists. They, and not the Federalists, may have been the real harbingers of the moral and political world we know—the liberal, democratic, commercially advanced world of individual pursuits of happiness.

If this is true—if indeed the Founders did not stand for modernity—then it should not be surprising that they are now so lost to us that they should have become, as we continually lament, "a galaxy of public leaders we have never been able remotely to duplicate since."[2] Instead of being the masters, were they really the victims of events? Is it possible that their Constitution failed, and failed miserably, in what they wanted it to do?

Naturally, we are reluctant to admit that the Constitution may have failed in what it set out to do, and consequently we have difficulty in fully understanding its origins. To be sure, we readily accept the necessity for a new central government in 1787. Unable to imagine the United States as ever existing without a strong national government, we regard the creation of the new structure in 1787 as inevitable. (For us it is the Articles of Confederation that cannot be taken seriously.) But the new central government seems inevitable to us only for reasons that fit our modern preconceptions. As long as people in the 1780s explain the movement for the Constitution in terms of the weaknesses of the Confederation, we can easily understand and accept their explanations. But when people in the 1780s explain the movement for the Constitution in terms other than the palpable weaknesses of the central government—in terms of a crisis in the society—we become puzzled and skeptical. A real crisis? It hardly seems believable. The 1780s were, after all, a time of great release and expansion:

the population grew as never before, or since, and more Americans than ever before were off in pursuit of prosperity and happiness. "There is not upon the face of the earth a body of people more happy or rising into consequence with more rapid stride, than the Inhabitants of the United Stares of America," Charles Thomson told Jefferson in 1786. "Population is encreasing, new houses building, new lands clearing, new settlements forming, and new manufactures establishing with a rapidity beyond conception."³ The general mood was high, expectant, and far from bleak. No wonder then that historians of very different persuasions have doubted that there was anything really critical happening in the society.⁴

Yet, of course, we have all those statements by people in the 1780s warning that "our situation is critical and dangerous" and that "our vices" were plunging us into "national ruin." Benjamin Rush even thought that the American people were on the verge of "degenerating into savages or devouring each other like beasts of prey." But if we think that Rush is someone with a hyperactive imagination, here is the 1786 voice of the much more sober and restrained George Washington: "What astonishing changes a few years arc capable of producing. . . . From the high ground we stood upon, from the plain path which invited our footsteps, to be so fallen! so lost! it is really mortifying."⁵

What are we to make of such despairing and excited statements— statements that can be multiplied over and over and that were often made not in the frenzy of public debate, but in the privacy of letters to friends? Many of those historians who, like Charles Beard, believe that such statements are a gross exaggeration can conclude only that the sense of crisis was "conjured up" by the Federalists, since "actually the country faced no such emergency." But such a conspiratorial interpretation of the Constitution is hardly satisfying and tells us nothing of what such statements of alarm and foreboding meant. Why did some men, members of the elite—those who saved their letters for us to read—think America was in a crisis?⁶

Certainly it was not the defects of the Articles of Confederation that were causing this sense of crisis. These defects of the Confederation were remediable and were scarcely capable of eliciting horror and despair. To be sure, these defects did make possible the calling of the Philadelphia Convention to amend the Articles. By 1787 almost every political leader in the country, including most of the later Anti-Federalists, wanted something done to strengthen the Articles of Confederation. The Confederation had no power to pay its debts, no power to tax, and no power to regulate commerce, and it was daily being humiliated in its international relationships. Reform of the Articles in some way or other—particularly by granting the Congress a limited authority to tax and the power to regulate commerce—was in the air. This desire to do something about the central government was the Federalists' opportunity: it explains the willingness of people to accede to the meeting at Annapolis and the subsequent convening of delegates at Philadelphia. In fact, so acceptable and necessary seemed some sort of change in the Confederation that later Anti-Federalists were remarkably casual about the meeting at Philadelphia. William Findley of western Pennsylvania, for example, later claimed he was selected to go to the Convention but declined when he learned that "the delegates would have no wages." Thus the seven delegates Pennsylvania sent to the Convention were all residents of the city of Philadelphia (including even one, Gouverneur Morris, who was really a New Yorker), and no one at the time complained.[7]

Thus the defects of the Confederation were widely acknowledged, and many looked to the Philadelphia Convention for a remedy. But these defects do not account for the elite's expression of crisis, nor do they explain the ambitious nature of the nationalists' Virginia Plan that formed the working model for the Convention's deliberations. The nationalists' aims and the Virginia Plan went way beyond what the weaknesses of the Articles demanded. Granting Congress the authority to raise revenue, to regulate trade, to pay off its debts, and to deal effectively in international affairs did not require the total scrapping of the Articles and the creation of an extraordinarily powerful and distant national government, the like of which was virtually inconceivable to Americans a decade earlier. The Virginia Plan was the remedy for more than the obvious impotence of the Confederation; it was a remedy—and an aristocratic remedy—for what were often referred to as the excesses of American democracy. It was these excesses of democracy that lay behind the elite's sense of crisis.

What excesses of democracy? What on earth could have been happening to provoke fear and horror? Not Shays's Rebellion that broke out in the winter of 1786–1787. That was an alarming clincher for many Federalists, especially in Massachusetts, but it was scarcely the cause of the Federalists' pervasive sense of crisis, which existed well before they learned of Shays's Rebellion.[8] No, it was not mobs and overt disorder that really frightened the Founders. They knew about popular rioting, and had taken such occurrences more or less in stride for years. What bothered them, what they meant by the excesses of democracy, was something more insidious than mobs. It was something that we today accept as familiar, ordinary, and innocuous, but the Founders did not—good old American popular politics. It was popular politics, especially as practiced in the state legislatures, that lay behind the Founders' sense of crisis. The legislatures were unwilling to do "justice," and this, said Washington, is "the origin of the evils we now feel." The abuses of the state legislatures, said Madison, were "so frequent and so flagrant as to alarm the most stedfast friends of Republicanism," and these abuses, he told Jefferson in the fall of 1787, "contributed more to that uneasiness which produced the Convention, and prepared the public mind for a general reform, than those which accrued to our national character and interest from the inadequacy of the Confederation to its immediate objects."[9] Hard as it may be for us today to accept, the weaknesses of the Articles of Confederation were not the most important reasons for the making of the Constitution.

Throughout the whole period of crisis, Madison, the father of the Constitution if there ever was one, never had any doubt where the main source of the troubles lay. In his working paper drafted in the late winter of 1787 entitled "Vices of the Political System of the United States," Madison spent very little time on the impotence of the Confederation. What was really on his mind was the deficiencies of the state governments: he devoted more than half his paper to the "multiplicity," "mutability," and "injustice" of the laws passed by the states.[10] Particularly alarming and unjust in his eyes were the paper money acts, stay laws, and other forms of debtor-relief legislation that hurt creditors and violated individual property rights. And he knew personally what he was talking about. Although we usually think of Madison as a bookish scholar who got all his thoughts from his wide reading, he did not develop his ideas about the democratic excesses of the state governments by poring through the bundles of books that Jefferson was sending him from Europe. He learned about popular politics and legislative abuses firsthand—by being a member of the Virginia Assembly.

During the years 1784 through 1787 Madison attended four sessions of the Virginia legislature. They were perhaps the most frustrating and disillusioning years of his life, but also the most important years of his life, for his experience as a Virginia legislator in the 1780s was fundamental in shaping his thinking as a constitutional reformer.

Although Madison in these years had some notable legislative achievements, particularly with his shepherding into enactment Jefferson's famous bill for religious freedom, he was continually exasperated by what Jefferson years later (no doubt following Madison's own account) referred to as "the endless quibbles, chicaneries, perversions, vexations, and delays of lawyers and demi-lawyers" in the assembly. Really for the first time, Madison found out what democracy in America might mean. Not all the legislators were going to be like him or Jefferson; many of them did not even appear to be gentlemen. The Virginia legislators seemed so parochial, so illiberal, so small-minded, and most of them seemed to have only "a particular interest to serve." They had no regard for public honor or honesty. They too often made a travesty of the legislative process and were reluctant to do anything that might appear unpopular. They postponed taxes, subverted debts owed to the subjects of Great Britain, and passed, defeated, and repassed bills in the most haphazard ways. Madison had enlightened expectations for Virginia's port bill in 1784, but the other legislators got their self-serving hands on it and perverted it. It was the same with nearly all the legislative proposals he sought to introduce, especially those involving reform of the legal code and court system. "Important bills prepared at leisure by skilful hands," he complained, were vitiated by "crudeness and tedious discussion." What could he do with such clods? "It will little elevate your idea of our Senate," he wrote in weary disgust to Washington in 1786, to learn that the senators actually defeated a bill defining the privileges of foreign ambassadors in Virginia "on the principle . . . that an Alien ought not to be put on better ground than a Citizen."[11] This was carrying localism to absurdity.

It was not what republican lawmaking was supposed to be. Madison continually had to make concessions to the "prevailing sentiments," whether or not such sentiments promoted the good of the state or nation. He had to agree to bad laws for fear of getting worse ones, or give up good bills "rather than pay such a price" as opponents wanted. Today legislators are used to this sort of political horse-trading. But Madison simply was not yet ready for the logrolling and the pork-barreling that would eventually become the staples of American legislative politics. By 1786 he had "strong apprehensions" that his and Jefferson's hope for reforming the legal code "may never be systematically perfected." The legislature was simply too popular, and appealing to the people had none of the beneficial effects good republicans had expected. A bill having to do with court reform was, for example, "to be printed for consideration of the public"; but "instead of calling forth the sanction of the wise and virtuous," this action, Madison feared, would only "be a signal to interested men to redouble their efforts to get into the Legislature." Democracy was no solution to the problem; democracy was the problem. Madison repeatedly found himself having to beat back the "itch for paper money" and other measures "of a popular cast." Too often Madison had to admit that the only hope he had was "of moderating the fury," not defeating it.[12]

Madison, like other enthusiastic Revolutionary idealists, emerged from his experience with democratic politics in the mid-1780s a very chastened republican. It was bad enough, he wrote in his "Vices of the Political System of the United States," that legislators were often interested men or dupes of the sophistry of "a favorite leader" (like Patrick Henry).

Even more alarming for the fate of republican government, however, was the fact that such legislators were only reflecting the partial interests and parochial outlooks of their constituents. Too many of the American people could not see beyond their own pocketbooks or their own neighborhoods. "Individuals of extended views, and of national pride," said Madison (and he knew whom he meant), might be able to bring public proceedings to an enlightened cosmopolitan standard, but their example could never be followed by "the multitude." "Is it to be imagined that an ordinary citizen or even an assembly man of R. Island in estimating the policy of paper money, ever considered or cared in what light the measure would be viewed in France or Holland; or even in Massts or Connect? It was a sufficient temptation to both that it was for their interest."[13]

Madison's experience with the populist politics of the state legislatures was especially important because of his extraordinary influence in the writing of the federal Constitution. But his experience was not unusual; indeed, the Federalists could never have done what they did if Madison's experience was not widely shared. By the mid-1780s gentlemen up and down the continent were shaking their heads in disbelief and anger at the "private views and selfish principles" of the men they saw in the state assemblies, "men of narrow souls and no natural interest in the society." Selfish, ignorant, illiberal state legislators—"Characters too full of Local attachments and Views to permit sufficient attention to the general interest"—were bringing discredit upon popular government. They were promoting their own or their locality's particular interest, pandering "to the vulgar and sordid notions of the populace," and acting as judges in their own causes. "Private convenience, paper money, and ex post facto laws" were the "main springs" of these state lawmakers. Many of the delegates to the Philadelphia Convention were so ready to accept Madison's radical Virginia Plan and its proposed national authority to veto all state laws precisely because they shared his deep disgust with the localist and interest-ridden politics of the state legislatures. "The vile State governments are sources of pollution which will contaminate the American name for ages. . . . Smite them," Henry Knox urged Rufus King sitting in the Philadelphia Convention, "smite them, in the name of God and the people."[14]

We today can easily appreciate the concerns of the Founders with the weaknesses of the Confederation government: these seem real and tangible to us, especially in light of what we know our national government has become. But we have more difficulty in appreciating the fears the Founders expressed over the democratic politics of the state legislatures—the scrambling of different interest groups, the narrow self-promoting nature of much of the lawmaking, the incessant catering to popular demands. Surely, this behavior cannot be accurately described as the "wilderness of anarchy and vice." This "excess of democracy" is, after all, what popular politics is about, and it is not different from what Americans in time came to be very used to.[15]

It may not have been different from what Americans came to be used to, and it may not even have been different from what some of the Revolutionary leaders had occasionally experienced in their colonial assemblies. But for most of the Founding Fathers, popular political behavior in the states during the 1780s was very different from what they expected from their republican Revolution, and for them that difference was what made the 1780s a genuine critical period.

REPUBLICANISM WAS NOT SUPPOSED TO stimulate selfishness and private interests, but was to divert and control them. But in states up and down the continent various narrow factional interests, especially economic, were flourishing as never before, and, more alarming still, were demanding and getting protection and satisfaction from the democratically elected state legislatures. Although interest groups and factionalism had been common in the colonial legislatures, the interests and factions of post-Revolutionary politics were different: more numerous, less personal and family-oriented, and more democratically expressive of new, widespread economic elements in the society. The Revolution, it appeared, had unleashed acquisitive and commercial forces that no one had quite realized existed.

We are only beginning to appreciate the immense consequences that the Revolution and, especially, wartime mobilization had on American society. When all the articles and monographs are in, however, I think that we will find that the Revolutionary War, like the Civil War and the two World Wars, radically transformed America's society and economy. The war effort was enormous. The war went on for eight years (the longest in American history until that of Vietnam); it eventually saw one hundred thousand or more men under arms, and it touched the whole of American society to a degree that no previous event ever had. The inexhaustible needs of the army—for everything from blankets and wagons to meat and rum—brought into being a host of new manufacturing and entrepreneurial interests and made market farmers out of husbandmen who before had scarcely ever traded out of their neighborhoods. To pay for all these new war goods, the Revolutionary governments issued huge sums—four hundred million to five hundred million dollars—of paper money that made its way into the hands of many people who had hitherto dealt only in a personal and bookkeeping barter economy.[16] Under the stimulus of this wartime purchasing, speculative farmers, inland traders, and profiteers of all sorts sprang up by the thousands to circulate these goods and paper money throughout the interior areas of America. By 1778, wrote Henry Laurens, "the demand for money" was no longer "confined to the capital towns and cities within a small circle of trading merchants, but spread over a surface of 1,600 miles in length, and 300 broad." The war and rapidly rising prices were creating a society in which, as one bitter commissary agent complained, "Every Man buys in order to sell again."[17] No event in the eighteenth century accelerated the capitalistic development of America more than did the Revolutionary War. It brought new producers and consumers into the market economy, it aroused latent acquisitive instincts everywhere, it stimulated inland trade as never before, and it prepared the way for the eventual momentous shift of the basis of American prosperity from external to internal commerce.

The paper money and the enormous amounts of debts that all these inland entrepreneurs, traders, shopkeepers, and market farmers thrived on were the consequences neither of poverty nor of anticommercial behavior. Debt, as we of all generations in American history ought to know, was already emerging as a symptom of expansion and enterprise. Farmers, traders, and others in these Revolutionary years borrowed money, just as they married earlier and had more children than ever before, because they thought the future was going to be even better than the present. Common people had been increasingly buying consumer goods since at least the middle of the eighteenth century, but the Revolutionary War now gave many more ordinary farmers, often for the first time in their lives, the financial ability to purchase luxury goods that previously had been the preserve of the gentry—everything from lace finery to china dishware. It was this prospect of raising their standard of living and increasing their "pleasures and diversions" that got farmers to work harder and produce "surpluses" during the war, and there is evidence that when the availability of these "luxury" goods diminished during the war the farmers' productivity and their "surpluses" diminished too.[18] For ages men had thought that industry and frugality among the common people went together. Now suddenly in America the industriousness of ordinary people seemed dependent not on the fear of poverty, but on the prospect of luxury.[19]

The economic troubles of the 1780s came from the ending of the war and government purchasing. Too many people had too many heightened expectations and were into the market and the consumption of luxuries too deeply to make any easy adjustments to peace. The collapse of internal markets and the drying up of paper money meant diminished incomes, overextended businesses, swollen inventories of imported manufactures, and debt-laden farmers and traders. The responses of people hurt by these developments were very comprehensible; they simply wanted to continue what they had done during the war. The stay laws and other debtor-relief legislation and the printing of paper money were not the demands of backward-looking and uncommercial people. They were the demands of people who had enjoyed buying, selling, and consuming and desired to do more of it. In order to have prosperity, argued one defender of paper money in 1786, it was not enough to have an industrious people and a fertile territory; money was essential too. And for many ordinary people in the 1780s money—in the absence of gold and silver coin—meant paper money issued by governments or government loan offices. "By anticipating the products of several years labor," farmers were able to borrow loan office certificates based on land in order "to accelerate improvements" and "so to augment industry and multiply the means of carrying it on" and thereby "enrich" both themselves and the state.[20]

These calls for paper money in the 1780s were the calls of American business. The future of America's entrepreneurial activity and prosperity lay not with the hundreds of well-to-do creditor-merchants who dominated the overseas trade of the several ports along the Atlantic seaboard. Rather, it lay with the thousands upon thousands of ordinary traders, petty businessmen, aspiring artisans, and market farmers who were deep in debt and were buying and selling with each other all over America. For these people, unlike the overseas merchants who had their private bills of exchange, publicly created paper money was the only means "capable of answering all the *domestic* and *internal* purposes of a *circulating medium* in a nation" that lacked specie. The prosperity of a country, it was now argued, involved more than external commerce, more than having a surplus of exports over imports. "The *internal* commerce of the country must be promoted, by increasing its *real riches*," which were now rightly equated with the acquisitions, improvements, and entrepreneurial activity of ordinary people.[21]

There is no exaggerating the radical significance of this heightened awareness among Americans of the importance of domestic trade. Hitherto most Americans had thought of internal trade, as William Smith of New York put it in the 1750s, as publicly worthless—a mere passing of wealth around the community from hand to hand. Such exchanging, said Smith, "tho' it may enrich an Individual," meant that "others must be poorer, in an exact proportion to his Gains; but the collective Body of the People not at all."[22] Such was the traditional zero-sum mercantilist mentality that was now being challenged by the increased entrepreneurial activity of thousands of ordinary people. Farmers "in a new and unimproved country," it was now said, "have continual uses for money, to stock and improve their farms" or, as Madison noted, to "extend their consumption as far as credit can be obtained." And they now wanted more money than could be gotten by the old-fashioned means of applying "to a monied man for a loan from his private fortune." Consequently these farmers and other small-time entrepreneurs in state after state up and down the continent were electing representatives to their legislatures who could supply them with paper money, paper money which, as the preamble to a 1785 Pennsylvania statute establishing a loan office stated, was designed "to promote and establish the interests of internal commerce, agriculture and mechanic arts."[23] Not the defects of the Articles of Confederation, but this promotion of entrepreneurial interests by ordinary people—their endless buying and selling, their bottomless passion for luxurious consumption—was what really frightened the Federalists.

The Federalists in the 1780s had a glimpse of what America was to become—a scrambling business society dominated by the pecuniary interests of ordinary people—and they did not like what they saw. This premonition of America's future lay behind their sense of crisis and their horrified hyperbolic rhetoric. The wholesale pursuits of private interest and private luxury were, they thought, undermining America's capacity for republican government. They designed the Constitution in order to save American republicanism from the deadly effects of these private pursuits of happiness.

THE FOUNDERS DID NOT INTEND the new Constitution to change the character of the American people. They were not naive utopians; they were, as we have often noted, realistic about human nature. They had little or no faith in the power of religion or of sumptuary or other such laws to get people to behave differently. To be sure, they believed in education, and some of them put great stock in what it might do in reforming and enlightening American people. But still they generally approached their task in the 1780s with a practical, unsentimental appreciation of the givenness of human beings. They knew they lived in an age of commerce and interests. Although some of the landed gentry like Jefferson might yearn wistfully at times for America to emulate China and "abandon the ocean altogether," most of the Founders welcomed America's involvement in commerce, by which, however, they commonly meant overseas trade.[24] They believed in the importance of such commerce, saw it as a major agent in the refining and civilizing of people, and were generally eager to use the power of government to promote its growth. They knew too all about "interest," which Madison defined "in the popular sense" as the "immediate augmentation of property and wealth." They accepted the inevitability and the prevalence of "interest" and respected its power. "Interest," many of them said, "is the greatest tie one man can have on another." It was, they said, "the only binding cement" for states and peoples. Hamilton put it more bluntly: "He who pays is the master."[25]

Since 1776 they had learned that it was foolish to expect most people to sacrifice their private interests for the sake of the public welfare. For the Federalists there was little left of the Revolutionary utopianism of Samuel Adams. Already by the 1780s, Adams's brand of republicanism seemed archaic and Adams himself a figure from another time and place. Soon people would be shaking their heads in wonderment that such a person as Adams should have ever existed in America. "Modern times," it was said, "have produced no character like his." He was "one of Plutarch's men," a character out of the classical past. He was a Harvard-educated gentleman who devoted himself to the public. He had neither personal ambition nor the desire for wealth. He refused to help his children and gloried in his poverty. He was without interests or even private passions. Among the Revolutionary leaders he was unique. No other leader took classical republican values quite as seriously as Adams did.[26]

In fact, the other Revolutionary leaders were very quick to expose the unreality and impracticality of Adams's kind of republican idealism. As early as 1778 Washington realized that the Revolution would never succeed if it depended on patriotism alone. "It must be aided by a prospect of interest or some reward."[27] All men could not be like Samuel Adams.

It was too bad, but that was the way it was. Human beings were like that, and by the 1780s many of the younger Revolutionary leaders like Madison were willing to look at the reality of interests with a very cold eye. Madison's *Federalist* No. 10 was only the most famous and frank acknowledgment of the degree to which interests of various sorts had come to dominate American politics.

The Founders thus were not dreamers who expected more from the people than they were capable of. We in fact honor the Founding Fathers for their realism, their down-to-earth acceptance of human nature. Perhaps this is part of our despairing effort to make them one with us, to close that terrifying gap that always seems to exist between them and us. Nevertheless, in our hearts we know that they are not one with us, that they are separated from us, as they were separated from every subsequent generation of Americans, by an immense cultural chasm. They stood for a classical world that was rapidly dying, a world so different from what followed—and from our own—that an act of imagination is required to recover it in all its fullness. They believed in democracy, to be sure, but not our modern democracy; rather, they believed in a patrician-led classical democracy in which "virtue exemplified in government will diffuse its salutary influence through the society." For them government was not an arena for furthering the interests of groups and individuals but a means of moral betterment. What modern American politician would say, as James Wilson said in the Philadelphia Convention, that "the cultivation and improvement of the human mind was the most noble object" of government? Even Jefferson, who of all the Founders most forcefully led the way, though inadvertently, to a popular liberal future, could in 1787 urge a Virginia colleague: "Cherish . . . the spirit of our people, and keep alive their attention. Do not be too severe upon their errors, but reclaim them by enlightening them." All the Founding Fathers saw themselves as moral teachers.[28] However latently utilitarian, however potentially liberal, and however enthusiastically democratic the Founders may have been, they were not modern men.

Despite their acceptance of the reality of interests and commerce, the

Federalists had not yet abandoned what has been called the tradition of civic humanism—that host of values transmitted from antiquity that dominated the thinking of nearly all members of the elite in the eighteenth-century Anglo-American world. By the late eighteenth century this classical tradition was much attenuated and domesticated, tamed and eaten away by modern financial and commercial developments. But something remained, and the Federalists clung to it. Despite their disillusionment with political leadership in the states, the Federalists in 1787 had not yet lost hope that at least some individuals in the society might be worthy and virtuous enough to transcend their immediate material interests and devote themselves to the public good. They remained committed to the classical idea that political leadership was essentially one of character: "The whole art of government," said Jefferson, "consists of being honest."[29] Central to this ideal of leadership was the quality of *disinterestedness*—the term the Federalists most used as a synonym for the classic conception of civic virtue: it better conveyed the increasing threats from interests that virtue now faced.

Dr. Johnson defined "disinterested" as being "superior to regard of private advantage; not influenced by private profit"; and that was what the Founding Fathers meant by the term.[30] We today have lost most of this older meaning. Even educated people now use "disinterested" as a synonym for "uninterested," meaning indifferent or unconcerned. It is almost as if we cannot quite conceive of the characteristic that disinterestedness describes: we cannot quite imagine someone who is capable of rising above a pecuniary interest and being unselfish and unbiased where an interest might be present. This is simply another measure of how far we have traveled from the eighteenth century.

This eighteenth-century concept of disinterestedness was not confined either to Commonwealthmen or to the country tradition (which makes our current preoccupation with these strains of thought misleading). Nor did one have to be an American or a republican to believe in disinterestedness and the other classical values that accompanied it. Virtue or disinterestedness, like the concept of honor, lay at the heart of all prescriptions for political leadership in the eighteenth-century Anglo-American world. Throughout the century Englishmen of all political persuasions—Whigs and Tories both—struggled to find the ideal disinterested political leader amid the rising and swirling currents of financial and commercial interests that threatened to engulf their societies. Nothing more enhanced William Pitt's reputation as the great patriot than his pointed refusal in 1746 to profit from the perquisites of the traditionally lucrative office of paymaster of the forces. Pitt was living proof for the English-speaking world of the possibility of disinterestedness—that a man could be a governmental leader and yet remain free of corruption.[31]

This classical ideal of disinterestedness was based on independence and liberty. Only autonomous individuals, free of interested ties and paid by no masters, were capable of such virtue. Jefferson and other republican idealists might continue to hope that ordinary yeoman farmers in America might be independent and free enough of pecuniary temptations and interests to be virtuous. But others knew better, and if they did not, then the experience of the Revolutionary War soon opened their eyes. Washington realized almost at the outset that no common soldier could be expected to be "influenced by any other principles than those of Interest." And even among the officer corps there were only a "few . . . who act upon Principles of disinterestedness," and they were "comparatively speaking, no more than a drop in the Ocean."[32]

Perhaps it was as Adam Smith warned: as society became more commercialized and civilized and labor more divided, ordinary people gradually lost their ability to make any just judgments about the varied interests and occupations of their country; and only "those few, who, being attached to no particular occupation themselves, have leisure and inclination to examine the occupations of other people." Perhaps then in America, as well as in Britain, only a few were free and independent enough to stand above the scramblings of the marketplace. As "Cato" had written, only "a very small Part of Mankind have Capacities large enough to judge of the Whole of Things." Only a few were liberally educated and cosmopolitan enough to have the breadth of perspective to comprehend all the different interests, and only a few were dispassionate and unbiased enough to adjudicate among these different interests and promote the public rather than a private good. Virtue, it was said as early as 1778, "can only dwell in superior minds, elevated above private interest and selfish views." Even Jefferson at one point admitted that only those few "whom nature has endowed with genius and virtue" could "be rendered by liberal education worthy to receive, and able to guard the sacred rights and liberties of their fellow citizens."[33] In other words, the Federalists were saying that perhaps only from among the tiny proportion of the society the eighteenth century designated as "gentlemen" could be found men capable of disinterested political leadership.

This age-old distinction between gentlemen and others in the society had a vital meaning for the Revolutionary generation that we have totally lost. It was a horizontal cleavage that divided the social hierarchy into two unequal parts almost as sharply as the distinction between officers and soldiers divided the army; indeed, the military division was related to the larger social one. Ideally the liberality for which gentlemen were known connoted freedom—freedom from material want, freedom from the caprice of others, freedom from ignorance, and freedom from manual labor. The gentleman's distinctiveness came from being independent in a world of dependencies, learned in a world only partially literate, and leisured in a world of workers.[34] Just as gentlemen were expected to staff the officer corps of the Continental army (and expected also to provide for their own rations, clothing, and equipment on salaries that were less than half those of their British counterparts), so were independent gentlemen of leisure and education expected to supply the necessary disinterested leadership for government.[35] Since such well-to-do gentry were "exempted from the lower and less honourable employments," wrote the philosopher Francis Hutcheson, they were "rather more than others obliged to an active life in some service to mankind. The publick has this claim upon them." Governmental service, in other words, was thought to be a personal sacrifice, required of certain gentlemen because of their talents, independence, and social preeminence.[36]

In eighteenth-century America it had never been easy for gentlemen to make this personal sacrifice for the public, and it became especially difficult during the Revolution. Which is why many of the Revolutionary leaders, especially those of "small fortunes" who served in the Congress, continually complained of the burdens of office and repeatedly begged to be relieved from these burdens in order to pursue their private interests. Periodic temporary retirement from the cares and commotions of office to one's country estate for refuge and rest was acceptable classical behavior. But too often America's political leaders, especially in the North, had to retire not to relaxation in the solitude and leisure of a rural retreat, but to the making of money in the busyness and bustle of a city law practice.[37]

In short, America's would-be gentlemen had a great deal of trouble in maintaining the desired classical independence and freedom from the marketplace. There were not many American gentry who were capable of living idly off the rents of tenants as the English landed aristocracy did. Of course, there were large numbers of the Southern planter gentry whose leisure was based on the labor of their slaves, and these planters obviously came closest in America to fitting the classical ideal of the free and independent gentleman. But some Southern planters kept taverns on the side, and many others were not as removed from the day-to-day management of their estates as their counterparts among the English landed gentry. Their overseers were not comparable to the stewards of the English gentry; thus the planters, despite their aristocratic poses, were often very busy, commercially involved men. Their livelihoods were tied directly to the vicissitudes of international trade, and they had always had an uneasy sense of being dependent on the market to an extent that the English landed aristocracy, despite its commitment to enterprising projects and improvements, never really felt. Still, the great Southern planters at least approached the classical image of disinterested gentlemanly leadership, and they knew it and made the most of it throughout their history.[38]

In northern American society such independent gentlemen standing above the interests of the marketplace were harder to find, but the ideal remained strong. In ancient Rome, wrote James Wilson, magistrates and army officers were always gentleman farmers, always willing to step down "from the elevation of office" and reassume "with contentment and with pleasure, the peaceful labours of a rural and independent life." John Dickinson's pose in 1767 as a "Pennsylvania Farmer" is incomprehensible except within this classical tradition. Dickinson, the wealthy Philadelphia lawyer, wanted to assure his readers of his gentlemanly disinterestedness by informing them at the outset that he was a farmer "contented" and "undisturbed by wordly hopes or fears."[39] Prominent merchants dealing in international trade brought wealth into the society and were thus valuable members of the community, but their status as independent gentlemen was always tainted by their concern for personal profit.[40] Perhaps only a classical education that made "ancient manners familiar," as Richard Jackson once told Benjamin Franklin, could "produce a reconciliation between disinterestedness and commerce; a thing we often see, but almost always in men of a liberal education." Yet no matter how educated merchants were or how much leisure they managed for themselves, while they remained merchants they could never quite acquire the character of genteel disinterestedness essential for full acceptance as political leaders, and that is why most colonial merchants were not active in public life.[41]

John Hancock and Henry Laurens knew this, and during the imperial crisis each shed his mercantile business and sought to ennoble himself. Hancock spent lavishly, bought every imaginable luxury, and patronized everyone. He went through a fortune, but he did become the single most popular and powerful figure in Massachusetts politics during the last quarter or so of the eighteenth century. Laurens especially was aware of the bad image buying and selling had among Southern planters. In 1764 he advised two impoverished but aspiring gentry immigrants heading for the backcountry to establish themselves as planters before attempting to open a store. For them to enter immediately into "any retail Trade in those parts," he said, "would be mean, would Lessen them in the esteem of people whose respect they must endeavour to attract." Only after they were "set down in a Creditable manner as Planters" might they "carry on the Sale of many specie of European and West Indian goods to some advantage and with a good grace." In this same year, 1764, Laurens himself began to curtail his merchant operations. By the time of the Revolution he had become enough of an aristocrat that he was able to sneer at all those merchants who were still busy making money. "How hard it is," he had the gall to say in 1779, "for a rich, or covetous man to enter heartily into the kingdom of patriotism."[42]

For mechanics and others who worked with their hands, being a disinterested gentleman was impossible. Only when wealthy Benjamin Franklin retired from his printing business, at the age of forty-two, did "the Publick," as he wrote in his *Autobiography*, "now considering me as a Man of Leisure," lay hold of him and bring him into an increasing number of important public offices. Other artisans and petty traders who had wealth and political ambitions, such as Roger Sherman of Connecticut, also found that retirement from business was a prerequisite for high public office.[43]

Members of the learned professions were usually considered gentlemen, particularly if they were liberally educated. But were they disinterested? Were they free of the marketplace? Were they capable of virtuous public service? Hamilton for one argued strongly that, unlike merchants, mechanics, or farmers, "the learned professions . . . truly form no distinct interest in society"; thus they "will feel a neutrality to the rivalships between the different branches of industry" and will be most likely to be "an impartial arbiter" between the diverse interests of the society. But others had doubts. William Barton thought "a few individuals in a nation may be actuated by such exalted sentiments of public virtue, . . . but these instances must be rare." Certainly many thought lawyers did not stand above the fray. In fact, said Barton, "professional men of every description arc necessarily, as such, obliged to pursue their immediate advantage."[44]

Everywhere, men struggled to find a way of reconciling this classical tradition of disinterested public leadership with the private demands of making a living. "A Man expends his Fortune in political Pursuits," wrote Gouverneur Morris in an introspective unfinished essay. Did he do this out of "personal Consideration" or out of a desire to promote the public good? If he did it to promote the public good, "was he justifiable in sacrificing to it the Subsistence of his Family? These are important Questions; but," said Morris, "there remains one more," and that one question of Morris's threatened to undermine the whole classical tradition: "Would not as much Good have followed from an industrious Attention to his own Affairs?" Hamilton, for one, could not agree. Although he knew that most people were selfish scavengers, incapable of noble and disinterested acts, he did not want to be one of them. Thus he refused to make speculative killings in land or banking "because," as he put it in one of his sardonic moods, "there must be some *public fools* who sacrifice private to public interest at the certainty of ingratitude and obloquy—because my *vanity* whispers I ought to be one of those fools and ought to keep myself in a situation the best calculated to render service." Hamilton clung as long and as hard to this classical conception of leadership as anyone in post-Revolutionary America.[45]

Washington too felt the force of the classical ideal and throughout his life was compulsive about his disinterestedness. Because he had not gone to college and acquired a liberal education, he always felt he had to live literally by the book. He was continually anxious that he not be thought too ambitious or self-seeking; above all, he did not want to be thought greedy or "interested." He refused to accept a salary for any of his public services, and he was scrupulous in avoiding any private financial benefits from his governmental positions.

Perhaps nothing more clearly reveals Washington's obsession with these classical republican values than his agonized response in the winter of 1784–1785 to the Virginia Assembly's gift of 150 shares in the James River and Potomac canal companies. Acceptance of the shares seemed clearly impossible. The shares might be "considered in the same light as a pension," he said. He would be thought "a dependant," and his reputation for virtue would be compromised. At the same time, however, Washington believed passionately in what the canal companies were doing; indeed, he had long dreamed of making a fortune from such canals. He thought the shares might constitute "the foundation of the *greatest* and most *certain* income" that anyone could expect from a speculative venture. Besides, he did not want to show "disrespect" to his countrymen or to appear "ostentatiously disinterested" by refusing the gift of the shares.[46]

What should he do? Few decisions in Washington's career called for such handwringing as this one did. He sought the advice of nearly everyone he knew. Letters went out to Jefferson, to Governor Patrick Henry, to William Grayson, to Benjamin Harrison, to George William Fairfax, to Nathanael Greene, to Henry Knox, even to Lafayette—all seeking "the best information and advice" on the disposition of the shares. "How would this matter be viewed then by the eyes of the world[?]" he asked. Would not his reputation for virtue be tarnished? Would not accepting the shares "deprive me of the principal thing which is laudable in my conduct?"—that is, his disinterestedness.

The story would be comic if Washington had not been so deadly earnest. He understated the situation when he told his correspondents that his mind was "not a little agitated" by the problem. In letter after letter he expressed real anguish. This was no ordinary display of scruples such as government officials today show over a conflict of interest: in 1784–1785 Washington was not even holding public office.[47]

These values, this need for disinterestedness in public officials, were very much on the minds of the Founding Fathers at the Philadelphia Convention, especially James Madison's. Madison was a tough-minded thinker, not given to illusions. He knew that there were "clashing interests" everywhere and that they were doing great harm to state legislative politics. But he had not yet given up hope that it might be possible to put into government, at the national if not at the state level, some "proper guardians of the public weal," men of "the most attractive merit, and most diffusive and established characters." We have too often mistaken Madison for some sort of prophet of a modern interest-group theory of politics. But Madison was not a forerunner of twentieth-century political scientists such as Arthur Bentley, David Truman, or Robert Dahl. Despite his hardheaded appreciation of the multiplicity of interests in American society, he did not offer America a pluralist conception of politics.

He did not see public policy or the common good emerging naturally from the give-and-take of hosts of competing interests. Instead he hoped that these clashing interests and parties in an enlarged national republic would neutralize themselves and thereby allow liberally educated, rational men, "whose enlightened views and virtuous sentiments render them superior to local prejudices, and to schemes of injustice," to promote the public good in a disinterested manner. Madison, in other words, was not at all as modern as we make him out to be."[48] He did not expect the new national government to be an integrator and harmonizer of the different interests in the society; instead he expected it to be a "disinterested and dispassionate umpire in disputes between different passions and interests in the State." Madison even suggested that the national government might play the same superpolitical, neutral role that the British king had been supposed to play in the empire.[49]

The Federalists' plans for the Constitution, in other words, rested on their belief that there were some disinterested gentlemen left in America to act as neutral umpires. In this sense the Constitution became a grand—and perhaps in retrospect a final desperate—effort to realize the great hope of the Revolution: the possibility of virtuous politics. The Constitution thus looked backward as much as it looked forward. Despite the Federalists' youthful energy, originality, and vision, they still clung to the classical tradition of civic humanism and its patrician code of disinterested public leadership. They stood for a moral and social order that was radically different from the popular, individualistic, and acquisitive world they saw emerging in the 1780s.

THE ANTI-FEDERALISTS, OF COURSE, saw it all very differently. Instead of seeing enlightened patriots simply making a Constitution to promote the national good, they saw groups of interested men trying to foist an aristocracy onto republican America. And they said so, just as the Federalists had feared, in pamphlets, newspapers, and the debates in ratifying conventions. Fear of aristocracy did become the principal shibboleth and rallying cry of the opponents of the Constitution. Already during the 1780s the classical demand that government should be run by rich, leisured gentlemen who served "without fee or reward" was being met by increasing contempt: "Enormous wealth," it was said even in aristocratic South Carolina, "is seldom the associate of *pure* and *disinterested virtue.*"[50] The Anti-Federalists brought this popular contempt to a head and refused to accept the claim that the Federalists were truly disinterested patriots. In fact, many of them had trouble seeing anyone at all as free from interests. If either side in the debate therefore stood for the liberal, pluralistic, interest-ridden future of American politics, it was the Anti-Federalists. They, not the Federalists, were the real modern men. They emerged from the confusion of the polemics with an understanding of American society that was far more hardheaded, realistic, and prophetic than even James Madison.

There were, of course, many different Anti-Federalist spokesmen, a fact that complicates any analysis of the opposition to the Constitution. Yet some of the prominent Anti-Federalist leaders, such as Elbridge Gerry, George Mason, and Richard Henry Lee, scarcely represented, either socially or emotionally, the main thrust of Anti-Federalists. Such aristocratic leaders were socially indistinguishable from the Federalist spokesmen and often were as fearful of the excesses of democracy in the state legislatures as the Federalists. Far more representative of the paper money interests of the 1780s and the populist opposition to the "aristocracy" of the Federalists was someone like William Findley—that pugnacious Scotch-Irishman from western Pennsylvania. Gerry, Mason, and Lee did not really point the way to the liberal, interest-ridden democracy of nineteenth-century America, but Findley did. Until we understand the likes of William Findley, we won't understand either Anti-Federalism or the subsequent democratic history of America.

Findley came to the colonies from northern Ireland in 1763, at age twenty-two, in one of those great waves of eighteenth-century emigration from the northern parts of the British islands that so frightened Dr. Johnson. After trying his hand at weaving, the craft to which he had been apprenticed, Findley became a schoolmaster and then a farmer—until he was caught up in the Revolutionary movement, moved through the ranks to a militia captaincy, and became a political officeholder in Pennsylvania. Findley was the very prototype of a later professional politician and was as much a product of the Revolution as were the more illustrious patriots like John Adams or James Madison. He had no lineage to speak of, he went to no college, and he possessed no great wealth. He was completely self-taught and self-made, but not in the manner of a Benjamin Franklin who acquired the cosmopolitan attributes of a gentleman: Findley's origins showed, and conspicuously so. In his middling aspirations, middling achievements, and middling resentments, he represented far more accurately what America was becoming than did cosmopolitan gentlemen like Franklin and Adams.[51]

By the middle eighties this red-faced Irishman with his flamboyant white hat was becoming one of the most articulate spokesmen for those debtor–paper money interests that lay behind the political turbulence and democratic excesses of the period. As a representative from the West in the Pennsylvania state legislature, he embodied that rough, upstart, individualistic society that eastern squires like George Clymer hated and feared. In the western counties around Pittsburgh, gentry like Clymer could see only avarice, ignorance, and suspicion, and a thin, weak society where there were "no private or publick associations for common good, every Man standing single."[52] Findley never much liked Clymer, but he reserved his deepest antagonism for two others of the Pennsylvania gentry—Hugh Henry Brackenridge and Robert Morris.

Findley's political conflicts with these two men in the Pennsylvania legislature in the 1780s foreshadowed and, indeed, epitomized the Anti-Federalists' struggle with the Federalists. It is perhaps not too much to say that Findley came to see the Constitution as a device designed by gentry like Brackenridge and Morris to keep men like himself out of the important affairs of government. This was especially galling to Findley because he could see no justification for the arrogance and assumed superiority of such men. Brackenridge and Morris were in reality, he believed, no different from him, and during the 1780s he meant to prove it.

Hugh Henry Brackenridge, born in 1748, was seven years younger than Findley. He was a Princeton graduate who in 1781 moved to western Pennsylvania because he thought the wilds of Pittsburgh offered greater opportunities for advancement than crowded Philadelphia. As the only college-educated gentleman in the area, he saw himself as an oasis of cultivation in the midst of a desert. He wanted to be "among the first to bring the press to the west of the mountains," so he helped establish a newspaper in Pittsburgh for which he wrote poetry, bagatelles, and other things.[53] He was pretty full of himself, and he never missed an opportunity to sprinkle his prose with Latin quotations and to show off his learning. This young, ambitious Princeton graduate with aristocratic pretensions was, in fact, just the sort of person who would send someone like William Findley climbing the walls.

William Findley was already a member of the state legislature in 1786 when Brackenridge decided that he too would like to be a legislator. Brackenridge ran for election and won by promising his western constituents that he would look after their particular interests, especially in favoring the use of state certificates of paper money in buying land. But then his troubles began. In Philadelphia he inevitably fell in with the well-to-do crowd around Robert Morris and James Wilson, who had cosmopolitan tastes more to his liking. Under the influence of Morris, Brackenridge voted against the state certificates he had promised to support and identified himself with the eastern establishment. He actually had the nerve to write in the *Pittsburgh Gazette* that the "eastern members" of the assembly had singled him out among all the "Huns, Goths and Vandals" who usually came over the mountains to legislate in Philadelphia and had complimented him for his "liberality." But it was a dinner party at Chief Justice Thomas McKean's house in December 1786, at which both he and Findley were guests, that really did him in. One guest suggested that Robert Morris's support for the Bank of North America seemed mainly for his own personal benefit rather than for the people's. To this Brackenridge responded loudly, "The people are fools; if they would let Mr. Morris alone, he would make Pennsylvania a great people, but they will not suffer him to do it."[54]

Most American political leaders already knew better than to call the people fools, at least aloud, and Findley saw his chance to bring Brackenridge down a peg or two. He wrote a devastating account of Brackenridge's statement in the *Pittsburgh Gazette* and accused him of betraying the people's trust by his vote against the state certificates. It was all right, said Findley sarcastically, for a representative to change his mind if he had not solicited or expected the office, "which is the case generally with modest, disinterested men." But for someone like Brackenridge who had openly sought the office and had made campaign promises—for him to change his vote could only arouse the "indignation" and the "contempt" of the people. Brackenridge may have professed "the greatest acquired abilities, and most shining imagination," but he was in fact a self-seeking and self-interested person who did not have the public good at heart.

Brackenridge vainly tried to reply. At first he sought to justify his change of vote on the classical humanist grounds that the people could not know about the "complex, intricate and involved" problems and interests involved in legislation. "The people at home know each man his own wishes and wants." Only an educated elite in the assembly could see the problems of finance whole; it required "the height of ability to be able to distinguish clearly the interests of a state." But was Brackenridge himself a member of this disinterested elite? Did he really stand above the various interests of the state? He admitted under Findley's assault that he had a "strong *interest* to prompt me to *offer* myself" for election, but his private interest was the same interest with that of the western country where he lived. "My object was to advance the country, and thereby advance myself."[55]

It was a frank and honest but strained answer, a desperate effort by Brackenridge to reconcile the presumed traditional disinterestedness of a political leader with his obvious personal ambition. The more he protested, the worse his situation became, and he never recovered from Findley's attack. The two men crossed swords again in the election of delegates to the state ratifying convention in 1788, and Brackenridge as an avowed Federalist lost to the Anti-Federalist Findley. Brackenridge then abandoned politics for the time being and turned his disillusionment with the vagaries of American democracy into his comic masterpiece, *Modern Chivalry.*

Findley sent Brackenridge scurrying out of politics into literature by attacking his pretensions as a virtuous gentlemanly leader. He attacked Robert Morris in a similar way, with far more ruinous consequences for Morris. Findley and Morris first tangled while they were both members of the Pennsylvania legislature in the 1780s. During several days of intense debate in 1786 over the rechartering of the Bank of North America, Findley mercilessly stripped away the mask of superior classical disinterestedness that Morris had sought to wear. This fascinating wide-ranging debate— the only important one we have recorded of state legislative proceedings in the 1780s—centered on the role of interest in public affairs.

Findley was the leader of the legislative representatives who opposed the rechartering of the bank. He and others like John Smilie from western Pennsylvania were precisely the sorts of legislators whom gentry like Madison had accused throughout the 1780s of being illiberal, narrow-minded, and interested in their support of debtor farmers and paper money. Now they had an opportunity to get back at their accusers, and they made the most of it. Day after day they hammered home one basic point: the supporters of the bank were themselves interested men. They were directors or stockholders in the bank, and therefore they had no right in supporting the rechartering of the bank to pose as disinterested gentlemen promoting the public good. The advocates of the bank "feel interested in it personally." Their defense of the bank, said Findley, who quickly emerged as the principal and most vitriolic critic of the bank's supporters, revealed "the manner in which disappointed avarice chagrins an interested mind."

Morris and his fellow supporters of the bank were embarrassed by these charges that they had a selfish interest in the bank's charter. At first, in George Clymer's committee report on the advisability of rechartering the bank, they took the overbearing line that the proponents of the bank in the general community "included the most respectable characters amongst us," men who knew about the world and the nature of banks. But as the charges of their selfishness mounted, the supporters of the bank became more and more defensive. They insisted they were men of "independent fortune and situations" and were therefore "above influence or terror" by the bank. Under the relentless criticism by Findley and others, however, they one by one grew silent, until their defense was left almost entirely in the hands of Robert Morris, who had a personal, emotional involvement in this debate that went well beyond his concern for the bank.[56]

Morris, as the wealthiest merchant in Pennsylvania and perhaps in all of North America, had heard it all before. The charges of always being privately interested had been the plague of his public career. No matter that his "Exertions" in supplying and financing the Revolution were "as disinterested and pure as ever were made by Mortal Man," no matter how much he sacrificed for the sake of the public, the charges of using public office for personal gain kept arising to torment him. No prominent Revolutionary leader had ever been subjected to such "unmeritted abuse," such bitter and vituperative accusations of selfishness, as he had.[57]

Now in 1786 he had to hear it all over again: that his support of the bank came solely from his personal interest in it. What could he do? He acknowledged that he was a shareholder in the bank, but he tried to argue that the bank was in the interest of all citizens in the state. How could he prove that he was not self-interested? Perhaps if he sold his bank stock? If he did, he assured his fellow legislators that he would be just as concerned with the bank's charter. At one point he gave up and said he would leave the issue of his self-interestedness to the members of the house to determine. But he could not leave it alone, and was soon back on his feet. Members have said "my information is not to be trusted, because I am interested in the bank: but surely," he pleaded, "I am more deeply interested in the state." He hoped, "notwithstanding the insinuation made, that it will never be supposed I would sacrifice the interest and welfare of the state to any interest I can possibly hold in the bank." Why couldn't his arguments for the bank be taken on their merits, apart from their source? he asked. Let them "be considered, not as coming from parties interested, but abstractedly as to their force and solidity."

Such nervous arguments were symptoms of his mounting frustration, and he finally exploded in anger and defiance. Once more he stated categorically: "I am not stimulated by the consideration of private interest, to stand forth in defence of the bank." If people supposed that he needed this bank, they were "grossly mistaken." He was bigger than the bank. If the bank should be destroyed, he on his "own capital, credit, and resources" would create another one; and even his enemies ("and God knows I seem to have enough of them") would have to deal with him, if only "for the sake of their own interest and convenience."[58]

It was an excruciating experience for Morris. At one point in the debate he expressed his desire to retire from office and become a private citizen, "which suits both my inclination and affairs much better than to be in public life, for which I do not find myself very well qualified." But the lure of the public arena and what it represented in the traditional aristocratic terms of civic honor were too great for him, and instead he retired once and for all from his merchant business and like Hancock and Laurens before him sought to ennoble himself. In the late eighties and early nineties, he shifted all his entrepreneurial activities into the acquisition of speculative land—something that seemed more respectable for an aristocrat than trade. He acquired a coat of arms, patronized artists, and hired L'Enfant to build him a huge marble palace in Philadelphia. He surrounded himself with the finest furniture, tapestry, silver, and wines and made his home the center of America's social life. Like a good aristocrat, he maintained, recalled Samuel Breck, "a profuse, incessant and elegant hospitality" and displayed "a luxury . . . that was to be found nowhere else in America." When he became a United States senator in 1789, he—to the astonishment of listeners—began paying himself "compliments on his manner and conduct in life," in particular "his disregard of money." How else would a real aristocrat behave?[59]

For Morris to disregard money was not only astonishing, however; it was fatal. We know what happened, and it is a poignant, even tragic story. All his aristocratic dreams came to nothing; the marble palace on Chestnut Street went unfinished; his dinner parties ceased; his carriages were seized; and he ended in debtors' prison. That Morris should have behaved as he did says something about the continuing power of the classical aristocratic ideal of disinterestedness in post-Revolutionary America. It also says something about the popular power of William Findley, for it was Findley, more than anyone else in the debate over the bank, who had hounded Morris into renouncing his interests in commerce.

Findley in the debate knew he had Morris's number and bore in on it. "The human soul," Findley said, "is affected by wealth, in almost all its faculties. It is affected by its present interest, by its expectations, and by its fears." All this was too much for Morris, and he angrily turned on Findley. "If wealth be so obnoxious, I ask this gentleman why is he so eager in the pursuit of it?" If Morris expected a denial from Findley, he did not get it. For Findley's understanding of Morris's motives was really based on an understanding of his own. Did he love wealth and pursue it as Morris did? "Doubtless I do," said Findley. "I love and pursue it—not as an end, but as a means of enjoying happiness and independence," though he was quick to point out that he had wealth "not in any proportion to the degree" Morris had. Not that this made Morris in any way superior to Findley. Indeed, the central point stressed by Findley and the other western opponents of the bank was that Morris and his patrician Philadelphia crowd were no different from them, were no more respectable than they were. Such would-be aristocrats simply had "more money than their neighbours." In America, said Findley, "no man has a greater claim of special privilege for his £100,000 than I have for my £5." That was what American equality meant.

Morris, like all aspiring aristocrats in an egalitarian society, tried to stress that social distinctions were not based on wealth alone. "Surely," he said in desperate disbelief, "persons possessed of knowledge, judgment, information, integrity, and having extensive connections, are not to be classed with persons void of reputation or character." But Morris's claims of superiority were meaningless as long as he and his friends were seen to be interested men, and on that point Findley had him. Findley and his western legislative colleagues had no desire to establish any claims of their own to disinterestedness. In fact they wanted to hear no more spurious patrician talk of virtue and disinterestedness. They had no objection to Morris's and the other stockholders' being interested in the bank's rechartering: "Any others in their situation . . . would do as they did." Morris and other legislators, said Findley, "have a right to advocate their own cause, on the floor of this house." But then they could not protest when others realize "that it is their own cause they are advocating; and to give credit to their opinions, and to think of their votes accordingly." In fact, said Findley, such open promotion of interests meant an end to the archaic idea that representatives should simply stand and not run for election. When a candidate for the legislature "has a cause of his own to advocate, interest will dictate the propriety of canvassing for a seat." Who has ever put the case for special-interest elective politics any better?[60]

These were the arguments of democratic legislators in the 1780s who were sick and tired of being told by the aristocratic likes of James Madison that they were "Men of factious tempers" and "of local prejudices" and "advocates and parties to the causes which they determine." If they were interested men, so too were all legislators, including even those such as Morris and Brackenridge who were supposed to be liberal-thinking genteel men of "enlightened views and virtuous sentiments." "The citizens," Findley later wrote, by which he meant citizens like himself, "have learned to take a surer course of obtaining information respecting political characters," particularly those who pretended to disinterested civic service. They had especially learned how to inquire "into the local interests and circumstances" of such characters and to point out those with "pursuits or interests" that were "inconsistent with the equal administration of government." Findley had seen the gentry up close, so close in fact that all sense of the mystery that had hitherto surrounded aristocratic authority was lost.[61]

The prevalence of interest and the impossibility of disinterestedness inevitably became a central argument of the Anti-Federalists in the debate over the Constitution. Precisely because the Constitution was designed to perpetuate the classical tradition of disinterested leadership in government, the Anti-Federalists felt compelled to challenge that tradition. There was, they said repeatedly, no disinterested gentlemanly elite that could feel "sympathetically the wants of the people" and speak for their "feelings, circumstances, and interests." Would-be patricians like James Wilson, declared William Findley, thought they were "born of a different race from the rest of the sons of men" and "able to conceive and perform great things." But despite their "lofty carriage," such gentry could not in fact see beyond "the pale of power and worldly grandeur." No one, said the Anti-Federalists, however elevated or educated, was free of the lures and interests of the marketplace. As for the leisured gentry who were "not . . . under the necessity of getting their bread by industry," far from being specially qualified for public leadership, they were in fact specially disqualified. Such men contributed nothing to the public good; their "idleness" rested on "other men's toil."[62]

But it was not just the classical tradition of leisured gentry leadership the Anti-Federalists challenged. Without realizing the full implications of what they were doing, they challenged too the whole social order the Federalists stood for. Society to the Anti-Federalists could no longer be a hierarchy of ranks or even a division into two unequal parts between gentlemen and commoners. Civic society should not in fact be graded by any criteria whatsoever. Society was best thought of as a heterogeneous mixture of "many different classes or orders of people, Merchants, Farmers, Planter Mechanics and Gentry or wealthy Men," all equal to one another. In this diverse egalitarian society, men from one class or interest could never be acquainted with the "*Situation* and Wants" of those from another. Lawyers and planters could never be "adequate judges of trademens concerns." Legislative representatives could not be just *for* the people; they actually had to be *of* the people. It was foolish to tell people that they ought to overlook local interests. Local interests were all there really were. "No man when he enters into society, does it from a view to promote the good of others, but he does it for his own good." Since all individuals and groups in the society were equally self-interested, the only "fair representation" in government, wrote the "Federal Farmer," ought to be one where "every order of men in the community . . . can have a share in it." Consequently, any American government ought "to allow professional men, merchants, traders, farmers, mechanics, etc. to bring a just proportion of their best informed men respectively into the legislature." Only an explicit form of representation that allowed Germans, Baptists, artisans, farmers, and so on each to send delegates of its own kind into the political arena could embody the pluralistic particularism of the emerging society of the early Republic.[63]

Thus in 1787–1788 it was not the Federalists but the Anti-Federalists who were the real pluralists and the real prophets of the future of American politics. They not only foresaw but endorsed a government of jarring individuals and interests. Unlike the Federalists, however, they offered no disinterested umpires, no mechanisms at all for reconciling and harmonizing these clashing selfish interests. All they and their Republican successors had was the assumption, attributed in 1806 to Jefferson, "that the public good is best promoted by the exertion of each individual seeking his *own good* in his own way."[64]

As early as the first decade of the nineteenth century it seemed to many gentlemen, like Benjamin Latrobe, the noted architect and engineer, that William Findley and the Anti-Federalists had not really lost the struggle after all. "Our representatives to all our Legislative bodies, National, as well as of the states," Latrobe explained to Philip Mazzei in 1806, "are elected by the majority *sui similes,* that is, *unlearned.*"

> For instance from Philadelphia and its environs we send to congress not *one* man of letters. One of them indeed is a lawyer but of no eminence, another a good Mathematician, but when elected he was a Clerk in a bank. The others are plain farmers. From the next county is sent a Blacksmith and from just over the river a Butcher. Our state legislature does not contain one individual of superior talents. The fact is, that superior talents actually excite distrust, and the experience of the world perhaps does not encourage the people to trust men of genius.[65]

This was not the world those "men of genius," the Founding Fathers, had wanted. To the extent therefore that the Constitution was designed to control and transcend common ordinary men with their common, ordinary pecuniary interests, it was clearly something of a failure. In place of a classical republic led by a disinterested enlightened elite, Americans got a democratic marketplace of equally competing individuals with interests to promote. Tocqueville saw what happened clearly enough. "Americans are not a virtuous people," he wrote, "yet they are free." In America, unlike the classical republics, "it is not disinterestedness which is great, it is interest." Such a diverse, rootless, and restless people—what could possibly hold them together? "Interest. That is the secret. The private interest that breaks through at each moment, the interest that moreover, appears openly and even proclaims itself as a social theory." In America, said Tocqueville, "the period of disinterested patriotism is gone . . . forever."[66]

No wonder the Founding Fathers seem so remote, so far away from us. They really are.

POSTSCRIPT

Were the Anti-Federalists right? Was no one in government without interests? Perhaps Brackenridge and Morris had interests, but did other Federalists? Were the "men of intelligence and uprightness" and "enlightened views and virtuous sentiments" that Federalists like James Wilson and James Madison spoke of also interested? Were such liberally educated cosmopolitans really no different from the debtor farmers of western Pennsylvania? These were essentially Charles Beard's questions, and they are still good ones.[67]

Most Federalist leaders certainly saw themselves as different from the likes of William Findley, and to a large extent they were different. They certainly had wealth and property; otherwise they could not have been the leisured gentlemen they aspired to be. But what was the nature of that property? How did most of them make their incomes? The Founding Fathers' sources of income is not a subject we know much about. How, for example, did Franklin actually support his genteel living through all those years of retirement? Merchants lived off the profits of their overseas trade, and Southern planters earned money by selling in transatlantic markets. Some gentry were landlords living off the earnings of tenants, and many others were professionals who earned money from fees. A few relied on the emoluments of government offices, though in the Revolutionary years this was not easy.

But with the exception of rents from property, most such direct sources of income were defiled by interest. That is, the income of most American gentlemen did not come without work and participation in commerce, as Adam Smith suggested it ought to for leaders to be truly disinterested. The "revenue" of the English landed aristocrats was unique, said Smith; their income from rents "costs them neither labour nor care, but comes to them as it were, of its own accord, and independent of any plan or project of their own." Thus would-be disinterested American public leaders struggled to find an equivalent, a reliable source of income that was not stained by marketplace exertion and interest. Many gentlemen of leisure found such a source in the interest from money they had lent out. It is not surprising that so many of the gentry used their wealth in this way. After all, what were the alternatives for investment in an underdeveloped society that lacked banks, corporations, and stock markets? Land, of course, was a traditional object of investment, but in America, as John Witherspoon pointed out in an important speech in the Continental Congress, rent-producing land could never allow for as stable a source of income as it did in England. In the New World, said Witherspoon, where land was more plentiful and cheaper than it was in the Old World, gentlemen seeking a steady income "would prefer money at interest to purchasing and holding real estate."[68]

The little evidence we have suggests that Witherspoon was correct. The probate records of wealthy individuals show large proportions of their estates out on loan. In fact, it was often through such loans to friends and neighbors that great men were able to build networks of dependents and clients. In 1776 Cadwallader Colden was the creditor of seventy-three different people. All sorts of persons lent money, said John Adams: merchants, professionals, widows, but especially "Men of fortune, who live upon their income." Because earning interest from loans was considered more genteel than most other moneymaking activities, John Dickinson reinforced the disinterestedness of his persona, the "Pennsylvania Farmer," by having him living off "a little money at interest." When merchants and wealthy artisans wanted to establish their status unequivocally as leisured gentlemen, they withdrew from their businesses and, apart from investing in property, lent their wealth out at interest. Franklin did it. So did Roger Sherman, John Hancock, and Henry Laurens. By 1783 Hancock had more than twelve thousand pounds owed him in bonds and notes. As soon as the trader Joseph Dwight of Springfield, Massachusetts, had any profits, he began removing them from his business and lending them out at interest. By the time of his death in 1768 he had more than 60 percent of his assets out on loan.[69]

As Robert Morris pointed out, in the years before the Revolutionary War, "monied men were fond, of lending upon bond and mortgage: it was a favourite practice; was thought perfectly safe." Even many of the great planters of the South earned more from such ancillary activities as lending money at interest than they did from selling their staple crops. Charles Carroll of Maryland had twenty-four thousand pounds on loan to his neighbors. A large landowner in the Shenandoah Valley, James Patton, had 90 percent of his total estate in the form of bonds, bills, and promissory notes due him. In this context all the bonds and loan office certificates sold by the state and congressional governments during the Revolution became just one more object of investment for gentlemen looking for steady sources of income.[70]

For these sorts of creditors and investors, inflation caused by the excessive printing of paper money could have only devastating consequences. "A depreciating Currency," warned John Adams, "will ruin Us." Indeed, for all those local creditors who were at the same time urban merchants or

Southern planters dealing in overseas trade with transatlantic obligations, excessive paper currency was doubly harmful: they received cheapened money from their debtors but had to pay their overseas creditors in rising rates of exchange. Washington was both a planter and a banker. In the 1780s he was angry at what his debtors and the promoters of inflation through paper money emissions had done to him while he was away fighting the Revolution. Such scoundrels, he complained more than once, had "taken advantage of my absence and the tender laws, to discharge their debts with a shilling or six pence in the pound," while to those whom he owed money, he now had "to pay in specie at the real value." Rather than enter into litigation, "unless there is every reason to expect a decision in my favor," he reluctantly agreed to accept paper money in place of specie for his rents and debts, "however unjustly and rascally it has been imposed." No wonder then, said Robert Morris, that wealthy men, at least those who had survived the Revolution, had stopped taking up bonds and mortgages; they were "deterred from lending again by the dread of paper money and tender laws."[71]

We have always known that the skyrocketing inflation fueled by the excessive printing of paper money during these years was devastating to creditors, but we have not always appreciated precisely what this meant socially and morally. Credit was the principal sinew of the society and was absolutely essential for the carrying on of any form of commerce. Establishing one's creditworthiness in this personally organized society was nearly equivalent to establishing one's existence as a person, which is why letters of recommendation were so important. The relationships between creditors and debtors were not supposed to be merely impersonal legal contracts. Such engagements, even when they spanned continents and oceans, depended ultimately, it seemed, on personal faith and trust. Debts were thus thought by many to be more than legal obligations; they were moral bonds tying people together. That is why defaulting debtors were still thought to be more than unfortunate victims of bad times; they were moral failures, violators of a code of trust and friendship who deserved to be punished and imprisoned.[72]

It is not surprising therefore that many of those whom George Clymer called "honest gentry of intrinsic worth" tended to see all actions interfering with this relationship between creditor and debtor as morally abhorrent. Inflation artificially induced by Rhode Island's printing of paper money threatened, said a Boston gentleman, nothing less than "the first principles of society." Paper money, Madison told his fellow Virginia legislators, was unjust, pernicious, and unconstitutional. It was bad for commerce, it was bad for morality, and it was bad for society: it destroyed "confidence between man and man." Thus most Federalists who stood up for credit and the honest payment of debts did not see themselves as just another economic interest in a pluralistic society. They were defending righteousness itself. "On one side," said Theodore Sedgwick, "are men of talents, and of integrity, firmly determined to support public justice and private faith, and on the other there exists as firm a determination to institute tender laws, paper money, . . . land in short to establish iniquity by law."[73]

The federal Constitution's abolition of the states' power to emit paper money was therefore welcomed by most gentry as the righting of a moral and social wrong. The wickedness of such inflationary state policies was so much taken for granted by the members of the Convention that this prohibition of the states' authority in Article I, Section 10 of the Constitution was scarcely debated. Even a proposal to grant authority to the federal Congress to emit bills of credit was thrown out by the Convention, nine states to two. The truth is there were almost no real Anti-Federalists such as William Findley present in the Convention to defend the states' paper money emissions of the 1780s. Of the delegates present, only eccentric Luther Martin spoke out against the prohibition of the states' emitting bills of credit. The Federalists morally controlled the debate over paper money in 1787–1788 and browbeat most potential defenders of it into silence. As William R. Davie pointed out to the North Carolina ratifying convention, gentlemen in their speeches attached such dishonesty and shame to paper money that even "a member from Rhode Island" (which was defiantly excessive in emitting paper money) "could not have set his face against such language."[74] So dominant were classical values and so disturbing seemed the moral and social consequences of paper money that even those who defended paper emissions in the 1780s often did so in terms that conceded the Federalists' traditional argument against ordinary people's earning and spending money beyond their station.[75] Only in time, with the spread of paper-issuing banks and a new understanding of the economy, would Americans find the arguments to legitimate the position of men like William Findley.

Whatever the confusion of the Anti-Federalists, most Federalists believed they understood what their opponents were like. "Examine well the characters and circumstances of men who are averse to the new constitution," warned David Ramsay of South Carolina. Many of them may be debtors "who wish to defraud their creditors," and therefore, for some of them at least, Article I, Section 10 of the Constitution may be "the real ground of the opposition. . . . though they may artfully cover it with a splendid profession of zeal for state privileges and general liberty."[76] But even if this were not true, the Federalists at least knew that the end of the states' printing of paper money would be of "real service to the honest part of the community." If the new Constitution, said Benjamin Rush in 1788, "held forth no other advantages [than] that [of] a future exemption from paper money and tender laws, it would be eno' to recommend it to honest men." This was because "the man of wealth realized once more the safety of his bonds and rents against the inroads of paper money and tender laws."[77] That was putting it about as selfishly as it could be put.

Yet in the end it should not be put that way. To rest something as monumental as the formation of the federal Constitution on such crude, narrow, and selfish motives was Beard's mistake, and it should not be repeated. The Federalists certainly had far more fundamental concerns at stake in 1787 than their personal credit and their social status. They were defending not their personal interests (for they were often debtors as well as creditors), but rather a moral and social order that had been prescribed by the Revolution and the most enlightened thinking of the eighteenth century. So committed were they to these classical humanist values that they were scarcely capable of understanding, let alone admitting the legitimacy of, the acquisitive and enterprising world that paper money represented. They saw themselves, as sincerely and thoroughly as any generation in American history, as virtuous leaders dedicated to promoting the good of the nation. However strong and self-serving their underlying interests may have been, the Federalists always described their ideals and goals in the language of classical republican disinterestedness; and this language, these ideals and goals, repeated endlessly in private correspondence and public forums up and down the continent, inevitably controlled and shaped their behavior. Washington's agony over the canal shares and Morris's abandonment of his mercantile career are object lessons in the power of this culture to affect behavior. Self-interest that could not be publicly justified and explained was self-interest that could not be easily acted upon.

The Founders thus gave future Americans more than a new Constitution. They passed on ideals and standards of political behavior that helped to contain and control the unruly materialistic passions unleashed by the democratic revolution of the early nineteenth century. Even today our aversion to corruption, our uneasiness over the too-blatant promotion of special interests, and our yearning for examples of unselfish public service suggest that such ideals still have great moral power. Yet in the end we know that it was not the Federalists of 1787 who came to dominate American culture. Our wistful celebration of their heroic greatness, our persistent feelings that they were leaders the likes of whom we shall never see again in America, our ready acceptance of parties and interest-group politics—all tell us that it was William Findley and the Anti-Federalists who really belonged to the future. They, and not the Federalists, spoke for the emerging world of egalitarian democracy and the private pursuit of happiness.

AFTERWORD TO CHAPTER 4

This piece began as a lecture at a conference held in Philadelphia in October 1984 in preparation for the bicentennial celebration of the formation of the Constitution three years later. It was extensively revised and en-larged for publication in the 1987 volume that came out of the conference.

I probably made a mistake with the too-cute suggestion that maybe the Anti-Federalists were the ones who stood for the future of American politics better than did the Federalists. Many readers have tended to be very literal-minded, and they have taken me to task for trying to reverse our understanding of who was more important in the future development of American politics, the Federalists or the Anti-Federalists. Trying to assess individuals' or groups' responsibility for the future in this manner is probably not a very good way to write history. The historical process is too complicated for that sort of assessment.

CHAPTER FIVE

The ORIGINS of AMERICAN CONSTITUTIONALISM

THE CONSTITUTIONALISM OF THE UNITED STATES is rather old hat these days. Since the country has the oldest written national constitution in the world, there doesn't seem to be much that is new and peculiar about it. Certainly the fact that the American Constitution is written is not unusual. Most constitutions these days are written, many of them during the past three decades. When people talk about a country like Afghanistan or Iraq getting a new constitution, they assume it will be a written one; it now seems that writing one out on paper is the only way to create a constitution these days. (I should point out that most newly written constitutions are a good deal longer than the eight thousand words of the American Constitution. Actually, the U.S. Constitution today has become as "unwritten" as those of Israel or Great Britain.)

It used to be that America's separation of powers was unusual, if not unique, among governments. Not anymore. Lots of governments now have independent judiciaries and presidents who are not members of their legislatures. But the parliamentary system of cabinet responsibility to the legislature still dominates in the world, and thus the American system of separation of powers still seems unusual.

There was a time when judicial review was peculiarly American, but no longer. Many states in the world now have judiciaries that review legislation and have the authority to declare statutes null and void. (Parenthetically, however, it is important to point out that many of these courts, unlike the American courts, are specialized constitutional courts.) Even the English courts, which have always been respectful of parliamentary sovereignty, have recently begun trying to use the European Convention on Human Rights as a basis for interpreting or limiting parliamentary statutes.

Foreign courts now routinely deal with the same issues that American courts deal with—right-to-life, freedom of speech, and equality. In fact, foreign courts sometimes critically scrutinize and use American court decisions in reaching their own decisions. Some judiciaries in the European states now declare more statutes void than does the U.S. Supreme Court. Many of these foreign courts, such as the Israeli Supreme Court, even consider cases justiciable that the American courts have avoided, especially those dealing with military matters. It is very unlikely that the U.S. Supreme Court would have taken on a case similar to one concerning the amount of food being provided to those holed up in the Church of the Nativity in Bethlehem while surrounded by the Israeli army. But the Israeli Supreme Court did, even without a written constitution!

Americans used to be known for their obsession with rights, but that obsession now seems to be shared more and more by other countries in the developed world. Most of the new constitutions of the past three decades have a core of basic rights and liberties to which judges can refer in their court decisions. Even the idea of separation of church and state, which Americans pioneered, has spread to other nations struggling with religious diversity. Federalism may have been a modern American invention, but it has been much copied. Indeed, federalism is so common throughout the world today that America's example is scarcely illuminating anymore. America may, in fact, be the most centralized of the many federal states and thus the least interesting model.

Despite all these modern similarities between the U.S. Constitution and other national constitutions, however, there are important differences. To better understand those differences and perhaps to make some sense of Americans' habitual ignorance of other constitutions in the world, it may be helpful to look at the origins of America's constitutionalism.

The first thing to emphasize is the fact that the Founders who created America's constitutional structure at the end of the eighteenth century were Englishmen with a strong sense that they were heirs of the English tradition of freedom. Although England had become corrupted during the eighteenth century, Americans believed that at one time it had been the dominant source of liberty and popular government in the world, its constitution celebrated by liberal intellectuals everywhere. Thus it was fitting that Anglo-Americans (the title most Europeans gave to Americans in the early nineteenth century) should become the beneficiaries of this popular tradition of English rights and English liberty. Americans thought that the torch of English freedom had been passed to them and that they had a responsibility to make it shine brighter and more enduringly than the English had been able to do.

The Americans were intent on avoiding the corruption they believed plagued the English constitution, and that meant that they had to deviate from the English constitutional tradition in a number of ways. In fact, comparing the Americans' constitutional developments at the end of the eighteenth century with the English constitutional system that they broke away from can help to illuminate just what is distinctive about American constitutionalism.

The most obvious difference between eighteenth-century English and American constitutionalism was the American Revolutionaries' conception of a constitution as a written document, as a fundamental law circumscribing the government. Before the American Revolution, a constitution was rarely distinguished from the government and its operations. Traditionally in English culture, a constitution referred both to the way the government was put together, or constituted, and to the fundamental rights the government was supposed to protect. The eighteenth-century English constitution was an unwritten mixture of laws, customs, principles, and institutions.

By the end of the Revolutionary era, however, the Americans' idea of a constitution had become very different. A constitution was now seen to be no part of the government at all: it was a written document distinct from and superior to all the operations of government. A constitution was, as Thomas Paine said in 1791, "a thing *antecedent* to a government; and a government is only the creature of a constitution." And, said Paine, it was "not a thing in name only; but in fact."

For Americans, a constitution was something fundamental. It was a written document, possessed by every family, and carried about like the Bible to be quoted and cited article by article. Such a constitution could never be an act of the legislature; it had to be the act of the people themselves, declared James Wilson—one of the principal framers of the Constitution of 1787—and "in their hands it is clay in the hands of a potter; they have the right to mould, to preserve, to improve, to refine, and to furnish it as they please." If eighteenth-century Britons thought this American idea of a constitution was, as the British writer Arthur Young caustically suggested in 1792, "a pudding made from a recipe," the Americans had become convinced that the English had no constitution at all.

As much as we now take for granted this idea of a constitution as written fundamental law, the idea was not easily arrived at. The American colonists began the debate with Great Britain in the 1760s thinking about constitutional issues in much the same way as their fellow Britons. Like the English, they believed that the principal threat to the people's ancient rights and liberties had always been the prerogative powers of the king— those vague and discretionary but equally ancient rights of authority that the king possessed in order to carry out his responsibility for governing the realm. Indeed, the eighteenth-century English saw their history as essentially a struggle between these ancient conflicting rights—between power and liberty, between an encroaching monarchy on one hand and the freedom-loving people on the other. Time and again in the colonial period, Americans, like their fellow Englishmen at home, had been forced to defend themselves against the intrusions of royal prerogative power. They relied for their defense on their colonial assemblies, their rights as English subjects, and what they called their ancient charters.

In the seventeenth century, many of the colonies had been established by crown charters—corporate or proprietary grants made by the king to groups such as the Massachusetts Puritans or to individuals such as William Penn and Lord Baltimore to found colonies in the New World. In subsequent years these charters gradually lost their original meaning in the eyes of the colonists and took on a new importance, both as prescriptions for government and as devices guaranteeing the rights of the people against their royal governors. In fact, the whole of the colonial past was littered with such charters and other written documents of various sorts to which the colonial assemblies repeatedly appealed in their squabbles with royal power.

In turning to written documents as confirmation of their liberties, the colonists acted no differently from other Englishmen. From almost the beginning of their history, the English had continually invoked written documents and charters in defense of their rights against the crown's power. "Anxious to preserve and transmit" their rights "unimpaired to posterity," declared a Connecticut clergyman on the eve of the Revolution, the English people had repeatedly "caused them to be reduced to writing, and in the most solemn manner to be recognized, ratified and confirmed," first by King John, then Henry III and Edward I, and "afterwards by a multitude of corroborating acts, reckoned in all, by Lord Cook, to be thirty-two, from Edw. 1st. to Hen. 4th. and since, in a great variety of instances, by the bills of right and acts of settlement." All of these documents, from the Magna Carta to the Bill of Rights of the Glorious Revolution of 1688–1689, were merely written evidence of those fixed principles of reason from which the English believed their constitution was derived.

Although the eighteenth-century English talked about the fundamental law of the English constitution, few of them doubted that Parliament, as the representative of the nobles and people and as the sovereign lawmaking body of the nation, was the supreme guarantor and interpreter of these fixed principles and fundamental law. Parliament was in fact the bulwark of the people's liberties against the crown's encroachments; it alone defended and confirmed the people's rights. The Petition of Right, the act of Habeas Corpus, and the Bill of Rights were all acts of Parliament, statutes not different in form from other laws passed by Parliament.

For the English, therefore, as William Blackstone, the great eighteenth-century jurist, pointed out, there could be no distinction between the "constitution or frame of government" and "the system of laws." All were of a piece: every act of Parliament was part of the constitution and all law, both customary and statute, was thus constitutional. "Therefore," concluded the English theorist William Paley, "the terms *constitutional* and *unconstitutional*, mean *legal* and *illegal*."

Nothing could be more strikingly different from what Americans came to believe. Indeed, it was precisely on this distinction between "legal" and "constitutional" that the American and English constitutional traditions diverged at the time of the Revolution. During the 1760s and 1770s the colonists came to realize that although acts of Parliament, like the Stamp Act of 1765, might be legal—that is, in accord with the acceptable way of making law—such acts could not thereby be automatically considered constitutional, or in accord with the basic principles of rights and justice that made the English constitution what it was. It was true that the English Bill of Rights and the Act of Settlement of 1701 were only statutes of Parliament, but surely, the colonists insisted, they were of "a nature more sacred than those which established a turnpike road."

Under this kind of pressure, the Americans came to believe that the fundamental principles of the English constitution had to be lifted out of the lawmaking and other institutions of government and set above them. "In all free States," said Samuel Adams in 1768, "the Constitution is fixed; and as the supreme Legislature derives its Powers and Authority from the Constitution, it cannot overleap the Bounds of it without destroying its own foundation." Thus in 1776, when Americans came to make their own constitutions for their newly independent states, they inevitably sought to make them fundamental and write them out in documents. These state constitutions of 1776–1777, which were immediately translated into several European languages, captured the imagination of the enlightened everywhere.

It was one thing, however, to define the constitution as fundamental law, different from ordinary legislation and circumscribing the institutions of government; it was quite another to make such a distinction effective. Since the state constitutions were created by the legislatures, they presumably could also be changed or amended by the legislatures. Some of the constitution makers in 1776 realized the problem and tried to deal with it. Delaware provided for a supermajority, five-sevenths of the legislature, when changing its constitution. Maryland said that its constitution could be amended only by a two-thirds vote of two successive legislatures. Most states, however, simply enacted their constitutions as if they were regular statutes. Clearly, everyone believed that the constitutions were special kinds of law, but no one knew quite how to make them so.

In the years following the Declaration of Independence, Americans struggled with this problem of distinguishing fundamental from statutory law, none more persistently than Thomas Jefferson. In 1779 Jefferson knew from experience that no legislature "elected by the people for the ordinary purposes of legislation only" could restrain the acts of succeeding legislatures. Thus he realized that to declare his great Statute for Religious Freedom in Virginia to be "irrevocable would be of no effect in law; yet we are free," he wrote into his 1779 bill in frustration, "to declare, and do declare, that . . . if any act shall be hereafter passed to repeal the present [act] or to narrow its operation, such act will be an infringement of natural right." In effect, he was placing a curse on the future legislators of Virginia.

But Jefferson realized that such a paper declaration was not enough and that something more was needed. By the 1780s both he and his friend James Madison were eager "to form a real constitution" for Virginia; the existing one, they said, was merely an "ordinance" with "no higher authority than the other ordinances of the same session." They wanted a constitution that would be "perpetual" and "unalterable by other legislatures." The only way that could be done was to have the constitution created, as Jefferson put it, "by a power superior to that to the legislature." By the time Jefferson came to write his *Notes on the State of Virginia* in the early 1780s, the answer had become clear. "To render a form of government unalterable by ordinary acts of assembly," wrote Jefferson, "the people must delegate persons with special powers. They have accordingly chosen special conventions or congresses to form and fix their governments."

Massachusetts in 1780 had shown the way. It had elected a convention specially designated to form a constitution and had then placed that constitution before the people for ratification. When the Philadelphia Convention drew up a new constitution for the nation in 1787, it knew what to do. It declared that the new Constitution had to be ratified by the people meeting in state conventions called for that purpose only. Constitutional conventions and the process of ratification made the people themselves the actual constituent power. As enlightened Europeans realized, these devices were some of the most distinctive contributions the American Revolution made to world politics.

But these were not the only contributions. With the conception of a constitution as fundamental law immune from legislative encroachment more firmly in hand, some state judges during the 1780s began cautiously moving in isolated cases to impose restraints on what the assemblies were enacting as law. In effect, they said to the legislatures—as George Wythe, judge of the Virginia supreme court, did in 1782—"Here is the limit of your authority; and hither shall you go, but no further." These were the hesitant beginnings of what would come to be called judicial review—that remarkable practice by which judges in the ordinary courts of law have the authority to determine the constitutionality of acts of the state and federal legislatures.

The development of judicial review came slowly. It was not easy for people in the eighteenth century, even those who were convinced that many of the acts of the state legislatures in the 1780s were unjust and unconstitutional, to believe that unelected judges could set aside acts of the popularly elected legislatures; this seemed to be an undemocratic usurpation of power. But as early as 1787, James Iredell, soon to be appointed an associate justice of the newly created Supreme Court of the United States, saw that the new meaning Americans had given to a constitution had clarified the responsibility of judges to determine the law. A constitution in America, said Iredell, was not only "a fundamental law" but also a special, popularly created "law in writing . . . limiting the powers of the Legislature, and with which every exercise of those powers must necessarily be compared." Judges were not arbiters of the constitution or usurpers of legislative power. They were, said Iredell, merely judicial officials fulfilling their duty of applying the proper law. When faced with a decision between "the *fundamental unrepeatable* law" made specially by the people, and an ordinary statute enacted by the legislature contrary to the constitution, they must simply determine which law was superior. Judges could not avoid exercising this authority, concluded Iredell, for in America a constitution was not "a mere imaginary thing, about which ten thousand different opinions may be formed, but a written document to which all may have recourse, and to which, therefore, the judges cannot witfully blind themselves."

Although Iredell may have been wrong about the number of different opinions that could arise over a constitution, he was certainly right about the direction judicial authority in America would take. The way was prepared for Supreme Court Justice John Marshall's decision in *Marbury v. Madison* in 1803 and the subsequent but bitterly contested development of the practice of judicial review—a practice that Europeans soon became aware of.

Unlike the European and Israeli constitutional courts, the American federal courts are not special courts with constitutional responsibilities separate from ordinary law adjudication. This is an important point of distinction whose implications are not easy to spell out. Because the European and Israeli constitutional courts are so special, they are usually protected from partisanship by elaborate mechanisms of appointment. The Israeli system of appointment is indirect and largely removed from the politics of the Knesset. As we know only too well from recent events,

Americans have no such indirect method of appointing judges. Thus the filibustering of appointments by the U.S. Senate becomes a crude requirement of a supermajority for federal court appointments. Of course, this is simply a measure of how significant judges have become in our constitutional system.

As important as the idea of a written constitution distinguishable from ordinary statute law was in the eighteenth century, however, it was not the most significant constitutional deviation the Americans made from their inherited English traditions. More important in distinguishing American constitutionalism from that of the English, and most other democratic nations in the world today, was the idea of separation of powers.

Montesquieu, in his *Spirit of the Laws*, had praised the English constitution for separating the executive, legislative, and judicial powers of government. But Montesquieu did not understand precisely what was happening to the English constitution in the eighteenth century. The legislature (that is, Parliament) and the executive (that is, the king's ministry) were in fact becoming blurred as England stumbled into what eventually became its modern parliamentary system of responsible cabinet government. The key to the British system is the fact that the ministers of the crown are simultaneously members of Parliament. It was this linkage, which the American colonists labeled "corruption" and David Hume called "influence," that the Americans in 1776 were determined to destroy.

Thus, in their state constitutions of 1776, they excluded from their assemblies all members of the executive branch, so that, as the New Jersey constitution declared, "the legislative department of this Government may, as much as possible, be preserved from all suspicion of corruption." This separation was repeated in the federal Constitution in Article I, Section 6—preventing the development of responsible cabinet government in America. In this respect, at least, American constitutionalism has not been influential at all, for most democratic governments in the world have tended to follow the British parliamentary model of government.

But beneath these obvious differences between the constitutionalism of Great Britain and of America are even more fundamental deviations that help to make America's conception of government and politics different from nearly every other nation in the world. These differences began with the concept of representation.

During the debates over the nature of the empire in the 1760s and 1770s, the British vainly tried to justify Parliament's taxation of the colonies. They argued that the American colonists, like Britons everywhere, were subject to acts of Parliament through a system of what they called "virtual" representation. Even though the colonists, like "nine-tenths of the people of Britain, did not in fact choose any representative to the House of Commons," they said, they were undoubtedly "a part, and an important part of the Commons of Great Britain: they are represented in Parliament in the same manner as those inhabitants of Britain are who have not voices in elections."

To most of the mainstream English at home, this argument made a great deal of sense. Centuries of history had left Britain with a confusing mixture of sizes and shapes of its electoral districts. Some of the constituencies were large, with thousands of voters, but others were small and more or less in the pocket of a single great landowner. Many of the electoral districts had few voters, and some so-called rotten boroughs had no inhabitants at all. One town, Dunwich, continued to send representatives to Parliament even though it had long since slipped into the North Sea. At the same time, some of England's largest cities, such as Manchester and Birmingham, which had grown suddenly in the mid-eighteenth century, sent no representatives to Parliament. The British justified this hodgepodge of representation by claiming that each member of Parliament represented the whole British nation and not just the particular locality he supposedly came from. Parliament, as Edmund Burke said, was not "a *congress* of ambassadors from different and hostile interests, which interests each must maintain, as an agent and advocate, against other agents and advocates; but Parliament is a deliberative assembly of *one* nation, with *one* interest, that of the whole." Requirements that the members of Parliament (MPs) reside in the constituencies they represented had long since been ignored and of course are still not necessary for MPs today. According to this idea of virtual representation, people were represented in England not by the process of election, which was considered incidental to representation, but rather by the mutual interests that members of Parliament were presumed to share with all Britons for whom they spoke—including those, like the colonists, who did not actually vote for them.

The Americans strongly rejected these British claims that they were "virtually" represented in the same way that the nonvoters of cities like Manchester and Birmingham were. They challenged the idea of virtual representation with what they called "actual" representation. If the people were to be properly represented in a legislature, the colonists declared, not only did the people have to vote directly for the members of the legislature, but they also had to be represented by members whose numbers were proportionate to the size of the population they spoke for. What purpose is served, asked James Otis of Massachusetts in 1765, by the continual attempts of the English to defend the lack of American representation in Parliament by citing the examples of Manchester and Birmingham, which returned no members to the House of Commons? "If those now so considerable places are not represented," said Otis, "they ought to be."

What was meaningful in England made no sense in America. Unlike in England, electoral districts in the New World were not the products of history that stretched back centuries, but rather were recent and regular creations that were related to changes in population. When new towns in Massachusetts and new counties in Virginia were formed, new representatives customarily were sent to the respective colonial legislatures. This system of actual representation stressed the closest possible connection between the local electors and their representatives. Unlike the English, Americans believed that representatives had to be residents of the localities they spoke for and that people of the locality had the right to instruct their representatives. The representatives were to be in effect what Burke had said they should never be, ambassadors from their localities. Since Americans thought it only fair that their localities be represented more or less in proportion to their population, they wrote that requirement into their Revolutionary constitutions. In short, the American belief in actual representation pointed toward the fullest and most equal participation of the people in the process of government that the modern world had ever seen.

Since this actual representation was based on the people's mistrust of those they elected, they pushed for the most explicit and broadest kind of consent, which generally meant voting. The mutuality of interests that made virtual representation meaningful in England was in America so weak and tenuous that the representatives could not be trusted to speak for the interests of their constituents unless those constituents actually voted for them. Actual representation thus made the process of election not incidental but central to representation.

Actual representation became the key to the peculiarities of American constitutionalism and government. People wanted elected officials that were like them in every way, not only in ideas but in religion, ethnicity, or social class. The people in Philadelphia in 1775 called for so many Presbyterians, so many artisans, and so many Germans on the Revolutionary committees. Already Americans were expressing the idea that the elected representatives not only had to be *for* the people, they also had to be *of* the people.

Mistrust became the source of American democracy. Indeed, the mistrust at times became so great that the representative process itself was brought into question, and mobs and extralegal associations emerged to claim to speak more authentically for the people than their elected representatives. The people, it seemed, could be represented in a variety of ways and in a variety of institutions. But no officials, however many votes they received, could ever fully represent the people.

Ultimately, these contrasting ideas of representation separated the English and American constitutional systems. In England Parliament came to possess sovereignty—the final, supreme, and indivisible lawmaking authority in the state—because it embodied the whole society, all the estates of the realm, within itself, and nothing existed outside of it.

In America, however, sovereignty remained with the people themselves, and not with any of their agents or even with all their agents put together. The American people, unlike the British, were never eclipsed by the process of representation.

When Americans referred to the sovereignty of the people, they did not just mean that all government was derived from the people. Instead, they meant that the final, supreme, and indivisible lawmaking authority of the society remained with the people themselves, not with their representatives or with any of their agents. In American thinking, all public officials became delegated and mistrusted agents of the people, temporarily holding bits and pieces of the people's power out, so to speak, on always recallable loan.

It may be important to point out why the Constitutional Convention failed to include a bill of rights with the Constitution it drafted in 1787. At the end of the Convention one delegate suggested that one was required. But the motion was defeated by every state delegation. The rationale for not having a bill of rights was that—unlike in England, where the crown's prerogative power preexisted and had to be limited by a bill of rights—all power in America existed in the people, who doled out only scraps of it to their various agents, so no such fence or bill of rights was necessary. This was a bit too precious an argument for many, however, and Madison and other supporters eventually had to concede the need for amendments, the first ten of which became the Bill of Rights.

By thinking of the people in this extraordinary way, Americans were able to conceive of federalism—that is, the remarkable division of power between central and provincial governments. By creating two legislatures with different powers operating over the same territory—the Congress and the separate state legislatures—the Americans offered the world a new way of organizing government. In subsequent decades, nineteenth-century libertarian reformers everywhere in Europe and Latin America, struggling to put together central governments in the face of strong local loyalties, appealed to the American example of federalism. German reformers in 1848 cited the American example in their efforts to build a confederation, and liberal reformers in Switzerland called the United States Constitution "a model and a pattern for the organization of the public life of republics in general, in which the whole and parts shall both be free and equal. . . . The problem," they said, with more enthusiasm than accuracy, given America's growing federal crisis that resulted in the Civil War, "has been solved by the new world for all peoples, states and countries."

Only by conceiving of sovereignty remaining with the people could Americans make sense of their new constitutional achievements, such as the idea of special constitution-making conventions and the process of popular ratification of constitutions. In America the notion that sovereignty rested in the people was not just a convenient political fiction; the American people, unlike the English, retained an actual lawmaking authority. The English did not need conventions and popular ratifications to change their constitution because Parliament was fully and completely the people and the people did not exist politically or constitutionally outside of it, except at the moment of election.

Once election became for Americans the sole criterion of representation, it was natural to think of all elected officials as somehow representative of the people. As early as the 1780s, many Americans were referring to their elected senates as double representations of the people; some began claiming that their governors, because they were elected by all the people, were the most representative officials in the state. Soon all elected officials were being designated representatives of the people, and the term originally applied to the various "houses of representatives" in the state constitutions and the federal Constitution became an awkward reminder that Americans had once thought of representation as the English had: as confined to the lower houses of their legislatures.

The people inevitably included even judges as their various agents. When, in order to justify judicial review, Alexander Hamilton in *The Federalist* No. 78 referred to judges as agents of the people and not really inferior to the people's other agents in the legislature, he opened up a radically new way of thinking of the judiciary. If judges were indeed the people's agents, as many soon concluded, then rightfully they ought to be elected, especially since election had become the sole measure of representation. Consequently, it was only a matter of time before the states began electing their judges. Conceiving of judges as just another one of their agents perhaps helps explain why Americans eventually became so accepting of judicial review, including even having the Supreme Court decide who will be president.

Since in the American system the people were never fully embodied in government, all sorts of strange political institutions and practices could and did emerge. The primaries, referendums, processes of recall, and ballot initiatives introduced by Progressive reformers at the beginning of the twentieth century were only extensions of the ideas of popular sovereignty and acute actual representation created at the Founding of the United States. These efforts to reach beyond actual representation to some kind of pure democracy were based on popular mistrust of elected officials, as were the original ideas of actual representation. As one account of 1896 put it, California had "only one kind of politics and that was corrupt politics. It didn't matter whether a man was a Republican or Democrat. The Southern Pacific Railroad controlled both parties."

In the past several decades the number of ballot initiatives in some of the western states has soared, to the point where they seem to rival the number of statutes passed by the legislatures. Ironically, the Southern Pacific Railroad, now just another special-interest group, in 1990 promoted a ballot initiative to issues billions in bonds in support of rail transportation. Although Oregon has had more ballot initiatives than California, California's have become the most notorious. The recall of Governor Gray Davis and the election of Arnold Schwarzenegger as governor of California in 2003 are the kinds of popular actions not likely to be duplicated in any other developed democracy in the world today (with the possible exception of Switzerland). But once we grasp the peculiar American idea of the sovereignty of the people, based on a deeply rooted mistrust of all elected officials, these extraordinary political events begin to make some sense. Whether these efforts at direct democracy are sensible ways of running a modern democratic state, however, remains to be seen.

Like many of these collected essays, this one began as a lecture presented at a conference on constitutionalism at the University of Chicago Law School in January 2004. Although it has never previously been published, it highlights themes that have been part of my thinking and writing over the past half century.

The history of American constitutionalism in the eighteenth century is very important, if only because of recent events. Over the past two decades or so, sixty-nine countries—from the nations of post-communist Central and Eastern Europe, to South Africa, to Afghanistan and Iraq— have drafted constitutions. At the same time many other states have revised their constitutions on paper, and even the European Union has tried to get a written constitution ratified. Consequently, only a few states in the world are without written constitutions. Indeed, it is almost impossible for many people today to conceive of a constitution as anything but a written document. And it all essentially began with America a little over two centuries ago.

For more on the influence of American constitutionalism over the past two centuries, see the monumental study by George Athan Billias, *American Constitutionalism Heard Round the World, 1776–1789: A Global Perspective* (New York: New York University Press, 2009).

A German scholar, Horst Dippel, is in the midst of a huge project of editing and publishing all constitutions written between the period 1776 and 1860. Entitled *Modern Constitutionalism and Its Sources*, it will be an enormously helpful resource when completed.

CHAPTER SIX

The MAKING *of*
AMERICAN DEMOCRACY

*O*NE OF THE MOST PROFOUND REVOLUTIONS of the past two centuries or so has been the introduction of ordinary people into the political process. For America and the rest of Western Europe this revolution was most dramatically expressed at the end of the eighteenth century—"the age of the democratic revolution," as historian R. R. Palmer once called it.[1] This bringing of the people into politics took place in the several decades following the American Revolution, while in Europe it took much longer, requiring for many nations the greater part of the nineteenth century. And for the rest of the world the process is still going on. Indeed, since the end of World War II we have witnessed what has been called a "participation explosion"—the rapid incorporation into the political process of peoples who hitherto had been outside of politics— in hurried, sometimes even desperate, efforts by underdeveloped nations to catch up with the modern developed states.[2] During the first decade of the twenty-first century various organizations have estimated that the great majority of all the states in the world have become electoral democracies, with the number of presumed democracies hovering around 120 or so. Of course, these democracies differ greatly from one another. Indeed, *The Economist* puts the number of full-fledged democracies at only twenty-eight, with eighty-four considered to be either flawed democracies or hybrid regimes. *The Economist* labels the governments of fifty-five countries as authoritarian.

Still, the growth of democracies throughout the world over the past six or seven decades is impressive. In fact, this incorporation of common people into politics is what sets the modern world apart from what went on before. Eighteenth-century Revolutionary Americans were in the vanguard of this modern development. Within decades following the Declaration of Independence, Americans were calling their government a democracy; they legitimated the term and set the rest of the world on the path of democratization.

To be sure, it was the ancient Greeks who had actually invented democracy—that is, rule directly by the people themselves—and who had passed the word on to the eighteenth-century Western world. But the Greek idea of democracy inherited by the West was regarded with suspicion and hostility. The great Greek writers whose works the Western Europeans most read—Thucydides, Plato, and Aristotle—had found democracy wanting to one degree or another. They believed that the people trying to rule by themselves would inevitably lead to anarchy and violence, ending in dictatorship and tyranny. At best, Aristotle had contended, democracy might be part of a mixed government, acceptable if it were balanced by monarchy and aristocracy.

And that is how the eighteenth-century English on both sides of the Atlantic tended to employ the word "democracy": as a term almost always used in conjunction with "monarchy" and "aristocracy"—as an essential part of a mixed or balanced constitution. Indeed, the eighteenth-century English constitution was so famous precisely because it mixed or balanced the three pure types of government—monarchy, aristocracy, and democracy—in its crown, House of Lords, and House of Commons.

By itself a pure democracy—"a government of all over all," as James Otis called it—was not much valued.[3] It meant not a government electorally derived from the people, but one actually administered by the people themselves. Enlightened Britons might agree that ideally the people ought to govern themselves directly, but they realized that democracy in this literal sense had been approximated only in the Greek city-states and in the New England towns; actual self-government or simple democracy was not feasible for any large community. As one American polemicist stated in 1776, even the great radical Whig Algernon Sidney had written that he had known of "no such thing" as "in the strict sense, . . . a pure democracy, where the people in themselves and by themselves, perform all that belongs to government," and if any had ever existed in the world, he had "nothing to say for it."⁴ Neither Alexander Hamilton nor James Madison in *The Federalist* had any good words for the kind of pure democracy that existed in antiquity. "Such Democracies," wrote Madison in *The Federalist* No. 10, "have ever been spectacles of turbulence and contention; have ever been found incompatible with personal security, or the rights of property; and have in general been as short in their lives, as they have been violent in their deaths." Consequently, most eighteenth-century Britons in both the mother country and the colonies were so uneasy over the impracticality and instability of pure democracy that the term "democracy" was commonly used vituperatively to discredit any untoward tendency toward popular government.

The English had invented the idea of representation, imagining their elected House of Commons to be the democratic part of the mixed constitution. But, as we have seen in the previous essay, it was the Americans who expanded the idea of representation to all parts of their federal and state governments. This expansion did not happen immediately. The original Revolutionary state constitutions of 1776 were intended to be republican versions of the mixed or balanced constitution of the former mother country. This is why we call the lower houses of our federal and state legislatures "houses of representatives" and set them against our senates, executives, and judiciaries, as if they were the only representative bodies in our governments. But eventually, in the several years following the Declaration of Independence, Americans came to think of all their elected governmental institutions as representative of the people, and the term "republic," which meant government derived from the people, became identified with the term "democracy." By the first decade or so of the nineteenth century the two terms became interchangeable.

Because representation of the people was based so exclusively on popular election, voting in America, as we have noted, became the sole criterion of representation. Americans believed that unless they actually voted for their agents, they could not be adequately represented by them. This peculiar notion of actual representation in turn made the suffrage seem to be the necessary and sufficient measure of democratic politics—which accounts for our often naive notion that simply giving people the vote in a developing country is tantamount to creating a democracy. Although the right to vote is clearly a prerequisite for democratic politics, it is hardly all there is to it. In fact, voting is only the exposed tip of an incredibly complicated political and social process. How this process came about and how the people became involved in politics are questions that lie at the heart of the American Revolution.

The American Revolution was both a consequence and a cause of democracy. It marked a decisive change in the way political activity was carried on in America and gave new legitimacy to the involvement of common people in politics. It was not, however, simply a matter of enfranchising new voters. The franchise in most colonies prior to the Revolution was already extensive. Although the right to vote in colonial America was restricted by property qualifications (usually a personal estate worth forty pounds or a freehold worth forty shillings a year) as it was in eighteenth-century England, property owning was so widespread in America that the colonists enjoyed the broadest suffrage of any people in the world: perhaps as many as 60 to 80 percent of adult white males in the colonies could legally vote. The legal exclusion of the propertyless from the franchise was based not on the fear that these people without property might confiscate the wealth of the aristocratic few, but on the opposite fear: that the aristocratic few might manipulate and corrupt the poor for their own ends. Only men who were independent, owned stable amounts of property, and were free from influence should have the vote. The same reasoning lay behind the exclusion from the franchise of women, minors, and others who were considered to be dependent and to have no will of their own.

Despite the breadth of suffrage in colonial America, however, the fact remains that most of those legally enfranchised did not exercise their right to vote. And when they did vote, they usually voted for the same prominent families. It turns out that the property holders in colonial America were not as independent and as free from influence as the law presumed. The social structure and social values were such that colonial politics, at least when compared to politics in post-Revolutionary America, was remarkably stable; the percentage of people actually voting and participating in politics remained small, and the political leadership remained in a remarkably limited number of hands.

Established social leaders expected deference from those below them and generally got it, and were habitually reelected to political office. Yet this acquiescence that people gave to those who by their wealth, influence, and independence were considered best qualified to rule was based not simply on traditional habits of deference but, more important, on the substantial dependency that patronage and economic and social power created. In 1773 in the Mohawk district of Tryon County, New York, at least four hundred men had the franchise. Yet in an election for five constables, only fourteen electors turned out to vote; all fourteen were closely tied by interest or patronage to Sir William Johnson, the local grandee of the area, and all fourteen naturally voted for the same five candidates.[5]

Translating the personal, social, and economic authority of the leading gentry into political patronage and power was essentially what eighteenth-century politics was about. The process was self-intensifying: social authority created political power, which in turn created more social influence. Some members of the gentry, such as the Tidewater planters of Virginia or the wealthy landholders of the Connecticut River valley, had enough patronage and influence to overawe entire communities. Connecticut River valley gentry like Israel Williams and John Worthington, so imposing as to be called "river gods," used their power to become at one time or another selectmen of their towns, representatives to the

Massachusetts General Court, members of the Massachusetts Council, provincial court judges, justices of the peace, and colonels of their county regiments. It became impossible to tell where the circle of their authority began: the political authority to grant licenses for taverns or mills, to determine the location of roads and bridges, or to enlist men for military service was of a piece with their wealth and social influence.

It was likewise substantial paternalistic and patronage power, and not merely the treating of the freeholders with toddy at election time, that enabled the great Virginia planters to mobilize their "interest" and to maintain law and order over their local communities without the aid of police forces. The leading Virginia gentry were the vestrymen of their parishes and the lay leaders of the Anglican Church, so that the sacredness of religion and the patronage of poor relief further enhanced the hierarchy of authority. All this was the stuff of which aristocracies were made.

Colonial society had no organized political parties and no professional politicians in today's sense of these terms. Large planters, established merchants, and wealthy lawyers held the major offices and ran political affairs as part of the responsibility of their elevated social position. It was rare for a tavern keeper or a small farmer to gain a political office of any consequence. Men were granted political authority in accord not with their seniority or experience in politics but with their established economic and social superiority. Thus Thomas Hutchinson, scion of a distinguished Boston mercantile family, was elected to the Massachusetts House of Representatives at the age of twenty-six and almost immediately became its speaker. So too could Jonathan Trumbull, an obscure country merchant, be catapulted in 1739 into the speakership of the Connecticut assembly at age twenty-eight and into the prestigious Council of Assistants the following year simply by the fact that his marriage into the ancient and esteemed Robinson family had given him, as eighteenth-century historian Samuel Peters put it, "the prospect of preferment in civil life."[6] Social and political authority was indivisible, and men moved horizontally into politics from society rather than (as is common today) moving up vertically through an exclusively political hierarchy.

Yet politics in eighteenth-century colonial America was unstable enough in many areas that members of the elite struggled for political power and precedent among themselves. The social hierarchy was often sufficiently confused at the top that it was never entirely clear who was destined to hold political office and govern. It was obvious that well-to-do lawyers or planters from distinguished families were superior to, say, blacksmiths, but within the group of well-to-do lawyers or wealthy planters, superiority was not so visible and incontestable. Indeed, in some colonies social superiority was so recent and so seemingly arbitrary that contesting it was inevitable. These contests for office and power created the grinding factionalism—the shifting competing congeries of the leading gentry's personal and family "interests"—that characterized much of eighteenth-century colonial politics.[7]

Before the 1730s and 1740s, many of these contests were transatlantic in character and focused on the metropolitan center of the empire (London). In the early decades of the eighteenth century, elite factions opposed to the royal governors often sought political leverage from the imperial arena; in other words, they resorted to the use of imperial interests and transatlantic connections in order to win local political battles in their colonies. They used extralegal channels in the home country, such as merchant groups in London, in order to undermine the royal governors' political positions from the rear. Or they formed alliances with other imperial agents, such as those representing the Church of England, in order to bypass the governors. Colonial opposition leaders even made personal journeys to London to lobby for the reversal of gubernatorial decisions or even the removal of a governor. This kind of Anglo-American politics was open-ended. Since there were many transatlantic avenues of influence and connection and many appeals over the heads of local officials to Whitehall, few decisions made in the colonies themselves could be final.[8]

But after 1740 or so this open-ended character of American politics began to close up, and the colonists' ability to influence English politics sharply declined. Communications to the mother country became more formal, and personal appeals declined. The colonial lobbying agents who earlier had been initiators of colonial policy were now hard put to head off colonial measures begun by others in Britain. As the earlier transatlantic channels and avenues of influence clogged up or closed off, the royal governors were left as the only major link between the colonies and Great Britain. If opposition groups in the colonies were going to contest their governors, they would have to find leverage within their own colonies.[9]

Under these changed circumstances dissident factions in the colonies were forced to turn inward, toward the only source of authority other than the king recognized by eighteenth-century Anglo-American political theory: the people. Opposition groups now began to mobilize the electorate in their colonies as never before, using the popular elective assemblies as their main instrument of opposition against the royal governors. Consequently, the number of contested elections for the colonial assemblies rapidly multiplied. In Boston, for example, in the decade of the 1720s, only 30 percent of elections were contested; by the 1750s, 60 percent were. With the growth of contested elections came greater voter participation and more vitriolic political rhetoric and propaganda. Groups began forming tickets, caucuses, and political clubs, and hiring professional pamphleteers to attack their opponents for being overstuffed men of wealth and learning. In these mid-eighteenth-century developments we can see the beginnings of what would eventually become typically American egalitarian electoral propaganda and modern political campaigning.[10]

But of course nobody had the future in mind. By appealing to the people, these elite families and factions were not trying to create the democratic world of the nineteenth century; they were simply using whatever weapons they had at their disposal—together with inflammatory popular Whig rhetoric—to get at their opponents. All of their appeals to the people were merely tactical devices for gaining office. The colonial assemblies that earlier had been virtual closed clubs now became more sensitive to the public out-of-doors. In the 1750s they began publishing compilations of their laws and revealing how their members voted on particular issues. In the 1760s they began building galleries in the legislative halls to allow the people to witness debates. Some even began calling for a widening of the franchise. Those who opposed these measures were labeled "enemies of the people."[11]

Democracy in America thus began not as the result of the people arousing themselves spontaneously and clamoring from below for a share in political authority. Instead, democracy was initially created from above. The people were cajoled, persuaded, even sometimes frightened into getting involved. Although normally many of the towns of Massachusetts—sometimes as many as one-third—did not even bother to send their representatives to the General Court, they "have it in their power upon an extraordinary Emergency," warned Governor William Shirley in 1742, "to double and almost treble their numbers [of representatives], which they would not fail to do if they should be desirous of disputing any point with His Majesty's governor which they might suspect their ordinary members would carry against his influence in the House."[12] Each competing faction tried to outdo its opponents in posing as a friend of the people, defending popular rights and advancing popular interests against those of the crown. Yet over time what began as a pose eventually assumed a reality that had not been anticipated. The people once mobilized could not easily be put down.

Thus by the 1760s American politics were already primed for the Revolutionary transformation from monarchy to republicanism. As patriot leaders began contesting the authority of the English government, the earlier practices of mobilizing the people into politics increased dramatically. As we have seen, the imperial debate not only challenged traditional British authority but compelled Americans to articulate an idea of actual representation that they have never lost. This idea of actual representation led to heightened demands to expand the franchise and to the unprecedented conviction that representation in government ought to be equal and more or less in proportion to population. Initially provided for in the Revolutionary state constitutions of 1776, this conviction resulted in the federal Constitution's mandate that a census be taken every ten years. Eventually, as we have noted in the previous essay on "The Origins of American Constitutionalism," the belief inherent in the concept of actual representation that voting itself was the sole criterion of representation tended to transform all elected officials, including governors and members of upper houses, into other kinds of representatives of the people, placing them, at least in name, in an awkward relationship to the original houses of representatives.

Actual representation had more than constitutional importance for American politics. It had social significance as well. Even before the Revolutionary turmoil had settled, some Americans, as we have seen, began arguing that mere voting by ordinary men was not a sufficient protection of ordinary men's interests if only members of the elite continued to be the ones elected. It was coming to be thought that in a society of diverse and particular interests, men from one class or group, however educated and respectable, could not be acquainted with the needs and interests of other classes and groups. Wealthy college-educated lawyers or merchants could not know the concerns of poor farmers or small tradesmen. As we have seen, the logic of actual representation required that ordinary men be represented by ordinary men, indeed, by men of the same religion, ethnic group, or occupation.

Such an idea—lying at the heart of the radicalism of the American Revolution—constituted an extraordinary transformation in the relationship between society and government. It expressed egalitarian forces released by the Revolution that could not be easily contained.

At the outset of the Revolution, equality to most Americans had meant an equality of legal rights and the opportunity to rise by merit through clearly discernible ranks. But in the hands of competing politicians seeking to diminish the credentials of their opponents and win votes, the idea of equality was soon expanded in ways that few of its supporters had originally anticipated—to mean that one man was as good as another. This meaning of equality soon dissolved the identity between social and political leadership and helped to give political power to the kinds of men who hitherto had never held it. Politics was transformed, and political upstarts—obscure men with obscure backgrounds who had never been to college—launched vigorous attacks on the former attributes of social superiority (names, titles, social origins, family connections, even education) and bragged that their own positions were based not on relatives or friends but only on what their hard work and money had made for them.

The confrontation in the 1780s between John Rutledge, a distinguished social and political leader in South Carolina, and William Thompson, an unknown Charleston tavern keeper, graphically illustrates the new emerging post-Revolutionary culture. Rutledge had sent a female servant to Thompson's tavern to watch a fireworks display from the roof. Thompson denied the servant admittance and sent her back to Rutledge. Rutledge was infuriated and demanded that Thompson come to his house and apologize. Thompson refused and, believing that his honor had been affronted by Rutledge's arrogant request, challenged Rutledge to a duel. Since the social likes of Rutledge did not accept challenges from tavern keepers, Rutledge went to the South Carolina House of Representatives, of which he was a member, and insisted that it pass a bill banishing Thompson from the state for insulting an officer of its government. Thompson took to the press for his defense and in 1784 made what can only be described as a classic expression of American resentment against social superiority—a resentment voiced, said Thompson, not on behalf of himself but on behalf of the people generally, or "those more especially, who go at this day under the opprobrious appellation of the Lower Orders of Men."

In his newspaper essays Thompson did not merely attack the few aristocratic "nabobs" who had humiliated him; he actually assaulted the very idea of a social hierarchy ruled by a gentlemanly elite. In fact, he turned traditional eighteenth-century opinion upside down and argued that the social aristocracy was peculiarly unqualified to rule politically. In other words, social authority should have no relation to political authority; it was in fact harmful to political authority. Rather than preparing men for political leadership in a free government, said Thompson, "signal opulence and influence," especially when united "by intermarriage or otherwise," were really "calculated to subvert Republicanism." The "persons and conduct" of the South Carolina nabobs like Rutledge "in private life may be unexceptionable, and even amiable, but their pride, influence, ambition, connections, wealth, and political principles ought in public life," Thompson contended, "ever to exclude them from public confidence." Since in a republican government "consequence is from the public opinion, and not from private fancy," all that was needed in republican leadership, said Thompson, was "being good, able, useful, and friends to social equality."

Thompson sarcastically went on to recount how he, a mere tavern keeper, "a wretch of no higher rank in the Commonwealth than that of Common-Citizen," had been debased by what he called "those self-exalted characters, who affect to compose the grand hierarchy of the State, . . . for having dared to dispute with a John Rutledge, or any of the NABOB tribe." The experience had been degrading enough to Thompson as a man, but as a former militia officer it had been, he said, "insupportable"—indicating how Revolutionary military service had affected social mobility and social expectations. Undoubtedly, wrote Thompson, Rutledge had "conceived me his inferior." But like many others in these years—tavern keepers, farmers, petty merchants, small-time lawyers, former militia officers—Thompson could no longer "comprehend the inferiority."[13]

Many new politicians in the following years, likewise not being able to comprehend their inferiority, began using the popular and egalitarian ideals of the Revolution to upset the older hierarchy and bring ordinary people like themselves into politics. This was not always easy, for as some politicians complained, "the poorer commonality," even when they possessed the legal right to vote, seemed apathetic to appeals and too accepting of traditional authority. Their ideas of government had too long been "rather aristocratical than popular." "The rich," said one polemicist, "having been used to govern, seem to think it is their right," while the common people, "having hitherto had little or no hand in government, seemed to think it does not belong to them to have any."[14] To convince the people that they rightfully had a share in government became the task of hustling egalitarian politicians in the decades following the Revolution.

Everywhere, but especially in the North, these middling politicians urged the people to shed their political apathy and "keep up the cry against Judges, Lawyers, Generals, Colonels, and all other designing men, and the day will be our own." They demanded that they do their "utmost at election to prevent all men of talents, lawyers, rich men from being elected."[15]

The increased competition between candidates and parties in the early nineteenth century meant more and more contested elections for both federal and state officials, which sent the turnout of voters skyrocketing. In many places, especially in the North, the participation of eligible voters went from 20 percent or so in the 1790s to 80 percent or more in the first decade of the nineteenth century.[16]

As voting took on a heightened significance, the states that had not already done so began to expand the franchise by eliminating property qualifications or transforming the requirement into the mere paying of taxes. In the eighteenth century, landed property had been a justifiable qualification for voting because it had been seen as a source of independence and authority. But as property in the fast-moving economy of the early Republic became more and more a commodity to be exchanged in the marketplace, property as a requirement for officeholding and suffrage steadily lost its meaning. Who could believe that "property is . . . any proof of superior virtue, discernment or patriotism"? asked the New York Democratic-Republicans in 1812.[17] By 1825, under this kind of popular pressure, every state but Rhode Island, Virginia, and Louisiana had more or less achieved universal white male suffrage; by 1830 only Rhode Island, which had once been the most democratic place in North America, retained the old forty pounds–forty shillings freehold qualification for voting. With the exception of a brief period in New Jersey (1790–1807) no state granted women suffrage. By modern standards the system was far from democratic, but by the standards of the early nineteenth century, America possessed the most popular electoral politics in the world.[18]

Many of the spokesmen for popular interests who emerged in these

years made no pretense to having any special personal or social qualifications to rule. They were not wealthy men, they had not gone to Harvard
or Princeton, and they were often proud of their parochial and localist
outlook. When Simon Snyder, the ill-educated son of a poor mechanic,
ran successfully for governor of Pennsylvania in 1808, opponents mocked
his obscure origins and called him and his followers "clodhoppers." Snyder and his supporters quite shrewdly picked up the epithet and began
proudly wearing it. Being a clodhopper in a society of clodhoppers became
the source of much of Snyder's political success. Like other such popular political figures, his claim to office was based solely on his ability to
garner votes and satisfy the interests of his constituents. No longer could
political office be the consequence of a gentleman's previously established
wealth and social authority. If anything, holding office in America was
becoming the source of that wealth and social authority.

In the 1780s James Madison had hoped that government might
become a "disinterested & dispassionate umpire in disputes between different passions & interests in the State."[19] But this hope seemed increasingly visionary. Few elected officials sought to stand above the competing
interests of the marketplace and, like an umpire, make impartial judgments about what was good for the whole society. In fact, elected officials
were bringing the partial, local interests of their constituents, and sometimes even their own interests, right into the workings of government.
State legislators often became what Madison in the 1780s had most feared:
judges in their own causes. In Connecticut the subscription list of the
Hartford Bank, suggested one shrewd subscriber in 1791, had to be left
open, or seem to be open—that is, if the bank hoped to be incorporated
by the Connecticut legislature. There were "a number in the Legislature
who would wish to become subscribers, and would, of course, advocate
the bill while they supposed they could subscribe, and, on the contrary, if
it was known the subscription was full, they would oppose it violently."[20]

Everywhere legislators responded to the interests of those who elected
them. Since every town in the country seemed to want a bank, banks proliferated. In 1813 the Pennsylvania legislature in a single bill authorized

the incorporation of twenty-five new banks. After the governor vetoed this bill, the legislature in 1814 passed over the governor's veto another bill incorporating forty-one banks. By 1818 Kentucky had forty-three new banks, two of them in towns that had fewer than one hundred inhabitants.

Early nineteenth-century politics increasingly assumed modern characteristics, and partisanship and parties—using government to promote partial interests—acquired a legitimacy that they had not had before. Congressmen began referring to those who sought to influence them as "a commanding lobby," and the term "lobbyist" took on its modern meaning. The word "logrolling" in the making of laws (that is, the trading of votes by legislators for each other's bills) likewise began to be used for the first time, to the bewilderment of conservative Federalists. "I do not well understand the Term," said an Ohio Federalist, "but I believe it means bargaining with each other for the little loaves and fishes of the State." The modern problem of taxation in a democracy had already emerged. As one Virginia congressman complained in 1814, "Everyone is for taxing every body, except himself and his Constituents."[21]

If representatives were elected to promote the particular interests and private causes of their constituents, then the idea that such representatives were simply disinterested gentlemen, squire worthies called by duty to shoulder the burdens of public service, became archaic. Many now began running for office, not, as earlier, simply standing for election. The weakening of the older social hierarchy and the erosion of the traditional belief in elite rule made the rise of political parties both necessary and possible. Indeed, the United States was the first nation to develop modern political parties dealing with mass electorates. Individuals cut loose from traditional ties to the social hierarchy were now forced to combine in new groups for political ends. Political office was no longer set by social ascription, but rather was won by political achievement within the organization of the party and through the winning of votes.

In time new arts of persuasion, using cheap newspapers and mass meetings, were developed, and politics assumed carnival-like characteristics that led during the nineteenth century to participation by higher percentages of the legal electorate than ever again was achieved in American politics. In such an atmosphere of stump-speaking and running for office, the members of the older gentry were frequently at a considerable disadvantage. In fact, by the early nineteenth century, being a gentleman or professing the characteristics of a gentleman, even having gone to college, became a liability in elections in some parts of the country.

In his Jeffersonian Republican campaign for governor of New York in 1807, Daniel Tomkins, prosperous lawyer and graduate of Columbia College, knew that portraying himself as a simple "farmer's boy" would contrast successfully with the character of his opponent, Morgan Lewis, who was an in-law of the aristocratic Livingston family. In 1810 the New York Federalists tried to retaliate and combat Tomkins and the Jeffersonian Republicans with their own plebeian candidate, Jonas Platt, "whose habits and manners," said the Federalists, "are as plain and republican as those of his country neighbors." Unlike Tompkins, Platt was not "a city lawyer who rolls in splendor and wallows in luxury."[22]

By the middle decades of the nineteenth century, this kind of popular antielitism coming out of the Revolution was as strong as ever, as the 1868 election campaign for the fifth congressional district of Massachusetts vividly demonstrates. The fifth congressional district—Essex County—was the former center of Massachusetts Brahmin Federalism, but by the mid-nineteenth century it was increasingly filled with Irish immigrants. The campaign was essentially between Richard Henry Dana Jr., a well-to-do and Harvard-educated descendent of a distinguished Massachusetts family and author of *Two Years Before the Mast*, and Benjamin Butler, son of boardinghouse keeper who had never been to college and was one of the most flamboyant demagogues American politics has ever produced. (One gets some idea of Butler's standing with the Massachusetts elite by realizing that he was the first governor of Massachusetts in over two centuries not invited to a Harvard College commencement.) In the congressional campaign, Butler showed Dana what nineteenth-century electoral politics was all about. While Dana was talking to tea groups about bond payments, Butler was haranguing the Irish shoe workers of

Lynn, organizing parades, turning out the fire and police departments, hiring brass bands, distributing hundreds of pamphlets, and charging his opponent with being a Beau Brummel in white gloves. Dana was simply no match for him.

When Dana was finally forced to confront audiences of workingmen, he gave up talking about bonds and tried desperately to assure his audiences that he too worked hard. All the while, Butler mocked his wearing of white gloves and his efforts to make common cause with the people. During one speech Dana told the Irish shoe workers that when he spent two years before the mast as a young sailor he too was a worker who didn't wear white gloves. "I was as dirty as any of you," he exclaimed. With such statements it is not surprising that Dana ended up with less than 10 percent of the vote in a humiliating loss to Butler.[23]

By vying for political leadership and competing for votes, new men— not necessarily as colorful as Butler but having the same social obscurity and doomed in any other society to remain in obscurity—became part of the political process. The most important criterion of their leadership was their ability to appeal to voters.

It was the American Revolution that had helped to make possible and to accelerate these changes in our politics. As a result of the republican revolution, Americans essentially denied any other status than citizen. The people were all in politics and all of the people were equal. Any sort of unequal restrictions on the rights of citizenship—on the right to run for office or to vote, for example, theoretically were anomalies, relics of an older society that now had to be eliminated. In the early decades of the nineteenth century, competing political parties searched out groups of people hitherto uninvolved in politics and brought them in: renters initially denied the franchise because they were not freeholders, poor men who lacked the necessary property qualifications, and newly arrived immigrants—anyone who might become a voter and supporter of the party, or even one of its leaders. If they could not yet legally vote, the vote could be given them. If they could legally vote but did not bother, then they could be persuaded that they ought to. In these ways American politicians in the decades following the Revolution worked to establish universal male suffrage and democratic politics.

We take these developments for granted and easily forget how far ahead of the rest of the world the United States was in the early nineteenth century. Tavern keepers and weavers were sitting in our legislatures while most European states were still trying to disentangle voting and representation from an incredible variety of estate and corporate statuses. In 1792 Kentucky entered the Union with a constitution allowing universal suffrage for all free adult males. A generation later the English were still debating whether voting was a privilege confined to a few; in fact, England had to wait until 1867 before workingmen got the vote and became, in William Gladstone's words, "our fellow subjects." In many parts of the world today people are still waiting to become citizens and full participants in the political process.

Yet, as we know all too well, America's record in integrating the people into politics has not been an untainted success story. The great aberration amidst all the Revolutionary talk of equality, voting, and representation was slavery. Indeed, it was the Revolution itself, not only with its appeal to liberty but with its idea of citizenship of equal individuals, that made slavery in 1776 suddenly seem anomalous to large numbers of Americans. What had been taken for granted earlier in the eighteenth century as part of the brutality and inequality of life—regarded as merely the most base and degraded status in a society of numerous degrees and multiple ranks of freedom and unfreedom—now seemed conspicuous and peculiar. In a republic, as was not the case in a monarchy, there could be no place for subjection and degrees of freedom or dependency. In the North, where slavery was considerable but not deeply rooted, the exposure of the anomaly worked to abolish it. By 1804 all the Northern states had legally ended slavery, and by 1830 there were fewer than 3,000 black slaves remaining out of a Northern black population of over 125,000.[24] In the South the suddenly exposed peculiarity of slavery threw Southern whites, who had been in the vanguard of the Revolutionary movement and among the most fervent spokesmen for its libertarianism, onto the defensive. Although the South was able to maintain dominance over much of the federal government in the antebellum period by manipulating the Constitution, its leadership was hollow, increasingly desperate, and without firm foundation in the country as a whole; in time, the peculiarity of slavery gradually separated the section from the mainstream of America's egalitarian developments.

Yet the very egalitarianism of America's republican ideology—the egalitarianism that undercut the rationale of slavery—worked at the same time to inhibit integrating the free black man into the political process. Since republican citizenship implied equality for all citizens, a person once admitted as a citizen into the political process was put on a level with all other citizens and regarded as being as good as the next man—uneducated tavern keepers were as good as wealthy college-educated planters. With the spread of these republican assumptions, Northern whites began to view black voters with increasing apprehension, unwilling to accept the equality that suffrage and citizenship dictated. In the 1790s in several states of the North, free blacks possessed the right to vote (often as a result of the general extension of the franchise that took place during the Revolution), and they exercised it in some areas with particular effectiveness. But in subsequent years, as the white electorate continued to expand through changes in the laws and the mobilization of new voters, blacks found themselves being squeezed out.

There is perhaps no greater irony in the democratization of American politics in the early nineteenth century than the fact that as the poor white man gained the right to vote, the free black man lost it. By the heyday of Jacksonian democracy, white popular majorities in state after state in the North had moved to eliminate the remaining property restrictions on white voters while at the same time concocting new restrictions taking away the franchise from black voters who in some cases had exercised it for decades. No state admitted to the Union after 1819 allowed blacks to vote. By 1840, 93 percent of Northern free blacks lived in states that completely or practically excluded them from suffrage and hence from the participation in politics.[25]

This exclusion of blacks from politics was largely a consequence of white fears of the equality that republican citizenship demanded. But it was also a product of competitive democratic politics. In some states, like Pennsylvania, black exclusion was the price paid for lower-class whites gaining the right to vote, universal male suffrage having been opposed on the grounds that it would add too many blacks to the electorate. In other states, like New York, exclusion of blacks from the franchise was an effective way for Democratic Party majorities to eliminate once and for all blocs of black voters who too often had voted first for Federalist and then for Whig candidates. Since the Democratic Party—as the spokes-man for the popular cause against elitism and aristocracy—was in the forefront of the effort to expand suffrage, it seemed to be good politics for the party not only to attract new voters to its ranks but to take away voters who supported its opponents. It was this kind of political pressure that led to the peculiar situation in some states in which immigrant aliens were granted the right the vote before they had become citizens while blacks who had been born and bred in the United States had their right to vote abolished—a development often based on a shrewd assessment by politi-cians of what particular party new immigrants and blacks would support. Such were the strange and perverse consequences of democracy.

For a republican society it was an impossible situation, and Ameri-cans wrestled with it for decades. Federal officials in the first half of the nineteenth century could never decide the precise status of free blacks, sometimes arguing that blacks were not citizens in possessing the right to vote but were citizens in having the right to secure passports. Others tried to discover some sort of intermediate legal position for free blacks as denizens standing between aliens and citizens. But the logic of republi-can equality would not allow these distinctions, and sooner or later many sought to escape from the dilemma posed by black disfranchisement by denying citizenship to all blacks, whether slave or free, a position Chief Justice Roger Taney and the Supreme Court tried to establish in the *Dred Scott* decision of 1857. Suffrage had become sufficiently equated with rep-resentation in America that if a person was not granted the right to vote then he was not represented in the community; and not being represented in a republican community was equivalent to not being a citizen. In the end, enslaved blacks without liberty and free blacks without citizenship were such contradictions of the Revolutionary ideals that sooner or later they had to tear the country apart.

When Northerners came to debate methods of Southern reconstruction at the end of the Civil War, they moved often reluctantly but nonetheless steadily toward black enfranchisement, impelled both by the logic of the persisting ideals of the Revolution and by the circumstances of politics. Although some historians have believed that the Republican Party's espousal of black suffrage in the aftermath of the war was based on a cynical desire to recruit new voters to the party, it was obviously based on much more than that. In terms of political expediency alone, the Republicans' sponsorship of black suffrage ran the risk even in the North of what we later came to call "white backlash." Many advocates of black suffrage sincerely believed, as Wendell Phillips put it, that America could never be truly a united nation "until every class God has made, from the lakes to the Gulf, has its ballot to protect itself."[26]

Nevertheless, there can be little doubt that black enfranchisement after the Civil War was bolstered, like all reforms, by political exigencies, and that many Northerners and Republicans favored it grudgingly and only as a means of preventing the resurgence of an unreconstructed South controlled by a Democratic Party that would threaten the dominance of the Republican Party. Hence there resulted an awkward gap between the Fourteenth Amendment, which defined citizenship for the first time and gave it a national emphasis that it had hitherto lacked, and the Fifteenth Amendment, which enfranchised blacks but unfortunately linked their enfranchisement not to their citizenship but to their race. This linkage allowed a state to impose any voting qualifications it chose as long as they were not based on race. This created a tangled situation that Americans only began to unravel a century later.

Although Americans have hesitated to make the connection between citizenship and the right to vote explicit and unequivocal, everything in American history has pointed to that connection. During the 1960s, largely under the impetus of the civil rights movement but going beyond that, Americans became more and more interested in political and voting rights, and the logic of principles concerning suffrage and the representation first articulated in the Revolution were finally drawn out. The voting rights acts and the anti–poll tax amendment were based on a deeply rooted belief that no nation like ours could in conscience exclude any of its citizens from the political process. That same legacy from the Revolution led the Supreme Court in a series of reapportionment decisions to apply the idea of "one person, one vote" to congressional and state legislative districting. As a result, senates in many states finally became the fully representative bodies they had not been intended to be in 1776. Of course, as one wag has observed, our periodic redistricting can sometimes turn democracy on its head. Instead of the voters choosing their political leaders, the leaders get to choose their voters.[27]

Many Americans became concerned with large and unequal campaign contributions precisely because they seemed to negate the effects of equal suffrage and violate the equality of participation in the political process. Despite an electorate that at times seems apathetic, interest in suffrage and in the equality of consent has never been greater than it has over the past generation. Such a concern naturally puts a terrific burden on our political system, but it is a burden we should gladly bear (and many other nations would love to have it), for it bespeaks an underlying popular confidence in the processes of politics that surface events and news headlines tend to obscure.

In fact, our concern with suffrage and with the formal rights of consent has assumed such a transcendent significance that it has sometimes concealed the substance of democratic politics and has tended to exaggerate the real power of the legal right to vote. Suffrage has become such a symbol of citizenship that its possession seems necessarily to involve all kinds of rights. Thus acquiring the vote has often seemed to be an instrument of reform or a means of solving complicated social problems. The women's rights movement of the nineteenth century—premised on the belief, as one woman put it in 1848, that "there is no reality in any power that cannot be coined into votes"—came to focus almost exclusively on the gaining of suffrage.[28] And when the Nineteenth Amendment granting women the franchise was finally ratified in 1920 and did not lead to the promised revolution, the sense of failure set the feminist movement back at least half a century. As late as the 1960s, this formal integration into the political process through suffrage continued to be regarded as a panacea for social ills. Certainly this assumption lay behind the response to the youth rebellions of the late 1960s and the eventual adoption of the Twenty-sixth Amendment giving eighteen-year-olds the vote.

This special fascination with politics and this reliance on political integration through voting as a means of solving social problems are legacies of our Revolution, and they are as alive now as they were then. The Revolution not only brought ordinary people into politics; it also created such confidence in suffrage as the sole criterion of representation that we have too often forgotten just what makes the right to vote workable in America. In our dealings with newly developing nations, we are too apt to believe that the mere institution of the ballot in a new country will automatically create a viable democracy, and we are often confused and disillusioned when this rarely happens.

The point is that we have the relationship backward. It is not suffrage that gives life to our democracy; it is our democratic society that gives life to suffrage. American society is permeated by the belief in (and, despite extraordinary differences of income, in the reality of) equality that makes our reliance on the ballot operable. It was not the breadth of the franchise in the nineteenth century that created democratic politics. The franchise was broad even in colonial times. Rather, it was the egalitarian process of politics that led to the mobilization of voters and the political integration of the nation. It was the work of countless politicians recruited from all levels of society and representing many diverse interests, attempting to win elections by exhorting and pleading with their electors, that in the final analysis shaped our democratic system. Any state can grant suffrage to its people overnight, but it cannot thereby guarantee to itself a democratic polity. As American history shows, such a democracy requires generations of experience with electoral politics. More important, it requires the emergence of political parties and egalitarian politicians none of whom have too much power and most of whom ought to run scared—politicians whose maneuvering for electoral advantage, whose courting of the electorate, and whose passion for victory result, in the end, in grander and more significant developments than they themselves can foresee or even imagine. Politicians are at the heart of our political system, and insofar as it is democratic, they have made it so.

AFTERWORD TO CHAPTER 6

This essay is a much-revised and updated version of a lecture originally given before the Kentucky legislature in Frankfort, Kentucky, on January 9, 1974, which perhaps accounts for the rather exuberant paean to politicians at the end. The event was arranged by the American Enterprise Institute, which sponsored a series of lectures by scholars and other intellectual figures at different venues as part of the bicentennial celebration of the American Revolution.

These lectures were collected and published as *America's Continuing Revolution: An Act of Conservation* (Washington, D.C.: American Enterprise Institute, 1975).

CHAPTER SEVEN

The RADICALISM *of* THOMAS JEFFERSON *and* THOMAS PAINE CONSIDERED

B Y 1792 THOMAS PAINE already sensed that the world might not give him as much credit for his endeavors on behalf of the American Revolution as he thought he deserved, and thus he thought he ought to set the world straight. "With all the inconveniences of early life against me," he wrote in *The Rights of Man: Part the Second*, "I am proud to say that with a perseverance undismayed by difficulties, a disinterestedness that compelled respect, I have not only contributed to raise a new empire in the world, founded on a new system of government, but I have arrived at an eminence in political literature, the most difficult of all lines to succeed and excel in, which aristocracy with all its aids, has not been able to reach or to rival." Paine sensed the future correctly. By 1800 there were few Americans left who were willing to recognize Paine's contribution to their Revolution. Thomas Jefferson was the great exception. Paine, he said in 1801, had "steadily labored" on behalf of liberty and the American Revolution "with as much effect as any man living."[1]

Naturally, it was Jefferson who celebrated Paine when everyone else was scorning him, for he and Paine thought alike. Indeed, no two prominent American Revolutionaries shared so many ideas as did Jefferson and Paine. Yet no two Revolutionaries were more different in background and temperament.

Jefferson was a wealthy slaveholding aristocrat from Virginia who was as well connected socially as anyone in America. His mother was a Randolph, perhaps the most prestigious family in all of Virginia, and positions in his society came easy to him. Personally, he was cool, reserved, and self-possessed. He disliked personal controversy and was always charming in face-to-face relations with both friends and enemies. Although he played at being casual, he was utterly civilized and genteel. He mastered several languages, including those of antiquity, and he spent his life trying to discover (and acquire) what was the best and most enlightened in the world of the eighteenth century. He prided himself on his manners and taste; indeed, he became an impresario for his countrymen, advising them on what was proper in everything from the arts to wine. There was almost nothing he did not know about. "Without having quitted his own country," this earnest autodidact with a voracious appetite for learning had become, as the French visitor Chevalier de Chastellux noted in the early 1780s, "an American who . . . is at once a Musician, a Draftsman, Surveyor, Astronomer, Natural Philosopher, Jurist, and Statesman."[2]

By contrast, Paine was a free-floating individual who, as critics said, lacked social connections of any kind. He came from the ranks of the middling sorts, and unlike, say, Benjamin Franklin, he never really shed his obscure and lowly origins. He had some education but did not attend college, and he knew no languages except English. He spent the first half of his life jumping from one job to another, first a stay maker like his father, then a teacher, next a failed businessman, then back to stay making, followed by two failed attempts as an excise collector; he also tried running a tobacco shop. He was slovenly and lazy and was described as "coarse and uncouth in his manners."[3] His temperament was fiery and passionate, and he loved his liquor and confrontations of all sorts. He came to America at age thirty-seven full of anger at a world that had not recognized his talents.

Yet as dissimilar as Jefferson and Paine were from one another, they shared a common outlook on the world. As a British dinner partner observed in 1792, Jefferson in conversation was "a vigorous stickler for revolutions and for the downfall of an aristocracy. . . . In fact, like his friend T. Payne, he cannot live but in a revolution, and all events in Europe are only considered by him in the relation they bear to the probability of a revolution to be produced by them."[4]

Jefferson and Paine were good republicans who believed in the rights of man. They thought that all government should be derived from the people and that no one should hold office by hereditary right. No American trusted the people at large or outside of government more than did these two radicals, Jefferson and Paine.

This confidence flowed from their magnanimous view of human nature. Both men had an extraordinary faith in the moral capacity of ordinary people. Being one of the ordinary people, Paine had a natural tendency to trust them. But even Jefferson, the natural aristocrat, on most things trusted ordinary people far more than he trusted his aristocratic colleagues, who, he believed, were very apt to become wolves if they could. Unlike the elite, common people were not deceptive or deceitful; they wore their hearts on their sleeves and were sincere. An American republican world dominated by common folk would end the deceit and dissembling so characteristic of courtiers and monarchies. "Let those flatter who fear: it is not an American art," said Jefferson.[5]

Paine agreed that everyone shared a similar social or moral sense. Appeals to common sense, he said, were "appeals to those feelings without which we should be incapable of discharging the duties of life or enjoying the felicities of it."[6] Reason might be unevenly distributed throughout society, but everyone, even the most lowly of persons, had senses and could feel. In all of his writings, Paine said, his "principal design is to form the disposition of the people to the measures which I am fully persuaded it is their interest and duty to adopt, and which need no other force to accomplish them than the force of being felt."[7]

But Paine and Jefferson went further in their trust in common people. By assuming that ordinary people had personal realities equal to their own, Paine and Jefferson helped to give birth to what perhaps is best described as the modern humanitarian sensibility—a powerful force that we of the twenty-first century have inherited and further expanded. They, like most other Revolutionary leaders, shared the liberal premises of Lockean sensationalism: that all men were born equal and that only the environment working on their senses made them different. These premises were essential to the growing sense of sympathy for other human creatures felt by enlightened people in the eighteenth century. Once the liberally educated came to believe that they could control their environment and educate the vulgar and lowly to become something other than what the traditional society had presumed they were destined to be, then the enlightened few began to expand their sense of moral responsibility for the vice and ignorance they saw in others and to experience feelings of common humanity with them.

Thus, despite their acceptance of differences among people, both Jefferson and Paine concluded that all men were basically alike, that they all partook of the same common nature. It was this commonality that linked people together in natural affection and made it possible for them to share each other's feelings. There was something in each human being—some sort of moral sense or sympathetic instinct—that made possible natural compassion and affection. Indeed, wrote Paine, "[i]nstinct in animals does not act with stronger impulse, than the principles of society and civilization operate in man." Even the lowliest of persons, even black slaves, Jefferson believed, had this sense of sympathy or moral feeling for others. All human beings, said Jefferson, rich and poor, white and black, had "implanted in their breasts" this "moral instinct," this "love of others." Everyone, whatever their differences of education, instinctively knew right from wrong. "State a moral case to a ploughman and a professor," said Jefferson; the ploughman will decide it as well, and often better, than the professor, "because he has not been led astray by artificial rules."[8]

This belief in the equal moral worth and equal moral authority of every individual was the real source of both Jefferson's and Paine's democratic equality, an equality that was far more potent than merely the Lockean idea that everyone started at birth with the same blank sheet.

Jefferson's and Paine's assumption that people possessed an innate moral or social sense had important implications. It lay behind their belief in the natural harmony of society and their advocacy of minimal government. People, they claimed, had an inherent need to socialize with one another and were naturally benevolent and affable. This benevolence and sociability became a modern substitute for the ascetic and Spartan virtue of the ancient republics. This new modern virtue, as David Hume pointed out, was much more in accord with the growing commercialization and refinement of the enlightened and civilized eighteenth century than the austere and severe virtue of the ancients.

The classical virtue of antiquity had flowed from the citizen's participation in politics; government had been the source of the citizen's civic consciousness and public-spiritedness. But the modern virtue of Jefferson, Paine, and other eighteenth-century liberals flowed from the citizen's participation in society, not in government. Society to eighteenth-century liberals was harmonious and compassionate. We today may believe that society—with its class antagonisms, business and capitalist exploitation, and racial prejudices—by itself breeds the ills and cruelties that plague us. But for eighteenth-century radicals, society was benign; it created sympathy, affability, and the new domesticated virtue. By mingling in drawing rooms, clubs, and coffeehouses, by partaking in the innumerable interchanges of the daily comings and goings of modern life, people developed affection and fellow feeling, which were all the adhesives really necessary to hold an enlightened people together. Some even argued that commerce, that traditional enemy of classical virtue, was in fact a source of modern virtue. Because it encouraged intercourse and confidence among people and nations, commerce actually contributed to benevolence and fellow feeling.

The opening paragraph of Thomas Paine's *Common Sense* articulated brilliantly this distinction between society and government. Society and government were different things, said Paine, and they have different origins. "Society is produced by our wants and government by our wickedness." Society "promotes our happiness *positively* by uniting our affections"; government affects us *"negatively* by restraining our vices. The one encourages intercourse, the other creates distinctions. . . . Society in every state was a blessing; but government even in its best state was but a necessary evil; in its worst state an intolerable one."[9] The most devout republicans like Paine and Jefferson believed that if only the natural tendencies of people to love and care for one another were allowed to flow freely, unclogged by the artificial interference of government, particularly monarchical government, society would prosper and hold itself together.

These liberal ideas that society was naturally autonomous and self-regulating and that everyone possessed a common moral and social sense were no utopian fantasies but the conclusions of what many enlightened thinkers took to be the modern science of society. While most clergymen continued to urge Christian love and charity upon their ordinary parishioners, many other educated and enlightened people sought to secularize Christian love and find in human nature itself a scientific imperative for loving one's neighbor as oneself. There seemed to be a natural principle of attraction that pulled people together, a moral principle that was no different from the principles that operated in the physical world. "Just as the regular motions and harmony of the heavenly bodies depend upon their mutual gravitation towards each other," said the liberal Massachusetts preacher Jonathan Mayhew, so too did love and benevolence among people preserve "order and harmony" in the society.[10] Love between humans was the gravity of the moral world, and it could be studied and perhaps even manipulated more easily than the gravity of the physical world. Enlightened thinkers like Lord Shaftesbury, Francis Hutcheson, and Adam Smith thus sought to discover these hidden forces that moved and held people together in the moral world—forces, they believed, that could match the great eighteenth-century scientific discoveries of the hidden physical forces (gravity, magnetism, electricity, and energy) that operated in the physical world. Out of such dreams was born modern social science.

Their complete reliance on "a system of social affections" is what made Paine and Jefferson such natural republicans.[11] Republics demanded far more morally from their citizens than monarchies did of their subjects. In monarchies each man's desire to do what was right in his own eyes could be restrained by fear or force, by patronage or honor, by the distribution of offices and distinctions, and by professional standing armies. By contrast, republics could not use the traditional instruments of government to hold the society together; instead, they had to hold themselves together from the bottom up, ultimately, from their citizens' willingness to sacrifice their private desires for the sake of the public good—their virtue. This reliance on the moral virtue of their citizens, on their capacity for self-sacrifice and their innate sociability, was what made republican governments historically so fragile.

Jefferson and Paine had so much confidence in the natural harmony of society that they sometimes came close to denying any role for government at all in holding the society together. To believe that government contributed to social cohesion was a great mistake, said Paine. "Society performs for itself almost every thing which is ascribed to government." Government had little or nothing to do with civilized life. Instead of ordering society, government "divided it; it deprived it of its natural cohesion, and engendered discontents and disorder, which otherwise would not have existed."[12] Both Paine and Jefferson believed that all social abuses and deprivations—social distinctions, business contracts, monopolies and privileges of all sorts, even excessive property and wealth, anything and everything that interfered with people's natural social dispositions—seemed to flow from connections to government, in the end from connections to monarchical government. Everywhere in the Old World, said Paine, we "find the greedy hand of government thrusting itself into every corner and crevice of industry, and grasping the spoil of the multitude."[13]

Both Jefferson and Paine believed deeply in minimal government—not as nineteenth-century laissez-faire liberals trying to promote capitalism, but as eighteenth-century radicals who hated monarchy, which was the only kind of government they had known. Calling them believers in minimal government is perhaps too tame a way of describing their deep disdain for hereditary monarchical government. Monarchy for Paine was "a silly contemptible thing" whose fuss and formality, when once exposed, became laughable. Jefferson felt the same; when he was president he went out of his way to mock the formalities and ceremonies of the court life of the European kings. His scorn of the European monarchs knew no bounds. They were, he said, all fools or idiots. "They passed their lives in hunting, and dispatched two couriers a week, one thousand miles, to let each other know what game they had killed the preceding days."[14]

But what really made Jefferson and Paine hate monarchy was its habitual promotion of war. As far as they were concerned, as Paine put it, "all the monarchical governments are military. War is their trade, plunder and revenue their objects."[15] Angry liberals everywhere in the Western world thought that monarchy and war were intimately related. Indeed, as the son of the Revolutionary War general Benjamin Lincoln declared, "Kings owe their origin to war."[16] This recent Harvard graduate, like Jefferson and Paine, spoke out of a widespread eighteenth-century liberal protest against developments that had been taking place in Europe over the previous three centuries.

From the sixteenth century through the eighteenth century, the European monarchies had been busy consolidating their power and marking out their authority within clearly designated boundaries while at the same time protecting themselves from rival claimants to their power and territories. They erected ever-larger bureaucracies and military forces in order to wage war, which is what they did through most decades of these three centuries. This meant the building of more centralized governments and the creation of more elaborate means for extracting money and men from their subjects. These efforts in turn led to the growth of armies, the increase in public debts, the raising of taxes, and the strengthening of executive power.

Such monarchical state building was bound to provoke opposition, especially among the English who had a long tradition of valuing their liberties and resisting crown power. The country-Whig-opposition ideology that arose in England in the late seventeenth and early eighteenth centuries was directed against these kinds of monarchical state-building efforts taking place rather belatedly in England. When later eighteenth-century British radicals, including Thomas Paine, warned that the lamps of liberty were going out all over Europe and were being dimmed in Britain itself, it was these efforts at modern state formation that they were talking about.

Liberals and republicans like Jefferson and Paine assumed that kings brought their countries into war so frequently because wars sustained monarchical power. The internal needs of monarchies—the requirements of their bloated bureaucracies, their standing armies, their marriage alliances, their restless dynastic ambitions—lay behind the prevalence of war. Eliminate monarchy and all its accoutrements, many Americans believed, and war itself would be eliminated. A world of republican states would encourage a different kind of diplomacy, a peace-loving diplomacy—one based not on the brutal struggle for power of conventional diplomacy but on the natural concert of the commercial interests of the people of the various nations. "If commerce were permitted to act to the universal extent it is capable," said Paine, "it would extirpate the system of war, and produce a revolution in the uncivilized state of governments."[17] In other words, if the people of the various nations were left alone to exchange goods freely among themselves—without the corrupting interference of selfish monarchical courts, irrational dynastic rivalries, and the secret double-dealing diplomacy of the past—then, as Jefferson, Paine, and other radical liberals hoped, international politics would become republicanized, pacified, and ruled by commerce alone, and a universal peace might emerge. Old-fashioned political diplomats might not even be necessary in this new commercially linked world.

Both men naturally and enthusiastically supported the French Revolution; indeed, both of them were close to Lafayette and his liberal circle and participated in the early stages of that Revolution. They had no doubt that the republican ideals of the American Revolution were simply spreading eastward and would eventually republicanize all of Europe. Although Paine became a member of the French National Convention and participated in its affairs, he turned out to be somewhat less fanatical than Jefferson. Paine never said anything comparable to Jefferson's comment of January 1793, in which the American secretary of state declared that he "would have seen half the earth desolated" rather than have the Revolution in France fail. "Were there but an Adam and an Eve left in every country, and left free, it would be better than as it is now." Indeed, while Paine bravely argued in the National Convention that the life of King Louis XVI ought to be spared, Jefferson viewed the king's execution as "punishment like other criminals." He hoped that France's eventual triumph would "bring at length kings, nobles and priests to the scaffolds which they have been so long deluging with human blood."[18]

For hardheaded realists like Alexander Hamilton, these radical ideas of Jefferson and Paine were nothing but "pernicious dreams." By abandoning the main instruments by which eighteenth-century monarchical governments held their turbulent societies together and ruled—patronage, ceremonies and rituals, aristocratic titles, and force—dreamers like Jefferson and Paine, said a disgruntled Hamilton, were offering "the bewitching tenets of the illuminated doctrine, which promises men, ere long, an emancipation from the burdens and restraints of government." By the early 1790s Hamilton was alarmed by the extraordinarily utopian idea coming out of the French Revolution "that but a small portion of power is requisite to Government." And some radicals like William Godwin believed that "even this is only temporarily necessary" and could be done away with once "the bad habits" of the ancien régime were eliminated. Unfortunately, said Hamilton, there were wishful thinkers in both France and America who assumed that, "as human nature shall refine and ameliorate by the operation of a more enlightened plan" based on a common moral sense and the spread of affection and benevolence, "government itself will become useless, and Society will subsist and flourish free from its shackles."[19]

With all the "mischiefs . . . inherent in so wild and fatal a scheme," Hamilton had hoped that "votaries of this new philosophy" would not push it to its fullest. But the new Jefferson administration that took over the federal government in 1801 was trying to do just that. "No army, no navy, no *active* commerce—national defence, not by arms but by embargoes, prohibition of trade &c.—as little government as possible." These all added up, said Hamilton in 1802, to "a most visionary theory."[20] Consequently, Hamilton and the other opponents of the Jefferson administration never tired of ridiculing the president and his supporters as utopians who walked with their heads in the clouds trying to extract sunbeams from cucumbers. Jefferson, the quixotic president, may have been ideally suited to be a college professor, they declared, but he was not suited to be the leader of a great nation.

But like many college professors, both Jefferson and Paine were optimists, believing in the promise of the future rather than in the dead hand of the past. Both loved inventions, like Paine's iron bridge, that made life and commerce easier. Both detested primogeniture and other aristocratic inheritance laws that treated new generations of children unequally. They hated charters and corporations that gave the few monopoly privileges that were not shared by the many. They were, said Paine, "charters, not of rights, but of exclusion."[21] The idea that corporate charters were vested rights that were unalterable by subsequent popular legislatures was, said Jefferson, a doctrine inculcated by "our lawyers and priests" that supposed "that preceding generations held the earth more freely than we do; had a right to impose laws on us, unalterable by ourselves, and that we, in like manner, can make laws and impose burdens on future generations, which they will have no right to alter; in fine, that the earth belongs to the dead and not the living."[22] Neither Jefferson nor Paine, in other words, had any patience with the sophisticated defense of prescription set forth by Edmund Burke.

Even the two men's religious views were similar—as radical as the enlightened eighteenth century allowed. Although Jefferson never publicly attacked orthodox religion in the extreme way Paine did in his *Age of Reason* (1794)—"Of all the systems of religion that ever were invented," Paine declared, "there is none more derogatory to the Almighty, more unedifying to man, more repugnant to reason, and more contradictory in itself than this thing called Christianity"—Jefferson privately shared Paine's scorn for traditional Christianity. Members of the "priestcraft," he wrote to friends he could trust, had turned Christianity "into mystery and jargon unintelligible to all mankind and therefore the safer engine for their purposes." The Trinity was nothing but "Abracadabra" and "hocus-pocus . . . so incomprehensible to the human mind that no candid man can say he has any idea of it." Ridicule, he said, was the only weapon to be used against it. But because he had been badly burned by some indiscreet remarks about religion in his *Notes on the State of Virginia*, he had learned to share his religious thoughts with only those he could rely on. "I not only write nothing on religion," he told a friend in 1815, "but rarely permit myself to speak on it, and never but in a reasonable society."[23]

Paine's outrageous statements about Christianity in his *Age of Reason* helped to destroy his reputation in America. These views, coupled with his vicious attack on George Washington, meant that when he returned from Europe to America in 1802, he had few friends left in the country, but Thomas Jefferson was one of them.

Jefferson was the president and a political figure and that made all the difference between the two men. On nearly every point of political and religious beliefs the two enlightened radicals were in agreement. Where they differed was in Paine's need to voice his ideas publicly and in Jefferson's need to confine them to private drawing rooms composed of reasonable people. Paine was America's first modern public intellectual, an unconnected social critic, who knew, he said, "but one kind of life I am fit for, and that is a thinking one, and of course, a writing one."[24] By aggressively publishing his ideas, Paine aimed to turn the contemplative life into an active one. Jefferson could not do this. Since he had a political career that depended on popular elections, he could not afford to spell out his radical ideas in pamphlets and books in the forceful way Paine could. Yet if he had written out in any systematic manner what he believed about politics, it would have resembled Paine's *The Rights of Man: Part the Second*. As a politician, Jefferson continually had to compromise his beliefs—on minimal government, on banks, on the debt, on patronage, and perhaps on slavery. When he was speaking with his liberal friends abroad, he certainly took the correct line in opposition to slavery, but he was unable to become the kind of outspoken opponent of slavery that Paine became. Yet the intensity with which Jefferson enforced his embargo—his grand experiment in "peaceful coercion" as an alternative to war—reveals just how dedicated a radical he could be on some issues.

Although Jefferson was certainly cosmopolitan in an enlightened eighteenth-century manner, he was at heart a Virginian and an American deeply attached to his country. Paine was different. By the time he left America to return to the Old World in 1787, he had emotionally cut loose from his adopted home and had turned into an intellectual progenitor of revolutions. "It was neither the place nor the people [of America], but the Cause itself that irresistibly engages me in its support," he told the president of the Continental Congress as early as 1779, "for I should have acted the same part in any other country could the same circumstance have arisen there which have happened here." He had come to see himself as little better than "a refugee, and that of the most extraordinary kind, a refugee from the Country I have befriended." In the end he became a man without a home, without a country, and literally, as he said, "a citizen of the world."[25]

Because Paine after 1787 became as eager to reform the Old World as he had the New, his writings eventually took on issues that he had not dealt with earlier. Thinking of England and its huge numbers of landless people and its extremes of wealth and poverty, he proposed systems of public welfare and social insurance financed by progressive taxation in his *Rights of Man: Part the Second* and in his *Agrarian Justice.* Jefferson, as the patriot who believed that agrarian America was already an egalitarian paradise, felt no need to express such radical views publicly. Yet as early as 1785 he privately suggested various measures to ensure that property in a state not become too unequally divided. Indeed, he declared, so harmful was gross inequality of wealth that "legislators cannot invent too many devices for subdividing property." In addition to proposing that all children inherit property equally, he, like Paine, advocated the progressive taxation of the rich and the exemption of the poor from taxes. Even in America, he said, "it is not too soon to provide by every possible means that as few as possible shall be without a little portion of land. The small landholders are the most precious part of a state."[26]

In the end, Americans treated the two men who shared so many ideas very differently. Although Americans have erected a huge memorial to Jefferson in Washington, D.C., and celebrated him as the premier spokesman for democracy, they have scarcely noticed Thomas Paine. He died in obscurity in the United States in 1809 and ten years later William Cobbett took his bones away to England. Although Jefferson declared in 1801 that Paine had labored on behalf of liberty and the American Revolution "with as much effort as any man living," Paine still remains a much-neglected Founder.[27] Perhaps it is time for that to change.

AFTERWORD TO CHAPTER 7

This was a paper presented at a conference in London in 2009 celebrating the bicentennial of Thomas Paine's death. Although not written with that intent, the paper may help refurbish the reputation of Jefferson in some small way. It is not easy, since Jefferson has come in for some very brutal and often deserved bashing by historians over the past half century. Although he has traditionally been seen as America's premier spokesman for democracy, he was an aristocratic slaveholder, and the irony of that conjunction has been too much for many historians to bear, especially as historians have made slavery the central fact in the founding of the nation. Jefferson seems to be the ultimate hypocrite, and because he has been such a symbol of America, his hypocrisy has tainted the nation's reputation as well.

Although it took courage for young Jefferson, raised in a slave society, to speak out against the institution, there is ultimately no defending Jefferson on slavery or race. He did indeed oppose slavery as a young man, and he even tried to do something about limiting it, but his suspicions of black inferiority and racial distinctiveness expressed in his *Notes on the State of Virginia* are so abhorrent that his moral credentials appear to be fatally compromised. Yet despite his repugnant views on race, Jefferson still has something to say to us Americans today. Indeed, I think that he deserves his traditional reputation as America's supreme apostle of democracy.

Paine may be able to help redeem Jefferson. Since it is clear that Jefferson and Paine thought alike on virtually every issue, Paine's radical and democratic credentials may allow historians, especially those of the left, to see Jefferson in a somewhat more favorable light, or at least see him in light of the eighteenth century, and not in today's light.

So taken with Jefferson's hypocrisy are recent historians that some of them have even suggested that Jefferson's advocacy of minimal government was merely a device for defending slavery. Since a small government presumably would have less opportunity to interfere with the institution of slavery, some Southern Jeffersonian Republicans certainly found minimal government appealing. But that was not Jefferson's motive or the motive of his many Northern followers. Jefferson's ideas of minimal government were widely shared by eighteenth-century radicals such as Paine, William Godwin, and others who certainly had no brief for slavery. The fact of the matter is that late eighteenth-century Anglo-American radicalism demanded a belief in minimal government, and historians who do not appreciate that fact reveal their ignorance of the period.

Jefferson's standing as the spokesman for democracy rests on his belief in equality. It is why Lincoln paid "all honor to Jefferson." He and others subsequently have drawn inspiration from the Declaration of Independence and its claim that all men are created equal. But Jefferson went much further than simply claiming that all men were created equal—that was a cliché among the enlightened in the late eighteenth century. As I try to point out in this article, both he and Paine believed that people were not just created equal but were actually equal to everyone else throughout their lives. Not that Jefferson and Paine denied the obvious differences among individuals that exist—how some individuals are taller, smarter, more handsome than others—but rather both radicals posited that at bottom, every single individual, men and women, black and white, had a common moral or social sense that tied him or her to other individuals. None of the other leading Founders believed that—not Washington, not Hamilton, not Adams. And since no democracy can intelligibly exist without some such magnanimous belief that at heart everyone is the same, Jefferson's position as the apostle of American democracy seems not only legitimate but necessary to the well-being of the nation.

PART III

THE *Early Republic*

CHAPTER EIGHT

MONARCHISM *and* REPUBLICANISM
in EARLY AMERICA

*D*URING THE DEBATE over the new proposed Constitution in 1787–1788, many Americans were fearful that the entire Revolutionary project of 1776 was being threatened. Opponents thought that the Constitution threatened to undermine the republican experiment and create a monarchical tyranny that would eventually take away America's liberty. They especially objected to "the mighty and splendid President," who possessed power "in the most unlimited manner" that could be easily abused.[1]

It was true that the Convention had decided on an extraordinarily strong and single executive. The president was to stand alone, unencumbered by an executive council except one of his own choosing. With command over the armed forces, with the authority to direct diplomatic relations, with power over appointments to the executive and judicial branches that few state governors possessed, and with a four-year term of office (longer than that of any state governor) and perpetually reeligible for reelection, the president was a magistrate who, as Patrick Henry charged, could "easily become king."[2] Many of the opponents of the Constitution believed that the country was being led down the garden path to monarchy.

These opponents of the new Constitution were not entirely wrong. By 1787–1788 many of those who supported the new Constitution—the Federalists, as they called themselves—did have aspects of monarchy on their minds. By the time the Constitutional Convention met in Philadelphia in 1787, many members of the elite had lost faith in the Revolutionary dream of 1776—that America could exist as a confederation of thirteen states with a minimum of government. Some New England Federalists, "seeing and dreading the evils of democracy," according to one English traveler at the time, were even willing to "admit monarchy, or something like it." The wealthy New England merchant Benjamin Tappan, father of the future abolitionists, was not alone in thinking that a good dose of monarchism was needed in 1787 to offset the popular excesses of the American people. Even though Henry Knox, Washington's close friend, had given Tappan "a gentle check" for openly voicing such an opinion, Tappan told Knox that he "cannot give up the Idea that monarchy in our present situation is become absolutely necessary to save the states from sinking into the lowest abyss of misery." Since he had "delivered my sentiment in all companies" and found it well received, he believed that "if matters were properly arranged it would be easily and soon effected," perhaps with the aid of the Society of the Cincinnati, the fraternal organization of former Revolutionary War officers. Even if nothing were done, Tappan intended to continue to be "a strong advocate for what I have suggested."[3]

There were many more Americans in 1787 thinking like Tappan than we have been prepared to admit. This new federal government marked as great a change as the Revolution itself. Such a strong national government as the Constitution prescribed had certainly not been anticipated by anyone in 1776. No one in his wildest dreams had even imagined such a powerful government.

In 1776 the Revolutionaries had established not a single republic but thirteen of them. The Declaration of Independence was in fact a declaration of thirteen separate states. All of these states in 1776 had immediately set about constructing their own constitutions. These Revolutionary constitutions were modeled on what Americans thought the mixed or balanced constitution of the so-called English commonwealth ideally ought to have been. Thus most of the state constitution makers created mixtures of governors, senates, and houses of representatives, which they identified with the monarchy, aristocracy, and democracy of the English constitution. The new republican governors may have been elected, but they were still thought to embody the monarchical element in society. In the same way, the senates or upper houses of the legislatures were thought to embody the aristocratic element.

Of course, the American constitution makers wanted to avoid the corruption of the English constitution, which they believed flowed from the misuse of patronage by the crown. Hence they forbade members of the legislatures from simultaneously holding office in the government or executive branch. This prohibition, repeated in Article I, Section 6 of the federal Constitution, prevented the development of ministerial responsibility to the legislatures and, as we saw in a previous essay, sent Americans off on a very different constitutional path from the English.

Although Americans in 1776 attempted to model their republican state constitutions on the balanced English monarchical constitution, they knew only too well that republican and monarchical governments were designed for very different societies. Republicanism put a premium on the homogeneity and cohesiveness of its society. By contrast, monarchies could comprehend large territories and composite kingdoms and peoples with diverse interests and ethnicities. Monarchies had their unitary authority, kingly honors and patronage, hereditary aristocracies, established national churches, and standing armies to hold their diverse societies together. Republics had none of these adhesive elements. Instead, republics were supposed to rely for cohesion on the moral qualities of their people—their virtue and their natural sociability. Monarchy imagined its society in traditional and prenational terms, as a mosaic of quasicorporate communities, and thus had little trouble in embracing African slaves and Indians as subjects. But republicanism created citizens, and since citizens were all equal to one another, it was difficult for the Revolutionaries to include blacks and Indians as citizens in the new republican states they were trying to create. This emphasis on republican homogeneity and equal citizenship meant that republics, as Montesquieu had indicated, should be small in size.

For this reason, none of the Revolutionaries in 1776 had had any idea of making the thirteen United States anything other than a confederation. Hence they created in 1777 and ratified in 1781 the Articles of Confederation. It was a league of friendship among thirteen independent states, in character not all that different from the present European Union. In this Confederation each of the states had equal representation and a single vote. The individual states may have been republics, but the Confederation government was something else—a union of republics. Although the Confederation Congress was not a king, it was designed to play the same role the former king had been supposed to play in the empire. It inherited most of the prerogative powers that the British king had exercised over the colonies—namely, the powers to conduct foreign policy, to declare and wage war and to make peace, to handle Indian affairs, and to settle disputes between the states. The Congress, composed of equal representation from each state, was not intended to be a legislature but rather a superintending executive of the Confederation. It became in effect a stand-in for the former monarchy, which is why it was not given the powers to tax or regulate trade: these powers were not prerogative powers and had not been exercised unilaterally by the king.

By the early 1780s the vicissitudes of the war forced the Congress to create separate departments of war, finance, and foreign affairs, with single individuals appointed to head them; in other words, the Congress created something akin to modern executive departments. This development turned the Congress, which was supposed to play the central magisterial role the crown had played in the empire, into something resembling a legislature. And when this happened, many began complaining that now this congressional legislature did not proportionally represent the people in the various states. All of this prepared the way for the disposing of the Articles and the creation of an entirely new government with the Constitution of 1787—the present existing government of the United States.

In the decade following the Declaration of Independence, many of the Revolutionary leaders had become increasingly disillusioned with the consequences of their republican revolution. The Confederation lacked the powers to tax and to regulate trade and was unable to stand up for the United States in international affairs. But, more important, the states themselves were not behaving as the leaders had expected. By the mid-1780s, as we have seen, many of them had become convinced that not only was the Confederation too weak to accomplish its tasks, but, more alarming, the states themselves were unable to function as stable and just republics.

James Madison and other leaders had concluded that legislative majorities in the states were acting irresponsibly, flooding the states with poorly drafted and mutable laws that victimized minorities and violated individual rights. Most alarming, these state legislators were simply acting in accord with the sentiments of the voters who elected them. Such abuses of popular power, these excesses of democracy, were not easily remedied, for they struck at the heart of what the Revolution was about. These legislative evils, said Madison, "brought into question the fundamental principle of republican Government, that the majority who rule in such governments are the safest Guardians both of public Good and private rights."[4] To Madison and to other leaders it thus seemed as if the entire American experiment in republicanism was at stake.

Thus the crisis of the 1780s was a real one for many of the country's leaders. There was too much democracy in the states, and this excessive democracy had to be curbed—without doing violence to republican principles. At first many reformers had concentrated on changing the Revolutionary state constitutions. They urged taking power back from the houses of representatives and giving it to the senates and the governors—the aristocratic and monarchical elements of their constitutions. Although Americans in 1776 had created their mixed or balanced state governments in emulation of the famed English constitution, the reformers soon discovered that they could no longer justify strengthening their governors and senates by talking in traditional terms of infusing more monarchy and aristocracy into their state constitutions. Since any public reference to monarchy and aristocracy was vehemently denounced as unrepublican and un-American, reformers had to find new justifications for the senates and the governors. Within a few years they began describing all parts of the original mixed state governments—governors and senators, and not just the houses of representatives—as representative agents of the people. As we have seen, this forced Americans into an entirely new understanding of the sovereign people and the people's relationship to government.

Many reformers, however, soon realized that even changing the state constitutions would not solve the problems of majoritarian factionalism and minority rights in the state legislatures. They soon began to look beyond the state level for what Madison called "a republican remedy for those diseases most incident to republican government." Those who wanted to reform the states were able to come together with the growing numbers of those who were urging reform of the Confederation. Indeed, by the mid-1780s nearly the entire political nation agreed that some specific powers needed to be added to the Confederation Congress—namely, the powers to levy customs duties and to regulate trade.

Thus almost everybody welcomed the calling of the Convention in Philadelphia in May 1787 in order to amend the Articles of Confederation. But the Convention offered an opportunity as well to those who were most concerned with the problems of democracy in the states. Although it was the widespread desire to reform the Confederation that made the calling of the Convention possible, it was the problems of democracy in the states that actually drove the plans of the Convention's leaders, including Madison, who more than anyone was responsible for the new Constitution. It was, Madison told his friend Jefferson, the abuses of the state legislatures, "so frequent and so flagrant as to alarm the most stedfast friends of Republicanism," that "contributed more to that uneasiness which produced the Convention, and prepared the public mind for a general reform, than those which accrued to our national character and interest from the inadequacy of the Confederation to its immediate objects."[5] Instead of merely adding some powers to the Articles of

Confederation, the Convention, under Madison's leadership, scrapped the Articles and drew up an entirely new Constitution. Which, of course, it had no authority to do.

The new Constitution created not a confederation of separate states but a new powerful national republic operating directly on the people; in other words, it created a nation instead of a union, although the supporters scrupulously avoided using the terms "nation" and "national" in the Constitution. Given the prevailing assumption that republics were supposed to be small in size and homogeneous in character, justifying this huge extended republic posed some problems. All experience and all theory were against the kind of extended national republic that Americans in 1787 were attempting to erect. Not only did Americans know from their experience under the British Empire what far-removed central power could mean, but they also knew that conventional wisdom required that republics be small and homogeneous.

The new nation was hardly that. By 1787 Americans were already a very large and diverse people with a dazzling variety of ethnicities and religions. Not only were over 20 percent of the population of African descent, but the white population was composed of virtually every European nationality. Only about half the population was English in origin. Yet, unlike today, the defenders of the Constitution could scarcely stress America's multicultural diversity—not in the face of the conventional wisdom that republics were supposed to have a homogeneous society. So in order to justify their new extended republic, they had to stretch the truth in emphasizing that Americans were actually one people with one destiny.

Although most supporters of the new Constitution stressed the homogeneity of the American people, some of them sought to turn conventional wisdom on its head. Some, including Madison, argued (following David Hume) that perhaps a large republic with many varying interests was better able to sustain itself than a small republic—largely because the varying interests would neutralize one another and allow for a common good to emerge.

Whatever the nature of the arguments, however, all the Federalists knew that if democracy were to be curbed, then what was needed in the new government was more power. And power in eighteenth-century Anglo-American political theory essentially meant monarchy. In the conventional thinking of an eighteenth-century balanced or mixed constitution, too much democracy required the counterbalancing of some more monarchy.

Just as the state reformers had been inhibited from speaking frankly about the need for more monarchical and aristocratic principles in the state constitutions, so too were the Federalists unwilling to say openly that the new national government required more aristocratic and monarchical elements. Nevertheless, there is little doubt that many of them had come to believe that some aristocracy and especially some monarchism were needed to offset the democratic excesses of the American people. In 1790 Benjamin Rush described the new government as one "which unites with the vigor of monarchy and the stability of aristocracy all the freedom of a simple republic."[6] Even Madison, who was as devoted to republicanism as any of the Founders, was in 1787 sufficiently disillusioned with the democratic consequences of the Revolution to see some advantages in monarchy. With his dream of "the purest and noblest characters" of the society in power in his new extended republic, he expected that the new federal government would play the same superpolitical neutral role that the British king had been supposed to play in the empire. Like a good constitutional monarch, he wrote, the new national government would be "sufficiently neutral between the different interests and factions, to control one part of the society from invading the rights of another, and at the same time sufficiently controlled itself, from setting up an interest adverse to that of the whole society."[7]

That a moderate like Madison should see some benefits to monarchy was a measure of the crisis of the 1780s. Other Federalists like Alexander Hamilton were even more disillusioned with the democratic consequences of the Revolution and wanted even stronger doses of monarchy injected into the body politic. In fact, Hamilton and other high-toned

Federalists, who in the 1790s clung to the name of the supporters of the Constitution, wanted to create a centralized fiscal-military state that would eventually rival the great monarchical powers of Europe on their own terms. Yet they knew that whatever aspects of monarchy they hoped to bring back into America would have to be placed within a republican framework. Perhaps, as some historians have suggested, the Federalists really intended to create another Augustan Age. Augustus had, after all, sought to incorporate elements of monarchy into the Roman Empire while all the time talking about republicanism.

If some monarchical power were to be instilled in the new system, the energetic center of that power would be the presidency. For that reason it was the office of the president that made many Americans most suspicious of the new government. The executive or chief magistracy was, after all, the traditional source of tyranny and, as Benjamin Franklin pointed out, the source in America from which monarchy would naturally emerge.

Although Americans were used to congresses, the presidency was a new office for them. A single, strong national executive was bound to remind them of the king they had just cast off. When James Wilson at the Philadelphia Convention had moved that the executive "consist of a single person," a long, uneasy silence had followed. The delegates knew only too well what such an office implied. John Rutledge complained that "the people will think we are leaning too much towards Monarchy." The creation of the presidency, warned Edmund Randolph, "made a bold stroke for monarchy."[8] But the Convention resisted these warnings and went on to make the new chief executive so strong, so kinglike, precisely because the delegates expected George Washington to be the first president.

Many people, including Jefferson, expected that Washington might be president for life, that he would be a kind of elective monarch—something not out of the question in the eighteenth century.[9] Indeed, we will never understand events of the 1790s until we take seriously, as contemporaries did, the possibility of some sort of monarchy developing in America. From our vantage point, the idea of America becoming a monarchy may seem absurd, but in 1789 it did not seem so at all. After all, Americans had been raised as subjects of monarchy and, in the opinion of some, still seemed emotionally to need to look up to a single patriarchal figure. Republicanism was new and untried. Monarchy still prevailed almost everywhere; it was what much of the world was used to, and history showed that sooner or later most republics tended to develop into kingly governments. As ancient Rome had shown, the natural evolution of societies and states seemed to be from simple republican youth to complex monarchical maturity.

William Short, viewing the new Constitution from France, was not immediately frightened by the power of the executive. But he thought that "the President of the eighteenth century" would "form a stock on which will be grafted a King in the nineteenth." Others, like George Mason of Virginia, believed that the new government was destined to become "an elective monarchy," and still others, like Rawlins Lowndes of South Carolina, assumed that the government so closely resembled the British form that everyone naturally expected "our changing from a republic to monarchy."[10] To add to the confusion, the line between monarchical and republican governments in the eighteenth century was often hazy at best, and some were already talking about monarchical republics and republican monarchies.

From the outset, Washington's behavior often savored of monarchy. His journey from Mount Vernon to the capital in New York in the spring of 1789, for example, took on the air of a royal procession. He was saluted by cannons and celebrated in elaborate ceremonies along the way. Everywhere he was greeted by triumphal rejoicing and acclamations of "Long live George Washington!" With Yale students debating the advantages of an elective over a hereditary king, suggestions of monarchy were very much in the air. "You are now a King, under a different name," James McHenry told Washington in March 1789, and wished that he "may reign long and happy over us."[11] It was not surprising therefore that some people referred to his inauguration as a "coronation."[12]

So prevalent was the thinking that Washington resembled an elected monarch that some people even expressed relief that he had no heirs.[13] Washington was sensitive to these popular anxieties about monarchy, and for a while he had thought of holding the presidency for only a year or so and then resigning and turning the office over to Vice President John Adams. In the initial draft of his inaugural address he pointed out that "the Divine Providence hath not seen fit, that my blood should be transmitted or name perpetuated by the endearing though sometimes seducing channel of immediate offspring." He had, he wrote, "no child for whom I could wish to make a provision—no family to build in greatness upon my country's ruins." Madison talked him out of this draft, but Washington's desire to show the public that he harbored no monarchical ambitions remained strong.[14] His protests testified to the widespread sense that monarchy was a distinct possibility for America.

Sensitive to charges that he had royal ambitions, Washington was often uncertain about the role he ought to play as president. He realized that the new government was fragile and needed dignity, but how far in a monarchical European direction ought he to go to achieve it? Aware that whatever he did would become a precedent for the future, Washington sought the advice of those close to him, including the vice president and the man he would soon make his secretary of the treasury, Alexander Hamilton.

How often should he meet with the public? How accessible should he be? Should he dine with members of Congress? Should he host state dinners? Could he ever have private dinners with friends? Should he make a tour of the United States? The only state ceremonies that late eighteenth-century Americans were familiar with were those of the European monarchies. Were they applicable to the young republic?

Hamilton thought that most people were "prepared for a pretty high tone in the demeanour of the Executive," but probably not as high a tone as Hamilton thought desirable. "Notions of equality," he said, were as "yet . . . too general and too strong" for the president to be properly distanced from the other branches of the government. (Note the "yet"; Federalists thought time was on their side.) In the meantime, suggested

Hamilton, the president ought to follow the practice of "European Courts" as closely as he could. Only department heads, high-ranking diplomats, and senators should have access to the president. "Your Excellency," as Hamilton referred to Washington, might hold a half-hour levee no more than once a week, and then only for invited guests. He could give up to four formal entertainments a year, but must never accept any invitations or call on anyone.[15] Vice President John Adams for his part urged Washington to make a show of "splendor and majesty" for his office. The president needed an entourage of chamberlains, aides-de-camp, and masters of ceremonies to conduct the formalities of his office.[16]

Washington realized that he had to maintain more distance from the public than the presidents of the Confederation Congress had. They had reduced their office to "perfect contempt," having been "considered in no better light than as a maitre d'hotel . . . for their table was considered as a public one and every person who could get introduced conceived that he had a right to be invited to it." He knew that too much familiarity was no way "to preserve the dignity and respect that was due to the first magistrate."[17]

As uncomfortable as he often was with ceremony, Washington knew that he had to make the presidency "respectable," and when he became president he spared few expenses in doing so. Although he was compelled to accept his $25,000 presidential salary—an enormous sum for the age—he spent nearly $2,000 of it on liquor and wine for entertaining. In his public appearances he rode in an elaborately ornamented coach drawn by four and sometimes six horses, attended with four servants in livery, followed by his official family in other coaches.[18] In his public pronouncements he referred to himself in the third person, and he sat for dozens of state portraits, all modeled on those of European monarchs; these were hung in prominent public places throughout the nation with the hope of thereby encouraging respect for the new regime. Indeed, much of the iconography of the new nation, including its civic processions, was copied from monarchical symbolism.[19] Washington may have been a simple republican—at heart just a country gentleman who was in bed every night by 9:30—but there is no doubt that he was concerned with "the style proper for the Chief Magistrate." He conceded that a certain monarchical tone had to be made part of the government, and he was willing up to a point to play the part of a republican king. He was, as John Adams later caustically remarked, "the best actor of presidency we have ever had."[20]

Obsessed with the new government's weakness, other Federalists were even more eager than Washington to bolster its dignity and respectability. Most believed that this could be best done by adopting some of the ceremony and majesty of monarchy—by making, for example, Washington's birthday celebrations rival those of the Fourth of July. Like the king of England speaking to Parliament from the throne, the president delivered his inaugural address personally to the Congress, and like the two houses of Parliament, both houses of Congress formally responded and then waited upon the president at his residence.

The English monarchy was the model for the new republican government in other respects as well. The Senate, the body in the American government that most closely resembled the House of Lords, voted that writs of the federal government ought to run in the name of the president—just as writs in England ran in the name of the king. Although the House refused to go along, the Supreme Court used the Senate's form for its writs. The Senate also tried to have all American coins bear the head of the president, as was the case with the European monarchs.

Although the high-toned Federalists eventually lost this proposal to put the president's impression on the coins, they made many such attempts to surround the new government with some of the trappings of monarchy. They drew up elaborate monarchlike rules of etiquette at what soon came to be denounced as the "American Court."[21] They established formal levees for the president where, as critics said, Washington was "seen in public on Stated times like an Eastern Lama."[22] Led by Vice President Adams, the Senate debated for a month in 1789 the proper title for the president. He could not be called simply "His Excellency," for governors of the states were called that. "A royal or at least a princely title," said

Adams, "will be found indispensably necessary to maintain the reputation, authority, and dignity of the President." Only something like "His Highness, or, if you will, His Most Benign Highness" would do.[23] Eventually, under Adams's prodding, a Senate committee reported the title "His Highness the President of the United States of America, and Protector of their Liberties." When Jefferson learned of Adams's obsession with titles and the Senate's action, he could only shake his head and recall Benjamin Franklin's now-famous characterization of Adams as someone who was always an honest man, often a wise one, but sometimes on some things absolutely out of his mind.[24]

But apparently not the only one out of his mind, for Washington himself had supposedly initially favored for a title "His High Mightiness, the President of the United States and Protector of Their Liberties."[25] But when the president heard the criticism that such titles smacked of monarchy, he changed his mind and was relieved when the House of Representatives under Madison's leadership succeeded in fixing the simple title of "Mr. President." Still, the talk of royalizing the new republic continued and heightened the fears of many Americans. The financial program of Secretary of the Treasury Hamilton, with its funded debt and Bank of the United States, was modeled on that of the British monarchy. Indeed, like the British ministers of His Majesty George III's government, Hamilton sought to use patronage and every other source of influence to win support for his and Washington's programs. To many other Americans, however, it looked as if British monarchical corruption had spread to America.

Because of these very real apprehensions of monarchy and monarchical corruption, the first decade or so under the new American Constitution could never be a time of ordinary politics. In fact, the entire period was wracked by a series of crises that threatened to destroy the national government that had been so recently and painstakingly created. The new expanded republic of the United States was an unprecedented political experiment, and everyone knew that. No similar national republic in modern times had ever extended over such a large extent of territory. Since all theory and all history were against the success of this republican experiment, the political leaders worried about every unanticipated development. With even President Washington's having suggested at the conclusion of the Constitutional Convention that the new federal government might not last twenty years, most political leaders in the 1790s had no great faith that the Union would survive. In such uneasy and fearful circumstances, politics could never be what we today regard as normal.

The political parties that emerged in the 1790s—the Federalists and the Republicans—were not modern parties, and competition between them was anything but what some scholars used to call "the first party system." No one thought that the emergence of parties was a good thing; indeed, far from building a party system in the 1790s, the nation's leaders struggled to prevent one from developing. The Federalists under the leadership of Washington, Adams, and Hamilton never saw themselves as a party but as the beleaguered legitimate government beset by people allied with Revolutionary France out to destroy the Union. Although the Republicans, under the leadership of Jefferson and Madison, did reluctantly describe themselves as a party, they believed they were only a temporary one, designed to prevent the United States from becoming a Federalist-led British-backed monarchy. Since neither the Federalists nor the Republicans accepted the legitimacy of the other, partisan feelings ran very high, making the bitter clash between Hamilton and Jefferson, for example, more than just personal. Indeed, the 1790s became one of the most passionate and divisive decades in American history.

This is the best context for understanding the 1790s and Jefferson's election as president in 1800. Otherwise we can never make full sense of the extraordinary events and behavior of people in the period: the many riots and the burning of officials in effigy; the viciousness of the press; the many duels; the fighting and wrestling in the halls of Congress; the Alien and Sedition Acts that gave the government extraordinary powers to deal with aliens and to prosecute libel against federal officials; the astonishingly improper and indiscreet actions of officials in dealing with foreign powers, actions that in our own time might be labeled treasonous. Only by taking seriously the feeling of many Americans that the

Federalists in the 1790s were well on their way to reintroducing monarchy in America can we understand the significance of the election of Thomas Jefferson as president in 1800. Jefferson sincerely believed that his "revolution of 1800" was, as he later said, "as real a revolution in the principles of our government as that of 1776 was in its form."[26] He thought, with some justification, that he had saved the republic from monarchy.

From our present perspective, it is hard to take seriously Jefferson's belief in the revolutionary significance of his election (especially since the kind of fiscal-military quasimonarchical state the Federalists wanted for the United States has actually come into being; Hamilton surely would have loved the Pentagon and the CIA, and America's huge standing army). From our viewpoint, then, Jefferson's election does not seem all that bold and radical. At the outset he struck a note of conciliation: We are all republicans—we are all federalists, he said; and some Federalists were soon absorbed into the Republican Party. Jefferson's administration, as historian Henry Adams delighted in pointing out, did deviate from strict Republican principles. Thus the continuities are impressive, and the Jefferson "revolution of 1800" has blended nearly imperceptibly into the main democratic currents of American history.

However, compared to the consolidated and centralized state that the Federalists wanted to build in the 1790s, the Republicans after 1800 proved that something akin to a real revolution did take place. Jefferson radically reduced the power of the federal government. He turned it into something resembling the Articles of Confederation more than the European-type state the Federalists desired. In fact, the Jeffersonian Republicans sought to create a general government that would rule without the traditional attributes of power.

From the outset Jefferson was determined that the new government would lack even the usual rituals of power. He purposefully set a new tone of republican simplicity in contrast to the stiff formality and regal ceremony with which the Federalists, in imitation of European court life, had surrounded the presidency. Since the Federalist presidents (Washington and Adams), like the English monarch, had personally delivered their addresses to the legislature "from the throne," Jefferson chose to submit his in writing (a practice that was continued until the presidency of Woodrow Wilson). Unlike Washington and Adams, he made himself easily accessible to visitors. In order to contrast his administration with those of his predecessors, he sought greater casualness in the White House, even to the point of greeting the British minister in carpet slippers. He replaced the protocol and distinctions of European court life with egalitarian rules of pell-mell, or "first into their seats."

Jefferson left unbuilt Washington's plans for a magnificent capital befitting the new American empire. Jefferson wanted the national government to be insignificant. The federal government, he declared in his first message to Congress in 1801, was "charged with the external affairs and mutual relations only of these states." All the rest—the "principal care of persons, our property, and our reputation, constituting the great field of human concerns"—was to be left to the states. He and his Republicans set about reversing a decade of Federalist policy. Although the Federalist establishment was minuscule by even eighteenth-century standards (the War Department, for example, consisted of only the secretary, an accountant, fourteen clerks, and two messengers), Jefferson thought the bureaucracy had become "too complicated, too expensive," and offices under the Federalists had "unnecessarily multiplied."[27] Thus the roll of federal officials was severely cut back. All tax inspectors and collectors were eliminated. The diplomatic establishment was reduced to three missions—to Britain, France, and Spain. The Federalist dream of creating a European-type army and navy disappeared; the military budget was cut in half. The army, stationed only in the West, was reduced to 3,000 men and 172 officers. The navy was cut back to several hundred gunboats for defensive purposes only. Hamilton's financial program was dismantled or allowed to lapse and all federal taxes were eliminated. For most people, the national government's presence was reduced to the delivery of the mail.

When the Republicans under President James Madison came to fight the War of 1812 with Great Britain, they refused to strengthen the government's capacity to wage it. Better that the enemy burn the nation's capital than surrender to a Hamiltonian enhancement of federal power. Thus the Republicans sought to fight the war without having to raise taxes, increase the debt, enlarge the military forces, or expand the executive. They wanted to prove that even war could be waged without the usual instruments of power.

When Andrew Jackson became president in 1828, the republican principles of the United States seemed so secure that the Jacksonian Democrats felt they could reassert some the older aspects of monarchism inherent in the presidency without fear of political retribution. Perhaps the Jacksonian era is less the era of the common man and more the era of consolidation and reintegration than we have usually allowed. The Jacksonians developed the use of patronage—the "spoils system"—to a fine art; they built up the federal bureaucracy, and under Jackson's leadership they turned the presidency into the most popular and powerful office in the nation. Jackson's opponents, in retaliation, called him "King Andrew" and called themselves Whigs, invoking the old English name for the opponents of bloated crown power. But the earlier fear of monarchy was now gone, and the Whigs could never really capitalize on their antimonarchical ideology.

Yet monarchism was latent in the powerful office of the presidency and it has been revived by various presidents over the subsequent decades of American history. Article II of the Constitution is so vague that many presidents under wartime conditions have expanded executive authority to unanticipated lengths. Much of the so-called unitary executive was there at the outset. It may even be possible to argue that the presidency created in 1787 inherited all the prerogative powers of the English king save those that were explicitly assigned to the Congress, such as the powers to declare war, erect courts, and coin money. As we know from the history of the past half century, even the power to declare war has slipped back into the president's hands.

Thus the imperial presidency of the twentieth century and early twenty-first century was built into the office from the beginning. One could argue that republicanism has survived in the United States not by repudiating but by absorbing some of the essential elements of monarchy. Vice President John Adams may have had little sense of political correctness, but he was honest to the core and maybe very accurate indeed when he called the United States a republican monarchy.

AFTERWORD TO CHAPTER 8

This paper began as the Bernard Bailyn Lecture given at La Trobe University in Australia in 2000 and was published separately by La Trobe University. It has been much revised since then. In addition to the expansion of the president's powers during wartime mentioned in the essay, the president's role in domestic affairs from the New Deal on has grown as well. Sometimes the Congress has fought back against this executive aggrandizement, creating its own budget office, for example, to counter the executive's dominance over finance. But the crisis-ridden nature of modern life makes resisting the expansion of executive energy difficult. Over the past seven decades the president, like a royal monarch, has taken the country into war six times without the formal congressional declaration of war that is mandated by the Constitution. More recently the president has moved aggressively into the economy, asserting, for example, unprecedented control over the automobile and banking industries. The monarch-like character of the United States government seems more evident today than ever before.

CHAPTER NINE

ILLUSIONS *of* POWER *in* *the* AWKWARD ERA *of* FEDERALISM

*T*HE NATIONAL GOVERNMENT created by the Constitution was inaugurated in 1789 with more optimism and more consensus among the American people than at any time since the Declaration of Independence. A common enthusiasm for the new Constitution momentarily obscured the deep differences that existed among the national leaders and the states and sections they represented. The unanimous election of Washington as the first president gave the new government an immediate respectability it otherwise would not have had. A sense of beginning anew, of putting the republican experiment on a new and stronger foundation, ran through communities up and down the continent. By 1789 even the leading opponents of the Constitution, the Anti-Federalists, had come to accept it, though of course with an expectation of its soon being amended. In fact, none of the Anti-Federalists in 1787 had been opposed to some sort of strengthening of the national government; they simply had not anticipated as strong a central government as the Constitution had created. Consequently, the former opponents of the Constitution were really in no position to oppose the new national government without giving it a chance.

It was a liberal, humanitarian, and cosmopolitan age. The country's leaders saw America's "rising empire" fulfilling at long last the promises of the Enlightenment. Freemasonry flourished, and orators everywhere promised an end to ignorance and superstition and the beginnings of a new era of reason, benevolence, and fraternity. It was a heroic age in which men talked of the aristocratic passions—of greatness, honor, and the desire for fame. It was a neoclassical age, an Augustan Age, as historian Linda K. Kerber has called it, an age of stability following a revolutionary upheaval in which art and literature would thrive.[1] Never in American history have the country's leaders voiced such high expectations for the cultural achievements of the nation as did Americans in the 1790s. The arts and sciences were inevitably moving across the Atlantic to the New World and bringing America into a golden age.

By whatever term the Federalist age might be called, it was in fact a very brief one. It disappeared so fast that we have a hard time recovering or understanding it. The consensus and optimism of 1789 quickly evaporated, and the decade that had begun so hopefully turned into one of the most passionate and divisive periods of American history. By the end of the 1790s the United States was on the verge of civil war, and the "whole system of American Government," in the opinion of the British foreign secretary, was "tottering to its foundations."[2]

The decade of the 1790s is the most awkward in American history. It seems unrelated to what preceded or followed it, a fleeting moment of heroic neoclassical dreams that were unsupported by American reality. The self-conscious, self-molded, self-controlled character of George Washington was the perfect symbol for the age, for, like Washington himself, the entire Federalist project was a monumental act of will in the face of contrary circumstances. The Federalists stood in the way of popular democracy as it was emerging in the United States, and thus they became heretics opposed to the developing democratic faith. Everything seemed to turn against them. They thought they were creating a classically heroic state, and they attempted everywhere to symbolize these classical aims. Instead they left only a legacy of indecipherable icons, unread poetry, antique place names, and a proliferation of Greek and Roman temples. They despised political parties, but parties nonetheless emerged to shatter the remarkable harmony of 1789. They sought desperately in the 1790s to avoid conflict with the former mother country to the point that they appeared to be compromising the independence of the new nation, only to discover in the end that the war with Great Britain they had avoided was to be fought anyway in 1812 by the subsequent administration of their opponents. By the early nineteenth century, Alexander Hamilton, the brilliant leader of the Federalists, who more than anyone pursued the heroic dreams of the age, was not alone in his despairing conclusion "that this American world was not meant for me."[3]

The Federalist age was awkward because so many of America's leaders were heroically confident they were in control of events. No generation in American history was so acutely conscious that what it did would affect future generations, or, in the common phrase of the day, "millions yet unborn." The leaders felt an awesome responsibility not only for America's governments and political institutions but for its art, literature, and manners—indeed, for the entire culture.

But of course they were never in charge of events or circumstances. Everything was moving and changing much too fast. Indeed, it is the gap between the leaders' pretensions of control and the dynamic reality of the forces they were attempting to deal with that accounts for the strangeness and awkwardness of the decade. Subsequent generations of American leaders usually have had a much less heroic attitude about themselves. Mid-nineteenth-century leaders always had a sense of being caught up by forces larger than themselves, of being carried along by inevitable elements—whether called providence, progress, public opinion, or simply the popular masses. But most American leaders of the 1790s still clung to an older hierarchical-gentry world that assumed that a few men at the top could control and manipulate events and shape circumstances. The decade of the 1790s was the last gasp of an American eighteenth-century patrician world quickly lost and largely forgotten—a world of aristocratic assumptions, heroic leadership, and powdered wigs and knee breeches. It was a world soon to be overwhelmed by the most popular, most licentious, and most commercially ridden society history had ever known.

Most of what happened in the period was unanticipated and unwanted by the Founding Fathers. The sudden transformation of the electoral college in the election of the president, which had been the consequence of complicated and painstaking compromises by the Philadelphia Convention, was only the most graphic example of the best-laid plans gone amiss.

It may be hard for us today to see how much in the decade turned out differently from what the leaders at the time expected, for many of their hopes and dreams did eventually get realized, even if decades or centuries after being formulated. Consequently, we tend to give the Federalists and other leaders of the decade credit for foresight and for laying the proper foundations for the future even if they were unable to bring about much in their own lifetimes. The city of Washington, D.C., is a good example. The plans for it were truly monumental, but the implementation of those plans was a long time coming. For a good part of the nineteenth century the national capital remained the butt of jokes, a city of open spaces and long distances, "bearing," as one observer said, "the marks of partial labour and general desertion."[4] Only after mid-century, or perhaps only at the beginning of the twentieth century—some might say only in the past fifty years—did the Federal City begin to resemble what L'Enfant and others originally had hoped for it. Other dreams of the 1790s have likewise been gradually realized in time. But the fact that many of the hopes and aspirations of the Federalist era have eventually come to pass should not obscure the extent of disillusionment and unfulfilled expectation that dominated that bizarre and stormy decade.

Many of the issues of the decades reveal to one degree or another the gap that existed between the leaders' plans and purposes on one hand and the reality of dynamic social circumstances on the other. Few of the public decision makers, whether Hamilton or Jefferson, whether Federalist or Republican, clearly understood the complicated historical forces they were dealing with, or if they did, were able to control or manipulate those forces.

The problem can be most fully seen in the ways in which the national government was created in the 1790s. Certainly the political leaders had high hopes for the launching of the ship of state. But though they commonly resorted to a nautical image of launching a new ship, they also realized that in 1789 much of their ship existed only on the drawing boards. Not only was the ship of state largely unbuilt, but the plans and blueprints for it were general and vague enough that the size and shape of the ship still remained uncertain; it was not even clear what the ship would be designed to do. Everyone realized that the nature, purposes, and strength of the new national government all had to be worked out, and beneath the outward consensus of 1789 nearly everyone had his own ideas about what these ought to be.

Because the government was so unformed and the future so problematical, the stakes were high, and men knew that precedents were being set. Consequently, every issue, no matter how trivial, seemed loaded with significance. Many members of the Senate did not think they were wasting their time in spending a month debating the proper title for addressing the president. From that title, whether "His Highness" or simply "Mr. President," might flow the very character of the future government and state.

In such uncertain circumstances the advantage lay with those whose vision was clearest, whose purposes were most certain, and this meant the Federalist leaders, and in particular Alexander Hamilton, the secretary of the treasury. From 1787 the most nationally minded of the Federalists had wanted the United States to be no mere confederation of disparate states but a republican government in its own right with the power to act energetically in the public sphere—to be a mercantilist state. In building such an integrated national state, the Federalist leaders saw their principal political problem as one of adhesion: how to keep people in such a large sprawling republic from flying apart in pursuit of their partial local interests. This, of course, as Montesquieu had said, was the central problem for any republic, but it was especially a problem for a huge extended republic like the United States. Republics were supposed to rely for cohesion on the moral qualities of their people—their virtue and their natural sociability; unlike monarchies they had to be held together from below, by their natural affection and benevolence and by their willingness to sacrifice their partial and private interests for the sake of the public good.

In today's language, what was essential for republics was the existence of a civil society—all those voluntary associations and institutions that stand between the state and the individual. In our own time it has been the new states of Eastern Europe and the Middle East that have revived this Scottish Enlightenment emphasis on the importance of a civil society. In light of efforts of the ex-communist states of Eastern Europe and the states of the Middle East to erect viable democratic societies, we today can perhaps more fully understand the significance of a civil society to the workings of a popular government. Certainly we are in a better position than previous generations of Americans to appreciate the weaknesses of republics and the advantages of monarchies and authoritarian governments in holding peoples of diverse backgrounds, interests, and ethnicities together.

By 1789 many of the Federalists, particularly Hamilton, had no confidence whatsoever left in the virtue or the natural sociability of the American people as adhesive forces: to rely on such wild schemes and visionary principles, as radicals like Jefferson and Paine did, to tie the United States together, the Federalists said, was to rely on nothing. Hence Hamilton and the other Federalist leaders had to find things other than republican virtue and natural sociability to make the American people a single nation.

Tying people together, creating social cohesiveness, making a single nation out of disparate sections and communities without relying on idealistic republican adhesives—this was the preoccupation of the Federalists, and it explains much of what they did—from Washington's proposals for building canals to Hamilton's financial program. As we saw in the previous essay, many of the Federalists actually thought in terms of turning the government of the United States into a surrogate monarchy, of devising substitutes for traditional monarchical ligaments and placing them within a republican framework.[5]

In place of the impotent confederation of separate states that had existed in the 1780s, the Federalists envisioned a strong, consolidated, and prosperous national state, united, as Hamilton said, "for the accomplishment of great purposes" and led by an energetic government composed of the best and most distinguished men in the society.[6] As we have seen, they aimed to bolster the dignity of this government by adopting some of the ceremony and majesty of monarchy. Many of the Federalists, in short, aimed to make the United States in time a grand, illustrious nation and a rival of the great monarchies of Europe. Hamilton especially envisioned the new national government in traditional European fashion as a great military power. The federal government for him was not to be, as it was for James Madison, simply a disinterested umpire making judicial-like decisions among a number of competing interests. Hamilton wanted to use central state power positively in order to turn the United States into "something noble and magnificent." He and some other Federalists dreamed of making the United States the equal of the European monarchies on their own terms—terms that, as Washington said, were "characteristic of wise and powerful Nations."[7] This meant a strong central government that reached to all parts of an integrated nation with a powerful army and navy that commanded the respect of all the world.

Hamilton's model was England, and he consciously set out to duplicate the great English achievement of the eighteenth century. England had emerged from the chaos and civil wars of the seventeenth century that had killed one king and deposed another to become the most dominant power in the world. That this small island on the northern edge of Europe with a third of the population of France was able to build the biggest empire since the fall of Rome was the miracle of the century, even surpassing the astonishing achievement of the Netherlands in the previous century. The English "fiscal-military state," in John Brewer's apt term, could mobilize wealth and wage war as no state in history ever had. Its centralized administration had developed an extraordinary capacity to tax and borrow from its subjects without impoverishing them.[8] Hamilton saw that the secret of England's success was its system of funded debt together with its banking structure and its market in public securities. He aimed to do for the United States what English ministers had done for the former mother country. His financial program followed directly from this aim.

Hamilton was undoubtedly concerned with the commercial prosperity of the United States—with furthering "the interests of a great people"—but he was scarcely the capitalist promoter of America's emerging business culture that he is often described as being. He was a traditional eighteenth-century statesman, willing to allow ordinary people their profits and property, their interests and their petty pursuits of happiness, but wanting honor and glory for himself and his country. He was very much the mercantilist who believed deeply in the "need" in government for "a common directing power." He had only contempt for those who believed in laissez-faire and thought that trade and interests could regulate themselves. "This," he said, "is one of those wild speculative paradoxes which have grown into credit among us, contrary to the uniform practice and sense of the most enlightened nations. . . . It must be rejected by every man acquainted with commercial history."[9]

Of course, he accepted the prevalence of interests—indeed, he thought there could be no other tie but interest between most people in the society. He himself, however, was extraordinarily scrupulous as secretary of the treasury in maintaining his personal disinterestedness and freedom from corruption. Let others, including congressmen, become "speculators" and "peculators," but not he. He was determined to stand above all the interested men and try to harness and use them. He agreed with the eighteenth-century British economic philosopher Sir James Steuart that "self-interest . . . is the main spring and only motive which a statesman should make use of, to engage a free people to concur in the plans which he lays down for their government." Although he later and rather defensively denied that he had ever made self-interest "the weightiest motive" behind his financial program, there is no doubt that he thought the debt and other financial measures would strengthen the national government "by increasing the number of ligaments between the Government and the interests of Individuals."[10]

In effect, in the opposition language of the eighteenth-century Anglo-American world, Hamilton set out to "corrupt" American society, to use monarchical-like governmental influence to tie existing commercial interests to the government and to create new hierarchies of interest and dependency that would substitute for the absence of virtue and the apparently weak republican adhesives existing in America. In local areas, Hamilton and the Federalist leaders built up followings among Revolutionary War veterans and members of the Society of the Cincinnati. They appointed important and respectable local figures to the federal judiciary and other federal offices. They exploited the patronage of the treasury department and its seven hundred or more customs officials, revenue agents, and postmasters with particular effectiveness. By 1793 or so the Federalists had formed groups of "friends of government" in most of the states. Their hierarchies of patronage and dependency ran from the federal executive through Congress down to the various localities. It was as close to monarchy and a British system of corruption and influence made famous by Prime Minister Robert Walpole as America was ever to have.

At the same time the Federalists sought to wean the people's affections away from their state governments and to get them to feel the power of what they hoped would become a consolidated national government. The Constitution had attempted to reduce drastically the power of the states. Article I, Section 10, among other things, had forbidden the states from levying tariffs or duties on imports or exports and had barred them from issuing paper money or bills of credit. As these were the principal means by which premodern governments raised money, their prohibition cut deeply into the fiscal competency of the state governments. Some Federalists hoped to go further and eventually reduce the states to mere administrative units of the national government. Hamilton, at the time the Constitution was drafted, had hoped that the new federal government would "triumph altogether over the state governments and reduce them to an intire subordination, dividing the larger states into smaller districts."[11] Washington thought that the states might in time have no occasion for taxes and "consequently may abandon all the subjects of taxation to the Union." The federal excise taxes, especially the tax on whiskey, were designed to make people feel the authority of the national government. In a like way, the raising of nearly 15,000 militiamen by the national government to put down the Whiskey Rebellion flowed from Hamilton's assumption, voiced in 1794, that "government can never [be] said to be established until some signal display, has manifested its power of military coercion."[12]

But the national government could not rely on military force to keep people in line. Other more subtle and more ostensibly republican means were needed to control the surging democratic passions of the people. The Federalists found one answer in the judiciary. They were eager to make judges a bulwark against the unruly democratic consequences of the Revolution. Since the 1780s, those concerned about rampaging state legislatures and their abuses of private property and minority rights, particularly those of creditors, had conducted a propaganda campaign to strengthen the judiciary.

Judges in colonial America had been relatively insignificant members of government; they had been viewed largely as appendages or extensions of the royal governors or chief magistrates, who usually appointed them at the pleasure of the crown. At the time of the Revolution, Americans had done little to enhance the judiciary's negligible status. In their Revolutionary state constitutions of 1776 they had taken away the appointment of judges from the governors and had given it to the state legislatures, and through codification schemes they had tried further to reduce the importance of judges by turning them into what Jefferson called "a mere machine."[13]

In the following decades all this was reversed. Suddenly in the 1780s and 1790s, the judiciary in America emerged out of its earlier insignificance to become a full-fledged partner in what was now defined as the tripartite system of American government—sharing power equally with legislatures and executives. Many, in fact, thought that the judiciary had become the principal means for controlling popular legislatures and protecting private rights. The most dramatic institutional transformation in the early Republic was this rise of what was commonly referred to as an "independent judiciary." It is a fascinating story still not fully told.

It is not surprising, therefore, that the Federalists should have been concerned with creating strong judiciaries, not only in the states but especially in the new federal government. No institution of the new national government would be less susceptible to popular democratic pressure and yet touch the lives of ordinary people in their localities more than a federal court system. Thus the Federalists fought hard to create a separate national court structure in which, they hoped, the common law of crimes would run. The Judiciary Act of 1789, which gave concurrent original jurisdiction to the state courts, was scarcely satisfactory to the more nationally minded Federalists, and throughout the 1790s they struggled to expand the power and jurisdiction of the federal courts. The Judiciary Act of 1801 and the broadened and constructive interpretations of national law by federal judges in the 1790s, including that of treason, were manifestations of these efforts. The actions of the Marshall Court in subsequent years—as its repudiation of the idea that the common law of crimes ran in the federal courts and its limited definition of treason in the Burr trial show—were far from being extensions of national power and were in fact retreats from the advanced and exposed positions that the Federalists of the 1790s attempted to stake out for the national judiciary.[14]

All these grand and grandiose aims of the Federalist leaders, particularly of the high-toned Federalists, are a measure of their disillusionment with what the Revolution had done to American society and their confidence that they now had the national solution to the problems of the country. Their disillusionment had in fact been widely shared among America's gentry leadership in 1787 and had helped create the Constitution. But the degrees of disillusionment were vastly different among even fervent supporters of the Constitution. James Madison, for example, certainly shared Hamilton's misgivings about democracy and his desire to reduce popular state power; and he surely wanted a commercially strong mercantilist national government that would be able both to pass navigation acts and protect minority creditor rights in the several states. But he and others who had created and supported the Constitution, particularly in the Southern and mid-Atlantic states, did not share Hamilton's vision of the United States becoming a consolidated European-like "fiscal-military" power. Nor did they ever really doubt the popular basis of America's governments.[15] Indeed, Madison, Jefferson, and the Republicans never accepted the newly emerging European idea of the modern state, with its elaborate administrative structures, large armies and navies, high taxes, and huge debts. The Republicans' rejection of this modern state had immense implications for America's future.

The high-toned High-Federalists' attempts to impose such a state on America eventually divided the gentry-leaders of the nation and led to passionate factional splits throughout the country. Jefferson and the Republicans came to believe quite sincerely that Hamilton and the Federalists were out to create a monarchy in America. Although Hamilton with equal sincerity denied that that was ever his aim, popular Republican resistance to his projects only made him and the High-Federalists more desperate. By the end of the decade the Federalists had become truly frightened by the popular direction of events and felt compelled to pass alien and sedition acts and to make plans for war involving the creation of armies in the tens of thousands and the calling of Washington back into uniform as commander of these troops. Hamilton even toyed with the idea of dismantling the states.

We know how it all turned out—with Jefferson's election in 1800 and peaceful accession to power in 1801—and consequently we find it hard to take the fears of either the Federalists or the Republicans very seriously. But both had good reason to be frightened, for there were forces at work in the 1790s that neither the Federalists nor the Republicans fully understood or could control. The consequence was that many of their best intentions went awry.

The men who wrote the Constitution had expected to attract to the national government the best people, "men who possess the most attractive merit and the most diffusive and established characters," in Madison's words, or "men of discernment and liberality," as Washington described them.[16] They knew whom they meant even if we have a hard time defining such people. They meant men pretty much like themselves, gentlemen of talent and distinction, with all that the term "gentlemen" implied in the eighteenth century. Such gentlemen should ideally be educated in the liberal arts at a good college like Harvard or Princeton, or if not, at least self-cultivated and with sufficient wealth and independence that they did not have to earn a living in too blatant or mercenary a fashion. Madison was apprehensive that the First Congress was going to be composed of the same sorts of illiberal and narrow-minded men who had sat in the state legislatures, and he was relieved at the character of most of the congressmen he met. But it soon became evident that his elevated republic was not going to be high enough to keep out permanently the middling and other ordinary and interested people who had caused so much difficulty in the state legislatures in the 1780s. In the northern parts of America, at least, all levels of government were steadily being democratized and occupied by people with interests to promote. By the Second Congress, even William Findley, an ex-weaver from Pennsylvania and a prototype of the plebeian Anti-Federalists, made it into the elevated national government that was designed to keep his type out.

The problem was that Washington's "men of discernment and liberality" were hard to find and even when found lacked sufficient income to behave as disinterested gentlemen in government were supposed to behave. By 1795 President Washington was having trouble recruiting proper men for the highest federal offices, including the cabinet. Federalists in the House of Representatives charged that Jefferson, Hamilton, and Henry Knox had all resigned from the cabinet "chiefly for one reason, the smallness of the salary."[17] Although this was not at the case with Jefferson, both Knox and Hamilton did have trouble maintaining a genteel standard of living on their government salaries. There were of course plenty of claimants for the middle and lower offices of the government, but these were lesser sorts of men who were quite openly seeking the offices in order to make a living from them.

The truth was that the entire Federalist scheme rested on a false understanding of America's gentry. Washington, like other Federalists, conceived of his "men of discernment and liberality" in classically republican terms, as gentlemen of leisure and independence who were generally free of direct market interests and who therefore could take up the burden of public office as a disinterested obligation of their social rank. By proposing in the Philadelphia Convention that all members of the executive be barred from receiving any salaries or fees, Benjamin Franklin was simply expressing an extreme version of this classical republican view of officeholding. But the fact of the matter was that members of the American aristocracy, with the exception of a few wealthy individuals like Franklin and many Southern gentry like Washington and Jefferson, were incapable of living up to the classical image of a leisured patriciate serving in public office without compensation.

Heaven knows many of them tried to live up to the classical image, often with disastrous consequences for themselves and their families. Merchants who wanted to hold high public office usually had to ennoble themselves and put their mercantile property into a rentier form—John Hancock and Robert Morris being notable examples. As we have seen, the goal was to get enough wealth, preferably in the form of land, so that one did not have to work at accumulating money on a regular basis and in an acquisitive manner. All the desperate efforts of men like Morris, James Wilson, and Henry Knox to find genteel independence for themselves through land speculation—efforts that ended in ruin and sometimes debtors' prison—are measures of the power of that classical image of a leisured patriciate. For it was evident to the eighteenth-century gentry, even if not to us, that one could not acquire real independence of the marketplace without having that independence based on what historian George V. Taylor, in reference to eighteenth-century France, calls "proprietary wealth."[18]

Such proprietary wealth was composed of static forms of property— "unearned income," as we might call it: rents from tenants, bonds, interest from money out on loan—that allowed its holders sufficient leisure to assume the burdens of public office without expecting high salaries. These kinds of proprietary property holders were those Washington had in mind when he used the term "the monied gentry."[19] These monied gentry, with their static proprietary wealth, were of course very vulnerable to inflation, which is why the printing of paper money was so frightening to them. Although these proprietary gentry, like their counterparts in England, were often involved in various commercial ventures, they were not risk-taking entrepreneurs or businessmen in any modern sense. Instead, they were social leaders whose property was the source of their personal authority and independence; inflation therefore threatened not simply their livelihood but their very identity and social position. Until we grasp this point, we will never appreciate the depth of moral indignation behind the gentry's outcry against paper money and other debtor-relief legislation in the 1780s.

Of course, not only was this kind of proprietary wealth very hard to come by in America—where, compared to England, land was so plentiful and tenantry so rare—but commerce and trade were creating new forms of property that gave wealth and power to new sorts of people. This new property was anything but static: it was risk-taking, entrepreneurial capital—not money out on loan, but money borrowed. It was in fact all the paper money that enterprising people clamored for in these years. It was not "unearned income" that came to a person, as Adam Smith defined the rents of the English landed gentry, without exertion, but "earned income" that came *with* exertion—indeed, came with labor, production, and exchange. This was the property of businessmen and protobusinessmen—of commercial farmers, artisan-manufacturers, traders, shopkeepers, and all who labored for a living and produced and exchanged things, no matter how poor or wealthy they might be.

The increasing distinctions drawn in these years between, in the words of the uneducated New England farmer William Manning, "those that labour for a Living and those that git a Living without Bodily Labour," which included all gentry-professionals, expressed the rise of this new kind of property.[20] Unlike proprietary wealth, this new kind of dynamic, fluid, and evanescent property could not create personal authority or identity; it was, said Joseph Story, "continually changing like the waves of the sea."[21] Hence it was meaningless to rely on it as a source of independence. Once this was understood, then property qualifications for participation in public life either as voters or officeholders lost their relevance and rapidly fell away. The William Mannings and the William Findleys who spoke for these new kinds of entrepreneurial and labor-produced property—for "earned income"—were precisely the sorts of illiberal and parochial men that liberal gentry like Madison in the 1780s had condemned.[22]

But Madison, Jefferson, and other Southern gentry leaders of the Republicans no more understood what was happening to American society and to property than did Hamilton and the Federalists. Nor did Hamilton and Jefferson understand very clearly the direction the American economy was taking. Both assumed that the future prosperity of the United States lay essentially with foreign trade, and they were both wrong: it lay mainly with domestic or internal trade, with the United States becoming "a world within themselves."[23] Eighteenth-century leaders had difficulty putting great value on internal trade because of their lingering zero-sum mercantilist assumption that a nation's wealth as a whole could grow only at the expense of another nation; that is, the country as a whole could prosper only by selling more abroad than it bought.[24]

Domestic trade was thought to benefit only individuals or regions but not the country as a whole; it simply moved wealth about without increasing its total. Those involved in domestic commerce, however, had a different sense of where the future prosperity of the country lay, but they needed paper money to carry on their internal trading—lots of it. Article I, Section 10 of the Constitution had prohibited the states from printing bills of credit, but the needs and desires of all the protobusinessmen and domestic traders were too great to be stymied by a paper restriction. So the states, under popular pressure, got around the constitutional prohibition by chartering banks, hundreds upon hundreds of them, which in turn issued the paper money people wanted. Hamilton no more predicted or wanted this proliferation of banks and paper money than did Jefferson;

he and other Federalists had in fact thought the Bank of the United States would absorb the state banks and have a monopoly on banking and the issuing of currency.[25]

Both Hamilton and Jefferson equally underestimated the importance of artisan-manufacturing. As historian Joyce Appleby has told us, Jefferson and the Republican Party benefited from artisan and business support in the mid-Atlantic states, but Jefferson never fully grasped this point; he never appreciated the nature of the popular commercial forces he was presumably leading.[26] Hamilton's biggest political mistake was to ignore the interests of the artisan-manufacturers. Despite his 1791 "Report on Manufactures," which presumably recognized the importance of domestic commerce, Hamilton, as John R. Nelson has told us, never had his heart in manufacturing and never pushed to implement his report; instead, his program actually favored moneyed men and import merchants at the expense of domestic producers and traders.[27] Consequently, artisans in the mid-Atlantic states who had been fervent Federalists in 1787–1788 were eventually driven into the ranks of the Republican Party—except in New England. The exception is illuminating. Too many of the New England artisans were too closely tied to patron-client relationships with wealthy overseas merchants in New England's port cities to develop as sharp a sense of their separate interests as that possessed by the mid-Atlantic artisans. From 1793 to 1807 New England's interests and prosperity were almost entirely absorbed in overseas trade. As a result, the emphasis Hamilton's program placed on overseas trade skewed Federalist support toward New England and helped to mask the fact that the future prosperity of the United States lay largely in the development of domestic commerce and not in international shipping.

In other areas as well, gentry leaders of all sections and both parties lived with illusions and misunderstood the realities of American society. Many leaders in the 1790s, for example, thought that slavery was on its way to ultimate extinction. The American Revolution had unleashed enlightened principles of liberty that seemed to make the disappearance of slavery just a matter of time: David Ramsay of South Carolina thought there would "not be a slave in these states fifty years hence."[28] Liberal opinion everywhere in the world condemned the institution. When even Southerners like Jefferson, Patrick Henry, and Henry Laurens deplored the injustice of slavery, from "that moment," many believed, "the slow, but certain, death-wound was inflicted upon it."[29]

Of course, as we know, such predictions could not have been more wrong: far from being doomed, slavery in the United States in the 1790s was on the verge of its greatest expansion. But such self-deception, such mistaken optimism, among the Revolutionary leaders was understandable, for they wanted to believe the best, and there was some evidence that slavery was dying away. The Northern states, where slavery was not inconsequential, were busy trying to eliminate the institution, and by 1804 all had done so. There were indications that the same thing was happening in the Southern states, especially in the Upper South. More antislave societies existed in the South than in the North, and manumissions in the South were becoming more frequent.

Virginia, being the richest and most populous state in the nation, not only dominated the presidency but seemed to be setting the tone for the country. In Virginia alone the number of free blacks increased from 3,000 in 1780 to 13,000 by 1790. Between 1790 and 1810 the free black population in the United States grew faster than the slave population. By the 1790s all the states, including South Carolina, had ended the international slave trade. Many hoped that abolishing the importation of slaves from abroad would eventually kill off the institution of slavery. But faith in the future was not enough: the Founding Fathers had simply not counted on the remarkable demographic capacity of the old slave states themselves, especially Virginia, to produce slaves for the expanding areas of the Deep South and Southwest. Believing that slavery was dying a natural death was the most fatal of the Founders' many illusions.

Perhaps we can muster some sympathy for the Founding Fathers' difficulty in predicting the future when we take into account the breathtaking speed of events and complexity of circumstances in the 1790s. Nowhere was this speed and complexity more obvious than in the settlement of the

West, and nowhere was the gap between the leaders' illusions and reality more conspicuous than in the way they dealt with the West.

The Federalists at least were not mistaken in their sense of the fragility of the United States. It was the largest republic since ancient Rome, and as such it was continually in danger of falling apart. Indeed, fear for the integrity of the United States lay behind the Continental Congress's passage of the Northwest Ordinance of 1787. Despite its progressive promises, this plan for the colonization of American territories was actually quite reactionary. Its proposals for garrison governments with authoritarian leadership for the new western colonies resembled nothing so much as those failed seventeenth-century English efforts at establishing military governments over the obstreperous colonists.[30] The ordinance was an indication of how fearful eastern leaders were of the unruly westerners leaving the union, lured away perhaps by one European power or another.

These fears that westerners could be separated from the United States by European powers were not entirely illusory—not when popular societies were toasting the right of everyone to "remove out of the limits of these United States" at will.[31] There were indeed conspiracies involving Britain and Spain on the western borders. In fact, some British officials in Canada were convinced that they could reverse the Revolution and put the North American British Empire back together again. American fears of foreign influence help account both for the hasty admission into the Union in the 1790s of Vermont, Kentucky, and Tennessee, and for the later violations of the Northwest Ordinance's procedures for orderly territorial advancement to statehood. Since Britain in Canada was regarded as by far the more dangerous power, Americans felt they had to organize the Northwest Territory as soon as possible. Spain, on the other hand, was thought to be so decrepit, its hold on its empire so weak, that its Southern and Southwestern territories could be left to fall into American hands like so many ripe fruit. Natural demographic pressures would see to that, it being a common assumption in the 1790s that most western migrants would come from the burgeoning Southern states. This was one of several mistaken ideas that American leaders had about the future of the West.

The Federalists' western policy, including the working of the North-west Ordinance and treatment of the Indians, rested on the assumption that settlement of the western territories would be neat and orderly. Many of the Federalist leaders were scrupulously concerned for the fate of the Indians; indeed, the statements of Secretary of War Henry Knox about the need for just treatment of the native Americans might even be deemed politically correct by a modern anthropologist. But purchasing the Indians' rights to the land and assimilating or protecting them in a civilized manner depended on an orderly and steady pace of white settlement.

So too did both the hopes for governmental revenue from the land and the plans of land speculators depend on gradual, piecemeal, and well-regulated settlement of the West. The federal government hoped to gain steady revenues by selling its western land to land companies and speculators. The speculators in turn counted on the settlers slowly filling in the territory surrounding the land they held, which would raise its value and bring them the promised returns on their investments.

Everything was built on illusions.[32] The people moving west ignored the federal government's Indian policies and refused to buy land at the expensive prices at which it was being offered. They shunned the speculators' land, violated Indian treaty rights, and moved irregularly, chaotically, unevenly, jumping from place to place and leaving huge chunks of unsettled land and pockets of hemmed-in Indians behind them. The government responded, and continued to respond until the Homestead Act of 1863, in a series of desperate efforts to keep up with popular pressures. It continually lowered the price of land, increased the credit it offered, and reduced the size of the parcels of land people had to buy; and still people complained and ignored the laws. Eventually the federal government recognized the rights of squatters to preempt the land, and finally it just gave the land away. It took more than a half century for governmental leaders to come to terms fully with the reality of popular settlement of the West.

For the Federalists of the 1790s it took less than that for most of their heroic plans and dreams to be exploded. Even if Jefferson had been somehow technically denied the presidency in 1800, most of the Federalists' blueprints for America were already doomed. They were too out of touch with the surging popular and commercial realities of American life. The demographic and economic forces at work were too powerful for any gentry leadership to overcome or any election to reverse. The secret of Jefferson's success, insofar as he had any, was his unwitting surrender to these popular commercial forces. He abandoned the Federalist goals of creating a strong, mercantilist, European-like state, reduced the power of the national government in a variety of ways, and in effect left everyone free to pursue his happiness as he saw fit. It remained for later generations of Americans—in some cases even the generation following World War II—to fulfill many of the dreams and schemes of the Federalists of the 1790s.

Perhaps our history since 1800 has been one long effort to do in two centuries what the Federalists unsuccessfully tried to do in a decade: bring under control the powerful and unruly popular and commercial forces unleashed by the Revolution and create a strong integrated nation. When we look at the huge, prosperous, and unitary fiscal-military state that we have built—the most powerful state the world has ever known—we might conclude that Hamilton and the Federalists of the 1790s have had the last laugh after all.

AFTERWORD TO CHAPTER 9

This began as a lecture opening the symposium on "Launching the 'Extended Republic'" held in the early 1990s under the auspices of the United States Capitol Historical Society. It was later published in Ronald Hoffman and Peter J. Albert, eds., *Launching the "Extended Republic": The Federalist Era* (Charlottesville: University Press of Virginia, 1996). By creating and organizing their extraordinarily successful project, *Perspectives on the American Revolution* (supported by the United States Capitol Historical Society), Hoffman and Albert have made an enormous contribution to our understanding of the Revolution and the early Republic.

For nearly twenty years, from the early 1980s to the end of the twentieth century, Hoffman and Albert, supplemented by occasional guest editors, brought out almost a dozen and a half volumes on various important issues connected with the American Revolution and its aftermath—everything from women, slavery, and Indians to religion, social developments, and patterns of consumption. It is a stunning achievement.

CHAPTER TEN

The AMERICAN ENLIGHTENMENT

*T*HE RATIFICATION OF the United States Constitution in 1788 was greeted with more excitement and more unanimity among the American people than at any time since the Declaration of Independence a decade earlier. "'Tis done!" declared Benjamin Rush in July 1788. "We have become a nation." This was an extravagant claim, to say the least. Yet Rush thought the new United States had become a nation virtually overnight. Everywhere in America, he said, there was "such a tide of joy as has seldom been felt in any age or country. . . . Justice has descended from heaven to dwell in our land, and ample restitution has at last been made to human nature by our new Constitution of all the injuries she has sustained in the old world from arbitrary government, false religions, and unlawful commerce." The new nation represented the "triumph of knowledge over ignorance, of virtue over vice, and of liberty over slavery."[1]

What gave Revolutionaries like Rush confidence in America's instant nationhood was their belief in America's enlightenment. As early as 1765 John Adams had declared that all of previous American history had pointed toward the eighteenth-century Enlightenment. The seventeenth-century settlement of America, he said, had opened up "a grand scene and design in Providence for the illumination of the ignorant, and the emancipation of the slavish part of mankind all over the earth."[2] The Revolution had become the climax of this great historic drama. Enlightenment was spreading everywhere in the Western world, but nowhere more so than in America. With the break from Great Britain complete and the Constitution ratified, many Americans in the 1790s thought that the United States had become the "most enlightened" nation in the world.[3]

For the people of these obscure provinces—"so recently," as Samuel Bryan of Pennsylvania declared, "a rugged wilderness and the abode of savages and wild beasts"—for these provincial people to claim to be the most enlightened nation on earth and to have "attained to a degree of improvement and greatness . . . of which history furnishes no parallel" seemed scarcely credible.[4] The United States in 1789, in comparison with the former mother country, was still an underdeveloped country. Americans had no sophisticated court life, no magnificent cities, no great concert halls, no lavish drawing rooms, and not much to speak of in the way of the fine arts. Its economy was primitive. There was as yet nothing comparable to the Bank of England; there were no stock exchanges, no large trading companies, no great centers of capital, and no readily available circulating medium of exchange. Nineteen out of twenty Americans were still employed in agriculture, and most of them lived in tiny rural communities. In 1790 there were only twenty-four towns in the entire United States with a population of 2,500 or more, and only five of these urban areas were cities with populations over 10,000. It took over two months for news of a foreign event in London to reach Philadelphia.[5] No wonder many Europeans thought of the United States as a remote wilderness at the very edges of Christendom, three thousand miles from the centers of Western civilization.

Nevertheless, as far removed from the centers of civilization as they were, many Americans persisted in believing not only that they were the most enlightened people on earth but also that because they were enlightened they were by that fact alone a nation. Indeed, America became the first nation in the world to base its nationhood solely on Enlightenment values. Gertrude Stein may have been right when she said that America was the oldest country in the world.

It was a strange kind of nationalism Revolutionary Americans asserted. For Americans to identify their nation with the Enlightenment was to identify it with transnational—indeed, universal and ecumenical— standards. They had little sense that their devotion to the universal principles of the Enlightenment was incompatible with loyalty to their state or to the country as a whole. Historian David Ramsay claimed he was "a citizen of the world and therefore despise[d] national reflections." Nevertheless, he did not believe he was being "inconsistent" in hoping that the professions would be "administered to my country by its own sons." Joel Barlow did not think he was any less American just because he was elected to the French National Convention in 1792–1793. The many state histories written in the aftermath of the Revolution were anything but celebrations of localism and the diversity of the nation. Indeed, declared Ramsay, these histories were testimonies to the American commitment to enlightened nationhood; they were designed to "wear away prejudices— rub off asperities and mould us into an homogeneous people."[6]

Homogeneous people! This is a phrase that seems to separate us most decisively from that different, distant eighteenth-century world. Because we today can take our nationhood for granted, we can indulge ourselves in the luxury of celebrating our multicultural diversity. But two hundred years ago Americans were trying to create a nation from scratch and had no such luxury. They were desperately trying to make themselves one people, and the best way they could do that was to stress their remarkable degree of enlightenment. Since the Enlightenment emphasized the value of homogeneity and of being a single people, by describing themselves as the most enlightened people in the world Americans assumed that they would thereby be a nation. More than anything else, their deep desire to be a nation is what accounts for their impassioned insistence that they were especially enlightened.

But why would they assume that they were especially enlightened? Of course, they had many European radicals like Richard Price filling their heads with the idea that they had actually created the Enlightenment. "A Spirit" that had originated in America, Price told Benjamin Franklin in 1787, was now spreading throughout the Atlantic world. This spirit, said Price, promised "a State of Society more favourable to peace, virtue, Science, and liberty (and consequently to human happiness and dignity) than has yet been known. . . . The minds of men are becoming more enlighten'd, and the silly despots of the world are likely to be forced to respect human rights and to take care not to govern too much lest they should not govern at all."[7]

But it was not simply compliments like Price's that made Americans believe that they were the most enlightened people on earth. They thought they had ample reason for their confidence. They may not have been correct in their reasoning, but it is important for us to know why they thought as they did. By doing so we can understand not only something about the origins of the United States but also something of what the Enlightenment meant to many people in the eighteenth-century Atlantic world.

Americans had no doubt that they were living in an age of Enlightenment. Everywhere the boundaries of darkness and ignorance were being pushed back and light and reason were being extended outward. More than most people in the Atlantic world, Americans were keenly aware that savagery and barbarism were giving way to refinement and civilization. Precisely because they were provincials living on the periphery of civilization, living, as historian Franco Venturi once pointed out, in a place "where the contact between a backward world and modern world was chronologically more abrupt and geographically closer," they knew what the process of becoming enlightened really meant.[8] The experience of becoming refined and civilized was more palpable and immediate for them than it was for those living in the metropolitan centers of the Old World.

Americans told themselves over and over that they were a young and forming people. And because they inhabited a New World and were in a plastic state, they were more capable of refinement and education than people stuck in the habits and prejudices of the Old World. In writings, orations, poetry—in every conceivable manner and in the most extravagant and rapturous rhetoric—Revolutionary Americans told themselves that they were more capable than any people in the world of making themselves over.

As republicans attempting to build a state from the bottom up, they were necessarily committed to Lockean sensationalism—that knowledge came less from reason and more from sense experience. Not only did such Lockean sensationalism give a new significance to the capacities of ordinary people, since all people had senses, but it also opened up the possibility of people being educated and improved by changing the environments that operated on their senses.

These views lay behind the enlightened assumption that all men were created equal. Even those as aristocratic as William Byrd and Governor Francis Fauquier of Virginia now conceded that all men, even men of different nations and races, were born equal and that, as Byrd wrote, "the principal difference between one people and another proceeds only from the differing opportunities of improvement." "White, Red, or Black; polished or unpolished," declared Governor Fauquier in 1760, "Men are Men."[9] The American Revolutionary leaders were primed to receive these ideas that culture was socially constructed and that only education and cultivation separated one man from another. In fact, their receptivity to these explosive ideas, which became the basis of all modern thinking, helps explain why they should have become the most remarkable generation of leaders in American history. Because they were men of high ambition and yet of relatively modest origins, they naturally were eager to promote the new enlightened standards of gentility and learning in opposition to the traditional importance of family and blood. They saw themselves sharply set apart from the older world of their fathers and grandfathers. They sought, often unsuccessfully but always sincerely, to be what Jefferson called "natural aristocrats"—aristocrats who measured their status not by birth or family but by enlightened values and benevolent behavior. To be a natural aristocrat meant being reasonable, tolerant, honest, virtuous, and candid. It implied as well being cosmopolitan, standing on elevated ground in order to have a large view of human affairs, and being free of the prejudices, parochialism, and religious enthusiasm of the vulgar and barbaric. It meant, in short, having all those characteristics that we today sum up in the idea of a liberal arts education.

Almost all the Revolutionary leaders—including the second and third tiers of leadership—were first-generation gentlemen. That is to say, almost all were the first in their families to attend college and to acquire a liberal arts education that was now the new mark of an enlightened eighteenth-century gentleman. Jefferson's father, Peter Jefferson, was a wealthy Virginia planter and surveyor who married successfully into the prestigious Randolph family. But he was not a refined and liberally educated gentleman: he did not read Latin, he did not know French, he did not play the violin, and, as far as we know, he never once questioned the idea of a religious establishment or the owning of slaves.

His son Thomas was very different. Indeed, all the Revolutionaries knew things that their fathers had not known, and they were eager to prove themselves by what they believed and valued and by their virtue and disinterestedness.

Most important, these Revolutionary leaders felt a greater affinity with the people they spoke for than did elites in Europe. Not for them "the withdrawal of the upper classes" from the uncultivated bulk of the population that historian Peter Burke speaks about. Because the American gentry were establishing republics, they necessarily had to have a more magnanimous view of human nature than their European counterparts. As we have seen, monarchies could comprehend large territories and composite kingdoms and rule over people who were selfish, corrupt, and diverse in interests and ethnicities. But republics required societies that were not only enlightened but were cohesive, virtuous, and egalitarian. It seemed as if the American people were ideally suited for republicanism; they necessarily possessed a unanimity and a oneness that other peoples did not have. As Joel Barlow noted in 1792, the "people" had come to mean something very different in America from what it did in Europe.

In Europe the people remained only a portion of the society; they were the poor, the rabble, the *misérables*, the *menu peuple*, the *Pöbel*.[10] But in America the people were the whole society. In republican America there could be no subjects, no orders, no aristocracy, no estates separate from the people. The people had become everything.

Perhaps some American gentry in the privacy of their dining rooms continued to express the traditional elitist contempt for ordinary folk. But it was no longer possible in public for an American leader to refer to the people as the common "herd." During the Virginia ratifying convention in June 1788, Edmund Randolph had used just this term in reference to the people, and Patrick Henry immediately jumped on him. By likening the people to a "herd," said Henry, Randolph had "levelled and degraded [them] to the lowest degree," reducing them "from respectable independent citizens, to abject, dependent subjects or slaves." Randolph was forced to rise at once and defensively declare "that he did not use that word to excite any odium, but merely to convey an idea of a multitude."[11]

From this moment no American political leader ever again dared in public to refer to the people in such disparaging terms. Instead, in their orations and writings they exulted in the various ways the American people as a whole were more enlightened than the rest of mankind.

In these attempts to justify their enlightenment, Americans created the sources of their belief in their exceptionalism, in their difference from the peoples of the Old World. Americans, they told themselves, were without both the corrupting luxury of Europe and its great distinctions of wealth and poverty. "Here," said the French immigrant and author Hector St. John de Crèvecoeur in one of his typical ecstatic celebrations of the distinctiveness of the New World, "are no aristocratical families, no courts, no kings, no bishops, no ecclesiastical dominion, no invisible power giving to a few a very visible one, no great manufactures employing thousands, no great refinements of luxury. The rich and the poor are not so far removed from each other as they are in Europe." There was nothing in America remotely resembling the wretched poverty and the gin-soaked slums of London. America, continued Crèvecoeur, was largely made up of "cultivators scattered over an immense territory," each of them working for himself. Nowhere in America, he said, ignoring for the moment the big houses of the Southern planters and the slave quarters of hundreds of thousands of black Africans, could one find "the hostile castle and the haughty mansion, contrasted with the clay-built hut and miserable cabin, where cattle and men help to keep each other warm and dwell in meanness, smoke and indigence."[12]

Precisely because Americans were separated from Europe and, as Jefferson said in 1787, "remote from all other aid, we are obliged to invent and execute; to find means within ourselves, and not to lean on others." The result of this American pragmatism, this ability, said Jefferson, "to surmount every difficulty by resolution and contrivance," was a general prosperity.[13] White Americans enjoyed the highest standard of living in the world, and goods of all sorts were widely diffused throughout the society. Indeed, the enlightenment of a society could be measured by the spread of material possessions, by seeing whether most people possessed what Jefferson called those things "applicable to our daily concerns." Did people eat with knives and forks instead of with their hands? Did they sleep on feather mattresses instead of straw? Did they drink out of china cups instead of wooden vessels? These were signs of prosperity, of happiness, of civilization. Jefferson believed that to know the real state of a society's enlightenment one "must ferret the people out of their hovels, . . . look into their kettle, eat their bread, loll on their beds under pretence of resting yourself, but in fact to find out if they are soft."[14]

The Revolution had made Americans a more intelligent people. It had given "a spring to the active powers of the inhabitants," said David Ramsay in 1789, "and set them on thinking, speaking, and acting far beyond that to which they had been accustomed."[15] Three-quarters of all the books and pamphlets published in America between 1640 and 1800 appeared in the last thirty-five years of the eighteenth century. By eighteenth-century standards, levels of literacy, at least for white Americans in the North, were higher than almost any other place on earth and were rapidly climbing, especially for white women. All their reading made them enlightened. Jefferson was convinced that an American farmer rather than an English farmer had conceived of making the rim of a wheel from a single piece of wood. He knew it had to be an American because the idea had been suggested by Homer, and "ours are the only farmers who can read Homer."[16]

Unlike in England where conservative aristocrats opposed educating the masses for fear of breeding dissatisfied employees and social instability, American elites wholeheartedly endorsed education for ordinary people. American leaders issued a torrent of speeches and writings on the importance of popular education that has rarely been matched in American history or in the history of any other country. Their goal, as Benjamin Rush put it, was not to release the talents of individuals as much as it was to produce "one general and uniform system of education" in order to "render the mass of the people more homogeneous, and thereby fit them more easily for uniform and peaceable government."[17]

Formal schooling was only part of the educational process of rendering the people more homogeneous and enlightened. Because information of all sorts had to be spread throughout the sprawling nation, Americans began creating post offices faster than any other people in the world. One of the consequences of this expanding postal system was an astonishing increase in the circulation of newspapers. "In no other country on earth, not even in Great Britain," said Noah Webster, "are Newspapers so generally circulated among the body of the people, as in America." By 1810 Americans were buying over twenty-two million copies of 376 newspapers annually—even though half the population was under the age of sixteen and one-fifth was enslaved and prevented from reading. This was the largest aggregate circulation of newspapers of any country in the world.[18]

Because republics, as Benjamin Rush said, were naturally "peaceful and benevolent forms of government," Americans inevitably took the lead in promoting humane reforms. Jefferson in fact thought that America was the most compassionate nation in the world. "There is not a country on earth," he said, "where there is greater tranquillity, where the laws are milder, or better obeyed . . . , where strangers are better received, more hospitably treated, & with a more sacred respect."[19] In the several decades following the Revolution, Americans took very seriously the idea that they were peculiarly a people of sentiment and sensibility, more honest, more generous, more caring than other peoples.

They eagerly began creating charitable and humanitarian societies by the hundreds and thousands. Indeed, there were more such societies formed in the decade following the Revolution than were created in the entire colonial period. These multiplying societies treated the sick, aided the industrious poor, housed orphans, fed imprisoned debtors, built huts for shipwrecked sailors, and, in the case of the Massachusetts Humane Society, even attempted to resuscitate those suffering from "suspended animation"—that is, those such as drowning victims who appeared to be dead but actually were not. The fear of being buried alive was a serious concern at this time. Many, like Washington on his death bed, asked that their bodies not be immediately interred in case they might be suffering from suspended animation.

The most notable of the humanitarian reforms coming out of the Revolution involved new systems of criminal punishment. Jefferson and other leaders drew up plans for liberalizing the harsh and bloody penal codes of the colonial period. Since people learned from what they saw, the cruel and barbaric punishments of monarchies carried out in public, said Thomas Paine, hardened the hearts of their subjects and made them bloodthirsty. "It is [monarchy's] sanguinary punishments which corrupt mankind."[20] Maybe it was sensible for Britain to have over two hundred crimes punishable by death, for monarchies were based on fear and had to rely on harsh punishments. But, said Paine, republics were different. They were capable of producing a kinder and gentler people.

People were not born to be criminals, it was now said; they were taught to be criminals by sensuously experiencing the world around them. If the characters of people were produced by their environments, as Lockean liberal thinking suggested, perhaps criminals were not entirely responsible for their actions. Maybe impious and cruel parents of the criminal were at fault, or maybe even the whole society was to blame. "We all must plead guilty before the bar of conscience as having had some share in corrupting the morals of the community, and levelling the highway to the gallows," declared a New Hampshire minister in 1796.[21] If criminal behavior was learned, then perhaps it could be unlearned. "Let every criminal, then, be considered as a person laboring under an infectious disorder," said one writer in 1790. "Mental disease is the cause of all crimes."[22] If so, then it seemed that criminals could be salvaged, and not simply mutilated or executed.

These enlightened sentiments spread everywhere and eroded support for capital punishment in the new republican states. Not that the reformers had become soft on crime. Although Jefferson's code called for the death penalty only for treason and murder, he did propose the lex talionis, the law of retaliation, for the punishment of other crimes. So the state would poison the criminal who poisoned his victim, and would castrate men guilty of rape or sodomy; guilty women would have a half-inch hole bored through their noses. In Massachusetts in 1785 a counterfeiter was no longer executed. Instead, he was set in the pillory, taken to the gallows where he stood with a rope around his neck for a time, whipped twenty stripes, had his left arm cut off, and finally was sentenced to three years' hard labor.

Although most states did something to change their codes of punishment, Pennsylvania led the way in the 1780s and 1790s in the enlightened effort, as its legislation put it, "to reclaim rather than destroy," "to correct and reform the offenders" rather than simply to mark or eliminate them. Pennsylvania abolished all bodily punishments such as "burning in the hand" and "cutting off the ears" and ended the death penalty for all crimes except murder. In their place the state proposed a scale of punishments based on fines and years of imprisonment. Criminals were now to feel their personal guilt by being confined in prisons apart from the excited environment of the outside world, in solitude where, declared a fascinated French observer, the "calm contemplation of mind which brings on penitence" could take place.[23]

Out of these efforts was created the penitentiary, which turned the prison into what Philadelphia officials called "a school of reformation." By 1805 New York, New Jersey, Connecticut, Virginia, and Massachusetts had followed Pennsylvania in constructing penitentiaries based on the principle of solitary confinement. Nowhere else in the Western world, enlightened philosophers recognized, were such penal reforms carried as far as they were in America.[24]

Not only did the Americans believe that they possessed a more intelligent, more equal, more prosperous, and more compassionate society than those of other countries, they also thought that they were less superstitious and more rational than the peoples of the Old World. They had actually destroyed religious establishments and created a degree of religious liberty that European liberals could only dream about. Many Americans thought that their Revolution, in the words of the New York constitution of 1777, had been designed to end the "spiritual oppression and intolerance wherewith the bigotry and ambition of weak and wicked priests" had "scourged mankind."[25]

Although it was the proliferation of different religious groups that made possible this religious freedom, Americans generally did not celebrate their religious diversity; indeed, the fragmentation of religion in America appalled most people. Most Americans accepted differences of religion only insofar as these differences made toleration and freedom of conscience possible. Even an enlightened reformer like Jefferson hoped that eventually everyone would become a Unitarian.

Since refugees from the tyrannies of Britain and Europe were entering the United States in increasing numbers in the 1790s, Americans had every reason to believe that their country had become the special asylum of liberty. In the spring of 1794 the United Irishmen of Dublin sent the renowned scientist Joseph Priestley their best wishes as he fled from persecution in England to the New World. "You are going to a happier world—the world of Washington and Franklin. . . . You are going to a country where science is turned to better uses."

All of this immigration meant that representatives of all the peoples of Europe were present in America, which in turn helped to fulfill the fraternal dream of the Enlightenment, as Benjamin Rush described it, of "men of various countries and languages . . . conversing with each other like children of one father."[26] Not that American leaders celebrated the ethnic diversity of America in any modern sense. Far from it. What impressed the Revolutionary leaders was not the multicultural diversity of these immigrants but rather their remarkable acculturation and assimilation into one people. John Jay lived in New York City, the most ethnically and religiously diverse place in all America, and was himself three-eighths French and five-eighths Dutch, without any English ancestry. Nevertheless, Jay could declare with a straight face in *The Federalist* No. 2 that "Providence has been pleased to give this one connected country to one united people—a people descended from the same ancestors, speaking the same language, professing the same religion, attached to the same principles of government, very similar in their manners and customs and who, by their joint counsels, arms, and efforts . . . have nobly established general liberty and independence."[27]

The Revolutionary leaders' idea of a modern state, shared by enlightened British, French, and German eighteenth-century reformers as well, was one that was homogeneous, not one that was fractured by differences of language, ethnicity, and religion. Much of Europe in the eighteenth century was still a patchwork of small duchies, principalities, and city-states—nearly 350 of them. Even those nation-states that had begun consolidating were not yet very secure or homogeneous. England had struggled for centuries to bring Wales, Scotland, and Ireland under its control. Only in the Act of Union in 1707 had it created the entity known as Great Britain, and as events showed, its struggle to create a single nation was far from over. France was even worse off. Its eighteenth-century ancien régime was a still a hodgepodge of provinces and diverse peoples and by modern standards scarcely a single nation at all. Spain had just recently begun assimilating the kingdoms of Castile and Aragon into a single state, but the Basque provinces and Navarre still maintained an extraordinary degree of independence from the central monarchy.

European reformers everywhere wanted to eliminate these differences within their national boundaries and bind the people of their state together in a common culture. The American Revolutionary leaders were no different. They thought that Americans had become the most enlightened nation in the world precisely because they were a more rational and homogeneous society. They had done away with the various peasant customs, craft holidays, and primitive peculiarities—the morris dances, the charavaries, the bear-baiting, and other folk practices—that characterized the societies of the Old World. The New England Puritans had banned many of these popular festivals and customs, and elsewhere the mixing and settling of different peoples had worn most of them away. In New England, all that remained of Old World holidays was Pope's Day, November 5—the colonists' version of Guy Fawkes Day. Since enlightened elites everywhere regarded most of these different plebeian customs and holidays as remnants of superstition and barbarism, their relative absence in America seemed to be another sign of the new nation's enlightenment and oneness.[28]

In various ways, Americans appeared to be more of a single people than the nations of Europe. Nothing made enlightened eighteenth-century Americans prouder than the fact that most people in America spoke the same language and could understand one another everywhere. That this was not true in the European nations was one of the great laments of enlightened reformers in the Old World. Europeans, even those within the same country, were cut off from one another by their regional and local dialects. A Yorkshireman could not be understood in Somerset and vice versa. On the eve of the French Revolution, the majority of people in France did not speak French.

Americans by contrast could understand each other from Maine to Georgia. It was very obvious why this should be so, said John Witherspoon, president of the College of New Jersey (later Princeton). Since Americans were "much more unsettled, and mov[ed] frequently from place to place, they are not as liable to local peculiarities, either in accent or phraseology."[29]

In England, said Noah Webster, language was what divided the English people from one another. The court and the upper ranks of the aristocracy set the standards of usage and thus put themselves at odds with the language spoken by the rest of the country. America was different, said Webster. Its standard was fixed by the general practice of the nation, and therefore Americans had "the fairest opportunity of establishing a national language, and of giving it [more] uniformity and perspicuity . . . [than] ever [before] presented itself to mankind." Indeed, Webster was convinced that Americans already "speak the most pure English now known in the world." Within a century and a half, he predicted, North America would be peopled with a hundred million citizens, "all speaking the same language." Nowhere else in the world would such large numbers of people "be able to associate and converse together like children of the same family."[30]

Others had even more grandiose visions for the spread of America's language. John Adams was among those who suggested that American English would eventually become "the next universal language." In 1789 even a French official agreed; in a moment of giddiness he actually predicted that American English was destined to replace diplomatic French as the language of the world. Americans, he said, "tempered by misfortune," were "more human, more generous, more tolerant, all qualities that make one want to share the opinions, adopt the customs, and speak the language of such a people."[31] We can only assume that this Frenchman's official career was short-lived.

It was understandable that American English might conquer the world, because Americans were the only true citizens of the world. To be enlightened was to be, as Washington said, "a citizen of the great republic of humanity at large." The Revolutionary generation was more eager to demonstrate its cosmopolitanism than any subsequent generation in American history. Intense local attachments were common to peasants and backward peoples, but educated and enlightened persons were supposed to be at home anywhere in the world. Indeed, to be free of local prejudices and parochial ties was what defined an enlightened gentleman.

One's humanity was measured by one's ability to relate to strangers, to enter into the hearts of even those who were different. Americans prided themselves on their hospitality and their treatment of strangers. In America, as Crèvecoeur pointed out, the concept of "stranger" scarcely seemed to exist. "A traveller in Europe becomes a stranger as soon as he quits his own kingdom; but it is otherwise here. We know, properly speaking, no strangers; this is every person's country; the variety of our soils, situations, climates, governments, and produce hath something which must please everyone."[32]

The truth, declared Thomas Paine in *Common Sense*, was that Americans were the most cosmopolitan people in the world. They surmounted all local prejudices. They regarded everyone from different nations as their countrymen and ignored neighborhoods, towns, and counties as "distinctions too limited for continental minds."[33] Because they were free men, they were brothers to all the world.

These were the enlightened dreams of Americans two hundred years ago. Looking back from our all-knowing postmodern perspective, we can only marvel at the hubris and hypocrisy involved in the building of their enlightened empire of liberty. Precisely because the United States today has become the greatest and richest empire the world has ever known, we can see only the limits of their achievement and the failures of their imaginations. All their talk of enlightenment and the promise of America seems hypocritical in light of their unwillingness to abolish slavery, promote racial equality, and treat the native peoples fairly. But in fact it was the Americans' commitment to being enlightened that for the first time on a large scale gave them both the incentive and the moral capacity to condemn their own treatment of the Indians and Africans in their midst. However brutally white Americans treated Indians and Africans in the decades following the Revolution—and no one can deny the brutality—that treatment was denounced as a moral evil by more and more enlightened Americans in ways that had not been done in premodern pre-Enlightenment times.

Since these Enlightenment ideals still constitute the source of American nationhood, we need to understand them and their origins. Despite all our present talk of diversity and multiculturalism, we are, because of these Enlightenment ideals, still in the best position among the advanced democracies to deal with the massive demographic changes and movements taking place throughout the world. All the advanced democracies of Europe are finding it very difficult to assimilate immigrants and are experiencing serious crises of national identity. Whatever problems we have in this respect pale in comparison with those of the European nations.

We, of course, are not the only country to base its nationhood on Enlightenment values. France also claims to be grounded in universal Enlightenment principles. But, ironically, the French have taken the Enlightenment desire for a single homogeneous nation so seriously that their collective sense of national oneness leaves little room for the existence of Arab and other ethnic minorities. Precisely because America ultimately came to conceive of itself not as a single entity but as a nation of individuals—in our better moments, open to anyone in the world—it is better able to handle this explosive demographic future. The coming decades will test just how much of an enlightened nation of immigrants we Americans are willing to be.

AFTERWORD TO CHAPTER 10

In recent years historians have been approaching the Anglo-American Enlightenment in new ways. They have tended to conceive of it as much more than a movement involving reason and deism and the works of high-level philosophers like David Hume and Adam Smith. Instead, they have taken seriously what contemporaries thought being enlightened meant. It turns out contemporaries talked a great deal about the growth of what they called politeness and civility. Thus historians of eighteenth-century Anglo-American life have given a new significance to such mundane subjects as tea parties and letter writing. On this expanded conception of the Enlightenment, see Richard L. Bushman, *The Refinement of America: Persons, Houses, Cities* (1992); David S. Shields, *Civil Tongues and Polite Letters in British America* (1997); and Lawrence E. Klein, *Shaftesbury and the Culture of Politeness: Moral Discourse and Cultural Politics in Early Eighteenth-Century England* (1994).

This paper began as a lecture at the Institute of United States Studies at the University of London in 2002. It was revised and later published in *America and Enlightenment Constitutionalism*, edited by Gary L. McDowell and Johnathan O'Neill (New York: Palgrave Macmillan, 2006).

A HISTORY *of* RIGHTS *in* EARLY AMERICA

E AMERICANS TODAY talk all the time about rights—everyone has rights—and we believe that they trump all other claims and values. Much of the time we seem to regard our preoccupation with rights as something new, something recent, something that began with, say, the Warren Court and the civil rights movement. But our obsession with rights is not new at all. From the very beginning of our history we have been very rights conscious.

The history of rights in America began, as much of our history did, in England. It is not very fashionable these days to talk about the contributions of Western Europeans to American culture, but in the case of our preoccupation with rights, we owe most of our consciousness to our English heritage. The English had a concern for rights and a Bill of Rights long before our Bill of Rights of 1791. As Chief Justice Thomas Hutchinson told a Massachusetts grand jury in 1769, "The bare Mention of the Word *Rights* always strikes an Englishman in a peculiar manner."[1] Medieval and early modern Englishmen valued their rights to their personal liberty and property—rights that were embedded in their common law. The common law had deeply held principles, including, for example, the notions that no one could be a judge in his own cause and that no one, even the king, could legally take another's property without that person's consent. These rights and liberties belonged to all the people of England, and they adhered in each person as a person. Their force did not depend on their written delineation; they existed in the customary or unwritten law of England that went back to time immemorial.

It was not just the people who had rights; the king did too, usually referred to as the king's prerogatives. These prerogatives, or royal rights, to govern the realm were as old and sacred as the privileges and liberties of the people. In that distant medieval world, the king had sole responsibility to govern, to provide for the safety of his people, and to see that justice was done—that is, that the people's rights were protected. The king's courts were expected to adjudicate the law common to those courts and to the realm, hence the development of the term "common law."

The king's highest court of all—Parliament—arose sometime in the thirteenth century and was composed both of the feudal nobles that eventually became the House of Lords and of agents from the boroughs and counties of the realm that eventually became the House of Commons. Unlike the modern English Parliament, its medieval predecessor was convened by the king only sporadically and did not have as yet any direct responsibility for governing the country. Instead, its responsibility was mainly limited to voting supplies to the king to enable him to govern, presenting petitions to the king for the redress of popular grievances, and, as the highest court in the land, correcting and emending the common law so as to ensure that justice was done. This correcting and emending of the law was not regarded as legislation in any modern sense, for medieval men thought of law not as something invented but as something discovered in the customs and precedents of the past. The modern idea of law as the command of a legislative body was as yet inconceivable; indeed, law was equated with justice, and its purpose was to protect the rights of people from each other and from the king.

Thus the king had his rights to govern, and the people had their equally ancient and equally legitimate rights to their liberties and their property. Indeed, it is perhaps not too much to say that the whole of

English constitutional history can be seen as a struggle between these two competing sets of rights. The courts, including the high court of Parliament, were supposed to adjudicate between these conflicting sets of rights. Because the king, in trying to fulfill his responsibility of governing the realm, often infringed upon the customary rights of the people, the English periodically felt the need to have the king recognize their rights and liberties in writing. These recognitions in the early Middle Ages took the form of coronation oaths and assizes and charters issued by the crown. In 1215 the barons compelled King John to sign what became the most famous written document in English history—the great charter, or Magna Carta. In it the king explicitly acknowledged many of the customary rights of the English people, including the right of a freeman not to be imprisoned, exiled, or executed "unless by the lawful judgment of his peers, or by the law of the land." This meant a judgment by the common-law courts or by Parliament, the highest court in the land.

The succeeding centuries of English history saw more struggles over rights and more attempts by the English people to place limits on their kings. These struggles came to a climax in the seventeenth century. When, in 1627, King Charles I attempted to raise money by forced loans, five English knights resisted, and Charles had the resisters arbitrarily imprisoned. This in turn led to the popular reinvocation of the Magna Carta and the reiteration of the rights of a subject to his property and to no imprisonment without the legal judgment of his peers. In 1628 the House of Commons presented these grievances in a Petition of Right, which the king was compelled to accept.

Yet this hardly resolved the conflict between the rights of the king and the liberties of the people. Only after a bloody civil war and one king had been beheaded and another driven from his throne was the struggle between king and people finally settled, in the Glorious Revolution of 1688–1689. In 1688–1689 the Convention-Parliament set forth a Declaration of Rights that quickly became enshrined in English constitutionalism. In this listing of rights, which became a statute or a Bill of Rights when the new king, William III, approved them, Parliament declared illegal certain actions of the crown, including its dispensing with laws, using prerogative power to raise money, and maintaining a standing army without the consent of Parliament. At the same time, Parliament asserted certain rights and freedoms possessed by the English, including the right to bear arms, to petition the king, to have free elections and frequent Parliaments in which speech would be free, and to have no excessive bail or fines.[2]

It is important to understand that this delineation of rights in 1689 was an act of Parliament consented to by the king. The English Bill of Rights was designed to protect the subjects not from the power of Parliament but from the power of the king. Indeed, it was inconceivable that Parliament could endanger the subjects' rights. Only the crown could do that. As the highest court in the land, Parliament was therefore the bulwark and guardian of the people's rights and liberties; there was no point in limiting it. Consequently, there were no legal or constitutional restrictions placed on the actions of the English Parliament, and, despite the efforts of some British judges to invoke the declarations of the European Union, there are still none today, which makes the English Parliament one of the most powerful governmental institutions in the world.

So convinced were the English, in the decades following 1689, that tyranny could come only from a single ruler that they could hardly conceive of the people tyrannizing themselves. Once Parliament became sovereign, once the body that represented and spoke for them—the House of Commons—had gained control of the crown authority that had traditionally threatened their liberties, the English people lost much of their former interest in codifying and listing their personal rights. Since the people themselves now controlled the government, charters defining the people's rights, and contracts between the people and government, no longer made sense. If the high court of Parliament represented or embodied the whole nation, then its judgments became in effect the sovereign commands of the whole nation, and what formerly had been adjudication now became legislation binding everyone and encompassing everyone's rights. Since Parliament was the protector of the people's rights, it could be no threat to them.

. . .

BY THE TIME OF the American Revolution, most educated Britons had become convinced that their rights existed only against the crown. Against their representative and sovereign Parliament, which was the guardian of these rights, they existed not at all. Although the American colonists did not have quite the same confidence in Parliament that the English at home did, they did equally fear the powers of the crown and saw their own local representative assemblies as the bulwarks of their rights. Like the English in relation to Parliament, very few colonists saw any need to protect their rights from their colonial assemblies. Following the Zenger trial in 1735, for example, no royal governor dared bring a case of seditious libel against anyone. But the colonial assemblies, which presumably spoke for the people, continued to punish individuals for seditiously libeling the legislatures under the common law. In other words, liberty of the press existed against the crown but not against the representatives of the people; any libel against them was ipso facto seditious.[3]

In the 1760s and 1770s, during the crisis that eventually tore apart the British Empire, the American colonists had the long English heritage of popular rights to draw upon. Like all Britons, they were familiar with the persistent struggle of the English people to erect written barriers against encroaching crown power. Their own colonial past was littered with written documents delineating their rights. From the "Laws and Liberties" of Massachusetts Bay in 1648 to New York's "Charter of Liberties and Privileges" in 1683, the early colonial assemblies had felt the need to acknowledge in writing what William Penn called "those rights and privileges . . . which are the proper birth-right of Englishmen."[4]

As government and law stabilized in the eighteenth century, however, the need in the colonies for these sorts of explicit codifications of rights declined just as they had in the mother country. But the Englishman's instinct to defend his rights against encroachments of the governmental power of the crown was always latently present and was easily aroused. And getting the ruler to recognize these rights on paper was part of that instinct. By the time of the imperial crisis, it was natural for colonists like Arthur Lee of Virginia to call in 1768 for "a bill of rights" that would "merit the title of the Magna Carta Americana."[5]

Indeed, as historian John Reid has reminded us, the colonial resistance movement of the 1760s and 1770s was all about the colonists' defense of their rights as Englishmen.[6] By the eve of the Revolution, the charters that the crown had granted to many of the colonies in the previous century had come to be seen as just so many miniature Magna Cartas, designed, as one New Englander declared, "to reduce to a certainty the rights and privileges we were entitled to" and "to point out and circumscribe the prerogatives of the crown." Their several charters (or, where these were lacking, "their commissions to their governors have ever been considered as equivalent securities") had become transformed into what, "from their subject matter and the reality of things, can only operate as the evidence of a compact between an English King and the American subjects." These charters, continued Joseph Hawley of Massachusetts, were no longer franchises or grants from the crown that could be unilaterally recalled or forfeited: "Their running in the stile of a grant is mere matter of form and not of substance." They were reciprocal agreements "made and executed between the King of England, and our predecessors," contracts between ruler and people, outlining the rights of each but particularly the rights of the people.[7]

This imagined contract between the rights of the king and the people was not John Locke's contract, which was a contract among the people to form a society; instead, it was the Whig contract that ran through much of eighteenth-century English thinking and justified the people's obeying the prerogative decrees and edicts of the king. This contract was an agreement, legal or mercantile in character, between rulers and people—equal parties with equal sets of rights—in which protection and allegiance were the considerations. "Allegiance," wrote James Wilson in 1774, "is the faith and obedience, which every subject owes to his prince. This obedience is founded on the protection derived from government: for protection and allegiance are the reciprocal bonds, which connect the prince and his subjects." This allegiance was not the same as consent. "Allegiance to the king and obedience to the parliament," said Wilson, "are founded on very different principles. The former is founded on protection, the latter on representation. An inattention to this difference," said Wilson, "has produced . . . much uncertainty and confusion in our ideas concerning the connexion, which ought to subsist between Great Britain and the American colonies."[8]

ALL OF THIS CONTRACTUAL IMAGERY between two equal parties, not to mention the familial imagery of a patriarchal king and the mother country, suggested that for many eighteenth-century Anglo-Americans the public and private realms were still largely indistinguishable. Indeed, the colonists never regarded the struggle between the rights of the crown and the rights of the people as one between public and private rights. For even as late as the eve of the Revolution, the modern distinction between public and private was still not clear. The people's ancient rights and liberties were as much public as private, just as the king's rights—his prerogatives—were as much private as they were public. So-called public institutions had private rights and private persons had public obligations. The king's prerogatives, or his premier rights to govern the realm, grew out of his private position as the wealthiest of the wealthy and the largest landowner in the society; his government had really begun as an extension of his royal household. But in a like manner all private households or families—"those small subdivisions of Government," one colonist called them—had public responsibilities to help the king govern.[9]

All of this meant that the colonists were used to a great deal of communal or "public" control and management of what we today would call "private" rights. Governments in this premodern colonial society regulated all sorts of personal behavior, especially the moral and religious behavior of people, without any consciousness that they were depriving people of their private liberty or rights. Of the nearly 2,800 prosecutions in the superior and general sessions courts of Massachusetts between

1760 and 1774, over half involved sexual and religious offenses, such as fornication and using profanity. Many of the other prosecutions involved drunkenness, slander, and various violations of decency and good manners. At the same time, the colonial governments spent very little time on what we today would call public matters. Royal governors did not have legislative policies, and assemblies did not enact legislative programs. Many of the governments' activities were private, local, and adjudicative. The colonial assemblies still saw themselves more as courts making judgments rather than as legislatures making law. They spent a good deal of their time hearing private petitions, which often were the complaints of one individual or group against another. In historian William Nelson's survey of the Massachusetts General Court in 1761 ("as typical a year as any," he says), he could find "only three acts that were arguably legislative in the sense that they changed law or made new law."[10]

Indeed, to the colonists the separation of legislative, executive, and judicial powers that we value so greatly was far from clear. Since there was no modern bureaucracy and few modern mechanisms of coercion—a few constables and sheriffs scarcely constituted a police force—it was often left to the courts to exercise what governmental coercion there was and to engage in an extraordinary number of administrative and even legislative tasks, usually drawing on the communities for help.

Much of this judicial or magisterial activity—in fact, much of the government—was carried on without direct compensation. No one as yet conceived of politics as a paid profession or a permanent civil service. Most officeholding was still regarded, with varying degrees of plausibility, as a public obligation that private persons *"serving gratis or generously"* owed the community.[11] Every private person in the society had an obligation to help govern the realm commensurate with his social rank—the king's being the greatest because he stood at the top of the social hierarchy.

As legal historian Hendrik Hartog has written, all government in the colonial period was regarded essentially as the enlisting and mobilizing of the power of private persons to carry out public ends. "Governments," writes Hartog, "did not so much act as they ensured and sanctioned the actions of others."[12] If the eighteenth-century city of New York wanted its streets cleaned or paved, for example, it did not hire contractors or create a "public works" department; instead, it issued ordinances obliging each person in the city to clean or repair the street abutting his house or shop. In the same way, if the colony of Connecticut wanted a college, it did not build and run the college itself, but instead gave legal rights to private persons to build and run it—in short, creating what were called corporations.

Most public action—from the building of wharves and ferries to the maintaining of roads and inns—depended upon private energy and private funds. Governments were always short of revenue and instead tended to rely mostly on their legal authority to mobilize the community and compel private persons to fulfill public obligations. They issued sanctions against private persons for failure to perform their public duties, and they enticed private persons into fulfilling public goals by offering corporate charters, licenses, and various other legal immunities together with fee-collecting offices.[13] Since the government, including the king, was only one property holder in a world of property holders, it could not take "private" property for "public" purposes without the consent of the owner of that property; in other words, it had no modern power of eminent domain.

The Revolution was designed to dramatically change all this. By creating republics, Americans brought into play the tradition of neo-Roman Whig thinking that emphasized the collective public liberty of the people.[14] In stressing the power of the republican commonwealth in this way, Americans suddenly became much more conscious of private individual rights and interests that stood in opposition to the public good. Since the earlier mobilizing of "private" power for "public" ends was now viewed as "corruption"—that is, the exploitation of the "public" for "private" gain—it had to cease. It was now hoped that governments would no longer grant monopoly charters, licenses, and fee-collecting offices to private individuals in order to induce them to carry out public goals. Instead, the new republican leaders expected select individuals to become public servants working for the state and generally for a salary. State power in America began assuming some of its modern character as an autonomous entity capable of hiring agents to carry out public tasks. The Revolutionaries now claimed the primacy of the public good over all private individual rights and interests; indeed, it sought to separate the public from the private in a new manner and to prevent the former intrusion of private rights and interests into what was now seen as a distinct public realm. With such goals, Revolutionary Americans had to conceive of state power and individual liberty in radically new ways.

It would be difficult to exaggerate what this new idea of republican state power meant. No longer could government be seen as the exercise of someone's personal authority, as the assertion of prerogative rights or of the rights of those with economic and social superiority. Rulers suddenly lost their traditional personal rights to rule, and personal allegiance as a civic bond became meaningless. The long-existing Whig image of government as a contract between rulers and ruled disappeared virtually overnight. The Revolutionary state constitutions eliminated the crown's prerogatives outright or re-granted them to the state legislatures. These constitutional grants of authority, together with the expanded notion of consent underlying all government, gave the new state legislatures a degree of public power that the colonial assemblies had never claimed or even imagined. Although the new state assemblies, to the chagrin of many leaders, continued to act in a traditional courtlike manner— interfering with and reversing judicial decisions and passing private acts affecting individuals—they now became as well sovereign embodiments of the people with legislative responsibility for exercising an autonomous public authority.

In republican America, government would no longer be merely private property and private interests writ large as it had been in the colonial period. Public and private spheres that earlier had been mingled were now presumably to be starkly separated. *Res publica* became everything.

The new republican states saw themselves promoting a unitary public interest that was to be clearly superior to the many private interests and rights of the people.

At the beginning of the Revolution, few Americans imagined that there could be any real conflict between this unitary public good expressed by the representative state legislatures and the rights of individuals. When in 1775 a frightened Tory warned the people of Massachusetts that a popular revolutionary legislature could become as tyrannical as the crown and deprive the people of their individual liberties, John Adams dismissed the idea out of hand. That the people might tyrannize themselves and harm their own rights and liberties was illogical, declared Adams. "A democratic despotism is a contradiction in terms."[15]

With their new heightened sense of the public good, the Revolutionary republican legislatures were determined to bring what were seen as the private rights of selfish individuals under communal control. Many Americans now viewed with suspicion the traditional monarchical practice of enlisting private wealth and energy for public purposes. Especially objectionable was the issuing of corporate privileges and licenses to private persons. In a republic, it was said, no person should be allowed to exploit the public's authority for private gain. Indeed, several of the states wrote into their Revolutionary constitutions declarations, like that of New Hampshire, that "government is instituted for the common benefit, protection, and security of the whole community, and not for the private interest or emolument of any one man, family, or class of men." And some of the states, like North Carolina, declared that "perpetuities and monopolies are contrary to the genius of a State, and ought not to be allowed."[16]

Because they wanted to avoid any taint of corruption by allowing private individuals to undertake public tasks, the new republican state governments sought to assert their newly enhanced public power in direct and unprecedented ways—doing for themselves what they had earlier commissioned private persons to do. The state assemblies began legislating—making and changing law—as never before. Indeed, as Madison complained in

1787, the states passed more laws in the single decade following independence than they had in the entire colonial period. And these laws had less and less to do with private matters (moral and religious issues) and more and more with public matters (economic development and commercial convenience).

"Improvement" was on every Revolutionary's mind, and most leaders naturally assumed that the new state governments would take the lead in promoting it. The states now carved out exclusively public spheres of action and responsibility where none had existed before. They drew up plans for improving everything from trade and commerce to roads and waterworks and helped to create a science of political economy for Americans. And they formed their own public organizations with paid professional staffs supported by tax money, not private labor. The city of New York, for example, working under the authority of the state legislature, now set up its own public workforce to clean its streets and wharves instead of relying, as in the past, on the private residents to do these tasks. By the early nineteenth century, as Hartog has told us in a brilliant work of legal history, the city of New York had become a public institution financed primarily by public taxation and concerned with particularly public concerns. Like other post-Revolutionary governments, New York City acquired what it had not had before: the modern power of eminent domain—the authority to take private property for the sake of the public good without the consent of the particular property owner.[17]

Many thought that the new state legislatures, as the representatives of the people, could do for the public whatever the people entrusted them to do. Some argued that the needs of the public could even override the rights of individuals. Did not the collective power of the people expressed in their representative legislatures supersede the rights of the few? Of course, under monarchy the people could legitimately defend their rights against encroachments from the prerogative rights and privileges of the king. But in the new republics, where there were no more prerogative rights, could the people's personal rights meaningfully exist apart from the people's sovereign power expressed in their assemblies? In other words, did it any longer make sense to speak of negative liberty where the people's positive liberty was complete and supreme? To be sure, as the Pennsylvania constitution and other Revolutionary constitutions declared, "no part of a man's property can be justly taken from him, or applied to public uses, without his consent," but this consent, in 1776 at least, meant "that of his legal representatives."[18]

IN 1776 IT WAS NOT at all clear that people had rights against their own representatives. Five states drew up bills of rights in 1776, and several other states listed the people's rights in the bodies of their constitutions. But because the Revolutionary constitutions so circumscribed the governors or rulers, many of the states felt no need any longer to protect the people's rights by separately listing them; their popular legislatures were surely no danger to individual liberties. This accounts for the confusion Americans in 1776 had in not being entirely sure against whom their state bills of rights were directed. In English history, declarations of rights had been directed against the crown and its prerogatives. But in republican America, where there was no longer any crown or any prerogatives, did bills of rights make sense? What was the need of protecting the people's rights from themselves? Monarchies might become despotic, but democracies, when they ran to excess, could only become anarchical and licentious. Or so everyone since the ancient Greeks had assumed.

We know what happened. Within a decade, the democratic despotism and the threat to individual rights from popular legislatures that had seemed so illogical and contradictory to John Adams and other American Whigs in 1775–1776 had become only too real—at least for many gentry leaders. Consequently, many of these leaders were faced with the great constitutional dilemma of limiting popular government and protecting private property and individual rights without, at the same time, denying the sovereign public power of the majority of the people.

This dilemma led some Americans to think freshly about a number of constitutional issues, including those that justified the creation of a new federal Constitution in 1787. Most difficult of all was the formulating of a defense of individual rights and liberties against the people themselves—against Parliament, so to speak. There were no precedents for this in English history or in their own colonial histories. And they had to do all this in the face of their own republican revolutionary ideology—their belief in the autonomous power of the republican community to determine the public good.

It was not easy limiting the popular legislatures without denigrating the people and everything the American Revolution had been about. If the people weren't capable of protecting their own rights and liberties, then what was the value of republican government? Many realized only too keenly that the violations of individual rights in the 1780s did not arise because the people had been forsaken by their legislative representatives, but, as a Boston newspaper declared, those violations occurred because the people's "transient and indigested sentiments have been too implicitly adopted."[19]

James Madison certainly agreed. The rampaging legislatures of the 1780s, he said in 1787, were not acting against the will of the people; they were acting on behalf of that will. Unfortunately, the legislators were only too representative, only too democratic, reflecting only too accurately the narrow views and parochial outlooks of their constituents. Good republicans had not expected this at the outset of the Revolution. "According to Republican Theory," said Madison, "Right and power being both vested in the majority, are held to be synonimous." But experience since 1776 had shown the contrary. "Wherever the real power in a Government lies," he told his friend Thomas Jefferson, residing in Paris, "there is the danger of oppression. In our Governments the real power lies in the majority of the Community, and the invasion of private rights is chiefly to be apprehended, not from any acts of Government contrary to the sense of its constituents, but from acts in which the Government is the mere instrument of the major number of the constituents." As we have seen, that was why for Madison the crisis of the 1780s was truly frightening. The legislative abuses and the many violations of individual rights, he said, "brought into question the fundamental principle of republican Government, that the majority who rule in such governments are the safest Guardians both of public Good and private rights."²⁰

From his post in France, Jefferson scarcely grasped what Madison was saying. His confidence in the people was too great for him ever to question their judgment. Instead, in his mind he drew a distinction between the representative legislatures and the people themselves. Jefferson had no doubt that all officials in government, even the popularly elected representatives in the lower houses of the legislatures, could act tyrannically; "173 despots would surely be as oppressive as one," he said of the Virginia House of Delegates in 1785. "An *elective despotism* was not the government we fought for."²¹ But this kind of tyranny was not really the people's fault. Jefferson always thought that the people themselves, if undisturbed by demagogues like Patrick Henry, would eventually set matters right. He saw little potential conflict between positive and negative liberty, between the people at large and individual rights. He was one of those who paid no attention to what Madison called that "essential distinction, too little heeded, between assumptions of power by the General Government, in opposition to the will of the constituent body, and assumptions by the constituent body through the Government as the organ of its will."²² For Jefferson, it could never be the people themselves but only their elected agents that were in error.

Whatever doubts American leaders had privately about the virtue or good sense of the people, few of them by 1787 were willing to express such doubts publicly. Questioning the judgment of the people themselves had become too politically risky for most. Hence publicly, at least, they began drawing the same distinction between the people and their elected delegates as Jefferson had, and sought to exploit that distinction in their efforts to curb the state legislatures. Indeed, that distinction became the basis of all the major arguments mounted by the defenders of the new Constitution in 1787–1788, or the Federalists, as they called themselves. Confronted with arguments from the opponents of the Constitution, or the Anti-Federalists, that raised the question of where sovereignty—the final supreme indivisible lawmaking authority—would lie under the new

Constitution, the Federalists, as we have seen, denied that sovereignty would be taken away from the state legislatures and given to the Congress. Unlike Britain, where sovereignty rested with the king-in-Parliament, sovereignty in America, they said, belonged to no institution of government, including the so-called houses of representatives, or even to all of the institutions together; it remained with the people themselves. In America, representative government could never fully embody the people.

By opening up and exaggerating the distinction between the sovereign people and their elected governments, the Federalists tended to homogenize political power and turn all government officials, in both the state and federal governments, into equally mistrusted agents of the people. Once people came to regard all political power as essentially similar, once they came to view all governmental officials, whether executive, judicial, or even legislative, as, in Jefferson's words, "three branches of magistracy," equally mistrusted, then it became possible to protect individual rights from the popularly elected legislatures without doing violence either to the Americans' republican theory or even to their English heritage. For hadn't the English always sought to protect their rights from the magistracy of the crown?[23]

Leaders anxious about individual liberties and the rights of property could now identify the popular legislatures with the former monarchical or magisterial power (which is what they meant by the term "democratic despotism"), and they could invoke the traditional language of the rights of the English in these new republican circumstances.

Not every American, of course, was willing to follow this line of thinking, and many opponents of the Constitution rose in defense of the peculiar popular character of the state legislatures and denied that their will could be limited in any way. After all, they represented the people. But now the Federalists had a ready answer to this traditional argument. In *The Federalist*, Alexander Hamilton rebuked these defenders of the state legislatures by caustically observing that "the representatives of the people, in a popular assembly, seem sometimes to fancy that they are the people themselves." And he went on to suggest ways the people's rights embodied in the constitutions could be protected from the legislatures—by relying on other agents of the people, the courts. Since the people created constitutions, not the legislatures, it could never "be supposed," he said, "that the constitution could intend to enable the representatives of the people to substitute their *will* to that of their constituents. It is far more rational to suppose that the courts were designed to be an intermediate body between the people and the legislature, in order, among other things, to keep the latter within the limits assigned to their authority."[24]

Already many others besides Hamilton had begun looking to the once-feared judiciary as a principal means of restraining the rampaging and unstable popular legislatures. Why not? It was just another kind of agent of the people, after all, ideally situated to protect the people's rights against the oppressive actions of some of their other agents in the legislatures. As early as 1786, William Plummer, a future U.S. senator and a governor of New Hampshire, concluded that the very "existence" of America's elective governments had come to depend upon the judiciary: "That is the only body of men who will have an effective check upon a numerous Assembly."[25]

Thus was launched the massive rethinking out of which in a matter of decades emerged America's strong independent judiciary, a judiciary that became primarily concerned with protecting individual rights. In the years following the Revolution, judges shed their earlier broad and ill-defined political and magisterial roles and adopted ones that were much more exclusively legal. They withdrew from politics, promoted the development of law as a mysterious science known best by trained experts, and restricted their activities to the regular courts, which became increasingly professional and less burdened by popular juries. Many of those who were suspicious of democracy thought that this withdrawal from politics made the judiciary a far better protector of the rights of individuals than the popular legislatures could ever hope to be. As early as 1787, Alexander Hamilton argued in the New York assembly that the state constitution prevented anyone from being deprived of his rights except "by the law of the land" or, as a recent act of the assembly had put it, "by due process of law," which, said Hamilton, in an astonishing and novel twist, had "a precise technical import": these words were now "only applicable to the process and proceedings of the courts of justice; they can never be referred to an act of legislature," even though the legislature had written them.[26]

The view expressed by Hamilton did not, of course, immediately take hold. The attorney general of North Carolina, for example, argued in 1794 that the clauses of the state constitution referring to due process and the law of the land were not limitations on the legislature; they were "declarations the people thought proper to make of their rights, not against a power they supposed their own representatives might usurp, but against oppression and usurpation in general . . . by a pretended prerogative against or without the authority of law." Thus the phrase that no one could be deprived of his property except by the law of the land meant simply "a law for the people of North Carolina, made or adopted by themselves by the intervention of their own legislature." This view was accepted by the North Carolina superior court.[27]

It is not surprising that the argument Hamilton put forth in 1787 was opposed by others, for his argument was truly extraordinary, to say the least—one of the first of many imaginative readings in our history to be given to that important phrase "due process of law." Parliament, which included the House of Commons, had always protected the rights of the English, including their property rights, from the crown's encroachments. That was what the Bill of Rights of 1689 had been all about. But the English had never thought it necessary to protect these rights from the power of the people themselves—that is, from the legislative power of Parliament. Blackstone had agreed that one of the absolute rights of an individual was "the right of property: which consists in the free use, enjoyment and disposal of all his acquisitions, without any control or diminution, *save only by the laws of the land.*"[28]

Of course, for Blackstone the laws of the land included those laws enacted by the legislature (Parliament). Not so any longer for Hamilton and many other Americans. As far as many Americans were concerned, the legislatures had become legally or constitutionally no different from the former crown. But, as brilliant as some of the Federalists' arguments were, it was never easy to see popularly elected legislatures as threats to individual rights. And since the Federalists tended to be conventional supporters of strong government, they themselves were confused. Because their opponents, the Jeffersonian Republicans, had so often invoked the "rights of man" against the oppressions of government, some Federalists could only conceive of retaliating in traditional terms—by seeking a strengthening of government against the licentiousness of the people whose rights had run amok. But other shrewder Federalists saw that they might be better off appropriating the rights talk of their Jeffersonian opponents and using it in their own behalf against the popular power of the state legislatures. Indeed, they perceived that the liberties of individuals—that is, negative liberty—could actually be turned against positive liberty or self-government. In the United States, the laws of the land were not just what the popular legislatures commanded; indeed, some laws, it seemed, were not under the purview of the legislatures at all.

Many Federalists now argued that the laws of the land concerning individual rights belonged exclusively to the courts. And the reason they belonged exclusively to the courts was that they involved private matters, not public, and private matters concerning individual rights required adjudication, not legislation. As legal historian William Nelson has pointed out, the courts in the early Republic became eager to leave "to legislatures the resolution of conflicts between organized social groups"—that is, conflicts of politics—and instead to concentrate on protecting the rights of individuals.[29]

Those Federalists and even those Republicans who were worried about democratic despotism and the legislative abuses of private rights argued that the popular state legislatures should stick to the great public responsibilities of being a republic and not "take up private business, or interfere in disputes between contending parties," as the colonial assemblies had habitually done. The evils of such legislative meddling were "heightened when the society is divided among themselves;—one party praying the assembly for one thing, and opposite party for another thing. . . . In such circumstances, the assembly ought not to interfere by any exertion of legislative power, but leave the contending parties to apply to the proper tribunals [that is, to the judiciary] for a decision of their differences."[30]

These efforts to separate private issues from public ones, to remove some questions from legislative politics and transform them into contests of individual rights, contributed to the emergence of a powerful independent judiciary in the early Republic. Almost overnight the judiciary in America became not only the principal means by which popular legislatures were controlled and limited but also the most effective instrument for sorting out individual disputes within a private sphere that the other institutions of government were forbidden to enter.

BY CARVING OUT an exclusively public sphere for the promotion of republican state power, the Revolutionaries had necessarily created a private sphere as well—a private sphere of individual rights that was to be the domain solely of judges. The idea that there was a sphere of private rights that lay absolutely beyond the authority of the people themselves, especially in a republican government, was a remarkable innovation. Few colonists had ever believed that there were individual rights that could stand against the united will of the community expressed in its representative assemblies. But the Revolution had prepared Americans to accept this innovation in their conception of rights. And it had done so with its radical commitment to the right of religious freedom. Once Americans were able to limit state authority in religious matters—an area of such importance that no state had hitherto ever denied itself the power to regulate— they set in motion the principle that there were some realms of private rights and individual liberties into which executives and legislatures had no business intruding. If formerly public religious corporations created by the state became private entities immune from further state tampering, then why couldn't other formerly public corporations be treated in a like manner?[31]

Indeed, that's what happened, as the economy of the early Republic became privatized, which meant turning public responsibilities into private rights. As Oscar and Mary Handlin, Louis Hartz, and others pointed out six or seven decades ago, the new Revolutionary states had expected to involve themselves directly in the economy. But the states attempted to do more than they could handle. As Hartz wrote in reference to Pennsylvania, "[T]he objectives of the state in the economic field were usually so broad that they were beyond its administrative powers to achieve."[32] And not just beyond its administrative powers, but its fiscal powers as well. Because the new democratically elected legislatures were often unwilling to raise taxes to pay for all that the governmental leaders desired to do, the states were forced to fall back on the traditional premodern monarchical practice of enlisting private wealth to carry out public ends. Instead of doing the tasks themselves, as many devout republicans had expected, the states ended up doing what the crown and all premodern governments had done, granting charters of incorporation to private associations and groups to carry out a wide variety of endeavors presumably beneficial to the public: in banking, transportation, insurance, and other enterprises. The states did not intend to abandon their republican responsibility to promote the public good; they simply lacked the money to do it directly. And, of course, there were many private interests that were only too eager to acquire these corporate privileges.

Yet because of the republican aversion to chartered monopolies, the creation of these corporations did not take place without strenuous opposition and heated debate. As a consequence, these corporations were radically transformed. The popular state legislatures began giving out these charter rights freely to a variety of clamoring interests, religious groups as well as business groups. If a group in Boston received a bank charter, then a group in Newburyport wanted one too; and then other groups in both cities requested and received bank charters as well. Before long there were chartered banks all over the state of Massachusetts. Not only did the number of corporations rapidly multiply, but their earlier monopolistic privileged character changed as well. Whereas all the colonies together had chartered only about a half dozen business corporations, the new states began creating them in astonishing numbers, numbers that were unmatched anywhere else in the world. From an exclusive privilege granted at the behest of the state to a few highly visible, socially distinguished recipients to carry out a public purpose, corporate charters eventually became an equal right available to virtually everyone. The states issued 11 charters of incorporation between 1781 and 1785, 22 more between 1786 and 1790, and 114 between 1791 and 1795. Between 1800 and 1817 they created nearly 1,800 corporate charters. With this multiplication not only was the traditional exclusivity of the corporate charters destroyed, but the public power of the state governments was also dispersed. If "government, unsparingly and with an unguarded hand, shall multiply corporations, and grant privileges without limitation," then, declared a concerned Governor Levi Lincoln of Massachusetts, sooner or later "only the very shadow of sovereignty" would remain.[33]

At the same time as these corporations increased in number and shed their exclusivity, they lost much of their earlier public character as well and were more and more regarded as private property. As private property—as rights vested by the legislatures in private individuals—these corporations now became exempt from further legislative interference. This idea that the corporate charter was a species of private property was expressed early. "In granting charters," declared William Robinson in the Pennsylvania assembly in 1786 in defense of the charter of the Bank of North America, "the legislature acts in a ministerial capacity"; that is, it acted as the crown had acted in mobilizing private resources for public purposes. This bestowing of charters, said Robinson, "is totally distinct from the power of making laws, and it is a novel doctrine in Pennsylvania that they can abrogate those charters so solemnly granted." There was a difference between laws and charters. Laws were general rules for the whole community; charters "bestow particular privileges upon a certain number of people. . . . Charters are a species of property. When they are obtained, they are of value. Their forfeiture belongs solely to the courts of justice."[34] This argument did not convince the Pennsylvania assembly in 1786, but it was a brilliant anticipation of what was to come.

The more the state legislatures could be demonized as monarch-like tyrants, the more their grants could be regarded as rights vested in individuals that could not be taken back by the legislatures. "The proposition that a power to do, includes virtually, a power to undo, as applied to a legislative body," wrote Hamilton in 1802, "is generally but not universally true. All *vested* rights form an exception to the rule."[35] This protection of vested rights, as Edward S. Corwin once pointed out, became "the basic doctrine of American constitutional law."[36] So much had legislative grants seem to have become contracts that Senator Gouverneur Morris used the analogy to oppose the Jeffersonian Republicans' elimination of the circuit court positions created by the Federalists' Judiciary Act of 1801. When you give an individual the right to make a toll road or bridge, said Morris, "can you, by a subsequent law, take it away? No; when you make a compact, you are bound by it."[37] This thinking prepared the way for the argument that corporations were actually contracts immune from state tampering by the contract clause in Article I, Section 10 of the Constitution, a position eventually endorsed by the Supreme Court in the *Dartmouth College* case in 1819.

Of course, many resisted these efforts to turn chartered corporations into species of private property. Jefferson may have been especially dedicated to equal rights, but he did not believe that a corporate charter was one of those rights. To his dying day he never accepted the idea that corporations were private property that could not be touched or modified by the legislative body that chartered them. That idea, he said, "may perhaps be a salutary provision against the abuses of a monarch, but is most absurd against the nation itself." Others agreed. "It seems difficult to conceive of a corporation established for merely private purposes," declared a North Carolina judge in 1805. "In every institution of that kind the ground of the establishment is some public good or purpose to be promoted."[38] This increasing stress on the need for a "public purpose" behind the state's activity, however, only worked to further privatize the business corporations. Eventually people felt compelled to distinguish between corporations such as banks, bridges, and insurance companies that were now considered private because they were privately endowed, and those such as towns or counties that remained public because they were tax-based. Even in Massachusetts, which retained its established church until 1833, religious dissenters transformed religious corporations into private voluntary associations that acted beyond the state but were entitled to legal recognition and protection by the state.[39]

There was a curious paradox in these developments. Just as the public power grew in these years of the early Republic, so too did the private rights of individuals. Those who sought to protect the rights of individuals did not deny the public prerogatives of the states. Instead, they drew boundaries around the rights of private individuals, including business corporations, which judges eventually transformed into private, rights-bearing "persons." In fact, the heightened concern for the private vested rights of persons was a direct consequence of the enhanced public power the republican Revolution had given to the states and municipalities. The bigger the public domain, the bigger the private domain of private rights had to be to protect itself. Although the power of the federal government certainly declined in the decades following Jefferson's election as president, the public authority and the police powers and regulatory rights of the states and their municipalities grew stronger.

Separating the political from the legal, the public from the individual, actually allowed for more vigorous state action as long as that action served what was called a "public purpose." Individuals may have had rights, but the public had rights as well—rights that grew out of the sovereignty of the state and its legitimate power to police the society. The state of New York, for example, remained deeply involved in the society and economy. Not only did the state government of New York distribute its largess to individual businessmen and groups in the form of bounties, subsidies, stock ownership, loans, corporate grants, and franchises, but it also assumed direct responsibility for some economic activities, including building the Erie Canal.[40] Even when the states, lacking sufficient tax funds, began dissipating their modern public power by reverting to the premodern practice of enlisting private wealth to carry out public ends by issuing increasing numbers of corporate charters, they continued to use their ancient police power to regulate their economies. Between 1780 and 1814, the Massachusetts legislature, for example, enacted a multitude of laws regulating the marketing of a variety of products—everything from lumber, fish, tobacco, and shoes, to butter, bread, nails, and firearms. The states never lost their inherited responsibility for the safety, economy, morality, and health of their societies.[41] The idea that there was a public good that could interfere with some private rights remained very much alive.

Despite all this state police power legislation and municipal regulation, however, it was usually left to the courts to sort out and mediate the conflicting claims of public authority and the private rights of individuals. The more the state legislatures enacted statutes to manage and regulate the economy, the more judges found it necessary to exert their authority in order to do justice between individuals and to make sense of what was happening. Following the lead of William Blackstone and Lord Mansfield in eighteenth-century England, American judges in the early Republic interpreted the common law flexibly in order to mitigate and correct the harm done by the profusion of conflicting statutes passed by unstable democratic legislatures.[42] Judges were often able to play down the importance of precedents and to emphasize instead reason, equity, and convenience in order to bring the law into accord with changing commercial circumstances.[43]

They were able to do this and to expand their authority by transforming many public issues of the economy into private ones, turning political questions into questions of individual rights that could only be judicially determined. If an enterprising and improving society needed certainty in the law, then the courts seemed more capable than popular legislatures in assuring it. The success of the courts in promoting commercial and economic development in the early Republic was due in large part to their ability to separate the legal issues of individual rights from the tumultuous and chaotic world of democratic politics. As Chief Justice John Marshall said in his *Marbury* decision of 1803, some questions were political; "they respect the nation, not individual rights," and thus were "only politically examinable" by elected legislatures. But questions involving the vested rights of individuals were different; they were in their "nature, judicial, and must be tried by the judicial authority."[44] But these efforts to protect the rights of individuals from political abuse were not just Federalist-inspired. Even the strongly Jeffersonian Virginia court of appeals in 1804 took the position that the state legislature could do many things, but it could not violate private and vested rights of property.[45]

In the late 1780s, Madison had yearned for some enlightened and impartial men who would somehow transcend the interest-group politics that plagued the state legislatures. In *The Federalist* No. 10 he had used judicial imagery in describing the problems of America's legislative politics. Madison accepted the fact that the regulation of different commercial interests had become the principal task of modern legislation. This meant, he wrote, that in the future the spirit of party and faction was likely to be involved in the ordinary operations of government. Since in traditional fashion he continued to think of all legislative acts as "so many judicial determinations, not indeed concerning the rights of single persons, but concerning the rights of large bodies of citizens," he could only conclude pessimistically that legislators would become "both judges and parties at the same time." The best solution he could offer to prevent these parties from becoming judges in their own causes and violating the rights of individuals and minorities was to enlarge the arena of politics so that no party could dominate, thus allowing only disinterested and impartial men to exercise power and make decisions. He hoped against hope that the new elevated federal government might assume a judicial-like character and become a "disinterested and dispassionate umpire in disputes between different passions and interests" within the individual states.[46] By the early decades of the nineteenth century, he, along with many other Americans, came to the conclusion that perhaps the judiciary was the only governmental institution that even came close to playing this role. It is a conclusion that in our history we have reached time and time again.

AFTERWORD TO CHAPTER II

This paper is actually a revised composite of several different lectures and articles. It began as a lecture at the American Antiquarian Society in October 1991 celebrating the bicentennial of the Bill of Rights. This lecture was later published in the *Proceedings of the American Antiquarian Society*, 101, Part 2 (1992), 255–274. Some of the material in that paper found its way into the McCorkle Lecture given at the University of Virginia School of Law in March 1999, and was later published as "The Origins of Vested Rights in the Early Republic" in the *Virginia Law Review*, 85 (1999), 1421–1445. This article was in turn heavily revised and presented as a lecture at Colgate University in 2001 and published as "The History of Rights in Early America" in *The Nature of Rights at the American Founding and Beyond*, edited by Barry Alan Shain (Charlottesville: University of Virginia Press, 2007), 233–257. Anyone interested in the development of rights in early America can do no better than to consult the other papers in this volume, all written by distinguished political scientists and historians.

The AMERICAN REVOLUTIONARY TRADITION, *or* WHY AMERICA WANTS *to* SPREAD DEMOCRACY AROUND *the* WORLD

THE REVOLUTION BEGAN on April 19, 1775, with, as Emerson put it in the mid-nineteenth century, a "shot heard round the world." That, in fact, was how the nineteenth century saw the Revolution—as an event of worldwide significance. It was an event that opened up a new era in politics and society, not just for Americans but eventually for everyone in the world. It is a perspective on the American Revolution not always grasped, even by Americans, and it is the perspective of this essay.

It was "America's destiny," said the Hungarian patriot Louis Kossuth in 1852, "to become the cornerstone of Liberty on earth." "Should the Republic of America ever lose this consciousness of this destiny," Kossuth went on in a speech given while he was in the United States trying to raise money for the 1848 Hungarian revolution, "that moment would be just as surely the beginning of America's decline as the 19th of April 1775 was the beginning of the Republic of America."

I don't know if that moment of decline is at hand or not, but in the aftermath of September 11 and our involvement in Iraq and Afghanistan, we are certainly at a significant moment in our history. We now dominate the world as no nation in history ever has. Our military expenditures are nearly equal to those of all the other nations in the world put together. We have over a million men and women under arms and we have troops in at least forty countries. This may not be an empire in the traditional meaning of that term, but it is an extraordinary degree of dominance over the world that we are exercising. Is this the fulfillment of our destiny, as Kossuth saw it, to build liberty everywhere? Or is it a repudiation of our destiny? Have we lost our consciousness of being the bearers of liberty? Have we become just another great imperial power? Did our invasion of Iraq in order to bring democracy to the Middle East mark the end of our Revolutionary tradition, or, instead, was it the fulfillment of it?

It is hard for many people to think of the United States as a revolutionary nation operating out of a revolutionary tradition. For the past six or seven decades or more the United States has so often stood on the side of established governments and opposed to revolutionary movements that to describe America as a revolutionary state seems to be an oxymoron. So reactionary did many intellectuals think American policy was during the Cold War that they could only conclude that our involvement in the world was due solely to American capitalism and its needs. Many people continue to believe that our involvement in the Middle East can be explained simply in terms of oil. No doubt such economic explanations can make sense of particular events at particular times, but they cannot do justice to the incredibly complicated and ideological relationship we have had with the rest of the world throughout our history. Economic considerations, for example, can never adequately explain America's tragic involvement in Vietnam. But America's revolutionary tradition can.

The Revolution is important to us Americans for many reasons, not least because it gave us our obsessive concern with our own morality and our messianic sense of purpose in the world. In short, the Revolution made us an ideological people.

We do not like to think of ourselves as an ideologically minded people. Ideology seems to have no place in American thinking. The word even sounds European. It conjures up systems of doctrinaire ideas and dogmatic, abstract theories. It could hardly have much to do with the practical, pragmatic people we Americans have generally thought ourselves to be. And certainly ideology, it used to be thought, could not have been involved in that most practical of revolutions—the American Revolution.

Few historians of the Revolution believe that anymore. It now seems clear that the Revolution was very much an ideological movement, involving a fundamental shift in ideas and values. In fact, I would go so far as to say that the American Revolution was as ideological as any revolution in modern Western history, and as a consequence, we Americans have been as ideological-minded as any people in Western culture.

Of course, we Americans have vaguely known all along that we are peculiarly dedicated to intellectual principles, and that adherence to these intellectual principles has been the major adhesive holding us together. We Americans do not have a nationality the way other peoples do. Our sense of being a distinct ethnicity was not something we could take for granted, the way most Europeans could—which of course is why we can absorb immigrants more easily than they can. A nation like ours, made up of so many races and ethnicities, could not assume its identity as a matter of course. The American nation had to be invented or contrived.

At the end of the Declaration of Independence, the members of the Continental Congress mutually pledged to each other their lives, their fortunes, and their sacred honor. There was nothing else but themselves they could dedicate themselves to—no patria, no fatherland, no nation as yet.

In comparison with the 235-year-old United States, many European states are new, some created in the twentieth century. Yet these European states, new as they may be, are undergirded by peoples who had a preexisting sense of their own distinctiveness, their own nationhood. In the United States, the process was reversed. We Americans created a state before we were a nation, and much of our history has been an effort to define the nature of that nationality. In an important sense, we have never been a nation in any traditional meaning of the term. It is the state, the Constitution, the principles of liberty, equality, and free government that make us think of ourselves as a single people. To be an American is not to be someone, but to believe in something.

What is the nature of this ideology created by the American Revolution? Looking back from our vantage point at the beginning of the twenty-first century, what strikes me as most extraordinary about the Revolution is the world-shattering significance the Revolutionaries gave to it. In light of the fact that we did eventually become the greatest power the world has ever seen, it requires an act of imagination to recover the audacity and presumptuousness of Americans in 1776 in claiming that their little colonial rebellion possessed universal importance. After all, those thirteen colonies made up an insignificant proportion of the Western world, numbering perhaps two million people, huddled along a narrow strip of the Atlantic coast, three thousand miles from the centers of civilization. To believe that anything they did would matter to the rest of the world was the height of arrogance. Yet the Revolutionaries and their heirs in the nineteenth century sincerely believed that they were leading the world toward a new libertarian future. Our conception of ourselves as the leader of the free world began in 1776.

What made this presumptuous attitude possible, what made Americans in 1776 think they were on the edge of a new era in history, pointing the way toward a new kind of politics and society and a new sort of world, what, in short, transformed their Revolution into something more than a colonial rebellion was the revolutionary ideology of republicanism.

It has been only in the past generation or so that we have come to understand just how ideologically charged with republicanism the eighteenth century was. (For the term "republicanism" we today have to substitute the word "democracy," or we won't understand what was meant in the eighteenth century. After all, the Chinese today live in a republic, as do the Syrians and the Cubans. And for monarchy we have to think of authoritarian governments, since a good proportion of the states of Western Europe are monarchies.) Where republicanism today is taken so much for granted and where much of the monarchy that remains seems so benign, it is difficult to appreciate the power republicanism had for eighteenth-century intellectuals. Indeed, republicanism was as radical for the eighteenth century as Marxism was for the nineteenth. Republicanism and the republican tradition framed for all sorts of political and social critics of eighteenth-century Europe the moral perspective with which they confronted the dominant monarchism and materialism of the age.

This republicanism was not an indigenous ideology peculiar only to Americans, but was in fact a product of a long-existing heritage of civic humanism, originating in the classical Latin literature of antiquity—with Livy, Cicero, Tacitus, Sallust, and others—revived by Machiavelli and others in the Renaissance and carried into the eighteenth century by nearly everyone who claimed to be enlightened. These republican values articulated most vociferously but not exclusively by the popularizers and heirs of the seventeenth-century republicans—Harrington, Milton, and Sidney—promised far more than the elimination of kings and new elective governments. Republicanism, in fact, promised an entirely new morality. It necessarily involved the character and culture of the society and thus possessed immense significance for any people who should decide to become republican.

Everyone in the eighteenth century knew that republicanism required a special kind of people, a people who possessed virtue, who were willing to surrender their private interests for the sake of the whole. As we have seen in the earlier essays in this collection, monarchy or authoritarian governments were so prevalent because they were based on the assumption that people were incapable of this kind of virtue. Monarchy presumed that people were selfish and corrupt and that without the existence of the strong, unitary authority of monarchy, the society would fall apart. Theorists of the eighteenth century like Montesquieu would have understood perfectly what happened in the Soviet Union and in Yugoslavia in the 1990s when a strong unitary authority was removed. They would have understood too why the states of Iraq and Afghanistan and elsewhere are having such trouble sustaining themselves. People assert their various selfish ethnicities, religions, and interests, and the society cannot hold together and falls apart. Montesquieu would have said that the people of these states lacked sufficient virtue to hold their societies together.

Monarchies thus had advantages that republics lacked, which is why they have existed everywhere since the beginning of history and why authoritarian governments still flourish around the world. Monarchies were utterly realistic or cynical about human nature. Supporters of monarchy did not expect humans to be anything but corrupt and selfish. Authoritarian kings possessed a number of means for holding their diverse and corrupt societies together. Monarchies had powerful single executives, a multitude of offices, complicated social hierarchies, titles of honor, standing armies, and established churches to maintain cohesion.

But republics possessed few of the adhesive attributes of monarchies. Therefore, order, if there were to be any in republics, would have to come from below, from the virtue or selflessness of the people themselves. Yet precisely because republics were so utterly dependent on the people, they were also the states most sensitive to changes in the moral character of their societies. In short, republics were the most delicate and fragile kinds of states. There was nothing but the moral quality of the people themselves to keep republics from being torn apart by factionalism and division. Republics were thus the states most likely to experience political death.

To the eighteenth century the decay and death of states seemed as scientifically grounded as the decay and death of human beings. "It is with states as it is with men" was a commonplace of the day. "They have their infancy, their manhood, and their decline." The study of the life cycle of states, focusing on political disease, was of central concern to the Enlightenment, for through such political pathology, people could further their knowledge of political health and prevent the process of decay. With these kinds of concerns, the whole world, including the past, became a kind of laboratory in which the sifting and evaluating of empirical evidence would lead to an understanding of social sickness and health. Political science became a kind of diagnostics, and history became an autopsy of the past. Those states that had died would be cut open, so to speak, and examined in order to discover why they had died.

Of course, the most important states that had died were the republics of antiquity, especially the ancient republic of Rome. The death of Rome fascinated eighteenth-century thinkers. Almost every intellectual, including Montesquieu, tried his hand at writing about the decline and fall of Rome. Reading the great Latin writers of antiquity, the eighteenth century came to realize that the Roman republic became great not simply by the force of its arms; nor was it destroyed by military might. Both Rome's greatness and its eventual fall were caused by the character of its people. As long as the Roman people maintained their love of virtue, their simplicity and equality, their scorn of great distinctions, and their willingness to fight for the state, they attained great heights of glory. But when they became too luxury-loving, too obsessed with refinements and social distinctions, too preoccupied with money, and too effeminate to take up arms on behalf of the state, their politics became corrupted, selfishness predominated, and the dissolution of the state had to follow. Rome fell not because of the invasions of the barbarians from without, but because of decay from within.

The lesson for the Revolutionaries in 1776 was obvious. If their experiment in republicanism were to succeed, the American people had to avoid the luxury and corruption that had destroyed ancient Rome. They had to be a morally virtuous people.

Americans had good reason to believe that they were ideally adapted for republican government. Most of them, at least the white portion, were independent yeoman farmers, Jefferson's "chosen people of God," who were widely regarded as the most incorruptible sorts of citizens and the best foundation for a republic. There were no titled aristocrats in America and none of the legal distinctions and privileges that encumbered the European states. All in all, Americans in 1776 thought they were the special kind of simple, austere, egalitarian, and virtuous people that enlightened social science said was essential for the sustenance of a republic. Their moral quality thus became a measure of their success as a society, and this inevitably gave their new Republic an experimental and problematical character.

The Americans thus began their Revolution in a spirit of high adventure. They knew they were embarking on a grand experiment in self-government. That experiment remained very much in doubt during the first half of the nineteenth century, especially during the Civil War, when monarchy still dominated all of Europe. Hence we can understand the importance of Lincoln's Gettysburg Address, in which he described the Civil War as a test of whether a nation conceived in liberty could long endure. This idea that republican government was a perilous experiment was part of America's consciousness from the beginning.

All of this republican ideology assumed tremendous moral force. When fused with Protestant millennialism, it gave Americans the sense that they were chosen people of God, possessing peculiar qualities of virtue, with a special responsibility to lead the world toward liberty and republican government.

Americans began their experiment in republicanism with very high hopes that other peoples would follow their lead in throwing off monarchy. But they also knew that it wouldn't be easy, since republicanism required a particular moral quality in its people. Naturally, at first they saw the French Revolution as a copy of their own Revolution, and they welcomed the effort. Lafayette sent the key to the Bastille to Washington in gratitude for America's having inspired the French Revolution. But its rapid perversion and excesses, ending in Napoleonic despotism, disillusioned many Americans about the ability of Europeans to emulate them in becoming republican. They came to see the French Revolution as simply an abortive attempt to imitate the successful American effort at establishing republicanism. Far from changing things for the better in Europe, the French Revolution had failed. And thus the Americans' optimism about the future was tempered by doubts.

These doubts soon played into American attitudes toward the Latin

American colonial rebellions that broke out in the early decades of the nineteenth century. If any revolutions were emulations of the American Revolution, these certainly seemed to be. And, of course, Americans like John Adams and Thomas Jefferson welcomed them. But at the same time they were skeptical of the South Americans' ability to create free republican governments. Did they have the stuff, the virtue, that republicans were made of? "I feared from the beginning," wrote Jefferson in 1821, "that these people were not as yet sufficiently enlightened for self-government; and that after wading through blood and slaughter, they would end in military tyrannies, more or less numerous. Yet as they wished to try the experiment [in republicanism], I wish them success in it."

Thus Americans from the outset had an ambiguous attitude toward republican revolutions in other parts of the world. Naturally there was no hostility, only sympathy and enthusiasm mixed with some skepticism, a well-wishing mingled with a kind of patronizing pessimism bred of an anxiety that other peoples would not have the sort of social and moral qualities necessary to carry through a successful republican revolution. Nevertheless, Americans continued to believe that they, and not the French, were the revolutionary nation par excellence.

And some Europeans agreed with them. Count Metternich, the chief minister of the Austrian-Hungarian Empire, excoriated the United States for proclaiming in 1823 the Monroe Doctrine, which told the Europeans that they no longer had any role to play in the New World:

> In their indecent declarations [these United States] have cast blame and scorn on the institutions of Europe most worthy of respect. . . . In permitting themselves these unprovoked attacks, in fostering revolutions wherever they show themselves, in regretting those which have failed, in extending a helping hand to those which seem to prosper, they lend new strength to the apostles of sedition and re-animate the courage of every conspirator. If this flood of evil doctrines and pernicious examples should extend over the whole of America, what would become of

our religious and political institutions, of the moral forces of our governments, and of the conservative system which has saved Europe from complete dissolution?

Despite promising not to intervene in Europe's internal affairs and expressing a desire to have no entangling alliances with Europe, most Americans remained very concerned with what went on there. Yet they were reluctant to get directly involved in any revolutionary ventures that might endanger their own republican experiment. Believing that people who were ready for republicanism would sooner or later become republicans as they had, Americans in the nineteenth century concluded that they could best accomplish their mission of bringing free governments to the rest of the world simply by existing as a free government, by being an exemplar to the world.

William Wirt of Virginia put this very nicely in a speech in Baltimore in 1830. "We stand under a fearful responsibility to our Creator and our fellow citizens," Wirt told his audience. "It has been his divine pleasure that we should be sent forth as the harbinger of free government on the earth, and in this attitude we are now before the world. The eyes of the world are upon us; and our example will probably be decisive of the cause of human liberty."

So Americans watched and encouraged all the nineteenth-century revolutions. They did not intervene in deed, but they did in every other way. Individuals raised money for the rebels and some went off to fight on behalf of revolutionary movements. In all the European revolutions of the century—the Greek revolt of 1821, the French constitutional transformation of 1830, the general European insurrections of 1848, and the overthrow of the Second French Empire and the establishment of the Third French Republic in 1870—the United States was usually the first state in the world to extend diplomatic recognition to the new revolutionary regimes.

After all, in the Americans' eyes these European revolutions were simply efforts by oppressed peoples to become like them, all species of the same revolutionary *genus Americanus*. Americans never felt threatened by these revolutions and had no fear whatsoever of the spread of revolutionary ideas. There was, of course, one exception to this enthusiasm for revolution: the Haitian revolution that created in 1804 the second republic in the New World. We did not recognize the Haitian republic until Lincoln's administration. But we welcomed all the others and toasted those revolutionary patriots like Kossuth when they came to America in search of money and support.

Naturally, this encouragement of revolution did not endear us to the European monarchies. But nineteenth-century Americans in their geographical separation simply did not care. We were proud of our revolutionary example and simply assumed that we were the cause of all the revolutionary upheavals in nineteenth-century Europe. When the Hapsburg monarchy protested American sympathy with the Hungarian revolution of 1848, Secretary of State Daniel Webster did not resort to any traditional polite diplomatic evasion. Quite the contrary—he claimed nothing less than full American responsibility for the upheavals. He told the Austrian Hungarian minister in Washington "that the prevalence on the other continent of sentiments favorable to republican liberty is the result of the reaction of America upon Europe; and the source and center of that reaction has doubtless been, and now is, in these United States." Webster then went on to add, in one of those gratuitous insults for which American diplomatic messages in the nineteenth century were famous, that in comparison with the great extent of the United States, the Hapsburg monarchy was "but a patch on the earth's surface."

Because nineteenth-century Americans frequently resorted to such spread-eagled bombast but actually did very little to aid the revolutions, many historians have concluded that America's revolutionary sympathy was something of a fraud. But I think such a conclusion misunderstands the peculiar character of America's nineteenth-century revolutionary tradition. Because of their republican assumptions, Americans believed that any revolution in Europe would have to come from the oppressed peoples themselves and from the moral force of America's example as a republic.

But they never had any doubt that America was the center of the international revolution. This American ethnocentricity is mind-boggling. The best example I know of is a message from President Grant to the French government sent in response to the French overthrow of the Second Empire and the establishment of the Third Republic in 1870. Despite America's determination not to intervene in Europe's affairs, President Grant told the French, "We cannot be indifferent to the spread of American political ideas in a great and civilized country like France." It was as if France had no revolutionary tradition of its own to call on. One wonders what the officials at the French foreign office thought of this extraordinary message.

Because of the slowness with which republicanism spread, however, nineteenth-century Americans increasingly concluded that they were destined to be the only successful republican state in a corrupt world. Millions of people in the world seemed to think so too. The migration to the United States between 1820 and 1920 of over thirty-five million refugees from monarchism gave the Americans' conception of themselves as a chosen people a less divine and more literal meaning and confirmed for them their preeminence as a revolutionary people.

It is within this nineteenth-century context, this revolutionary tradition of republicanism, and this belief of Americans that they were in the vanguard of history leading the world toward liberty that we can begin to comprehend the extraordinary American reaction to the Russian Revolution of 1917. In the full sweep of American history up to that time, no foreign event had such a dramatic and searing effect on Americans as did the Bolshevik revolution of November 1917. After that momentous event, our understanding of ourselves and the world became very confused.

At first, with the March 1917 overthrow of the tsar and the formation of the provisional government, Americans welcomed the Russian Revolution as they had welcomed earlier antimonarchical European revolutions. Seven days after the tsar abdicated, the United States extended diplomatic recognition to the new Russian government, the first power in the world to do so. President Wilson now thought he had "a fit partner for a league of honor," a league which Wilson hoped would be a means for the worldwide extension of republicanism. In May 1917 the American ambassador in Moscow wrote back to the United States that he expected Russia to come out of its ordeal "as a republic, and with a government . . . founded on correct principles"—that is to say, principles similar to those of the American Republic.

Yet with the Bolshevik takeover of the revolution in the fall of 1917, all this initial American enthusiasm quickly disappeared. Instead of the Russian Revolution's firmest friend, the United States suddenly became its most bitter enemy. Instead of quickly extending diplomatic recognition to the new republican regime, as American governments had traditionally done throughout the nineteenth century, the United States withheld diplomatic recognition from the Soviet Union for sixteen years and four American presidencies, making the United States not the first but the last major Western power to recognize the revolutionary regime.

In light of America's earlier revolutionary tradition, this was a remarkable turnabout—a turnabout, however, that is explicable only in terms of that earlier revolutionary tradition. What was now different, what caused this abrupt change of attitude, was the nature of the Bolshevik appeal, the new character of the communist ideology. The Russian Revolution was not another species of the revolutionary *genus Americanus*; it was a new revolutionary genus altogether. The Bolsheviks claimed not simply to be leading another antimonarchical republican revolution in emulation of the American or French models of the late eighteenth century. The Bolsheviks said that their communist revolution represented a totally new departure in world history. Others saw what this meant. The Swiss playwright and essayist Herman Kesser said in 1918 that "it is [now] certain that mankind must make up its mind either for Wilson or for Lenin."

The great antagonism that immediately sprang up between the United States and the Soviet Union rested not simply on the exigencies of power politics, or the circumstances of contrasting marketing systems, but, more important, on the competitiveness of two very different revolutionary traditions. The Cold War really began in 1917. The Soviet Union threatened nothing less than the displacement of the United States from the vanguard of history. The Russians, not the Americans, now claimed to be pointing the way toward the future (and, more alarming still, there were some American intellectuals in the 1920s and 1930s who agreed with that claim).

For the first time since 1776, Americans were faced with an alternative revolutionary ideology with universalist aspirations equal to their own. This ideological threat was far more serious to us than anything the Russians did technologically, either in developing the H-bomb or in launching Sputnik. For it seemed to make America's heritage irrelevant. If we Americans were not leading the world toward liberty and free government, what then was our history all about?

With this dramatic emergence of an opposing revolutionary ideology, Americans in the twentieth century grew more and more confused about themselves and their place in history. They could not very well stand against the idea of revolution, but at the same time they could no longer be very enthusiastic about revolutions that they assumed would be communist. With the enunciation of the Truman Doctrine in 1947, the United States for the first time in its history committed itself to supporting established governments of "free peoples" against the threat from subversion from "armed minorities"—presumably communist—within the state. Our Cold War struggle with the Soviet Union eventually culminated in our disastrous intervention in Vietnam in the 1960s. Most Americans thought they were simply following President Kennedy's call in 1961 to "pay any price, bear any burden, meet any hardship, support any friend or oppose any foe to assure the survival and the success of liberty." Only this time, support for liberty meant supporting an existing government against revolution.

The fundamental threat to the meaning of our history posed by a rival revolutionary ideology blinded us to the nationalistic and other ethnocultural forces at work in the world. In such an atmosphere it became difficult for us not to believe that every revolution was in some way communist, and consequently our definition of "free" governments was stretched to extraordinary lengths to cover eventually any government that was noncommunist. The ironies, of course, are abundant: we Americans spent ten years between 1979 and 1989 helping the Taliban in Afghanistan withstand a Soviet takeover.

It would be a mistake, however, to see our support of corrupt or reactionary regimes as the direct response of American capitalism or as the result of some deep-rooted abhorrence of revolution. Many of our Cold War actions, clumsy and misguided as they often may have been, represented our confused and sometimes desperate efforts to maintain our universalist revolutionary aspirations in the world.

Our Point Four Program accompanied the Truman Doctrine; the Peace Corps coincided with our involvement in Vietnam. All were linked; all were cut from the same ideological cloth; all were expressions of what was becoming an increasingly dimly perceived sense of America's revolutionary mission in the world.

Suddenly, in 1989, this all changed. The Soviet Union collapsed; with it, its revolutionary aspirations to make the world over as communist collapsed as well. Joel Barr, an American engineer who had defected to the Soviet Union in 1950, told a *Los Angeles Times* reporter in 1992 that he had been wrong about communism. "I believe that now history will show that the Russian Revolution was a tremendous mistake. It was a step backward," he said. "The real revolution for mankind that will go down for many, many years was the American Revolution."

We're living at an extraordinary moment in our history. It is not at all clear what the consequences of the momentous events we're living through will be. At first September 11 seemed to have increased, not weakened, our desire to dominate the world. President George W. Bush came into office opposed to nation building. Then he became determined to do just that in Iraq. Lots of intelligent Americans, like Tom Friedman of the *New York Times* and the editors of the *New Republic*, initially welcomed the idea of bringing democracy to the Middle East. But after a long, frustrating struggle, we are now merely hoping against hope that as we get out of Iraq, it will become perhaps not a democracy but at least a functioning state. In Afghanistan we don't even talk about democracy. All we can hope for there is the establishment of a reasonably stable state capable of resisting the Taliban, or perhaps not even that—just a state capable of resisting Al Qaida. These Middle East wars seem to have drained away most of our idealism about changing the world. Yet what is happening in Egypt and elsewhere in the Middle East is reviving the hope of democracy re-emerging in the region, however tenuously.

We seem to be very much an all-or-nothing people. It is very difficult for us to maintain a *realpolitik* attitude toward the world. We have to be either saving the world or shunning it. In the 1990s some intellectuals were bitterly opposed to any of the messianic impulses coming out of our revolutionary tradition. Some, including Irving Kristol, thought that we had become a middle-aged nation not all that different from the nations of Europe. But still others, such as Secretary of State Madeleine Albright, contended that we were still the indispensable nation. Now, at the beginning of the second decade of the twenty-first century, we seem to be in a quandary about what to do, about what our role in the world ought to be. We remain the sole superpower but still unsure of quite how to use that power.

What the future will be is impossible to tell. All we can do with our history is to remember that the United States has always been to ourselves and to the world primarily an idea. However many troops we can muster around the world will mean little if, in using them, we erode that idea, that moral authority which is the real source of our strength and our ability to gain the admiration and support of other peoples.

Our revolutionary heritage still commands the attention of many people in the world—our devotion to liberty and equality, our abhorrence of privilege, our fear of abused political power, our faith in constitutionalism and individual liberties. This was brought home to me over three decades ago at a talk I gave in Warsaw in 1976—during the bicentennial of the American Revolution. It was an incident that I will never forget. It was well before the end of the Cold War, even several years before the emergence of Solidarity, the movement in 1980 that was the beginning of the end of communism in Poland.

At the end of my very ordinary lecture on the American Revolution, a young Polish intellectual rose to tell me that I had left out the most important part. Naturally, I was stunned. She said I had not mentioned the Bill of Rights—the constitutional protection of individual liberties against the government. It was true. I had taken the Bill of Rights for granted. But this young Polish woman living under a communist regime could not take individual rights for granted.

We forget—we take for granted—the important things. This example of the Polish intellectual showed me that our republic was still a potent experiment in liberty worth demonstrating to the rest of the world. We can only hope that that idea of America will never die.

ACKNOWLEDGMENTS

Since these essays were written at various times over the past half century,
I have incurred a host of debts that I can never adequately repay. The
individuals who have helped over the decades are too many to name, but
they certainly include the administrative staff of the History Department
at Brown University; I am grateful to all of the staff through the years,
and most recently Karen Mota, Cherrie Guerzon, Mary Beth Bryson,
and Julissa Bautista. My former editor at Penguin and now agent, Scott
Moyers, has been especially helpful. He is a brilliant editor, and he is
responsible for the titles of several of my books, including this one. I
can't thank him enough. Laura Stickney, my new editor at Penguin, has
been encouraging and patient, with a keen eye for what's appropriate and
what's not, and I am grateful for her able assistance in bringing out this
book. I am grateful too for Cathy Dexter's excellent copyediting. I am also
very grateful to Barbara Campo at Penguin for all of her help in seeing the
book into production. Of course, I owe the most to my editor in chief, my
wife, Louise, who has borne with me all these years.

NOTES

INTRODUCTION

1. Isaiah Berlin, *The Hedge and the Fox: An Essay on Tolstoy's View of History* (New York: Simon and Schuster, 1953), 1–2.

2. James H. Broussard, "Historians and the Early Republic: SHEAR's Origins and Prospects," *Journal of the Early Republic*, II (1982), 66.

3. Winthrop D. Jordan, *White Over Black: American Attitudes Toward the Negro, 1550–1812* (Chapel Hill: University of North Carolina Press, 1968); James M. Banner Jr., *To the Hartford Convention: The Federalists and the Origins of Party Politics in Massachusetts, 1789–1815* (New York: Knopf, 1970).

4. Broussard, "Historians and the Early Republic," 66.

5. William Nesbit Chambers, *Political Parties in a New Nation: The American Experience, 1776–1809* (New York: Oxford University Press, 1963); Seymour Martin Lipset, *The First New Nation: The United States in Historical and Comparative Perspective* (New York: Basic Books, 1963).

6. On the differing historical views of the early Republic, see Gordon S. Wood, "The Significance of the Early Republic," *Journal of the Early Republic*, VIII (1988), 1–20, from which some of this introduction is derived.

7. Jim Cullen, review of Gordon Wood's *Empire of Liberty: A History of the Early Republic, 1789–1815* (New York: Oxford University Press, 2009), on *History News Network*, December 1, 2009.

8. See in particular Richard Hofstadter, *The Progressive Historians: Turner, Beard, Parrington* (New York: Knopf, 1968). Before his untimely death in 1970, Hofstadter planned a multivolume history of the late eighteenth through early nineteenth centuries—the very period that fascinated his mentors. What he completed of his first volume was published posthumously as *America in 1750: A Social Portrait* (New York: Knopf, 1971).

9. Among the best of these was Dixon Ryan Fox, *The Decline of Aristocracy in the Politics of New York* (New York: Columbia University Press and Longmans, Green and Co., 1919).

10. For a summary of this anti-Progressive literature, see Bernard Bailyn, "Political Experience and Enlightenment Ideas in Eighteenth-Century America," *American Historical Review*, LXVII (1962), 339–351.

11. Edward Pessen, *Most Uncommon Jacksonians: The Radical Leaders of the Early Labor Movement* (Albany: State University of New York Press, 1967); Douglas T. Miller, *Jacksonian Aristocracy: Class and Democracy in New York, 1830–1860* (New York: Oxford University Press, 1967).

12. Richard Hofstadter, *The American Political Tradition and the Men Who Make It* (New York: Knopf, 1951), esp. 44–66; Bray Hammond, *Banks and Politics in America: From the Revolution to the Civil War* (Princeton: Princeton University Press, 1957).

13. Louis Hartz, *The Liberal Tradition in America* (New York: Harcourt, Brace, 1955).

14. Richard D. Brown, *Modernization: The Transformation of American Life, 1600–1865* (New York: Hill and Wang, 1976).

15. It was these headline events of politics and diplomacy that Henry Adams concentrated on in his classic account of the period. Henry Adams, *History of the United States of America During the*

Administrations of Thomas Jefferson and James Madison, 9 vols. (New York: Charles Scribner's Sons, 1889–1891).

16. See, for example, Mary Beth Norton, *Liberty's Daughters: The Revolutionary Experience of American Women, 1750–1800* (Boston: Little, Brown, 1980); Nancy F. Cott, *The Bonds of Womanhood: "Woman's Sphere" in New England, 1780–1835* (New Haven, CT: Yale University Press, 1977); Lee Chambers-Schiller, *Liberty, a Better Husband: Single Women in America: The Generations of 1780–1840* (New Haven, CT: Yale University Press, 1984); Joan M. Jensen, *Loosening the Bonds: Mid-Atlantic Farm Women, 1750–1850* (New Haven, CT: Yale University Press, 1986); Donald M. Scott, *From Office to Profession: The New England Ministry, 1750–1850* (Philadelphia: University of Pennsylvania Press, 1978); Gerard W. Gawalt, *The Promise of Power: The Emergence of the Legal Profession in Massachusetts, 1760–1840* (Westport, CT: Greenwood Press, 1979); W. J. Rorabaugh, *The Craft Apprentice: From Franklin to the Machine Age in America* (New York: Oxford University Press, 1986); Patricia Cline Cohen, *A Calculating People: The Spread of Numeracy in Early America* (Chicago: University of Chicago Press, 1982); Carl F. Kaestle, *Pillars of the Republic: Common Schools and American Society, 1780–1860* (New York: Hill and Wang, 1983); W. J. Rorabaugh, *The Alcoholic Republic: An American Tradition* (New York: Oxford University Press, 1979); Paul G. Faler, *Mechanics and Manufacturers in the Early Industrial Revolution: Lynn, Massachusetts, 1780–1860* (Albany: State University of New York Press, 1981); Sean Wilentz, *Chants Democratic: New York City and the Rise of the American Working Class, 1788–1850* (New York: Oxford University Press, 1984); Cynthia J. Shelton, *The Mills of Manayunk: Industrialization and Social Conflict in the Philadelphia Region, 1787–1837* (Baltimore: Johns Hopkins University Press, 1986); Paul Gilje, *The Road to Mobocracy: Popular Disorder in New York City, 1763–1834* (Chapel Hill: University of North Carolina Press, 1987); James H. Merrell, *The Indians' New World: Catawbas and Their Neighbors from European Contact Through the Era of Removal* (Chapel Hill: University of North Carolina Press, 1989); David Brion Davis, *The Problem of Slavery in the Age of Revolution, 1770–1823* (Ithaca, NY: Cornell University Press, 1975); Richard R. John, *Spreading the News: the American Postal System from Franklin to Morse* (Cambridge, MA: Harvard University Press, 1995); William E. Nelson, *Americanization of the Common Law: The Impact of Legal Change in Massachusetts Society, 1760–1830* (Cambridge, MA: Harvard University Press, 1975); Morton J. Horwitz, *The Transformation of American Law, 1780–1860* (Cambridge, MA: Harvard University Press, 1977); Donald A. Hutslar, *The Architecture of Migration: Log Construction in the Ohio Country, 1750–1850* (Athens, OH: Ohio University Press, 1986).

17. On the topics of research emerging in the historiography of the early Republic, see John Lauritz Larson and Michael A. Morrison, eds., *Whither the Early Republic: A Forum on the Future of the Field* (Philadelphia: University of Pennsylvania Press, 2005).

18. James Henretta, "Families and Farms: Mentalité in Pre-Industrial America," *William and Mary Quarterly*, 3rd ser., 35 (1978), 3–32; Christopher M. Jedrey, *The World of John Cleaveland: Family and Community in Eighteenth-Century New England* (New York: W. W. Norton, 1979); Allan Kulikoff, *The Agrarian Origins of American Capitalism* (Charlottesville: University Press of Virginia, 1992). Crucially important for dating the changes in the Northern economy is Winifred Barr Rothenberg, *From Market-Places to a Market Economy: The Transformation of Rural Massachusetts, 1750–1850* (Chicago: University of Chicago Press, 1992).

19. Daniel T. Rodgers, "Republicanism: The Career of a Concept," *Journal of American History*, LXXIX (1992), 25.

20. T. H. Breen, *American Insurgents, American Patriots: The Revolution of the People* (New York: Hill and Wang, 2010), 11.

21. Sir Lewis Namier, *Personalities and Powers* (London: Hamish Hamilton, 1955), 2.

22. For a fuller explanation of the view of the role of ideas in human experience, see Gordon S. Wood, "Intellectual History and the Social Sciences," in John Higham and Paul K. Conkin, eds., *New Directions in American Intellectual History* (Baltimore: Johns Hopkins University Press, 1979), 27. My approach to the role of ideas has been very much influenced by the work of Quentin Skinner. See James Tully, ed., *Meaning and Context: Quentin Skinner and His Critics* (Princeton: Princeton University Press, 1988). For concrete examples of Skinner's approach applied to history, see "The Principles and Practice of Opposition: The Case of Bolingbroke versus Walpole," in Neil

McKendrick, ed., *Historical Perspectives: Studies in English Thought and Society in Honour of J. H. Plumb* (London: Europa, 1974), 93–128, and John Brewer, *Party Ideology and Popular Politics at the Accession of George III* (Cambridge, UK: Cambridge University Press, 1976), 26–38.

23. Claude G. Bowers, *Jefferson and Hamilton: The Struggle for Democracy in America* (Boston: Houghton Mifflin, 1925), vi, 140.

24. For a major example, see Garry Wills, *"Negro President": Jefferson and the Slave Power* (Boston: Houghton Mifflin, 2003).

25. Doron Ben-Artar and Barbara B. Oberg, eds., *Federalists Reconsidered* (Charlottesville: University of Virginia Press, 1998), 10, 11. Of course, there were Southern Republicans who favored Jefferson's ideas of minimal government because they tended to lessen the threat to slavery, but to contend that the liberal late eighteenth-century Anglo-American belief in minimal government was fed by that concern alone is to grossly misunderstand the period. Radicals like Thomas Paine and William Godwin believed deeply in minimal government, and no one has accused them of being front men for slavery.

26. Gordon S. Wood, "The Creative Imagination of Bernard Bailyn," in James A. Henretta et al., eds., *The Transformation of Early American History: Society, Authority, and Ideology* (New York: Knopf, 1991), 38.

27. For examples of heavy-handed present-mindedness in histories of the early Republic, see Lawrence Goldstone, *Dark Bargain: Slavery, Profits, and the Struggle for the Constitution* (New York: Walker, 2005); and Robin L. Einhorn, *American Taxation, American Slavery* (Chicago: University of Chicago Press, 2006). For my review of these two works, see Gordon S. Wood, *The Purpose of the Past: Reflections on the Uses of History* (New York: Penguin, 2008), 293–308.

28. Thomas Jefferson to Benjamin Waterhouse, June 26, 1822, in Merrill D. Peterson, ed., *Thomas Jefferson: Writings* (New York: Library of America, 1984), 1459.

CHAPTER I, RHETORIC AND REALITY IN THE AMERICAN REVOLUTION

1. This is the title of a recent essay by Edmund S. Morgan in Arthur M. Schlesinger Jr. and Morton White, eds., *Paths of American Thought* (Boston: Houghton Mifflin, 1963), 11–33.

2. Samuel E. Morison, ed., "William Manning's *The Key of Libberty*," *William and Mary Quarterly*, 3rd ser., XIII (1956), 208.

3. Edmund S. Morgan, "The American Revolution: Revisions in Need of Revising," *William and Mary Quarterly*, 3rd ser., XIV (1957), 14.

4. William Vans Murray, *Political Sketches, Inscribed to His Excellency John Adams* (London: C. Dilly, 1787), 21, 48.

5. Daniel Leonard, *The Origin of the American Contest with Great-Britain...[by] Massachusettensis...* (New York: James Rivington, 1775), 40; Douglass Adair and John A. Schutz, eds., *Peter Oliver's Origin and Progress of the American Rebellion: A Tory View* (San Marino: Huntington Library, 1961), 159.

6. Simeon Baldwin, *An Oration Pronounced Before the Citizens of New-Haven, July 4th, 1788...* (New Haven, CT: J. Meigs, 1788), 10; [Murray], *Political Sketches*, 48; David Ramsay, *The History of the American Revolution* (Philadelphia: R. Aitken & Son, 1789), I, 350.

7. Thomas Paine, *Letter to the Abbé Raynal...* (1782), in Philip S. Foner, ed., *The Complete Writings of Thomas Paine* (New York: Citadel Press, 1945), II, 243; John Adams to H. Niles, February 13, 1818, in Charles Francis Adams, ed., *The Works of John Adams* (Boston: Little, Brown, 1850–1856), X, 282.

8. William Pierce, *An Oration, Delivered at Christ Church, Savanah, on the 4th of July, 1788...* (Savannah, GA: James Johnston, [1788]), 6; Enos Hitchcock, *An Oration; Delivered July 4th, 1788...* (Providence, RI: Bennett Wheeler, [1788]), 11.

9. Petition to the King, October 1774, in Worthington C. Ford, ed., *Journals of the Continental Congress, 1774–1789* (Washington, DC: U.S. Government Printing Office, 1904–1937), I, 118.

10. Samuel Williams, *The Natural and Civil History of Vermont...* (Walpole, NH: Isaiah Thomas and David Carlisle Jr., 1794), vii, 372–373; Pierce, *Oration...4th July, 1788*, 8.

11. Moses Coit Tyler, *The Literary History of the American Revolution, 1763–1783* (New York: G. P. Putnam's Sons, 1897), I, 8–9.

12. For a bald description of the assumptions with which this generation of historians worked, see Graham Wallas, *Human Nature in Politics*, 3rd ed. (New York: Knopf, 1921), 5, 45, 48–49, 83, 94, 96, 118, 122, 156.

13. Charles A. Beard, *An Economic Interpretation of the Constitution* (New York: Macmillan, 1935), x, viii.

14. While the Progressive historians were attempting to absorb and use the latest scientific techniques of the day, nonbehaviorists in government departments and others with a traditional approach to political theory—men like Andrew C. McLaughlin, Edwin S. Corwin, William S. Carpenter, Charles M. McIwain, and Benjamin F. Wright—were writing during this same period some of the best work that has ever been done on Revolutionary constitutional and political thought. However, because most of them were not, strictly speaking, historians, they never sought to explain the causes of the Revolution in terms of ideas.

15. Carl L. Becker, *The Declaration of Independence: A Study in the History of Political Ideas* (New York: Harcourt, Brace, 1922), 133, 203, 207.

16. Quoted in Philip Davidson, *Propaganda and the American Revolution, 1763–1783* (Chapel Hill: University of North Carolina Press, 1941), 141, 150, 373.

17. Arthur M. Schlesinger Jr., *Prelude to Independence: The Newspaper War on Britain, 1764–1776* (New York: Knopf, 1958), 34. For examples of the scientific work on which the propagandist studies drew, see note 1 in Sidney I. Pomerantz, "The Patriot Newspaper and the American Revolution," in Richard B. Morris, ed., *The Era of the American Revolution* (New York: Columbia University Press, 1939), 305.

18. Davidson, *Propaganda*, 59; Schlesinger, *Prelude to Independence*, 20.

19. Davidson, *Propaganda*, xiv, 46.

20. Schlesinger, *Prelude to Independence*, 44; Arthur M. Schlesinger Jr., *New Viewpoints in American History* (New York: Macmillan, 1922), 179.

21. Edmund S. Morgan, "Colonial Ideas of Parliamentary Power, 1764–1766," *William and Mary Quarterly*, 3rd ser., V (1948), 311, 341; Edmund S. Morgan and Helen M. Morgan, *The Stamp Act Crisis: Prologue to Revolution*, rev. ed. (New York: Collier Books, 1963), 306–307; Page Smith, "David Ramsay and the Causes of the American Revolution," *William and Mary Quarterly*, 3rd ser., XVII (1960), 70–71.

22. Jack P. Greene, "The Flight from Determinism: A Review of Recent Literature on the Coming of the American Revolution," *South Atlantic Quarterly*, LXI (1962), 257.

23. This revisionist literature of the 1950s is well known. See the listings in Bernard Bailyn, "Political Experience and Enlightenment Ideas in Eighteenth-Century America," *American Historical Review*, LXVII (1961–1962), 341n; and in Greene, "Flight from Determinism," 235–259.

24. Greene, "Flight from Determinism," 237, 257; Thad W. Tate, "The Coming of the Revolution in Virginia: Britain's Challenge to Virginia's Ruling Class, 1763–1776," *William and Mary Quarterly*, 3rd ser., XIX (1962), 323–343, esp. 340.

25. Bailyn, "Political Experience and Enlightenment Ideas," 339–351.

26. Bernard Bailyn, ed., assisted by Jane N. Garrett, *Pamphlets of the American Revolution, 1750–1776* (Cambridge, MA: Belknap Press of Harvard University Press, 1965–), I, viii, 60, x, 20. The 200-page general introduction is entitled "The Transforming Radicalism of the American Revolution."

27. This is not to say, however, that work on the Revolutionary ideas is in any way finished. For examples of the reexamination of traditional problems in Revolutionary political theory, see Richard Buel Jr., "Democracy and the American Revolution: A Frame of Reference," *William and Mary Quarterly*, 3rd ser., XXI (1964), 165–190; and Bailyn's resolution of James Otis's apparent inconsistency in *Revolutionary Pamphlets*, I, 100–103, 106–107, 121–123, 409–417, 546–552.

28. Smith, "Ramsay and the American Revolution," 72.

29. Morgan, "Revisions in Need of Revising," 13.

30. Adair and Schutz, eds., *Peter Oliver's Origin*, ix. In the present neo-Whig context, Sidney S. Fisher, "The Legendary and Myth-Making Process in Histories of the American Revolution," in *American Philosophical Society, Proceedings*, LI (Philadelphia: American Philosophical Society, 1912), 53–75, takes on a renewed relevance.

31. Bailyn, *Revolutionary Pamphlets*, I, 87, ix.

32. [Moses Mather], *America's Appeal to the Impartial World…* (Hartford, CT: Ebenezer Watson, 1775), 59; [John Dickinson], *Letters from a Farmer in Pennsylvania to the Inhabitants of the British Colonies* (Philadelphia: William and Thomas Bradford, 1768), in Paul L. Ford, ed., *The Writings of John*

Dickinson (Historical Society of Pennsylvania, *Memoirs*, XIV [Philadelphia: Historical Society of Pennsylvania, 1895]), II, 348. Dickinson hinged his entire argument on the ability of the Americans to decipher the "intention" of parliamentary legislation, whether for revenue or for commercial regulation. Ibid., 348, 364.

33. See Herbert Davis, "The Augustan Conception of History," in J. A. Mazzeo, ed., *Reason and the Imagination: Studies in the History of Ideas, 1600–1800* (New York: Columbia University Press, 1962), 226–228; W. H. Greenleaf, *Order, Empiricism and Politics: Two Traditions of English Political Thought, 1500–1700* (New York: University of Hull/Oxford University Press, 1964), 166; R. N. Stromberg, "History in the Eighteenth Century," *Journal of the History of Ideas*, XII (1951), 300. It was against this "dominant characteristic of the historical thought of the age," this "tendency to explain events in terms of conscious action by individuals," that the brilliant group of Scottish social scientists writing at the end of the eighteenth century directed much of their work. See Duncan Forbes, "'Scientific' Whiggism: Adam Smith and John Millar," *Cambridge Journal*, VII (1954), 651, 653–654. While we have had recently several good studies of historical thinking in seventeenth-century England, virtually nothing has been done on the eighteenth century. See, however, J. G. A. Pocock, "Burke and the Ancient Constitution—A Problem in the History of Ideas," *Historical Journal*, III (1960), 125–143; and Stow Persons, "The Cyclical Theory of History in Eighteenth Century America," *American Quarterly*, VI (1954), 147–163.

34. [Dickinson], *Letters from a Farmer*, in Ford, ed., *Writings of Dickinson*, 388.

35. Bailyn has noted that Oliver M. Dickerson, in chapter 7 of his *The Navigation Acts and the American Revolution* (Philadelphia: University of Pennsylvania Press, 1951), "adopts wholesale the contemporary Whig interpretation of the Revolution as the result of a conspiracy of 'King's Friends.'" Bailyn, *Revolutionary Pamphlets*, I, 724.

36. Morgan, "Revisions in Need of Revising," 7, 13, 8; Greene, "Flight from Determinism," 237.

37. Edmund S. Morgan, *The Birth of the Republic, 1763–89* (Chicago: University of Chicago Press, 1956), 51.

38. Greene, "Flight from Determinism," 258; Morgan, *Birth of the Republic*, 3.

39. Bailyn, *Revolutionary Pamphlets*, I, vii, ix.

40. Ibid., vii, viii, 17.

41. J. G. A. Pocock, "Machiavelli, Harrington, and English Political Ideologies in the Eighteenth Century," *William and Mary Quarterly*, 3rd ser., XXII (1965), 550.

42. Sir Lewis Namier, *England in the Age of the American Revolution*, 2nd ed. (London: Macmillan, 1961), 131.

43. Ibid., 129.

44. Bailyn, *Revolutionary Pamphlets*, I, 90, x, 169, 140. See Hannah Arendt, *On Revolution* (New York: Viking, 1963), 173: "American experience had taught the men of the Revolution that action, though it may be started in isolation and decided upon by single individuals for very different motives, can be accomplished only by some joint effort in which the motivation of single individuals...no longer counts...."

45. See Sir Lewis Namier, *The Structure of Politics at the Accession of George III*, 2nd ed. (London: Macmillan, 1961), 16; Sir Lewis Namier, "Human Nature in Politics," in *Personalities and Power: Selected Essays* (New York: Harper & Row, 1965), 5–6.

46. Bailyn, *Revolutionary Pamphlets*, I, 22. The French Revolutionaries were using the same group of classical writings to express their estrangement from the ancien régime and their hope for the new order. Harold T. Parker, *The Cult of Antiquity and the French Revolutionaries: A Study in the Development of the Revolutionary Spirit* (Chicago: University of Chicago Press, 1937), 22–23.

47. The relation of ideas to social structure is one of the most perplexing and intriguing in the social sciences. For an extensive bibliography on the subject, see Norman Birnbaum, "The Sociological Study of Ideology (1940–60)," *Current Sociology*, IX (1960).

48. Jacob Duché, *The American Vine, A Sermon, Preached... Before the Honourable Continental Congress, July 20th, 1775...* (Philadelphia: James Humphreys, 1775), 29.

49. For recent discussions of French and Puritan Revolutionary rhetoric, see Peter Gay, "Rhetoric and Politics in the French Revolution," *American Historical Review*, LXVI (1960–1961), 664–676; Michael Walzer, "Puritanism as a Revolutionary Ideology," *History and Theory*, III (1963), 59–90. This entire

issue of *History and Theory* is devoted to a symposium on the uses of theory in the study of history. In addition to the Walzer article, I have found the papers by Samuel H. Beer, "Causal Explanation and Imaginative Re-enactment," and Charles Tilly, "The Analysis of a Counter-Revolution," very stimulating and helpful.

50. Bryan A. Wilson, "Millennialism in Comparative Perspective," *Comparative Studies in Society and History*, VI (1963–1964), 108. See also Neil J. Smelser, *Theory of Collective Behaviour* (London: Routledge and Kegan Paul, 1962), 83, 120, 383.

51. Tate, "Coming of the Revolution in Virginia," 324–343.

52. Robert E. Brown and B. Katherine Brown, *Virginia, 1705–1786: Democracy or Aristocracy?* (East Lansing: Michigan State University Press, 1964), 236; Alexander White to Richard Henry Lee, 1758, quoted in J. R. Pole, "Representation and Authority in Virginia from the Revolution to Reform," *Journal of Southern History*, XXIV (1958), 23.

53. Purdie and Dixon's *Virginia Gazette* (Williamsburg), April 11, 1771; Rind's *Virginia Gazette*, October 31, 1771. See Lester J. Cappon and Stella F. Duff, eds., *Virginia Gazette Index, 1736–1780* (Williamsburg, VA: Institute of Early American History and Culture, 1950), I, 351, for entries on the astounding increase in essays on corruption and cost of elections in the late 1760s and early 1770s.

54. *The Defence of Injur'd Merit Unmasked; or, the Scurrilous Piece of Philander Dissected and Exposed to Public View. By a Friend to Merit, wherever found* (n.p., 1771), 10. Robert Carter chose to retire to private life in the early 1770s rather than adjust to the "new system of politicks" that had begun "to prevail generally." Quoted in Louis Morton, *Robert Carter of Nomini Hall: A Virginia Tobacco Planter of the Eighteenth Century* (Williamsburg: Colonial Williamsburg Inc., 1941), 52.

55. Jay B. Hubbell and Douglass Adair, "Robert Munford's *The Candidates*," *William and Mary Quarterly*, 3rd ser., V (1948), 238, 246. The ambivalence in Munford's attitude toward the representative process is reflected in the different way historians have interpreted his play. Cf. ibid., 223–225, with Brown, *Virginia*, 236–237. Munford's fear of "men who aim at power without merit" was more fully expressed in his later play, *The Patriots*, written in 1775 or 1776. Courtlandt Canby, "Robert Munford's *The Patriots*," *William and Mary Quarterly*, 3rd ser., VI (1949), 437–503, quotation from 450.

56. [John Randolph], *Considerations on the Present State of Virginia* ([Williamsburg], 1774), in Earl G. Swem, ed., *Virginia and the Revolution: Two Pamphlets, 1774* (New York, 1919), 16; Purdie and Dixon's *Virginia Gazette*, November 25, 1773.

57. Rind's *Virginia Gazette*, September 8, 1774; Brown, *Virginia*, 252–254; Morton, *Robert Carter*, 231–250.

58. See George Washington to George Mason, April 5, 1769, in John C. Fitzpatrick, ed., *The Writings of George Washington* (Washington, DC: U.S. Government Printing Office, 1931–1944). II, 502; Carl Bridenbaugh, *Myths and Realities: Societies of the Colonial South* (New York: Atheneum, 1963), 5, 10, 14, 16; Emory G. Evans, "Planter Indebtedness and the Coming of the Revolution in Virginia," *William and Mary Quarterly*, 3rd ser., XIX (1962), 518–519.

59. Rind's *Virginia Gazette*, August 15, 1766. See Carl Bridenbaugh, "Violence and Virtue in Virginia, 1766: or The Importance of the Trivial," Massachusetts Historical Society, *Proceedings*, LXXVI (1964), 3–29.

60. Quoted in Bridenbaugh, *Myths and Realities*, 27. See also Morton, *Robert Carter*, 223–225.

61. John A. Washington to R. H. Lee, June 20, 1778, quoted in Pole, "Representation and Authority in Virginia," 28.

62. Evans, "Planter Indebtedness," 526–527.

63. Julian P. Boyd et al., eds., *The Papers of Thomas Jefferson* (Princeton: Princeton University Press, 1950–), I, 560. Most of our knowledge of entail and primogeniture in Virginia stems from an unpublished doctoral dissertation, Clarence R. Keim, "Influence of Primogeniture and Entail in the Development of Virginia" (University of Chicago, 1926). Keim's is a very careful and qualified study and conclusions from his evidence—other than the obvious fact that much land was held in fee simple—are by no means easy to make. See particularly pp. 56, 60–62, 110–114, 122, 195–196.

64. Emory S. Evans, "The Rise and Decline of the Virginia Aristocracy in the Eighteenth Century: The Nelsons," in Darrett B. Rutman, ed., *The Old Dominion: Essays for Thomas Perkins Abernethy* (Charlottesville: University Press of Virginia, 1964), 73–74.

65. Max Farrand, ed., *The Records of the Federal Convention of 1787* (New Haven, CT: Yale University Press, 1911), I, 56; Bridenbaugh, *Myths and Realities*, 14, 16.

66. John Adams, "Novanglus," in Charles Francis Adams, ed., *The Works of John Adams* (Boston: Little, Brown, 1850–1856), IV, 14.

67. Arthur F. Bentley, *The Process of Government: A Study of Social Pressures* (Chicago: University of Chicago Press, 1908), 152.

AFTERWORD TO CHAPTER I

1. Rhys Isaac, *The Transformation of Virginia, 1740–1790* (Chapel Hill: University of North Carolina Press, 1982); T. H. Breen, *Tobacco Culture: The Mentality of the Great Tidewater Planters on the Eve of the Revolution* (Princeton: Princeton University Press, 1985); Richard R. Beeman, *The Evolution of the Southern Backcountry: A Case Study of Lunenburg County, Virginia, 1746–1832* (Philadelphia: University of Pennsylvania Press, 1984); Jack P. Greene, "Society, Ideology, and Politics: An Analysis of the Political Culture of Mid-Eighteenth Century Virginia," in Richard M. Jellison, ed., *Society, Freedom, and Conscience: The Coming of the Revolution in Virginia, Massachusetts, and New York* (New York: W. W. Norton, 1976), 14–57; Jack P. Greene, " *'Virtus et Libertas'*: Political Culture, Social Change, and the Origins of the American Revolution in Virginia, 1763–1766," in Jeffery J. Crow and Larry E. Tise, eds., *The Southern Experience in the American Revolution* (Chapel Hill: University of North Carolina Press, 1978), 55–65; Jack P. Greene, "Character, Persona, and Authority: A Study of Alternative Styles of Political Leadership in Revolutionary Virginia," in W. Robert Higgins, ed., *The Revolutionary War in the South: Power, Conflict, and Leadership* (Durham, NC: Duke University Press, 1979), 3–42.

CHAPTER 2, THE LEGACY OF ROME IN THE AMERICAN REVOLUTION

1. R. R. Palmer, *The Age of the Democratic Revolution: A Political History of Europe and America, 1760–1800*, 2 vols. (Princeton: Princeton University Press, 1959, 1964); Franco Venturi, *Utopia and Reform in the Enlightenment* (Cambridge, UK: Cambridge University Press, 1971), 90.

2. 1 Samuel 8:19–20.

3. John Adams to Richard Cranch, August 2, 1776, in L. H. Butterfield et al., eds., *Adams Family Correspondence* (Cambridge, MA: Harvard University Press), II, 74; see also Gordon S. Wood, *The Creation of the American Republic, 1776–1787* (Chapel Hill: University of North Carolina Press, 1969), 49–51; John Adams to Mercy Otis Warren, July 20, 1807, Massachusetts Historical Society, *Collections*, 5th ser., IV (1878), 353; Adams to J. H. Tiffany, April 30, 1819, Charles Francis Adams, ed., *Works of John Adams*, X, 378.

4. Montesquieu, *The Spirit of the Laws*, Franz Neumann, ed., pt. I, bk. ix, ch. 13 (New York: Hafner Press, 1949), 167; James William Johnson, *The Formation of English Neo-Classical Thought* (Princeton: Princeton University Press, 1967), 91–105; Richard Jenkyns, ed., *The Legacy of Rome: A New Appraisal* (Oxford: Oxford University Press, 1992), 26.

5. Peter Gay, *The Enlightenment: An Interpretation—The Rise of Modern Paganism* (New York: Knopf, 1966).

6. Wood, *The Creation of the American Republic*, 52, 414; Johnson, *Formation of English Neo-Classical Thought*, 239–240.

7. Johnson, *Formation of English Neo-Classical Thought*, 93, 246; Gay, *Enlightenment: Rise of Paganism*, 109; Bernard Bailyn, *The Ideological Origins of the American Revolution* (Cambridge, MA: Harvard University Press, 1967), 25.

8. J. G. A. Pocock, *The Machiavellian Moment: Florentine Political Thought and the Atlantic Republican Tradition* (Princeton: Princeton University Press, 1975); Johnson, *Formation of English Neo-Classical Thought*, 222–224; Meyer Reinhold, *Classica Americana: The Greek and Roman Heritage in the United States* (Detroit: Wayne State University Press, 1984), 30–31.

9. David Hume, "The British Government," in Eugene Miller, ed., *Essays: Moral, Political, and Literary* (Indianapolis: Liberty Classics, 1985), 51; Linda Colley, "The Apotheosis of George III: Loyalty, Royalty and the British Nation, 1760–1820," *Past and Present*, 102 (1984), 94–129; Jeffrey Merrick, *The Desacralization of the French Monarchy in the Eighteenth Century* (Baton Rouge: Louisiana State University Press, 1990)

10. Harold T. Parker, *The Cult of Antiquity and the French Revolutionaries* (Chicago: University of Chicago Press, 1937), 35, 39.

11. *South Carolina Gazette*, July 29, 1749, quoted in Hennig Cohen, *The South Carolina Gazette, 1732–1775* (Columbia: University of South Carolina Press, 1953), 218.

12. James Thomson, "Liberty," v, in *The Poetical Works of James Thomson* (Edinburgh: J. Nichol, 1863), 369.

13. Adams to Warren, July 20, 1807, 353; Adams to J. H. Tiffany, April 30, 1819, 378; Venturi, *Utopia and Reform in the Enlightenment*, 71.

14. Simon Schama, *Citizens: A Chronicle of the French Revolution* (New York: Knopf, 1989), 172; William L. Vance, *America's Rome*, 2 vols. (New Haven, CT: Yale University Press, 1989), i, 17, 15; John Barrell, *The Dark Side of the Landscape: The Rural Poor in English Painting, 1730–1840* (Cambridge, UK: Cambridge University Press, 1980), 7; Conyers Middleton, *The History of the Life of Marcus Tullius Cicero*, 2 vols. (London: James Bettenham, 1741), I, ix.

15. Caroline Robbins, *The Eighteenth-Century Commonwealthman: Studies in the Transmission, Development, and Circumstance of English Liberal Thought from the Restoration of Charles II Until the War with the Thirteen Colonies* (Cambridge, MA: Harvard University Press, 1959); Issac F. Kramnick, *Bolingbroke and His Circle: The Politics of Nostalgia in the Age of Walpole* (Cambridge, MA: Harvard University Press, 1968).

16. Edward Gibbon, *The Decline and Fall of the Roman Empire* (New York: Modern Library, 1931), I, 164–165; W. Jackson Bate, *Samuel Johnson* (New York: Harcourt Brace Jovanovich, 1975), 171–172.

17. William L. Grant, *Neo-Latin Literature and the Pastoral* (Chapel Hill: University of North Carolina Press, 1965), 255; Howard D. Weinbrot, *Augustus Caesar in "Augustan" England: The Decline of a Classical Norm* (Princeton: Princeton University Press, 1978), 47–48, 53, 62, 64; Howard Erskine-Hill, *The Augustan Idea in English Literature* (London: Edward Arnold, 1983), 249–266; Carl J. Richard, "A Dialogue with the Ancients: Thomas Jefferson and Classical Philosophy and History," *Journal of the Early Republic*, IX (1989), 445; Meyer Reinhold, ed., *The Classick Pages: Classical Readings of Eighteenth-Century Americans* (University Park, PA: American Philological Association, 1975), 100; Johnson, *Formation of English Neo-Classical Thought*, 226, 297, Hume, "Of the Parties of Great Britain," *Essays*, Miller, ed., 72.

18. Alexander Pope, "An Essay on Criticism," in Aubrey Williams, ed., *Poetry and Prose of Alexander Pope* (Boston: Houghton Mifflin, 1969), 41, lines 118–121.

19. Bertrand A. Goldar, *Walpole and the Wits: The Relation of Politics to Literature, 1722–1742* (Lincoln: University of Nebraska Press, 1976), 3, 22–23, 26, 135, 147–148, 158–159; Johnson, *The Formation of English Neo-Classical Thought*, 95–105; Reed Browning, *Political and Constitutional Ideas of the Court Whigs* (Baton Rouge: Louisiana State University Press, 1982), 5.

20. Johnson, *Formation of English Neo-Classical Thought*, 168.

21. Quentin Skinner, "The Idea of Negative Liberty: Philosophical and Historical Perspectives," Richard Rorty, et al., eds., *Philosophy in History* (Cambridge, UK: Cambridge University Press, 1984), 193–221; Michael Ignatieff, "John Millar and Individualism," in Istvan Hont and Michael Ignatieff, eds., *Wealth and Virtue: The Shaping of Political Economy in the Scottish Enlightenment* (Cambridge, UK: Cambridge University Press, 1983), 329–330.

22. David Hume, *A Treatise on Human Nature*, L. A. Selby-Bigge and P. N. Nidditch, eds. (Oxford: Clarendon Press, 1978), 587; Benjamin Franklin to Cadwallader Colden, October 11, 1750, Labaree, et al., eds., *Papers of Franklin*, IV, 68.

23. Gregory H. Nobles, *Divisions Throughout the Whole: Politics and Society in Hampshire County, Massachusetts, 1740–1775* (Cambridge, UK: Cambridge University Press, 1983), 182.

24. Thomas Jefferson, *Notes on the State of Virginia*, William Peden, ed. (Chapel Hill: University of North Carolina Press, 1954), 165.

25. Wood, *Radicalism of the American Revolution*, 240; Cicero, *Selected Works*, Michael Grant, ed. (Harmondsworth, UK: Penguin, 1960), 188.

26. Robert R. Livingston, quoted in Bernard Friedman, "The Shaping of the Radical Consciousness in Provincial New York," *Journal of American History*, LVI (1970), 786. For a discussion of Cicero's distinction between gentlemanly and vulgar callings, see Neal Wood, *Cicero's Social and Political Thought* (Berkeley: University of California Press, 1988), 95–100.

27. Adam Smith, *An Inquiry into the Nature and Causes of the Wealth of Nations*, ed., R. H. Campbell and A. S. Skinner (Oxford: Oxford University Press, 1976), I, 50–51; II, 781–783; Francis Hutcheson, *A System of Moral Philosophy in Three Books . . .* (London: R. and A. Foulis, 1755), II, 113.

28. Wood, *Radicalism of the American Revolution*, 83, 287–88, 290–92.
29. James Wilson, "On the History of Property," in McCloskey, ed., *Works of James Wilson*, II, 716; James Thompson, *The Seasons and the Castle of Indolence*, James Sambrook, ed. (Oxford: Oxford University Press, 1972), x; Virginia C. Kenny, *The Country-House Ethos in English Literature, 1688–1750: Themes of Personal Retreat and National Expansion* (New York: St. Martin's Press, 1984), 8–9; Jack P. Greene, *Landon Carter: An Inquiry into the Personal Values and Social Imperatives of the Eighteenth-Century Virginia Gentry* (Charlottesville: University Press of Virginia, 1965), 86–87.
30. William C. Dowling, *Poetry and Ideology in Revolutionary Connecticut* (Athens: University of Georgia Press, 1990).
31. John Dickinson, "Letters of a Farmer in Pennsylvania" (1768), in Paul L. Ford, ed., *The Writings of John Dickinson: I, Political Writings, 1764–1774* (Pennsylvania Historical Society, Memoirs, XIV [Philadelphia: Pennsylvania Historical Society, 1895]), 307.
32. Andrew R. L. Cayton, *The Frontier Republic: Ideology and Politics in the Ohio Country, 1780–1825* (Kent, OH: Kent State University Press, 1986), 12–32; Gibbon, *Decline and Fall of the Roman Empire*, I, 32; Tamara Platkins Thornton, *Cultivating Gentlemen: The Meaning of Country Life Among the Boston Elite, 1785–1860* (New Haven, CT: Yale University Press, 1989), 31.
33. Reinhold, *Classica Americana*, 98.
34. David Humphreys, "A Poem on the Industry of the United States of America," in Vernon L. Parrington, ed., *The Connecticut Wits* (New York: Thomas Y. Crowell, 1954), 401.
35. Ronald Paulson, *Representations of Revolution (1789–1820)* (New Haven, CT: Yale University Press, 1983), 12; Stephen Botein, "Cicero as Role Model for Early American Lawyers: A Case Study in Classical Influence," *The Classical Journal*, LXXIII (1977–1978), 313–321; Pauline Maier, *The Old Revolutionaries: Political Lives in the Age of Samuel Adams* (New York: Knopf, 1980), 33, 34, 47; Garry Wills, *Cincinnatus: George Washington and the Enlightenment* (New York: Doubleday, 1984).
36. Ezra Stiles, *Election Sermon* (1783), in John Wingate Thornton, ed., *The Pulpit of the American Revolution* (Boston: D. Lothrop, 1876), 460; John Adams to Abigail Adams, April 25, 1778, in L. H. Butterfield et al., eds., *The Book of Abigail and John: Selected Letters of the Adams Family* (Cambridge, MA: Harvard University Press, 1975), 210; Benjamin Rush to ———, April 16, 1790, in L. H. Butterfield, ed., *Letters of Benjamin Rush* (Princeton: Princeton University Press, 1951), I, 550.
37. Neil Harris, *The Artist in American Society: The Formative Years, 1790–1860* (New York: George Braziller, 1966), 42.
38. Eleanor Davidson Berman, *Thomas Jefferson Among the Arts: An Essay in Early American Esthetics* (New York: Philosophical Library, 1947), 84; Jefferson, *Notes on the State of Virginia*, 153; Jefferson to Madison, Sept. 20, 1785, in Julian P. Boyd et al., eds., *Papers of Thomas Jefferson* (Princeton: Princeton University Press, 1950–); VIII, 535; Jefferson to William Buchanan and James Hay, Jan. 26, 1786, in *Papers of Jefferson*, IX, 221.
39. Reinhold, *Classica Americana*, 129; Benjamin Rush to James Hamilton, June 27, 1810, in Butterfield, ed., *Letters of Benjamin Rush*, II, 1053.
40. Edward Everett, "An Oration Pronounced at Cambridge . . . 1824," in Joseph L. Blau, ed., *American Philosophic Addresses, 1700–1900* (New York: Columbia University Press, 1946), 77.

AFTERWORD TO CHAPTER 2

1. Bernard Bailyn, *The Ideological Origins of the American Revolution* (Cambridge, MA: Harvard University Press, 1967), 23–26.

CHAPTER 3, CONSPIRACY AND THE PARANOID STYLE

1. Jack P. Greene, "Search for Identity: An Interpretation of the Meaning of Selected Patterns of Social Response in Eighteenth-Century America," *Journal of Social History*, III (1970), 189–220.
2. Kenneth S. Lynn, *A Divided People* (Westport, CT: Greenwood Press, 1977), 105. Cf. Philip Greven, *The Protestant Temperament: Patterns of Child-Rearing, Religious Experience and the Self in Early America* (New York: Knopf, 1977).
3. The best and most restrained of these efforts is Edwin G. Burrows and Michael Wallace, "The American Revolution: The Ideology and Psychology of National Liberation," *Perspectives in*

American History, VI (1972), 167–306. See also Winthrop D. Jordan, "Familial Politics: Thomas Paine and the Killing of the King, 1776," *Journal of American History*, LX (1973), 294–308.

4. Fawn M. Brodie, *Thomas Jefferson: An Intimate History* (New York: W. W. Norton, 1974); Peter Shaw, *The Character of John Adams* (Chapel Hill: University of North Carolina Press, 1976), and *American Patriots and the Rituals of Revolution* (Cambridge, MA: Harvard University Press, 1981); John J. Waters, "James Otis, Jr.: An Ambivalent Revolutionary," *History of Childhood Quarterly*, I (1973), 142–150; Bruce Mazlish, "Leadership in the American Revolution: The Psychological Dimension," in *Leadership in the American Revolution*, Library of Congress Symposia on the American Revolution (Washington, DC: Library of Congress, 1974), 113–133.

5. Jack P. Greene, "An Uneasy Connection: An Analysis of the Preconditions of the American Revolution," in Stephen G. Kurtz and James H. Hutson, eds., *Essays on the American Revolution* (Chapel Hill: University of North Carolina Press, 1973), 60; Greven, *Protestant Temperament*, 351.

6. Jack P. Greene, "Search for Identity," *Journal of Social History*, III (1970), 219; James H. Hutson, "The American Revolution: The Triumph of a Delusion?" in Erich Angermann et al., eds., *New Wine in Old Skins: A Comparative View of Socio-Political Structures and Values Affecting the American Revolution* (Stuttgart, Germany: Klett, 1976), 179–194.

7. Bailyn's introduction was entitled "The Transforming Radicalism of the American Revolution," in *Pamphlets of the American Revolution*, I (Cambridge, MA: Belknap Press of Harvard University Press, 1965), 3–202; Richard Hofstadter, *The Paranoid Style in American Politics and Other Essays* (New York: Vintage, 1965).

8. Bernard Bailyn, *The Origins of American Politics* (New York: Knopf, 1968), 13, and *The Ideological Origins of the American Revolution* (Cambridge, MA: Harvard University Press, 1967), 94–95.

9. For a typical example of the sociological studies of the early 1950s, see Daniel Bell, ed., *The New American Right* (New York: Criterion, 1955).

10. Hofstadter, *Paranoid Style*, 7.

11. Ibid., ix, 4, 6.

12. Ibid., ix.

13. Richard O. Curry and Thomas M. Brown, eds., *Conspiracy: The Fear of Subversion in American History* (New York: Holt, Rinehart & Winston, 1972), ix, x; David Brion Davis, ed., *The Fear of Conspiracy: Images of Un-American Subversion from the Revolution to the Present* (Ithaca, NY: Cornell University Press, 1971), xiv.

14. David Brion Davis, *The Slave Power Conspiracy and the Paranoid Style* (Baton Rouge: Louisiana State University Press, 1909), 29; Davis, ed., *Fear of Conspiracy*, 23.

15. James Kirby Martin, *Men in Rebellion: Higher Governmental Leaders and the Coming of the American Revolution* (New Brunswick, NJ: Rutgers University Press, 1973), 34; Daniel Sisson, *The American Revolution of 1800* (New York: Knopf, 1974), 130, 131, 132; Hutson, "American Revolution," in Angermann et al., eds., *New Wine in Old Skins*, 179, 180.

16. Lance Banning, "Republican Ideology and the Triumph of the Constitution, 1789 to 1793," *William and Mary Quarterly*, 3rd ser., XXXI (1974), 171.

17. Greven, *Protestant Temperament*, 349, 352.

18. Hutson, "American Revolution," in Angermann et al., eds., *New Wine in Old Skins*, 177, 180, 181, 182. In a more recent unpublished essay, "The Origins of 'the Paranoid Style in American Politics': Public Jealousy from the Age of Walpole to the Age of Jackson," Hutson has virtually repudiated his earlier psychological interpretation. He now suggests that "the special position the Revolution occupies in our national life" has inhibited historians from following him in making the Revolution "the first link on Hofstadter's paranoid chain." Perhaps other historians were quietly filling in behind him more than he realized. At any rate, he has retreated from his exposed position and returned to one not very different from Bailyn's. In this paper he describes the Americans' "paranoid style" as a product of their long tradition of jealousy and suspicion of governmental power. Such fears of abused political power, Hutson now concedes, made American conspiratorial views "altogether credible," at least up to 1830 or so. Only after that date, when American suspicions and jealousy were transferred from the government to nongovernmental agencies and groups, such as the Masons and the Roman Catholic Church, for which there was no tradition of past abuse, is it "possible," says Hutson, "to speak of these fears veering off towards pathology."

19. "The British ministers of the Revolutionary Era," writes Hutson, "were shifting coalitions whose principal discernible goal was the preservation of power. How could reasonable people believe them capable of fiendish malevolence, cunningly concerted and sustained, year in, year out?" ("American Revolution," in Angermann et al., eds., *New Wine in Old Skins*, 177.) Although not as boldly as Hutson, other historians trying to explain the Revolutionaries' conspiratorial beliefs in effect seem to be asking the same question.

20. Daniel Defoe, quoted in Maximillian E. Novak, ed., *English Literature in the Age of Disguise* (Berkeley: University of California Press, 1977), 2; George Farquhar, *The Beaux' Stratagem*, Charles N. Fifer, ed. (Lincoln: University of Nebraska Press, 1977), act 4, sc. 1; Swift, *Gulliver's Travels*, pt. III, chap. 6, in *The Writings of Jonathan Swift*, Robert A. Greenberg and William Bowman Piper, eds. (New York: W. W. Norton, 1973), 162–163.

21. Bailyn, *Ideological Origins*, 144–159, quotation on p. 153; Ira D. Gruber, "The American Revolution as a Conspiracy: The British View," *William and Mary Quarterly*, 3rd ser., XXVI (1969), 360–372; David T. Morgan, "'The Dupes of Designing Men': John Wesley and the American Revolution," *Historical Magazine of the Protestant Episcopal Church*, XLIV (1975), 121–131; J. M. Roberts, *The Mythology of the Secret Societies* (London: Secker and Warburg, 1972), 24; Georges Lefebvre, *The Great Fear of 1789: Rural Panic in Revolutionary France*, Joan White, trans. (New York: Pantheon Books, 1973), 60–62, 210; Jack Richard Censer, *Prelude to Power: The Parisian Radical Press, 1789–1791* (Baltimore: Johns Hopkins University Press, 1976), 99.

22. Johnson, *A Dictionary of the English Language . . .*, 12th ed. (Edinburgh: A. M. Knapton, 1802); Hofstadter, *Paranoid Style*, 36, 32, 27.

23. Erich Auerbach, *Mimesis: The Representation of Reality in Western Literature*, Willard Trask, trans. (Princeton: Princeton University Press, 1953), 463.

24. Niccolo Machiavelli, "Discourses on the First Decade of Titus Livius, Book 3," in *The Chief Works and Others*, Allan Gilbert, trans., 3 vols. (Durham, NC: Duke University Press, 1965), I, 428. See also letter CII in Montesquieu's *The Persian Letters*, George R. Healy, trans. (Indianapolis: Bobbs-Merrill, 1964), 170.

25. *American Museum, or, Universal Magazine*, XII (1792), 172; Samuel Kinser, ed., *The Memoirs of Philippe de Commynes*, Isabelle Cazeaux, trans., I (Columbia: University of South Carolina Press, 1969), 361.

26. Thomas Preston Peardon, *The Transition in English Historical Writing, 1760–1830* (New York: Columbia University Press, 1933), 35. See also Peter Burke, *Popular Culture in Early Modern Europe* (New York: Harper & Row, 1978), 173.

27. Myron P. Gilmore, *Humanists and Jurists: Six Studies in the Renaissance* (Cambridge, MA: Belknap Press of Harvard University Press, 1963), 59–60.

28. Keith Thomas, *Religion and the Decline of Magic* (New York: Charles Scribner's Sons, 1971), 78–112.

29. Increase Mather, *The Doctrine of Divine Providence Opened and Applyed* (Boston: Richard Pierce, 1684), quoted in Lester H. Cohen, *The Revolutionary Histories: Contemporary Narratives of the American Revolution* (Ithaca, NY: Cornell University Press, 1980), 27–29. Cohen's book is richly imaginative and by far the best work we have on early American historical thinking.

30. Halifax, quoted in Thomas, *Religion and the Decline of Magic*, 109. On the scientific revolution, see Herbert Butterfield, *The Origins of Modern Science, 1300–1800* (London, 1949), and J. Bronowski, *The Common Sense of Science* (Cambridge, MA: Harvard University Press 1953).

31. Bronowski, *Common Sense of Science*, 40; Smith, *The Lectures . . . on the Subjects of Moral and Political Philosophy* (Trenton, NJ: Daniel Fenton, 1812), I, 9, 122.

32. Steven Shapin, "Of Gods and Kings: Natural Philosophy and Politics in the Leibniz-Clarke Disputes," *Isis*, LXXII (1981), 192; M. B. Foster, "The Christian Doctrine of Creation and the Rise of Modern Natural Science," in Daniel O'Connor and Francis Oakley, eds., *Creation: The Impact of an Idea* (New York: Charles Scribner's Sons, 1969), 29–53; Francis Oakley, "Christian Theology and the Newtonian Science: The Rise of the Concept of the Laws of Nature," ibid., 54–83; P. M. Heimann, "Voluntarism and Immanence: Conceptions of Nature in Eighteenth-Century Thought," *Journal of the History of Ideas*, XXXIX (1978), 271–292; Roy N. Lokken, "Cadwallader Colden's Attempt to Advance Natural Philosophy Beyond the Eighteenth-Century Mechanistic Paradigm," American Philosophical Society, *Proceedings*, CXXII (1978), 365–376; Margaret C. Jacob, *The Newtonians and the English Revolution, 1689–1720* (Ithaca, NY: Cornell University Press, 1976).

33. The best brief discussion of the search for a science of human behavior in the eighteenth century is Gladys Bryson, *Man and Society: The Scottish Inquiry of the Eighteenth Century* (Princeton: Princeton University Press, 1945).

34. Smith, *Lectures*, II, 22; Warburton and Volney are quoted in R. N. Stromberg, "History in the Eighteenth Century," *Journal of the History of Ideas*, XII (1951), 300; Richard H. Popkin, "Hume: Philosophical Versus Prophetic Historian," in Kenneth R. Merrill and Robert W. Shahan, eds., *David Hume: Many-Sided Genius* (Norman: University of Oklahoma Press, 1976), 83–95.

35. On the effects of the new causal thinking on the development of the novel see Edward M. Jennings, "The Consequences of Prediction," in Theodore Besterman, ed., *Studies on Voltaire and the Eighteenth Century* (Oxford: Oxford University Press, 1976), CLIII, 1148–1149, and Martin C. Battestin, "'Tom Jones': The Argument of Design," in Henry Knight Miller et al., eds., *The Augustan Milieu: Essays Presented to Louis A. Landa* (Oxford: Oxford University Press, 1970), 289–319.

36. Bolingbroke, *Historical Writings*, Isaac Kramnick, ed. (Chicago: University of Chicago Press, 1972), 18, 21, 22; Gibbon, "Essai sur L'Etude de la Litterature," in *Miscellaneous Works of Edward Gibbon . . .* , John, Lord Sheffield, ed. (London, 1796), II, 477. These enlightened assumptions about man's responsibility for what happened led naturally to historical explanations that R. G. Collingwood thought were "superficial to absurdity." It was the Enlightenment historians, wrote Collingwood, "who invented the grotesque idea that the Renaissance in Europe was due to the fall of Constantinople and the consequent expulsion of scholars in search of new homes." For Collingwood, who usually had so much sympathy for the peculiar beliefs of the past, such personal sorts of causal attribution were "typical . . . of a bankruptcy of historical method which in despair of genuine explanation acquiesces in the most trivial causes for the vastest effects" (*The Idea of History* [Oxford: Oxford University Press, 1946], 80–81). Elsewhere, Collingwood of course recognized the historical differentness of the eighteenth century (ibid., 224).

37. David Kubrin, "Newton and the Cyclical Cosmos: Providence and the Mechanical Philosophy," *Journal of the History of Ideas*, XXVIII (1967), 325–346; P. M. Heimann and J. E. McGuire, "Newtonian Forces and Lockean Powers: Concepts of Matter in Eighteenth-Century Thought," *Historical Studies in the Physical Sciences*, III (1971), 233–306.

38. Arthur O. Lovejoy, *Reflections on Human Nature* (Baltimore: Johns Hopkins Press, 1961), 153; [John Trenchard and Thomas Gordon], *Cato's Letters: Or Essays on Liberty, Civil and Religious, and Other Important Subjects*, 5th ed. (London, 1748), IV, 86; Hans Kelsen, *Society and Nature: A Sociological Inquiry* (London: Kegan Paul, 1946), 42. On the ways in which Arminian-minded Protestants reconciled individual responsibility with God's sovereignty, see Greven, *Protestant Temperament*, 217–243.

39. Lokken, "Cadwallader Colden," American Philosophical Society, *Proceedings*, CXXII (1978), 370; Heimann, "Voluntarism and Immanence," *Journal of the History of Ideas*, XXXIX (1978), 273, 378–379.

40. David Hume, "An Enquiry Concerning Human Understanding," sec. VIII, pt. I, in *Essays, Moral, Political, and Literary*, T. H. Green and T. H. Grose, eds. (New York: Longmans, Green, 1912), II, 72, 77; Reid, quoted in S. A. Grave, *The Scottish Philosophy of Common Sense* (Oxford: Clarendon Press, 1960), 216.

41. [James Dana], *An Examination of the Late Reverend President Edwards's "Enquiry on Freedom of Will," . . .* (Boston: Daniel Kneeland, 1770), 81, 89; Stephen West, *An Essay on Moral Agency . . .* , 2nd ed. (Salem, MA: Thomas C. Cushing, 1794), 73–74.

42. George L. Dillon, "Complexity and Change of Character in Neo-Classical Criticism," *Journal of the History of Ideas*, XXXV (1974), 51–61; Warren, quoted in Cohen, *Revolutionary Histories*, 193–194; Bryson, *Man and Society*, 109.

43. [Dana], *Examination*, xi, 50, 62, 66. See Jonathan Edwards, *Freedom of the Will*, Paul Ramsey, ed. (New Haven, CT: Yale University Press, 1957), 156–162.

44. Merle Curti and William Tillman, eds., "Philosophical Lectures by Samuel Williams, LL. D., on the Constitution, Duty, and Religion of Man," American Philosophical Society, *Transactions*, N.S., LX, pt. 3 (1970), 114. Since the moral effects of human behavior were determined by the causes or motives of the actors, James Wilson devoted a large section of his "Lectures on Law" to an attempt to demonstrate that "the common law measures crimes chiefly by the intention." Such intention, he said, presupposed the operation of both understanding and will. "If the operation of either is wanting," as in the case of lunatics, children, and other dependents, "no crime can exist" ("Of the

Persons Capable of Committing Crimes; and of the Different Degrees of Guilt Incurred in the Commission of the Same Crime," in Robert Green McCloskey, ed., *The Works of James Wilson*, II [Cambridge, MA: Harvard University Press, 1967], 677). "In every moral action," wrote Samuel Stanhope Smith, "the principal ground on which we form a judgment of its rectitude or pravity is the disposition or intention with which it is performed" (*Lectures*, I, 313).

45. [Dana], *Examination*, 50, 66, 96; Hume, "Concerning Human Understanding," sec. VIII, pt. I, in *Essays*, Green and Gross, eds., 74.

46. Bernard Mandeville, *Free Thoughts on Religion, the Church, and Natural Happiness* (1720), quoted in H. T. Dickinson, "Bernard Mandeville: An Independent Whig," in Besterman, ed., *Studies on Voltaire*, CLII, 562–563.

47. Curti and Tillman, eds., "Lectures by Williams," American Philosophical Society, *Transactions*, N.S., LX, pt. 3 (1970), 121.

48. Bernard Mandeville, *The Fable of the Bees: Or, Private Vices, Publick Benefits*, F. B. Kaye, ed. (Oxford: Clarendon Press, 1924), 239; J. A. W. Gunn, "Mandeville and Wither: Individualism and the Workings of Providence," in Irwin Primer, ed., *Mandeville Studies; New Explorations in the Art and Thought of Dr. Bernard Mandeville (1670–1733)* (The Hague: Martinus Nijhoff, 1975), 101.

49. John Adams to Ebenezer Thayer, September 24, 1765, in Robert J. Taylor et al., eds., *Papers of John Adams* (Cambridge, MA: Belknap Press of Harvard University Press, 1977), I, 135.

50. Jonathan Edwards, *The Mind: A Reconstructed Text*, Leon Howard, ed. (Berkeley: University of California Press, 1963), 76–78. The mind is "informed by means of observed motion, of design," wrote the British scientist James Hutton in 1792, "for when a regular order is observed in those changing things, whereby a certain end is always attained, there is necessarily inferred an operation somewhere, an operation similar to that of our mind, which often premeditates the exertion of a power and is conscious of design" (quoted in Heimann and McGuire, "Newtonian Forces and Lockean Powers," *Historical Studies in Physical Sciences*, III [1971], 283).

51. Samuel Sherwood, *The Church's Flight into the Wilderness: An Address on the Times* . . . (New York: S. Loudon, 1776), 9, 13, 26, 29, 30, 38, 40, and *A Sermon, Containing Scriptural Instructions to Civil Rulers and All Free-born Subjects* . . . (New Haven, CT: T. and S. Green, 1774), vi; Nathan O. Hatch, *The Sacred Cause of Liberty: Republican Thought and the Millennium in Revolutionary New England* (New Haven, CT: Yale University Press, 1977), 56; James West Davidson, *The Logic of Millennial Thought: Eighteenth-Century New England* (New Haven, CT: Yale University Press, 1977).

52. [Moses Mather], *America's Appeal to the Impartial World* . . . (Hartford, CT, 1775), 59; Izrahiah Wetmore, *A Sermon, Preached Before the Honorable General Assembly of the Colony of Connecticut* . . . (Norwich, CT: Judah P. Spooner, 1775), 4, 11; Henry C. Van Schaack, *The Life of Peter Van Schaack* . . . (New York: D. Appleton, 1842), 56; Thomas Jefferson, A *Summary View of the Rights of British America* . . . (Williamsburg, VA: Clementine Rind, 1774), in Julian P. Boyd et al., eds., *The Papers of Thomas Jefferson*, I (Princeton: Princeton University Press, 1950), 125.

53. [Dickinson], *Letters from a Farmer in Pennsylvania* . . . (Philadelphia: William and Thomas Bradford, 1768), in Paul Leicester Ford, ed., *The Writings of John Dickinson* (Historical Society of Pennsylvania, *Memoirs*, XIV [Philadelphia: Historical Society of Pennsylvania, 1895]), 349, hereafter cited as Ford, ed., *Writings of Dickinson*; Griffith J. McRee, ed., *Life and Correspondence of James Iredell* . . . , I (New York: D. Appleton, 1857), 312. "If the American public had not penetrated the intentions of the English government," noted Jefferson's Italian friend Philip Mazzei in 1788, "there would have been no revolution, or it would have been stillborn" (*Researches on the United States*, Constance D. Sherman, trans. and ed. [Charlottesville: University Press of Virginia, 1976], 125).

54. Adams, "Misanthrop, No. 2" (January 1767), in Taylor et al., eds., *Adams Papers*, I, 187. "There is not an emotion or thought which passes through the mind," wrote Smith, "that does not paint some image of itself on the fine and delicate lines of the countenance" (*Lectures*, I, 30). Beliefs such as this led to the faddish science of physiognomy promoted by the Swiss J. K. Lavater. See Samuel Miller, *A Brief Retrospect of the Eighteenth Century* . . . , I (New York: T. and J. Swords 1803), 433–434.

55. Richardson, *The History of Clarissa Harlowe*, William Lyon Phelps, ed., IV (New York: Croscup & Sterling, 1902), 112 (Letter XXVIII); Defoe, quoted in Novak, ed., *Age of Disguise*, 2; Dillon, "Complexity and Change," *Journal of the History of Ideas*, XXXV (1974), 51–61.

56. Lord Chesterfield to his son, August 21, 1749, in Bonamy Dobrée, ed., *The Letters of Philip Dormer Stanhope, 4th Earl of Chesterfield*, IV (London: Eyre and Spottiswoode, 1932), 1382–1383. On the issue of sincerity see the engaging and learned article by Judith Shklar, "Let Us Not Be Hypocritical," *Daedalus* (Summer 1979), 1–25.

57. John Adams, August 20, 1770, in L. H. Butterfield et al., eds., *Diary and Autobiography of John Adams*, I (Cambridge, MA: Belknap Press of Harvard University Press, 1961), 363; *Am. Museum*, XII (1792), 172; Warren, quoted in Cohen, *Revolutionary Histories*, 207, 208.

58. Henry Fielding, "An Essay on the Knowledge of the Characters of Men," in *The Works of Henry Fielding*, XI (New York: Charles Scriber's Sons, 1899), 190; William Henry Drayton, *The Letters of Freeman, Etc.: Essays on the Nonimportation Movement in South Carolina*, Robert M. Weir, ed. (Columbia: University of South Carolina Press, 1977), 34; David Hume, *The History of England . . .* , VI (New York: Harper & Brothers, 1879 [originally published Edinburgh: Hamilton, Balfour, and Neill, 1754–1762]), chap. 65, 16; Alan Heimert, *Religion and the American Mind: From the Great Awakening to the Revolution* (Cambridge, MA: Harvard University Press, 1966), 308; Ian Watt, *The Rise of the Novel* (London: Penguin, 1970), 283–287; Smith, *Lectures*, I, 10, 314. "In Truth," wrote Trenchard and Gordon, "every private Subject has a Right to watch the Steps of those who would betray their Country; nor is he to take their Word about the Motives of their Designs, but to judge of their Designs by the Event" (*Cato's Letters*, I, 86).

59. Adams, "A Dissertation on the Canon and the Feudal Law" (1765), in Taylor et al., eds., *Adams Papers*, I, 127; Cooke, *A Sermon Preached at Cambridge . . . May 30th, 1770* (Boston: Edes and Gill, 1770), in John Wingate Thornton, ed., *The Pulpit of the American Revolution. Or, the Political Sermons of the Period of 1776* (Boston: Gould and Lincoln; Sheldon, 1860), 167; [Dickinson], *Letters from a Farmer*, in Ford, ed., *Writings of Dickinson*, 348. The eighteenth-century fascination with power, both in physics and in politics, was enhanced by this need to infer causes from their effects. Power or causation, "which," said Joseph Priestley, "is only the same idea differently modified," was not found in our sensory experience. "We all see events one succeeding another," wrote Thomas Reid, "but we see not the power by which they are produced." Locke had called power a "mysterious quality," and it remained such for Americans well into the nineteenth century. Power was something observable only from its effects. Whether from a magnet attracting iron, from a charged electrical jar giving a shock, or from a series of tax levies, men got the idea that some sort of cause or agent was at work. Power, said James Hutton, was "a term implying an unknown thing in action" (Heimann and McGuire, "Newtonian Forces and Lockean Powers," *Historical Studies in Physical Sciences*, III [1971], 266, 280, 286; Thomas Brown, "Inquiry into the Relation of Cause and Effect," *North American Review*, XII [1821], 401).

60. Hume, "Concerning Human Understanding," sec. VIII, pt. I, in *Essays*, Green and Grose, eds., 71. See also ibid., sec. VI, 48–49.

61. Smith, *Lectures*, I, 254. The colonists, writes Bailyn, had "a general sense that they lived in a conspiratorial world in which what the highest officials professed was not what they in fact intended, and that their words masked a malevolent design" (*Ideological Origins*, 98).

62. Jay Fliegelman, *Prodigals and Pilgrims: The American Revolution Against Patriarchal Authority, 1750–1800* (Cambridge, UK: Cambridge University Press, 1982), chap. 1; [Trenchard and Gordon], *Cato's Letters*, III, 330, 334; Priestley, quoted in Robert Darnton, *Mesmerism and the End of the Enlightenment in France* (Cambridge, MA: Harvard University Press, 1968), 16.

63. William Livingston, *The Independent Reflector: Or Weekly Essays on . . . the Province of New-York*, Milton M. Klein, ed. (Cambridge, MA: Belknap Press of Harvard University Press, 1963), 218; Courtlandt Canby, ed., "Robert Munford's *The Patriots*," *William and Mary Quarterly*, 3rd ser., VI (1949), 492; Tillotson, quoted in Leon Guilhamet, *The Sincere Ideal: Studies on Sincerity in Eighteenth-Century English Literature* (Montreal: McGill-Queen's University Press, 1974), 16. American Protestantism was always preoccupied with the problem of deception and hypocrisy. While seventeenth-century New England Puritans had recognized man's ultimate inability to discover who was saved or not and had accepted the possibility of some hypocrites being within the visible church, early nineteenth-century Christian perfectionists were sure they could tell who the deceivers were, for those "who bear a bold and living testimony against all sin, and confirm the same by their works" could not feign; their behavior thus "puts a period eventually, to all the contentions and

debates, about Who is a christian and who is not" (Perry Miller, *The New England Mind: From Colony to Province* [Cambridge, MA: Harvard University Press, 1953], 68–81; John Dunlavy, *The Manifesto, or a Declaration of the Doctrines and Practice of the Church of Christ* [Pleasant Hill, KY: P. Bertrand, 1818], 268, 283, 284–285).

64. Henrick Hartog, "The Public Law of a County Court: Judicial Government in Eighteenth-Century Massachusetts," *American Journal of Legal History*, XX (1976), 321–322. For some even the administration of all criminal justice could be reduced to the unmasking of deception. James Wilson thought that the word "felony"—"the generical term employed by the common law to denote a crime"—was derived from both Latin and Greek meaning "to deceive." It was not an injurious action alone that causes a crime, said Wilson; instead, the action revealed that the actor had a dispostion unworthy of the confidence of the community, "that he is false, deceitful, and treacherous: the crime is now completed" ("Law Lectures," in McClosky, ed., *Works of Wilson*, II, 622).

65. P. K. Elkin, *The Augustan Defence of Satire* (Oxford: Clarendon Press, 1973); Maynard Mack, "The Muse of Satire," in Richard C. Boys, ed., *Studies in the Literature of the Augustan Age: Essays Collected in Honor of Arthur Ellicott Case* (New York: Gordian Press, 1966); Basil Willey, *The Eighteenth Century Background: Studies on the Idea of Nature in the Thought of the Period* (New York: Columbia University Press, 1940), 100, 106.

66. [Adams], "U" to the *Boston Gazette*, August 29, 1763, in Taylor et al., eds., *Adams Papers*, I, 78, 79.

67. So Eustache LeNoble wrote in the preface to his novel *Abra-Mule* (1696): "The actions of sovereigns always have two parts, one is the public element which everyone knows and which forms the material of gazettes and the greater part of histories; the other, which these sovereigns hide behind the veil of their policy, are the secret motives of intrigue which cause those events, and which are known or revealed only to those who have had some part in these intrigues, or who by the penetration of their genius know how the one part becomes the other" (quoted in Rene Godenne, *Historie de la Nouvelle Française aux XVIIe et XVIIIe Siècles* [Geneva: Droz, 1970], 96).

68. Hume, *History of England*, VI, 64–65. In the years between the Restoration and the era of George III, the modern English notion of the criminal law of conspiracy was essentially formed. Basic to this notion was the belief that the criminality of conspiracy lay in the intent, which was revealed by the acts done. A justice in *Rex v. Sterling* (1664) had suggested that "the particular facts" were "but evidence of the design charged." A century later Lord Mansfield in *Rex v. Parsons et al.* elaborated the point by instructing the jury "that there was no occasion to prove the actual fact of conspiring, but that it might be collected from collateral circumstances" (James Wallace Bryan, *The Development of the English Law of Conspiracy*, Johns Hopkins University Studies in Historical and Political Science, XXVII [Baltimore: Johns Hopkins Press, 1909], 77, 78–79, 81. I owe this reference to Stanley N. Katz).

69. Edmund Burke, "Thoughts on the Cause of the Present Discontents" (1770), in *The Works and Correspondence of . . . Edmund Burke*, Charles William and Richard Bourke, eds. (London: Francis and John Rivington, 1852), III, esp. 112–114, 130–131. For the prevalence of the belief in a "double cabinet" operating "behind the curtain" in the era of George III, see Ian R. Christie, *Myth and Reality in Late-Eighteenth-Century British Politics and Other Papers* (London: Macmillan, 1970), 27–54.

70. Henry Laurens to John Brown, October 28, 1765, in George C. Rogers Jr., et al., eds., *The Papers of Henry Laurens*, V (Columbia: University of South Carolina Press, 1976), 30; Staughton Lynd, ed., "Abraham Yates's History of the Movement for the United States Constitution," *William and Mary Quarterly*, 3rd ser., XX (1963), 231, 232.

71. Richard Henry Lee to ———, May 31, 1764, in James Curtis Ballagh, ed., *The Letters of Richard Henry Lee*, I (New York: Macmillan, 1911), 7; James Boswell, *Life of Samuel Johnson*, Modern Library ed. (New York, 1945), 532. Even someone as enlightened and prone to conspiratorial thinking as John Adams repeatedly fell back on the "inscrutable" designs of "providence" in order to account for strange turns of events. This providential tradition, associated especially with Protestantism, was the only means in the eighteenth century, other than conspiracies, to account for events that seemed inconsistent with their causes (Taylor et al., eds., *Adams Papers*, II, 84, 236).

72. Nathanael Emmons, *A Discourse, Delivered on the National Fast, April 25, 1799* (Wrentham, MA: Nathaniel and Benjamin Heaton, 1799), 23.

73. *Boston Evening-Post*, December 29, 1766. See Lovejoy, *Reflections on Human Nature*, 129–215, and Albert O. Hirschman, *The Passions and the Interests: Political Arguments for Capitalism Before Its Triumph* (Princeton: Princeton University Press, 1977).

74. Duncan Forbes, "'Scientific' Whiggism: Adam Smith and John Millar," *Cambridge Journal*, VII (1954), 651, 653–654; Adam Ferguson, *An Essay on the History of Civil Society* (1767), Duncan Forbes, ed. (Edinburgh: Edinburgh University Press, 1966), 122, 123.

75. M. H. Abrams, *Natural Supernaturalism: Tradition and Revolution in Romantic Literature* (New York: W. W. Norton, 1971), 328; William Wordsworth, "The Borderers," in William Knight, ed., *The Poetical Works of William Wordsworth*, I (Edinburgh: William Patterson, 1882), 109. François Furet notes the differing views of the two French Revolutionary leaders, Brissot de Warville and Robespierre, over what was happening. Brissot, writes Furet, argued publicly in 1792 that "it was impossible to foresee the turn of events and that human intentions and the course of history were two separate matters." This "kind of historical objectivity, which made it possible to disregard the possibility—indeed, in this case, the probability—that evil intentions were at work, was by definition totally alien to Robespierre's political universe, in which it was implicitly assumed that intentions are perfectly coherent with the actions they prompt and the effects they aim at. . . . In such a universe, action never had unforeseeable consequences, nor was power ever innocent." The difference that Furet finds between the thinking of Brissot and Robespierre is precisely the difference between our modern conception of reality and that of the American Revolutionaries (*Interpreting the French Revolution*, trans. Elborg Forster [Cambridge, UK: Cambridge University Press, 1981], 67–68).

76. See esp. Roberts, *Secret Societies*, 160–167. On April 17, 1798, the recent immigrant to America Benjamin Henry Latrobe wrote to his Italian friend Giambattista Scandalla of the unprecedented turmoil of the French Revolution. "At the present moment the great convulsions of empires and nations, are so violent, that they lay hold of, and move individuals with an effect unknown in the former wars of kings. The surface—the great men of every nation—were once the only part of the mass really interested. The present storm is so violent, that the ocean is moved to the very depth, and you and I who inhabit it, feel the commotion" (John C. Van Horne and Lee W. Formwalt, eds., *The Correspondence and Miscellaneous Papers of Benjamin Henry Latrobe*, I [New Haven, CT: Yale University Press, 1988]).

77. Gouverneur Morris, "Political Enquiries," in Willi Paul Adams, ed., "'The Spirit of Commerce Requires that Property Be Sacred': Gouverneur Morris and the American Revolution," *Amerikastudien/American Studies*, XXI (1976), 328. Adams dates Morris's unpublished essay at 1776, but the content suggests that it was more likely written a decade or so later.

78. The fullest account of the Illuminati scare is Vernon Stauffer, *New England and the Bavarian Illuminati* (New York, 1967 [originally published 1918]). On conspiratorial thinking in the early Republic, see J. Wendell Knox, *Conspiracy in American Politics, 1787–1815* (New York: Arno Press, 1972).

79. David Tappan, *A Discourse Delivered in the Chapel of Harvard College, June 19, 1798* (Boston: Manning & Loring, 1798), 13, 19–21.

80. Ibid., 6; Dwight, *The Duty of Americans, at the Present Crisis, Illustrated in a Discourse Preached, on the Fourth of July* . . . (New Haven, CT: Thomas and Samuel Green, 1798), 16. It was this traditional assumption about the cause-effect relationship between beliefs and behavior that lay behind the Federalists' enactment of the Sedition Act of 1798. They could scarcely appreciate the emerging notion set forth by some Republicans that Americans should be free to believe and express whatever opinions they pleased.

81. Abraham Bishop, *Connecticut Republicanism. An Oration on the Extent and Power of Political Delusion* . . . (Albany, NY: John Barber, 1801), 8, and *Oration Delivered in Wallingford on the 11th of March 1801* . . . (New Haven, CT: William W. Morse, 1801), 24. I owe some of these citations relating to the Illuminati conspiracy to David C. Miller, "The Ideology of Conspiracy: An Examination of the *Illuminati* Incident in New England" (seminar paper, Brown University, 1977).

82. Bishop, *Proofs of a Conspiracy, Against Christianity, and the Government of the United States* . . . (Hartford, CT: John Babcock, 1802), 10–12, and *Oration Delivered in Wallingford*, 25, 26.

83. By avowing that "'holiness' is no 'guarantee for political rectitude,'" Bishop, wrote a stunned Federalist David Daggett, was undermining the moral order of society. "What security then," asked

Daggett, "have we for 'political rectitude'?" (*Three Letters to Abraham Bishop* . . . [Hartford, CT: Hudson and Goodwin, 1800], 27).

84. *Monthly Magazine and American Review*, I (1799), 289; Charles Brockden Brown, "Walstein's School of History," in *The Rhapsodist and Other Uncollected Writings*, Harry R. Warfel, ed. (New York: Scholars Facsimiles and Reprints, 1943), 147. In discussing the conspiratorial interpretation that saw the Order of the Bavarian Illuminati bringing about the French Revolution, Hofstadter wrote that "what is missing [in it] is not veracious information about the organization, but sensible judgment about what can cause a revolution" (*Paranoid Style*, 37). The basic question is why we think one judgment "sensible" and another not.

85. Robert K. Merton, "The Unanticipated Consequences of Purposive Social Action," *American Sociological Review*, I (1936), 894–904. Fisher Ames, the most pessimistic of Federalists, was one of the few Americans of these years who came to think like a European about revolutions and the "stream" of history. "Events," he wrote, "proceed, not as they were expected or intended, but as they are impelled by the irresistible laws of our political existence. Things inevitable happen, and we are astonished, as if they were miracles, and the course of nature had been overpowered or suspended to produce them" ("The Dangers of American Liberty" [1805], in Seth Ames, ed., *Works of Fisher Ames* . . . , II [Boston: Little, Brown, 1854], 345).

86. See W. B. Berthoff, " 'A Lesson on Concealment': Brockden Brown's Method in Fiction," *Philological Quarterly*, XXXVII (1958), 45–57; Michael Davitt Bell, " 'The Double-Tongued Deceiver': Sincerity and Duplicity in the Novels of Charles Brockden Brown," *Early American Literature*, IX (1974), 143–163; John Clemen, "Ambiguous Evil: A Study of Villains and Heroes in Charles Brockden Brown's Major Novels," ibid., X (1975), 190–219; Mark Seltzer, "Saying Makes It So: Language and Event in Brown's *Wieland*," ibid., XIII (1978), 81–91; and David H. Hirsch, *Reality and Idea in the Early American Novel* (The Hague: Mouton, 1971), 74–100.

87. Charles Brockden Brown, *Wieland; or, the Transformation* (Philadelphia: McKay, 1889 [originally published 1798]), 234, *Edgar Huntly, or Memoirs of a Sleep Walker* (Philadelphia: McKay, 1887 [originally published 1799]), 267, and "Walstein's School of History," in *Rhapsodist*, Warfel, ed. 152, 154.

88. Jeremy Bentham, *An Introduction to the Principles of Morals and Legislation* (Oxford: University of London, 1907 [originally published London, 1789]), 102. Utilitarianism has often been used rather loosely by historians and equated simply with utility or happiness. Although late eighteenth- and early nineteenth-century Americans were centrally interested in the usefulness of behavior, most did not mean by it what Bentham did: the abandonment of a concern with motives in favor of consequences. This sort of Benthamite utilitarianism had very little influence in America. See Paul A. Palmer, "Benthamism in England and America," *American Political Science Review*, XXXV (1941), 855–871; Morton White, *The Philosophy of the American Revolution* (New York: Oxford University Press, 1978), 230–239; and Wilson Smith, "William Paley's Theological Utilitarianism in America," *William and Mary Quarterly*, 3rd ser., XI (1954), 402–424. Even in criminal legislation, where, through the influence of Beccaria, utilitarianism was rampant, an ultimate concern with motives insinuated itself. In designating punishments for various offenses, wrote New York penal reformer Thomas Eddy, modern legislators could scarcely take into account "the moral condition" of the criminals; they could "regard only the tendency of actions to injure society, and distribute those punishments according to the comparative degrees of harm such actions may produce." Yet this stark utilitarianism in criminal legislation was justified in Eddy's mind only because it gave the supervisors of the penitentiaries the opportunity of "distinguishing the shades of guilt in different offenders" and thus of effecting the moral reformation of the criminals (*An Account of the State Prison or Penitentiary House, in the City of New York* [New York: Isaac Collins and son, 1801], 51–52).

89. "Introduction," *United States Magazine and Democratic Review*, I (October 1837), in Joseph L. Blau, ed., *Social Theories of Jacksonian Democracy: Representative Writings of the Period 1825–1850* (New York: Bobbs Merrill, 1954 [originally published 1947]), 28.

90. George Washington (1788), quoted in Paul C. Nagel, *One Nation Indivisible: The Union in American Thought, 1776–1861* (New York: Oxford University Press, 1964), 149.

91. Jacob Viner, *The Role of Providence in the Social Order: An Essay in Intellectual History* (Philadelphia: American Philosophical Society, 1972), 111. "God governs the world by the laws of a general

providence," observed Peres Fobes in 1795. Things did not happen in violation of these laws, for "this would introduce such a train of miraculous events, as would subvert the whole constitution of nature, and destroy that established in connexion between cause and effect, which is now the principal source of human knowledge and foresight" (*A Sermon Preached before His Excellency Samuel Adams . . . Being the Day of General Election* [Boston: Young and Minns, 1795], 12).

92. Charles Stewart Davies, *An Address Delivered on the Commemoration at Fryeburg, May 19, 1825* (Portland, ME: J. Adams Jr., 1825), in Blau, ed., *Social Theories*, 40.

93. On the romantic historians' view of the progressive patterning of events that sometimes transcended individual motives see David Levin, *History as Romantic Art: Bancroft, Prescott, Motley and Parkman* (Stanford, CA: Stanford University Press, 1959), 40–43.

94. Timothy Dwight, quoted in Marie Caskey, *Chariot of Fire: Religion and the Beecher Family* (New Haven, CT: Yale University Press, 1978), 39; see also Lyman Beecher, *Sermons, Delivered on Various Occasions*, II (Boston: John P. Jewitt, 1852), 156–158. Although Beecher and the other New Haven theologians believed that people had free wills, they also believed that the law of cause and effect operated in the moral as in the natural world, "the laws of mind, and the operation of moral causes, being just as uniform as the laws of matter." This made revivalism a science like engineering (Conrad Cherry, "Nature and the Republic: The New Haven Theology," *New England Quarterly*, LI [1978], 518–520).

95. John Taylor, *An Inquiry into the Principle and Policy of the Government of the United States* (New Haven, CT: Yale University Press, 1950 [originally published 1814]), 96; Tocqueville, *Democracy in America*, Phillips Bradley, ed., II (New York: Knopf, 1945), 85. "It is evidently a general constitution of providence," wrote Nathaniel Chipman as late as 1833, "that the general tendency of *vice* is to produce misery to the agent, of *virtue*, to produce happiness, connected in both by the relation of cause and effect" (*Principle of Government; a Treatise on Free Institutions . . .* [Burlington, VT: Edward Smith, 1833], 22).

96. Everett, *An Oration Delivered at Concord, April the Nineteenth 1825* (Boston: Cummings, Hilliard, 1825), 3–4; Cohen, *Revolutionary Histories*, 86–127.

97. Haskell, *The Emergence of Professional Social Science: The American Social Science Association and the Nineteenth-Century Crisis of Authority* (Urbana: University of Illinois Press, 1977), 40.

CHAPTER 4, INTERESTS AND DISINTERESTEDNESS IN THE MAKING OF THE CONSTITUTION

1. Gladstone, quoted in Douglass Adair, "The Tenth Federalist Revisited," in Trevor Colbourn., ed., *Fame and the Founding Fathers* (New York: W. W. Norton, 1974), 81.

2. Henry Steele Commager, *Jefferson, Nationalism, and the Enlightenment* (New York: George Braziller, 1975), xix.

3. Charles Thomson to Thomas Jefferson, April 6, 1786, in Julian P. Boyd et al., eds., *The Papers of Thomas Jefferson* (Princeton: Princeton University Press, 1950–), IX, 380. On the demographic explosion of the 1780s, see J. Potter, "The Growth of Population in America, 1700–1860," in D. V. Glass and D. E. C. Eversley, eds., *Population in History: Essays in Historical Demography* (Chicago: Aldine, 1965), 640.

4. For examples of the various historians who have minimized the criticalness of the 1780s, see Charles A. Beard, *An Economic Interpretation of the Constitution of the United States* (New York: Free Press, 1913), 48; E. James Ferguson, *The Power of the Purse: A History of American Public Finance, 1776–1790* (Chapel Hill: University of North Carolina Press, 1961), 337; Merrill Jensen, *The New Nation: A History of the United States During the Confederation, 1781–1790* (New York: Harper and Brothers, 1950), 348–349; Bernard Bailyn, "The Central Themes of the American Revolution: An Interpretation," in Stephen G. Kurtz and James H. Hutson, eds., *Essays on the American Revolution* (Chapel Hill: University of North Carolina Press, 1973), 21.

5. "Amicus Republicae," *Address to the Public . . .* (Exeter, N.H., 1786), in Charles S. Hyneman and Donald S. Lutz, eds., *American Political Writing During the Founding Era, 1760–1805* (Indianapolis: Liberty Fund, 1983), 1, 644; Rush to David Ramsay, [March or April 1788], in L. H. Butterfield, ed., *Letters of Benjamin Rush* (Princeton: Princeton University Press, 1951), I, 454; Washington to John Jay, August 1, 1786, May 18, 1786, in John C. Fitzpatrick, ed., *The Writings of George Washington . . .* (Washington, DC: U.S. Government Printing Office, 1931–1944), XXVIII, 431–432, 503.

6. Jackson Turner Main, *The Antifederalists: Critics of the Constitution, 1781–1788* (Chapel Hill: University of North Carolina Press, 1961), 177–178.

7. William Findley to Gov. William Plumer of New Hampshire, "William Findley of Westmoreland, Pa.," *Pennsylvania Magazine of History and Biography*, V (1881), 444; Jerry Grundfest, *George Clymer: Philadelphia Revolutionary, 1739–1813* (New York: Arno Press, 1982), 293–294; John Bach McMaster and Frederick D. Stone, eds., *Pennsylvania and the Federal Constitution, 1787–1788* (Philadelphia: Pennsylvania Historical Society, 1888), 115.

8. On this point, see Robert A. Feer, "Shays's Rebellion and the Constitution: A Study in Causation," *New England Quarterly*, XLII (1969), 388–410.

9. George Washington to John Jay, May 18, 1786, in Fitzpatrick, ed., *Writings of Washington*, XVIII, 432; James Madison to Thomas Jefferson, October 24, 1787, in Boyd et al., eds., *Papers of Jefferson*, XII, 276.

10. Robert A. Rutland, editorial note to "Vices of the Political System of the United States," in William T. Hutchinson et al., eds., *The Papers of James Madison* (Chicago, Charlottesville: University of Chicago Press, University Press of Virginia, 1962–), IX, 346.

11. Thomas Jefferson quoted in Ralph Ketcham, *James Madison; A Biography* (New York: Macmillan 1971), 162; Drew R. McCoy, "The Virginia Port Bill of 1784," *Virginia Magazine of History and Biography*, LXXXIII (1975), 294; James Madison to Edmund Pendleton, January 9, 1787, to George Washington, December 24, 1786, in Hutchinson et al., eds., *Papers of Madison*, IX, 225, 244; A. G. Roeber, *Faithful Magistrates and Republican Lawyers: Creators of Virginia Legal Culture, 1680–1810* (Chapel Hill: University of North Carolina Press, 1981), 192–202.

12. McCoy, "Virginia Port Bill," 292; James Madison to George Washington, December 7, 1786, to Edmund Pendleton, January 9, 1787, to George Washington, December 24, 1786, to Thomas Jefferson, December 4, 1786, in Hutchinson et al., eds., *Papers of Madison*, IX, 200, 244, 225, 191; Ketcham, *Madison*, 172.

13. "Vices," in Hutchinson et al., eds., *Papers of Madison*, IX, 354, 355–356.

14. George Washington to Henry Lee, April 5, 1786, in Fitzpatrick, ed., *Writings of Washington*, XXVIII, 402; Grundfest, *Clymer*, 164, 165; E. Wayne Carp, *To Starve the Army at Pleasure: Continental Army Administration and American Political Culture, 1775–1783* (Chapel Hill: University of North Carolina Press, 1984), 209; Knox quoted in William Winslow Crosskey and William Jeffrey Jr., *Politics and the Constitution in the History of the United States* (Chicago: University of Chicago Press, 1980), III, 420, 421.

15. Benjamin Rush to Jeremy Belknap, May 6, 1788, in Butterfield, ed., *Letters of Rush*, I, 461; Elbridge Gerry, in Max Farrand, ed., *The Records of the Federal Convention of 1787* (New Haven, CT: Yale University Press, 1911, rev. ed., 1937), I, 48.

16. The best study of wartime mobilization in a single state is Richard Buel Jr., *Dear Liberty: Connecticut's Mobilization for the Revolutionary War* (Middletown, CT: Western University Press, 1980). For an insightful general assessment of the effects of mobilization, see Janet Ann Riesman, "The Origins of American Political Economy, 1690–1781" (Ph.D. diss., Brown University, 1983), 302–338.

17. Laurens quoted in Albert S. Bolles, *The Financial History of the United States from 1774 to 1789: Embracing the Period of the American Revolution*, 4th ed. (New York: D. Appleton, 1896), 61–62 (I owe this citation to Janet Riesman); Carp, *To Starve the Army*, 106.

18. Nathanael Greene to Jacob Greene, after May 24, 1778, in Richard K. Showman ed., *The Papers of General Nathanael Greene* (Chapel Hill: University of North Carolina Press, 1976–), II, 404; Richard Buel Jr., "Samson Shorn: The Impact of the Revolutionary War on Estimates of the Republic's Strength," in Ronald Hoffman and Peter J. Albert, eds., *Arms and Independence: The Military Character of the American Revolution* (Charlottesville: University Press of Virginia, 1984), 157–160. On the growth of commercial farming in the middle of the eighteenth century, see especially Joyce Appleby, "Commercial Farming and the 'Agrarian Myth' in the Early Republic," *Journal of American History*, LXVIII (1982), 833–849. There is nothing on eighteenth-century America's increased importation of "luxuries" and "comforts" resembling Neil McKendrick et al., *The Birth of a Consumer Society: The Commercialization of Eighteenth-Century England* (Bloomington: Indiana University Press, 1982). But see the articles of Carole Shammas, especially "The Domestic Environment in Early Modern England and America," *Journal of Social History*, XIV (1980), 3–24; Lois Green Carr and Lorena S. Walsh, "Inventories and the Analysis of Wealth and Consumption Patterns in St. Mary's County,

Maryland, 1658–1777," *Historical Methods*, XIII (1980), 81–104; and Gloria L. Main, *Tobacco Colony: Life in Early Maryland, 1650–1720* (Princeton: Princeton University Press, 1982).

19. For examples of the new thinking about luxury as an inducement to industry, see Drew R. McCoy, *The Elusive Republic: Political Economy in Jeffersonian America* (Chapel Hill: University of North Carolina Press, 1980), 97.

20. [William Barton], *The True Interest of the United States, and Particularly of Pennsylvania Considered . . .* (Philadelphia: M. Carey, 1786), 12.

21. Ibid., 4, 25–26.

22. [William Smith], *The Independent Reflector . . . by William Livingston and Others*, Milton M. Klein, ed. (Cambridge, MA: Belknap Press of Harvard University Press, 1963), 106. See J. E. Crowley, *This Sheba, Self: The Conceptualization of Economic Life in Eighteenth-Century America* (Baltimore: Johns Hopkins University Press, 1974), 38–39, 44, 49, 87, 97–99.

23. *Remarks on a Pamphlet, Entitled, "Considerations on the Bank of North-America"* (Philadelphia: John Steele, 1785), 14; James Madison to James Monroe, April 9, 1786, in Hutchinson et al., eds., *Papers of Madison*, IX, 26; [Barton], *True Interest*, 20; Pennsylvania Statute of 1785, cited in E. A. J. Johnson, *The Foundations of American Economic Freedom: Government and Enterprise in the Age of Washington* (Minneapolis: University of Minnesota Press, 1973), 43n.

24. Thomas Jefferson, *Notes on the State of Virginia*, William Peden, ed. (Chapel Hill: University of North Carolina Press, 1955), Query XXII, 175; Thomas Jefferson to G. K. van Hogendorp, October 13, 1785, in Boyd et al., eds., *Papers of Jefferson*, VIII, 633.

25. Madison to Monroe, October 5, 1786, in Hutchinson et al., eds., *Papers of Madison*, IX, 141; *Carlisle Gazette* (Pa.), October 24, 1787, quoted in Herbert J. Storing, ed., *The Complete Anti-Federalist* (Chicago: University of Chicago Press, 1981), II, 208; George Washington to James Warren, October 7, 1785, in Fitzpatrick, ed., *Writings of Washington*, XXVIII, 291; Hamilton, in Farrand, ed., *Records of the Federal Convention*, I, 378. On the nature and role of interests in eighteenth-century British politics, see Michael Kammen, *Empire and Interest: The American Colonies and the Politics of Mercantilism* (Philadelphia: J. B. Lippincott, 1970).

26. Pauline Maier, *The Old Revolutionaries: Political Lives in the Age of Samuel Adams* (New York: Knopf, 1980), 3–50, quotation at 47.

27. George Washington, quoted in Lester H. Cohen, *The Revolutionary Histories: Contemporary Narratives of the American Revolution* (Ithaca, NY: Cornell University Press, 1980), 273.

28. Joseph Lathrop (1786), in Hyneman and Lutz, eds., *American Political Writing*, I, 660; Wilson, in Farrand, ed., *Records of the Federal Convention*, I, 605; Thomas Jefferson to Edward Carrington, January 16, 1787, in Boyd et al., eds., *Papers of Jefferson*, XI, 49. See also Ralph Ketcham, *Presidents Above Party: The First American Presidency, 1789–1829* (Chapel Hill: University of North Carolina Press, 1984).

29. Jefferson, "Summary View of the Rights of British America" (1774), in Boyd et al., eds., *Papers of Jefferson*, I, 134.

30. Johnson, *A Dictionary of the English Language . . .* (London: W. Strahan, 1755); Charles Royster, *A Revolutionary People at War: The Continental Army and American Character, 1775–1783* (Chapel Hill: University of North Carolina Press, 1979), 22–23.

31. John Brewer, *Party Ideology and Popular Politics at the Accession of George III* (Cambridge, UK: Cambridge University Press, 1976), 97.

32. George Washington to John Hancock, September 24, 1776, in Fitzpatrick, ed., *Writings of Washington*, VI, 107–108.

33. Adam Smith, *An Inquiry into the Nature and Causes of the Wealth of Nations*, R. H. Campbell and A. S. Skinner, eds. (Oxford: Oxford University Press, 1976) (V.i.f. 50–51), II, 781–783; [John Trenchard and Thomas Gordon], *Cato's Letters; or, Essays on Liberty, Civil and Religious, and Other Important Subjects*, 5th ed. (London: T. Woodward et al., 1748), III, 193; Phillips Payson, "A Sermon Preached before the Honorable Council . . . at Boston, May 27, 1778," in John Wingate Thornton, ed., *The Pulpit of the American Revolution . . .* (Boston, New York: Gould and Lincoln, Sheldon and Co., 1860), 337; Jefferson, "A Bill for the More General Diffusion of Education" (1779), in Boyd et al., eds., *Papers of Jefferson*, II, 527. On the eighteenth-century British developments out of which "Cato," Smith, and others wrote, see the illuminating discussion in John Barrell, *English Literature in History, 1730–80: An Equal Wide Survey* (London: Hutchinson, 1983), 17–50.

34. The best discussion of the distinctiveness of the gentry in colonial America is Rhys Isaac, *The Transformation of Virginia, 1740–1790* (Chapel Hill: University, of North Carolina Press, 1982), esp. 131–132.

35. Royster, *Revolutionary People at War*, 86–95; John B. B. Trussell Jr., *Birthplace of an Army: A Study of the Valley Forge Encampment* (Harrisburg: Pennsylvania Historical and Museum Commission, 1976), 86.

36. Francis Hutcheson, *A System of Moral Philosophy in Three Books* . . . (London: R. and A. Foulis 1755), II, 113. "Let not your Love of Philosophical Amusements have more than its due Weight with you," Benjamin Franklin admonished Cadwallader Colden at midcentury. Public service was far more important. In fact, said Franklin, even "the finest" of Newton's "Discoveries" could not have excused his neglect of serving the commonwealth if the public had needed him (Franklin to Colden, October 11, 1750, in Leonard W. Labaree et al., eds., *The Papers of Benjamin Franklin* [New Haven, CT: Yale University Press, 1959–], IV, 68).

37. Jack N. Rakove, *The Beginnings of National Politics: An Interpretative. History of the Continental Congress* (New York: Knopf, 1979), 216–239, quotation by William Fleming to Jefferson, May 10, 1779, at 237; George Athan Billias, *Elbridge Gerry, Founding Father and Republican Statesman* (New York: McGraw-Hill, 1976), 138–139.

38. See William R. Taylor, *Cavalier and Yankee: The Old South and American National Character* (New York: George Braziller, 1961).

39. Wilson, "On the History of Property," in Robert Green McCloskey, ed., *The Works of James Wilson* (Cambridge, MA: Harvard University Press, 1967), II, 716; Dickinson, "Letters of a Farmer in Pennsylvania" (1768), in Paul Leicester Ford, ed., *The Writings of John Dickinson*, vol. I, *Political Writings, 1764–1774* (Pennsylvania Historical Society, *Memoirs*, XIV [Philadelphia: Pennsylvania Historical Society, 1895]), 307 (hereafter cited as Ford, ed., *Writings of Dickinson*).

40. "We have found by experience, that no dependence can be had upon *merchants*, either at *home*, or in *America*," Charles Chauncy told Richard Price in 1774, "so many of them are so mercenary as to find within themselves a readiness to become slaves themselves, as well as to be accessory to the slavery of others, if they imagine they may, by this means, serve their own private separate interest" (D. C. Thomas and Bernard Peach, eds., *The Correspondence of Richard Price* [Durham, NC: Duke University Press, 1983], I, 170). For Adam Smith's view that the interest of merchants and indeed of all who lived by profit was "always in some respects different from, and even opposite to, that of the publick," see Smith, *Wealth of Nations*, Campbell and Skinner, ed. (I.xi.p.10), I, 267.

41. Richard Jackson to Benjamin Franklin, June 17, 1755, in Labaree et al., eds., *Papers of Franklin*, VI, 82. On the colonial merchants' "detachment from political activity," see Thomas M. Doerflinger, "Philadelphia Merchants and the Logic of Moderation, 1760–1775," *William and Mary Quarterly*, 3rd ser., XL (1983), 212–213; and Edward Countryman, *A People in Revolution: The American Revolution and Political Society in New York, 1760–1790* (Baltimore: Johns Hopkins University Press, 1981), 113.

42. William M. Fowler Jr., *The Baron of Beacon Hill: A Biography of John Hancock* (Boston: Houghton Mifflin, 1980); Charles W. Akers, *The Divine Politician: Samuel Cooper and the American Revolution in Boston* (Boston: Northeastern University Press, 1982), 121, 128, 130, 141, 176, 311; Henry Laurens to Richard Oswald, July 7, 1764, in Philip M. Hamer et al., eds., *The Papers of Henry Laurens* (Columbia: University of South Carolina Press, 1968–), IV, 338 (see also Rachel N. Klein, "Ordering the Backcountry: The South Carolina Regulation," *William and Mary Quarterly*, 3rd ser., XXXVIII [1981], 667); David Duncan Wallace, *The Life of Henry Laurens* . . . (New York: Russell and Russell, 1915), 69–70, quotation at 335. In the 1780s Elbridge Gerry likewise retired from mercantile business and "set himself up as a country squire" (Billias, *Gerry*, 135–136).

43. Leonard W. Labaree et al., eds., *The Autobiography of Benjamin Franklin* (New Haven, CT: Yale University Press, 1964), 196; Christopher, Collier, *Roger Sherman's Connecticut: Yankee Politics and the American Revolution* (Middletown, CT: Wesleyan University Press, 1971), 14, 21–22.

44. Jacob E. Cooke, ed., *The Federalist* No. 35 (Middletown, CT, 1961) [Barton], *True Interest*, 27. For arguments in pre-Revolutionary Virginia whether lawyers were practicing "a grovelling, mercenary trade" or not, see Roeber, *Faithful Magistrates and Republican Lawyers*, 156–157. Some conceded that lawyers were members of one of the "three genteel Professions," but that they were guilty of more "petit Larceny" than doctors and clergymen. Madison was not convinced of the disinterestedness of lawyers (ibid., 157, 147, Ketcham, *Madison*, 145). On the efforts of some nineteenth-century thinkers

to make professional communities the repositories of disinterestedness against the selfishness and interestedness of businessmen, see Thomas L. Haskell, "Professionalism *versus* Capitalism: R. H. Tawney, Emile Durkheim, and C. S. Peirce on the Disinterestedness of Professional Communities," in Thomas L. Haskell, ed., *The Authority of Experts: Studies in History and Theory* (Bloomington: Indiana University Press, 1984), 180–225.

45. Morris, "Political Enquiries," in Willi Paul Adams, ed., "'The Spirit of Commerce, Requires that Property Be Sacred': Gouverneur Morris and the American Revolution," *Amerikastudien/American Studies*, XXI (1976), 329; Alexander Hamilton to Robert Troup, April 13, 1795, in Harold C. Syrett, et al., eds., *The Papers of Alexander Hamilton* (New York: Columbia University Press, 1961–1979), XVII, 329.

46. George Washington to Benjamin Harrison, January 22, 1785, to George William Fairfax, February 27, 1785, in Fitzpatrick, ed., *Writings of Washington*, XXVIII, 36, 85.

47. George Washington to Benjamin Harrison, January 22, 1785, to William Grayson, January 22, 1785, to Lafayette, February 15, 1785, to Thomas Jefferson, February 25, 1785, to George William Fairfax, February 27, 1785, to Governor Patrick Henry, February 27, 1785, to Henry Knox, February 28, 1785, June 18, 1785, to Nathanael Greene, May 20, 1785, in Fitzpatrick, ed., *Writings of Washington*, XXVIII, 36, 37, 72, 80–81, 85, 89–91, 92–93, 146, 167. The only friend whose advice on the disposition of the canal shares Washington did not solicit was Robert Morris, perhaps because he feared that Morris might tell him to keep them. Instead he confined his letter to Morris to describing the commercial opportunities of the canals. To Morris, February 1, 1785, ibid., 48–55.

48. Cooke, ed., *The Federalist* No. 10; Gordon S. Wood, "Democracy and the Constitution," in Robert A, Goldwin and William A. Schambra, eds., *How Democratic Is the Constitution?* (Washington, DC: American Enterprise Institute, 1980), 11–12. On the tendency to misread Madison, see Robert J. Morgan, "Madison's Theory of Representation in the Tenth Federalist," *Journal of Politics*, XXXVI (1974), 852–885; and Paul F. Bourke, "The Pluralist Reading of James Madison's Tenth *Federalist*," *Perspectives in American History*, IX (1975), 271–295.

49. James Madison to George Washington April 16, 1787, to Edmund Randolph, April 8, 1787, in Hutchinson et al., eds., *Papers of Madison*, IX, 370, 384; John Zvesper, "The Madisonian Systems," *Western Political Quarterly*, XXXVII (1984), 244–247.

50. Jerome J. Nadelhaft, "'The Snarls of Invidious Animals': The Democratization of Revolutionary South Carolina," in Ronald Hoffman and Peter J. Albert, eds., *Sovereign States in an Age of Uncertainty* (Charlottesville: University Press of Virginia 1981), 77.

51. On Findley, see his letter to Governor William Plumer of New Hampshire, February 27, 1812, "William Findley of Westmoreland, Pa.," *Pennsylvania Magazine of History and Biography*, V (1881), 440–50; and Russell J. Ferguson, *Early Western Pennsylvania Politics* (Pittsburgh: University of Pittsburgh Press, 1938), 39–40.

52. Grundfest, *Clymer*, 141.

53. Claude Milton Newlin, *The Life and Writings of Hugh Henry Brackenridge* (Princeton: Princeton University Press, 1932), 71.

54. Ibid., 78, 80–81; Ferguson, *Early Western Pennsylvania*, 66–69.

55. Newlin, *Brackenridge*, 79–80, 83–84; Ferguson, *Early Western Pennsylvania*, 70–72.

56. Mathew Carey, ed., *Debates and Proceedings of the General Assembly of Pennsylvania on the Memorials Praying a Repeal or Suspension of the Law Annulling the Charter of the Bank* (Philadelphia: Carey and Co., Seddon and Pritchard, 1786), 19, 64, 10, 30.

57. Robert Morris to George Washington, May 29, 1781, E. James Ferguson et al., eds., *The Papers of Robert Morris, 1781–1784* (Pittsburgh: University of Pittsburgh Press, 1973–), I, 96; Ellis Paxson Oberholtzer, *Robert Morris, Patriot and Financier* (New York: Macmillan, 1903), 52–56, 70–71.

58. Carey, ed., *Debates*, 33, 79–80, 98 (quotations on 80, 98).

59. Ibid., 81; Oberholtzer, *Morris*, 285–286, 297–299, 301–303; Eleanor Young, *Forgotten Patriot: Robert Morris* (New York: Macmillan, 1950–), 170; Barbara Ann Chernow, *Robert Morris, Land Speculator, 1790–1801* (New York: Arno Press, 1978); H. E. Scudder, ed., *Recollections of Samuel Breck . . .* (Philadelphia: Porter & Coates, 1877), 203: *The Journal of William Maclay* (New York: Albert & Charles Boni, 1927 [orig. pub, 1890]), 132.

60. Carey, ed., *Debates*, 66, 87, 128, 21, 130, 38, 15, 72–73.

61. Cooke, ed., *The Federalist* No. 10; [William Findley], *A Review of the Revenue System Adopted at the First Congress under the Federal Constitution* ... (Philadelphia: Bailey, 1794), 117.

62. Jonathan Elliot, ed., *The Debates in the Several State Conventions on the Adoption of the Federal Constitution* ... (Philadelphia: J. B. Lippincott, 1896), II, 13, 260; [Findley], "Letter by an Officer of the Late Continental Army," *Independent Gazette* (Philadelphia), November 6, 1787, in Storing, ed., *Complete Anti-Federalist*, III, 95; Ruth Bogin, *Abraham Clark and the Quest for Equality in the Revolutionary Era, 1774–1794* (East Brunswick, NJ: Fairleigh Dickinson University Press, 1982), 32.

63. Philip A. Crowl, "Anti-Federalism in Maryland, 1787–88," *William and Mary Quarterly*, 3rd ser., IV (1947), 464; Richard Walsh, *Charleston's Sons of Liberty: A Study of the Artisans, 1763–1789* (Columbia: University of South Carolina Press, 1959), 132; [James Winthrop] "Letters of Agrippa," *Massachusetts Gazette*, December 14, 1787, in Storing, ed., *Complete Anti-Federalist*, IV, 80; "Essentials of a Free Government," in Walter Hartwell Bennett, ed., *Letters from the Federal Farmer to the Republican* (Tuscaloosa: University of Alabama Press, 1978), 10.

64. Benjamin Latrobe to Philip Mazzei, December 19, 1806, in Margherita Marchione et al., eds., *Philip Mazzei: Selected Writings and Correspondence* (Prato, Italy: Cassa di Risparmi e Depositi di Prato, 1983), III, 439 (I owe this reference to Stanley J. Idzerda).

65. Ibid.

66. James T. Schleifer, *The Making of Tocqueville's "Democracy in America"* (Chapel Hill: University of North Carolina Press, 1980), 242, 243; Tocqueville to Ernest de Chabrol, June 9, 1831, in Roger Boesch, ed., *Alexis de Tocqueville: Selected Letters on Politics and Society* (Berkeley: University of California Press, 1985), 38; Tocqueville, *Democracy in America*, ed. Phillips Bradley (New York: Vintage Books, 1954), I, 243. It was not, of course, as simple as Tocqueville made it out to be. The ideal of disinterested politics did not disappear in the nineteenth century, and even today it lingers on here and there. It formed the basis for all the antiparty and mugwump reform movements and colored the thinking of many of the Progressives. For Theodore Roosevelt in 1894, "the first requisite in the citizen who wishes to share the work of our public life ... is that he shall act disinterestedly and with a sincere purpose to serve the whole commonwealth" (Roosevelt, *American Ideals and Other Essays, Social and Political* [New York: G.P. Putnam's Sons, 1897], 34 [I owe this reference to John Patrick Diggins]). Of course, at almost the same time, John Dewey was telling Americans that it was psychologically impossible for anyone to act disinterestedly. See John Patrick Diggins, *The Lost Soul of American Politics: Virtue, Self-Interest, and the Foundations of Liberalism* (New York: Oxford University Press, 1984), 341–343. See also Stephen Miller, *Special Interest Groups in American Politics* (New Brunswick, NJ: Transaction Books, 1983).

67. Wilson, in Farrand, ed., *Records of the Federal Convention*, I, 154; Cooke, ed., *The Federalist* No. 10. Vernon Parrington asked the same questions. If ordinary men were motivated by self-interest, as the Federalists believed, why would "this sovereign motive" abdicate "its rule among the rich and well born? ... Do the wealthy betray no desire for greater power? Do the strong and powerful care more for good government than for class interests?" (*Main Currents in American Thought: An Interpretation of American Literature from the Beginnings to 1920* [New York: Harcourt, Brace, 1927], I, 302).

68. John Witherspoon, "Speech in Congress on Finances," *The Works of John Witherspoon* ... (Edinburgh: John Turnbull, 1805), IX, 133–134.

69. Robert J. Taylor, *Western Massachusetts in the Revolution* (Providence, RI: Brown University Press, 1954), 20; Robert A. East, *Business Enterprise in the American Revolutionary Era* (New York: Columbia University Press, 1938), 20–22; Dickinson, "Letters of a Farmer," in Ford, ed., *Writings of Dickinson*, 307; Fowler, *Baron of Beacon Hill*, 251; Margaret E. Martin, *Merchants and Trade of the Connecticut River Valley, 1750–1820* (*Smith College Studies in History*, XXIV [Northampton, MA: Smith College, 1938–1939]), 159. See also Alice Hanson Jones, *Wealth of a Nation to Be: The American Colonies on the Eve of the Revolution* (New York: Columbia University Press, 1980), 145–153.

70. Carey, ed., *Debates*, 96; Aubrey C. Land, "Economic Base and Social Structure: The Northern Chesapeake in the Eighteenth Century," *Journal of Economic History*, XXV (1965), 650; Isaac, *Transformation of Virginia*, 133; East, *Business Enterprise*, 19; Robert D. Mitchell, *Commercialism and Frontier: Perspectives on the Early Shenandoah Valley* (Charlottesville: University Press of Virginia, 1977), 116, 123.

71. John Adams to James Warren, February 12, 1777, in Robert J. Taylor et al., eds., *Papers of John Adams* (Cambridge, MA: Belknap Press of Harvard University Press, 1983), V, 83; Riesman, "Origins of American Political Economy," 135–136, 144; Norman K. Risjord, *Chesapeake Politics, 1781–1800* (New York: Columbia University Press, 1978), 124; George Washington to Governor George Clinton, April 20, 1785, to Battaile Muse, December 4, 1785, in Fitzpatrick, ed., *Writings of Washington*, XXVIII, 134, 341; Carey, ed., *Debates*, 96.

72. Roy A. Foulke, *The Sinews of American Commerce* (New York: Dun & Bradstreet, 1941), 66–68, 74–75, 89; William E. Nelson, *Americanization of the Common Law: The Impact of Legal Change on Massachusetts Society, 1760–1830* (Cambridge, MA: Harvard University Press, 1975), 44–45. For a sensitive analysis of the Virginia planters' etiquette of debt, see T. H. Breen, *Tobacco Culture: The Mentality of the Great Tidewater Planters on the Eve of the Revolution* (Princeton: Princeton University Press, 1985), esp. 93–106.

73. Grundfest, *Clymer*, 177; *Providence Gazette*, August 5, 1786, quoted in David P. Szatmary, *Shays' Rebellion: The Making of an Agrarian Insurrection* (Amherst: University of Massachusetts Press, 1980), 51; Madison, "Notes for Speech Opposing Paper Money" [November 1, 1786], in Hutchinson et al., eds., *Papers of Madison*, IX, 158–159; Taylor, *Western Massachusetts*, 166.

74. Farrand, ed., *Records of the Federal Convention*, II, 310, III, 350.

75. Ruth Bogin, "New Jersey's True Policy: The Radical Republican Vision of Abraham Clark," *William and Mary Quarterly*, 3rd ser., XXXV (1978), 105.

76. David Ramsay, "An Address to the Freemen of South Carolina on the Subject of the Federal Constitution" (1787), in Paul Leicester Ford, ed., *Pamphlets on the Constitution of the United States* (Brooklyn, NY: Historical Printing Club, 1888), 379–380. Madison thought that the Anti-Federalist pamphlets omitted "many of the true grounds of opposition" to the Constitution. "The articles relating to Treaties, to paper money, and to contracts, created more enemies than all the errors in the System positive and negative put together" (James Madison to Thomas Jefferson, October 17, 1788, in Boyd et al., eds., *Papers of Jefferson*, XIV, 18).

77. Benjamin Rush to Jeremy Belknap, February 28, 1788, quoted in John P. Kaminski, "Democracy Run Rampant: Rhode Island in the Confederation," in James Kirby Martin, ed., *The Human Dimensions of Nation Making: Essays on Colonial and Revolutionary History* (Madison: State Historical Society of Wisconsin, 1976), 267; Rush to Elias Boudinot, July 9, 1788, in Butterfield, ed., *Letters of Rush*, I, 471.

CHAPTER 6, THE MAKING OF AMERICAN DEMOCRACY

1. R. R. Palmer, *The Age of the Democratic Revolution: A Political History of Europe and America, 1760–1800*, 2 vols. (Princeton: Princeton University Press, 1959, 1964).

2. Gabriel A. Almond and Sidney Verba, *The Civic Culture: Political Attitudes and Democracy in Five Nations* (Boston: Little, Brown, 1965), 2.

3. James Otis, *Right of the British Colonies Asserted and Proved* (Boston: Edes and Gill, 1764), in Bernard Bailyn, ed., *Pamphlet of the American Revolution, 1750–1776* (Cambridge, MA: Harvard University Press, 1965), 427.

4. Philadelphia *Pennsylvania Gazette*, April 24, 1776.

5. Edward Countryman, *A People in Revolution: The American Revolution and Political Society in New York, 1760–1790* (Baltimore: John Hopkins University Press, 1981), 33.

6. Clifford K. Shipton, "Jonathan Trumbull," in *Sibley's Harvard Graduates: Biographies of Those Who Attended Harvard College* (Boston: Massachusetts Historical Society, 1951), 8: 269.

7. Bernard Bailyn, *The Origins of American Politics* (New York: Knopf, 1968).

8. On the politics of the imperial relationship, see the works by Alison Gilbert Olson, *Anglo-American Politics, 1660–1775: The Relationship Between Parties in England and Colonial America* (New York: Oxford University Press, 1973), and Olson, *Making the Empire Work: London and American Interest Groups, 1690–1790* (Cambridge, MA: Harvard University Press, 1992).

9. On the increasing difficulties of colonial communication in the empire on the eve of the Revolution, see Michael Kammen, *A Rope of Sand: The Colonial Agents, British Politics, and the American Revolution* (Ithaca, NY: Cornell University Press, 1968).

10. Gary B. Nash, "The Transformation of Urban Politics, 1700–1764," *Journal of American History*, LX (1973), 605–632.

11. J. R. Pole, *The Gift of Government: Political Responsibility from the English Restoration to American Independence* (Athens, GA: University of Georgia Press, 1983).

12. *Acts and Resolves, Public and Private, of the Province of Massachusetts Bay* (Boston: Secretary of the Commonwealth, 1878), III, 70.

13. *South Carolina Gazette* (Charleston), May 13, April 29, 1784.

14. Philadelphia *Pennsylvania Evening Post*, July 30, 1776, quoted in David Hawke, *In the Midst of Revolution* (Philadelphia: University of Pennsylvania Press, 1961), 187.

15. Alfred Young, "The Mechanics and the Jeffersonians: New York, 1789–1801," *Labor History*, 5 (1964), 274; Donald H. Stewart, *The Opposition Press of the Federalist Period* (Albany: State University of New York Press, 1969), 389; Richard E. Ellis, *The Jeffersonian Crisis: Courts and Politics in the Young Republic* (New York: Oxford University Press, 1971), 173.

16. Philip Lampi's *Collection of American Election Data, 1787–1825*, for presidential, congressional, gubernatorial, and state legislative elections shows how popular and competitive American politics became during the first two decades of the nineteenth century. In other words, America did not have to wait for Andrew Jackson in order to become democratic. Lampi's *Collection* is available online via the American Antiquarian Society's Web page "A New Nation Votes: American Election Returns, 1787–1825."

17. Harvey Strum, "Property Qualifications and the Voting Behavior in New York, 1807–1816," *Journal of the Early Republic*, I (1981), 359.

18. Chilton Williamson, *American Suffrage: From Property to Democracy, 1760–1860* (Princeton: Princeton University Press, 1960); and Alexander Keyssar, *The Right to Vote: The Contested History of Democracy in the United States* (New York: Basic Books, 2000). Many states continued to maintain taxpaying requirements for voting.

19. James Madison to George Washington, April 16, 1787, in Jack N. Rakove, ed., *James Madison: Writings* (New York: Library of America, 1999), 81.

20. Walter R. Fee, *The Transition from Aristocracy to Democracy in New Jersey, 1789–1829* (Somerville, NJ: Somerset Press, 1933), 146; Joseph S. Davis, *Essays in the Earlier History of American Corporations, IV, Eighteenth-Century Business Corporations in the United States* (Cambridge, MA: Harvard University Press, 1917), 321; P. H. Woodward, *One Hundred Years of the Hartford Bank . . .* (Hartford: CT: Case, Lockwood & Brainard, 1892), 50.

21. Jeffrey L. Pasley, "Private Access and Public Power: Gentility and Lobbying in the Early Congress," in Kenneth R. Bowling and Donald R. Kennon, eds., *The House and Senate in the 1790s: Petitioning, Lobbying, and the Institutional Development* (Athens: Ohio University Press, 2002), 74–76; Donald J. Ratcliffe, *Party Spirit in a Frontier Republic: Democratic Politics in Ohio, 1793–1821* (Columbus: Ohio State University Press, 1998), 79; Donald Hickey, *The War of 1812* (Urbana: University of Illinois Press, 1980), 122.

22. Strum, "Property Qualifications and the Voting Behavior in New York, 1807–1816," *Journal of the Early Republic*, I (1981), 350, 369.

23. Samuel Shapiro, " 'Aristocracy, Mud, and Vituperation': The Butler-Dana Campaign," *New England Quarterly*, XXXI (1958), 340–360.

24. Arthur Zilversmit, *The First Emancipation: The Abolition of Slavery in the North* (Chicago: University of Chicago Press, 1967), 222.

25. Leon F. Litwack, *North of Slavery: The Negro in the Free States, 1790–1860* (Chicago: University of Chicago Press, 1961), 75.

26. James M. McPherson, "The Ballot and Land for the Freedman, 1861–1865," in Kenneth M, Stampp and Leon F. Litwack, eds., *Reconstruction: An Anthology of Revisionist Writings* (Baton Rouge: Louisiana State University Press, 1969), 138.

27. *New York Times*, September 8, 2010.

28. Chilton Williamson, *American Suffrage from Property to Democracy, 1760–1860* (Princeton: Princeton University Press, 1960), 279.

CHAPTER 7, THE RADICALISM OF THOMAS JEFFERSON AND THOMAS PAINE CONSIDERED

1. Thomas Paine, *The Rights of Man: Part the Second* (1792), in Philip S. Foner, ed., *The Complete Writings of Thomas Paine* (New York: Citadel, 1969), I, 405–406; Thomas Jefferson to Thomas Paine,

March 18, 1801, in Barbara Oberg et al., eds., *The Papers of Thomas Jefferson* (Princeton: Princeton University Press, 2006), 33, 359.

2. Marquis de Chastellux, *Travels in North America in the Years 1780, 1781 and 1782*, Howard C. Rice, ed. (Chapel Hill: University of North Carolina Press, 1963), 2, 391.

3. John Keane, *Tom Paine: A Political Life* (Boston: Little, Brown, 1995), 211.

4. S. W. Jackman, "A Young Englishman Reports on the New Nation: Edward Thornton, to James Bland Burges, 1791–1893," *William and Mary Quarterly*, XVIII (1961), 110.

5. Thomas Jefferson, "A Summary View of the Rights of British Colonists (1774)," in Julian P. Boyd et al., eds., *The Papers of Thomas Jefferson* (Princeton: Princeton University Press, 1950–), I, 134.

6. Thomas Paine, *Common Sense* (1776), in Foner, ed., *Complete Writings of Thomas Paine*, I, 23.

7. Thomas Paine, "The Crisis Extraordinary," October 4, 1780, in Foner, ed., *Complete Writings*, I, 182.

8. Thomas Paine, *The Rights of Man: Part the Second* (1792), in Foner, ed., *Complete Writings*, I, 363; Thomas Jefferson to T. Law, June 13, 1814, in A. A. Lipscomb and Albert Ellery Bergh, eds., *The Writings of Thomas Jefferson* (Washington, DC: Thomas Jefferson Memorial Association, 1903), XIV, 141–142; Thomas Jefferson to Peter Carr, August 12, 1787, in Boyd et al., eds., *Papers of Jefferson*, XII, 15.

9. Thomas Paine, *Common Sense*, in Foner, ed., *Complete Writings*, I, 4.

10. Jonathan Mayhew, *Seven Sermons upon the Following Subjects . . .* (Boston: Alden Bradford, 1749), 126.

11. Thomas Paine, *The Rights of Man: Part the Second* (1792), in Foner, ed., *Complete Writings*, I, 357.

12. Ibid., 359.

13. Ibid., 355.

14. Ibid., 373; Thomas Jefferson to Governor John Langdon, March 5, 1810, in Merrill D. Peterson, ed., *Thomas Jefferson: Writings* (New York: Library of America, 1984), 1221.

15. Thomas Paine, *The Rights of Man: Part the Second*, in Foner, ed., *Complete Writings*, I, 355–356.

16. [Benjamin Lincoln Jr.], "The Free Republican No. III," Boston *Independent Chronicle*, December 8, 1785.

17. Thomas Paine, *The Rights of Man: Part the Second*, in Foner, ed., *Complete Writings*, I, 400.

18. Thomas Jefferson to Joseph Fey, March 18, 1793, in Boyd et al., eds., *Papers of Jefferson*, XXV, 402; Thomas Jefferson to William Short, January 3, 1793, in Peterson, ed., *Jefferson: Writings*, 1004; Thomas Jefferson to Tench Coxe, May 1, 1794, in Boyd et al., eds., *Papers of Jefferson*, XXVIII, 67.

19. Alexander Hamilton to Rufus King, June 3, 1802, in Joanne B. Freeman, ed., *Alexander Hamilton: Writings* (New York: Library of America, 2001), 993; Alexander Hamilton, "Views on the French Revolution (1794)," Harold C. Syrett et al., eds., *The Papers of Alexander Hamilton* (New York: Columbia University Press, 1962–), XXVI, 739–740.

20. Alexander Hamilton, "Views on the French Revolution (1794)," Syrett et al., eds., *Papers of Alexander Hamilton*, 739–740; Alexander Hamilton to Rufus King, June 3, 1802, in Freeman, ed., *Hamilton: Writings*, 993.

21. Thomas Paine, *The Rights of Man: Part the Second*, in Foner, ed., *Complete Writings*, I, 408.

22. Thomas Jefferson to William Plumer, July 21, 1816, in Lipscomb and Bergh, eds., *Writings of Jefferson*, XV, 46–47.

23. Thomas Paine, *The Age of Reason* (1794), in Eric Foner, ed., *Thomas Paine: Collected Writings* (New York: Library of America, 1995), 825; Thomas Jefferson to Horatio Spafford, March 17, 1814, Thomas Jefferson to James Smith, December 8, 1822, in James H. Hutson, ed., *The Founders on Religion: A Book of Quotations* (Princeton: Princeton University Press, 2005), 68, 218; Thomas Jefferson to Charles Clay, January 29, 1815, in Lipscomb and Bergh, eds., *Writings of Jefferson*, XIV, 233.

24. Thomas Paine to Henry Laurens, September 14, 1779, in Foner, ed., *Complete Writings of Paine*, II, 1178.

25. Ibid.; Thomas Paine to Robert Livingston, May 19, 1783, quoted in Keane, *Paine*, 242.

26. Thomas Jefferson to James Madison, October 18, 1785, in Peterson, ed., *Jefferson: Writings*, 841–842.

27. Thomas Jefferson to Thomas Paine, March 18, 1801, in Boyd et al., eds., *Papers of Jefferson*, XXXIII, 359.

CHAPTER 8, MONARCHISM AND REPUBLICANISM IN EARLY AMERICA

1. Patrick Henry, in Bernard Bailyn, ed., *The Debate on the Constitution* (New York: Library of America, 1993), II, 629, 675.

2. Patrick Henry, in Jonathan Elliot, ed., *The Debates in the Several State Conventions on the Adoption of the Federal Constitution* (Washington, 1854), III, 58, 491.

3. Benjamin Tappan to Henry Knox, April 1787, Henry Knox Papers, Massachusetts Historical Society. (I owe this citation to Brendan McConville.)

4. James Madison, cited in Gordon S. Wood, *The Creation of the American Republic, 1776–1787* (Chapel Hill: University of North Carolina Press, 1969), 410.

5. James Madison to Thomas Jefferson, October 24, 1787, in Julian P. Boyd et al., eds., *The Papers of Thomas Jefferson* (Princeton: Princeton University Press, 1950–), XII, 276.

6. Benjamin Rush, "To ———: Information to Europeans Who Are Disposed to Migrate to the United States," April 16, 1790, L. H. Butterfield, ed., *Letters of Benjamin Rush* (Princeton: Princeton University Press, 1951), II, 556.

7. James Madison, "Vices of the System of the United States," in Hutchinson et al., eds., *Papers of Madison*, IX, 352, 357.

8. Max Farrand, ed., *The Records of the Federal Convention* (New Haven, CT: Yale University Press, 1937), I, 65, 119; II, 513.

9. Thomas Jefferson to David Humphreys, March 18, 1789, in Boyd et al., eds., *Papers of Jefferson*, XIV, 679.

10. Louise B. Dunbar, *A Study of "Monarchical" Tendencies in the United States, from 1776 to 1801* (Urbana: University of Illinois Press, 1923), 99–100.

11. James McHenry to George Washington, March 29, 1789, in W. W. Abbot et al., eds., *Papers of Washington: Presidential Series* (Charlottesville: University Press of Virginia, 1983–), I, 461.

12. Winifred E. A. Bernard, *Fisher Ames: Federalist and Statesman, 1758–1808* (Chapel Hill: University of North Carolina Press, 1965), 92.

13. David W. Robson, *Educating Republicans: The College in the Era of the American Revolution, 1758–1800* (Westport, CT: Greenwood Press, 1985), 149; Thomas E. V. Smith, *The City of New York in the Year of Washington's Inauguration, 1789* (New York: Anson D. F. Randolph, 1889, reprint ed., Riverside, CT, 1972), 217–219; Barry Schwartz, *George Washington: The Making of an American Symbol* (New York: Free Press, 1987).

14. William B. Allen, ed., *George Washington: A Collection* (Indianapolis: Liberty Classics, 1988), 446.

15. Alexander Hamilton to George Washington, May 5, 1789, in Syrett et al., eds., *Papers of Alexander Hamilton*, V, 335–337.

16. John Adams to George Washington, May 17, 1789, in Abbot et al., eds., *Papers of Washington: Presidential Series*, II, 312.

17. James Thomas Flexner, *George Washington and the New Nation (1783–1793)* (Boston: Little, Brown, 1970), 195.

18. Leonard D. White, *The Federalists: A Study in Administrative History* (New York: Greenwood, 1948), 108.

19. David Waldstreicher, *In the Midst of Perpetual Fetes: The Making of American Nationalism, 1776–1820* (Chapel Hill: University of North Carolina Press, 1997), 120–122.

20. George Washington to James Madison, March 30, 1789, in John Rhodehamel, ed., *George Washington: Writings* (New York: Library of America, 1997), 723; John Adams to Benjamin Rush, June 21, 1811, in John A. Schutz and Douglass Adair, eds., *The Spur of Fame: Dialogues of John Adams and Benjamin Rush, 1805–1813* (San Marino, CA: Huntington Library, 1966), 181.

21. Kenneth R. Bowling and Helen E. Veit, eds., *The Diary of William Maclay and Other Notes on Senate Debates: Documentary History of the First Federal Congress of the United States of America, 4 March 1789–3 March 1791* (Baltimore: Johns Hopkins University Press, 1988), IX, 21; Schwartz, *Washington*, 62.

22. Bowling and Veit, eds., *Diary of Maclay*, 21.

23. Page Smith, *John Adams* (New York: Doubleday, 1962), II, 755.

24. Thomas Jefferson to James Madison, July 29, 1789, in Boyd et al., eds., *Papers of Jefferson*, XV, 316.

25. White, *Federalists*, 108.

26. Thomas Jefferson to Spencer Roane, September 6, 1819, in Paul L. Ford, ed., *The Writings of Thomas Jefferson* (New York: G. P. Putnam's Sons, 1899), X, 140.

27. Jefferson, First Annual Message, December 8, 1801, in Merrill Peterson, ed., *Thomas Jefferson: Writings* (New York: Library of America, 1984), 504.

CHAPTER 9, ILLUSIONS OF POWER IN THE AWKWARD ERA OF FEDERALISM

1. Linda K. Kerber, *Federalists in Dissent: Imagery and Ideology in Jeffersonian America* (Ithaca, NY: Cornell University Press, 1970), 1–22.

2. Manning J. Dauer, *The Adams Federalists* (Baltimore: Johns Hopkins University Press, 1953), 241.

3. Alexander Hamilton to Gouverneur Morris, February 29, 1802, Harold C. Syrett and Jacob E. Cooke, eds., *The Papers of Alexander Hamilton* (New York: Columbia University Press, 1961–1967), XXV, 544.

4. James Sterling Young, *The Washington Community, 1800–1828* (New York: Columbia University Press, 1966), 41.

5. The talk of the United States becoming more monarchical in these years was much more prevalent than we have generally admitted. The only significant study we have is Louise Burnham Dunbar, *A Study of "Monarchical" Tendencies in the United States from 1776 to 1801* (New York: Da Capo Press, 1970, [originally published 1922]).

6. Hamilton, Speech at New York Ratifying Convention, June 28, 1788, Syrett et al., eds., *Papers of Hamilton*, V, 118.

7. Alexander Hamilton, quoted in Thomas K. McCraw, "The Strategic Vision of Alexander Hamilton," *American Scholar* (Winter 1994), 40; George Washington to Henry Knox, February 28, 1785, in John C. Fitzpatrick, ed., *The Writings of George Washington* (Washington, DC: U.S. Government Printing Office, 1938), XXVIII, 93.

8. John Brewer, *The Sinews of Power: War, Money and the English State, 1688–1783* (New York: Routledge, 1989).

9. Hamilton, Speech at the New York Ratifying Convention, June 27, 1788, and in *The Continentalist*, no. V, April 18, 1782, in Syrett et al., eds., *Papers of Hamilton*, V, 96; III, 76.

10. Alexander Hamilton to Robert Troup, April 13, 1795, Syrett et al., eds., *Papers of Hamilton*, XVIII, 329; Sir James Steuart (1767), quoted in Stephen Copley, *Literature and the Social Order in Eighteenth-Century England* (London and Dover, NH: Croom Helm, 1984), 120; Alexander Hamilton, "The Defence of the Funding System, July 1795," Syrett et al., eds., *Papers of Hamilton*, XIII, 349.

11. Alexander Hamilton, "Conjectures about the New Constitution," Syrett et al., eds., *Papers of Hamilton*, IV, 276.

12. George Washington, quoted in Leonard D. White, *The Federalists: A Study in Administrative History* (New York: Greenwood, 1948), 404n; Alexander Hamilton, quoted in Richard H. Kohn, *Eagle and Sword: The Federalists and the Creation of the Military Establishment in America, 1783–1802* (New York: Free Press, 1975), 171.

13. Thomas Jefferson to Edmund Pendleton, August 26, 1776, in Julian Boyd et al., eds., *The Papers of Thomas Jefferson* (Princeton: Princeton University Press, 1950–), I, 505.

14. For two revisionist interpretations of the origins of judicial review, see J. M. Sosin, *The Aristocracy of the Long Robe: The Origins of Judicial Review in America* (New York: Greenwood Press, 1989); and Robert L. Clinton, *Marbury v. Madison and Judicial Review* (Lawrence: University Press of Kansas, 1989). For attempts to describe the judicial and legal climates out of which judicial review arose, see Gordon S. Wood, "The Origins of Judicial Review," *Suffolk Law Review*, XXII (1988), 1293–1307; and Wood, "Judicial Review in the Era of the Founding," in Robert Licht, ed., *Is the Supreme Court the Guardian of the Constitution?* (Washington, DC: AEI Press, 1993), 153–166.

15. This is the gist of Lance Banning's book *The Sacred Fire of Liberty: James Madison and the Founding of the Federal Republic* (Ithaca, NY: Cornell University Press, 1995).

16. *The Federalist* No. 10.

17. White, *The Federalists*, 301.

18. George V. Taylor, "Noncapitalist Wealth and the Origins of the French Revolution," *American Historical Review*, LXII (1967), 469–496; William Doyle, *Origins of the French Revolution* (Oxford: Oxford University Press, 1980), 17–18.

19. George Washington to Thomas Johnson, July 20, 1770, Fitzpatrick, ed., *Writings of Washington*, 3:18. On the efforts of some Boston gentry to set themselves up as country farmers, georgic style, see Tamara Platkins Thornton, *Cultivating Gentlemen: The Meaning of Country Life Among the Boston Elite, 1785–1860* (New Haven, CT: Yale University Press, 1989).

20. Samuel Eliot Morison, ed., "William Manning's *The Key of Liberty*," *William and Mary Quarterly*, 3rd ser., XIII (1956), 202–254.

21. Merrill Peterson, ed., *Democracy, Liberty, and Property: The State Constitutional Conventions of the 1820s* (Indianapolis: Bobbs-Merrill, 1966), 79–82. On the new democratic understanding of property as the product of labor, see Alan Taylor, *Liberty Men and Great Proprietors: The Revolutionary Settlement on the Maine Frontier, 1760–1820* (Chapel Hill: University of North Carolina Press, 1990), 25, 28.

22. Although Michael Merrill and Sean Wilentz have recently tried to portray Manning as someone opposed to capitalism, they admit that he was no "injured little yeoman" uninvolved in a commercial economy. He was more than a farmer in his little developing town of Billerica; he was as well an improver and a small-time entrepreneurial hustler. He ran a tavern off and on, erected a saltpeter works making gunpowder during the Revolutionary War, helped build a canal, bought and sold land, constantly borrowed money, and urged the printing of money by state-chartered banks, seeking (not very successfully, it seems) every which way to better his and his family's condition. By themselves Manning's commercial activities may not have been much, but multiply them many thousandfold throughout the society and we have the makings of an expanding capitalist economy. Michael Merrill and Sean Wilentz, eds., *The Key of Liberty: The Life and Democratic Writings of William Manning, "A Laborer," 1747–1814* (Cambridge, MA: Harvard University Press, 1993), 31–32.

23. Cathy Matson and Peter Onuf, "Toward a Republican Empire: Interest and Ideology in Revolutionary America," *American Quarterly*, XXXVII (1985), 496–531. Fanny Wright, in her *Views of Society and Manners in America*, Paul R. Baker, ed. (Cambridge, MA: Harvard University Press, 1963), 208, used the same phrase to describe American society a generation later. Although Hamilton's "Report on Manufactures" suggests that he understood the importance of domestic trade, in fact, as John R. Nelson has argued, he never fully appreciated nor supported the interests of manufacturers and those involved in domestic commerce. Insofar as he supported manufacturing, it was the manufacturing of goods for export. John R. Nelson Jr., *Liberty and Property: Political Economy and Policymaking in the New Nation, 1789–1812* (Baltimore: John Hopkins University Press, 1987), 37–51.

24. As John E. Crowley has shown, Americans were not very good students of Adam Smith: they tended to ignore his support for domestic trade over foreign trade and remained mercantilists a lot longer than the British; that is to say, they "slight[ed] or countermand[ed] the imperatives of market relations in the name of political imperatives." John E. Crowley, *The Privileges of Independence: Neomercantilism and the American Revolution* (Baltimore: Johns Hopkins University Press, 1993), xii–xiii, 133, 207.

25. Bray Hammond, *Banks and Politics in America from the Revolution to the Civil War* (Princeton: Princeton University Press, 1957), 126–127.

26. Joyce Appleby, *Capitalism and a New Social Order: The Republican Vision of the 1790s* (New York: New York University Press, 1984).

27. John R. Nelson, "Alexander Hamilton and American Manufacturing: A Reexamination," *Journal of American History*, LXV (1979), 971–995.

28. Jack P. Greene, *The Intellectual Construction of America: Exceptionalism and Identity from 1492 to 1800* (Chapel Hill: University of North Carolina Press, 1993), 189.

29. E. H. Smith, *A Discourse Delivered April 11, 1798 . . .*, quoted in Duncan J. MacLeod, *Slavery, Race and the American Revolution* (Cambridge, UK: Cambridge University Press, 1974), 29.

30. On "garrison governments," see the work of Stephen Saunders Webb (who coined the term) especially *The Governors-General: The English Army and the Definition of Empire, 1569–1681* (Chapell Hill: University of North Carolina Press, 1979).

31. Eugene Perry Link, *Democratic-Republican Societies, 1790–1800* (New York: Columbia University Press, 1942), 136–137. Jefferson had a very relaxed idea of the modern state and was never worried about Americans leaving the territorial boundaries of the United States. He always conceived of his "empire of liberty" as one of like principles, not like boundaries—similar to the way some eighteenth-century German and Italian intellectuals conceived of their nations. As long as Americans believed certain things, they remained Americans, regardless of the territorial boundaries of the government they happened to be in. At times he was remarkably indifferent to the possibility that a western confederacy might break away from the eastern United States. What did it matter? he asked in 1804. "Those of the western confederacy will be as much our children and descendents as those of

the eastern." Thomas Jefferson to Dr. Joseph Priestley, January 29, 1804, *Thomas Jefferson: Writings*, Merrill Peterson, ed. (New York: Library of America, 1984), 1142.

32. For some of these illusions about the West, see Andrew R. L. Cayton, *The Frontier Republic: Ideology and Politics in the Ohio Country, 1780–1825* (Kent, OH: Kent State University Press, 1986). "Neither the Federalist not the Republican vision of the future of the Ohio Valley was foolish or naive. The problem with both was that they were inappropriate for the kind of society emerging in Ohio." Ibid., 153.

CHAPTER 10, THE AMERICAN ENLIGHTENMENT

1. Benjamin Rush to Elias Boudinot?, "Observations on the Federal Procession in Philadelphia," July 9, 1788, in L. H. Butterfield, ed., *Letters of Benjamin Rush* (Princeton: American Philosophical Society, 1951), I, 470–475.

2. John Adams, "Dissertation on the Feudal and Canon Law" (1765), in Gordon S. Wood, ed., *The Rising Glory of America, 1760–1820* (New York: George Braziller, 1971), 29.

3. Charles S. Hyneman and George W. Carey, eds., *A Second Federalist: Congress Creates a Government* (New York: Appleton-Century-Crofts, 1967), 24.

4. "Centinel" [Samuel Bryan], in Bernard Bailyn, ed., *The Debate on the Constitution* (New York: Library of America, 1993), I, 686.

5. Allen R. Pred, *Urban Growth and the Circulation of Information: The United States System of Cities, 1790–1840* (Cambridge, MA: Harvard University Press, 1973), 26.

6. Evarts B. Greene, *The Revolutionary Generation, 1763–1790* (New York: Macmillan, 1943), 418; Colin Bonwick, *English Radicals and the American Revolution* (Chapel Hill: University of North Carolina Press, 1977), 13–14; Alan D. McKillop, "Local Attachment and Cosmopolitanism: The Eighteenth-Century Pattern," in Frederick W. Hilles and Harold Bloom, eds., *From Sensibility to Romanticism: Essays Presented to Frederick A. Pottle* (New York: Oxford University Press, 1965), 197; David Ramsay to John Eliot, August 11, 1792, in Robert L. Brunhouse, ed., *David Ramsay . . . Selections from His Writings* (Philadelphia: American Philosophical Society, 1965), 133.

7. Richard Price to Benjamin Franklin, September 17, 1787, Papers of Benjamin Franklin (unpublished).

8. Franco Venturi, *Utopia and Reform in the Enlightenment* (Cambridge, UK: Cambridge University Press, 1971), 133.

9. Julie Richter, "The Impact of the Death of Governor France Fauquier on His Slaves and Their Families," *Colonial Williamsburg Interpreter*, XVIII, no. 3 (Fall 1997), 2.

10. Joel Barlow, *Advice to the Privileged Orders in the Several States of Europe* (1792; repub. Ithaca, NY: Cornell University Press, 1956), 17; Harry C. Payne, *The Philosophes and the People* (New Haven, CT: Yale University, Press, 1976), 7–17.

11. Virginia Ratifying Convention, in John P. Kaminski and Gaspare J. Saladino, eds., *The Documentary History of the Ratification of the Constitution* (Madison: State Historical Society of Wisconsin, 1999), IX, 1044–1045.

12. Hector St. John de Crèvecoeur, *Letters from an American Farmer*, Letter III (New York: Penguin, 1981), 67.

13. Thomas Jefferson to Martha Jefferson, March 28, 1787, in Julian P. Boyd et al., eds., *The Papers of Thomas Jefferson* (Princeton: Princeton University Press, 1950–), XI, 251.

14. Thomas Jefferson to Lafayette, April 11, 1787, in Boyd et al., eds., *Papers of Jefferson*, XI, 285.

15. David Ramsay, *The History of the American Revolution*, Lester H. Cohen, ed. (1789; repub. Indianapolis: Liberty Press, 1989), II, 630.

16. Edwin T. Martin, *Thomas Jefferson: Scientist* (New York: Henry Schuman, 1952), 54.

17. Benjamin Rush, "Of the Mode of Education Proper in a Republic," in Dagobert D. Runes, ed., *The Selected Writings of Benjamin Rush* (New York: Philosophical Library, 1947), 88, 90.

18. Frank L. Mott, *A History of American Journalism in the United States . . . 1690–1940* (New York: Macmillan, 1941), 159, 167; Merle Curti, *The Growth of American Thought*, 3rd ed. (New York: Harper & Row, 1964), 209; Donald H. Stewart, *The Opposition Press of the Federalist Period* (Albany: State University of New York Press, 1969), 15, 624.

19. Thomas Jefferson to Maria Cosway, October 12, 1786, in Boyd et al., eds., *Papers of Jefferson*, X, 447–448.

20. Thomas Paine, *The Rights of Man* (1791), in Philip S. Foner, ed., *The Complete Writings of Thomas Paine* (New York: Citadel, 1969), I, 265–266.

21. Louis P. Masur, *Rites of Execution: Capital Punishment and the Transformation of American Culture, 1776–1865* (New York: Oxford University Press, 1989), 37.

22. Ibid., 77; *American Museum* (March 1970), 137.

23. Masur, *Rites of Execution*, 82.

24. Michael Meranze, *Laboratories of Virtue: Punishment, Revolution, and Authority in Philadelphia, 1760–1835* (Chapel Hill: University of North Carolina Press, 1996), 71; Masur, *Rites of Execution*, 65, 71, 80–82, 87, 88; Adam J. Hirsch, "From Pillory to Penitentiary: The Rise of the Criminal Incarceration in Early Massachusetts," *Michigan Law Review*, LXXX (1982), 1179–1269; Linda Kealey, "Patterns of Punishment: Massachusetts in the Eighteenth Century," *American Journal of Legal History*, XXX (1986), 163–176; Michael Meranze, "The Penitential Ideal in Late Eighteenth-Century Philadelphia," *Pennsylvania Magazine of History and Biography*, 108 (1984), 419–450; Bradley Chapin, "Felony Law Reform in the Early Republic," *Pennsylvania Magazine of History and Biography*, 113 (1989), 163–83.

25. Greene, *Revolutionary Generation*, 80.

26. Rush to Elisabeth Graeme Ferguson, July 16, 1782, in *Letters of Benjamin Rush*, L. H. Butterfield, ed., 280.

27. John Jay, *The Federalist* No. 2.

28. Richard L. Bushman, "American High Style," in Jack P. Greene and J. R. Pole, eds., *Colonial British America: Essays in the New History of the Early Modern Era* (Baltimore: Johns Hopkins University Press, 1984), 371–372.

29. John Witherspoon, "The Druid, No. V," in *The Works of the Rev. John Witherspoon*, 2nd ed. (Philadelphia: W. W. Woodward, 1802), IV, 417.

30. Noah Webster, *Dissertations on the English Language* (Boston: Isaiah Thomas, 1789), 36, 288. See Michael P. Kramer, *Imagining Language in America: From the Revolution to the Civil War* (Princeton: Princeton University Press, 1992).

31. Andrew Burstein, *Sentimental Democracy: The Evolution of America's Romantic Self-Image* (New York: Hill and Wang, 1999), 152.

32. Crèvecoeur, *Letters from an American Farmer*, Letter III, 80.

33. David Ramsay to Benjamin Rush, April 8, 1777, Brunhouse, ed., *Ramsay . . . Selections from His Writings*, 54; Arthur L. Ford, *Joel Barlow* (New York: Twaine, 1971), 31; Paine, *Common Sense*, in Foner, ed., *Writings of Paine*, I, 20.

CHAPTER II, A HISTORY OF RIGHTS IN EARLY AMERICA

1. John Phillip Reid, *Constitutional History of the American Revolution: The Authority of Rights* (Madison: University of Wisconsin Press, 1986), 3.

2. Lois G. Schwoerer, *The Declaration of Rights, 1689* (Baltimore: Johns Hopkins University Press, 1981).

3. Leonard Levy, *Legacy of Suppression: Freedom of Speech and Press in Early American History* (Cambridge, MA: Belknap Press of Harvard University Press, 1960).

4. William Penn, *England's Present Interest Considered* (1675), in Philip B. Kurland and Ralph Lerner, eds., *The Founders' Constitution* (Chicago: University of Chicago Press, 1987), I, 429.

5. Lee, quoted in Bernard Bailyn, *The Ideological Origins of the American Revolution* (Cambridge, MA: Harvard University Press, 1967), 189.

6. Reid, *Constitutional History: Authority of Rights*.

7. Gordon S. Wood, *The Creation of the American Republic, 1776–1787* (Chapel Hill: University of North Carolina Press, 1969), 268–269.

8. James Wilson, *Considerations on the Authority of Parliament* (1774), in Robert G. McCloskey, ed., *Works of James Wilson* (Cambridge, MA: Harvard University Press, 1967), II, 736–737.

9. Gordon S. Wood, *The Radicalism of the American Revolution* (New York: Knopf, 1992), 81.

10. William E. Nelson, *Americanization of the Common Law: The Impact of Legal Change on Massachusetts Society, 1760–1830* (Cambridge, MA: Harvard University Press, 1975), 37–38, 14.

11. William Douglass, *A Summary, Historical and Political, of the First Planting, Progressive Improvements, and Present State of the British Settlements in North America* (Boston London: R. Baldwin, 1749), I, 507.

12. Hendrik Hartog, *Public Property and Private Power: The Corporation of the City of New York in American Law, 1730–1870* (Chapel Hill: University of North Carolina Press, 1983), 62–68.
13. Ronald E. Seavoy, "The Public Service Origins of the American Business Corporation," *Business History Review*, LII (1978), 30–36.
14. Quentin Skinner, *Liberty Before Liberalism* (Cambridge, UK: Cambridge University Press, 1998).
15. John Adams, quoted in Wood, *Creation of the American Republic*, 62–63.
16. Wood, *Radicalism of the American Revolution*, 188.
17. Hartog, *Public Property and Private Power*, 155; Harry N. Scheiber, "The Road to Munn: Eminent Domain and the Concept of Public Purpose in the State Courts," *Perspectives in American History*, V (1971), 363; Horst Dippel, "Human Rights: From Societal Rights to Individual Rights," *Boletim Da Faculdade de Direito*, LXXXIV (Coimbra: Universidade de Coimbra, 2008), 343–348.
18. J. A. C. Grant, "The 'Higher Law' Background of the Law of Eminent Domain," *Wisconsin Law Review*, VI (1930–31), 70; William Michael Treanor, "The Origins and Original Significance of the Just Compensation Clause of the Fifth Amendment," *Yale Law Journal*, XCIV (1985), 694–716.
19. Wood, *Creation of the American Republic*, 410.
20. James Madison, "Vices of the Political System of the United States," April 1787, in Jack N. Rakove, ed., *James Madison: Writings* (New York: Library of America, 1999), 71; James Madison to Thomas Jefferson, October 17, 1788, in Rakove, ed., *Madison: Writings*, 421.
21. Thomas Jefferson, *Notes on the State of Virginia*, William Peden, ed. (Chapel Hill: University of North Carolina Press, 1955), 120.
22. Drew R. McCoy, *The Last of the Fathers: James Madison and the Republican Legacy* (Cambridge, UK: Cambridge University Press, 1989), 115.
23. Jefferson, *Notes on Virginia*, Peden, ed., 121.
24. *The Federalist* No. 71, No. 78, Jacob E. Cooke, ed. (Middletown, CT: Wesleyan University Press, 1961).
25. Lynn W. Turner, *William Plumer of New Hampshire, 1759–1850* (Chapel Hill: University of North Carolina Press, 1962), 34–35.
26. Alexander Hamilton, "Remarks in New York Assembly," February 6, 1787, in Harold C. Syrett et al., eds., *The Papers of Alexander Hamilton* (New York: Columbia University Press, 1961–1967), IV, 35.
27. Edward S. Corwin, "The Doctrine of Due Process of Law Before the Civil War," *Harvard Law Review*, XXIV (1911), 371–372.
28. Edward S. Corwin, "The Basic Doctrine of American Constitutional Law," *Michigan Law Review*, XII (1914), 254.
29. William E. Nelson, "Changing Conceptions of Judicial Review," *University of Pennsylvania Law Review*, CXX (1972), 1176.
30. Philadelphia *Pennsylvania Packet*, September 2, 1786.
31. On this point, see Barry Shain, *Myth of American Individualism: The Protestant Origins of American Political Thought* (Princeton: Princeton University Press, 1994); and Johann N. Neem, "Politics and the Origins of the Nonprofit Corporation in Massachusetts and New Hampshire, 1780–1820," *Nonprofit and Voluntary Sector Quarterly*, XXXII (2003), 344–365.
32. Louis Hartz, *Economic Policy and Democratic Thought: Pennsylvania, 1776–1860* (Cambridge, MA: Harvard University Press, 1948), 292.
33. Pauline Maier, "Revolutionary Origins of the American Corporation," *William and Mary Quarterly*, L (1993), 68–70.
34. Mathew Carey, ed., *Debates and Proceedings of the General Assembly of Pennsylvania . . .* (Philadelphia: Seddon and Pritchard, 1786), 11–12.
35. Hamilton, "The Examination," February 23, 1802, in Syrett et al., eds., *Papers of Hamilton*, XXV, 533.
36. Corwin, "The Basic Doctrine of American Constitutional Law."
37. Debates in the Senate of the United States on the Judiciary During the First Session of the Seventh Congress (Philadelphia: Thomas Smith, 1802), 39. (I owe this citation to Kurt Graham.)
38. R. Kent Newmyer, *Supreme Court Justice Joseph Story: Statesman of the Old Republic* (Chapel Hill: University of North Carolina Press, 1985), 132; Harry N. Scheiber, "Public Rights and the Rule of Law in American Legal History," *California Law Review*, LXXII (1984), 217–251.
39. Neem, "Politics and the Origins of the Nonprofit Corporation in Massachusetts and New Hampshire, 1780–1820," *Nonprofit and Voluntary Sector Quarterly*, XXXII (2003), 358.

40. L. Ray Gunn, *The Decline of Authority: Public Economic Policy and Political Development in New York, 1800–1860* (Ithaca, NY: Cornell University Press, 1988).

41. William J. Novak, *People's Welfare: Law and Regulation in Nineteenth-Century America* (Chapel Hill: University of North Carolina Press, 1996), 15, 88.

42. David Lieberman, *Province of Legislation Determined: Legal Theory in Eighteenth-Century Britain* (Cambridge, UK: Cambridge University Press, 1989).

43. Nelson, *Americanization of the Common Law*, 171–172.

44. *Marbury v. Madison* (1803), William Cranch, ed., *U.S. Supreme Court Reports . . .* (Washington, DC, 1804), 165, 177.

45. George L. Haskins, "Law Versus Politics in the Early Years of the Marshall Court," *University of Pennsylvania Law Review*, CXXX (1981), 19–20.

46. James Madison to George Washington, April 16, 1787, in Robert Rutland et al., eds., *Papers of James Madison* (Chicago: University of Chicago Press, 1975), IX, 384.

INDEX

to make professional communities the repositories of disinterestedness against the selfishness and interestedness of businessmen, see Thomas L. Haskell, "Professionalism *versus* Capitalism: R. H. Tawney, Emile Durkheim, and C. S. Peirce on the Disinterestedness of Professional Communities," in Thomas L. Haskell, ed., *The Authority of Experts: Studies in History and Theory* (Bloomington: Indiana University Press, 1984), 180–225.

45. Morris, "Political Enquiries," in Willi Paul Adams, ed., "'The Spirit of Commerce, Requires that Property Be Sacred': Gouverneur Morris and the American Revolution," *Amerikastudien/American Studies*, XXI (1976), 329; Alexander Hamilton to Robert Troup, April 13, 1795, in Harold C. Syrett, et al., eds., *The Papers of Alexander Hamilton* (New York: Columbia University Press, 1961–1979), XVII, 329.

46. George Washington to Benjamin Harrison, January 22, 1785, to George William Fairfax, February 27, 1785, in Fitzpatrick, ed., *Writings of Washington*, XXVIII, 36, 85.

47. George Washington to Benjamin Harrison, January 22, 1785, to William Grayson, January 22, 1785, to Lafayette, February 15, 1785, to Thomas Jefferson, February 25, 1785, to George William Fairfax, February 27, 1785, to Governor Patrick Henry, February 27, 1785, to Henry Knox, February 28, 1785, June 18, 1785, to Nathanael Greene, May 20, 1785, in Fitzpatrick, ed., *Writings of Washington*, XXVIII, 36, 37, 72, 80–81, 85, 89–91, 92–93, 146, 167. The only friend whose advice on the disposition of the canal shares Washington did not solicit was Robert Morris, perhaps because he feared that Morris might tell him to keep them. Instead he confined his letter to Morris to describing the commercial opportunities of the canals. To Morris, February 1, 1785, ibid., 48–55.

48. Cooke, ed., *The Federalist* No. 10; Gordon S. Wood, "Democracy and the Constitution," in Robert A, Goldwin and William A. Schambra, eds., *How Democratic Is the Constitution?* (Washington, DC: American Enterprise Institute, 1980), 11–12. On the tendency to misread Madison, see Robert J. Morgan, "Madison's Theory of Representation in the Tenth Federalist," *Journal of Politics*, XXXVI (1974), 852–885; and Paul F. Bourke, "The Pluralist Reading of James Madison's Tenth *Federalist*," *Perspectives in American History*, IX (1975), 271–295.

49. James Madison to George Washington April 16, 1787, to Edmund Randolph, April 8, 1787, in Hutchinson et al., eds., *Papers of Madison*, IX, 370, 384; John Zvesper, "The Madisonian Systems," *Western Political Quarterly*, XXXVII (1984), 244–247.

50. Jerome J. Nadelhaft, "'The Snarls of Invidious Animals': The Democratization of Revolutionary South Carolina," in Ronald Hoffman and Peter J. Albert, eds., *Sovereign States in an Age of Uncertainty* (Charlottesville: University Press of Virginia 1981), 77.

51. On Findley, see his letter to Governor William Plumer of New Hampshire, February 27, 1812, "William Findley of Westmoreland, Pa.," *Pennsylvania Magazine of History and Biography*, V (1881), 440–50; and Russell J. Ferguson, *Early Western Pennsylvania Politics* (Pittsburgh: University of Pittsburgh Press, 1938), 39–40.

52. Grundfest, *Clymer*, 141.

53. Claude Milton Newlin, *The Life and Writings of Hugh Henry Brackenridge* (Princeton: Princeton University Press, 1932), 71.

54. Ibid., 78, 80–81; Ferguson, *Early Western Pennsylvania*, 66–69.

55. Newlin, *Brackenridge*, 79–80, 83–84; Ferguson, *Early Western Pennsylvania*, 70–72.

56. Mathew Carey, ed., *Debates and Proceedings of the General Assembly of Pennsylvania on the Memorials Praying a Repeal or Suspension of the Law Annulling the Charter of the Bank* (Philadelphia: Carey and Co., Seddon and Pritchard, 1786), 19, 64, 10, 30.

57. Robert Morris to George Washington, May 29, 1781, E. James Ferguson et al., eds., *The Papers of Robert Morris, 1781–1784* (Pittsburgh: University of Pittsburgh Press, 1973–), I, 96; Ellis Paxson Oberholtzer, *Robert Morris, Patriot and Financier* (New York: Macmillan, 1903), 52–56, 70–71.

58. Carey, ed., *Debates*, 33, 79–80, 98 (quotations on 80, 98).

59. Ibid., 81; Oberholtzer, *Morris*, 285–286, 297–299, 301–303; Eleanor Young, *Forgotten Patriot: Robert Morris* (New York: Macmillan, 1950–), 170; Barbara Ann Chernow, *Robert Morris, Land Speculator, 1790–1801* (New York: Arno Press, 1978); H. E. Scudder, ed., *Recollections of Samuel Breck . . .* (Philadelphia: Porter & Coates, 1877), 203: *The Journal of William Maclay* (New York: Albert & Charles Boni, 1927 [orig. pub, 1890]), 132.

60. Carey, ed., *Debates*, 66, 87, 128, 21, 130, 38, 15, 72–73.

34. The best discussion of the distinctiveness of the gentry in colonial America is Rhys Isaac, *The Transformation of Virginia, 1740–1790* (Chapel Hill: University, of North Carolina Press, 1982), esp. 131–132.

35. Royster, *Revolutionary People at War*, 86–95; John B. B. Trussell Jr., *Birthplace of an Army: A Study of the Valley Forge Encampment* (Harrisburg: Pennsylvania Historical and Museum Commission, 1976), 86.

36. Francis Hutcheson, *A System of Moral Philosophy in Three Books . . .* (London: R. and A. Foulis 1755), II, 113. "Let not your Love of Philosophical Amusements have more than its due Weight with you," Benjamin Franklin admonished Cadwallader Colden at midcentury. Public service was far more important. In fact, said Franklin, even "the finest" of Newton's "Discoveries" could not have excused his neglect of serving the commonwealth if the public had needed him (Franklin to Colden, October 11, 1750, in Leonard W. Labaree et al., eds., *The Papers of Benjamin Franklin* [New Haven, CT: Yale University Press, 1959–], IV, 68).

37. Jack N. Rakove, *The Beginnings of National Politics: An Interpretative. History of the Continental Congress* (New York: Knopf, 1979), 216–239, quotation by William Fleming to Jefferson, May 10, 1779, at 237; George Athan Billias, *Elbridge Gerry, Founding Father and Republican Statesman* (New York: McGraw-Hill, 1976), 138–139.

38. See William R. Taylor, *Cavalier and Yankee: The Old South and American National Character* (New York: George Braziller, 1961).

39. Wilson, "On the History of Property," in Robert Green McCloskey, ed., *The Works of James Wilson* (Cambridge, MA: Harvard University Press, 1967), II, 716; Dickinson, "Letters of a Farmer in Pennsylvania" (1768), in Paul Leicester Ford, ed., *The Writings of John Dickinson*, vol. I, *Political Writings, 1764–1774* (Pennsylvania Historical Society, *Memoirs*, XIV [Philadelphia: Pennsylvania Historical Society, 1895]), 307 (hereafter cited as Ford, ed., *Writings of Dickinson*).

40. "We have found by experience, that no dependence can be had upon *merchants*, either at *home*, or in *America*," Charles Chauncy told Richard Price in 1774, "so many of them are so mercenary as to find within themselves a readiness to become slaves themselves, as well as to be accessory to the slavery of others, if they imagine they may, by this means, serve their own private separate interest" (D. C. Thomas and Bernard Peach, eds., *The Correspondence of Richard Price* [Durham, NC: Duke University Press, 1983], I, 170). For Adam Smith's view that the interest of merchants and indeed of all who lived by profit was "always in some respects different from, and even opposite to, that of the publick," see Smith, *Wealth of Nations*, Campbell and Skinner, ed. (I.xi.p.10), I, 267.

41. Richard Jackson to Benjamin Franklin, June 17, 1755, in Labaree et al., eds., *Papers of Franklin*, VI, 82. On the colonial merchants' "detachment from political activity," see Thomas M. Doerflinger, "Philadelphia Merchants and the Logic of Moderation, 1760–1775," *William and Mary Quarterly*, 3rd ser., XL (1983), 212–213; and Edward Countryman, *A People in Revolution: The American Revolution and Political Society in New York, 1760–1790* (Baltimore: Johns Hopkins University Press, 1981), 113.

42. William M. Fowler Jr., *The Baron of Beacon Hill: A Biography of John Hancock* (Boston: Houghton Mifflin, 1980); Charles W. Akers, *The Divine Politician: Samuel Cooper and the American Revolution in Boston* (Boston: Northeastern University Press, 1982), 121, 128, 130, 141, 176, 311; Henry Laurens to Richard Oswald, July 7, 1764, in Philip M. Hamer et al., eds., *The Papers of Henry Laurens* (Columbia: University of South Carolina Press, 1968–), IV, 338 (see also Rachel N. Klein, "Ordering the Backcountry: The South Carolina Regulation," *William and Mary Quarterly*, 3rd ser., XXXVIII [1981], 667); David Duncan Wallace, *The Life of Henry Laurens . . .* (New York: Russell and Russell, 1915), 69–70, quotation at 335. In the 1780s Elbridge Gerry likewise retired from mercantile business and "set himself up as a country squire" (Billias, *Gerry*, 135–136).

43. Leonard W. Labaree et al., eds., *The Autobiography of Benjamin Franklin* (New Haven, CT: Yale University Press, 1964), 196; Christopher, Collier, *Roger Sherman's Connecticut: Yankee Politics and the American Revolution* (Middletown, CT: Wesleyan University Press, 1971), 14, 21–22.

44. Jacob E. Cooke, ed., *The Federalist* No. 35 (Middletown, CT, 1961) [Barton], *True Interest*, 27. For arguments in pre-Revolutionary Virginia whether lawyers were practicing "a grovelling, mercenary trade" or not, see Roeber, *Faithful Magistrates and Republican Lawyers*, 156–157. Some conceded that lawyers were members of one of the "three genteel Professions," but that they were guilty of more "petit Larceny" than doctors and clergymen. Madison was not convinced of the disinterestedness of lawyers (ibid., 157, 147, Ketcham, *Madison*, 145). On the efforts of some nineteenth-century thinkers

RT: *To my family*

MD: *To Rebecca*

Contents

Acknowledgments

THE AUTHORS EXPRESS sincere thanks to our agent, Leah Spiro of Riverside Creative Management, for her knowledge of the publishing world and her uncanny ability to find the right fit. We consider ourselves very lucky to have started out with the best of all possible agents.

Leah led us to many resources, one of the best is Anne Greenberg, whose sharp editorial eye and deep knowledge of many complex subjects proved critical for us more than once.

We also thank Neil Livingstone, chairman and CEO of Executive Action, LLC, a leading global security expert, for his guidance in helping us navigate through the secretive world of digital attacks. Thanks also go to Adam D'Luzansky for his insights into recent changes in digital technologies.

And we thank our long-suffering colleagues—Clark S. Judge, founder of The White House Writers Group; Edward A. Orgon, president, The Torrenzano Group; and everyone from our firms who were gracious with their help and understanding during our absence while researching and writing this book.

We are also deeply grateful to our editor, St. Martin's Press Editor in Chief George Witte, and especially John Murphy and the entire editorial, marketing, and PR team for their encouragement, support, and guidance.

DigitalAssassination

1 : // The Digital Mosh Pit

ON JUNE 5, 1968, for reasons known only to himself, Sirhan Sirhan fired a bullet into the head of Robert F. Kennedy at the Ambassador Hotel in Los Angeles, killing him.

In May 2005, a Nashville man, for reasons known only to himself, used Wikipedia to fire a bullet directly into the reputation of John Seigenthaler, former Kennedy aide, civil rights hero, and newspaper publisher, character assassinating him to the core.

The Wikipedia entry reported that Seigenthaler:

> was the assistant to Attorney General Robert Kennedy in the early 1960's. For a brief time, he was thought to have been directly involved in the Kennedy assassinations of both John, and his brother, Bobby. Nothing was ever proven. . . . John Seigenthaler moved to the Soviet Union in 1971, and returned to the United States in 1984.

Was the entry correct? Did it matter?

It did to Seigenthaler. "At age 78," he later wrote in *USA Today,* "I thought I was beyond surprise or hurt at any negative said about me. I was wrong. One sentence in the biography was true. I was Robert Kennedy's administrative assistant in the early 1960s. I also was his pallbearer."[1]

Did the entry really harm Seigenthaler?

At that time, one of the authors was asked to pen an introduction of Seigenthaler for a speaker at a charitable event. Though not fooled by the Wikipedia entry, the writer took pause, consuming valuable time and attention to sort out the story in advance of the event. There is no telling how many others linked to John Seigenthaler were similarly perplexed . . . or actually believed it.

The entry sat on Wikipedia's page for 132 days, and was picked up uncritically by two widely used information automatons, Reference.com and Answers.com.

For those 132 days, Seigenthaler's character was assassinated—not the man himself, but his reputation, his avatar constructed of words spoken and written. When such an assassination happens, however, more than a shadow self is murdered.

Digital assassination can murder opportunity—carefully cultivated brands or businesses, jobs or job offers, celebrity, and personal relationships. Character assassination has led to heartbreak . . . and even death by suicide.

The world witnessed a vivid example of character assassination in the digital arena on September 22, 2010, when Rutgers University freshman Tyler Clementi jumped from the George Washington Bridge into the Hudson River. Two students had used a webcam to secretly stream on the Internet Clementi's sexual encounter with a man.

"There might be some people who can take that type of treatment and deal with it, and there might be others, as this young man obviously was, who was much more greatly affected by it," New Jersey governor Chris Christie observed in the aftermath of the tragedy.[2]

Clementi's digital assassination relied on a media that is instantaneous, vivid, works 24/7, has global reach, an eternal memory, and can organize crowds to attack individuals. But we are wrong if we imagine the character attacks the Internet enables are something entirely new.

More than half a century before, in the McCarthy era, a group of Republican senators went to a Democratic colleague, Lester C. Hunt of Wyoming, and suggested that the arrest of Hunt's son in a homosexual prostitution sting could be kept quiet if Hunt were to announce his retirement from the Senate. Days later, Hunt sneaked a rifle under his coat into his Senate office and blew out his brains.[3]

> The malevolent can assassinate character, brand, reputation,
> celebrity, business, or life with emotional violence.

FOR DECADES, Steve Jobs was not just the cofounder of Apple. To millions, he *was* Apple, the most successful and visible CEO of our generation.

Years before Jobs took his most recent medical leave of absence in January 2011, equity market short sellers and other financial vultures tried to exploit Apple's stock by spreading rumors about his long struggle against pancreatic cancer, followed by a liver transplant.

Why has Jobs been so important? Apple is a company with a soul, dominating the market by meeting consumer cravings for a fusion of design and functionality—the essence of cool. Jobs and his team certainly know how to excite the 4G spot of millions of technophiles.

"Design," Jobs purportedly said, "is not just what it looks like and feels like. Design is how it works."

The soul of Apple, however, seemed to disappear in the mid-1980s when Steve Jobs was forced to step aside for a soda executive he had recruited. And the soul of Apple, their mojo, reappeared only when Jobs came back.

Will there be an Apple after Jobs? By the second decade of the century, Jobs had been at the helm so long, his DNA so instilled in the corporate culture, the company will almost certainly continue being the Apple we have come to know. For years, however, the best way to damage Apple was to try to digitally assassinate Jobs.

In 2008, a teenager on CNN's iReport, its "citizen journalism page," reported that Steve Jobs had suffered a heart attack. The result? This teenager's digital attack caused one of the world's best-known brands to lose millions of dollars in stock value within minutes. The traffic of rumors was so thick that Jobs publicly accused hedge funds and short sellers of profiting off Internet rumors about his health.[4]

"Millions of people, from hard-core computer geeks to high-finance Wall Street martini drinkers, hang on every word related to Apple," observed Tom Krazit of CNET News. "Sometimes that can have consequences."[5]

Like losing millions of dollars in a single day.

> The greedy can assassinate your brand, reputation, or stock with
> the lure of pure fiction propelled by the Internet's instant interna-
> tional reach.

WHEN WILLIAM SHAKESPEARE had Julius Caesar opine about the dangers of men with a "lean and hungry look," the Bard could have been describing James Carville, the political operator and organizing genius behind the successful presidential campaign of Bill Clinton. Carville, who fires deadly innuendos with a vulpine smile, is a good man to have in a foxhole—provided it's your foxhole and he's your man.

Needless to say, Carville has made his fair share of enemies in Washington, as has his wife, Mary Matalin, an equally acid-tongued Republican who once worked behind the scenes for both presidents named Bush.

Bipartisan couples are not rare in Washington. But pairing two operatives with so many years of back-alley political skulduggery against each other's bosses is exotic, a spectacle as alluring as if Lucrezia Borgia had matched up with Niccolò Machiavelli. Needless to say, the sparks fly between them—sparks of political anger and underlying attraction that makes for great theater. And so Carville and Matalin have become fixtures on television political talk shows.

One day it seemed as if the tension between them had spun out of control. The circuits of the nation's political gossip networks overloaded when it was reported that James Carville was arrested after firing a gun into a sofa, plunging a knife into a wall, and physically abusing Mary at the couple's Rockville, Maryland, home. The online story, under the byline of Lee Canular of the *Montgomery County Ledger,* was aired on a national radio syndicate and was e-mailed back and forth between every politically connected person in both parties.

A few facts began to surface. The Carvilles lived in Virginia at that time, not in Maryland. There is no *Montgomery County Ledger,* nor is there a reporter named Lee Canular—the last name is the same as the French word for hoax. Carville had not been arrested by the Rockville police or any other police for anything. And there is no reason to ask James Carville when he quit beating his wife.[6]

> Unknown people use the Internet for unknown reasons to muddy
> brands and reputations without fear of a reckoning.

DID YOU KNOW that "Roddy Boyd Sucks It Like He's Paying the Rent"? Or that he left *Fortune* magazine to "slither into his own unique and arrest-warrant-laden world (that's him, just above the child porn guy.)"?[7]

Roddy Boyd is a journalist whose reporting often appears in Time Warner's *Fortune* magazine. The person posting this diatribe is not a forty-year-old man in pajamas living in his mother's basement. The man who wrote this message—and many other entries of similar ilk—is Patrick Byrne, former Marshall Scholar (Cambridge), Stanford PhD in philosophy, and CEO of Overstock.com, the Utah-based online retailer represented by the sexy ads with German actress Sabine Ehrenfeld ("It's all about the O"). Overstock is a major player in Internet retail that competes with eBay and Amazon.com.

The arrest reference is in a blog linked to the police log in what appears to be from a *Greenwich Post* article on January 22, 2009. This item refers to Boyd's arrest over a failure to appear in court after a previous arrest for running a light while under a suspended license and allegedly without auto insurance. The reference to child pornography has nothing to do with Boyd, except that the next case listed in the Connecticut police log concerns a man charged with downloading numerous images of child pornography. This apparently was the worst thing that could be found out about Boyd.

"I am one of only two reporters—the other is my former *Fortune* magazine colleague Bethany McLean—apparently evil enough in his [Byrne's] eyes to warrant a reference to oral sex and ejaculation in his assessment of our ethics and reporting skills," Boyd drolly blogged on a Slate site.[8]

Byrne has called reporters lapdogs and hedge fund quislings. This CEO accused another reporter of being "on the take, and get[ting] paid off somewhere in order to do hatchet-jobs-to-order."[9]

Why is Byrne burning up his keyboard? The CEO seems convinced that he and his company are the victims of character assassination by equity short sellers and hedge funds that encourage the spread of negative media stories about his and other corporations, paving the way for quick and dirty profits. And to back it up, Byrne initially funded DeepCapture.com, though it is not part of Overstock. It purports to reveal, says its mission statement, "that powerful actors have been able to influence or take control of not just the regulators, but also law enforcement, elected officials, national media, and the intellectual establishment."[10]

Who is the assassin here and who is the victim?

Some observers believe Byrne has a point to make against some hedge funds and perhaps some journalists. Overstock did succeed in winning $5 million from one hedge fund, Copper River (formerly Rocker Partners), though the fund characterizes the settlement as a payoff to end years of meritless litigation.[11]

Opinions will differ about the merits of Byrne's underlying arguments. But it is hard to imagine Byrne's board of directors and shareholders of a NASDAQ-traded company are pleased with his aggressive and unorthodox approach to representing Overstock.

> The new social media environment enhances the vulgarization of business culture by airing vituperation among elites.

FINE INDEPENDENT FILMS have been made for less money than some production company's budget for their Oscar campaigns. About $20 million was lavished in 2000 promoting *Gladiator,* which eventually won five Oscars, including one for Best Picture.[12] By 2011, Sony's Oscar campaign for *The Social Network* had invested $55 million in ads and the re-release of the film in 603 theaters.[13]

Much more than vanity is at stake. Win an Oscar for Best Picture, and the global and digital rights to a film are worth many times more than the expense of such a campaign. Not surprisingly, some of the money is spent not just on raising the profile of a film, but promoting and spreading some disqualifying dirty linen—often a spun or distorted fact—about a competitor's film.

Was there ever a surer bet for the Academy Award's Best Picture than Steven Spielberg's 1998 *Saving Private Ryan*? At the time of its summer release by DreamWorks, *Saving Private Ryan* became an instant classic— managing to shock viewers into tears who considered themselves long since jaded by war-movie violence. When Oscar time came, *Ryan's* only real competition was *Shakespeare in Love,* a romp through an Elizabethan comedy of errors.

Cowritten by playwright Tom Stoppard, produced by brash mogul Harvey Weinstein of Miramax, *Shakespeare* was indeed a good film.

But it was a comedy (no comedy had won Best Picture since *Annie Hall* in 1978), and it was at times more than a little predictable.

"But journalists and critics on both coasts report that they were recipients of negative Miramax spin," Hollywood insider Nikki Finke wrote in *New York* magazine, "including comments from Weinstein himself, who opined to at least one major critic that *Ryan* 'peaks in the first twenty minutes.'"[14]

When *Shakespeare in Love* won Best Picture in 1999, the Hollywood elite grinned at what they saw as a triumph of publicity and politics over art.

By 2002, Oscar-season disparagement had migrated to the Internet when Universal's *A Beautiful Mind* came up against Weinstein and Miramax's *In the Bedroom*. *A Beautiful Mind* used startling reverses, plot twists, and animation to take us into the schizophrenic mind of John Forbes Nash Jr., a Nobel Prize–winning mathematician who lost—and regained—his grip on sanity. It was a tour de force for actor Russell Crowe, more well known for his physicality on screen and his brawling off screen than for his acting skill. Equipped with nothing more than dowdy clothes and a wax pencil on which to frantically scribble formulas on a bay window overlooking the Princeton University campus, Crowe made us believe that he possessed a vast and luminous intelligence that allowed him to peer deeply into the very fabric of reality. Director Ron Howard convinced us that we could follow Crowe as his character's hold on reality shatters and his mental phantoms slither into the full light of day.

As Oscar night approached, Hollywood was ablaze with ugly gossip from the Drudge Report, not about Russell Crowe or Ron Howard, but about the film's subject—the Nobel Prize winner, John Forbes Nash, who was rumored to have been a raving anti-Semite and a sexual weirdo. Matt Drudge reported that three academy members had changed their votes after learning that Nash was guilty of being a "Jew basher." Nash himself took this charge in stride, noting that when he was ill, he had said and done a great many strange things—he once believed he was the emperor of Antarctica. He allowed that he might very well have made some anti-Semitic utterances.[15]

Questions, fueled by bloggers, kept coming: Why wasn't this in the story? Why did Howard and screenwriter Akiva Goldsman choose to leave out details about Nash's complex sexual life? The answer, of course, is that like all moviemakers, Howard and Goldsman streamlined and skewed history, adapting it to the screen. Somehow, however, a campaign was under way in Hollywood to make this artistic choice seem as if it were some kind of sordid scam, if not an outright cinematic scandal.[16]

In the end, *A Beautiful Mind* was too good to be derailed. It won Best Picture. But Hollywood insiders said that the negative campaign from an interested source did real damage to the film's chances.

"This may not be the worst year in Oscar history, but it's pretty low," Pete Hammond, a film historian and consultant for American Movie Classics, told *The New York Times.* "To accuse the subject of a film of being anti-Semitic when you know that a lot of the people who will be voting on the Oscars are Jewish, well, that's really down and dirty. . . . It's getting nastier. It's like a political campaign now. You get these so-called Oscar consultants who go out there thinking, 'What kind of dirt can we dig up?' "[17]

In 2010, the Academy of Motion Picture Arts and Sciences banned *The Hurt Locker* producer Nicolas Chartier from attending the Oscars for sending out an e-mail disparaging competitor *Avatar,* while Hollywood insiders report that the little digs in Chartier's e-mail were mild compared to some of the sponsored attacks they were seeing every day.

> Powerful competitors knock worthy projects as easily as a race car can tip an opponent into a tailspin.

Something Old, Something New

Digital assassins gone mad with money, sex, power, and envy will use technology to fire a malicious story to weaken, wound, or kill you. But not all attacks are digital assassinations.

Brands, companies, products, and celebrities can be criticized and subjected to the rough-and-tumble of free speech—a truth made apparent when an Amarillo jury in 1998 found Oprah Winfrey not guilty of libeling the Texas beef industry for airing a show on mad cow disease.

Character assassination is certainly not to be confused with bad publicity based on wicked acts, hypocrisy, incompetence, or lack of due diligence. Representative Anthony Weiner of New York, Tiger Woods, former senator and presidential candidate John Edwards, former South Carolina governor Mark Sanford, and former New York governor Eliot Spitzer were not character assassinated. They self-destructed, killing their own reputations.

The same can be said for Toyota in its apparent lack of due diligence in the sudden-acceleration debacle, BP's repeated careless actions leading up to the Gulf oil spill, or the bad odor from the decision by Merrill Lynch CEO John Thain to spend $1,400 on a trash can as part of his million-dollar makeover of his office during the worst recession in seventy years.

These are clear examples of character suicide. So what then is digital character assassination?

Digital assassination begins as a willful act by someone who wishes to do harm through the Internet. It unfolds as a deliberate campaign to spread harmful lies that the assassin has concocted about you or as an attempt to take a fact about you grossly out of context or embellish it, making an ordinary shortcoming seem ghastly. Words are then forged into swords to be thrust into the gut.

Digital assassination is most effective when others—as knowing conspirators or unknowing parrots—are incited by social media to thrust swords of their own. The result is multiple slices and stabs, leaving a permanent, searchable Internet record that continues to harm your brand, fan base, business, or reputation among friends, customers, investors, or other media on a 24/7 basis.

This power of the new digital assassin to destroy is as powerful as YouTube, but as old as civilization. Character assassination was a weapon in the arsenal of the ancients, from palace intrigues against Jewish advisers to the king of Persia, to the philippics employed in the class struggles and civil warfare that consumed Rome in the time of Cicero and Mark Antony.

Character assassination is deeply woven into the fabric of American political life. America's revolutionary leaders, nostalgically remembered as our Founding Fathers, indulged in endless acrimonious backbiting. They used Latin pseudonyms and pamphlets to attack each other. They hired character assassins and subsidized vituperative partisan presses. The next chapter seeks lessons for the digital age from the savage, covert war Thomas Jefferson and Alexander Hamilton waged against each other through various journalistic outlets, flinging taunts that were well-understood references to each other's personal vulnerabilities in an effort to blackmail and dishearten.

This tendency to fling mud and ruin reputations was checked somewhat in the twentieth century by the rise of mainstream media—newspapers, wire services, magazines, radio news, and then television news—that relied on mass subscriptions and advertising to liberate editors and reporters from the tyranny of business and political patrons. The mainstream media had its biases. But it did something no character assassin has ever done. It tried to be fair and often succeeded.

The establishment media at its zenith illuminated all that could be seen. But the sun began to set on such media with the close of the twentieth century.

In this new century, we find ourselves surprisingly close to the nineteenth-century era of barbed commentary, slanted accounts, and subsidized attacks. The migration of these smears from paper pamphlets to screens, however, is about more than the evolution of print into more vivid media.

With the new technology, character assassins have more than a few new platforms from which to attack. Digital technology enables spontaneous groups to emerge instantly, bringing the power of social media to the age-old human tendency to character assassinate.

The Internet empowers a motley collection of anarchists, libertarians, leftists, and hackers known as Anonymous to spontaneously organize hundreds of sites to continue Julian Assange's cyber WikiLeaks campaign against Washington, D.C. Social media lets ordinary people do what tyrants and terrorists could not—make a frontal assault on the U.S. government and win.

Assassins with little effort and little cost can now contact your customers or stakeholders, employees and colleagues, lovers or friends, fans, and even former high school coaches and teachers, to contribute a few keystrokes that can add telling details to form a collective portrait of your monstrosity. Such smears then become a permanent part of your digital reputation—one you can subsume, but not hide from the world.

In the days of the old media, you had obvious ways to counter a bad story. There were ombudsmen, op-eds and letters to the editor, advertising opportunities and plenty of competitors willing to let you tell your side.

Now, when a negative thread appears about you on the Internet, you'll never know for sure who read it, how it was received, or whether a separate targeted campaign was mounted to directly deliver it to your friends, customers, clients, employers, and significant others. Today, in this new media, you may never know how deep the wound is until it manifests itself in the form of murdered opportunity, both personal and financial.

So then, what can be done?

We take an analytical and anecdotal approach to the new phenomenon of digital assassination. This is needed because many books today tend to get lost in technology, as well as its platforms—Twitter, Facebook, Yelp, and the rest—as if the basis of the problem was technology itself.

To be sure, new technology is transformative. And it is overwhelmingly good, improving the way we live, work, shop, educate, and romance. It changes societies with unprecedented transparency.

This technology, however, also has a dark side. We explore how that dark side can threaten your reputation, brand, and business from online attacks.

The first two chapters show how principles of human behavior, not technology, are the driving factors behind this dark side of the Internet. In chapters 3 through 9, we reveal the seven forms of digital attacks, how they can destroy business, career, and life.

In these chapters, we draw on stories from the left, the right, and the center—from ancient times; the American Founding Fathers; our experience working with world leaders, CEOs, and corporate boards; and pulp dramas right out of the tabloids—not to make you feel sorry for the victims, but to create object lessons useful for you.

We will explore what is timeless about the uses of this technology and what is new.

Many victims of digital assassination in these pages might include people whose personalities you find grating or whose politics you find offensive or both.

Never mind.

This is not a political book. It is about understanding the nature of attacks, as a basis to prepare you to act in your defense.

In chapter 11, we arm you with seven strategies, as well as tactics and keystrokes, you need to blunt and reverse attacks. This chapter presents ways to be ready for a surprise onslaught and to monitor your presence in cyberspace, and provides a simple game plan and actions to take when an attack occurs.

Whether you are a corporate executive or manager, doctor, lawyer, accountant, consultant with a large group or singular sensation, shop-keeper or restaurateur, model, designer, celebrity, parent, or grandparent, this book will help you understand the nature of these digital attacks and how to prepare for them and respond.

No one is bulletproof in the digital world. Take steps to show a digital assassin you are not an easy mark.

2:// America's First Bloggers

> One of our greatest presidents [Thomas Jefferson],
> our greatest Founding Father, is also the one we've got the
> goods on in terms of being a jerk.
>
> —**Stephen Colbert**, interview on "Monticello," *American Icons*

MILLIONS OF PEOPLE feel adrift on the Silicon Sea. There are no welcoming shores visible on this horizon, only mysterious kingdoms with fanciful names like Tumblr, Twitter, Digg, Delicious, Foursquare, Second Life.

If you are older, you might sometimes feel like you have been given the exhausting task of exploring these unfamiliar shorelines to classify a whole new zoology, as if it were up to you personally to define the ecological niche each distinctive new service occupies in the world of social media.

In truth, understanding the technology is the easy part. All you have to do is to Google, Bing, or Yahoo! anything you don't understand. Go to that site, and it will show you what it does. If you want to know more, read consumer or media reviews from leading sites like mashable.com, as well as the mainstream press. Clear answers in everyday language are at your fingertips.

If you are younger, you navigate the virtual world with ease. What is harder for all generations to grasp is that behind the technology is greed, malice, desire—the age-old motivations of money, sex, power, and envy.

Many take information from you—where you go, whom you talk to, what you decide to post—and commoditize it, even weaponize it.

So age needs to approach technology with greater skill, while youth needs to approach technology with greater wisdom. For everyone, the most difficult things to anticipate about new technologies are the possible creative uses for them and humans' myriad reasons to use them in spiteful ways.

How do we recognize age-old patterns of attack in the new media? And in which ways can technology endow human malice with awesome new muscle?

Too much of commentary about the misuses of Internet platforms gets lost in the power and breadth of this technology. True, the Internet, no less than the Industrial Revolution, is reshaping every aspect of our life. One in eight couples married in the United States met through social media. Facebook is the world's largest country.[1] User-generated content is forcing business to be responsive to the customer as never before. Adaptive information technology may be our best hope of educating the planet.

Digital technology is an enormous force for good. But the cyberutopians overlook the fact that because digital technology is woven into almost everything we do and think, this technology also has a raging dark side, which includes digital assassination.

Some current books tend to get lost in the modality of expression, as if the basis of the problem was the technological platforms themselves. Rather than get lost in these technologies and platforms, we must first understand the broader strategic patterns from which character attacks surface on digital platforms. This book starts with the insight that the underlying issue is not the proliferation of dangerous technologies, but the amplification of human meanness.

To fully understand how character assassination works in our digital world, we need to look to history. This chapter will examine a conflict from late 1700s America, when newspapers came damp with printer's ink. This struggle reveals seven key ways to destroy a target's character. We will examine each of these seven "swords" to understand how they are amplified by digital speed, magnitude, and the capacity for spontaneous organization.

Blackmail, Slaves, and Sex

Every day, millions of bloggers—some paid, some not; some tired, angry, or blowing off steam—fill the Internet with attacks on brands, products, companies, or individuals. It is all too easy to get hung up on the technology and forget that what we are dealing with are for the most part just words.

The practice of using words to slip a knife into the ribs of a rival is as old as Rome—and as American as Thomas Jefferson and Alexander Hamilton. This chapter takes an in-depth look at a historical struggle that involved power, sex, and skulduggery.*

This story reveals the seven swords of character assassination exposed by a feud between prominent early Americans, those we call America's first bloggers. Jefferson and Hamilton—each embodying an ideological polarity of early America—waged a long subterranean war that began in Washington's cabinet between the secretary of state and the secretary of the treasury. The weapon of choice in their duel was the exposure of each other's sex lives. What transpired in this early period provides a model for understanding the dangerous trends proliferating in our digital age.

Hamilton Sexposed

On a July day in 1791, in Philadelphia, Alexander Hamilton had a lapse in judgment that would become a gift to his enemies. He took a visit from Maria Reynolds, an attractive and vulnerable twenty-three-year-old mother abandoned by her husband James to fend for herself and their daughter. She sought help from the sensitive and sympathetic Hamilton, one of the young nation's most prominent men.

When Hamilton promised to give Maria $30, he made a point of delivering it personally. Maria pointedly invited Hamilton upstairs to her bedroom, where, he later admitted, "it was quickly apparent that other than pecuniary consolation would be accepted." In fact, for almost a year, Hamilton—married to Elizabeth Schuyler, one of the most beautiful and socially connected women in New York State—made regular visits to the young Maria, entering her rooming house through a back door.

Hamilton must have known of Maria's husband. James Reynolds was a hustler who was making a fortune swindling Revolutionary War

* For a detailed but riveting history, see Ron Chernow's *Alexander Hamilton* (New York: Penguin, 2004).

veterans and their widows out of their back pay. Returning to Philadelphia and to his young wife, Reynolds saw the married Hamilton as a new mark. He wrote a letter about "the poor Broken harted woman" that must have shot a bolt of fear through Hamilton's heart: "I would Sacrefise almost my life to make her Happy. but now I am determined to have satisfaction."

As it turned out, satisfaction could be had not in the form of a duel, but in the form of a government sinecure. Hamilton refused to install Reynolds in an office, but he did pay $1,000 in blackmail to James Reynolds, about $23,000 in today's money. There would be many more such "contributions."

After a brief attempt at restraint, Hamilton returned to the affections of the young Maria. As he did, more requests for payments came from James Reynolds. In effect, Hamilton was now paying Reynolds as both a blackmailer and a pimp.

In 1792, James Reynolds was arrested for, among other things, an early American version of identity theft, claiming to be the executor of a soldier's estate. From his jail cell, Reynolds got word of the affair to several political detractors of Hamilton, including future president James Monroe.

Hamilton came clean, admitting to the whole squalid arrangement to congressional inquirers. Monroe held on to the copies of the incriminating documents, which eventually found their way to his fellow Jeffersonians, including James Callender, the scurrilous smear artist secretly subsidized by Jefferson. Jefferson himself tried to get the U.S. House of Representatives to censure the Treasury Secretary for mixing up federal accounts, as well as other charges.

Hamilton survived by throwing himself into a prodigious effort to respond to each charge. This lunge for Hamilton's jugular was a mistake, for Thomas Jefferson's private life was at least as vulnerable as Hamilton's. And Hamilton knew just how to strike back at Jefferson.

Jefferson's Secret Desire

After leaving office, Hamilton took up writing under the pen name of Phocion in the *Gazette of the United States* in 1796, ridiculing the southern fear that emancipation would result in miscegenation, when in fact the slavemaster (unmistakably Jefferson) "must have seen all around him sufficient marks" of racial mixing. A few days later, Hamilton referred to "evidences of aristocratic splendor, sensuality, and epicureanism" on the plantation.

Four days later, Jefferson's allies anonymously referred to the Reynolds affair in the Republican *Aurora*. "Would a publication of the circumstances of that transaction redound to the honour or reputation of the parties and why has the subject been so long and carefully smothered up?"

In other words, Hamilton employed a front to tell Jefferson that he knew that the sage of Monticello was using a slave for sex. Jefferson, likely through the pen of an ally, was telling Hamilton, that he'd better shut up about that, or the whole world would know about Maria Reynolds.

For a time, both Jefferson and Hamilton had acceded to the reputational equivalent of mutually assured destruction. Jefferson's Charlottesville neighbors had long gossiped about the widower's closeness to his slave, Sally Hemings, and the resemblance of her children to the master of the house.

And here matters rested until Callender went public with the Reynolds story, using the sex angle to prop up the old charge that Hamilton had been cooking the federal books.

Under attack, Hamilton adopted the same response as he had done before Congress. He published ninety-five pages of personal confession, letters, and affidavits that led the reader through a thorough account of the affair, Hamilton's long slide into the grasping hands of James Reynolds, and documentation absolving him of any betrayal of his public duty.

Did it work? The Jeffersonian press had a field day, raising the question that if Hamilton admitted to being a rake, why should we not believe he was also swindler? Most readers saw something else. They recognized in Hamilton's confession the desire to obtain the respect of his countrymen for his achievements as a statesman at the expense of their opinion of his private behavior. Even then, there were sections of Hamilton's pamphlet that read almost like an eighteenth-century version of the Starr Report. It offered, in modern parlance, too much information.

Jefferson had little time to gloat. In this all-out war of character attack by paid partisans, neither party would escape unscathed. In Jefferson's case, it was not so much the hidden hand of Alexander Hamilton as it was the undependability of his own paid assassin.

The same James T. Callender who prospered on Jefferson's payroll became embittered when jailed under President Adams's Alien and Sedition Acts, and vengeful when Jefferson, now president himself, refused to pay off his potential blackmailer with a government appointment. The president did make a private "charity" payment. Callender was insulted but took the money.

In 1802, Callender accused Jefferson in the Richmond *Recorder* of fathering several of the six children of Sally Hemings. Callender's revelation came at the worst possible time for Jefferson, early in his first term as president.

The Reputational Fallout

Jefferson could have followed Hamilton's strategy of issuing a confession. He could have tried, like Nixon, a "limited hangout." He could have lied like Clinton. Instead, Jefferson maintained a dignified and glacial silence. Fourteen years later, Jefferson explained his approach to the scandal in a letter to a supporter: "I should have fancied myself half guilty had I condescended to put pen to paper in refutation of their falsehoods, or drawn to them respect by any notice from myself."

The scandal in our time, of course, is not that Jefferson likely loved a woman of color, but that he owned her and their children—and continued to own them when he could have given them their freedom. This personal failing throws into stark relief the contradiction of Jefferson, human liberator and slaveholder.

In matters of character, we are sometimes forced to choose between current comfort and damnation for posterity. Hamilton sullied his reputation while safeguarding his place in history. Jefferson protected his presidency at the expense of his reputation for all time.

Now, how is all this relevant today?

The Seven Swords of Digital Assassination

Digital attacks are more about words and strategy than media and technology.

The Internet has power that no other media has ever offered. Power in the form of instantaneity, 24/7 global reach, eternal memory, deep search capability, and instant retrieval. But what was the American Revolution if not a social media movement drummed up by newspapers, pamphlets, and polemical engravings, such as Paul Revere's rendition of the Boston Massacre?

As with the paper world, the digital world has its Facebook prostitutes and digital exposés. But out of the Jefferson–Hamilton stealth reputation war we can identify seven distinct strategies of attack, seven swords of character assassination augmented by the new power of the Internet age.

In the coming chapters, we will examine how each of these seven swords slash and wound in the twenty-first century.

The First Sword of Digital Assassination—New Media Mayhem

From the printing press to the personal digital assistant, new media has been a disruptive force that upends regimes and overturns authority of every kind. This can be seen in the eighteenth century, when mass circulation media in the form of paper pamphlets, magazines, and daily newspapers trafficked in gossip and skewered monarchs and presidents alike. This cacophony of anger helped inspire colonial rebellion in America, social turmoil in England, and bloody revolution in France.

Today, new media organizes leaderless revolutions in Libya, Tunisia, Egypt, and elsewhere, allowing WikiLeaks to set the U.S. government on its heels and bloggers to confront global corporations.

The Second Sword of Digital Assassination—Silent Slashers

Silent Slashers are severe cuts to one's reputation from anonymous attackers. In early America, anonymous pamphlets and leaflets aired personal and political attacks too venomous for attribution, freeing attackers from having to own up to their remarks. Federalist leaflets depicted Jefferson as a swindler, an atheist, and a Jacobin who wanted the streets to run red with revolution. Republican leaflets portrayed John Adams as planning to marry his sons into the British royal family in order to establish monarchies on either side of the Atlantic. Many of these broadsides were from Silent Slashers—anonymous, destructive, and well circulated.

Today Silent Slashers have instantaneous and global reach. They appear, disappear, and reappear with a new angle of attack.

The Third Sword of Digital Assassination—Evil Clones

Impersonators can create an evil caricature of you, an avatar self that revels in its faults. In early America, the Jeffersonians attributed bogus quotes to John Adams to create a false representation of him as a "champion of kings, ranks, and titles," just as Federalists exaggerated Jefferson's Enlightenment views so as to make him seem atheistic and as dangerously radical as Robespierre.

Today digital technology allows anyone to instantaneously spawn an evil clone, a perfectly believable avatar, of anyone else, in online images as well as words.

The Fourth Sword of Digital Assassination—Human Flesh Search Engines

Attackers can crowd-source private information, turning gossip into actionable intelligence, using these unearthed secrets to incite mobs ready to tar, feather, and even lynch. Callender teased out intelligence about Jefferson and, in casual conversation while in jail and, later, with Jefferson's neighbors over fence posts and in taverns. The story had already been put together for him: Crowds can perform investigations better than any individual.

Today digital assassins appeal to global audiences to collect secrets about individuals from old teachers, colleagues, and ex-lovers—and then call on the crowd to launch attacks on that target from every possible angle.

The Fifth Sword of Digital Assassination—Jihad by Proxy

Organizations with noble-sounding names and mission statements can disguise attacks for donors with less than the civic good in mind. Jefferson's campaign against President Adams was organized through Committees of Correspondence, modeled after the effective revolutionary political communications organs of the same name, that produced attacks and spread dirt from organizations that appeared to be citizens acting out of high motives.

Today there is a panoply of front organizations, nourished and funded by special interests, that launch online attacks on environmental, health, and patriotic grounds that are utterly disingenuous.

The Sixth Sword of Digital Assassination—Truth Remix

Ordinary human imperfection can be exaggerated, turning commonplace failings and vices into horrendous crimes. In the eighteenth century, Jefferson tried to transform Hamilton's personal scandal into a financial one, and Hamilton tried to link Jefferson's complicated life to the charge of being a dangerous radical. They reduced shades of gray into deepest black.

Today the traditional media has been replaced by a blogosphere that creates falsities out of truth in order to compete for ratings and clicks.

The Seventh Sword of Digital Assassination—Clandestine Combat

Throughout history, when all else fails, enemies or competitors simply purloin each other's secrets.

This was done to Hamilton by Jeffersonians who leaked the confidential investigation of the Reynolds affair, and by Hamilton who secretly interviewed cabinet officers, getting them to leak stories that portrayed President Adams as unstable and "mad." At the end, water seeks the lowest level. Character assassins are desperate enough to take what they cannot find.

Today, the open architecture of our critical technologies provide hackers unprecedented opportunities for outright stealing.

THESE SEVEN SWORDS are examined in the chapters ahead. We will reveal age-old patterns of attack and emerging new capabilities powered by technology in the digital age.

In *Thirteen Days*, a movie about the Cuban Missile Crisis, the Robert McNamara character looks at a war-room map of the U.S. Navy blockade of Cuba. McNamara tells a top admiral that a naval blockade at the brink of nuclear war is not a blockade. "This is language," he says. "A new vocabulary, the likes of which the world has never seen! This is President Kennedy communicating with Secretary Khrushchev!"[2]

This was eloquent but wrong.

Instead, what was being used was an old vocabulary of power projection that seemed new because it was transmitted instantly and for far higher stakes. What had changed was speed and magnitude. The same is true of digital technology today.

In a digital world, age needs to approach technology with greater skill. Youth needs to approach technology with greater wisdom.

3:// The First Sword

New Media Mayhem

> Clothes make the man. Naked people have little or no influence on society.
>
> —**Mark Twain**

NEW MEDIA is still evolving in fast-forward, shaped by Darwinian forces that mold increasingly lethal forms of digital assassination. This first sword of digital assassination, new media mayhem—from Gutenberg's printing press to Google's Android—is a disruptive force that roils governments and challenges authority in all its forms.

This new global media environment oddly takes us back to the level of a disgraced inhabitant of a small village of a prior era, condemned for life by gossip. It is impossible to doubt that we live in a global village of character assassination when:

- Fortune 500 companies and individuals alike rely on computer systems wide open to hacking and exploitation.
- Negative images are sticky, eternal, and prone to spread like kudzu in a Google environment.
- Nongovernmental organizations (NGOs) are often in cahoots with secret donors, the media, and ambitious prosecutors to target the successful.
- Media institutions that might have mitigated the damage have been replaced by the clowns and barking seals of a digital circus.
- Companies, brands, products, and people must monitor anything said about them through nights, weekends, and holidays

in order to keep pace with the tech-enabled demons inhabiting the Internet.
- We are surrounded by potential "shame famers" grasping for attention.
- Business competitors are as apt to inspire or spread the defamation about you as they are to rush to your defense.

The Global Bookie and the Hilton Effect

Exquisitely sensitive to customer needs, Google has tried to live up to its unofficial motto, "Don't Be Evil"—winning the applause of human rights activists by standing up to censorship by the People's Republic of China. Google is the first big Western company willing to risk abandoning the world's largest market over an issue of principle.

The problem with Google isn't its business ethics or its heart, but the way its algorithms wind up reinforcing the Internet's dark side. Google doesn't mean to be evil. It means to track billions of click-throughs to see how hot topics, sales, ads, and pricing trends fluctuate—information that is worth billions of dollars to marketers.

Google excels at this because it is a heuristic learner. That is, Google learns by its experience with you. It excels at seeking optimal solutions based on rough approximations of your somewhat inaccurate and sometimes misspelled search terms. As it learns what you like, Google hones in on your preferences to find more of what you like.

"Another light side of informatics is Amazon," says Leo Yakutis, an IT expert who started his career troubleshooting product support for Microsoft and is now a digital hound, a private investigator who detects breeches in corporate firewalls and traces attacks back to their source. "Amazon predicts and recommends things that you want for the future. That's what happens when what is out there about you is used for a productive purpose."[1]

Just as Amazon predicts what kind of book you'll want, and Google can track and remember your searches, so too can search engines follow the tastes of the crowd to rank search results by popularity. These capabilities are truly transformative, shifting the commercial paradigm from mass marketing to social media and putting unprecedented power in the hands of consumers.

But it isn't always the cream that rises to the top. It is the sensational that draws the most viewers and inspires them to link to one another. And negative emotions draw the most links of all. A razor-sharp attack in the Huffington Post or the National Review Online will immediately attract cross-links and chatter from a thousand blogs and Twitter accounts. Negative items that shock the most rise even faster.

In late 2009, people around the world who searched for an image of the First Lady of the United States found among the top results to come up was not one of Mrs. Obama's official and press portraits and candid shots, but a grotesque melding of her face with that of a chimpanzee.

"People gimmick the system to get their stuff up higher and higher," says James Lee, a social media expert and president of The Lee Strategy Group in Los Angeles. "Google keeps trying to improve its searches, but people keep finding ways to skew the system. If you want to intentionally defame someone, it's an easy process."[2]

The process is easy even when defamation may not be intended.

In a landmark case, Barbra Streisand unintentionally demonstrated how the sticky nature of the Internet can spread unwanted information even when no malicious force is at work. The diva was following the rules of old media when she sued to keep an environmental activist and Pictopia.com from posting aerial photos of her beachside mansion. At the time, the photo was sandwiched with more than 12,000 other coastline photographs.

The publicity from Streisand's lawsuit for $50 million in damages had the effect of blowing hard on a dandelion gone to seed—the obscure site soon had more than one million visitors.[3] The picture wafted all across the Internet, like so many dandelion seeds, into too many places to monitor or count. Since then, the tendency of cease-and-desist letters to spread unwanted or damaging information or images has been called the Streisand Effect.

So it is almost impossible for an offended person to compel the total removal of something off the web that has already achieved some notoriety without making it more widespread. Since Google's caching of the web gives it virtual omniscience, the effort at old-fashioned damage control also guarantees that the offending pictures, video, or words never really go away.

Two days after Tyler Clementi committed suicide, Yakutis checked to see how far the actual sex tape had circulated. "It was on over a thousand English-speaking servers," he says. "How are you going to clean that up?"

The media focuses on the catastrophic stories of Internet exposure and suicide like Clementi's. But there are many more young people who will pay a more subtle price. "Digitally defaming a grandma in her seventies is not really that effective if she doesn't use the media," says Yakutis. "But make a charge of assault against a young football player, no matter how little foundation for the charge, it can't go away for him—ever."

Nor does an inflammatory comment a young person makes online. "Young professional athletes have lots of testosterone, lots of ambition, lots of money, and low maturity," Yakutis says. "So say a young football player bad-mouths his coach on Facebook or Twitter. Every tweet from the beginning of Twitter in 2006 is now indexed at the Library of Congress."

"Your indiscretions will be able to be seen by generations and generations of graduate students," Stanford scholar Paul Saffo told *The New York Times*.[4]

And when a posting does start to fade, archival retrieval services like the Wayback Machine act as digital time capsules to make sure that everything that once was on the Internet can remain on the Internet. "You touch the Internet and it never forgets," says Bill Livingstone, a former high-level political operative turned security expert. "Your criminal record can be wiped clean in seven years, but not if you can still find it on the Internet."[5]

This Streisand Effect is what happens when you fail to understand how Google operates.

The Hilton Effect is what happens when you fail to understand who is in control of the pattern of attacks and counterattacks. Consider how Google's rating by popularity acts as fuel for salacious Internet destinations like that of Perez Hilton's Hollywood gossip site. This shock blogger until recently had a habit of drawing penises over the faces of celebrities he doesn't like. He also inserts snarky captions. One Hollywood celebrity, a picture posted of her looking out the window from the driver's seat of her car, has Hilton's added caption "Crack Is Wack," thus implying that she is a crack addict.[6]

The opening salvo of an attack on such a site may be highly clicked. If the public gets engaged in the story, the counter to the attack is thus also assured of high ratings, boosted by links and algorithms to a few keywords, which sets up even higher ratings for the next attack.

More dirt means more eyeballs, which means greater ad revenue.

The Hilton Effect was on full display in 2009, when a Miss USA judge, none other than Perez Hilton himself, asked California beauty contestant Carrie Prejean where she stood on gay marriage. No matter how you feel about gay marriage, the digital subtext of this media drama is perhaps the greater story, one that reveals new media as a force greater than any debate it amplifies.

Prejean replied with an answer that she later characterized as "biblically correct" rather than politically correct. Within minutes, the beauty queen's no to gay marriage became a top feature on Internet searches and YouTube clicks, propelled by both angry people passionately in favor of gay marriage and people who greatly opposed to same-sex unions.

Perez Hilton, the self-styled queen of all media, quickly responded with a video flaming Prejean as a "dumb bitch" who had made the biggest PR mistake in pageant history. Thus Hilton's attack became a top Internet search term; his vitriolic interpretation was laid on top of her answer, creating a negative context for it.

When Prejean appeared on NBC's *Today* show two days after the pageant, she shot back that she was being victimized for giving an honest answer that was close to those given by then presidential candidates Obama and Hillary Clinton. Prejean's response overlaid Hilton's comments, putting her back on top on YouTube.

Hilton and his allies subsequently revealed Prejean's old modeling pictures, which they argued were salacious (part of a nipple was showing), and exposed the evangelical Christian Prejean to the charge of being a hypocrite. Then Prejean responded with a detailed explanation of how the pictures came to be and added another counter about how she had been mistreated.

And so on, the Hilton Effect game continued, each hand grabbing a higher part of a seemingly endless stick. Whether they knew it or not, Prejean and Hilton were in business together, his gay, blue-state yin countering her straight, red-state yang, and vice versa, for months on end.

Who won?

Google won. The corporate giant serves as the smart bookie who wins both sides of every bet, selling ads all along the way.

> **Global Bookie and the Hilton Effect:** For people, brands,
> or companies attacked on the Internet, Google's algorithms
> assure that every defense will hype every attack—and every
> counterresponse—for as long as the sheer ugliness of a fight is
> interesting to onlookers.

A Pirate's Dream

Ever wonder how vulnerable you are to digital pirates?

By now, everyone has read about Russian gangs and brigades of sophisticated hackers organized by the People's Liberation Army of China. But do these sophisticated hackers really target individuals, brands, or businesses? Do I really have to be worried about the computers in my offices, in my home, as well as my accounts with companies I do business with?

The average American is exposed to about 34 gigabytes of data and information each day. The average American youth, eight to eighteen years, devotes 7 hours and 38 minutes a day to entertainment media (10 hours and 45 minutes, if you include multitasking).[7] As that data flows into your devices, data about you is constantly flowing out—and not always to benign sources.

Reported privacy breaches occur all the time on a monumental scale. In 2010, Facebook, MySpace, and other sites were discovered to be releasing vast amounts of personal information about millions of users through apps and advertisers.

Then there is the more sinister work of "black hat" hackers. A Data Breach Investigations Report issued in 2009 by Verizon's RISK team could account for 90 data breaches compromising 285 million records in 2008.[8] Reported breaches have occurred with T-Mobile, American Express, PepsiCo, and Merrill Lynch.[9]

Bank of America in 2011 found itself in the crosshairs of unwanted attention from WikiLeaks. Even video games are subject to mass exposure of personal information. In May 2011, Sony acknowledged that digital pirates waged a highly sophisticated attack that potentially compromised more than 100 million online-gaming accounts, including its popular PlayStation Gaming Network. Industry insiders concede there have been innumerable other breaches—likely tens of millions of them—that companies do not want to report or even acknowledge internally.

Some basic truth about your computer emerged when a major IT company told the authors it decided to investigate just how seriously cyberattacks had penetrated the average computer—*your* computer. The company's engineers purchased a garden-variety PC from a chain retailer. They installed in it the best off-the-shelf antivirus, anti-spyware protection, and firewall software packages available. Then they connected this PC to the Internet. They did not use it for anything. They just tracked the flow of code into and out of the machine.

Within four hours the engineers detected the first ping by a potential hacker. In two weeks more sophisticated software from a computer in Canada slowly embedded itself in the PC and started running its own software. The Canadian computer soon set up links between the enslaved zombie PC and a computer in Singapore, which used the PC to attack a network in Poland.

This wide-open nature of any computer attached to the Internet, whether wired or wireless, is something that many executives understand intellectually but do not incorporate into their actions. Witness John Deutch, a polymath who earned a PhD in chemistry at MIT and served as President Bill Clinton's director of the CIA. This supremely intelligent man—at a conference one of the authors saw him taking notes in the form of a string of calculus variables—apparently did not know or accept how a computer worked. He took a CIA computer home with him, one laden with classified files containing—judging from the government's subsequent reaction—some of America's most closely held sources and methods. Deutch became the subject of an intense investigation after a routine audit of his computers by the CIA showed that he had connected it to the Internet, and on occasion someone with access to his computer used it to visit pornography websites.[10] Deutch might as well have left a briefcase full of secrets in Tiananmen Square or on the front doorstep of the FSB in Moscow.

Bill Clinton pardoned Deutch on his last day in office.

Before WikiLeaks revealed the extent of the government's vulnerability to pirates from within, attacks from China accessed sensitive data in four computers used by a staffer to U.S. Representative Frank Wolf specializing in foreign policy and human rights, likely compromising the identity of human rights sources in China.[11] Long before Google objected to China's infiltration of its Gmail accounts and corporate information, an attack linked to the People's Liberation Army forced the Pentagon to shut down part of a computer system serving the office of Defense Secretary Robert Gates.[12]

While black hats can't match the prowess of foreign governments in accessing federal computers, they have more than enough skill to get into any digital device you own. So if you are wondering if your computer or laptop is compromised in some way, you can stop worrying.

It is.

The ease with which digital assassins and potential blackmailers can access your machines for damaging information to use against you is limited only to the extent that there is nothing in any message you have ever sent, any website you have ever visited, or any secret—including financial details, account numbers and PIN numbers—that you would not want anyone to know about, in any of your computers.

> **A Pirate's Dream:** You are not somewhat exposed. The open nature of computing allows our systems to be easily boarded by digital assassins.

Corporate Warfare

Corporate executives once adhered to a code similar to that of white-shoe law firms. They would refrain from running down one another's products, brands, ethics, or character in ads or anywhere else. The peace between corporate giants of postwar America mirrored the uneasy Cold War peace. The damage such conflict would create was seen as an unthinkable risk, the corporate version of mutually assured destruction.

In the twenty-first century, however, this code seems as outdated as the top hats presidents once wore to their inaugurals. We are now in the age of combative advertising that began with the cola wars of the 1980s. Some negative ads are good natured and jocular in tone. In a set of 2009 commercials, after a Verizon ad lampooned AT&T's coverage, AT&T responded with a lawsuit, then a humorous response with actor Luke Wilson slowly downloading himself with Verizon.[13]

Others are meant to draw blood. Jenny Craig made a little dig at its principal diet-industry competitor, Weight Watchers, on its website and in a 2010 TV ad in the critical post-holiday season in which actress Valerie Bertinelli donned a lab coat to claim that a major clinical trial showed that "Jenny Craig clients lost, on average, over twice as much weight as those on the largest weight-loss program!"[14]

This was a direct attack on the credibility of Weight Watchers spokeswoman Jenny McCarthy, who was boasting she had lost 75 pounds on the Weight Watchers program. Weight Watchers sued, claiming that Jenny Craig was lying. There had been, Weight Watchers claimed, no such "major clinical trial." The case was soon settled with Jenny Craig being forced to drop the ad.[15] These two corporations came off looking like two Roller Derby queens—Valerie and Jenny—throwing elbows and body slams.

Then there is Burt's Bees, the homespun maker of "Earth-friendly" personal care products. When Burt's Bees attacked its competitors, it did so not by attacking their brand, but by arousing fear about competitors' ingredients. One Burt's Bees Internet ad states that the lip balm from leading competitors (such as ChapStick) contains petroleum, which the ad helpfully adds is "a nonrenewable hydrocarbon made from crude oil . . . sometimes used to stop corrosion on car batteries."[16] Few customers realize that this eco-friendly brand with a logo that looks like it came straight from the *Farmers' Almanac* is in fact now a division of Clorox—a sign that even top Fortune 500 companies are willing to punch low and hard.[17]

In May 2011, Facebook was deeply embarrassed when it was caught using global PR firm Burson-Marsteller to pitch negative stories meant to put Google in hot water with the federal trade commission.[18]

Indeed, low-grade corporate warfare is constantly being waged between technology giants through patent trolls, insider blogs, and corporate talking points that company lobbyists thrust in front of senior congressional staffers and regulators. Time and again, it seems that technology companies that are against regulation as a matter of principle are more than willing to see harsh regulations imposed on their competitors.

What has changed is not just the willingness of companies to attack each other's products, but to launch real attacks on the lives of each other's brands or businesses.

> **Corporate Warfare:** When a brand, product, executive, or
> company are digitally assassinated, shots may very well have been
> fired by a peer competitor.

The Iron Rectangle

Political scientists have long written of an Iron Triangle between congressional committees, the bureaucracy, and special interests. The American political scene today is more of an Iron Rectangle made up of new players. Money and politics shape and define the digital conversation.

It works like this: Trial lawyers, many of them überrich, troll for deep-pocket corporate victims to attack with class-action lawsuits. These trial lawyers funnel large sums (often laundered through foundations) into the second corner of the rectangle, activist nongovernmental organizations (NGOs).

The activist "scholars" of these NGOs are then inspired to act as opposition researchers to level a debatable but explosive charge, whether environmental (killing rivers!), health (cancer clusters!), or other hot-button claim (sweatshop!), against the target company, brand, or executive. The NGO spreads around the dirt in slickly produced reports and video clips, often with a voice-over by a naive Hollywood celebrity. All this publicity stimulates the third corner of the rectangle—the media—to ring like a chuckwagon dinner bell.

NGOs such as the National Resources Defense Council or the Center for Science in the Public Interest are powerful and well funded. They have institutional agendas no less ambitious than those of Exxon or Citigroup. Yet many journalists and bloggers uncritically accept any claims these NGOs put before them as if these came from pure and objective sources.

The media, whether old mainstream or new online, are more than willing to trumpet these stories as scandals and raise the heat to create a basis for public action. This in turn engages the fourth and final corner of the rectangle, politicians—federal and state regulators, members of Congress angling for a TV or video bite, and especially state attorney generals, who (close to the trial bar, usually his or her biggest contributor and future employer) often hire on behalf of the state—surprise!—members of the trial bar who initiated the whole controversy.

Eliot Spitzer, long before his own disgrace and resignation as New

York governor in a sex scandal—a man many on Wall Street dubbed the worst character assassin of the last decade—perfected this game of state attorney general as avenging angel. The power behind this Iron Rectangle, however, begins and ends with the trial bar, which has revenues that far exceed those of Intel, Microsoft, or Coca-Cola.[19]

The tobacco settlements and successful asbestos class-action verdicts have left trial lawyers with billions of dollars more to invest in pioneering new charges with a coterie of bespoke scientists, oily PR firms, and pliable NGOs, thus pushing claims against new deep-pocket victims through corporate character assassination.

The Iron Rectangle: Ready-made character assassination machines driven by powerful and moneyed interests.

The Rise of the "Digital Estate" and Gossip Girls

Big media is often accused of being liberal, biased, and urbane. But if ABC, CBS, NBC, or CNN made an assertion, it was in the open. You knew who was reporting the allegation, even if they did quote unnamed sources. There was also a predictable cycle to the news in the last century that worked, in most instances, to ferret out the truth.

Wire services, radio network news, and newspapers gave more thoughtful analysis and local TV sent out reporters to validate information. In the end, major networks, *The New York Times,* and *The Washington Post* defined what was newsworthy.

It was a creaky and flawed system based on fallible, biased human beings. But it (mostly) worked.

Today the old networks continue to cover news largely as they always have, but with a rapidly shrinking audience. Fox News covers the news differently, with a conservative bias, but also with enough credibility to grow market share exponentially. In a sign of Fox's growing media dominance, in 2010 and May 2011, Bill O'Reilly went mano a mano with one of the great wits of the left, Jon Stewart of *The Daily Show*. It is impossible to imagine such ideological diversity, not to mention unrestrained debate, in the days of Dan Rather and John Chancellor.

While declining ad revenues have forced newspapers and TV stations to pull their last remaining news bureaus from state capitals and make deep cuts in their news staff, a new animal—online "sponsored news"—has begun to occupy this empty space. This is not the Fourth Estate we have long known. This is a new Digital Estate.

On the left, sponsored news is typified by the Huffington Post Investigative Fund, a group of online journalists sponsored by the left-wing Tides Center, the 501(c)3 with connections to the scandal-ridden ACORN.[20] On the right, sponsored news is supported by the Franklin Center for Government and Public Integrity, a 501(c)3 that supports investigative journalist watchdogs who reveal profligacy and conflicts of interest in state capitals.[21]

In both cases, these organizations are not required by law to reveal the identities of their ultimate donors—and they do not.

Journalists in both camps do profess adherence to the code of ethics of the Society of Professional Journalists. Both sides undoubtedly strive to report the truth as they see it. Franklin Center journalists broke the story that the Obama administration was bragging about saving or creating jobs with stimulus dollars in congressional districts that don't exist. The HuffPo investigative journalists broke the story that the payday lending industry spent record sums on lobbyists to try to stay out of Washington's various proposals for financial reform.

So both report with a given slant to expose a set of targets to satisfy the worldviews of their sponsors and readerships. The HuffPo Investigative Fund is not likely to go after a scandal in the Obama administration, and journalists supported by the Franklin Center are not likely to fact-check Sarah Palin.

As mainstream media retreats, there are fewer and fewer journalists who would be willing to go after sacred cows on either side of the ideological divide.

Meanwhile, on national TV, the signature news of today comes not from a magisterial network anchor, whether Fox, NBC, or the gray lady of *The New York Times,* but from biased stories from Gossip Girls like Extra, ET, and TMZ who serve every prurient taste ("who's gay and who's not," "fat celebrities on the beach!"). This is what is taking over the golden slot, the dinner hour that was once the province of Walter Cronkite and Peter Jennings.

People who once scoured the society pages of *The New York Times* turn to anonymous reviewers like Socialite Rank, with comment boards that offered unsourced descriptions of cocaine use and lurid sex.

The old major networks are often forced, sometimes with mock reluctance, to report gossip as news. So if TMZ or Perez Hilton drives a story far enough on the Internet, old media is forced to cover it with the fig leaf that the very spread of the gossip itself forces them to treat it as news.

Rising over the exotic creatures of this vast and ever-changing new media ocean is the sun, which is of course Google.

Gossip Girls: Victims of character assassination should expect little fairness and no ombudsmen from this new Digital Estate.

Damage at Light-Speed

"Everywhere you go, everyone has a camera," says comedian Robin Williams. "It's not Big Brother anymore, it's Little Snitch."[22] The Internet is the new camera of the twenty-first century. It is always on.

Little Snitch hides in video cameras, cell phone cameras, and tiny pinhole cameras disguised in pens or on lapels or in reading or sunglasses. It can arrive in your office in the hands of Michael Moore, or it can already be in your office. James O'Keefe, half of the "pimp and prostitute" hoax that brought down ACORN, pled guilty for masquerading as a telephone technician to get into the telephone exchange of Senator Mary Landrieu, Democrat of Louisiana.[23]

It is not enough to watch what you say. You have to be careful what you read. Representative John Conyers, a Democrat from Illinois, chairman of the House Judiciary Committee in 2010, was riding on an airplane when he was caught by another passenger's camera phone ogling photo spreads in an adult magazine.[24]

A device that weighs next to nothing can have the instant, broad, and permanent impact of a thousand-pound bomb. Remember the explosive impact online photos of prisoner abuse at Abu Ghraib had on Donald Rumsfeld and the Pentagon? Or the crushing impact on actor Alec Baldwin when his telephone tirade against his daughter went viral? Or the coup de grâce to Mel Gibson's reputation when his girlfriend leaked his rants to Radar Online? All it takes is a few sound bites or devastating images to fashion a "TubeBomb" on YouTube, a visual IED to take out you, your brand, your product, or your company.

Restaurants, who rely on the trust of easily turned-off customers, are particularly vulnerable to TubeBomb attacks. A KFC in California and a Burger King in Ohio were the first fast-food chains to be Tube-Bombed by employees taping themselves performing disgusting pranks (in these cases, workers filmed themselves soaking in restaurant kitchen sinks).[25]

Then in 2009 came the mother of all pranks, when two young Domino's Pizza employees in rural North Carolina filmed themselves sneezing and blowing their noses on Domino's food and other grotesque behavior. By the time 750,000 people had viewed the video, Domino's was reeling and struggling to get out the word that the two now-fired employees had not actually served the disgusting pizza to customers.

About forty-eight hours later, Domino's president Patrick Doyle posted a sincere YouTube response in which he thanked the online community for allowing him to take immediate action—issuing felony arrest warrants for the employees and sanitizing the store. He ended his two-minute apology with an impassioned talk about the damage to Domino's local, independent owners and the company's 125,000 employees.[26]

This was a bold move, a light-speed reaction according to the standards of classic media relations. In this new global, digital world, however, the authors advise clients to view eight hours as one digital day. By this standard, Doyle was late by five digital days. "The lag in response time left the online conversation to grow and fester, and the story continued to proliferate throughout social media channels," wrote Patrick Vogt in *Forbes* magazine.[27]

A truly effective response would have been mounted *within hours*.

Sales still sagged. Within months, Domino's unveiled a new humility campaign, launching a total repositioning of its product.

Damage at Light-Speed: Renders digital assassination a form of asymmetrical warfare with the attacker always having the ultimate advantage—surprise.

Shame Famers

Most people become celebrities because, like Tiger Woods or John Edwards, they do one thing exceptionally well. The fact that this preceding statement may have prompted you to giggle illustrates the extent to which scandal can utterly overshadow achievement.

The sexual predations of wayward people is matched by the publicity predators they seem to attract, for whom scandal is their only claim to fame. This was not true of the infamous women of history, from Cleopatra to Catherine the Great, who were resourceful queens who manipulated empires and commanded armies. Their sexual predations only inflamed their existing reputations. But in today's digital world Paris Hilton was what?—an "heiress"—when her sex video went viral and made her a household name.

That kind of viral shame fame would have been impossible without the Internet. For this new kind of celebrity, scandal is the only reason for fame—with big potential to inflict collateral damage on everyone they know. Few people who are publicly embarrassed like Paris Hilton actually find their shame to be a golden road to riches. But that doesn't keep thousands from trying.

Witness Duke University 2010 graduate Karen Owen, who created a multimedia "Fuck List" PowerPoint thesis of the men she had slept with, rating their attributes complete with a professional-looking case-study approach, including bar charts. The fact that she may have foolishly believed it would be shared with just a few friends did not stop it becoming a global sensation—with a flood of queries from agents, publishers, and movie producers.[28]

Or consider the women in the Tiger Woods scandal. There was a time not so long ago when being publicly identified as an adulteress was a badge of shame and would have had severe consequences for one's career or marriage prospects. At the very least, most women would have been mortified to have their parents, family, boss, and friends know that they engaged in this behavior.

Not Jaimee Grubbs, the cocktail waitress who sold her story to *US Weekly* and told it to VH1's *Tool Academy,* or any number of other women who came out of the woodwork of various golf clubs and bars to tell their Tiger tales. The willingness, even eagerness, to blithely disclose sordid details to millions of strangers is a new kind of exhibitionism that is a prime enabler of character assassination.

A record of sorts was set in this arena when YaVaughnie Wilkins, the former mistress of Charles Phillips, president of Oracle, made her announcement to the world. After Phillips broke off their relationship, Wilkins became famous—infamous being hard to achieve these days—by spending a fortune to post photos of her snuggling with the married Phillips on gigantic billboards in New York City, Atlanta, and San Francisco.

In years gone by, wives were most likely to go public to embarrass a wayward husband. Now it is the other woman.

Another source of shame fame comes from young men who lack any memory of the chivalric code that males were once taught by their fathers. Levi Johnston is a prime example of the new age of shame fame.

Soon after his wedding plans with Bristol Palin were scrapped, Johnston trashed his onetime fiancée and her family on the usual round of celebrity talk shows. He revealed a number of personal family secrets, posed nude for *Playgirl,* and shopped a book and a movie deal. It doesn't matter where you come down on the political spectrum or what you think of the Palins. Johnston has taken boorishness to a new level.

The likelihood is that most of these Shame Famers will live to regret their roll in the mud. Ten years from now when the easy money has long since run out, they will bitterly regret having defined themselves for life.

Or maybe not. For many people, having once been on national television and in the pages of *People* magazine is the definition of success, regardless of the reason. This exhibitionistic drive is more than a danger for the wayward. It is a positive danger for organizations, good and bad actors alike, that can be reduced to shambles by a character assassin posing as a whistle-blower.

It is not a far step from a Shame Famer to Mark E. Whitacre (memorably played by Matt Damon in Steven Soderbergh's *The Informant*), who alerted the FBI to price-fixing at Archer Daniels Midland and served as their undercover agent, while simultaneously defrauding the company of $9 million. Later, when Whitacre was stripped of his legal immunity as a whistle-blower, *New York Times* reporter Kurt Eichenwald reported in his masterful chronicle, on which the movie was based, Whitacre tried to implicate the FBI by falsely accusing agents of destroying tapes.

> **Shame Famers:** Suicide bombers who have nothing to protect can take out victims by the busload.

Blood and Sand in the New Digital Arena

Many people are somewhat knowledgeable about social media. Some are adept at using it for product publicity and promotion. But most still do not have solid plans and strategies to counter digital attacks.

The Internet is now a central feature of risk management for brands, products, or reputation. Yet most corporations have yet to become as sensitive to what is said about them online as many restaurants, doctors, and local businesses are to their reviews on Yelp. In the face of a digital onslaught, the prevailing instinct is still to circle the wagons . . . or Toyotas or BP tankers or Goldman Sachs trading desks.

In short, businesses or individuals, celebrities or nonprofits choose to stroll unprotected through this new war zone. Many sense but don't truly understand how the law treats digital media differently from offline media. Many still do not know that Section 230 of the Communications Decency Act of 1996 distinguishes between an interactive computer service provider—who is held harmless from liability—and an information content provider, who can be sued.

Take the case of a post on an AOL bulletin board that attached the phone number of an innocent man to cruel, sick humor about the bombing of the Alfred P. Murrah Federal Building (advertising T-shirts with the slogans, among others, "Visit Oklahoma City . . . It's a BLAST!!!" and "Putting the Kids to Bed . . . Oklahoma 1995").[29] The Fourth Circuit Court of Appeals upheld a lower court decision in favor of AOL.

One federal judge explained the logic behind this seemingly unfair law:

> Interactive computer services have millions of users. . . . The amount of information communicated via interactive computer services is therefore staggering. The specter of tort liability in an area of such prolific speech would have an obvious chilling effect. It would be impossible for service providers to screen each of

their millions of postings for possible problems. Faced with potential liability for each message republished by their services,
interactive computer service providers might choose to severely
restrict the number and type of messages posted.[30]

In other words, if interactive computer service providers—not just
AOL, but Google, Bing, Wikipedia, eHarmony, Facebook, and countless others—as defined by the Section 230 of the Communications
Decency Act, were held responsible for anything and everything posted,
the Internet as we know it and everything that depends on it would
shut down.

That is why you may be able to sue *The New York Times* for running
a letter to the editor that defames you, but you cannot successfully sue
nytimes.com for a slur someone posts on the comments section of an
article. In the digital world, only the content provider—the person who
posted the malicious comment—can be held responsible.

The rub is that this person in many cases can be almost impossible
to identify. While Section 230 keeps defamation suits from shutting
down the Internet, it also encourages many websites to take a lackadai-
sical attitude toward defamation, forcing victims to spend a lot of time,
anguish, and money to get their attention.

Most who are attacked on the Internet do not understand that assassins are playing under different rules from those in the offline world.
Victims do not comprehend the fight they face to protect their company, brand, reputation, careers, marriages, and livelihoods because,
being decent people themselves, they don't appreciate the many reasons
attackers attack.

Why do people digitally assassinate?

The facile answer is because they can.

And they can because new technology platforms today allow a
vengeful individual to have an impact as never before. The same power
of social media that enabled Barack Obama to raise $650 million in
small donations to run for the presidency also enables the nastier side of
democracy. Social media can awaken citizen power. But it can also create a digital lynch mob.

The old motivations of money, sex, power, and envy are at play.

Take the money motivation. This can include powerful interests
looking for profit: trial lawyers looking for a payout, ambitious politi-

cians looking for trial lawyer contributions, unions looking for raises, TMZ and other Gossip Girls looking for higher Google or TV ratings, or corporate competitors looking to clear space for themselves on shelves in their marketplace.

The attacker might also be looking for blackmail. At the high end are racial and environmental organizations that certify corporations for their good behavior, in effect indemnifying them from class-action lawsuits. Fail to pay and the certification may give way to one character attack after another, followed by class-action lawsuits from associated trial lawyers.

At the low end are defamation poachers, bloggers who complain knowing that a complaint to a responsive, customer-oriented company can often result in a free pass, voucher, or a new replacement item.

Others are out to shove you to the political left or right. They believe if they apply enough pressure, they can use your reputation or that of your company or brand to advance their political goals.

And then are old lovers, disgruntled or former employees, and irrationally incensed customers who want to deface your storefront and reputation. They want to flame you and the Internet provides an anonymous way to do it.

These attackers just want to create agita, Italian slang (from *acidus*), a term doctors now use for severe acid indigestion. Others seek to commit a little vandalism—perhaps to sever Tiger Woods from his sponsors; to humiliate, superimposing penises or wisecracks about crack cocaine on celebrity images; or to attack a man's heart, such as linking John Seigenthaler, friend of the Kennedys, to the Kennedy assassinations.

And some just want to kill. If digital assassination results in ruin or death, all the better.

In the movie *The Dark Knight*, Batman (Bruce Wayne) has trouble deciphering the motives of his nemesis, the Joker. Michael Caine's character, the butler Alfred Pennyworth, speaks of his past experience tracking a bandit.

> Alfred Pennyworth: A long time ago, I was in Burma, my friends and I were working for the local government. They were trying to buy the loyalty of tribal leaders by bribing them with precious stones. But their caravans were being raided in a

forest north of Rangoon by a bandit. So we went looking for the stones. But in six months, we never met anyone who traded with him. One day I saw a child playing with a ruby the size of a tangerine. The bandit had been throwing them away.

Bruce Wayne: So why steal them?

Alfred Pennyworth: Because he thought it was good sport. Because some men aren't looking for anything logical, like money. They can't be bought, bullied, reasoned, or negotiated with. Some men just want to watch the world burn.[31]

4 :// The Second Sword

Silent Slashers

> If you know the enemy and know yourself, you need
> not fear the result of a hundred battles. If you know
> yourself but not the enemy, for every victory gained
> you will also suffer a defeat. If you know neither the
> enemy nor yourself, you will succumb in every battle.
>
> —**Sun Tzu,** *The Art of War*

SILENT SLASHER ATTACKS are wounds that go unnoticed until you've walked ten paces past your attacker only to feel something warm and sticky soaking your shirt. Silent Slashers enjoy this advantage of wounding targets anonymously without exposing themselves to scrutiny.

Today the Internet empowers digital assassins, allowing undocumented charges and concocted images to ping around the globe at light-speed. But we make a mistake if we suppose that this represents something new in human nature.

Writings on the Wall

In HBO's acclaimed series *Rome,* Julius Caesar and his wife are being carried on litters by slaves when they encounter a wall crammed with offensive graffiti referring to Caesar's relationship with his mistress, Servilia. Several include messages that have ready cognates in English, "Caesar Servilia Futatrix," and "Servilia Caesaris fellator." Each of the graffiti, commissioned by an enemy, is underscored by an appropriately graphic line drawing. Caesar turns stiff and red-faced as onlookers glare at him and his wife while they are forced to pass beneath the offending messages.[1]

The scene, though fictional, is inspired. How many modern politicians have had to endure similar embarrassment in real time, not from graffiti on a wall but from a glowing screen?

Graffiti in particular can be seen as the ancient world's Silent Slasher equivalent of today's Internet message boards. Graffiti allowed anonymous artists to post digs at the rich and famous with impunity, spurned lovers to attack their rivals, the humblest to humble the powerful by scrawling on their walls or defacing their family's expensive mausoleum.

Just as the leaderless revolutions of Twitter today can rock regimes from Tunis to Tehran, so too did graffiti help undermine the Emperor Nero, especially after the great fire that swept Rome on July 18 in AD 64. As the Roman historian Suetonius records, disrespectful graffiti about the matricidal emperor began to appear on the walls of Rome.

> *Count the numerical values*
> > *Of the letters in Nero's name,*
> *And in "murdered his own mother":*
> > *You will find their sum is the same.*[2]

The legend that Nero sang of the sack of Troy while the city burned to the ground gained widespread circulation in graffiti that depicted him chanting "to the lyre with heavenly fire."

Resentment grew over the Golden Palace Nero was building in the cleared-out city.

> *The Palace is spreading and swallowing Rome!*
> *Let us all flee to Veii and make it our home.*
> *Yet the Palace is growing so damnably fast*
> *That it threats to gobble up Veii at last.*[3]

A portrait of the young emperor on one of his grand estates makes him a ridiculous figure, with a scruffy beard and fish eyes.[4] Though Nero tried to divert attention by scapegoating the Christians, it wasn't long before the relentless verbal attacks from the walls of Rome presaged a revolt across the empire that forced Nero to commit suicide much as Twitter and Facebook comments helped generate the political whirlwind sweeping the Muslim world today.

One of the richest sources on daily life, commerce, and politics in the ancient Roman world is from the walls of the excavated city of Pompeii. "I am amazed that you haven't fallen down, O wall / Loaded as you are with all this scrawl," scribbled one artist.[5] Some Pompeian graffiti read as if they were plucked from a modern-day chat room:

> If you bugger the fire, you burn your prick.

The Latin word for fire in this sentence, scholar Mary Beard tells us, can also mean the title of a minor municipal official.[6]

Some of the graffiti work like ancient world blog comments. One young man, Severus, wrote of a rival for the love of Iris:

> Successus, a weaver, loves the innkeeper's slave girl named Iris. She, however, does not love him. Still, he begs her to have pity on him. His rival wrote this. Goodbye.

Successus answered in terse, Instant Messaging style:

> Envious one, why do you get in the way? Submit to a handsomer man and one who is being treated very wrongly . . .

Severus gets the last word:

> I have spoken. I have written all there is to say. You love Iris, but she does not love you.[7]

It is a pity that Iris the slave girl herself never added her feelings to the wall. Imagine reading one graffito after another, as a fast-walking Pompeian might as she moved quickly through the side streets and byways of Pompeii, and the experience seems like reading a message board.

Read in sequence, they have the same bathroom-wall vulgarity and random flashes of wit as any chat room. Consider:

> Restitutus says: "Restituta, take off your tunic, please, and show us your hairy privates."

> Lovers are like bees in that they live a honeyed life.

> Antiochus hung out here with his girlfriend Cithera.

Theophilus, don't perform oral sex on girls against the city wall like a dog.

Blondie has taught me to hate dark-haired girls.

Whoever loves, let him flourish. Let him perish who knows not love. Let him perish twice over whoever forbids love.

I don't want to sell my husband, not for all the gold in the world.[8]

Many offered Yelp-like reviews on the outside walls of taverns on the quality of their food, wine, or service. Some of the messages are the same commonplace reportings that make up so many contemporary Facebook postings, such as the Pompeian who felt the need to declare, "On April 19th, I made bread."[9]

What comes through the ages to us is the same burning desire by spurned lovers, disappointed customers, and various favor seekers to find expression in venomous words, just as Internet users do today on a billion screens. Of course our human eye instantly perceives graffiti as the product of one individual hand. This is harder to remember in the twenty-first century, when any online post can have the same visual authority as *The New York Times*. Now, with the creation of tools like Google's Sidewiki—which allows visitors to scrawl comments across a sidebar on any website—graffiti is a fully digital phenomenon.

> In graffiti through the ages, words are weapons, anonymity is always available, and candor can be a vice.

Disfiguring Faces and Reputations

Liskula Cohen, a tall, blond New York City model, was enjoying drinks with friends one winter evening at the Ultra nightclub on January 14, 2007, when a friend of a twenty-five-year-old off-duty doorman, Samir Dervisevic, lifted a vodka bottle from her table and served himself. Cohen objected. Dervisevic threw a drink in her face. Then he called Cohen the c-word.

Cohen did what most women would—she tossed her drink in his

face. Dervisevic smashed the vodka bottle and ground it in her cheek, drenching her white Ralph Lauren minidress in blood. Cohen needed forty-six stitches to repair the quarter-size hole in her face. Dervisevic pleaded guilty. The lithe Canadian-born model was still stunningly photogenic, but in the world of flawless fashion photography, her bookings fell off.[10]

Cohen was attacked again a year later, only this time defaced by a Silent Slasher attack that also had the potential to affect her fashion-career prospects. This slash, however, came when she achieved un-wanted notoriety in a blog that—evidently unconcerned with its truth or falsity—awarded Cohen the title "Skankiest in NYC."[11]

> How old is this skank? 40 something? She's a psychotic, lying, whoring, still going to clubs at her age, skank.

> Yeah she may have been hot 10 years ago, but is it really attractive to watch this old hag straddle dudes in a nightclub or lounge? Desperation seeps from her soul, if she even has one.[12]

In the second assault, Cohen (who was actually in her thirties) was the victim of a Silent Slasher.[13] Until the advent of the telephone, voice mail, and then the Internet, graffiti could be read by only a few.

> New technology platforms provide graffiti artists with anonymity and global reach, while wikis give them a crowd to hide in.

Borat at Yale

One frequent source of Silent Slasher attackers is the message board of AutoAdmit, an online discussion forum for law school students founded by a young insurance broker in Allentown, Pennsylvania.[14] Amid the questions about appropriate shoes for a big law firm (which link to an image of a classic black shoe from a men's store) are observations, speculations, and verbal ejaculations about the sex lives of women attending some of the nation's most prestigious law schools.

One woman, an anonymous poster claimed, is a herpes-infected slut who got into Yale Law School through bribery and lesbian sex with an admissions officer. Another has gonorrhea, yet another post alleged, and won a passing grade in a class by performing oral sex on a dean. She also "deserves to be raped." An African American law student at Vanderbilt Law was said to have, of course, been "gangbanged" by four Cincinnati Bengals. All of these posts were fictional attacks.

Follow the threads, with their hundreds of "cunts," "fags," and "bitches," and you will quickly make out the jocular, frat-house gutter talk of young men. Something else is at work. Frequent racist rants against "niggers" and "rat-faced Jews" have the air of parody, as if the real joke is on anyone square enough to seriously imagine that these attacks represent real opinions.

Journalist David Margolick, in a sharply written 2009 profile piece in Portfolio.com, interviewed an academic who nailed the vicarious pleasures of AutoAdmit, which gives "its patrons a peculiar, vicarious kick: It allowed people who were straitlaced and risk-averse enough to want to be lawyers in the first place to become briefly, crazily irresponsible. They could spout outrageous lies, or, in the manner of Sacha Baron Cohen, invent entirely new personalities for themselves, invariably as homophobes, racists, or misogynists."[15]

So what's the big deal?

Google.

AutoAdmit's trolls posted their comments about the targeted women with enough frequency to put their rants at the very top of any search about them. Indeed, these postings seemed to have been deliberately designed to shove aside good material about the women and make sure that prominent keywords would make ugly falsehoods would be the first thing any prospective employer would see at the top of a search engine results page (SERP).

So what appears as offensive but juvenile tripe on AutoAdmit becomes deadly serious defamation when algorithms enable horrific sexual imagery to dominate background checks. It is for this reason, a later lawsuit alleged, that one of the Yale Law women, who had published in top legal journals and interned at prestigious law firms, interviewed with sixteen law firms for summer jobs but received no offers.[16] The African American law student who was supposedly "gangbanged" felt so intimidated that she changed law schools.[17]

> Harm comes in many ways. Most people don't see racist slurs in
> the light of post-racial irony.

Lighting Up Targets

Silent Slashers also can put individuals and whole countries in the cross-hairs of geopolitics. One recent senior U.S. official, deeply involved in the war on terror, was surprised to find that his Wikipedia biography had an unusual level of detail on his family members, listing the full names of his adult children and where they lived. It was of official concern that they were included in his Wikipedia page by political detractors in order to enhance the likelihood that his family members could be targeted by Al Qaeda.

Silent Slashers have an abundance of old techniques to draw from the predigital world.

The late Vasili Mitrokhin, the former chief archivist for the foreign intelligence arm of the KGB, revealed in a book that he wrote with Cambridge historian Christopher Andrew that one of the most success-ful disinformation campaigns ever mounted by the KGB was the plant-ing of the story that the United States had bioengineered HIV/AIDS, which the CIA subsequently spread throughout Africa. The Soviet Union may be long gone, but to this day many educated Africans be-lieve that HIV was born at the U.S. Army Medical Research Institute of Infectious Diseases at Fort Detrick, Maryland.[18]

Or consider the case of "Hitler's Pope." Over the last thirty years, a rising chorus of scholars and journalists have contributed to a portrait of Eugenio Pacelli, Pope Pius XII, as having at best mounted a timid response to Nazi persecution of Europe's Jews. Some go further, believ-ing Pacelli had a thinly veiled sympathy with the Third Reich's anti-Semitism and tacitly approved of Hitler's goals.

Now a growing body of counterscholarship is beginning to suggest that not only is this portrait off the mark, but that Pacelli himself was such an ardent defender of Jews and consistent opponent of Hitler that he deserves recognition by Israel as a non-Jew who took great risks to oppose the Nazi regime and save large numbers of Jews. The weight of the existing evidence is sufficient to convince Martin Gilbert, the Oxford-educated historian, official biographer of Winston Churchill and preeminent scholar of World War II and the Holocaust, to say: "I think the time has certainly come, in the light of what we now know, for the pope to be put forward for nomination at Yad Vashem in the Department of the Righteous."[19] (The complete Martin Gilbert

interview can be seen at http://www.barhama.com/PAVETHEWAY/
gilbert.html.)

The argument will not be settled until all the relevant documents in
the Vatican archives are released and fully assessed. But if the mainstream understanding of Pope Pius XII for forty-eight years has been a
monstrous and unjust inversion of the truth, how could so many get it
so wrong? Intellectual opinion first began to turn against Pius XII with
the enthusiastic international reception of a play, *The Deputy,* by a German writer, Rolf Hochhuth, that portrays Pius XII as so obsessed with
protecting church property that he agreed to look the other way as
Hitler completed the Holocaust—a play Martin Gilbert says he didn't
find "historical in any way."[20]

It has been alleged that *The Deputy* was part of a deliberate disinformation campaign. According to Ion Mihai Pacepa, a high-ranking
Romanian intelligence agent who defected during the Cold War, the
image of Pius XII as a coldhearted Nazi sympathizer was deliberately
disseminated in the West as part of a decades-long character assassination by the KGB, including its secret conception and production of *The
Deputy.* The apparent purpose of this assassination campaion was to drive
a wedge between two religions prominent in the West, and destroy the
reputation of the Vatican worldwide.[21]

> Whether or not this in fact occurred in *The Deputy,* the dark arts of
> disinformation on the Internet have the potential to insinuate any
> falsehood, provided it is lurid enough.

User Name Cowardice

The anonymity afforded by server farms and domain proxies allow Silent Slashers to go about their business. For more casual attacks on a
business, the pseudonymity of review sites can be enough.

When writer Andrew Ferguson went looking for information on
hotels, he wrote in *Forbes Life,* "I learned that the local Hilton was a
terrific bargain with pleasant service and an excellent central-city location, and that I would be charmed by the little sequined unicorns laid
by the maids on the pillows every night. It was also, I learned, scrolling
down, a hellhole manned by human ferrets, with overflowing toilets
and mephitic smells that had tragically ruined the honeymoon of

vox12populi and I wantmyrum, who were now exacting revenge by describing their nightmarish experience on every message board they could find . . . How seriously am I supposed to take the views of a person who identifies himself as 'boogerman'?"[22]

The nature of largely anonymous reviews can also be hell for the people on the other side of the check-in desk. When the business partner of one Detroit restaurateur entertained the client of a record label at the hotel bar, a guest mistook the musician for a prostitute. The guest posted an anonymous review describing the misunderstood scene on TripAdvisor. The restaurateur says reviews can sometimes be "a cesspool of negativity."[23]

> The worst aspect of Silent Slashers' negative comments is that they are read by Google's spiders, automated web crawlers that scuttle across websites to index pages for searches—boosting slander rankings.

Hackers' Paradise

With as little as a $100 digital video camera and a $400 laptop computer, Silent Slashers can post words, images, and video through such sites with little fear of being traced. Any small-time operator can set up a website and enjoy administration rights to control the site with complete anonymity. All it takes is a prepaid credit or debit card, which can then be used to purchase a website from a privacy service such as Domains by Proxy, affiliated with the domain registrar Go Daddy, which assures private registrants that "your identity is nobody's business but ours."

There are, to be fair, a number of legitimate reasons why someone might put up a website anonymously, including a desire to avoid domain-related spam, to hide from stalkers, and to enjoy more privacy. If you're trying to identify a Silent Slasher, however, consulting the public Whois directory of domain owners will often show only domainsbyproxy.com (or the relevant domain service) as the owner. In the United States, if a legal action is pending, a court can force a hosting company to reveal who is behind a given site. In Great Britain, where libel laws are strict, it is easier to use the law to identify someone hosted in that country. But it takes legal expenses to obtain discovery.

Sophisticated investigators with resources to burn can still locate website owners, even if they are not listed in WHOIS. "If you want to put up a website without fingerprints, there are so many pieces you have to be aware of to be anonymous, or else it won't work," says Bill Livingstone, the sought-after American security expert who works out of Europe. But hiring an investigator is also an expense.

Even then, Internet service providers under court order or digital investigators may still not be able to track the offender. In lax jurisdictions such as Australia, Iceland, and the Netherlands, authorities protect virtual identities from exposure or prosecution for anything short of child porn or snuff films. The international rise of server farms in these countries—where server capacity is clustered—makes it difficult to trace anonymous Internet attacks. "The Australians value freedom of speech above any other country," says Leo Yakutis, the digital hound. "Australia has truly anonymous servers. You can set something up, and it can't be taken down. You can try to block it or DoS [denial of service attack] it. But you can't take it down." The Netherlands is another country that attracts server farms criminal hackers use for phishing and other crimes.

Iceland is yet another hackers' paradise, where some prominent lawmakers are openly sympathetic to WikiLeaks. Walk along Reykjavik's urban waterfront, and you will encounter a fisherman's row, picturesque old wooden clapboard buildings with freshly painted trim and brass fixtures near wharves where most of the boats are pleasure craft. The fishing fleets may be gone, but that doesn't mean there isn't any fishing going on. "If you made a thermal image of these buildings, you would see that they are very hot, with big coolers," Yakutis says.

In California, such hot spots with high electrical use and coolers would indicate that someone is growing indoor marijuana. In Reykjavik, it means server farms. "Because Iceland has two Internet backbones going through it, it has become a haven for some very weird stuff," Yakutis says. Of course, a lot of the work being done on the servers at fisherman's row is legitimate. Some of it is gray, or at the edge of legality. Some of it is black.

Some of these international hosts, whose landing pages promise not to bow to lawyers or law enforcement, have information on servers from twelve different places around the world. Just determining the jurisdiction of a site by country can be impossible. And in the relevant place, the law may simply not exist. "A third of the world has a lot of laws, a third of the world has some laws, and a third of the world has no laws," Livingstone says. "Depending on where you are oriented, you can do a lot of things and not break the law. You have a lot more rope."

> There is no lack of remote caves in which Silent Slashers can hide, plan, and launch attacks.

Rumors and Google Bombs

On the Internet, even Netflix can be turned into a weapon. One jilted boyfriend, looking to get even with his ex-girlfriend, posted a screen shot from her Netflix account. Under the caption "My girlfriend cheated on me, so I rated movies in her Netflix account until I reached the desired result," he recommended the poster icons for movies he thought she would appreciate: *The Scarlet Letter, Unfaithful, Indecent Proposal, Whore,* and *Slutty Summer.*[24]

This technique of conflating names is a low-tech version of the practice of Google bombing, which manipulates search results so that a search for one person or thing leads the searcher to something satirical or defamatory.

Google bombs began as the manipulation of search engine algorithms as ridiculous broadsides. The classic Google bomb in 1999 yielded the top result "Microsoft" for the search "more evil than Satan himself."[25] Since 2003, the top result for the search "French military victories" leads you to a phony Google results page that asks, "Did you mean French military *defeats*?"

A humor magazine Google-bombed a site that sold merchandise for George W. Bush fans; in 2003 it was linked to the text "dumb motherfucker." This may be funny to Bush critics, but it wasn't a bit funny to the merchants who were trying to capitalize on that president's popularity in Red State America.[26]

French president Nicolas Sarkozy's Facebook page regularly comes up from a search for *trou de cou de Web* ("asshole of the Internet"). Other world leaders and political parties, from countries as disparate as the Philippines and Estonia, are hit with similar links. In 2007, humorist Stephen Colbert enlisted his audience to create enough links so that his website would rank number one in the search for "big brass balls," though he settled for "greatest living American."[27]

A similar technique, keyword stuffing, surrounds a victim's appearance on search engine result pages with defamatory URL names and troublesome descriptions. The nomenclature gets a bit fuzzy here—some also call this technique Google bombing—although the search company, for obvious reasons, doesn't like having its name linked to a shady practice.

Just before the 2010 midterm elections, Chris Bowers of the Daily Kos and Neil Stevens of RedState got into a heated exchange over the propriety of using tactics that Bowers calls "Grassroots SEO" and Stevens calls a "pagerank scam."[28]

The issue, once again, is Google bombing, which Bowers frankly admits he advocates, using the same anchor text to link many blogs and many websites together to make "the most damaging news article" about a Republican congressional candidate one of the first things on a potential voter's SERP.[29]

RedState's Stevens indignantly demanded that Google impose its digital "death penalty" on the Daily Kos for this behavior; although frankly, campaign operatives in both parties will tell you they would be committing political malpractice if they failed to use search techniques against their opponents.[30] Nor can Stevens expect much help from Google, though its spokesmen say the company does not condone Google bombing.

"If you look up Google's policies, Google bombing is legal," Leo Yakutis says. "There is no law against it. There is no Google policy against it."

What is against Google policy is to proliferate meaningless, repetitive anchor text and link it to artificially drive up the ranking of a given search term. "The Google search engine is a mathematical formula," Yakutis says. "In the same way that you hear about an Ivy League team that went to break Vegas, so too can you break Google because it is an index, very mathematical."

In these cases, Google does enact the "death penalty" on those who use link farms or other automated means to generate links, or who excessively link reciprocally or to sites with no real information just to artificially drive search results. But Google has no ability and really no desire to stop Silent Slashers from making organic links that reflect their interests. If that interest happens to be your defamation, then so be it.

▓ Google bombing can surround your name, brand, business, or
▓ product on search results with sheer ugliness.

Same Tricks, Different Day

Saul Alinsky, the left-wing Chicago organizer who godfathered Hillary
Clinton's entry into politics and who is often cited by Barack Obama
for having inspired him to get into politics, wrote a handbook, *Rules for
Radicals.* Though himself an anticommunist, he had a distinctly Lenin-
ist zest for psychological warfare and the employment of the threat of
defamation to wrest power from enemies.

Alinsky's rules would later be picked up and perfected for the other
side by Republican operatives, from Lee Atwater to Karl Rove.

"Pick the target," Alinsky wrote, "freeze it, personalize it, and polar-
ize it."[31] Alinsky's methods are ideal for the Internet age, where Silent
Slasher campaigns inspire a thousand cuts by creating a self-replicating
rumor. Rumors flourish best when the subject is important to the targeted "rumor public"—a subset of people who have reason to care about
your reputation, brand, product, or company, but must contend with
ambiguous information.

A famous 1947 study by psychologists Gordon Allport and Joseph
Postman reduced the power of a rumor to this equation:

$$R \sim i \times a$$

This equation holds that the circulation of a rumor (R) will increase
with the importance (i) of the rumor's subject to the listener *times* the
ambiguity (a) in reliable information about the subject. It is multiplica-
tive because if either of the two variables—i or a—reaches zero, the
rumor zeroes out and stops.[32] To take a trivial example, if Lindsay
Lohan is important to you and she disappears for a spell behind the
walls of a county correctional facility, the ambiguity—indeed, the
invisibility—of her situation will make you more susceptible to outlandish rumors about what happens to her behind bars.

Whole countries can be plunged into a stew of rumor. One of the
authors was a student in Greece during the 1974 revolution and that
country's limited war with Turkey over Cyprus. The bar of his hotel was
abuzz with "news"—that the deposed king of Greece had marshaled an

army in Yugoslavia and was marching through mountain passes south to take Athens. Another rumor held that the Turks had resigned from NATO and joined forces with the Soviet Union to mount an amphibious attack on Greece.

Each rumor had the ring of truth because in the absence of legitimate news under Greece's ruling junta, each was equally probable. "Rumor will race," Allport and Postman wrote, "when individuals distrust the news that reaches them."[33] When there is a vacuum of information, people will fill that vacuum with speculation, which can be taken as fact—a classic PR nightmare.

We are affected by rumors we know likely are not true, especially where food is concerned. In the late seventies, the McDonald's and Wendy's hamburger chains were reeling from stories that they used ground worms as additives in their hamburger patties. "Just the thought in the back of one's mind of worms in hamburgers was enough to steer one to a pizza parlor," sociologist Fredrick Koenig observed in the 1985 classic, *Rumor in the Marketplace*.[34]

With the spread of information technology, the ability of Silent Slashers to deliberately perpetuate rumors increased. Church newsletters spread the story that one CEO or another had confessed a corporate allegiance to Satan on national TV. The first recorded incidence of such a rumor being spread by computer occurred in 1982 when someone in Kansas with access to the computer system of the Union Pacific Railroad used it to send the message "Satan is afoot."[35]

In the Internet age, shadow groups harm people and companies by putting up unattributed sites that collate any defamatory thing said about a company on Twitter feeds and other sites.

≡ Digital assassins distribute rumors with unprecedented precision.

Trajectory of a Rumor

Who uses these tactics? In the 1980s, sociologist Koenig discounted the probability that business competitors are behind the generation of rumors. When the New York Stock Exchange had a larger, much more active trading floor, an observer standing in the press gallery could observe a rumor pass from one side of the room to other, rolling through the trading floor like a wave. As it did, the facial expressions of humor, sadness, or excitement passed along with the wave. "It is more difficult to 'start' a rumor by composing it and planting it somewhere than most people realize," Koenig wrote, adding that "it is more realistic to think of rumors as emerging and evolving than as being 'started.'"

Besides, he wrote, any business competitor that did engage in this behavior might victimize itself, for rumors "once they get started, they have a life of their own . . . The risk is much like that in using poison gas in warfare: The wind may force change and blow all the gas back over the initiating forces."[36] There is a tendency of similar businesses to get hit by the same rumor, as Wendy's and McDonald's both were by the ground-worm rumor.

Two caveats need to be added here. First, a sophisticated and deliberate smear campaign, backed by doctored documents or documents taken out of context, like the *dezinformatsia* efforts of the KGB, can start rumors. Two, Koenig's astute observation in the commercial world may no longer hold up in an age of information technology.

Consider the legendary case of Procter & Gamble and charges of satanism, which began as a Silent Slasher starting a rumor among churches. The rumor died out, only to be resurrected through technology by a competitor. How this case evolved over time shows how technology is changing our understanding of how rumors propagate.

In 1980, *The Washington Post* reported a rumor about P&G that "the crescent moon-faced logo with a cluster of stars is a symbol of witchcraft, Satan or both." The *Minneapolis Tribune* traced one of the sources of the occult rumor to a high school club division of the Youth for Christ. By 1982, church newsletters made much of the curls in the Man-in-the-Moon's beard, which were said to be a mirror image of 666, the number of the beast, while the thirteen stars evoked a passage from Revelations.[37]

P&G managed to stamp out the rumor with statements from the Reverend Billy Graham and other evangelical leaders in mass mailings to churches and with media campaigns.[38] It also threatened to sue. The last tactic, Koenig writes, was particularly important in calling "public attention to the company's strong legal stand against the rumor, not necessarily to obtain legal redress." The campaign and the P&G strategy succeeded—an analog strategy perfect for an analog world.

But in the mid-nineties, the rumor, stoked by technology, returned with a vengeance. Why? A federal jury in 2007 awarded P&G a $19.25

million judgment against distributors from its competitor Amway (though Amway itself was dismissed from the lawsuit). The cause of action was related to a series of messages distributed through a voice mail network reaching salesmen in many states.[39] The rumor should have been dead, but it was resurrected because of technology.

Of course social media can quickly correct bad information. Bloggers finding fault with a national news story caused Dan Rather to prematurely lose his anchor's seat. But social media can also perpetuate rumors—from Area 51 tales to Barack Obama's supposed lack of American citizenship.

> Competitors use technology to stoke rumors and spread them to the four winds.

"Positive Slander" and Google Bowling

An early twentieth-century psychologist noted that rumors are often spread by the "grandiose," those with "the desire to figure as a person of distinction, to occupy the center of the stage, to have the eyes and ears of the neighbors directed admiringly toward us."[40] When a Silent Slasher leaks sensitive political or corporate information, it is often to buy some measure of goodwill and admiration at the employer's expense.

When one of the authors served on the White House staff, more than once he read in the news the exact opposite of what had actually happened in the West Wing. Such malicious leaks are the currency of the White House. Often leakers can be identified by the way in which the reporter will put the leaker at the periphery of a bad event. Prolific leakers can sometimes be identified by profile puff pieces written about them by White House beat reporters. So every White House chief of staff is always on the lookout for descriptions of a staffer as strangely heroic.

This awareness makes another Silent Slasher technique even harder to spot—the malicious leaking of praise. Here's how this works in the White House: Imagine you are a high level staffer. After a meeting in the Oval Office, the president has initially bought into an ill-considered proposal. So you politely but firmly intervene, pointing out the flaws in the proposal to the president. The president listens to you, reverses course, and nixes the proposal. This happens every day in the fevered improvisational atmosphere of the White House.

A classic Silent Slasher technique, then, is to leak the story of the good staffer going to the mat to protect a dim-witted president from harming himself. For these purposes, it is okay if the story makes the Silent Slasher himself look like one of the dopes. In fact that is optimal—it insulates him from suspicion.

As for the Silent Slasher's victim, his mother may want to clip out the story and place it in the family album. But the poor chump will have been made to look to the president like a vainglorious bastard who is willing to sell out his chief executive in order to get a one-day bump in the press.

A digital analogue of this technique, called Google bowling, can knock down competitors like bowling pins. Google bowling harms brands and businesses by using technology to puff them up. Most businesses engage in search engine optimization (SEO), a technique to raise the rankings of one's own website. Google bowling works just the opposite way. When Google determines that a business or brand has been using automated spam to artificially raise its profile, it will ruthlessly kick its website down in the rankings, often with no appeal and little explanation.

One prominent website for black hat hackers makes a sales pitch:

> Google bowling is a tactic to consider only after you have exhausted all on site SEO.
>
> It will probably take more than a few infractions to affect a site[']s rankings. We don't recommend even trying to Google bowl a competitor with less than $2500 worth of search engine spam.
>
> It may take tens of thousands of dollars of **Google bowling** to affect all the sites that rank above you for a keyword phrase—with no guarantee of success. Some sites cannot be effectively Google bowled at all.
>
> But if you make a significant amount of money per sales, why not give it a try?[41]

A Silent Slasher can then procure a black hat to mount an obvious, automated Google bomb on behalf of a competitor. For a short time, the competitor will be deluded into thinking that his firm has bottled lightning as it zooms to the top of the rankings. Then the Silent Slasher can laugh into his sleeve when Google kicks that competitor down the rankings and punishes the website.

> . . . if your competitors [*sic*] starts using tactics like poorly cloaked doorway pages and buying site wide links, they may get **penalized, sandboxed or even banned.**

> So, why not take the initiative and buy this search engine spam for your competition??[42]

Character assassins have long known that good news can be deadly.

Wicked Wiki World

In Hawaiian, wiki means quick. A technologist in the mid-1990s saw the word on the Wiki-Wiki bus shuttle at Honolulu International Airport and applied it to a website that allowed for rapid open content creation and editing by a crowd. So a wiki today is any website that allows for open creation and editing.

The ability of strangers to spontaneously cooperate and create new software or content is a startling new power of social media, with consequences examined in chapter 6. Wikipedia—which self-assembles like Hoyle's proverbial tornado that sweeps through a junkyard to create a 747—is the one wiki that, after Google and Facebook, defines the digital domain.

John Seigenthaler's ordeal, which opens the first chapter, is worth examining in some detail, for it shows how easily Silent Slashers can hide among the palm trees in the wiki forest. A former editor of Nashville's daily the *Tennessean,* John Seigenthaler Sr. performed heroic work for Attorney General Robert F. Kennedy during the era of civil rights and the Freedom Rides. Seigenthaler had close calls, including one instance in which he was knocked unconscious with a lead pipe after being overrun by a mob of white supremacists. He later served as publisher of the *Tennessean* and founding editorial director of *USA Today* before founding the Freedom Forum's First Amendment Center at Vanderbilt University in Nashville.

Now in his eighties, still going to the office, John Seigenthaler plays the role of éminence grise with disarming humor. One September day in 2005, a leading Nashville businessman and longtime friend called Seigenthaler to ask if he had seen his Wikipedia post.

"No," Seigenthaler replied.

"Google yourself to the Wikipedia link and sue the bastards," the friend said with a laugh.

So Seigenthaler did.

The piece had been posted since late May. After he took in the sentences that linked him to the murders of John and Robert Kennedy, his initial reaction was to snort in disbelief. It wasn't until several days later that Seigenthaler got a demonstration in the reach and harm such a comment can do when he received a phone call from a young woman who had interned at the First Amendment Center and was now studying at the University of Hawaii.

She had told international students about her great experience with the First Amendment Center and John Seigenthaler. Naturally, the first thing the students did was to look up Seigenthaler's Wikipedia page. They were perplexed. The former intern was in tears. "You have to do something to get that down because these people believe it," she told him over the phone.

Another call from his son, also John Seigenthaler, the former weekend anchor for NBC News, forced him to take a harder look at the impact of the posting. "Look, Dad, you're not the only John Seigenthaler around, so don't take this lightly," he said. "Your son is John Seigenthaler and your grandson Jack is John Seigenthaler."

Reflecting on that conversation, John Seigenthaler acknowledges that his son understood the full reach of Wikipedia in a way he did not. The younger Seigenthaler told his father that there were twenty-four mirror sites that had picked up Wikipedia. "At that point, I got a little pissed off," Seigenthaler said.

A couple of weeks went by as the elder Seigenthaler struggled over what to do. He looked up an archive interview between Jimmy Wales, the cofounder of Wikipedia, with Brian Lamb at C-SPAN, "an old, close friend." In the interview, Wales had asserted that Wikipedia's thousands of volunteer editors correct mistakes within minutes.

Seigenthaler called Brian Lamb, who gave him Wales's telephone number in St. Petersburg, Florida. After listening to Seigenthaler's complaint,

Wales replied that he didn't happen to know of Seigenthaler, but was certain the entry was too outlandish to be true. He promised to retire the comment to Wikipedia's archives.

"Do you . . . have any way to know who wrote that?" Seigenthaler asked.

"No, we don't," Wales said, though he stressed that he wanted to. The comment came from an anonymous contributor, Wales said, although he could trace the contributor's Internet Protocol address, the online equivalent of a home address. Seigenthaler had already turned to a young, tech-savvy employee at the First Amendment Center who had traced the IP address to Bell South, but no further.

Seigenthaler told Wales he was not comfortable with having the Kennedy assassination smear even in Wikipedia's archives, given that thousands of Wikipedia administrators and editors could still see it. "We ended that conversation without much satisfaction on my part," Seigenthaler says. His lawyer, after talking with Bell South, came back with the news that Seigenthaler would have to file a "John Doe/Jane Doe" lawsuit, committing him to prosecuting the claim in order to get the identity of this "biographer."

"You know, if you are the founder of the First Amendment Center at Vanderbilt, you shouldn't be thinking of suing anybody for saying bad things about you," Seigenthaler said. "So it never really did cross my mind."

In investigating the posting, Seigenthaler learned a particularly galling fact. The biography had been posted on May 26. Soon after, an eagle-eyed editor saw that the first entry of the defamatory portion of his biography had spelled the word "early," as "e-a-l-r-y," and corrected it. "So Jimmy's administrator caught it the same day, corrected the misspelling, and left me a suspected assassin who had defected to the Soviet Union for thirteen years," Seigenthaler said.

Stymied, Seigenthaler decided to make his case on the more familiar turf of mainstream journalism. Six months after the post, Seigenthaler wrote a very personal piece in *USA Today* detailing his ordeal. "And so we live in a universe of new media with phenomenal opportunities for worldwide communications and research—but populated by volunteer vandals with poison-pen intellects," Seigenthaler concluded. "Congress has enabled them and protected them."[43]

After the editorial ran, "I was flooded immediately with e-mails and phone calls from people who had suffered, not always from Wikipedia, but suffered similar distress" from digital attacks. The editorial made Seigenthaler a Silent Slasher piñata. As for Wikipedia, Seigenthaler's friend the late writer David Halberstam said, "it's like somebody lifted the lid on a running sewer." One attacker wrote that Seigenthaler had raped Jacqueline Kennedy.

As Seigenthaler's article got media attention, *The New York Times* business editor Larry Ingrassia, known for incisive reporting, sent a memo to reporters reminding them not to rely on Wikipedia. In this midst of this ordeal, Seigenthaler soon heard from Daniel Brandt, the San Antonio editor of wikipediawatch.com, a site that documents Wikipedia's mistakes, shortcomings, and—in Brandt's eyes—its essentially flawed nature. Brandt is so tenacious that he finally wore down Wikipedia, forcing them to delete his own biography altogether.

Brandt went to work and called about two weeks later to say that he had found a "reverse page" on the Internet that revealed that the IP number also served a small delivery company. "I had never heard of [it]," Seigenthaler said. "I did what any run-down, aging investigative reporter would do, I ran to the city directory and there it was."

Word was passed to reporters, who flooded the little firm with a dozen or more calls from journalists. Soon after, a man walked into the First Amendment Center with a signed letter of apology.

Following Digital Bread Crumbs

Not everyone has a Daniel Brandt in their corner. Did Seigenthaler have any other options? Essentially one: Follow the advice of Seigenthaler's friend and "sue the bastards."

Of course, Section 230 would have prevented Seigenthaler from winning a lawsuit against Bell South and Wikipedia. Nothing, apart from Seigenthaler's conscience and sensibilities would have kept him from suing to get to the information content provider—the man who wrote the slur—and winning. Of course a sophisticated Silent Slasher who used anonymous web hosting paid for with a debit card or a public IP address with a cheap, toss-away computer would be beyond the realm of a subpoena.

"Many people have said that when they do it to enough members of Congress, that we'll get regulation," Seigenthaler said. "I go the other way on that. I deplore what is happening, but Jimmy [Wales] could have solved this a long time ago if he really wanted to be an editor. He calls it an 'intellectual democracy.' It's a libertarian approach. The last thing I would want to do is urge repeal of Section 230, although I will admit that after forty years as a journalist, the threat of a libel suit—it can sharpen the mind."

Golfer Frank Urban "Fuzzy" Zoeller Jr., former Masters and U.S. Open winner, was ready to sue after he was defamed by a malicious, untrue Silent Slasher Wikipedia entry describing him as an alcoholic who beats his wife and children after polishing off a fifth of Jack Daniel's chased with Vicodin. He traced the attack back to the IP address of a law firm in Miami. But the identity of the actual writer could not be found. It might have been someone who was visiting the office. Or, as in many of these cases, it could have been someone in close proximity to a company's wireless hot spot.[44]

As we will see in more detail in later chapters, attackers can always use proxy servers in wireless hot spots to hide their ID.

> You cannot sue those who you cannot find.

Wikipedia's Dirty Underwear

John Seigenthaler is far from being the most high-profile victim of Wikipedia. That particular honor would have to go to Jimmy Wales himself. One day in 2008, Rachel Marsden, a Canadian editorial writer and former Fox News commentator, whose tart prose in favor of conservative viewpoints often prompts reporters to dub her the "Ann Coulter of Canada," posed on eBay modeling a medium black T-shirt that she had put up for sale, along with another article of clothing. In the image, Marsden is looking straight into the camera, eyes fierce and set, a slight smile.

"Both of these items have been washed, twice, with Tide extra-strength liquid detergent," Marsden posted. "Otherwise, they would not be in salable condition. I took them out of GitMo style isolation from a plastic bag in my closet (where they were placed to prevent the ongoing terrorism of my olfactory senses) and washed them out for the purposes of this auction."[45]

Marsden said that Jimmy Wales, the cofounder of Wikipedia, had left the clothes in her New York City apartment, before he broke up with her "via announcement on Wikipedia." It was "such a classy move that I was inspired to do something equally classy myself"—sell Wales's undergarments on eBay.[46] She also posted this March 2008 response to Wales:

> I only have one thing to say to you: You are the sleazebag I always suspected you were, and should have listened more carefully to my gut instincts—and to my friends. No, in fact, you are much, much worse than I ever expected. You are an absolute creep, and it was a colossal mistake on my part to have gotten involved with you.[47]

The Marsden–Wales saga, a sensational story of a high-profile breakup in full view of a global audience (including the release by Marsden of steamy sexual Instant Messaging conversations), is as important to policy as it is to prurience. It raises significant questions about wikis and their policies.

Marsden, like Seigenthaler, had contacted Wales about her Wikipedia biography. Her biography as of 2011 still encapsulated a sexual harassment charge she leveled against a university swimming coach, which he countered by saying she stalked him. It also details Marsden's stormy relationships with men that ended in blizzards of accusations and legal complaints.

Whatever the truth (or lack of truth) of any of this, Marsden had contacted Wales—at that time separated from his wife—seeking what she insisted were necessary corrections to her biography. Her account and the IMs she released depict a more responsive reaction to Marsden than Seigenthaler ever received.

The IMs portray Wales as working with Marsden point by point in the disputed material with a chronological dissection of the charges. In messages released to the Gawker media blog, Valleywag, Wales was portrayed as responding.

jimbo.wales: but the correct timeline is
(1) wrote about him on the blog

me [Marsden]: hahhahaha

jimbo.wales: (2) he files harassment charges
(3) you post email messages to show how his harassment charges
are bullshit

me: you're a sh*tdisturber. :)
right

I only posted the emails after he went public trtying [*sic*] to create
trouble
NOT before that.

jimbo.wales: nod
so we can get that sorted
and then this makes the story clearer

me: that's good of you to do. really.

jimbo.wales: ok so then the other thing is . . .
in my email I said, here are some thoughts about this, things that
need fixing
and i may follow up if there are clarifications from her
but then I said I am recusing myself from it other than that
i explained that we became friends in IM and that I offered to give
advice about your website and that we would be meeting about
that

me: ahhhh so you qualified it, and left it "up to them". :)

jimbo.wales: and therefore not appropriate for me to directly edit
the article with a conflict of interest

me: which usually, actually, works better than the alternative

jimbo.wales: the truth is of course a much worse conflict of interest
than that :) but that will do

me: aaaaaaaaahahaha. lol

jimbo.wales: well this is an internal mailing list of people who
specialize in fixing this kind of stuff, so you are in good hands

me: awwww thank you.
how many people are on the list?

jimbo.wales: oh, huh
I have no idea.

me: hahaha so you told them the half-truth. :p

jimbo.wales: depends on what the meaning of "is" is

me: ahahahahahha[48]

Wales acknowledged that he had a relationship with Marsden. He posted that he had worked on her biography before they had met because he "found it not to be up to our standards. My involvement in cases like this is completely routine, and I am proud of it." He also states that after planning to meet Marsden, he disclosed his plans to the Wikipedia team that handles complaints and addresses concerns relating to the Biographies of Living Persons (BLPs). Then he posts he "recused myself from any further official action with respect to her biography."[49]

While the story resides in he-said/she-said land, the fact remains that some biographical entries of living persons will always cry out for correction—such as Seigenthaler's—while others will simply cry out—such as Marsden's. As for Wikipedia, it might take only one credible documentation of favoritism to step out of the role of host and into the role of content creator, and therefore into potential liability.

In the aftermath of the Seigenthaler and other debacles, Wikipedia in April 2009 set out a tighter standard for editors for BLPs that make it harder for Silent Slashers to weaponize them. "Wikipedia is an encyclopedia, not a tabloid," Wikipedia declares in its BLP guidelines. "[It] is not Wikipedia's job to be sensationalist, or to be the primary vehicle for the spread of titillating claims about people's lives, and the possibility of harm to living subjects must always be considered when exercising editorial judgment."[50]

An entry must therefore have a neutral point of view, be verifiable, and contain no original research. Facts must be anchored to publicly accepted sources of information. Contentious material about a living person that is unsourced or poorly sourced should be removed without waiting for discussion. Wikipedia's BLP standard also forbids "feedback loops" in which a contributor quotes his own material.

Wikipedia must still rely on the integrity and competence of armies of faceless volunteer administrators, editors, and contributors. Those who feel stymied in their efforts to add, correct, or defame still often resort to sock puppetry, the use of separate digital identities to reinforce an edit, as well as meat puppetry, the recruiting of proxies to do the same.

> Wikipedia remains only as good, or as bad, as the crowd that edits it.

Takeaway—Fighting Silent Slasher Attacks

In Roman times, one simply repainted the walls. Today it can cost thousands of dollars to hire a specialist to perform digital forensics, the kind of service that Daniel Brandt performed free for John Seigenthaler. Even when the identity of the attacker is obvious, one can easily spend $5,000, $25,000, or more to have such a company verify the identity of a posted statement and provide a technician to testify in court.

Of course not everyone is as reluctant as Seigenthaler to call in a lawyer. For most people, a lawsuit remains the easiest way to track down a Silent Slasher. This is the path chosen by the two Yale Law women who were subjected to AutoAdmit's campaign of abuse. With the help of Reputation Defender, they filed claims against almost thirty pseudonymous attackers. The use of a beauty contest photo of one of the women allowed the lawsuit to allege copyright infringement, which elevated the case to the tougher standards of federal court.[51]

Not all, but some of the men who made the postings were outed (the scofflaws were smart enough to make their IP addresses untraceable). Some of the men settled. One was eaten up with contrition. ("I said something really stupid on the fucking Internet, I typed for literally, like, 12 seconds, and it devastated my life," he told journalist David Margolick.)[52]

Perhaps most important, legal action forced AutoAdmit to clean out the threads, reducing most of the trash to distant search results. If you search these women's names now, most of the material at the top of the search highlights their ordeal and their response to it. Their names cleared, one woman headed to a top law firm in New York, the other to work for the International Criminal Court in the Hague.[53]

A legal but stealthy method to ferret out the identities of people who might be stalking or snooping around you is to set up a conspicuous website and use tracking software to capture the IP addresses of all visitors. "One of the advantages of having a website up is to see who's looking at you," Livingstone says. This works unless the visitor takes pains to hide his digital fingerprints.

More must be done than just combat Silent Slashers. One must counter the rumors they create. Remember the Allport and Postman rumor equation: If either the importance of a rumor or its ambiguity can be reduced to zero, the rumor itself evaporates. As P&G did by contacting churches, one must locate and address what Allport and Postman refer to as susceptible populations, or "rumor publics."

The opposite is true. You don't want to pack the rumor equation with even more weight. Dismissing the rumor without giving it new life and fresh color is harder than it seems. The exact wording of a response, then, is of maximum importance.

An extreme example of this was the task McDonald's faced in killing the rumor about ground-up worms being added to its patties. It wisely elected not to use the word "worm," but to deny rumors about "protein additives" and then launch a slick ad campaign about McDonald's "100% U.S. Government-inspected beef."[54] McDonald's approach succeeded brilliantly in reducing the rumor to zero.

A similarly nuanced approach is needed in confronting rumors today.

Tough response strategies that worked brilliantly in the offline world would evoke the Streisand Effect in a nanosecond today. When the Stroh Brewery Company came under fire for allegedly slipping cash under the table to bankroll the presidential run of the Reverend Jesse Jackson in 1984, Stroh's ran a newspaper ad offering $25,000 to the first person to identify who started the rumor, and left the number of a Chicago detective agency to call with any information or evidence. It is hard to imagine an Internet equivalent today without tremendous blowback.[55]

The AutoAdmit case reveals a superior strategy, that of public shaming and counter social media efforts. The power of AutoAdmit, after all, rested on a perverse incentive. Even those who were offended by it felt they had to read it to see what might be posted about them. This drove traffic, giving the defamations greater reach. Elena Kagan, Harvard Law's dean before President Obama appointed her to the U.S. Supreme Court, helped break this vicious cycle by asking her students in an e-mail to boycott this "new and highly efficient mechanism for malicious gossip."[56] It seems to have worked. Unique visitors to AutoAdmit are a fraction of what they were.

Whatever the response—a lawsuit against AutoAdmit or Amway distributors, a traditional media campaign against Wikipedia, or a counter social media campaign—victims must understand the potential lethality of a Silent Slasher attack.

In many attacks, attackers leave behind some kind of signature. Sometimes it is intentional, a fragment of themselves they place as a boast or a joke. Certainly the code writer of the Stuxnet virus, which caused the centrifuges in the Iranian nuclear program to go haywire, had a sense of humor, as well as a sense of history.

In 2010, discovered buried deep in the code of Stuxnet was an ancient word, "Myrtus."[57] Some scholars believe this is an allusion to the Hebrew name for the Biblical Esther. If the word was a deliberate clue or taunt, it was an appropriate one. Esther, the covertly Jewish queen to the Persian king Ahasuerus, had saved her people. She had detected and stopped court politicians who were generating a Silent Slasher attack, an anti-Semitic rumor campaign that had caused the king to assent to a pogrom.

Who did this? Israel's cyberwar Unit 8200? Another power seeking to point the finger at Israel?

> Whoever the code writers, they are people who appreciate the deadly, silent power of a rumor.

5:// The Third Sword:

Evil Clones

You are who Google says you are.

—**Anna Vander Broek**, "Managing Your Online Identity"[1]

IDENTITY THEFT IS AS OLD AS the story of Jacob and Esau, when one brother used a bit of goatskin to fool his blind father into giving him his shaggy twin's inheritance.

By now every consumer knows that Evil Twins flourish on the Internet in the form of phishing scams, those phony but official-looking websites that come complete with a company logo over photos of smiling employees. Many people are just becoming aware of Evil Twin wireless networks, rogue Wi-Fi base stations that jam legitimate wireless providers to con you into providing your confidential information. Some are still taken by surprise by a related tactic, Evil Clones, which can slam your brand, business, or personal reputation by stealing your identity to make it appear as if you have done something stupid, wrong, terrible.

Christianne Carafano, a voluptuous actress noted for appearances on *General Hospital* and *Star Trek: Deep Space Nine,*[2] was a victim of Evil Clones. For a beautiful woman, she had an unusually desperate profile on the dating site, Matchmaker.com.

The site's format involves sixty-two questions, for which the profiled person provides self-descriptive answers. Carafano's were unusually blunt and to the point.

"Main source of current events?"

Playboy, Playgirl, read Carafano's profile.

"Why did you call?"

Looking for a one-night stand.

In addition to alluring pictures of Carafano, the profile stated that she was looking for a "hard and dominant" man with a "strong sexual appetite," and that she "liked sort of being controlled by a man, in and out of bed."[3]

The worst aspect of Carafano's profile? It provided her home address (a violation of the site's policies) and a Yahoo! e-mail address with an autoresponder that, when contacted, replied, "You think you are the right one? Proof [sic] it!!" The e-mail provided her telephone number as well as her address again.[4]

For days, as sexually suggestive messages began to fill her voice mail, Carafano was unaware that this profile had been posted by someone using a computer in Berlin on Matchmaker's Los Angeles site. When she returned home from a trip, Carafano found a sexually explicit fax that threatened her and her son. Phone calls, voice mail messages, letters, and e-mail from anxious men began to flood into her house.

When she learned of the source of all this unwanted attention, Carafano had her assistant contact Matchmaker on a Saturday to demand the profile be taken down. The customer service representative initially said that only the person who posted the profile could do that. By Monday morning, presumably when higher management got involved, the profile was blocked and soon deleted. Feeling unsafe, Carafano and her son stayed locally in hotels and sometimes away from Los Angeles.

Carafano filed suit against Matchmaker for invasion of privacy, defamation, and other torts. An appellate judge found her to be the victim of "a cruel and sadistic identity theft"—but nothing more. The case, after a few twists and turns, was resolved before the U.S. Ninth Circuit Court of Appeals. In order for Matchmaker to be held liable under Section 230, the court held in *Carafano v. Metrosplash,* the company would have to have been considered an information content provider. Simply providing a template, even sixty-two detailed questions, the court found, was not enough to make Matchmaker a liable content creator.

When all was said and done, only the information content provider, the unidentified person in Berlin, was at fault.[5]

≣ Evil Clones attract hordes of attackers like ants on honey.

Fouling the Nest

The authors uncovered a struggle between a young man and a young woman, the scions of rich and powerful families, who dated while they worked for rival financial services firms in a major North American city. They were not, however, typical MBAs in love.[6] They were citizens of the People's Republic of China, highly educated, perfectly fluent in English. Each of their families had set them up at top American corporations to get experience for their future careers back in China.

The couple worked hard, played hard, and stayed close . . . until the boyfriend started showing signs of being too possessive.

After a period of tension, the young woman broke off their relationship. Rather than get drunk or write a hate letter, this ex-boyfriend, being a creature of his times, resorted to a twenty-first-century form of retaliation. He opened his laptop and set out to do a number on her. He invaded her office e-mail account to send catty comments about the personal foibles, physical appearance, and hygiene of her superiors at the firm to other workers, all under her name and IP address.

Fortunately for this young lady, she had a wealthy father in China with the resources to hire the best digital hounds to find out what had happened. At first glance, the e-mails appeared perfectly legitimate, coming straight from her office e-mail. After a little digging, however, the hounds discovered that the jilted boyfriend had made one critical mistake. Some of the e-mails went out from the young woman's IP in the United States address while she was visiting her parents in China.

Investigators were eventually able to track the e-mail back to the boyfriend. He had used one of the most common means to crack her e-mail. While they were still dating, the boyfriend had installed a simple key logger, software that recorded her every stroke.

Once exposed, the ex-boyfriend lawyered up. At first the young man's lawyer offered only counterthreats and indignation. When all the evidence was aired, a settlement was reached.

In this case, the young woman's father could afford to write a check for $50,000 to start the process of forensic investigation, an amount few could easily afford. But in truth, the stain of such an incident never truly rubs off a young person's career. "You have to ask what effect did this incident have on her?" says one person close to this case. "Even if everyone understood, it was not a positive event for her career. Everyone is going to remember she is the one who had the crazy boyfriend." At the very least, she exhibited poor judgment. And every superior who was targeted in the e-mails—likely from some real gossip the young woman once shared with her ex-boyfriend—will remain insulted.

≡ Even the exonerated pay a reputational price.

Candidate Clones

A recent victim of Evil Cloning is S. R. Sidarth, who between his junior and senior years at the University of Virginia followed the senatorial reelection campaign of George Allen with a video camera on behalf of Allen's opponent. Allen, the front-runner who at the time was also considered a leading Republican candidate for the presidency, famously referred to the American-born son of immigrants from India as a "macaca." This odd racial slur derailed Allen's political career and elected Sidarth's candidate, James Webb, to the Senate.

Two weeks later, a conservative blogger assailed Sidarth for his AutoAdmit postings in which the young man confessed to having sex with a transvestite while high on methamphetamines. Sidarth, of course, had posted no such thing. Someone had created an Evil Clone of Sidarth to digitally assassinate him.[7]

Similar Evil Cloning tactics have been used at one of the world's best universities. In 2010, as two young men ran against each other to head the Harvard Republican Club, an e-mail from McKinsey & Company arrived in the in-boxes of at least several Harvard undergraduates and members of the Republican club. This e-mail included an invitation to sign up for "one of 25 exclusive fast-track interview slots, available only to those who attend our event."[8]

For business-oriented undergraduates, as Gawker put it in its usual crass (but accurate) terms, "waving a McKinsey gig in front of Harvard College Republicans is like waving a crack salad with crack dressing in front of a crackhead."[9] Unfortunately the private gig, an exclusive recruiting event at MIT, happened to fall at the very same time as the Harvard Republican Club was to hold its election. A second, more important problem was that McKinsey had not sent the e-mail.

After one of the candidates accused the other of forging the e-mail, the accused dropped out of the race (while proclaiming his innocence). What is the truth? As in many of these kinds of investigations, the digital breadcrumbs thin out and disappear. As a board member of the Harvard Computing Society informed the *Harvard Crimson,* "messages sent from the Gmail web client usually show the IP address of the website's servers rather than the unique IP address of the sender."[10]

Evil Cloning also hit the 2008 presidential elections with the emergence of phony domains—RudyGiulianiForum.com, MittRomney forum.com, and the online Fred Thompson Forum. "Most posts adopt the persona of a supporter of the candidate, while offering views that amount to over-the-top parodies of genuine boosters," wrote Sarah Lai Stirland, a Wired News reporter, who determined that these phony forums used the same software, the same hosting company, and a common IP address. After Stirland exposed deceptive spam promoting Ron Paul's candidacy for president, it was her turn to be the victim. Someone made an Evil Clone of Stirland's digital identity confess that her story was a fraud paid for by Giuliani supporters. The impersonation of Stirland and her confession was believable enough to inspire a YouTube attack on *Wired* as a paid attack dog for Rudy Giuliani.[11]

Another new permutation of the Evil Clone is the concern troll. Here's how it works: A concerned Democrat under the user name IndieNH posted pieces in 2006 on liberal blogs in New Hampshire giving tepid support to Democrat Paul Hodes, set to oppose U.S. Representative Charlie Bass, a Republican, while expressing the concern that Hodes could not win. "I am going to look at the competitive race list to figure out where to send another donation and maybe help out in other ways," IndieNH posted. "Maybe CT or NY for me—they are at least close by."

When site managers traced the IP address, they found that the messages came from official computers inside the U.S. House of Representatives. After an investigation, Representative Bass, the Republican, fired a top aide for posting the phony Democratic blog entries.[12]

Evil Clones can also take more vivid form. Doctored Internet images of actor Jake Gyllenhaal show the actor stretching in a beefcake pose in white briefs. Legal action by Gyllenhaal, however, seems to be evoking the Streisand Effect. "We're keeping the photo up, since it hasn't been proven fake and because their letter bumped it from 'funny and cute' to 'actually newsworthy,'" Queerty.com told the press.[13] It is easy to do this to anyone's image with Photoshop, though close inspection reveals that the head in the picture is not quite matched to the body. With the exponential increase in the power of cheap digital imaging, within a few years these kinds of smears will become fully pornographic, incorporating realistic, full-motion video.

> Given the ease with which Evil Clones can be created, they now spill into all areas of modern life, from Harvard Yard to the boxing ring.

High Society Hit Parade

"Next time you think about skipping that certain gala, wearing that unknown designer, dating some weird band member, beware. We're watching. And your ranking is on the line!" So warned Socialite Rank, a website that the *New York Post* called "the hilariously bitchy anonymous cabal!"

A profile piece by Isaiah Wilner in *New York* magazine reported that the now-defunct site Socialite Rank not only elevated "unknown women to unlikely prominence" but also included comment boards "with catty and frequently venomous remarks," including allegations of cocaine abuse. "And what made it more eerie—like the voice of a Bitch God bellowing from the heavens—was that no one knew who was speaking," Wilner observed. "The Rankers hid behind their anonymity, as did the commenters who wrote in with their own harsh judgments."

One target of the site was Olivia Palermo. In 2007, Socialite Rank alleged that she had e-mailed a long list of people prominent on the New York social scene to beg "for acceptance, privacy, and forgiveness" for being such a desperate, raving sycophant. Socialite Rank gave Olivia its "final verdict," booting her from the website and its rankings. That Palermo herself quickly denied that she had sent the message was of far less interest.[14]

> Evil Clones often take the guise of penitents who want to publicly confess.

Evil Clone Stock Scams

On a spring day in 2007, Engadget, the slick and highly respected consumer electronics weblog, received a startling e-mail from a trusted
source within Apple. The company was issuing a bad-news release.
Apple announced a delay in the delivery of the new version of its Mac
OS X operating system, Leopard. Worse, Apple announced it was being
forced to delay the production of its iconic iPhone. "This one doesn't
bode well for Mac fans and the iPhone-hopeful," Engadget opined.
Leopard had already been delayed, so news of another delay sounded
credible. Apple's stock dived 2.2 percent.[15]

In truth, the product delay was as real as Steve Jobs's later "heart
attack" in 2008. Someone had used Apple's internal e-mail system to
spoof Engadget into producing a legitimate-sounding story that had
rocked the investment world.

The flaw in these kind of bear attacks, or short-and-distort securities
fraud, is that the trail often leads back to the perpetrator. The fraudster
has the problem of explaining to the SEC the remarkable coincidence of
his shorting stocks before the phony announcement. The classic case in
the Internet age was a bear attack on Emulex, which caused the California IT equipment maker in 2000 to lose $2.5 billion in value. Investiga-
tors quickly located the twenty-three-year-old intern for a wire news
service working out of a community college who had made $250,000
from short-selling Emulex shares—and secured a guilty plea and a multiyear prison sentence.[16]

A likelier scam is the pump and dump, which involves putting out
good news on a company, often an announcement that the company has
developed a breakthrough product ("promising cure for a wide variety of
cancers!") or news that it is being acquired at a high stock price ("Warren
Buffett invests millions!"). Small science-based companies whose stock
prices can be volatile are the most frequent pump-and-dump victims. In
such a scheme, the perpetrator, already holding shares for some period
and clever enough not to be linked to his phony news, simply dumps his
shares the instant the phony news bump ups share value. The perpetrator
can be harder for the SEC to find since pump-and-dumpers can be lost
amid the hordes of other people cashing out at the word of unexpected
good fortune.

Years ago, such scams were perpetrated through faxes and snail mail.

The news was not instant because of the nature of those communications. These schemes then worked as well for short sellers as for pump and dumps. While technology has made pump and dump the better play, the motive—greed—is exactly the same as it was in the days when traders gathered under Wall Street's buttonwood tree in 1792.

In 1987, Gordon Gecko in the first *Wall Street* movie said, "Greed is good."

It was not then. It is not today.

While new services are wising up, performing journalistic due diligence when presented with a market-moving news releases, some fraudsters are still managing to stay ahead of the curve. In June 2010, PR Newswire and Business Wire, two of the most prominent distributors of business news releases, fell prey to spoof releases. One phony release put up on PR Newswire read: "Obama Orders Full Investigation of General Mills Supply Chain Following Food Recalls"; it indicated that the administration was preparing a massive investigation and regulatory assault on General Mills.[17]

When a reporter from the Minneapolis–St. Paul *Star Tribune* was approached by the writer of the phony news release, the man said that his motive for the hoax was not financial but political. "It's not to manipulate stock prices, but to serve to discredit Obama," the "media contact" said.[18]

Another phony release—this one fallen for by Business Wire—seemed to support a pump-and-dump scheme, announcing that in a 5–4 decision, the U.S. Supreme Court had ruled in favor of Javelin Pharmaceuticals in a product liability suit. Adding a little novelistic detail, the phony release had Javelin thanking Justice Clarence Thomas, who "was particularly influential in swaying the vote our way."[19]

In both the General Mills and the Javelin attacks, the perpetrators posted almost at midnight.[20] Both General Mills and Javelin were quick to spot the releases and seek retractions. In the case of General Mills, however, human action could not beat the automated news links, with headlines and stories appearing on Dow Jones Newswire, WSJ.com, and Fox Business News.[21]

> The greedy manipulate financial markets with old ploys wrapped in new technology, making good news bad news, and bad news even worse news.

Fatal Masquerade

The Lancet medical journal reported that an eighteen-year-old Italian man was depressed over a breakup, a heartache that deepened when his ex-girlfriend "friended" many new young men while "unfriending" him. *The Lancet* found it interesting that when the young man connived to get back on her Facebook page, the sight of her photos exacerbated his asthma, causing him to experience a frightening shortness of breath. Perhaps the ex-girlfriend would have suffered shortness of breath if she had been aware that her ex was on her site masquerading under a new nickname.[22] Indeed, another young man might have sought a friend request from his ex-girlfriend using the photo of, say, an attractive girl plucked off the Internet, with an interesting profile that made imaginary connections to her school and work, all under a new name.

The creation of Evil Clone identities out of whole cloth has been the central feature in a number of high-profile cyberbullying cases, some ending in death.

The iconic cyberbullying case of Megan Meier is worth revisiting. A thirteen-year-old girl in Dardenne Prairie, Missouri, Megan was thrilled to make a new friend on her MySpace page, a sixteen-year-old boy named Josh Evans, in September 2006. Megan thought Josh, who had a pet snake and looked handsome in his posted photo, was cool. Josh thought Megan was "sexi." Megan responded: "aww sexi josh ur so sweet if u moved back u could see me up close and personal lol."[23]

Megan, who struggled with self-esteem issues and was on antidepressants, was elated to know that there was a boy sensitive enough to see her true worth. The relationship, however, remained online. Josh had moved and did not yet have phone service. Over time, however, Josh turned on Megan. His communications became more critical, more undermining. On October 5 he posted, "I don't like the way you treat your friends, and I don't know if I want to be friends with you." The fracas attracted other teens, who hurled obscene insults at Megan.

On October 16, 2006, Josh finally suggested that "the world would be a better place without you."[24] Megan went to her room, sobbing. Twenty minutes later, her parents found that the teen had hanged herself in a wardrobe closet. She died the next day in a hospital.

The ugly potential of Evil Cloning caught the attention of the American public when it came to light that Josh did not exist. He was a digital creation that prosecutors would later attribute to Lori Drew, then forty-seven, a neighbor of the Meiers. Drew's daughter and Megan had once been best friends, even vacationing with the Drews, before becoming estranged. Concerned that Megan was spreading rumors about her daughter, Lori Drew allegedly conspired with a teenage employee of her home-based business, Ashley Grills, to create the digital persona of Josh, in order to spoof Megan into revealing what she was saying about Drew's daughter.[25]

According to Ashley Grills, Lori Drew, her daughter, and Grills took turns concocting the messages from "Josh." Drew, through her attorney, denies that she created the Josh Evans MySpace account or directed anyone to do so, though "she was aware of it."[26] Drew says the project belonged to Ashley Grills, a defense that a repentant Grills denied on *Good Morning America*.

Under a grant of immunity, the teen co-conspirator, Ashley Grills, later testified that it was she who had sent the fatal cruel message. She sent the message, she later said, to make Megan so angry that she would quit communicating with Josh, allowing Ashley to close the book on the digital setup.[27] Soon after, Grills said Drew ordered her to shut down the account and to say nothing more about it. Lori Drew attended Megan's funeral and said not a word to her parents about what had happened. Had it not been for the contrition of Ashley Grills, who revealed the plot six weeks later, Megan's parents might never have known who prompted their daughter to commit suicide.

Lori Drew was prosecuted in a federal court in Los Angeles (where MySpace servers are located), only to be found guilty of a misdemeanor violation, which the judge later set aside. The prosecution had based its case on the Computer Fraud and Abuse Act aimed at hard-core hackings. The contention was that by violating MySpace's terms of service forbidding fake identities and harassment, Lori Drew had become in effect a hacker.[28]

What happened next shows how much leeway the law gives those who create Evil Clones. Ashley Grills testified that like almost everyone else, the little cabal that created "Josh" had not read MySpace's terms-of-service page before clicking the "I Agree" button.[29] U.S. District Judge George Wu dismissed the charges, noting that if Lori Drew could be convicted of being a hacker, the precedent "basically leaves it up to a website owner to determine what is a crime," criminalizing a mere breach of contract.[30] Internet free speech proponents breathed a sigh of relief. The State of Missouri passed a law that took a more modest stance, adding the Internet to written and telephone communications as the means of transmitting illegal harassment.[31]

And Lori Drew? It was her turn to be the victim of anonymous Internet attacks. A digital mob assembled Lori Drew's personal information, including her e-mail address and a satellite image of her house. Someone hurled a brick through her kitchen window.[32]

> An Evil Clone can be a wholly imaginary person and yet draw you to ruin.

Did I Write That?

Liberia is a country recovering its tranquility and reputation after being torn apart by rampaging armies of child soldiers. Since its founding by former American slaves, Liberia has often been in the grip of self-serving elites known to divert national wealth into private bank accounts.

The latest cycle of violence wound down slowly in the face of a broad-based reform movement led by courageous women, both Christian and Muslim. A fair election was held, one that brought Harvard-educated Ellen Johnson Sirleaf to the presidency. During her tenure, Sirleaf negotiated major reductions in Liberia's debt, began a national healing process with a Truth and Reconciliation Commission patterned after that of South Africa, and began to restore Liberia's reputation as a reliable business partner.

Liberia's flag itself is in a sense its major export. Liberian-flagged vessels encompass more than a tenth of the world's commercial fleets. Liberia gave a contract to the Virginia-based Liberian International Ship and Corporate Registry (LISCR) to manage the activities of 3,500 Liberian-flagged vessels that carry more than 112 million gross tons and bring more than one-third of the oil imported to the United States.

That contract for the Liberian Registry comes up for renewal every ten years. Run on the U.S. side by businessman Yoram Cohen in Northern Virginia, the contract has been estimated by outside experts to be worth $10 million to the foreign partner; for Liberia, it represents a very large percentage of its national revenue. When the contract was last up for renewal, the ship company and the Liberian government were attacked in a way that left both sides dumbstruck.

A raft of e-mails between Cohen and one of his aides to Willis Knuckles, a minister in Sirleaf's government, appeared in FrontPage Africa, a muckraking online journal dedicated to uncovering corruption in Africa. The e-mails were unambiguous in their meaning. So was their origin. They had come from the company's computers in Vienna, Virginia, to the computer in Knuckles's office in Monrovia.

On August 15, 2008, the press reported this e-mail was sent from a Cohen aide to Knuckles:

> You are the man! What would we do with out our PR man. It is only prove to me again that the issue of the pr men is extremely essential. Anyways please inform Madame President that her concerns will be addressed. Yoram told me that he has already informed you that the first payment of US$1 million will be made after our contract is signed.[33]

This revelation put Cohen at immediate risk of investigation and prosecution under the U.S. Foreign Corrupt Practices Act. Knuckles—whose pleas of innocence were not helped by the fact that by this time he had already been forced to resign from the cabinet after a pants-down photo of him having sex with two women went viral—faced prosecution under Liberia's Penal Code.

As FrontPage Africa reported this story, even President Sirleaf herself might have been in jeopardy. Africans seized on a message reported on the Internet in which Knuckles was reported to have written to Cohen and his aide:

> I have been assured by the President that the process will not be opened to bid. I was also told by her at the symposium some harsh words might be used at LISCR. But keep in mind, that in order for her to look transparent she has to be on the offensive don't take it personal its just for show.[34]

The story was picked up by the international press.

There is certainly no lack of muck for muckrakers to rake in Liberia. The editor of FrontPage Africa would spend a few days in Liberia's most notorious and dangerous prison in 2011 for contempt of court after publishing a letter questioning the ethics of a Liberian Supreme Court justice, before being released by the government.[35]

The IP addresses for the e-mails were legitimate. The messages had been sent from the respective computers of the holders of these accounts. But they were false. As reported in the media, Cohen called in investigators, who discovered a sophisticated act of industrial espionage, which they believe came from a jealous competitor corporation. "Somebody wanted a piece of that contract," a digital forensic investigator opined. "Somebody wanted to cut Yoram out. So they hacked his e-mail server, took e-mails from Willis Knuckles, took e-mails from Yoram, altered them, resent them, making them look like they were doing bribes and other things against U.S. laws in an attempt to defame them, so the Liberian government would not renew the contract."

Every e-mail has a mathematical value associated with it called a checksum, which serves as a kind of digital fingerprint. The press later reported that the James Mintz Group, an investigative firm contracted by the Liberian government to determine the veracity of the e-mails, confirmed that the e-mails had been altered. "But proving what's been altered and explaining that in a way that anyone would believe was a very difficult process," one digital hound observes of the publicized reports of this story. "Someone took a legitimate e-mail, added sentences and subtracted sentences to change both what it was stating and the tone in which it was stated. On the other hand, this is not a new approach . . . Forgery is a five-thousand-year-old pastime."

Although no one knows for sure, the forger who crafted the Evil Clone e-mails may have been acting for a corporate interest jealous of LISCR's contract. After the investigation cleared LISCR, the Liberian government renewed its ten-year contract with the American firm.

In the Liberian ship case, the American company recovered its business, but it was still—eighteen months after the cyberattack—working at a breakneck pace to safeguard its computer operations. The Liberian government had to spend $350,000 to conduct an independent investigation that included the Mintz Group to confirm what LISCR already knew—that the e-mails were fraudulent. With IT help, lawyers and detectives, it is likely that LISCR's cost also ranged in the hundreds of thousands of dollars.

The cost to the attacker? Not counting the hacker's time, close to zero.

Criminal Matryoshka Dolls

Some impersonators have the same criminal intent that forgers always have had. Just as every consumer is by now aware of phishing sites, so too are retailers worried about brandjackers who might use automated programs to search for a lapse in the renewal of their brand's website—with the intent of snatching up their brand equity to sell cheaper, knock-off merchandise.

Toward the end of the last decade, many top brands were facing up to 10,000 attempts at brandjacking a week.[36] Other programs catch those who misspell URLs. "A lot of that real negative stuff is coming out not just on the consumer side," social media expert James Lee says. "It is also coming out in the nonprofit world."[37]

Even a tragedy can be brandjacked. In the aftermath of the 2010 Haiti earthquake and the 2011 Japan earthquake and tsunami, sites appeared like mushrooms after a spring rain to lure the compassionate into donating to a phishing site. Crimes like these pay because cybercriminals are not bound by the physical location of their hardware.

"If you access a server from any place, it can leave a trace telling where you probably are," Bill Livingstone says of tactics used by those seeking to operate websites with anonymity. "But you can cloud the trail by going to Internet cafés, using secondhand computers when accessing the server where the website is hosting. And if you go to a Starbucks Wi-Fi in Vienna one day, London the next, you can be very hard, if not impossible, to accurately trace."[38]

For consultants who wish to wage opposition-issue campaigns for businesses without fingerprints or legal liability, there are more sophisticated methods to throw digital hounds off the scent. They might use mind tricks, such as Americans employing British spelling. Some use untraceable services that automatically switch servers around the planet, from Latin America to Europe to Asia.

Many campaigns are sponsored by shell companies. "You can also create companies in some parts of the world and you have no idea who they really are," Livingstone says. "In Russia and the more lawless countries that came out of the Soviet Union, they like to use cutouts, dozens of companies that own companies that own companies. Russians, for example, might use a local law firm, under client privilege, to set up a company in New Jersey."[39]

> Tracking an IP address can become an endless series of digital matryoshka dolls.

YouSuck.com

Cybersquatters register a corporate or trademark domain name in bad faith, snapping up a site so they can sell it to the owner at an inflated price. Name-jackers will go after a prominent professional, a lawyer, or a doctor, buying up adjacent permutations of his name—and again, make it available for a steep price.

The law mandates a dispute resolution process, which works well for brands and trademarks, but not so well for individuals. Actor Kevin Spacey had to go through extensive legal maneuvers to shut down a namesake domain, which linked to a commercial celebrity fan site.[40]

A related phenomenon is the use of "sucks" or "sux" after the name of a company or person, which represents legitimate criticism or the character assassination of a brand, depending on your point of view. This all started when William Porta flew Alitalia to India for a wedding, only to have Alitalia lose his luggage. Porta had to attend the wedding—as the best man—in ill-fitting, inappropriate local clothes instead of formal wear. When Porta was further angered by Alitalia's reneging on one promise after another for assistance, then compensation, in 2000 he founded the website www.alitaliasucks.com. This site has but one purpose, to tell you the many reasons the content provider believes that Italy's signature airline generates massive suction.

Alitalia sued. In a filing in Porta's defense, Public Citizen noted that "nobody looks for a company by going to 'www.companynamesucks. com' . . . Any consumer finding Porta's website in a search engine's list of relevant sites would see a description sufficient to inform them that his was a critical site, and not one sponsored by Alitalia."[41]

The courts had previously held that the First Amendment protects consumers who use trademark names to make critical comments. As a result, Alitalia's suit failed. More than ten years later, Alitialiasucks. com still comes up on the first search page for the airline.

Similar tactics can be used against an individual, without the obviously satirical "sucks." During his tenure as CEO of United Airlines, Glenn Tilton probably had little love for glenntilton.com, a site maintained by United airline pilots. It was a rich and multilayered site with bars that would lead you to what it termed Tilton's operational failures, his alleged customer service screwups, and the Air Line Pilots Association's call for Tilton to resign.[42] In fact it would have been better for Tilton if the site had had the word "sucks" in it. As offensive as that would be for him, at least visitors would not mistake it for Tilton's home page.

Also on the first page of glenntilton.com was a result that led you to Untied.com, which reproduces the look and feel of a United page. It tells you that "Unless you enjoy being eaten alive by bedbugs, you might have second thoughts about 'flying the friendly skies' with UAL." The site, which has been up since the late-1990s, collects customer complaints and tracks lawsuits against the airline.[43]

> Corporations today have to offer customer service as never before because individuals today have the power to punish as never before.

Social Media Satire Attacks

As with Google bombs, brandjacking easily lends itself to satire. In the aftermath of the Deepwater Horizon disaster that spurted millions of gallons of oil into the Gulf of Mexico, British Petroleum began issuing comments even stranger than then-CEO Tony Hayward's self-pitying comments such as "What the hell did we do to deserve this?" and "I'd like my life back."[44] Or the comments of BP Chairman Carl-Henric Svanberg, who doubled down on BP's image problems with a comment that characterized Gulf Coast residents as "small people" (despite an otherwise well-prepared statement for Svanberg's White House appearance).[45]

As America's outrage grew over the continuing coverage of the torrents of oil chugging up from the bottom of the ocean, a @BPGlobalPR Twitter feed began to pollute BP's reputation with quips so bad, they sounded as if they could have actually come from BP.

We regretfully admit that something has happened off the Gulf Coast. More to come.

Are people mad at us for drilling in the ocean? Maybe God shouldn't have put oil out there in the first place.

Here's the thing: we made $45 million A DAY in profits in 2009. This really isn't a big deal.

Catastrophe is a strong word, let's all agree to call it a whoopsie daisy.

And this:

At night the gulf doesn't really look that bad.[46]

BP was also hit with viral video skits purporting to be from the company that showed hapless BP employees stunned into inactivity by a spill of coffee across a desk. These skits about BP's response, which open with a shot of a BP building and its logo, was the handiwork of the Upright Citizens Brigade, an improvisational sketch comedy group. In another piece, a faux spokesman in front of a BP logo apologized for that "oil in the Gulf business."[47]

Facebook cofounder Mark Zuckerberg has also been a target of the Upright Citizens Brigade, which had his Evil Clone issue a snarky apology. "It must have come as a shock to realize," says a Zuckerbergish-looking actor, "that when you handed over that personal information to us, we then had that personal information. I am sorry that I took the personal and private data that you typed into your computers and sent to my company and showed it to other people, even when you told me to forget everything that you told me."[48]

Under American law, the obvious satiric nature of Upright Citizens Brigade's videos protect the use of trademarks as a form of critical speech. While the Twitter feeds of @BPGlobalPR can be mistaken for the real deal, it takes only a few seconds to realize that these pieces are comparable to *Saturday Night Live*'s skits depicting screaming people inside a runaway Toyota Prius.

Some of these takeoffs can be pointed, ending with a vicious crunch instead of a laugh. One viral video appeared to be a Kit Kat commercial in which an office worker in a soulless office takes a break by unwrapping the candy bar and taking a bite. Instead of a satisfying moment and the popular company jingle, however, blood starts to squirt from the man's mouth. He doesn't see that he has in fact bitten into the dismembered finger of an orangutan. The point of the video post, produced by Greenpeace, was to protest Nestlé's use of palm oil in Indonesia, which leads to the deforestation of the orangutan's native habitat.

Nestlé, which had already committed to shifting to environmentally certified palm oil, asked YouTube to remove the video. This of course activated the Streisand Effect to ensure it would go viral.[49]

> Countering Evil Clones that have migrated to Twitter and YouTube must be part of any basic crisis plan.

Spokesmen Trolls

Jude Finisterra, spokesman for Dow Chemical, appeared on BBC World TV from Paris, the Eiffel Tower behind him. The anchor was primed to question the spokesman about the thousands of deaths and injuries in the aftermath of the 1984 disaster at the Bhopal chemical plant owned by Dow's Union Carbide subsidiary. "Do you now accept responsibility for what happened?" the anchor asked in the interview that took place twenty years after the Bhopal tragedy.

"Today, I am very, very happy to announce that for the first time Dow is accepting full responsibility for the Bhopal catastrophe," said Finisterra, a trim man with short black hair in a dark suit, white shirt, and dark tie. "We have a $12 billion plan to finally at long last fully compensate the victims, including the 120,000 who may need medical care for their entire lives." Finisterra promised a swift and complete environmental remediation of the site. He then spoke of children who still play in playgrounds and drink water at sites drenched in tons of toxic waste. "It's a mess." The money would come, Finisterra said, from the liquidation of Union Carbide.[50]

By this point, one might think that the BBC would be wondering why a Fortune 100 executive was going to such great lengths to sound like a class-action attorney indicting his own company. He referred to Union Carbide as "this nightmare for the world and this headache for Dow," and offered for Dow to "take full responsibility," a term no general counsel of any corporation in the world would permit a spokesman to offer for a subsidiary's more-than-twenty-year-old actions.

Perhaps the producers at BBC might have connected a little grade-school Latin to the man's name: *finis,* meaning the end, and *terra,* the earth.

Mr. End of the Earth was, of course, a prankster. He was one of the Yes Men engaged in a practice the group calls "identity correction," "culture jamming," "subvertising"—and the rest of us would call a hoax.[51] In the case of the Dow Chemical hoax, the company lost $2 billion in market value before the story was discredited.[52] Journalists reported that the phony story had left residents of Bhopal in tears.

The Yes Men have engaged in brandjacking with dowethics.com, in which it offers a mission statement: "As a publicly owned corporation, Dow is unable, due to share-price concerns, to accept any responsibility for the Bhopal catastrophe caused by our fully owned subsidiary, Union Carbide."[53] The Yes Men also have a News Center with headlines such as "Chemicals are not only for external uses." They offer a devilishly ingenious "Acceptable Risk Calculator," as well as a PR prop, Gilda the golden skeleton.[54]

Sometimes they hit a droll approach that perfectly parodies the bland, button-down style of corporate communications. One Yes Men website, www.gatt.org, parodies the World Trade Organization with zany headlines, such as a phony Wharton Business School announcement of the creation of a new, much improved form of slavery for Africa.[55]

When the Yes Men step out of character, however, they come across as thin-skinned, distinctly unfunny ideologues who see all private enterprise as inherently corrupt. You can see this in their slickly produced knockoff of an Apple website that advertises the new iPhone 4CF, the C standing for "conflict-free" minerals, instead of what it describes as Apple's current sourcing from the violent extraction industry of the Democratic Republic of Congo.[56] When Apple responded with indignation over the Evil Clone, the Yes Men responded, "Apple's heavy-handed and humorless reaction just shows where their big mechanical (and conflict-mineral-rich) corporate heart is at."[57]

But the signature statements of the Yes Men are often made in character as Evil Clones in the flesh. Posing as spokesmen for the U.S. Chamber of Commerce in late 2009, the Yes Men announced the chamber had dropped its opposition to cap-and-trade climate change legislation and called for a carbon tax. The websites of *The New York Times* and *The Washington Post* picked up the phony story. This "news" also became the subject of a breathless Fox Business Network segment until the anchor, Brian Sullivan, was handed a piece of paper and, after an embarrassed silence, announced it was a hoax.[58]

In April 2011, the Yes Men put out a phony press release announcing that GE would "repay" a nonexistent $3.2 billion "refund" to the U.S. Treasury.[59]

In 2009, Yes Men volunteers handed out 100,000 phony copies of Rupert Murdoch's *New York Post,* reversing that publication's traditional skeptical approach to human-caused global warming to announce, "We're Screwed." The rest of the publication included thirty-two pages on climate change, complete with phony Page Six gossip that managed to pull in a green theme.[60] They have also impersonated *The New York Times* and its website.

In a seemingly innocuous keynote luncheon address before an audience in the petroleum industry in Calgary, a Yes Man appeared as spokesman for the National Petroleum Council. Amid the clatter of silverware and hum of an industry crowd, this Yes Man launched into what sounded at first like a boilerplate special. On occasion, heads would jerk back as the Yes Man's remarks became increasingly bizarre. We need "something as useful as whales, but infinitely more abundant," the supposed representative from the National Petroleum Council said. "Why wait millions of years," he asked, to make oil, when you can turn the billions of people who will be killed by climate change into oil? He then unveiled Vivoleum, a petroleum product made of rendered human flesh.[61]

The Yes Men's droll, understated manner for making offensive statements ("starvation is the new black") neatly skewers the corporate style. As with the antics of Sacha Baron Cohen and his Brüno character, the lack of dissent from the audience to the hoaxsters' heartless statements is depicted by the Yes Men as tacit agreement by the corporate community to moral depravity. The reality appears somewhat more benign. After a few dropped jaws, people in the corporate audience obviously clue in. They listen politely because they know that they are watching some kind of circus act. Such overly polite acquiescence helps the Yes Men put audience members in a bad light. It makes a wreck of corporate PR campaigns and press conferences.

When Chevron invested in a "We Agree" ad campaign, the Yes

Men teamed up with two environmental organizations to send e-mails resembling official Chevron corporate messages, directing media to chevron-weagree.com, that included phony news releases with headers like "Radical Chevron Ad Campaign Highlights Industry Problems." The phony site offered PDF files to download consisting of satirical street posters.[62] The Yes Men went on to promote "billboard alteration kits."[63]

As a result, Chevron's multimillion-dollar ad campaign was marred as the stream of approved and satirical information bled together in the reporting.

> Evil Clones, often flesh-and-blood avatars with agendas, use comedy to wreak havoc on brands and companies.

Anatomy of an Online Breakup

The saga of the digital breakup of a middle-aged professional couple shows how maneuvers on the Internet can escalate a domestic quarrel to the edge of violence and personal ruin. This complicated breakup shows how online impersonation techniques can create an Evil Clone to land someone behind bars.[64]

Let's call the couple "Steve" and "Linda." They are middle-aged, each divorced, attractive players on the lookout for something better. Linda works at an upscale specialty business. Steve heads his own small firm. He is burly, sardonic, frank, and profane. She is good looking and irreverent. The attraction was immediate. Their multiyear relationship was physical and fun.

Before they were done, Steve and Linda would both put each other in jail. Their story, told by documents and surprising candor from Steve's perspective, also shows how technology can make breaking up hard to do in a 24/7 Internet age that provides people with little cooling-off time.

One recent summer, Linda went on a business trip overseas. While she was gone, Steve corresponded with "Vicky," a woman he had met on a dating site. He sent her an e-mail and they agreed to meet for a drink. As soon as she returned to the United States, Linda called, "and she's absolutely livid," Steve says. "She wants to know who Vicky is. And throughout the discussion, it is obvious that she not only has access to my e-mails but has copies of spreadsheets, documents, and photographs that are all on my hard drive."

Steve has imported old data into one computer after another for several decades, each time adding fresh layers to the digital archaeology of his life. Buried deep in Steve's personal computer, which he also uses for business, is a folder that contains nude photos of old girlfriends and copies of old love letters. That folder also contains a "list as best as I can remember of women that I've slept with, not for bed-notching purposes, but in today's world for health reasons," Steve says. "Linda has this list. She has all these pictures. She's quoting me verbatim from letters I had sent long ago."

More alarming than the exposure of his private life was *how* Linda got into Steve's computer. Linda had once confided in Steve that a former lover was involved in shady international business deals. After they broke up her ex worried that Linda might report her suspicions about some of his business deals to the authorities. Later, Linda found out, a friend of her ex, a prolific black hat named "Harold," started hacking into her computer to see if there was anything his friend needed to worry about. This is how Harold discovered that Steve was the new man in Linda's life. So for good measure, he also started examining Steve's computer as well.

According to Linda, Harold was the one who alerted her to Steve's flirting. Harold confessed that he had been monitoring Linda's communications, all for the single purpose of keeping her ex at ease. Harold felt comfortable telling Linda this: His friend had already moved to another part of the world and had shifted all his accounts to offshore banks far from any likely investigator. So Harold told Linda that Steve's behavior was so treacherous that he felt an obligation to warn her about him.

Worried, Steve called in a local computer geek company, a consultancy that found that someone had imported a keystroke logger to follow Steve's every computer touch. The geeks encrypted Steve's networks, installed new firewalls, updated his passwords. Still, Steve says more than three years later, "it's in the back of my mind that somebody's always watching."

After weeks of estrangement, Steve and Linda started seeing each other again. Once they were back together, Steve says, Linda "did seem to have unerring knowledge if some woman had written me on some

online site." Every time it happened, Steve wondered if he was still being hacked or if Linda had simply gone through the search history on
Steve's computer.

One spring night, the couple started sniping at each other at a dinner party. The argument escalated when they returned to Steve's house;
early the next morning Linda announced that she wanted out. "You
want to go, fine!" Steve shouted at her. He flung the door open and
threw her bags out the front door. Linda called 911 and told the police
that she had not been physically assaulted but that she feared for her
safety.

"The next thing that I know, there are two cop cars at my house,"
Steve says. "And the cops are asking what's going on, and I'm telling
them, hey, we're breaking up, she wants to go, I want her the fuck out
of here. I didn't lay a hand on her, I tossed her stuff out. There it is, right
there."

The police gave Linda a Breathalyzer test that revealed she was legally intoxicated. They told Steve that if he wanted her off his property,
they would have had to tow her car and drive her to a hotel. "At first I'm
like, 'What the fuck do I care, get her the hell out of here,'" he says.
"Then I come to arguably the stupidest decision I've ever made in my
life, which is—I don't need to be *that* much of an asshole. I can just
make up the guest room for her. She can just sleep it off and then leave
in the morning."

Most people would say, however, that it was the next thing that
Steve did on the Internet that might have been the stupidest decision
he'd ever made in his life. Linda had confided personal secrets to him.
They were secrets no more. "Linda goes to sleep," Steve says. "So I get
on Facebook and I'm writing her best friend, Trudy, who didn't know
that Linda had been banging someone very close to her while he was
engaged to some other woman. I e-mailed some other friend of hers who
she worked with, saying, 'Hey, you know, I'm out of the picture, feel
free to nail her to your heart's content.' There was on old friend of hers
who was panting after her, despite being married and having kids. I
sent him the same sort of nasty e-mail. Nothing illegal. I wasn't hacking into her account. Just Facebook being what it is, if somebody is a
friend of somebody else, for the most part you can contact them."

In this digital age, however, many people are on social media when
they should be sleeping. One of them was Linda. "About three o'clock

in the morning she comes flying out of the guest room," Steve says. "She's getting either messages or notification of the messages on her BlackBerry and she knows what I've done. She's just rip-snorting mad, which was, you know, anticipated. I just didn't expect her to find out about it right then and there. But I wanted her [to find the messages] the next day when she got home [and] to be as pissed off at me as possible, so this would be the final nail in the coffin."

After an altercation, Linda could not find her car keys and accused Steve of hiding them. As Steve would later tell the police, Linda flew into a rage and snapped a windshield wiper from his car, smashed a bottle of wine and scattered the glass all over a table, then pushed the table over and broke it, knocked over a dresser drawer, and emptied filthy trash into his printer/fax. She flipped a coffee table, smashed CDs, and broke an inherited keepsake. She stomped on a computer mouse and splashed red wine on the wall.

Photographs submitted to the police do indeed appear to show this destruction. What no one could photograph, however, was Linda's feeling that Steve's e-mails and betrayal of confidence had also ransacked, broken, and smashed her personal life. "When she was out looking for her keys again, I closed the door and locked it behind her," Steve says. This time it was his turn to call 911 to get the police to take her out of his house.

The next morning, Steve decided to file charges for destruction of property. "My interest is not seeing her get arrested," he says. "It was consequences and seeing that I was compensated." That evening Steve speaks by phone with the officer in charge of the case. He doesn't relent, though Steve seeks an assurance that Linda wouldn't be embarrassed by being arrested at work like "a common criminal." It probably didn't seem that way to Linda, who after she surrendered herself was arrested, patted down, fingerprinted, and given a mug shot.

About one week later, the police officer asks Steve to come down to the station to discuss the case. "At this point," Steve says, "I have collected all of my estimates and such, and I've got them along with a list of all the line items, and I'm assuming that is what he wants to talk to me about."

Steve arrives at the station in early evening. To his surprise, the officer "starts giving me a hard time," disputing the extent of the damage. "Have you communicated with her?" the officer asks.

"We exchanged a few e-mails, and there was texting that went on back and forth," Steve replied.

"Well, what about these e-mails?"

The officer shows Steve two of three e-mails that had been sent from his account to hers. One read:

> I'm assuming by now you've had your tour of the County Detention Center and have concluded tat [*sic*] I was indeed successful in convincing them that you did all the damage. Might want to stop underestimating me. You do so at your peril.
>
> This all could have been avoided if you had just responded to me last week. No need to be so rude. What gives you the right to think you can ignore me like that? Or were you simply so consumed with whomever the newest interest might be. Like I said, my money is on "Hank." So sad really. Now you've brought all these problems on yourself.
>
> —S

In this one brief communication, Steve seemed to be congratulating himself for committing the crime of framing Linda with the damage to his house, as well as coercing her for not "responding" to him. In another, he seemed to threaten blackmail:

> Don't forget about all those pictures I have of you in various creative outfits, positions, etc. Wouldn't want them to end up in the wrong hangs [*sic*], now would you? Don't push me. It will not be pretty.
>
> Cheers!—S

A third e-mail from Steve to Linda notes that she blocked his ability to access her Facebook, LinkedIn, and MySpace profiles. Steve said that he had no intention of sending more messages "unless you fuck with me in some very severe and unexpected" way.

Steve stared at the e-mails and wondered if it was possible that he had gotten so angry he'd written these and forgotten that he had. He had definitely written the third message. But Steve's recollection was that he had not sent it, but had wisely (for once) held it in the "drafts" folder of his e-mail. Had he not been under so much pressure from the policeman, he would have remembered that he had accidentally left his laptop with the TSA at an airport security gate. He didn't. Perhaps remembering his Facebook tantrum, Steve instead allowed for the possibility that he had sent the e-mails in anger and suppressed the memory.

"It sounds like me, but I have no recollection of having sent these, and I am not senile," Steve says. "I'll get back to you, and I'll let you know what I find out. Are we done here?"

The policeman says that they are done, "except for one thing."

"What?'"

"Stand up and put your arms behind your back."

The policeman, swayed by the new e-mail evidence, is accepting Linda's insistence that Steve had in fact physically assaulted her the night of the breakup. Now it is Steve's turn before the magistrate. The policeman surprises him by testifying that Linda, on the night they had broken up and both called 911, had "scratches that appeared to be fresh."

When Steve is released, he calls in the computer geeks. In Steve's send box are the threatening e-mails sent to Linda from his account that he now fully realized he had never seen before, along with the angry e-mail he had written, but kept in the drafts folder. That e-mail too had been sent.

The computer consultant scrolled to the bottom of one suspicious message and clicked on "complete header." This revealed the IP address the message originated from, as well as the IP address it was delivered to.

The threatening e-mails Linda had presented to the police had the same origination IP address on it. Hers.

The messages were an Evil Clone tactic that had gotten Steve arrested. Steve believes that at this point Harold was not involved.

"I hadn't given Linda the password to my account, but in arguments over the dating sites, I had given her the password to the dating sites," he says. "In a naive sort of way, all my passwords were amalgams of my children's names plus their birthdays. So all she had to do was guess, and she quickly came up with the right one."

Steve changed his passwords again, this time to a more robust form Linda could not guess. He commissioned a digital forensic report from the computer consultant and had a subpoena sent to his Internet service provider asking for all the times and IP addresses of anyone who had accessed his account over a six-week period.

In the days to come, Linda had another digital ploy. She slapped a protective order against Steve. He was to have no communication by phone, by e-mail, or in person with Linda. Then she claimed he had IM-ed her and had him arrested again—twice.

"Now I am scared shitless," Steve says. "I am on a first-name basis with everyone in the magistrate's office. And I can't get anything done because I am looking out my window every six seconds expecting to see police cars there. She has offered no proof of this whatsoever, and all she has to do is pick up the phone and say, 'He sent me a text message or an IM,' and they're going to come and arrest me again."

Finally Steve got the result of the subpoena, which showed that Linda had remotely accessed Steve's e-mail account. A further subpoena showed that the vile e-mails were sent while Steve's laptop was still in the hands of the TSA. He presented his evidence to the authorities.

The cases against Steve and Linda were mutually dismissed, Steve being told he was no longer at risk of being arrested for violating the restraining order. During his legal preparations, Steve noticed that Linda has signed a statement under penalty of perjury that she had minimal assets in order to get a court-appointed attorney.

"I had been her ad hoc financial adviser for two years," Steve says. "I know this woman is sitting on six figures in savings."

Steve presents his evidence about Linda's true financial condition and her court-appointed attorney to a detective. The gambit works. Linda is arrested again.

Some time later, in the middle of the night, Steve receives one call after another from Linda. After the seventeenth call or so, at 4:00 A.M., Steve picks up the phone.

"She's calling mostly to remind me what an asshole I am," he says. "But she's also throwing in my face things about my personal life that I can't begin to imagine how she knows. She knows I'm seeing a new woman, she knows that my kids are not at home." Linda had gotten back in Steve's system.

The next morning, Steve found five e-mails from his phone company telling him that his PIN number, password, and secret question to his account have been changed. He also discovers a new e-mail address has been added to notifications tied to an old e-mail account. When he checks, the phone company tells him that the account was accessed from Linda's IP address.

"Now I know how she knows about all this stuff," Steve says. "She has deleted my 150 messages, most of which I am saving because there was business information in there that I needed." Steve took his case to the detective who was handling Linda's perjury case. The detective sent an e-mail, "Linda, this is a week before your trial. How is this going to help you? Do I need to add new charges here?"

The detective subpoenaed a number of Steve's digital accounts and all of them registered positive hits. After a plea agreement Linda was sentenced to time in jail—most but not all of it suspended—followed by probation. She could have spent more time in jail had she been prosecuted for malicious prosecution, defamation, and computer trespass.

What were Steve and Linda left with?

Largely due to an escalating feud enabled by technology, each of them been arrested. Although only Linda ultimately served jail time, it is likely that the forged e-mails represented for her a kind of rough justice approximating Steve's flaming of her reputation before her Facebook friends. Steve could have replaced the damaged goods in his house many times over with what he spent on forensic digital studies, the testimony of digital investigators, lawyers, and other court costs. Worst of all, he had suffered days of mental torment because he had been framed by a digital clone.

> In a bitter all-out flame war between ex-lovers determined to create
> Evil Clones, there are no winners.

Takeaway—Counters to Evil Clone Attacks

If someone is impersonating you, follow the example of General Mills and Javelin Pharmaceutical by immediately countering the deception. E-mail all your friends, contacts, and business acquaintances. Put up a notice on Facebook. Post a news release.

Don't let it sit for a moment.

As we have seen, some people—when confronted with e-mails they did not send—are at first not certain that they did not in fact send them. Keeping good records and asking a digital hound to compare the checksums of messages are not enough. If you are presented with a nasty e-mail bearing your name, you should be certain that it is not yours because you never send a nasty e-mail or one that is damaging in substance. While your e-mails may contain proprietary and personal information, there should be nothing so essentially wrong about them that you would be in danger of losing your job or getting in legal trouble to see them quoted on the Drudge Report.

If someone impersonates your company in person, follow the example of the U.S. Chamber of Commerce, which sent a spokesman to walk into the Yes Men's phony press conference, interrupt it, and set the record straight.

If someone impersonates you or presents himself as you or your company's spokesmen, you should file a civil suit and explore criminal charges. In January 2011, California enacted a new criminal law against someone who "knowingly and without consent credibly impersonates another actual person through or on an Internet Web site or by other electronic means with the intent to harm, intimidate, threaten or defraud."[65] Like so much else from California, this law is apt to be enacted in many other states, perhaps even on a federal level.

On the other hand, if you or your company is hit with an online satire, many things you could do in response will only make it worse. The courts give wide latitude where humor is used to make a point. There are, however, many fine distinctions to discuss with a lawyer where copyright violations and misuse of trademarks are concerned.

You might use the Digital Millennium Copyright Act to force the Internet service provider to take down the site—if it truly misuses your copyrighted material. Don't use the DMCA, however, if critics are merely using your trademark to criticize or satirize your company. And do not use the DMCA to take down material just because it is offensive to you. Such an Internet takedown order will be obeyed almost immediately. But if your opponent can prove that there was no copyright violation and that you invoked the DMCA without justification, you can be held liable—and the penalties can be severe.[66]

One key to protecting your reputation is to have the best and most up-to-date firewalls and software to protect confidential, personal, or corporate information. You have to be aware of whom you allow to use your computer. And don't provide passcode information to anyone but your spouse. Make those passcodes robust and change them periodically, particularly after any incident.

> Evil Clones can cause trouble with a mate, an employer, and the law. Safeguarding your technology is the best way to safeguard your identity. Quick response is the best way to unmask an Evil Clone.

6:// The Fourth Sword

Human Flesh Search Engines

The mob is the mother of tyrants.

—Diogenes

IN THE 2007 WESTERN *3:10 to Yuma,* Ben Wade, a character played by Russell Crowe, is being held in a hotel in the town of Contention by marshals waiting for a train to take Wade to trial. One of Wade's confederates surveys the seedy frontier town and realizes that it is populated by useful lowlifes. So he promises $200 to every man who kills a marshal. The offer instantly transforms the men of Contention from a crowd of ambling, shiftless drunks into an army out to liberate Ben Wade.

The difference between this scene and today's Internet is that one need not offer $200, just the chance to anonymously harm someone. The Human Flesh Search Engine, a Chinese netizen term that originated on an Internet bulletin board, began by singling out antisocial acts on social media, using crowd-sourcing to locate perpetrators and national shaming to punish them.

> The Human Flesh Search Engine draws on the power of social media, activating digital mobs to launch an attack on a target from multiple directions.

Social Media Gang Bang

The iconic example of the Human Flesh Search Engine occurred when Zhu Guang Bing, a Chinese netizen, in 2003 used crowd-sourcing to track a woman who posted a "crush" video of her spearing the head of a live kitten with her stiletto heel. Zhu and a horde of other outraged netizens tracked the website to a thirty-seven-year-old nurse, in part by connecting the handle of the person who had uploaded the video to the recent purchase of a pair of high-heeled shoes from an online auction site. Once exposed to a relentless barrage of Internet criticism, the woman lost her job and was forced to make a national apology.[1]

In 2005, a South Korean with a camera phone captured a young woman who refused to clean up after her dog. Her outrageous indifference to the complaints of others made the segment a viral video hit. It wasn't long before the Human Flesh Search Engine tracked down the woman, who became known from one end of the country to the other as "dog-shit girl." The human flesh attack went into overdrive, seeking as much personal and damaging information about the young woman as it could dig up, reportedly forcing her to withdraw in shame from her university studies.[2]

One doesn't have to be a scofflaw to become a victim of this fourth sword of the new media. On the comment board of Socialite Rank, Olivia Palermo's protestations that she was the victim of Internet impersonation only made her anonymous accusers circle into a full-fledged human flesh attack. "She's turning into the Anna Nicole Smith of the benefit circle," one vicious commenter posted. "A tawdry, trashy, white-trash circus freak." One of the self-described masterminds of the site told journalist Isaiah Wilner that Socialite Rank worked to reveal real secrets as well. "Once the girls got the fame, their friends revealed their dark demons, their secrets—drug use, sexual pasts."[3]

The Human Flesh Search Engine can easily turn on its creators. In the aftermath of the 2008 Sichuan earthquake, Zhu, the pioneer who had turned the human flesh attack against the kitten killer, learned that his Frankenstein's monster could turn on anyone, making summary judgments without the support of facts or any right of appeal. When Zhu tried to auction off websites for charitable relief, he was accused by social media vigilantes of cashing in on the tragedy. The result was a devastating bombardment. "They said I was going to try and keep the money myself and that I just wanted to get famous," Zhu told the media. "Because I posted my phone number, they hounded me day and night, dozens of calls at home and the office. I couldn't do my work, so I lost my job all because I was trying to do a good thing."[4]

A similar sense of outrage prompted the Human Flesh Search Engine to go after Megan Meier's tormentor, Lori Drew, enabling someone to locate her house and hurl a brick through her kitchen window (see chapter 5).[5]

This is all in keeping with the writings of Gustave Le Bon, a nineteenth-century social psychologist who drew many examples from France's tumultuous post-Bastille history of how crowds can be swept up into violence by their self-reinforcing sense of justice.

> Human Flesh Search Engine vigilantes feed off the irony of "live by the sword, die by the sword."

SHAC Attack

One summer evening Brian Cass, the fifty-three-year-old managing director of Huntingdon Life Sciences (HLS) in Cambridgeshire, England, drove home from work in the dark, and when exiting his car saw three people with pickaxe handles raised above their heads. The rain of blows that followed on his head, back, and forearm left Cass with a three-inch-long head wound. The police considered Cass, who was rescued by his partner and a neighbor, lucky to have survived the attack. A British court later convicted a thirty-four-year-old man, revved up by a human flesh engine attack, of leading the assault.[6]

The attack on Cass was just one episode in a war on HLS, the science-based company that performs animal testing. It shows how Internet incitement and virtual organization can promote violence, even terrorism, against an organization, its people, and anyone affiliated with it. HLS is a research organization that conducts scientific animal tests on medicines, as well as on agricultural and industrial chemicals, to ensure that they meet the United Kingdom's stringent safety standards. British law is among the strictest in the world on how animals may be tested, outlawing the testing of cosmetics, tobacco, and weapons on animals, as well as forbidding experiments on chimpanzees and other great apes.[7]

Although scientists are currently experimenting with replacing animal testing with human tissue cultures, animal testing remains essential to scientific and medical progress. Animal testing, for example, has led to the development of a brain pacemaker that can ease the symptoms of Parkinson's disease.[8]

By the turn of the century, HLS had found substitutes that allowed it to replace half of its tests with nonanimal methods. Even then, the BBC reported, its experiments consumed 75,000 animals a year, including 750 dogs and 190 primates for tests. All the animals used were eventually killed.[9]

This migration toward nonanimal testing couldn't come too soon after a 1997 documentary on Britain's Channel 4, *It's a Dog's Life*, taken by an undercover whistle-blower with a hidden camera. The exposé outraged the British public with scenes of laboratory technicians abusing an uncooperative beagle, punching it to get it to submit to a test, shaking it to force the animal to accept an injection. The televised report also showed that the chemicals being injected were incompetently measured, rendering the experiment valueless and making the dog's suffering without any moral purpose.[10]

In the ensuing firestorm of public outrage, HLS fired the three technicians. Two of them were arrested at their homes for animal cruelty.[11] HLS apologized, portrayed the beagle incident as an anomaly, and tightened up its management and training. It wasn't enough to satisfy the radical animal rights activists of Stop Huntingdon Animal Cruelty (SHAC), whose leaders turned to social media to activate a human flesh attack on HLS. The animal rights group published shareholders' names on the Internet, calling on supporters to "adopt a director" for harassment and intimidation. The attacks soon expanded to include hundreds of employees and executives at client organizations that contracted for the testing, especially those who worked in pharmaceutical companies.

Institutions that financially supported HLS were also listed, including the Bank of New York and the Bank of Scotland Branch Nominees, Ltd.[12] So many suppliers of HLS were scared off that the company had to build its own laundry, cleaning service, and cafeteria.[13]

Simply listing people for "adoption" was enough to make them targets of terror. The campaign of intimidation included late-night phone calls, hate mail, and the delivery of unwanted sex toys. The cars of affiliate executives were bombed with Molotov cocktails. Neighbors of the victims received letters that included a photo of a mutilated monkey (which had nothing to do with HLS), urging neighbors to "let them know what you think about animal cruelty."[14]

One pension fund manager, frightened by bomb threats, sold its 10 percent holdings in HLS.[15] SHAC bragged that its tactics forced Merrill Lynch, Charles Schwab, and Deloitte Touche to withdraw from doing any business with HLS.[16] The campaign of terror extended to the United States, where HLS had a lab in New Jersey.

The Internet was central to organizing human flesh attacks on HLS and its affiliates and vendors, allowing SHAC leaders to keep their hands as clean as possible by simply listing targets on a website. Describing the activists as cunning, a spokesman for Cambridgeshire police said, "These people often go right to the edge of what is legal, which can make it difficult for us to bring a charge."[17] Being on SHAC's Internet adoption list had real-world consequences, as Brian Cass found out.

The campaign of violence also extended to the home of a Japanese executive living in England who worked for a pharmaceutical client of HLS. Four hooded men smashed the windows of his home and tried to smash down his front door. They fled before the police could arrive. The executive and his family were terrorized, "shaken, drained, and utterly bewildered."[18]

While physical attacks tended to turn executives into sympathetic victims, smear campaigns turned out to be a much more effective way of attacking clients. Executives' wives and mothers had their phone numbers listed in swingers' magazines, advertising their services as prostitutes. In at least fifteen cases, letters were delivered to hundreds of neighbors of executives warning them that they were living next to convicted pedophiles.[19]

By 2007, with police now on full alert, the SHACtivists increasingly turned to encrypted e-mail, sharing the names and addresses of targeted HLS suppliers on a "backbite" website.[20] The Internet proved to be the best way to securely incite, organize, and take credit for acts of violence. "Your life is in danger whenever you go to your car after working in the torture chamber," one SHACtivist wrote in mass e-mails to HLS employees. In another e-mail, she added: "Don't even think that your children are safe, if you have any. It doesn't take us long to find out where they go to school and where they live."

After the woman was found responsible for these threats, she was sentenced to five months in prison and later claimed that she was just a "harmless animal lover." Soon activists were posting the "Internet death lists" of executives worthy of execution.[21]

Activists continue to Google bomb the company, surrounding the HLS website with sites offering heart-rending videos of animal cruelty.

Google bombs were especially effective in the United States in driving investment away from HLS. Another bonus: SHAC found that many of those drawn to the cause of animal rights in North America also happen to have computer skills on tap.

"So any company that got tied to Huntingdon, all of a sudden they touched the third rail and the extremists started to come after them," says a security expert who worked the case. "They wanted to make anything around Huntingdon radioactive." [22] As they did, the Internet became the safe place to post demands and take anonymous credit for acts of terror and vandalism.

In this mode, activists splashed red paint on the Manhasset Bay Yacht Club on Long Island, New York, and the Animal Liberation Front proclaimed on an Internet board: "Let this be a message to any other company who chooses to court HLS . . . If you trade in LSR [Life Science Research, parent company of HLS] shares, make a market, process orders, or purchase shares you can expect far worse treatment. The message is simple, don't touch HLS!" Carr Securities, which had been prepared to guide HLS in listing on the New York Stock Exchange, got the message. It put out a statement of capitulation. [23]

Eventually, though, the rule of law prevailed. If the British are well-known animal lovers, they are also tenacious upholders of the rule of law. The more the campaign escalated, the more HLS employees saw themselves as standing for something important. Most stayed on the job. "There is something of the Dunkirk spirit," an HLS spokesman told the press. "We are not going to let these bastards get us down." [24]

The full resources of Scotland Yard and the FBI were employed, and the trail of violence was traced back in 2008 to SHAC leaders, who were tried, convicted, and faced long jail sentences. [25]

Is the SHAC/HLS war a harbinger of digital wars to come, with the anonymity of the Internet facilitating terror? "If you have other options to invest your money, do you need the hassle of threats to your families?" one of the investigators asks. "Do you need to have security assessments to your house, having to monitor all of your facilities, dealing with stink bombs and protests?" [26]

Such experiences have become so commonplace that elaborate security is needed to protect management and the public posture of the company subjected to such tactics. One of the authors experienced this when he held two different senior corporate positions in the United States and

Europe in which he had to provide security to employees from activist terrorists. Employees were protected from attacks on the street and in their homes; the undercarriages of their cars were checked for bombs. In one case, he had to launch a worldwide recall of a popular drink, which an activist group had proudly claimed it had tampered with. This wasn't an idle threat. A number of bottles had in fact been laced with poison.

The power of such campaigns to terrorize are amplified by the reach and anonymity of the Internet, which allows terrorists to name victims, covertly coordinate actions without having to expose cells to discovery, and take credit for acts of mayhem.

> Human flesh engine attacks unleash terror simply by identifying targets on a comment board or website.

Clowns to the Left of Me . . .

In the fall of 2010, Christine O'Donnell's campaign to represent Delaware in the U.S. Senate was on the ropes. With the endorsement of Rush Limbaugh and Sarah Palin, O'Donnell had edged out a political giant, congressman and former governor Mike Castle, to win the GOP nomination.

From that point on, everything went wrong. A twelve-year-old clip of O'Donnell telling Bill Maher on *Politically Incorrect* that she had once dabbled in witchcraft solidified the notion that she was flighty and without substance. Her attempt at damage control—the infamous "I'm not a witch" ad—made her unelectable. That should have been enough to do her in. But somebody felt the need to pour the whole bucket of water on her.

An anonymous man, known only to be in his twenties and living in Philadelphia, posted a "I Had a One-Night Stand with Christine O'Donnell" piece. Gawker.com carried his claim that three years earlier an obviously tipsy O'Donnell lured the young man and his roommates to join her and a friend to go to a local bar on Halloween night. O'Donnell wore a ladybug costume—a claim backed by several digital photos of an apparently lit O'Donnell mugging around in just such a silly costume.[27]

If that had been all there was to the man's story, it would have been the kind of eleventh-hour embarrassment that every campaign faces. The piece did not stop there. Although there is no way to verify its credibility, it turned out nasty. "It really didn't take very long for Christine to make her move," the blogger wrote. "She'd grabbed my hand on the way from the apartment to South Street, so I can't say I was totally surprised when she leaned in to kiss me soon after we arrived at the bar." He noted that he was later surprised to learn that she was fourteen years older than him.

"I don't think I'd heard the word 'cougar' yet at that point, but that's probably what I'd call her," he wrote. "Things got physical on the couch pretty quickly. It wasn't long before we'd moved from the living room to my bed." He promised not to get into the "nitty-gritty details of what happened between the sheets that evening," then divulged that "it wasn't half as exciting as I'd been hoping it would be."

O'Donnell was "a decent kisser," but "as soon as her clothes came off and she was naked in my bed, Christine informed me that she was a virgin." He later came to understand that she was a "born-again virgin." He added the salacious centerpiece of the story, a commonplace anatomical observation that he used to heap ridicule on O'Donnell. Then the man rolled over and went to sleep without having sex with her.

The next morning, the blogger said, he had trouble getting her to leave his apartment before he went off to work. He ended the post by noting that O'Donnell later dated his roommate and likely did not have sex with him either.

Andrew Sullivan, the Oxford-educated, iconoclastic super-blogger now with the Daily Beast and no admirer of O'Donnell, called the post a "cowardly, brutal and misogynist invasion of privacy." Gawker, which had paid for the story in the low four figures, defended itself by saying that O'Donnell's championship of chastity and marriage made her a hypocrite, and therefore fair game.[28]

What were the underlying facts? O'Donnell wasn't married. And if the post is true, she did not have sex. Gawker's defense for such creepily caddish humiliation of a woman is that she, as a self-declared Christian, has on occasion been a hypocrite.

This Internet attack forces us to ask if the age of total transparency makes it possible for any living, breathing human being to champion a given moral standard. Most would agree that a fire-and-brimstone preacher who denounces adultery and homosexuality every Sunday from the pulpit while exploiting young men in his congregation is a hypocrite worth exposing. John Edwards, whose central campaign appeal to female voters was making displays of his unctuous infatuation with his wife while fathering a child with another woman, is clearly a hypocrite. Former Nevada Republican senator John Ensign, who called on President Clinton to resign and spoke of the sanctity of marriage as his reason for a measure barring same-sex marriage while carrying on an affair with the wife of a family friend and top aide, is certainly a hypocrite.

Christine O'Donnell is just an unmarried lady who got silly on one Halloween night, had too much good cheer, and may have let a man see her naked.

> Once a woman becomes a target, the Human Flesh Search
> Engine can crowd-source her entire private life—anyone who has
> ever known her—and strip her naked in the public square.

Jokers to the Right . . .

Reverend Carol Howard Merritt is a minister at the Western Presbyterian Church, a short walk from the Watergate building along the banks of the Potomac. A progressive who brings a liberal perspective to theology, Merritt is a voracious blogger, podcaster, and editorial contributor to the Huffington Post, with a significant following on Facebook and Twitter.

When Merritt started writing regularly in 2007, she says she was surprised "how quickly things spread. At first it was very positive, exciting, and interesting how, as a budding writer, I was being read."[29] As her pieces appeared on the Huffington Post, "pretty soon, I began to get nasty e-mails, comments which I tend to ignore."

Before long, Merritt was under attack by a group of people she did not know existed—atheist fundamentalists. Like many intellectual Christians, she had long cultivated many friends who are atheists, finding the give-and-take of ideas with other thinkers bracing. To her surprise, however, a fair number of atheists respond to digital debate with personal attacks.

"Often there is this sense of real woundedness that you can read in their comments," she says. "It's almost like they're oozing with pain from religion really hurting them in some ways."

The worst human flesh attacks, however, came from her fellow Christians, especially a group that has come to be called "heresy hunters." One evangelical preacher goes beyond criticism of Merritt's liberal theology to demonize her as a "pastrix"—a conflation of "pastor" and the sexually charged term "dominatrix."

"For a while he was reading every single thing on the Web I wrote and picking it apart," Merritt says. After Merritt posted a sharply worded critique entitled "Why Evangelicalism Is Failing a New Generation" on the Huffington Post, all hell broke loose.[30] A public campaign of shaming began, with critiques of Merritt from unknown posters taking on sexually charged terms—with "whore of Babylon" and "whore of Satan" taking top billing.

The rising tide of the human flesh attack culminated in a call to Merritt's husband, also a Presbyterian minister, with the unknown caller "starting out the conversation saying, 'You don't want to get your child hurt.'" To Merritt's surprise, online attacks come from even like-minded ministers interested in the progressive "emerging church" movement that conducts much of its dialogue via technology and blogs. "You're in conversation with these people, then all the sudden you'll say things they don't like," she says. "And this has happened with colleagues. Other ministers, they'll start attacking you. This emerging movement is kind of bad about that."

There seems, she says something about the terseness of Twitter that encourages misunderstanding and vicious group attacks. The attacks don't come, as you might imagine, on elevated terms about the nature of the Trinity or the relevance of the Westminster Confession of Faith. They are more along the lines of calling on targeted ministers to "suck a bag of dicks."

> Human flesh attacks on Twitter or other social media can rapidly transform bloggers with singular messages into human piñatas.

Global Opposition Research

When the board of Hewlett-Packard attempted to use a private detective to track a corporate leaker, it wound up costing CEO Patricia Dunn her job in the pretexting scandal. The private investigations used Evil Clone techniques to fish for information. These actions also resulted in a new federal law against using many phony pretexts to fish for confidential information. Even though Dunn was legitimately acting to protect corporate information, and was ultimately found to have committed no crime, the stigma attached to private detective work—no matter how legal—is daunting.[31]

Dirt diggers, however, no longer have to take such risks. Private investigation and its political sibling, opposition research, have moved out of the dark alley and onto center stage. Digital assassins can now draw on the power of social media to task the crowd to assemble secrets to ruin a target or force a change in policies.

The Old School method of opposition research, perhaps going back to James T. Callender, included digging through court records, rifling through trash, and scouring old divorce records. It was labor intensive and hit or miss.

The Human Flesh Search Engine crowd-sources intelligence, as it did with candidate O'Donnell, using social media to farm out the work of digging up dirt on people by everyone who has ever known them or who is in a position to obtain knowledge about them. Digital investigators and some PR firms also still use some forms of pretexting and other "social engineering" techniques. This later term involves hacking people, spoofing them into divulging secrets, often to gain access to their computer networks. In this way, they trick the companies that run web-based systems into giving hackers the keys to their private digital kingdoms.

The same techniques are increasingly being used by national intelligence agencies. China's People's Liberation Army (PLA) is a pioneer of the use of crowd-sourcing for espionage. One division of the Chinese military, says Tom Kellermann, who has served on the U.S. Commission on Cybersecurity, employs more than 30,000 computer scientists. But perhaps China's greatest intelligence asset is not in the PLA, but in the regime's ability to farm out espionage to eager freelance armies.[32]

"To be a nationalistic hacker is pretty much the coolest thing you can do as a child in China," Kellermann says. "They have competitions within their provinces for the best hacker. The winners and their families essentially get taken care of for life. They are given somewhere to live, a regular salary, and then they work for a shell company that allows them to do whatever they want, provided that when they find something interesting, they share it with the government.

"We see hacking as evil and we treat good hackers as evil," Kellermann continues. "They nurture them. The Chinese government has only one rule—and that rule is 'Don't hack us.' And if you do find something interesting, like a U.S.-owned system, or you can infiltrate something within the United States, let us know. There is a sense of nationalism around the tradecraft that is cyberespionage . . . The use of non-state actor proxies by regimes like China and Russia is overt."

Of course, if WikiLeaks ever revealed the innermost secrets of Beijing or Moscow, the worst persecution fantasies of Julian Assange would immediately come to pass as he quickly vanished from the Earth.

In the West, however, crowd-sourced intelligence works, and often for more trivial purposes than espionage. ChurchOuting.org, now gone dark, turned to the Human Flesh Search Engine for crowd-sourcing to collect the gay and straight sex secrets of Catholic priests as part of a campaign to nudge the archdiocese of Washington, D.C., to change its policies on gay marriage.[33] This website seemed to take a page out of Saul Alinsky's *Rules for Radicals*: "Make the enemy live up to their own book of rules," and adds, "You can kill them with this, for they can no more obey their own rules than the Christian church can live up to Christianity."

In the face-off between Jerry Brown and Meg Whitman for the governorship of California, a group calling itself "Level the Playing Field 2010" emerged, purporting to be interested in keeping Whitman from "buying the governor's office." It was funded by special interests, including the California Nurses Association PAC Committee. It established a platform called WikiMeg. This open source site asked "everyone and anyone with factual information to share—from laid off eBay workers and those frustrated with Whitman's eBay policies toward sellers to shareholders to regular voters—to help us fully vet Meg Whitman's job application."[34]

This was a clever use of crowd-sourcing to ferret out dirt on a political candidate. Although WikiMeg was just a sideshow (the most damaging event of the campaign was the claim that Whitman had hired an illegal alien, which came from attorney Gloria Allred), the likelihood is that this technique will become a standard tactic in every campaign.

Social media opposition research has even been used to light up targets for physical assassination. In 2010, ten aid workers—six Americans, two Afghans, a Briton, and a German—working with a nonpros-elytizing Christian aid group called International Assistance Mission, had just returned from a heroic 120-mile crossing by foot and horseback to bring medical relief to a remote Afghan village. While the aid work-ers were resting, a band of Taliban attacked, killing them with bullets, grenades, and crushing blows from Kalashnikov rifles. Intelligence sources later told the press that Taliban operatives on the Internet seemed to have tracked the group in real time on their Facebook page before they ever set foot in the village.[35]

> Attackers call on human flesh mobs to perform deep dives into personal backgrounds that exceed the best results of expensive detectives or even government "alphabet" agencies.

The 50-Cent Party

What makes the Human Flesh Search Engine such a potent force? It is a dark manifestation of the power of social media, which can organize cross-functional teams within an organization, set up a church picnic, or call up a flash mob. As a form of social media, however, it has en-ablers.

One enabler of the Human Flesh Search Engine is of course the power of bloggers. A vitriolic blog can provide the initial energy to stimulate and attract other bloggers, winds that swirl until a hurricane is formed. The immediacy and global reach of a blog can let loose the destructive hurricane to rip up governments, companies, and powerful individuals. This same force, however, can be sent spinning in the other direction by those very authorities to isolate their critics and punish them for speaking out.

For example, a Chinese citizen posted a criticism of the local police in the Henan province city of Jiaozuo, whereupon a flood of countercom-ments followed. Some 120 different bloggers eventually commented, all of them protesting the criticism, some of them attacking the complainer.[36]

Such bloggers are members of the "50-cent party," trained by the PRC and deemed to be ideologically in sync with the Communist Party establishment, paid spinners—legend has it that they are paid the equivalent of 50 cents per post—who are trained to look for criticism of the government and then change the terms of the debate. They are in effect the final defense the PRC employs against internal comments that make it past the "great firewall of China."[37]

In the United States, it is estimated that thousands of paid bloggers also put up phony opinions, mostly for commercial purposes, on a sliding bonus scale that can earn them $30,000 to $70,000 a year. Others provide news for websites such as Gawker Media, which give out retainers and bonuses for highly viewed posts. The competition to be the first to break news about products on technology sites is particularly intense.[38]

Western bloggers, however, have not proved as malleable or as excitable as their Chinese counterparts in using the human flesh engine to crack down on dissent. In the 2010 maritime dispute between China and Japan, a group of Chinese anti-Japanese protesters, perhaps stoked into action by nationalist bloggers paid by the government, made a media show of angrily smashing Japanese products.

A Chinese national, Hua Chunhui, sent a slightly sarcastic message that mocked this staged human flesh attack to his fiancée, Cheng Jianping, who retweeted it. For this, Cheng was sentenced to a year of hard labor.[39]

> Although Human Flesh Search Engines emerge out of anarchy, authoritarian regimes can turn them into a useful tool for repression.

Anonymous and Mirror Sites

A second enabler of the Human Flesh Search Engine is the relentless ability to use technology to disappear before any would-be tracker and perhaps reappear as someone else. In this game of international Whack-a-Mole, the mole rarely gets whacked.

The flesh engine extraordinaire, of course, is WikiLeaks, which managed to undermine, confound, and thwart the world's most powerful government. When the U.S. government pressured Amazon, PayPal, and other Internet sites to cut off server space and payment services for WikiLeaks, members of Anonymous and other informal activist groups created hundreds of mirror sites that cloned the original WikiLeaks site. Next a Swiss-Icelandic company, DataCell, picked up the slack to process donations from PayPal.[40] Like the many-headed

Hydra, WikiLeaks sprouted new sites as the effort to shut it down intensified.

> With no lack of people ideologically committed to thwarting any
> effort to shut down information, the Human Flesh Search Engine
> counts on the crowd to keep a hot thing going.

You Have Been Trolled

Being labeled dog-shit girl by one person is insulting. Having that label slapped on you by an entire nation is frightening and debilitating. Condemnation by an entire society and even the world is a punishment that outweighs most crimes. But the Human Flesh Search Engine does at least serve to reinforce social norms, much as public shaming once brought order to village life.

Another type of human flesh attack comes from people who reject all social norms. These commentators are, like the young men of Auto-Admit, firm in the belief that if you react with outrage to the vilest, darkest, racially and sexually charged language, then you really don't get the joke. These are trolls, the vandals of cyberspace, the id of the Internet.

For example, a Facebook page dedicated to being a memorial to teens who committed suicide is often defaced with comments about her being an "obese whore" and "skank who deserved to choke," or him being "a little fag who had it coming." One troll posted a cruel Megan Had It Coming blog. She was, the blogger posted, a "drama queen" who deserved ridicule for pining over a MySpace boy. "I mean yeah your [sic] fat so you have to take what you can get but still nobody should kill themselves over it."[41] The blogger falsely claimed to be Lori Drew.

Another troll site is dedicated to the lawsuit over the AutoAdmit case. Click it, and it will direct you to an image that—after you've taken a moment to make it out—is a photo from a car crash scene in which the head of a young woman has been pulverized into a red mush of brains and hair.

Such tricks are meant to elicit "lulz"—derived from the plural of "lol" (laugh out loud). Lulz is really something more. It's savoring other people's consternation, grief, horror, disgust, anger, and bewilderment.

And if the thought of inflicting fresh pain on bereaved parents leaves you livid, then that only shows the extent to which you are still a slave to words and the artificial constructs of society. If anything, some believe, your anguish is an object lesson in expressions that are inherently sentimentalized and therefore unreal.

Goatse Security, a small hacker group that reveals security flaws, stands at the intersection of the gray hacker and the troll. The name comes from a shock site that slaps the viewer with the image of a man using his fingers to open his rectum to full view (hence the group's slogan, "Gaping Holes Exposed"). One Goatse leader, "weev" (known in the straight world as Andrew Auernheimer, twenty-six), was arrested in 2010 when an FBI raid allegedly uncovered a stash of cocaine, ecstasy, LSD, and controlled pharmaceuticals.[42]

Some of the Goatse members seem to intersect with the small clique of trolls that calls itself the Gay Nigger Association of America, or GNAA. If the name offends you to the core, then YHBT: "You Have Been Trolled."

Why do they do it?

Again, for the lulz, which means the sheer joy of ruining your day. "Griefers" are a related, less sophisticated tribe, people who get their jollies from disrupting online multiplayer games.

If you are so clueless as to actually respond to such an attack with a lawsuit or with an editorial, as John Seigenthaler did, you will find yourself slashed by the piranhas in a human flesh attack of trolls, ideologues who believe that no one anywhere at any time should ever be held to account for what they say, write, or post.

Encyclopedia Dramatica, which is the Bizarro World troll version of Wikipedia ("In lulz we trust"), quotes Jon Postel, one of the architects of the Internet, who offered a Robustness Principle: "Be conservative in what you send; be liberal in what you accept." Postel's law, originally meant for technological application, has become the unstated attitude of wide tolerance most people bring to the Internet.

The troll's rule posted on Encyclopedia Dramatica overturns tolerance with anarchy, declaring, "You are not worthy of my understanding; I, therefore, will do everything I can to confound you."[43]

Jarret Cohen, the insurance broker who created AutoAdmit, took the time to write to Eugene Volokh, an eminent professor of law at UCLA. "One finds," Cohen wrote, "a much deeper and much more mature level of insight in a community where the ugliest depths of human opinion are confronted, rather than ignored."[44]

> Trolls lurk at the place where extreme libertarianism meets the evil heart of fascism.

Takeaway—Standing Up to the Crowd

The terror campaign against HLS left it with worthless stock and no creditworthiness. The company would have closed had it not been for the bold intervention of Prime Minister Tony Blair, who stepped in to uphold science and the rule of law. The government gave HLS a bank account, a large grant to the local police in Cambridgeshire to manage a gauntlet of protection that HLS employees had to endure every day to get to work.[45]

Huntingdon Life Sciences had become this vulnerable only in the aftermath of *It's a Dog's Life,* a documentary that left it with no reservoir of public goodwill.

In the age of Little Snitch, good behavior will not ensure goodwill. But it helps. As the authors advise their clients, companies need to enforce ethical behavior and "build a reputational cushion"[46]—seeding your search results in advance of any attack with credible demonstrations of the value of one's work. Ethical operating principles and proclaiming good deeds from the rooftops remain the best defense against demonization on the Internet.

Most victims are not as controversial as HLS, or the target of such well-orchestrated campaigns of terror. Most targets are somewhat like Reverend Merritt's church, which got a one-star review on Google maps. "Those who posted it had never been to our church, but they didn't like our stance on certain issues," she says. "So they left one star, commenting, 'I wish I could leave no stars in the review.'"

The danger here was that this review would attract likeminded heresy hunters, making the church the focus of a barrage of attacks. Merritt knew, however, that the same power of social media to turn a crowd against her could be used to create a crowd to come to her defense. She got on Facebook and asked all of her friends and followers to post. Naturally they posted praise for the church, postings that, she says, "drowned out the nastiness."

And how to respond to the vicious attacks? A little humor helps.

"Wow, don't drink and Twitter!" is one of Reverend Merritt's more effective responses.

And if your bad behavior, like dog-shit girl, lands you in the crosshairs of a human flesh attack? What if you become your very own wiki? The survivors apologize, explain what happened, point out the inequity of the punishment to crime, and draw on the power of social media to elicit friends to come to their defense.

> It is intimidating to face an angry crowd. With some initiative, you can work up a crowd of your own to stand behind you.

7:// The Fifth Sword

Jihad by Proxy

> Most of the errors of public life . . . come not because
> men are morally bad, but because they are afraid of
> somebody.
>
> **—Woodrow Wilson**

WHEN CAMPAIGNS ARE LAUNCHED against a brand, business, or
individual, digital assassins often attack through a front organization.
The cutout or front can be Nongovernmental organizations (NGOs), a
reasonable-sounding blog on the Internet, or a vendetta website masquerading as a high-minded news source. When these attacks from fronts are
organized against a target, you have the fifth sword of digital assassination, jihad by proxy.

This chapter also will examine several nondigital and predigital uses
of proxy groups. Why? Just as West Point still teaches lessons for future
warfare drawn from the Napoleonic era, so too in this Internet age, you
must understand how these groups form and work so you can grasp
how they now facilitate digital attacks.

Mothers Opposing Pollution

Jihad by proxy was exemplified in Australia in the 1990s with Mothers
Opposing Pollution (MOP), which billed itself as "the largest women's
environmental group in Australia with thousands of supporters across
the country." MOP presented an impressive facade. For an annual subscription of AU $39.95, supporters could get an environmental aware-
ness certificate, tree-growing instructions and seeds, and 10 percent off
MOP products such as soap or facial cleanser. The truly conscientious

could buy MOP badges through supermarkets to raise funds for turtle research.[1]

MOP's spokeswoman, Alana Maloney, also waged a public aware- ness campaign against plastic milk bottles for their supposed carcino- genic properties. She raised additional concerns about the degradation of milk by UV rays that can penetrate the plastic.

MOP operated for several years until investigative journalists for Brisbane's *Courier-Mail,* unable to locate the armies of outraged Aus- tralian women united against plastic milk bottles, unraveled its iden- tity. They found that Alana Maloney did not exist. She was a cutout, a stand-in for someone else and some other interest.

So who was behind Mothers Opposing Pollution? The Australian press traced it back to a PR professional, who while waging a phony environmental campaign against *plastic* milk cartons was found by jour- nalists to have business links to a firm that consulted for the *paper* milk- carton industry.[2]

Of course, in a digital age, creating a respectable facade to assassi- nate need not be elaborate. It can be done for a few shillings and key- strokes. "These tactics have filtered down to the bumpkin level," says one digital hound, who points to a website dedicated to local politics in one suburban county in the Deep South run by a 501(c)(4), a nonprofit that is allowed to engage in issue and lobbying activities. Handsomely designed with heartwarming images of families and green landscapes, this site uses an image of earnest, public-spirited people to send out e-mails defaming local county and school board candidates, often with grotesque financial, personal, and ethical charges.[3]

The law does not require that this site disclose its donors, and it does not. "This is small potatoes in a small potatoes field," says the investiga- tor, who was called in when victims sought out the identities of their anonymous attackers. "Yet they find money to do this. It tracks back to some of the richest families and one of the most successful politicians doing business in that state. So it's not just Washington.

"You think it's just the big players," he says. "It has infiltrated all the way down to county elections. You look at this and scratch your head. That's a lot of money for a whole lot of nothing. Proxy attacks are really now just part of the fabric of this country."

They are certainly part of the fabric of university life, where plazas are chock-full of proxy groups pushing petition drives. One of them is an old familiar, SHAC—Stop Huntingdon Animal Cruelty—the "animal rights" group members of which the British government prosecuted for terrorist activities, which presents perhaps the most sinister form of the laundering of motives to the extent it's terrorism masked behind a benign and compassionate public face.

SHAC's alleged association with the Animal Liberation Front (ALF), which is classified by the FBI as a domestic terrorist group, is a dichotomy that would allow it to raise money with a humanitarian facade while allowing the ALF brand to take credit for acts of violence, much as Sinn Féin once operated in public while leaving the violence to the Provisional Irish Republican Army.

Journalist and novelist Jo-Ann Goodwin, in an investigative piece for the London *Daily Mail,* described the benign public face of a particularly vicious motive launderer:

> [A]n unobtrusive stand—a trestle table, covered perhaps with a green blanket—manned by a well-meaning volunteer, sometimes an elderly lady.
>
> On display are pictures which are deliberately upsetting, pictures of miserable monkeys and suffering beagles destined to grab both the heart and the purse strings. Many of us have willingly signed petitions and given cash to the "worthy cause" which pledges to stamp out the torment animals endure because of needless scientific experimentation.[4]

Many of the photos on SHAC's tables are old and do not represent the actions of any current research organization. Nevertheless, the images are sufficiently powerful to open purses and wallets from Bristol to Edinburgh.

British police report that while these stands can take in tens of thousands of pounds, the petitions are typically discarded.[5] The money itself goes to a secretive organization with no published accounts or records.[6]

In short, the money seems to have been used for purposes that have nothing to do with the poor little monkeys and dogs bedeviled by needles and electrodes portrayed in SHAC's pictures. Similar shams exist all over the Internet today, from Haiti relief to orphans, puppies, and whales, because digital technology creates cutout groups with a few keystrokes.

Seemingly motherhood-and-apple-pie organizations may have hidden agendas.

Motive Laundering

Jihad by proxy occurs when a front group launches a publicity campaign of character assassination on behalf of an unidentified special interest for a purpose beyond its stated concerns and public charter. Cutouts such as Mothers Opposing Pollution exist precisely for this purpose of laundering the motive of kneecapping a competitor under the guise of concern for health and the environment. In some cases, organizations with well-deserved reputations for independent thinking or whistle-blowing sometimes cash out by allowing their hard-won credibility to be misused.

Why disguise motives? Jihad by proxy attacks can create or raise phony health or environmental issues to set the precedent for trial lawyers to launch class-action lawsuits. They can be attacks on behalf of a political operator whose real clients have interests too squalid to be publicly acknowledged. Or they can come from companies looking to heap regulatory burdens on their rivals.

As the national conversation goes digital, the lines between these planned shadow campaigns and spontaneous movements will inevitably blur. With social media, after all, all it takes is one tweet to enough followers to generate a spontaneous organization of people willing to send a coordinated message. Is that group spontaneous? Or is it organized? With billions of messages roiling around in cyberspace, does it really matter who starts a particular cascade of messaging?

Organizing like-minded people to convey a shared message is not jihad by proxy. If anything, this is the essence of democracy, even when the organizing begins with a corporation or union.

Both sides create phony grassroots campaigns, or "Astroturf." But not all efforts are phony. "With voters split fairly evenly down the middle on health care reform," blogger and op-ed contributor Ryan Sager wrote in *The New York Times,* "it seems presumptuous to label your side 'real' and the other synthetic. Considering today's 24-hour cable news babbling, down-and-dirty blog activism, and talk-radio-rabble rousing, it's worth asking if the Astroturf epithet still has meaning."[7]

In a social media world, there is often no need to pay people to feign interest in phony campaigns when many issues have a built-in following that can be inspired through Facebook or Twitter. When big organizations find their interests under challenge, they often use a digital thread to locate and activate people who are already in passionate agreement with them—the grassroots.

"You go back to the original Boston Tea Party, and I find it highly unlikely that you had 50 guys dress up like Indians, show up at a boat, bring the right tools, and then leave in an orderly fashion without any kind of organization," Adam Brandon, a spokesman for the conservative organization FreedomWorks, told Politico's Ben Smith.[8]

All true.

The Boston Tea Party would have been an example of motive laundering only if colonial Americans had been led to believe that the attack came from real Mohawks—and that the purpose of the raid was not to manifestly protest British tax policy, but to start a war with Native Americans.

Today many groups are willing to don war paint and engage in precisely that sort of motive laundering. And, there will be no lack of money to fund them or human resources to propel them.

In the political sphere, as a result of the U.S. Supreme Court's 2010 *Citizens United* decision, corporations and unions can fund independent political campaigns, with no legal limits on how much cash can enter into political wars. The court's decision will promote free speech and the First Amendment rights of organized groups. It will bring about more robust discussion of the issues. But this decision will also, as a side effect, inspire the creation of more front organizations.

How much more money will be available?

During the 2004 presidential race, the Swift Boat Veterans for Truth, the group that detracted from Senator John Kerry's war record and critized his protest statements, raised perhaps more than a few tens of millions of dollars in private donations.[9] Technology aided their coming together just for one election cycle. Their group ran a few ads, but mostly relied on the echo chamber of the media and the Internet.

After the U.S. Supreme Court lifted the cap on corporate and union funding of independent expenditures in *Citizens United*, the U.S. Chamber of Commerce raised and spent close to $75 million on congressional races in the 2010 midterm elections—on top of $190 million spent on lobbying in the first two years of the Obama administration.[10]

Not to be left behind, in November 2010 the top hundred donors to causes of the left held a private meeting at the lavish Mandarin Oriental hotel in Washington, D.C. Led by billionaires George Soros and Peter B. Lewis, they are bringing partners of the left-of-center Democracy Alliance to match the U.S. Chamber of Commerce and the conservative American Crossroads GPS advised by Karl Rove.[11]

As the floodgates of corporate, union, and foundation spending are opened, most of the money on both sides will go into ads in which the donors' intent is obvious. But with so much money sloshing around, a lot of corporate and union money is bound to find its way into independent-expenditure groups with facetious public agendas. "If you think that they're shoveling shit now, they're really going to be fertilizing the planet next year with that stuff," says one longtime political consultant looking ahead to the 2012 election.[12]

> Some groups use the new freedom to spend political money to enhance the digital debate. Others will hide behind digital cutouts in the age-old human quest for money and power.

Jack Be Nimble

One August day in 1998, former House majority whip Tom DeLay appeared on *Fox News Sunday* to launch a blistering critique of the International Monetary Fund, denouncing the global lending institution for running the fledgling Russian economy into the ground. "They are trying to force Russia to raise taxes at a time when they ought to be cutting taxes in order to get a loan from the IMF," DeLay said. "That's just outrageous."

DeLay was delighted to be known by his nickname, the Hammer. DeLay's meddling in Russian politics was supported by the U.S. Family Network (USFN), a public advocacy organization headed by DeLay's former chief of staff Edwin Buckham.

This story behind USFN and its related proxy groups, though not a digital example, reveals the hidden life of proxy groups now so prominent in the digital debate. The USFN was an excellent example of motive laundering. Founded in 1996, USFN set a goal of being an advocate for policies that would serve "economic growth and prosperity, social improvement, moral fitness, and the general well-being of the United

States." Tom DeLay called it "a powerful nationwide organization dedicated to restoring our government to citizen control." In fact, the tiny U.S. Family Network did little more than fund a Capitol Hill "safe house" for DeLay, employ DeLay's wife Christine, and pay Buckham a gigantic salary.

In a series of investigative pieces, *The Washington Post* in 2005 revealed that the U.S. Family Network received $1 million from a London law firm. The money, it was reported, originated from two oil and gas oligarchs with links to Gazprom, men described as being always surrounded by armed guards with machine guns, who wanted DeLay to attack the IMF in order to pressure it to bail out wealthy investors.

When DeLay's spokesman was asked about the trip, he said DeLay had gone to Moscow "to meet with religious leaders."[13] The facilitator in this and many other front organizations associated with DeLay was of course his friend Jack Abramoff.

As it turned out, Russia got the loan it wanted, without the strings it really didn't want.

The U.S. Family Network aided the moral fitness and well-being of the United States in other ways. It received half a million dollars from textile companies to stiff-arm Democratic investigations into the maltreatment of immigrant workers in the U.S. protectorate of the Mariana Islands, where products are tagged with a "Made in the USA" label. The U.S. Family Network also received about $250,000 from the Mississippi Band of Choctaw Indians to pressure conservatives in Congress to fight taxation of Indian gaming.[14]

The spider at the center of this web, Jack Abramoff, displayed a genius for creating front groups that waged proxy jihads on behalf of a number of clients. The bulk of Abramoff's manipulation of front groups came from the $45 million he received for lobbying and public affairs work over three years from four Indian tribes to support Indian gaming.[15] The operation, stunningly cynical, even by Washington standards, was well portrayed in the movie *Casino Jack*.

In lining up support concerning state measures on Indian casinos, Abramoff tapped evangelical Christians, including Ralph Reed, whose PR consultancy had on tap powerful networks Reed had developed as executive director of the Christian Coalition under Pat Robertson. Reed, with his eye on a possible future in electoral politics, ensured that his front organization be paid with money laundered through yet another front organization. One of them was the American International Center, a "premiere think tank" dedicated to "bringing great minds together from all over the globe." It was directed by a yoga instructor and a lifeguard.[16]

Abramoff also made adept use of existing organizations with real missions, transforming them into his front groups. He mobilized the Traditional Values Coalition, led by Reverend Louis P. Sheldon, a powerful evangelical in Orange County, California. This group attacked vulnerable Republican politicians for being soft on gambling, when in fact they were being attacked for supporting the Internet Gambling Prohibition Act.

Claiming to represent 43,000 churches coast to coast and in Puerto Rico, the Traditional Values Coalition is concerned with "religious liberties, marriage, the right to life, the homosexual agenda, pornography, family tax relief and education."[17] And apparently its concerns include helping an Abramoff client named eLottery defeat the Internet Gambling Prohibition Act so it could sell lottery tickets on the Internet.[18]

Abramoff served on the board of a think tank, the National Center for Public Policy Research, whose sponsorship he evoked when using clients' money to send DeLay and other powerful Washington officials on lavish golf outings in Scotland.[19] Another trip was paid for with money funneled through the Capital Athletic Foundation, which ostensibly used sports to instill character in inner-city youth.[20] And Abramoff used the Council of Republicans for Environmental Advocacy to seek help from the U.S. Department of the Interior to scuttle an Indian casino in Louisiana that would compete with Abramoff clients.[21]

In sum, the Abramoff machine shows that skillful motive laundering can channel concern for the environment, inner-city kids, the free market, and the Christian evangelical agenda to advance the interests of casinos and sweatshops.

> On digital platforms today, motive launderers similarly enlist the idealistic and the naive to serve squalid interests in the name of God and country.

Romanian Run-Around

Jihad by proxy is not just the domain of the right wing and business interests. It is also a favorite tool of foundations that pursue their agendas—sometimes hidden—through environmental and other activist organizations.

Gabriel Resources, a Toronto-based mining company, was at the receiving end of an NGO-based, social media campaign. The company thought it had made a sure bet when Gabriel invested in what promised to be one of the largest gold-mining operations in Europe located in the remote, mountainous Transylvania region of Romania.*

The site Gabriel settled on is near the village of Rosia Montana, or Red Mountain, whose name derives from the local rivers and streams turned into slurries of reddish-brown mud from centuries of careless mining that began under the Roman emperor Trajan. The Alburnus Maior mine, an archaeological site, still displays the chisel marks of slaves and the remains of wooden wheels used to pump out water.[22]

Rosia Montana today is a backwoods village in which Gabriel saw a golden opportunity to do well by doing good. The old state-run enterprise under the Communist government had left Rosia Montana hideously polluted, laden with heavy metals, including arsenic. So Gabriel promised the Romanian government it would take responsibility for this historic pollution by investing an estimated 35 million Euros to clean up the area.[23]

Though gold had been mined there from the Caesars to Ceaușescu, the gold never bothered to stay. Local unemployment is 80 percent.[24] Due to the area's pollution, a frigid climate, and forest-covered mountains, only potatoes grow well in the rocky soil between Rosia Montana's mountains. Half of the town's ramshackle dwellings have no running water. Two-thirds have outhouses.[25]

With vast deposits of gold to exploit, Gabriel came in with an offer it considered more than generous. To get to the land, it needed to clear away many houses. So it offered locals the once-in-a-lifetime chance to sell their homes at above-market rates, and relocate them to middle-class housing with all the modern amenities. People lined up to sell. By

* Disclosure: One of the authors provided about six hours of consultation for Gabriel Resources in 2007.

2007, 70 percent had sold and 98 percent of residents had their property surveyed.[26]

As envisioned by Gabriel, the project ultimately promised to infuse at least $4 billion into the Romanian economy and create 2,300 direct jobs during the construction phase of the mine, 800 of them high-wage jobs over the almost twenty-year-life of the project, leading to an indirect contribution of 3,000 jobs in the area.[27]

Gabriel also planned to provide the historic restoration that the government could not afford. As a show of good faith, it provided $10 million to fund a hundred-person team led by the best research archaeologists. It worked with the Romanian National History Museum to coordinate with leading experts. And it promised to restore the small historic center of Rosia Montana.[28]

Finally, the company promised that its use of cyanide—a necessary evil in most gold extraction—would be at levels below the rigorous standards of the European Union. This was a vital assurance. In 2000, an Australian-Romanian company reportedly allowed cyanide-laced water to flow out of a tailings dam into the Danube, destroying 1,200 metric tons of fish.[29]

Gabriel also developed a plan for the end of the project to restore the landscape to pristine condition, a state that this land hasn't known for many generations.

Gabriel set out its plans for the economic, environmental, and cultural rehabilitation of Rosia Montana and waited for the applause. The sound it heard instead was that of rocks hitting the windows.

Beginning in 2002, the Internet began to buzz with accusations and opposition from foreign environmentalists. Foremost among them was Stephanie Danielle Roth, a Swiss-French activist.[30] "Imagine yourself living in a small town surrounded by small farms," Roth told an adoring audience in San Francisco as she accepted the $150,000 Goldman Environmental Prize in 2005 for her work opposing Rosia Montana, in a speech now posted online. "Then one day a foreign mining company comes to your doorstep and tells you that you have to leave your home because it will be bulldozed over to make way for a commercial mine. And with it your neighborhood, where your best friends live . . . it will all be gone."[31]

When critical material began to spread throughout the web, Gabriel was puzzled. Most people were lining up to sell their shacks and live in modern housing.

Roth was also quoted as saying that foreign mining companies like Gabriel are "modern-day vampires; who in the name of progress aim to bleed Rosia Montana to death. Their lust for gold has already given rise to flagrant and crying injustices."[32]

Much was also made of the fact that Gabriel intended to use cyanide. Again, Gabriel was puzzled. The CEO, Alan Hill, claimed that more than four hundred other mines around the world use cyanide safely.[33] Gabriel said it would be setting a new standard in its use. Why were they being singled out?

Gabriel had many other questions. What about the pollution that no one else can afford to clean up? What about the archaeological artifacts no one else could afford to preserve?

What about the poor, desperate people of this hardscrabble region?

They would be fine, the project's opponents said. "It is part of the charm of Rosia Montana and this lifestyle," said Belgian environmentalist Françoise Heidebroek. "You know, people will use their horse and cart instead of using a car. They are proud to have a horse."[34]

It wasn't long before the campaign went viral, with Vanessa Redgrave and other celebrities from Los Angeles to London chiming in.[35]

With social media organizing activists and spreading every speech, quote, and protest online, the effect was to panic politicians in the Romanian capital of Bucharest against Gabriel. The campaign against the Rosia Montana mine accelerated, with a bewildering array of NGOs competing to top each other on the Internet with charges, some of them wild, even xenophobic. As the exacting environmental impact process for the project was under way, many Romanian politicians—who were originally ecstatic to have had such attention aimed at one of their poorest regions—began to talk of driving a stake through the heart of this foreign vampire.

Gabriel's executives were staggered because the attacks made little sense. This is not to say that the project was entirely immune to criticism: For example, the project included an open-pit mine, never something to put in a travel brochure. Still, to many observers the charges inverted any reasonable concern for the community and its environment. And the attacks appeared to be highly coordinated, including a network of new NGOs that seemed to enjoy lavish funding for what became a social media crusade.

The result was a win for the opponents, with the suspension of the environmental review process in 2007. Gabriel's stock plunged to a fifth of its former value.[36] The whole project and future of Rosia Montana was in danger.

In September 2007, then-CEO Alan Hill asked why the project was faced "with a persistent disinformation campaign that paints" the Rosia Montana project as a disaster for Romania? He wanted to know who was behind this opposition.[37]

Many of the NGOs were secretive about the sources of their funding. But there were hints. Hill claimed that in 2007 the local NGO, Alburnus Maior, which had indeed been set up by locals, had a website that was not registered in Romania. It was reportedly registered out of Budapest by a Hungarian NGO with ties to the Soros Foundation.[38]

Soon everywhere Gabriel looked, it saw connections to entities funded by George Soros, the Hungarian-American who had made a vast fortune in commodity and currency deals. Hill said he found that Alburnus Maior had the support of at least seventeen non-Romanian sources of support. He said that many of the NGO lawsuits designed to slow down the project were filed by lawyers from a center that also received funds from the Soros Foundation. When local anger began to grow at Alburnus because of alleged misrepresentations, the NGO turned to—where else?—the Soros Foundation to open an information center.[39]

While Soros-funded entities were allegedly exerting enormous pressure to slow down the political and regulatory approval of the Rosia Montana gold mine, the New York–based Soros Fund Management disclosed that it had substantial holdings in Freeport-McMoRan Copper & Gold, AngloGold Ashanti, Barrick Gold, and Newmont Mining, as well as Gammon Gold, Goldcorp, Imagold, Kinross, Northern Orion Resources, and NovaGold.[40]

Hill responded to the attacks with an angry speech in September 2007 that, if true, exposed the deeper motives behind what he claimed to be NGO and online proxy assaults.

"Mr. Soros, founder and funder of the Soros Foundation Romania and the Open Society network of NGOs, is not against mining," Hill said. "How could he be? He's made millions and millions investing [in] mining companies. He has made millions in a company that has moved a village and church to exploit a mine. He has made tens of millions investing in gold-mining companies that use cyanide . . . Yet Mr. Soros opposes our gold mine in Rosia Montana."[41]

Some cynics speculated George Soros funded an NGO-social media campaign against Gabriel's proposed gold-mining operation for the same reason that the fictional Auric Goldfinger wanted to detonate an atom bomb in Fort Knox—to make the value of his holdings soar. But others point out that the Soros gold investments, though large by most standards, are but a fraction of his holdings.

To skeptics, however, the spectacle of environmentalists mounting a social media campaign against a gold mine with money provided to them by a large investor in gold mines does at the very least bring to mind an old term from the ideological wars of the last century—the "useful idiot."

Gabriel pointed to another possible motivation: Hungarian nationalism. Gabriel accused its opposition of using environmental front groups to advance a secret agenda of irredentist claims over national borders. As proof, it circulated photos of protesters' signs that referred not to Rosia Montana, but to Verespatak—the Hungarian name for that area. Others, Gabriel noted, have gone to Rosia Montana to shout, "Keep Hungary's gold for Hungary!"[42]

Whatever the motivation of the project's opponents, or of George Soros—if indeed he was personally involved—it could well be something he regards as noble—Gabriel's project would not have excited as much social media opposition had it not been for the largesse of NGOs and foundations supported by the billionaire.

Soros is justly celebrated as a philanthropist who has done much good in the world. In the case of Rosia Montana, however, questions about undisclosed motives remain for claims made by environmental organizations his foundation funds.

> Environmental concern, empowered by social media, may be sincere but it can also be a cloak for other agendas.

Access to the Proxy

The U.S. Securities and Exchange Commission (SEC) is setting rules to bring more openness and access to proxy rules. This rite of spring requires shareholders to nominate and elect candidates for public company boards at annual meetings. The widening access to corporate proxies is a move many hail as a victory for shareholder democracy. No doubt, if it survives legal challenges, some good will come of it.[43] But many executives tell us they are bracing for a fight. They believe that this rule—at this writing it faces a court test—will create a Venetian ball of masked candidates representing groups with shadow agendas.

In years past, every annual meeting had a few obvious gadflies at the microphone who could be counted on for comic relief, before being dismissed with a witticism by the CEO. The authors have advised corporate insiders to prepare for months' long, perhaps year-long political campaigns against a new and different threat—attractive, business-savvy candidates who are publicly concerned about profitability, executive compensation, or dividends, but privately interested in something else. While few violins will be played on behalf of overpaid executives, there is a lot at stake. Such "shareholder democracy" could undermine the prime social function that corporations play—producing profits that fund taxes, salaries, and pensions.

In fact, many of these proxy candidates will be Trojan horses whose secret goal will be to open companies to unionization or to control by environmental or social organizers who could care less about shareholder value. If the rule is enacted, no matter how well they run their business, corporations will be forced to mount demonstrably different and difficult countercampaigns to fend off a range of well-funded players with ideological concerns, not business concerns. They will be besieged by institutional investors with grudges, union pension funds with political agendas, as well as powerful and perhaps extreme special interest groups.

Of course, the discussion will be about say on pay or global warming disclosure or sustainability reporting. The underlying substance—and the critical change in corporate governance—is about proxy groups placing people on boards who answer to constituents, not investors.

"Shareholder democracy" means the waters of Washington's Potomac River will mingle with New York's Hudson, making for turbulent sailing.

Takeaway—Do Your Own NGO CSI

Over time, the job of exposing front organizations and their real motives will likely become more difficult. Why? Because social media is going to spontaneously generate new organizations across the ideological spectrum; and, they will not be brick-and-mortar concerns that report their income on Form 990. They will be loose social media coalitions that may be genuine advocates one day and somebody's proxy the next.

For now, however, there are about a hundred major brick-and-mortar think tanks in America, not to mention legions of coalitions and associations, some of which will be willing to act as front groups. Starting a new one is largely a matter of a little legal paperwork.

When you are the digital victim of such a proxy attack, how can you identify their sponsors? How can you X-ray their motives?

Start with Cicero, who made famous the great question "Cui bono?" Who benefits?

Then ask: Who supports? It can be difficult to unravel support for front groups, even if you have the resources of a large organization at your disposal. Left-wing investigative hit pieces on corporations from The Huffington Post, or cancer-scare broadsides by the National Resources Defense Council could credibly be said to be sponsored by liberal foundations. On the other side of the ideological spectrum, proxy attacks by empty-shell "family" and "religious" conservative organizations of the sort evident in the Abramoff scandals have not gone away either.

Since many cutout organizations fall on the ideological left or right, you can use the resources of liberal and conservative muckrakers to expose proxy attackers from the other side.

- On the left, the Center for Media and Democracy's Source-Watch and PR Watch offers a "how to research front groups" web page that leads you to the various databases that can reveal the links, membership, and funding sources of conservative front groups.[44]
- On the right, former left-wing activist turned conservative David Horowitz runs DiscoverTheNetworks.org, which has detailed information on left-of-center groups, their funding, activities, and history. Another good source from the right is ActivistCash.com.

In most cases, you can also use public sources to find documentation from the national and state/provincial tax authority that leads back to at least a middleman. If that fails, you can put together clues—an IP address, the country location of websites, the affiliations of board members—and peel that back, from one front organization to another, to reveal the ultimate sponsor.

You can then challenge your attacker to match your transparency. Gabriel is a case in point. Armed with knowledge of their opponent, the CEO was able to issue a challenge: "Play by the same rules we do. Tell us the truth about why you oppose our project—because it cannot be based on the reasons you state publicly. Tell us who funds you. Do not demand transparency of everyone else—and operate from secrecy yourselves. And why won't you meet with us to debate the issue in public in a fair and transparent way? What do you have to hide?"[45]

Finally, once you know whom you are facing, expose the opposition. Gabriel asked a Northern Ireland journalist, Phelim McAleer, who had covered Eastern Europe for *The Financial Times* to write a brochure. McAleer replied that as a journalist he didn't do that kind of work. But he did say that he would take Gabriel's money to produce a documentary with his wife, Ann McElhinney, with the proviso that Gabriel would have no editorial control whatsoever.

If the story turned out to make the company look bad, so be it. With nowhere else to turn, Gabriel took a risk and gave McAleer the money, with no strings attached. McAleer also raised money from nonprofit foundations.[46]

The result was a critically acclaimed film, *Mine Your Own Business,* that demolished the claims of NGOs about local support with man-on-the-street interviews of Rosia Montana residents. One young man told McAleer that "without jobs, we would be dead here." A local doctor told him, "People from Rosia Montana don't need foreign advocates. We are smart enough to take our own fate in our hands." When McAleer relayed the notion promoted by NGOs that local residents were happier riding horses, the residents of Rosia Montana stared back, slack-jawed with incredulity.

In short, Gabriel's challenge and *Mine Your Own Business* began to change the uncritical nature of media reporting. The pushback had an even bigger impact in the blogosphere. As a result, as of early 2011,

Gabriel's project appears to be back on track, with renewed enthusiasm by Romanian leaders.

> When faced with a disingenuous attacker, unmask their motive and put them in the spotlight of transparency.

8 :// The Sixth Sword

Truth Remix

> All photographs are accurate. None of them is the truth.
>
> **—Richard Avedon**

TRUTH REMIX OCCURS when a fact about a target—often a mistake, shortcoming, or outright sin—has been exaggerated, distorted, and pulled into a direction that makes truth the basis of untruth. A new kind of truth emerges out of this remix—a gray truth that cannot be accepted or dismissed.

Therefore, truth remix.

Truth remix exists because some lies require a pedestal of truth to perch upon. "Man," the Huey Longish character in Robert Penn Warren's classic *All the King's Men* famously observed, "is conceived in sin and born in corruption and he passeth from the stink of the didie to the stench of the shroud. There is always something."

The problem with that something is that increasingly Google or some other search engine knows about it and promises never to forget it. Google's Eric Schmidt, later moved from CEO to executive chairman, famously observed that, "If you have something that you don't want anyone to know, maybe you shouldn't be doing it in the first place."[1]

The memory of the Internet ensures that digital assassins have no lack of material. Witness the AutoAdmit case. In addition to the base slander and juvenile sex talk, someone posted an old *Washington Post* article about the father of one of the targeted women, a World Bank official who had reportedly written forged checks to buy her a Thoroughbred horse when she was ten years old.[2]

The Internet's retention of any facts—especially negative ones—enables remixing of the truth, a slander that has some basis in reality. The loss of context that occurs when a negative fact is indiscriminately mixed in with the good—truth remix—is a tactic that occurs in Yelp reviews, in sexual harassment accusations, and in the premature release of information about technology products.

> It is no longer good enough to be truthful just in the eyes of God.
> You now have to be acceptable in the eye of Google.

Truth remix is helped along by the arbitrary and often inaccurate nature of search engine results pages, biased aggregator websites, and our own viral rants. Efforts at "social forgetting" and name-changing will always be defeated by technology and the human will to remember the worst about people. The result can be falsehood—polluting politics, distorting history, and perhaps inciting violent philippics that instigate real violence.

Stepping on the Dog

By April 2011, 50 million people a month were accessing Yelp's 17 million reviews of small businesses—restaurants and cafés, beauty shops and spas, veterinary clinics, dentists and doctors—all written by an army of volunteer contributors.[3] These reviews by people identified by their Yelp account profiles—"Molly T, Manhattan," and "Kevin C., New York"—give 83 percent of the businesses rated on Yelp three-star ratings or higher on its five-star scale.[4]

Simply put, Yelp is a social network that aggregates reviews of local business with search functions. If you are visiting San Francisco and looking for a French bistro near Nob Hill, Yelp will find it for you, tell you all about the place, and likely give you a few images. In almost all cases for businesses that are widely reviewed, the judgment that emerges from reading a wide sample of reviews gives a reliable portrait of their service.

To achieve this, Yelp necessarily relies on the trustworthiness of reviewers and the wisdom of crowds. For owners of small businesses, however, Yelp dishes out the good with the bad. The price of a three-star rating and glowing comments is the exposure to occasional snarky reviews.

For example, one Washington, D.C., dentist reports that a bad review came from a patient who claimed to have been given an unnecessary root canal at great cost and pain. When the dentist checked Yelp, she found that this same person had also posted many negative comments about dozens of other businesses.[5]

In response to such serial complainers, Yelp has instituted algorithms to screen out "suspicious" reviews, presumably those from competitors or the permanently and profanely disgruntled.[6] For some businesses, however, this is not enough. It is for that reason that 2010 was the year that made Yelp . . . yelp.

A class-action lawsuit centered around a Long Beach, California, veterinary clinic alleged that Yelp demanded the plaintiff pony up cash for Yelp ads to remove negative posts.[7] A pseudonymous comment on the message board of TechCrunch.com by one small business owner, johnny in baltimore, is typical of small businesses' worst suspicions that quitting an ad campaign on Yelp will automatically result in a rash of bad reviews: "The negative reviews didn't even make any sense. For example, one review said that 'the pool sucked.' Funny. Our gym doesn't have a pool."

According to the post, a Yelp representative contacted the gym owner "and said very cryptically if we ran an ad campaign they could talk to the 'person in charge of the algorithm' and see if the positive reviews could be spotlighted a little more. Honestly, I thought I was talking to a Tony Soprano in training."[8]

Yelp defenders say that the extortion charge is a misunderstanding. Many small businesses first notice bad reviews only after hearing from a Yelp representative selling ads, conflating the pitch with the review process. To improve the process, Yelp developed a category of "Elite" reviewers who provide their photos and real names, who are affirmed that the Yelp community trusts their "personal pizazz" and "Yelptitude."[9] Yelp now buries low-scoring reviews that get flagged by its "quality" algorithm. Since 2009, Yelp has allowed businesses to respond to negative reviews.[10]

> Review sites will always leave small business in fear that one bad interaction—a sandwich with too little cheese, a salesperson with a bad day, an off-color dye job—will overshadow years of great customer service and dedication.

Hurd on the Street

Charges of sexual harassment are breeding grounds for truth remix because they cover a multitude of sins, from the venal to the mortal. At its worst, many consider sexual harassment borderline rape, as it was in the Minnesota Iron Range mine portrayed in the movie *North Country*. At its crassest, it is like the nineties chief executive of a Fortune 500 company who was forced out of his job for his alleged unwanted nibbling of female employees' ears, his patting of their butts, and his atrocious habit of licking his fingers and inserting them in women's ears.[11]

The term might also, however, encompass misdemeanors, an off-color joke, or a thoughtless comment. More often than not, charges of sexual harassment leave us with some distasteful details but no real knowledge of what actually happened, as with Anita Hill, Clarence Thomas, and the misused Coke can, or Jenn Sterger, Bret Favre, and the sexting photo. Those Coke cans and digital photos will always haunt, fairly or not.

Consider the case of Mark V. Hurd, former CEO of Hewlett-Packard, a low-key but driven executive, who rises without an alarm clock every morning in Silicon Valley at 4:45 A.M. to get a jump on the East Coast.[12] He was brought in by the board to bring values and focus to HP after perceived strategic missteps under Carly Fiorina, and the pretexting scandal that forced Patricia Dunn to face down multiple felony charges.

Fix the company he did. Under Hurd's steady management, HP elbowed Dell out of PC leadership and generated revenues that passed those of IBM in 2008.[13] Just as HP investors were settling down to what they hoped was a return to normalcy, Hurd was fired in August 2010.

Facts began to emerge from the firing like the dots in a pointillist image. But the dots never amounted to a coherent portrait. Though digital technology was secondary in the reporting of this case, it clearly demonstrates the kind of mixed truth that is coming to the fore in our Internet age.

Hurd had been accused of sexual harassment by an HP marketing consultant and sometime actress named Jodie Fisher (*Intimate Obsession* and *Body of Influence 2*). Fisher hired Gloria Allred, the country's foremost klieg light litigator. There had been a personal settlement between Hurd and Fisher, but for what it is not exactly clear.[14]

When the HP board investigated, it reportedly found little evidence that sexual harassment had occurred. Fisher herself had publicly affirmed that she never had an "affair or intimate sexual relationship" with the married Hurd. In fact, she said, "I was surprised and saddened that Mark lost his job over this."[15]

There were meal, travel, and other receipts in the thousands of dollars over two years, which the board judged to be personal items improperly expensed.[16] But these expenses seemed to be related to CEO summits with top customers in which Fisher seemed to have acted as a corporate Vanna White.

Oracle chief Larry Ellison, a passionate defender of Hurd, told *The New York Times,* "The HP board just made the worst personnel decision since the idiots on the Apple board fired Steve Jobs many years ago."[17] The HP board acted on advice about disclosure from Washington-based APCO, a PR company that *The New York Times* reported "does not have a particularly strong reputation for crisis management or technology expertise."[18]

So one of the best CEOs in the country was fired for spending money on retreats for elite customers and a corporate hostess, against whom Hurd's own board believes that no sexual harassment occurred? "There is a missing piece here because it doesn't make sense," Shane Greenstein, a professor at Northwestern University's Kellogg School of Management, told a reporter.[19]

Next, to the amusement and consternation of Silicon Valley, Hurd accepted Ellison's offer to become president of Oracle, although he did have to relinquish $14 million in HP stock in response to what Ellison called a "vindictive" lawsuit by HP over trade secrets.[20]

Clearly something happened for the board to fire Hurd. But what was it?

In the absence of information, rumor will fill the void with the most salacious details, especially in cases of sexual harassment. New facts are remixed in everyone's imagination.

Rumors in Motion

When an Apple engineer left the prototype of the next generation iPhone 4 by a bar stool in the Gourmet Haus Staudt in Redwood City, California, a patron took it home, realized what it was, and sold it to Gizmodo .com for $5,000.[21] The result was the reporting, months in advance, of the characteristics of a prototype that was far from being ready for public release. The mistake also blew Apple's chance to reap the benefit of shaping the release of its information, worth millions of marketing dollars.

More deliberate leaks—those not involving beer—occur all the time for technology companies. When it is time to unveil a new consumer technology product, companies strive for the big reveal. With a vast colony of tech bloggers vying for a scoop and no lack of insiders willing to leak details, the big reveal is more often the long—and inaccurate—tease.

Witness the trouble Research In Motion has had in unveiling new permutations of its BlackBerry. Another site for premature releases months in advance through "unofficial sources" was Engadget, which sparked criticism of the device's perceived shortcomings in one new detail or another, without the context of the overall device. Cranky bloggers pick apart every new function and stylistic detail.

Or consider the Boy Genius Report. Founded in 2006 by a high school dropout, BGR managed to report on the BlackBerry Storm 2 months before RIM officially announced it.[22] BGR has provided lengthy reviews chock-full of technical minutiae of the second-generation Amazon Kindle, Palm Pre, and Nokia products before anyone else, as well as screen shots of Google's Android 2.0 while it was still in development. Given BGR's prominence, some of these leaks are no doubt authorized teases. Many are not, coming from inside tipsters who release details about mobile devices—like the changing interface of the Storm—before the company is ready to debut the product or make an announcement.

In this way, prematurely released facts about the product get remixed by the exaggeration of sour critics.[23]

Secret snapshots of a new product while still developing in the technological womb often mislead the media, investors, and customers.

Google Groping

Not all mixed truth is created as an intentional smear. Sometimes it is a matter of how the Internet perceives you. Eric Schmidt predicted that the search engine will know "roughly who you are, roughly what you

care about, roughly who your friends are."[24] This will likely be true someday, but is not true now.

One problem with any search engine is that its algorithmic mind,
lacking common sense and a proper respect for the nuances of human
behavior, often assembles raw facts to automatically remix the truth.
For example, television writer Seth Freeman received a Gmail from someone about "Holocaust deniers," only to later get an ad pitch for a holis-
tic dentist.[25]

When journalist Jessica Rose Bennett, twenty-nine, performed an
online search for herself for *Newsweek,* she found that her profile would
tell a prospective employer that she "spends 30 hours a week on social-
networking sites—while at work. She is an excessive drinker, a drug
user, and sexually promiscuous. She swears a lot, and spends way beyond her means shopping online." The negatives here come not from
her lifestyle, but from her reporting projects on drugs, polyamory, and
social networking. "The irony, of course, is that if this were a real job
search, none of this would matter—I'd have already lost the job," Bennett writes.[26]

Of course Bennett is a bold journalist who deliberately traffics in
outré topics. The skewed view of the Internet could be a big problem for
someone else. Seventy-five percent of recruiters and human-resource
professionals responded to a Microsoft-sponsored poll that the companies they serve require them to research their candidates online.[27]

Consider how search affected Stacy Snyder, a twenty-five-year-old in
Lancaster, Pennsylvania, when she was on the verge of graduating from
the Millersville University School of Education. College administrators
had come across a photo of her from a MySpace page wearing a pirate
hat with a drink in her hand. The caption under her photo, "Drunken
Pirate," was enough for the school to deny her a teaching degree, though
she was awarded an English degree. Snyder sued but lost. The courts
found Snyder, as an apprentice teacher who did unpaid classroom work,
fell under more stringent employment regulations. So she lost her ability
to become a teacher.[28]

And "drunken pirate" is the really tame stuff. So much more negative information is available on social media—especially that posted by
youth in their wilder moments—that Schmidt mused that it might
make sense to allow young people to change their identity.[29]

Harvard's Viktor Mayer-Schönberger argues exactly for this—a deliberate sunsetting of information in his intriguing 2009 book, *Delete: The Virtue of Forgetting in the Digital Age.* Most information, Mayer-Schönberger points out, is not timeless, but rooted to a certain time, place, and situation, like Stacy Snyder's costume party.

What some call social forgetting is a fine idea. But is it realistic to imagine that someone won't find a way to get around a data expiration date? Who is going to sunset the Wayback Machine? And how?

Eric Schmidt's suggestion that young people should be allowed to change their identity to escape the misadventures of their youth might not be technically feasible. (Although Spain's data Protection Agency is attempting to wipe out negative links on at least ninety people in an effort to enforce a "right to be forgotten.")[30] As facial recognition software develops, won't any effort at identity change be easily defeated for any post with a picture in it?

It is easy to imagine that the Internet, though not an organism and not sentient, acts as if it had a malevolent will of its own. The fact is, it is humans who bring all the will to do harm. Someone will always use technology to keep whatever can be kept. It is hard to imagine any law or technology that could make the Internet forget.

Meanwhile, we are set up to pay a price for e-mails or posts that could last a lifetime. There have been many examples of e-mails exploding months or years later, not unlike the Wall Street analysts who flogged financial products while privately writing about them in company e-mails as pigs with expensive lipstick.

Consider what may result from the blog of one prominent technical writer who created a stir when she reported that she was sexually assaulted at an Atlanta tech conference that began in a crowded room. She wrote of a wild evening of beer pong and networking laced with flirting. "I lay across the bed, sat on laps, generally tried to squish in to any available space and get time to talk to all the fabulous people thronging the place."[31]

When the party moved to an Irish pub, the blogger reports she went to the bathroom, where a young engineer tried to kiss and fondle her. She just didn't just tell the conference administrators and the Atlanta police and warn her friends. She did something that gave pause to many in her online community. She named the guy in her post.

"The real issue is that we have a baseless allegation in a very public place," writes one Reddit commenter. "And once that gun is fired, there's no pulling the bullet back."[32] The young man named in the blog has not been convicted of a crime, and indeed he may have done nothing wrong, but he may pay a subtle price for the allegation until he is an old man.

> Everyone using the Internet needs to think and pause before writing something just because it is "true." And think and pause again before pressing the send button.

Lightning and Lightning Bugs

On a winter's evening in 1912, boys from a local military academy in Bloomington, Illinois, put on a drill to entertain a party of friends in the home of a prominent family. They found an old repeating rifle, took out—they thought—all of the cartridges, and began to show how they could march and twirl the weapon. One twelve-year-old boy was showing off to an older girl, sixteen-year-old Ruth Merwin, when the gun went off, shooting her straight through the forehead.

The boy, Adlai Stevenson, grandson of a vice president, later to run for president himself, was described by *The New York Times* as "overcome with grief."[33] Had Stevenson been a political candidate in the twenty-first century, he would have been expected to repeatedly dissect the tragedy in media interviews and in broadcast. Though Stevenson did not discuss the incident as governor of Illinois and two-time presidential candidate, his biographers believe that it shaped his life—that from that moment on, Stevenson felt that he had an obligation "to live for two." So it came as news to the American people when leaflets began to appear in the 1952 presidential election informing the voters about the incident—and telling them that the Democratic nominee had killed the girl "in a jealous rage."[34]

A digital remixing of the truth was used in the 2010 midterm elections, when Representative Alan Grayson released an ad on TV and YouTube depicting his Republican opponent, state senator and former Florida House speaker Daniel Webster, as a religious fanatic whose Christian views made him "*Taliban* Dan." The ad devastatingly showed a video of Webster saying—four times—that the Bible orders wives to submit to their husbands.

When the independent FactCheck.org looked at the original video, however, it reported that he had been edited to sound as if he were saying the exact opposite of what he was saying: "In fact, Webster was cautioning husbands to avoid taking that passage as their own," and that husbands should *not* pick Bible verses that conveniently allow them to dominate their wives.[35]

In both cases, there was a degree of truth. It is a literal fact that Adlai Stevenson killed a girl. It is also a fact that Daniel Webster is the kind of Bible Belt politician prone to say things that make more secular voters squirm.

In both instances, these existing facts were used as platforms to sell a lie.

> Remixing the truth is a growing feature of our digital age, in which facts are often conditional, partial, and in varying shades of gray.

Deeper Capture, Wider Apertures

For many users, the pitiless gaze of a search engine is a catalog of human flaws. Some 46 percent of men reported that they would be embarrassed if someone saw their browsing history. And someone may well see it. A 2010 study by Stanford and Carnegie Mellon Universities finds that the privacy mode of the four major browsers is no absolute defense against having one's searches exposed from within the house or from without.[36]

Increasing exposure to embarrassment is a technological development that has been scaling up for more than a century. In 1890, jurists Louis Brandeis and Samuel Warren worried that "instantaneous photographs and newspaper enterprise have invaded the sacred precincts of private and domestic life; and numerous mechanical devices threaten to make good the prediction that 'what is whispered in the closet shall be proclaimed from the house-tops.'"[37]

The world moved on. Media that was once so alarming now seems quaint. In the twenty-first century, facial recognition software is advancing toward a state in which users will be able to snap a cell phone image of someone they pass by on the street, subject the image to a Google search, and receive all photos of that person on the Web.

The digital world is also acquiring hardware and extensions to actually follow us around. Personal drones are coming to market, small hovering UAVs that can carry onboard cameras and thermal imaging technology to track and record your every move. "If the Israelis can use them to find terrorists, certainly a husband is going to be able to track a wife who goes out at eleven o'clock at night and follow her," a New York divorce lawyer told a journalist.[38]

A similar compromise of privacy occurred when a Google Street View camera caught any number of men coming out of porn shops—not to mention the inexplicable shot of a naked German man rising out of the trunk of his Mercedes.

> Technology captures and immortalizes embarrassing facts, so truths are often remixed to look far worse.

Candid Camera Blackmail

A thirty-one-year-old man in Santa Ana, California, was arrested in 2010 for hacking into the computers of about 230 people, 44 of them minors. He had managed the difficult task of secretly viewing girls and women through their web cameras. The case affidavit states that he also offered audio files of in-demand songs on peer-to-peer networks that contained malware.

He hacked into the women's e-mail accounts in order to impersonate their boyfriends. He pleaded for the victims to send erotic pictures for his personal enjoyment. Once he was armed with videos of girls and young women performing sexually explicit acts, his Evil Clone impersonation of the boyfriends contacted them with an alias to demand more explicit videos, or else he would release the ones he had.[39] In this way, one questionable act—downloading free songs—led to a chain of ever more embarrassing exposures. These girls found themselves in a gray zone, compromised and therefore compromisable.

In the 2010 Nevada Senate race, the Tea Party candidate was upended when she tried make an insider Washington deal with a marginal candidate ("whatever juice I have, you have as well") who recorded their thirty-eight-minute conversation. It wound up in the hands of a journalist and then online.[40]

> The most common exposure to blackmail is from your own computer, or perhaps the person you are confiding in who has set an iPhone or other PDA to record.

True Lies

All across the Internet, phantom websites wink in and out of existence, like so many Cheshire cats. They often aggregate legitimate news—but selectively, in a way that is always negative to their targets.

Corporations often have surrogates create anonymous websites that aggregate real news stories on an issue of interest that, while fairly done by reputable sources, offer only one slant on a competitive or regulatory issue. The cumulative effect is to overwhelm the visitor with the sense that there is only one side to the case.

The vendetta website of HKLaw Investigation is an exemplar of what appears to be a high-minded investigative news site. It is complete with an inset picture of Sherlock Holmes in silhouette, when in fact it is the get-even tactic of a disgruntled insider or competitor who anonymously aggregates mixed-truth dirty laundry of a global law firm, Holland & Knight, its alleged internal disputes, sexual harassment claims, and personal gossip.[41]

Or take jewwatch.com. Beneath its ugly overlay of anti-Semitic agitprop, this site does the same thing in a much more disturbing way—aggregating many legitimate news stories in which the perpetrators just happen to be Jewish or Israeli citizens.

> The aggregation of a slanted selection of news creates an effective calumny. Selection bias, taken to the extreme, can enlist truth into a monstrous gray truth smear.

Viral Rants

Remixing the truth can be most damaging when you are captured in a moment of anger. When actress Lily Tomlin was filming *I ♥ Huckabees,* she got into several fights with her director, David O. Russell. During a moment of frustration over a scene, Tomlin expressed her exasperation over last-minute script changes. "I'm not as brilliant as you," she told Russell with unmistakable sarcasm. "I can't keep up with you."

The argument escalated, with Russell letting loose foul epithets, raking papers off a desk and kicking them. "Yeah, fuck yourself!" he screams.

"Why don't you fuck your whole movie," Tomlin says in a memorable retort. "Why don't you fuck your whole movie because that's what you're doing."

There was, of course, a video camera catching the whole scene, a scene posted by someone to become a TubeBomb for the amusement and mirth of millions.

The digital capturing of celebrities at their worst is now as common as the regularly televised car chases down the LA Freeway. The most devastating example, of course, is Mel Gibson's meltdown on the phone with the mother of his child, Oksana Grigorieva. Before that, there was Christian Bale's rant against a crew member who stepped into his scene, a rant later turned into a rhythmic song by DJ RevoLucian, with a splice-in of Barbra Streisand's voice on stage saying "Shut the fuck up— shut up if you can't take a joke" as a refrain. And of course before that was Alec Baldwin and his voice mail tirade at his daughter.

In most cases, it is not just the vehemence of the celebrities' anger, but the length of their diatribes that takes one aback. What is not captured on tape is the context—what pushed their button, who else was responsible, what they are like the rest of the time.

In the case of Christian Bale, he is now endlessly TubeBombed with images from *American Psycho* of his crazed, blood-splattered face to accompany his tirade. Alec Baldwin's screaming at his daughter is accompanied on one popular post with studio photos of him holding a gun, a baseball, and a blood-splattered axe.

It is likely that those who feast on these images would not recognize themselves if their worst moments were replayed with disturbing images. What most people don't realize is that the devices that captured Lily Tomlin, Mel Gibson, Christian Bale, and Alec Baldwin, not to mention South Korea's dog-shit girl, can mix the truth about you.

> Technology instantly immortalizes your worst moment into a tombstone epitaph.

Defining the Other Guy Down

Truth remix, more than any other of the seven swords of digital assassination, is the weapon of choice in politics. Truth remix does not include outright inventions, like the story that circulated to newspapers in the election of 1876 that Rutherford B. Hayes had shot his mother while insane from a night of drinking.[42] It does not include outright forgeries like the Morey letter, a phony missive leaked to the press that roiled the 1880 election by purporting to show that James A. Garfield secretly conspired to swell corporate profits by undercutting American workers with poorly paid Chinese immigrants.[43]

It does include the bigamy charge leveled against President Andrew Jackson, one so hurtful that it cut a man called Old Hickory to the core. Jackson's wife, Rachel, had been previously married to a violent man who promised to obtain a divorce but did not. This left the Jacksons to wander ignorantly, but temporarily, into a state of bigamy—a paperwork blunder the Jacksons fixed as soon as they could (even to the point of remarrying).

Enemies ran with this, calling Rachel a "whore" who was known for "open and notorious lewdness." One Republican paper asked if a "convicted adulteress and her paramour husband should be placed in the highest office of this free and Christian land?"[44]

For General Jackson's earlier signing of the execution warrants of six leaders of a militiamen mutiny, Republicans circulated a "Coffin Hand-bill" in the 1828 election, complete with a graphic of six coffins. When Jackson supporters learned that John Quincy Adams, as minister to the court of Czar Alexander I, had introduced his wife's servant girl to the court, they portrayed the diplomat as pimping American women to the Russian emperor.

By the late twentieth century, these tactics migrated to telephone "push polls"—phony polls that wrap smears in a facetious question about the opposition candidate. In the South Carolina 2000 Republican primary, operatives favoring George W. Bush used just such a tactic to plant the idea that rival John McCain had an illegitimate "black baby"—(the baby in question, now Bridget McCain, was a seriously ill Bangladeshi child adopted by the McCains from Mother Teresa's orphanage in Dhaka).[45]

Of all these cases, there is an element of truth to make the lie palatable. The fact of the matter is, the Jacksons were technically bigamists. Jackson had signed execution warrants. John Quincy Adams had introduced a young woman to the czar. The McCains had adopted a child of color, a remarkable act of love.

Concerning the latter, if such a fact can be turned into a weapon, almost any fact is subject to weaponization.

> In this century's second decade, the digital arena is the prime ground for this form of assassination . . . and nowhere is it used more viciously than in politics.

The Queen of Bithynia

The remixing of facts is such a constant in politics that it makes much of what we call history questionable. What do we really know for sure about, say, Julius Caesar? We know that as a young man, Caesar distinguished himself as a solider, winning the Roman equivalent of the Congressional Medal of Honor. He was also a young diplomat assigned to the court of Nicomedes IV, the Roman client king of Bithynia.

The king, recognizing something special in the young Roman, brought Caesar into his confidence and showed him the ins and outs of being a ruler, an experience that may explain the mature Caesar's appetite for kingly power. Caesar stayed so long under the king's mentorship that gossip began to spread.

So when he returned to Rome, Caesar was openly ridiculed as the "Queen of Bithynia." Years later, even after his conquest of Gaul, Caesar's soldiers, who had survived years of battle under their beloved commander, marred a triumphal procession through Rome with their ribald humor: "Home we bring our bald whoremonger; / Romans, lock your wives away! / All the bags of gold you lent him / Went his Gallic tarts to pay." It was a colorful if somewhat fair assessment.

But they also proclaimed, "Gaul was brought to shame by Caesar; / By King Nicomedes, he. / Here comes Caesar, wreathed in triumph / For his Gallic victory! / Nicomedes wears no laurels, / Though the greatest of the three."

Most modern historians believe it unlikely that Caesar shared the king's bed. Caesar himself denied the charge under oath. The problem for Caesar—and for us—is that this bit of mixed truth (mixed because the ever-promiscuous Caesar, as a young Roman, was unusually close to a foreign king) remains an indelible part of history, forever clouding the true image of the man (which was racy enough).[46]

Mixed truth permeates Roman history. Caligula and Nero, for example, were both without doubt unusually cruel and strange, even by the standards of Roman emperors. The few fragmentary histories we have of these two emperors are packed with many lurid details, however, that are probably remixed literary creations derived from later historians who had political and ideological biases.

So much of modern scholarship on ancient Rome must forever remain interpretative because we are forced to rely on source material that was poisoned by Rome's permanent atmosphere of character assassination and truth-twisting.

> How much of today's "history" is being distorted in real time by the Internet?

Verbal Violence

In modern America, the shooting of Congresswoman Gabrielle Giffords prompted endless media lectures and soul-searching about the link between caustic language and violence. In this case, there seems to be no connection between political rancor, mainstream or otherwise, to the mad inner dialogue of the Tucson gunman. Jared Lee Loughner's YouTube postings are a poignant and frightening portrayal of the disconnected logic of a sick mind. The fear, however, that personalized politics based on mixed truths can lead to violence should not be casually dismissed by anyone.

Words affect human emotions, which more often than not govern human actions. Nowhere is this social poison of casual character assassination more apparent than in Rome's late Republican era. Cicero, a Roman politician, orator, philosopher, and contemporary of Caesar, was the great litigator of his day. When standing for the prosecution, Cicero lustily employed coarse invective of the sort that thrives on the Internet today, calling his targets "swine," "filth," and "pest."

In one prosecution of a notorious defendant, Cicero said that the accused was "not only a thief, but a wholesale robber; not only an adulterer, but a ravisher of chastity; not only a sacrilegious man, but an open enemy to all sacred things and all religion; not only an assassin, but a most barbarous murderer of both citizens and allies; so that I think him the only criminal in the memory of man so atrocious, that it is even for his own good to be condemned."[47]

Cicero engaged in the orator's old parlor trick of promising not to disturb the sensibilities of his audience by telling them something is too vile, too awful, too stomach-turning for their delicate ears to hear, and then telling them anyway. "Nothing shall be said of his drunken nocturnal revels; no mention shall be made of his pimps, and dicers, and panders; his losses at play, and the licentious transactions."[48]

The man in this case was guilty of many horrendous crimes, including acts of murder. But he was also a prominent citizen well liked by many. The portrait Cicero paints is of a man so vile that it would be remarkable if his fellow citizens allowed him to walk down the street without stoning him to death. Cicero went on to employ his winning invective against the Catilinarian conspirators, many of whom wound up being frog-marched past the Roman Forum, thrown into a state dungeon, and strangled. After Caesar was assassinated, Cicero launched into a series of blistering philippics against Mark Antony.

When Antony came to power, he demanded Cicero's proscription. With all escape routes cut off, Cicero meekly submitted to execution, his orator's head and his writer's hands nailed up on display in the rostrum of the Forum—but not before Fulvia, the wife of Antony, pulled out the tongue of her husband's verbal tormentor to jab it repeatedly with a golden hairpin.

> Character assassins poison a political culture and prompt enemies to impeach, imprison, and even physically exterminate one another.

Unmixing the Facts Without Rancor

Another historical example shows us a better way. It shows how the remixing of truth can be faced down without rancor, much less violence. One of the worst gray truth attacks occurred in the election of 1884, one that sets a model for all time in responding to an embarrassing, complex charge. It all began with a sensational newspaper story:

A TERRIBLE TALE
A DARK CHAPTER IN A PUBLIC
MAN'S HISTORY

THE PITIFUL STORY OF MARIA
HALPIN AND GOVERNOR
CLEVELAND'S SON*

A child was born out of wedlock. Now ten years of age, this sturdy lad is named Oscar Folsom Cleveland. He and his mother have been supported in part by our ex-mayor, and now aspires to the White House. Astute readers may put the facts together and draw their own conclusion.[49]

The story depicted Grover Cleveland as fathering an illegitimate child, abandoning mother and child, and then conveniently hiding the poor woman in an insane asylum. Reverend George Ball, a Baptist minister and Republican Party mouthpiece, took it upon himself to spread the story across the East Coast and embellish it with depictions of Cleveland's debauchery.

The accusation of bad behavior went against what Americans thought they knew about the Democratic nominee for president. Cleveland had won a reputation as a tough reformer: first, as Erie County sheriff, who reluctantly pulled the gallows handle on two murderers, mayor of Buffalo; and then as reformist governor of New York. Up until that moment, the election of 1884 was going to be close. Any little thing could tip the margin of victory.

The story of the Cleveland baby was just such a tipping point. The article, which ran on the front page of *The Buffalo Evening Telegraph* that July, added to a portrait of Cleveland—a bachelor who enjoyed fishing and poker and was no stranger to saloons—as an amoral wastrel. It was the perfect way to undermine the case made by Democrats and their allies, Republican Mugwumps, that Cleveland was the reformer the nation needed to cleanse itself of a long Republican rule that had grown corrupt.

The Republicans made sure that a song, whose title made up the famous refrain "Ma! Ma! Where's My Pa?" was distributed by a national song company. "We do not believe that the American people will knowingly elect to the Presidency," wrote the ever-blunt Charles A. Dana of

---

* For a briskly written and colorful biography of Cleveland, see *An Honest President* by H. Paul Jeffers (New York: William Morrow, 2000).

The New York Sun, "a coarse debauchee who would bring his harlots with him to Washington and hire lodgings for them convenient to the White House."

The story left the Cleveland campaign in a panic. Grover Cleveland sent his instruction to a prominent supporter by telegram:

WHATEVER YOU DO, TELL THE TRUTH[50]

What was the truth?

In 1874, Maria Crofts Halpin had been a respectable widow, holding a position as head of the cloak department at a fashionable Buffalo dry goods store. Educated and fluent in French, Maria was tall, lively, attractive, and popular. She was also discreetly promiscuous, counting a number of suitors that included several married men, many of them friends of Cleveland, then a prominent lawyer. A flutter of fear, then, shot through a circle the city's leading men when she gave birth to a son one September day in 1874.

Halpin named Cleveland the father. Perhaps to protect the others in his circle, he stepped forward and took financial responsibility for the child, who was christened Oscar Folsom (after a friend and law partner who himself may have been a candidate for paternity) Cleveland. Suffering the stigma of being an unwed mother in late nineteenth-century America, Maria Halpin saw her tenuous place in respectable society slip away. She began to drink, neglect the boy, and show signs of mental instability.

Cleveland could have ignored the situation, buying distance from it with money. Instead, he turned to a county judge and friend to investigate. It was the judge on his own instigation who had Maria committed to an asylum run by the Sisters of Charity. Cleveland paid for the boy's commitment to the Protestant Orphan Asylum and paid his board through the judge. He helped Maria start a business in Niagara Falls. She sued to regain custody of her son and even tried to kidnap him. Thanks to Cleveland's network, the boy was adopted into a prominent family in Western New York.

Cleveland's supporters organized a legion of journalists and lawyers to nail down and publicize the facts. Foremost among them was a minister—Reverend Kinsley Twining—who neatly overturned the charges that Cleveland had abandoned Maria and the child, or that he had her sent her to an asylum as a coldhearted matter of convenience. When the facts were laid out, Twining said, it instead revealed that though the bachelor had a culpable irregularity, he had behaved in a way that was "singularly honorable." Twining proved that Maria, as she admitted to her lawyer, had never been led to believe that Cleveland would marry her.

Armed with the facts, Cleveland cultivated ministers with national reputations who could attest to his character. Cleveland turned a truth remix attack to his advantage by separating what was true, using respected third-party allies to painstakingly document those portions of the charges that were false, and deploying these allies to make sure everyone knew the difference. The result was blowback for the Republicans, exposing them as shrill benders of the truth while revealing Cleveland's essential honesty.

Cleveland later summed up his approach to the scandal in a letter to a friend as the policy of "no cringing."[51]

This is good advice today. Even when the charge is embarrassing, it pays to correct the false parts with documented evidence. Alexander Hamilton had done exactly this, but he had worked much of his defense alone with quill by candlelight. Cleveland was much more effective in recruiting friends and developing third-party support from respected people.

> This nineteenth-century example of defense by testimonials is ever more relevant today. The ease with which digital technology assembles crowds encourages like-minded people to go online, preferably on YouTube, to defend you, your brand, your company, or your product.

Takeaway—Pulling Out the Stingers

"Everyone has a break point where they take it personally," says Leo Yakutis. He cites a case he worked on in which the enemies of the head of a hedge fund tried to associate him with embezzlement. "We had to go out and counter this while someone on the other side was making sure that the bad information was being propagated to a couple of dozen websites that conspiracy theorists read, so they would remain very high in the search engine results," he says. "We had to break down those links and knock them off different pages, systematically, and also put correct information at top."[52]

If an Internet search brings up facts that add up to an erroneous portrait of you, then create positive websites, post positive items—your work with charity, your resume, a website with your blog—and then link those items together. Raise the profile of positive material to add to your reputational armor.

What should you do when truth about you is remixed? One way to address this issue comes from Snopes.com, run by the husband-and-wife team of Barbara and David Mikkelson, separates Internet fact, fiction, and urban legend on the Internet on a wide array of topics, including business. Snopes is candid when the facts cannot be nailed down and offers the visitor a color-coded range of reliability, from "true" to "false" "undetermined," and "unclassifiable veracity." One Snopes category, "multiple truth values," is especially useful in unmixing truth remix.

Ideally, Wikipedia's new Biographies of Living Persons policies should do the same for notable individuals. FactCheck.org polices the claims of politicians, and alerts visitors to sources of bad information, like viral e-mail rants.

When it comes to Yelp, businesses should not shrink from participating in the online discussion with customers. Yelp allows business owners who sign up to communicate with customers in public, apologizing for a mistake, explaining a shortcoming, or denying an unfounded comment.

Yelp also gives businesses tools to track how many view their page, add appealing photos, and announce special offers and upcoming events. As much as some businesspeople dislike Yelp, we should be grateful that it aggregates complaints and gives business a single platform on which to respond. Otherwise, businesses would have to contend with a Google soup of complaints.

The hard question about truth remix is how much to disclose. Alexander Hamilton provides the utmost example of providing excruciating detail in order to separate truth from untruth. This is utterly unlike the treatment of a ridiculous rumor in which victims, like McDonald's, avoid repeating lurid charges.

And perhaps we would all do well to set a better example, if not for Eric Schmidt, then for ourselves.

Grover Cleveland set an example when he was given a delicious chance at payback. He was presented with proof about problems in the marriage of his opponent. He purchased the evidence.

"Are all the papers here?" Cleveland asked.

Yes, he was told.

Cleveland slowly drew up a wastebasket, tore the sheets to pieces, and asked a servant to burn them in the fireplace.[53]

In truth remix, the worst details to our portraits are often added by ourselves. Whenever you speak, the person sitting across from you can easily be recording you on his PDA; whenever you send a message, the person receiving may post it in a public place.

9: // The Seventh Sword—
Clandestine Combat

In the twenty-first century it's not just about tanks and artillery.

—NATO spokesman, after cyber attack on Estonia[1]

THE KNOWLEDGE that our devices and data are insecure nags at us. Day by day we move forward, believing that there will be no adverse consequences to our exposure. Day by day, we live . . . in a fool's paradise?

We live, in fact, with the seventh sword of clandestine combat—the ease with which enemies or competitors can simply purloin secrets. "The head of one of the most profitable law firms in the country knows that his office, his house, and his mistress's apartment are all bugged," says one digital hound. "He doesn't care."

More often than not, however, even the most nonchalant victim of spying eventually discovers a breaking point.

The authors learned that the head of one national hotel chain knew that his office was bugged by another corporate interest reading his e-mail. He didn't get upset until he hired a firm to do an inventory of the intercepts and was told that his daughter's college dorm room had been bugged. Up until that time, he just said, "That's how we do business." When the competitor went after his daughter, it suddenly became very personal—and unacceptable.

He asked Leo Yakutis for protection. Yakutis is a bit of an anomaly in the IT world. With two master's degrees, one in history from the University of North Carolina at Charlotte and another in information science from the University of North Carolina at Chapel Hill, Yakutis has a combination of technical and human skills that make him popular with corporations in need of an investigator to trace a digital thread.

He often finds himself working for his clients to protect them from hackers and hacking firms paid to commit acts of corporate espionage and mayhem. "I only white-hat," he says. "I do not gray-hat. I do not black-hat. I can pass top secret with poly. That doesn't mean I don't know how the opposition works. In fact I *have* to know how the opposition works."[2]

Corporations and special interest groups resort to digital technology to undermine, blackmail, or demonize.

Tracking the Joker

In one assignment, Leo Yakutis came up against the most formidable group he has ever faced—"an intelligent group of fanatics" backed by a corporate interest that waged a wide-ranging digital war on a premier law firm in Washington, D.C. This confrontation demonstrates the lengths to which ideologically or financially driven people will go to in order to get the right information. That the firm was under assault became apparent after a senior partner sat down to type out draft legislation on a laptop to present to a U.S. senator friendly to a major client. This in itself was not unusual. Law firms routinely offer draft legislation on behalf of clients for Capitol Hill. The draft legislation was on nothing but the lawyer's laptop. "He didn't tell his wife, he didn't tell his son, he didn't tell his dog," Yakutis says. "It was only in his machine."

The day before the law partner was to present the legislation, he made a visit to the Hill on other business. A senior aide to another U.S. senator, known to be a leading opponent of the draft legislation, walked up to the law partner and asked him not to pass his draft bill on to any of his colleagues. The staffer for the opposition senator knew legislative details he could have learned of only by being informed by someone who had actually read the draft document.

"This guy [the law partner] just about strokes out on us," Yakutis says. "He doesn't understand what happened. He had a company come in and do a conventional sweep for wiretaps and bugs. Nothing. He checked the office access codes, and this guy has some nice equipment—nothing. He has months of videotape of his office to review that proved that no unauthorized person had gone into his office and taken anything. Nothing like that. That left the last vector—electronic."

When Yakutis investigated, he found that the law firm had a sophisticated firewall. As with all systems, however, it had a back door that was discovered after numerous probes by the intruders. The nature of the back door was simple. The law firm's software connected his phone and computer so voice mail messages would register in the partner's e-mail inbox. This link created a digital opening that the intruders were able to enter to place a payload on one such message. Once the payload detonated, the intruders were in the system, then had the means to take control of the partner's machine. And once in that machine, they spread malware from his laptop to other computers throughout the office.

"It allowed the opposition remote access to this guy's computer," Yakutis said. "Then they managed to go on his computer and other computers in the office and put more malware on there in order to destroy things and randomize things in an effort to make the attack look messy so that we wouldn't be able to track it back. Their hope was that there would be so much malware in the system that we wouldn't be able to see how they got in."

Once Yakutis learned the nature of the breach, he deployed sniffers to trace the traffic coming in and going out of the system. He found something even more disturbing. The intruder had not only broken into the system but had left the door wide open so that unrelated and less sophisticated hackers, "script kiddies," could embed malicious code that would propagate from machine to machine to commit random acts of digital mischief.

The intruder's strategy was akin to that of the Joker, Batman's nemesis, who often covers his tracks by throwing heaps of stolen cash into the air in order to escape through the confusion of a money-frenzied mob.

Only this Joker instigated a digital riot.

After a lot of painstaking work cleaning up the workplace, computer by computer, Yakutis was able to uncover the pathway by which the Joker was able to access the partner's laptop.

A funny thing happened in the hours Yakutis spent monitoring the digital code streaming in front of his face. An anomaly appeared, deliberate and in real time—too obvious, in fact, to be a covert effort. The

Joker had recognized that he was being watched, and he gave Yakutis a sort of digital wink. "We saw that it was somebody on a wireless network," Yakutis says. "We knew the approximate range of this network and knew that it was without amplification. And we knew that the only public wireless network around was coming from a Starbucks several stories below our office on the ground floor."

The Joker could be caught physically in the act.

Downstairs, there was only a coffeehouse on a workday in a busy downtown, a good dozen men and women standing in the coffee line or sitting on plush, overstuffed furniture, earnestly staring into laptops. All were dressed casually but had the look of well-groomed professionals.

The Joker might as well have been in a football stadium.

"So at least one of them was the perpetrator sitting downstairs three stories below in a coffeehouse laughing at us," Yakutis says. "It became obvious that this person was freakingly cheeky. He knew I was in there and he knew what I was doing, and he was having a little fun at my expense . . . I remember saying, 'Great, all right, we've got somebody with a sense of humor.'"

While the Joker hid among the coffeehouse crowd, a go-between who was paid to set up the hack was ultimately caught. He had once worked in the data center of a Fortune 500 IT company and used its equipment surreptitiously to create the platform for the intruder to use.

He was eventually exposed—not through technical means, but through his own greed and stupidity. "We found out when the hacker tried to generate more business for himself by boasting on hacker blog sites that he had gotten into this particular law firm using this methodology," Yakutis says. "We caught that. We validated it. If he hadn't had boasted, we probably wouldn't have known that last detail."

No one was arrested. There simply was not enough evidence for a prosecution. Eventually, however, enough information was compiled to confront the opposition and persuade them to call off the Joker's attacks, although the opposition intensified their efforts by other means.

For some competitors and ideological groups, hacking is a blood sport taken up with relish.

Everyone Pays

It's called "insurance.aes256."

It is a 1.4-gigabyte file large enough to hold hundreds of thousands of pages worth of information. It is protected by a 256-bit key encryption code. And perhaps by the time you have read this, the Anonymous friends of Julian Assange may have followed through on their threat to open it to the world with the push of a button.[3]

At this writing, what it contains is anybody's guess. The claim is that it is something so damaging to the United States that its leaders will back down before pursuing charges against Assange.

Insurance.aes256 may be a hoax. But the suggestion that it might be a credible threat represents a monumental change in our civilization—the ability of loosely, self-organized hackers to intimidate governments and large corporations. And yet the WikiLeaks phenomenon is only the public manifestation of the extreme vulnerability of personal, business, and governmental systems to the seventh sword of clandestine combat.

WikiLeaks' hundreds of thousands of purloined files are but a trickle compared to the Mississippi of data diverted by spies, black hats, and unscrupulous competitors. McAfee reported at the World Economic Forum that cybertheft cost people and businesses $1 trillion in 2009.[4] Organizations that suffered one or more data breaches in the United States in 2009, according to a Ponemon Institute study, lost an average of $6.75 million per incident, not including long-term litigation costs and possible penalties. Perhaps worst of all, these organizations lost on average 3.7 percent of their customer base. For pharmaceuticals, communications, and health care, the loss of customers was even worse—6 percent.[5] Heartland Payment Systems, a payment processor, disclosed what might have been the largest data breach on record in early 2009—losing at least 100 million credit and debit card records a month.[6]

Cybercrime continues to morph into ever more creative imitations of legitimate business. Long-discredited spam has become "spim," or instant messaging spam, used to trick you to clicking to a fraudulent phishing website for your personal or financial details. "Malvertising" camouflages malicious code as online ads. Now that more people are on to the legitimate-looking phisher websites, criminals have moved to "spear-phishing," e-mails with malicious payloads. The FBI reports that spear-phishing attacks are increasingly aimed at getting at corporations through their law firms and PR firms.[7]

> Criminals are not just looking for credit card numbers. They wish to do harm to reputations or commit informational blackmail.

Scraping Society

We accept an implicit bargain when we use web-based platforms. The various sites at our fingertips—our search engine, the sites we visit—offer an array of powerful services for free in exchange for the ability to track our wants and desires and report them to advertisers. For most people, this deal is acceptable, even if it does make one a little queasy, thanks to the use of pseudonymous identifiers. It allows Google and other big players to attach details about our interests and demographic information to a particular cookie, without correlating it with information that identifies us as individuals.

We have learned to delete our cookies, so companies now track computers' "fingerprints"—the unique time stamps and other settings that identify them, effectively, as you. So increasingly advertisers are following our devices, whether computers or cell phones, giving them "reputations" based on our searches, the things we buy, and matching them to our demographic information.

Even the apps in our cell phones can also follow us, telling advertisers which stores we visit in real time. In April 2011, it was revealed that Apple's iPhone and Google's Android are building massive databases on consumers' information by pinpointing cell phone locations and movements. Representative Edward Markey, Democrat from Massachusetts, issued a statement: "Apple needs to safeguard the personal location information of its users to ensure that an iPhone doesn't become an iTrack."[8] Tracking companies are also looking into "deep packet inspection," a peering into the actual data we send through the network. Again, the promise here is that any information gleaned won't be correlated with our real-world identities.[9]

The problem is that given the billions of dollars at stake, industry will be continually tempted to make the connection not to the device or to the unique identifier, but to the actual person.

A groundbreaking *Wall Street Journal* investigative series on online advertising found that many popular games like FarmVille (59 million users) and other apps on Facebook have been negligent at best in safeguarding consumers' identities, even those who choose the strictest privacy settings. About 70 percent of Facebook users enjoy one such app or another. The *Journal* reporters found that all of the ten most popular apps on Facebook were transmitting users' IDs to outside companies.[10] One of them, RapLeaf, uses its possession of real names to "build extraordinarily intimate databases on people by tapping voter-registration files, shopping histories, social-networking activities and real estate records, among other things."[11]

The technique of "scraping" personal information is so powerful that one Democratic political consultant used RapLeaf to target a key group of swing voters, 200,000 suburban women in Southern California over the age of forty. It helped him defeat a state ballot initiative on auto insurance rates.[12]

Facebook and companies that supply its apps are not devious. Many of the app developers seem not to have known that they were correlating this information, which after all was contrary to Facebook policy. Two weeks before the story broke, Facebook created a control panel that allows users to see "which apps are accessing which categories of information about them."[13]

The problem is that one way or another, what can be done will be done. And what can be done is a lot.

The *Journal* reported that the problem goes far beyond Facebook, which is at least transparent about making your Facebook user name and identifier searchable. In fact "the nation's 50 top websites on average installed 64 pieces of tracking technology onto the computers of visitors, usually with no warning. A dozen sites each installed more than a hundred."[14]

Tracking tools—cookies, "flash cookies" that reinstall, and "beacons" that can follow what you do on a website, including what you type—scan what you are doing on a website in real time, matching your activity to your location, income, shopping interests, and even medical conditions. "Some tools," the *Journal* reported, "surreptitiously re-spawn themselves even after users try to delete them."[15]

In a social network, of course, the compromise of one might mean the compromise of all. "If I have access to your Facebook profile password, I not only have access to your information, I have access to all your friends' information," says social media expert James Lee. Speaking of the thousands of followers of one digital guru, Lee says, "I could get all their birthdays, phone numbers, e-mail addresses, hometowns, anything that they made available to you under the privacy setting of friends. That's a huge treasure trove of data you're not able to get anywhere else. Same for LinkedIn, MySpace, all of those different sites . . . Mark Zuckerberg was right, though it may not have been good PR to say it—privacy as we know it is a dead concept on the Internet."*

Consider the finding of a joint team from Microsoft and Germany's Max Planck Institute that algorithms can intuit a person's sexuality and then effectively out them if they click on a gay- or lesbian-oriented ad, many perhaps still under the illusion that they were doing so in complete privacy. Any advertisers who collect data such as Facebook IDs could match a person's sexual preference with their unique ID and their name.[16]

While Facebook earnestly works to discipline its app providers and clarify its privacy policies, the evolving capability of the technology itself will continually outrace our ability to contain it. Already exchanges resembling stock markets are buying and selling masses of humanity's personal information by the gigabyte.[17]

> Eight out of ten children under the age of two in ten Western countries have their pictures online. They will be the first humans to be digitally tracked from cradle to grave.[18]

Street Stalkers

Breaches in our personal security can come from the street. When Google dispatched its vans around the world with 360-degree cameras for its Street View project (which matches local images to Google Maps), it picked up unencrypted information from Wi-Fi networks, including e-mail addresses, web page URLs, and passwords. Google, which promised it had not stored the data, apologized in 2010.[19] The scooping up of all this private data was in fact inadvertent, an example of robust technology outstripping customer relations. Again, what can be done will

---

* In a TechCrunch interview in the fall of 2010, when asked, "Where is privacy on the Web going?" Zuckerberg replied that Facebook would innovate to keep up as "social norms" evolved over time.

be done, if not by Google then by some other entity, competitor, or government.

There are other street dangers. Keep in mind that we might be tracked from the sky by that first generation of personal camera-equipped drones already on the market—indeed, tracked by means of gadgets in our own pockets. Cell towers have long allowed police to triangulate the position of a cell phone and its owner, solving kidnappings and finding missing children. GPS is now a standard feature of cell phones, helping with emergency services, enabling social mapping and other location-based services, including services that allow parents to use the phone to track their kids.

After *The News of the World* voicemail hacking scandal a lot of urban legends arose about how easy it is to "hack and track" through a cell phone. While it is unclear how easily cell phone hacking actually is, there is always the possibility of an inside job or those misrepresenting their right to know to use social engineering techniques to spoof phone companies or to persuade law enforcement to use your cell phone to follow you. "This is not uncommon with domestic disputes," one telecom executive told us.

An easier and more direct approach for eavesdropping is for a hacker to build, for about $1,500, a directional antenna of the sort already used by law enforcement to spoof a cell tower to collect outbound calls and data from callers.[20] This would in effect suck up all the calls and data in a local area for exploitation.

Even city speed cameras may be spying on you. In Great Britain, speed cameras check for speeding, tailgating, and seatbelts. They can also correlate with databases to ensure that you are up-to-date on your car insurance and taxes.[21]

≣ Getting tracked and hacked is no longer just an indoor sport.

The Burglar Sitting on Your Lap

A former National Security Agency (NSA) cyber expert has demonstrated that he can exploit security flaws in common web browsers to remotely gain control of a computer in under ten seconds. In one test, he opened the target's e-mail, activated his laptop's built-in camera, and took his picture.[22]

What do Scarlett Johansson, Miley Cyrus, Vanessa Hudgens, Emma Caufield, Addison Timlin, Busy Philipps, Renee Olstead, and Ali Larter have in common? TMZ broke the story that they're among fifty celebrities who've had compromising video and images taken from their mobile devices and computers by hackers.[23] Or consider what happened to the MySpace pages of Alicia Keys and two dozen other performers. Chinese hacking groups embedded malicious code in video software downloads on these celebrity pages that enabled the theft of credit card information.[24]

Of course your computer may itself already be enlisted as a soldier in a vast army of botnet cyber-thieves. By 2008, the FBI's Operation Botroast estimated that at least 1 million U.S. computers were infected.[25] The defense contractor's experiment with the quick infection rate and zombification of a plain vanilla computer described in chapter 3 suggests that the number of computers being used by unauthorized persons is by now likely much larger.

Another portal to turn Internet users into victims is through their embarrassment and guilt over downloading copyrighted material over file-sharing networks. Those who enjoy hentai—Japanese illustrated pornography—are sometimes encouraged to download what the user is led to believe is an illegal copy from a file-sharing network. Malware is also downloaded; it steals the victim's domain and computer name, software, search history and favorites, clipboard content and screen shots, all of which is posted on a website. Soon the victim receives an e-mail from a self-styled consumer defender warning the victim he is guilty of copyright infringement, not to mention the loss of privacy. This can all be fixed, of course, for a fee.[26]

> There are many ways into computers, some physical, some through emotional blackmail.

Corporate Info Wars

Elite hackers are winning enormous victories at the commanding heights of the world economy. Consider what happened to General Motors. In the first decade of the century, GM was crashing in the U.S. market but enjoying robust growth in Asia. The GM Daewoo brand in South Korea introduced the Spark, a car new to the Chinese market. As the Spark was being unveiled, China's Chery Automobile unveiled a new car of its own, the QQ.

GM executives were flabbergasted at what they saw in the showrooms. Chery hadn't bothered to make even a minor cosmetic disguise of its wholesale theft of the Spark. When examined by independent experts, the Spark and the QQ were found to be identical in body structure, exterior design, interior design, and key components. The two cars were so similar that parts were perfectly interchangeable. "This incident defies an innocent explanation," the U.S. secretary of commerce said in 2005.[27]

It seems apparent that the precise mathematical description of the Spark was taken by hacking into GM Daewoo's computers. Confronted with irrefutable evidence of intellectual property theft, Chery agreed to an undisclosed settlement between the two companies.[28]

In July 2010, a former GM worker, Shanshan Du, and her husband, Yu Qin, of Troy, Michigan, were charged with the unauthorized possession of trade secrets concerning hybrid car designs. They allegedly made an offer of design secrets, downloaded onto a hard drive, to . . . Chery Automobile (which denies knowing anything about the scheme).[29]

Other high-profile cases of alleged Chinese espionage involve Dow Chemical, DuPont, and Motorola, alleged inside jobs in which the alleged perpetrator often had to only download the data and hit send.[30]

Similar breaches are apt to happen in lawsuits in which nine or ten figures are on the table. One law firm involved in a major class-action lawsuit discovered that not only were its computers compromised but bugs had been installed in each office and in the homes of each partner involved in the lawsuit. A digital hound was able to source the attack back to an Asian firm owned by an American company in the lawsuit, making effective legal action all but impossible.[31]

> Hackers are more than just thieves or trolls. They can be effective strategic competitor-intelligence agents.

The Roots of Insecurity

No other system in human history has so quickly pervaded all aspects of our lives as computing while creating so much vulnerability. But *why* are we so vulnerable?

Most American industries and government agencies rely on COTS, commercial off-the-shelf technology designed to meet the Internet's high standard of interoperability, not security. Only banks and hospitals have devised their own closed loop systems that are reasonably secure.

"Banks get it because they have credit cards," Yakutis says. Despite the 2011 hacking of Citigroup credit card information, all the cyber experts interviewed for this book agree that if the rest of the U.S. infrastructure had the security protocols and secure links as strong as those of banks and other financial institutions, the nation's commerce would be much more secure. But they do not.

A good demonstration of the dark side of openness is regularly revealed by gray hats who purport to expose security flaws, usually in the commercial space, as a public service. A leader in this space in 2010 was Goatse Security. After exposing holes in the Mozilla and Apple Safari browsers, Goatse—of "Gaping Holes Exposed" fame—handed over to Gawker 114,000 e-mail addresses of early adopters of iPad 3G; these included Diane Sawyer of ABC News, movie producer Harvey Weinstein, and New York mayor Michael Bloomberg.[32] Clearly, the amorphous group of hackers who identify with Goatse have fun aiming their best shots at new security. What they reveal is just the tip of the iceberg of espionage, subterfuge, and theft that takes place in the corporate space.

Stealing can also be done physically. Slip into a hotel room or promise to guard someone's laptop while he or she goes to the airport restroom, and the quick insertion of a memory stick is enough to do the job.

Turning off a computer is no safeguard against expert thieves. When a computer is turned off or put into sleep mode, recent actions exist for a short time in its random access memory. Researchers at Princeton University, the Electronic Frontier Foundation, and Wind River Systems have demonstrated that with a can of compressed air or liquid nitrogen, a thief can mount a "cool boot attack" to restore residual data from a computer, including the decryption keys of disk-based encryption products.[33] One digital hound we interviewed practiced this technique and got it down to under five minutes.

Such elaborate, labor-intensive techniques are too dangerous for high-stakes corporate espionage. But there are far easier ways and legal ways to get high-level corporate information. For example, we learned that one senior executive at a top technology company regularly shares his digital calendar with employees in a way that outsiders can readily view. Whom he visits and when is proprietary information of the highest caliber, revealing potential customers to competitors. Despite repeated warnings by security consultants, he has yet to change his habits.[34]

> The Internet, spun out of a Cold War era research project, was given an open architecture to provide resiliency. Today the Internet's openness is our vulnerability.

The Hardware Store

In the early days of the Internet, anyone who wanted to use it had to master a certain amount of code. As information technology evolves toward an easy user interface, hacking is becoming user-friendly. This is good news for corporate spies, usually deployed by an upper mid-level executive under intense pressure to meet numbers. Such an executive can go to the online bazaar of hackers' websites and find illicit hacking firms for hire. For cyberespionage, the best can easily be recruited.

"There are websites where hacking is reduced to a tool chest, like being in a hardware store," security expert Bill Livingstone says. "All these different tools you can apply to hack into something. One might be a software program to break passwords. You don't have to write the program. You just take it off the shelf and apply it."[35]

More and more, cybercrime is organized by people who themselves are not hackers. This nefarious world works because there is a certain necessary amount of honor among thieves. Clients enter into a marketplace for services and software in which hackers are rated by their dependability in providing a product and clients are rated for paying on a full and timely basis, much like sellers are rated on eBay. As long as you don't get a reputation for being a "ripper," someone who does bad deals, you can choose from among an astonishing array of products.

"The way it will be done is that they will say, 'I need a Zero-Day exploit for Juniper routers,'" says Tom Kellermann. "And 'I need someone else who can give me the scanner that produces that exploit.' And then 'I need someone else to lease me a botnet so when I launch the attack, no one will know that it came from me.' And then 'I need someone else to datamine the information of whatever the code has gotten into and then find what it touches that is not me.' And lastly, 'I need someone else to be the command and control.'"[36] Thus an anonymous organizer can assemble a virtual army out of people who don't know each other, will never meet each other, and do not know—and do not want to know—the ultimate purpose of their work.

What can you buy on this market? For starters, you can buy the software to mount a Zero-Day attack.

"Zero-Day is an invincible weapon, it cannot be stopped by anything," Kellermann says. "It works when there's a vulnerability in the operating system itself that has never been seen before, so there's no patch or cure for it. And if you can hit the operating system with a Zero-Day, all of the security, firewalls, virus scanners, encryption, intrusion-protection devices, and forensics means jack shit because I literally own the foundation of your house."

The going rate for Zero-Day exploit for Windows 7, the latest Microsoft Operating System, is $75,000. A Zero-Day for Apple's Snow Leopard operating system goes for $25,000. To purchase a system rivaling the Stuxnet virus (which contains at least four Zero-Day applications), be prepared to pay a couple of hundred thousand dollars.

When you do a cost-benefit analysis, a system that can allow you to hack a bank's database in minutes could pay for your Zero-Day in the first thirty seconds of access.

It is for this reason that gifted hackers are like smash-and-grab artists who break the glass tops of jewelry store counters so they can run off with the biggest diamonds. Most hackers would rather get in and get out, hacking into a system and swiping the numbers of, say, 50,000 credit cards or stealing a priceless trade secret. They are often too impatient for the delayed satisfactions of a well-orchestrated smear campaign.

"For that reason, many corporate attacks are more direct," Yakutis says, explaining that many hackers won't take on corporate reputation smears unless the employer can show it will pay a lot of money. "But if someone has deep enough pockets, the hacker will do it."

When it comes to reputational warfare, one way to operate is to import material gleaned by hackers abroad. "I as an American cannot start hacking into a company website," says one digital investigator who wishes not to be named. "That is against the law. However, if someone from another part of the world hacks in to that site, and that illegally gathered information is brought into the United States and I use it, that is not against the law. And you have a lot of talented people outside of the United States who are doing a lot of interesting things."[37]

The good news is that once an attacker from a rival company is informed that he has been unmasked, he almost always backs down.

And what about the hackers themselves? One of the best ways for security experts to defeat hackers is to read their blogs. Being a successful hacker, after all, is somewhat like being Clark Kent. You may have flown to the ends of the Earth to defeat Lex Luthor, but as far as anyone around you can see, you're just another schlub with thick glasses. A hacker might have broken into the sanctum sanctorum of the CIA. But what good is it if no one knows?

So hackers need to brag. And they do, telling the world of their exploits. For example, we learned that at least one hacker actually did succeed in exploiting the penetration of a computer asset of the CIA. He did not go in directly. Instead, he followed a popular botnet that wormed inside the CIA-owned computer. Rather than follow it all the way in, the hacker waited outside the agency's digital firewall to catch the botnet as it exited. "He robbed the highway robber," someone close to this case says. It was a neat trick. It might have continued to work, except for the fact that the hacker bragged about it—and the agency noticed.

Harder to catch are the environmental and ideological groups that have begun, since 2009, to enlist millions of computers into botnets to mount data-flooding attacks to swamp sites, knocking companies offline. Perfume companies have been a particularly high-profile target for animal-rights activists.[38]

> Hackers hire their services like jobbers. Their weapons can be
> seen and purchased by anyone.

Cockroaches in the Cloud

The original Internet was, as Tom Kellermann says, a "giant, aquatic environment," a vast open ocean of information. It was not originally conceived to be a network that business, government, and the military could securely operate within. "So whoever the thought leaders were who said, 'Let's use this giant aquatic environment and put everything important on it,' kudos to them—because they're paying my salary right now," Kellermann, a highly paid security adviser, says with a wink.

Military and defense contractors worry about "trapdoors" built into the COTS hardware of our machines by the Chinese—tiny hard-to-notice anomalies in the design that can be remotely activated to turn over control. Kellermann says, "That's actually not the scariest part of supply chain. There is a virtual supply chain that makes it even more horrifying . . . the thing that everyone's talking about who wants to be hip, and that's the cloud—cloud computing." He calls cloud computing "giant apartment buildings in the sky."

Cloud computing is the practice of locating software applications and data in off-site, often distant data centers that store and manage your data. Its scalability brings powerful new efficiencies to computing. A prime feature of cloud computing is virtualization—using abstract computing platforms, with no need to immediately interact with a physical computer. The cloud is used to store data that we once stored in our machine or on backup memory or on a stick.

Why do this? The cloud gives us access to vastly more computing power at a reduced (or in some cases, almost no) cost. Microsoft raises three important questions every person and business should ask about a cloud host:

> —Are hosted data and applications within the cloud protected by suitably robust privacy policies?
> —Are the cloud computing provider's technical infrastructure, applications, and processes secure?
> —Are processes in place to support appropriate action in the event of an incident that affects privacy or security?[39]

In short, do we know where our organization's computer assets begin and end?

These are good questions, to which most people who are not chief information officers would answer, "I dunno." And yet we live in the clouds, even though we also know that breaches often come through third-party systems.

"Think of the national security and economic security implications of more than 50 percent of the Fortune 1000 and more than 50 percent of the federal government agencies that will be in a cohosted, multitenanted cloud environment by the end of 2011," Kellermann says. "What is the significance of polluting that supply chain and/or infiltrating that supply chain? Because in the cloud if your neighbor has cockroaches, so do you."

Kellermann says we should not be overconfident about the protection afforded us by encryption. "Encryption can and will be defeated, by technical innovation and human error," he says.

Most companies and people who use cloud computing enjoy significant levels of security. The benefits of cloud computing should not be underestimated.

> The cloud creates economy of scale for hackers as well as for clients.

Baking the Grid

Senate minority leader Mitch McConnell received a lot of criticism for rhetorical overkill for calling Julian Assange as "a high-tech terrorist." In fact, among the many secret State Department cables revealed by WikiLeaks is one that offers a helpful terrorist road map of overseas factories and infrastructure, from cables to pipelines, vital to the physical security of the United States.[40]

These are greater dangers from the cyberworld than damage to our reputation or bank accounts. Actions by hackers—whether by a group of lunatics, Al Qaeda, or a hostile nation-state—can kill. With Stuxnet-like viruses, an attacker can turn a power plant, in the words of one former U.S. national security official, "into a useless lump of metal," prompt the combustion chambers of chemical plants to fatally overheat, or ruin the turbines of a hydroelectric plant.[41] In a survey released in 2011, of two hundred IT executives in charge of oil, gas, and water utilities in fourteen countries reported that 80 percent of them had experienced large-scale denial of service attacks.[42]

Or an attacker could follow the example of Vitek Boden, a Queensland technician who commanded 300 systems governing sewage and drinking water from a stolen computer and radio transmitter in his car. He sluiced 800,000 liters of raw sewage into local parks, rivers, and the grounds of a luxury hotel.[43]

Aside from the closed systems of U.S. banks, the rest of the American infrastructure relies on public and easily accessed Internet connections. "The CEO likes to have the big shiny panel in his office he can show visitors by which he can track and control his facilities second by second," one security expert told us. "The problem is, any number of other people can reproduce that control panel on their laptop."

When most people think of a cyberattack on the electrical power grid, they think of blackouts. Less well known is the potential for push-button destruction. "Why think one direction here?" Kellermann asks. "Imagine if I were to cause a power surge. And instead of knocking out power, I were to pump too much power through the system. What happens then?" It might look something like the Aurora Project test at the Idaho National Labs, now on YouTube, of a hack attack on a twenty-seven-ton generator. In a few seconds, malicious code prompts the massive machine to destroy itself, sending bolts flying and smoke belching out. It would take months to replace such a generator, which would have to be ordered from overseas.[44] A smart grid of the sort touted by the Obama administration would only make the electrical system even more a creature of the vulnerable Internet.

Experts say that as much as 85 percent of all system relays in our electrical grid are digital. Kellermann says that a single exploitation of a vulnerability could be propagated across a cyber or power system network and potentially affect an entire class of assets at once. With a smart grid, an attacker wouldn't have to hack into a bay station. He could act from a house, causing a cascade of damage from relays to substations.

Most pernicious would be man-in-the-middle attacks, which operate within networks to attack central control rooms and push bad firmware out to remote field devices that won't be able to reboot or be recovered. "You can also actually hack into the system and maintain a presence within the system so you can cause surges at will by having remote access to command-and-control SCADA systems within it," Kellermann says. SCADA, or supervisory control and data acquisition systems, are controls that can be accessed over the Internet or phone lines.

In his 2010 book, *Cyber War,* former NSC official Richard Clarke writes that not only have both Russia and China deeply penetrated the U.S. electricity grid, but that the Chinese have "laced" the U.S. infrastructure with "logic bombs" capable of causing havoc on a similar scale of the Stuxnet attack on Iranian nuclear facilities.[45]

The Stuxnet worm is the first cyber weapon to demonstrate mass effects in the physical world. Its success against Iran's uranium enrichment facility and its nuclear reactor and elsewhere heralds things to come.

"When something succeeds spectacularly twice, it is ready for wider application," one cyber expert says.

Stuxnet can make robot arms go berserk, elevator doors close, and HVAC systems shut off.[46] It can open the valves of refineries, chemical plants, and water treatment facilities. "What keeps me up at night," Kellermann says, "is the fact that you no longer need to be there in person to kill or to maim or destroy."

One scenario he worries about is a pax mafioso between, say, former Soviet bloc mercenaries and terrorists or a hostile state to launch a two-prong attack. "The first prong is to play with the integrity of the information on which first responders rely," Kellermann says. "I don't mean turning it off. I mean playing with time, switching GPS coordinates, things like that. And then coupling that with a physical attack. There are so many ways you can kill a lot of Americans through cyberattacks on the infrastructure, it is unbelievable. And I don't just mean poisoning the water or turning off the electrical grid. Just look at the pharmaceutical industry." Kellermann worries that a hacker might turn off safety controls in an automated manufacturing facility to deliberately change computer formulas to mismeasure the amount of drug that goes into each capsule or pill.

Some cyber experts we interviewed believe that the nation's chemical plants are unconscionably vulnerable. Kellermann sees holes in plant security. "The problem is that the guys who run security at chemical plants are former FBI or Secret Service guys, not the cyber guys," Kellermann says. "They understand perimeter and physical security and . . . their generation was trained to believe that technology helps improve security, not that technology exacerbates security.

"And so these guys go wireless on everything, they use video everywhere, they connect those video camera systems into their primary systems, and they have all these wonderful widgets to protect themselves in a physical sense," Kellermann says. "But all those wonderful technological solutions meant to improve physical security actually create an Achilles' heel from a cybersecurity perspective."

Another set of worries is the hacking of the SCADA systems of chemical plants. A security expert who works with chemical companies told us that growing public awareness and the threat of fines have prompted the leading chemical companies to make big strides in security. In fact, several executives of large chemical companies told us that they have installed redundant physical systems that would use mechanical means to defeat an attempt to wreck a chemical plant over the Internet. Industry sources also conveyed that smaller companies have been less diligent and are more vulnerable.

Softer targets can also be attacked, including the results of an election. In the fall of 2010, the District of Columbia Board of Elections and Ethics opened an Internet-based voting system to the public for one week, inviting experts to mount exploitations to see what would happen. One University of Michigan professor did just that, unleashing his students on the system. Within days, rather than report the right election results, the system was playing, "The Victors," the fight song of the University of Michigan.[47]

What about the financial markets? Kellermann worries about hackers playing with the time stamps on trades in the New York central equities depository. If that could be done, it could cause serious disruption. Others question what would happen if a black hat got into large trading companies and started generating mass volumes of buy and sell orders.

When attacks happen, who is the most likely perpetrator? Two years ago, the eight major criminal syndicates of the world passed a major threshold. They derived 50 percent of their revenues from cybercrime, Kellermann reports. So in Kellermann's pax mafioso scenario, the actual work of committing cyberterrorism might be commissioned among any of a hundred criminal organizations, from the Japanese Yakuza to the Chinese Triads.

This is happening as the gang bosses, who are in their fifties or sixties, are increasingly turning to protégés in their thirties for advice. "If they are not tech savvy themselves, they are appreciative of it enough that they are going to coerce someone to work for them who does it really well," Kellermann says. "Or they are going to hire someone to do it really well. Or they are going to find someone who can barter online to get the capabilities they need, because in the end, who doesn't want to be omniscient?"

And the sweetest part is that for those who commission cybercrime, there is almost zero risk. "Only 1 percent of cases of hacking banks— cybercrime against financial institutions—are successfully prosecuted by either the Secret Service or FBI," Kellermann says.

Then there are attacks that have the unmistakable imprimatur of a state actor. Russia in 2007 launched a wave of cyberattacks on the

Estonian parliament and other institutions in a fit of anger over the removal of a Soviet-era war memorial. In 2008, Russia launched a cyber offensive against Georgia's Internet infrastructure in coordination with physical war.

The nation with the greatest demonstrated capability to attack the United States is of course the People's Republic of China. During an eighteen-minute period in April 2010, a state-owned Chinese firm hoovered the Internet, redirecting 15 percent of the Internet through Chinese servers, sweeping up U.S. government and military data. It caught data sent between the "dot.mil" branches of the U.S. armed services, as well as data from the U.S. Senate and Fortune 500 companies.[48]

Thanks to WikiLeaks, we now know that an inside source informed the U.S. embassy that the deep penetration of Google and the theft of its proprietary codes was ordered by the highest levels of the Chinese government, coordinated by the State Council Information Office, which reports directly to the PRC's Politburo Standing Committee.[49] It is rumored, but unconfirmed, that a senior Chinese official ordered the hack after seeing criticism of himself on sites that came up in a Google search result of his name.[50]

While launching these attacks, China also unveiled the creation of the world's most powerful supercomputer, the Tianhe-1A, which can manage 2,507 trillion calculations a second. Some experts see a connection between these two events, as if China is saying, "Not only do we have access to what you know, we can parse and distribute what you know with exceptional speed."

The greatest immediate source of physical danger is of course terrorists. While state-sponsored attacks can often be traced back to their source, terrorists are the most obvious candidates to mount a physical attack. Given their rootlessness and nihilism, they cannot be dissuaded or easily deterred. Al Qaeda offers an interesting example of how a hunted group, if it chooses to become a cyber-hunter, could mount attacks with attendant propaganda, without being found. Jihadists maintain online libraries in Egypt and Great Britain, resources for inspiration, propaganda, and fundraising. Those who are actually operational terrorists, however, have to be on the move. "Terrorists cannot openly operate a website for long without attracting the attention of government authorities," says Bill Livingstone. "So their sites are perpetually going up and coming down, changing addresses, locations."

We tend to think of cyber-warriors as sitting in a chair in front of a computer. Most of the developing world, however, doesn't use PCs. It communicates with mobile devices. The network for a terrorist act can be coordinated by cheap disposable cell phones. Terrorist videos and messages are sent in daisy-chain bursts, from cell phone to cell phone, from device to device.

While Al Qaeda doesn't have the sophistication of state-sponsored actors, it does have the will and the malice to carry out terror operations by remote control. Given the shifting topology of its network, it is hard to track and counter. Some experts believe, however, that Al Qaeda is currently too busy financing old-fashioned terrorist attacks with bombs and guns to use digital technology to mount digital attacks on critical infrastructure.

Besides criminals, nation-states, and terrorists, there is another source of deadly attacks against the United States—the individual, someone who might inflict on American infrastructure the same level of damage that twenty-three-year-old PFC Bradley Manning is accused of inflicting on American diplomacy by collecting secrets by the truck-load before offloading them on WikiLeaks. For months, Manning is believed to have sat at a terminal surrounded by fellow soldier/technicians, pretending to listen to a CD, lip-synching to Lady Gaga's "Telephone" while filling the disk with compressed files containing secrets by the gigabyte. In thinking of the damage he was going to inflict, Manning reportedly told hacker Adrian Lamo, "It's beautiful and horrifying."[51]

Like PFC Manning, some strange antisocial young person might mutter to himself "beautiful, horrifying" while watching smoke rise from the carnage of a city.

The Jesus Bar

We are dependent as never before on the digital devices that copy, store, and enact almost every transaction. An exabyte is a billion billion, or 1 followed by 18 zeros. By 2010, humanity required 40.8 exabytes of storage space for new data, or 2.7 gigabytes for every man, woman, and child on the planet.[52] And yet our deep and growing dependence is on systems that are utterly insecure. More than 221 million records containing individuals' personal data were compromised in 608 incidents in 2009.[53]

Tom Kellermann believes that the penetration of Internet and computer-enabled devices is pervasive in the United States. "From Grandma's computer at home to so many university computer systems that on a heat map it looks like it's all coming from here, but that just means the hackers have actually colonized more of our cyber infrastructure than anywhere else on the planet," he says.

Another expert with deep experience in national security systems invokes a simple handgrip in the cockpit that test pilots call the Jesus bar. It has a precise purpose. The Jesus bar allows a test pilot to do nothing. There are times in a stall in which anything a test pilot does will only worsen his predicament. He is better off toughing it out for a few seconds to see if the plane eases out on its own. In moments like these the Jesus bar allows the pilot to hang on for dear life and call out to Jesus.

The Jesus bar is a favorite metaphor of Dr. Eric Haseltine, who after he served as director of engineering at Hughes Aircraft managed technology projects and the virtual reality studio at Walt Disney Imagineering, then was recruited to be director of research for the National Security Agency. From 2005 to 2007, Haseltine was also associate director for science and technology, Office of the Director of National Intelligence (ODNI), a position he described to a journalist as "the CTO [chief technology officer] of the intelligence community." He oversaw the most sensitive computer systems of the CIA and much of the alphabet soup of intelligence agencies. He is now an author and a much sought after consultant and lecturer.

While at ODNI, Haseltine helped the federal government hone its offensive capabilities to deter and attack foreign governments and hacker clubs, as well as sharpen the government's means to defend its own systems. Through his experiences, Haseltine has had the world's best education in what could be achieved by offense and what was possible in the way of defense. His conclusion? "I think we're screwed," Haseltine says. "We're never going to be safe—and the situation is getting worse quickly."

How much worse can it get? According to some IT industry sources, there are more people in the world today devising malware than there are people writing software. Alarmed by the extent of penetration into federal systems and the vulnerability of major infrastructure, the Obama administration is pushing its own version of a Bush-era policy called the Comprehensive National Cybersecurity Initiative (CNCI), a federal program to unify the fragmented approach of federal agencies' approach to cybersecurity. Although it is a "black" budget program, journalists estimate CNCI's five-year budget at $40 billion.

While in government service, Dr. Haseltine was so impressed by the openness of federal systems and U.S. infrastructure to attack and was so discouraged about the prospects of defense that he believes that CNCI's colossal budget may be worse than a total waste of money. He wonders if federal cybersecurity efforts might actually be making us less safe, in much the same way a pilot's instant response might send a plane into a spiral, so that the best course of action for federal cyber administrators at this moment in history would be to grasp the Jesus bar, hang on for dear life, and do nothing at all—except perhaps scream.

> Governments are still sorting responses to cyberattacks at the most basic conceptual levels.

The Best and Brightest

The U.S. government is in action to restore cybersecurity. And when the government flies into action, new agencies are formed, each with their own shiny new emblems and shields. At the apex of cybersecurity is the newly formed U.S. Cyber Command, part of the U.S. Strategic Command and located at National Security Agency headquarters in Fort Meade, Maryland.

Although not charged with protecting commercial infrastructure, Cybercom is lending its expertise to the U.S. Department of Homeland Security, which has primary responsibility to protect critical private-sector networks in the United States. However, the head of Cybercom, General Keith Alexander, told Congress that "it is not my mission to defend today the entire nation."[54] He said that any defense of the power grid, for example, would have to rely on industry.

Industry is being asked to lead, but without clear guidelines to follow one has little reason to feel more secure. In May 2011, the Pentagon became so alarmed by the vulnerability of the United States that it announced that it would leave open the possibility that it might consider a large-scale cyber attack "an act of war," worthy of physical retaliation. Perhaps the most realistic, if fatalistic action being taken in 2011 is debate over a so-called Internet kill switch, legislation that would give the president the executive authority in a cyber emergency to shut down broad portions of the Internet that deal with critical infrastructure.

There is also a lot of emphasis on resiliency, which Kellermann fears is a sign that we learned the wrong lesson after 9/11. The problem with resiliency—hooking up remote users, putting up wireless LAN over fiber optics, setting up a backup data center—is that they "expand the target" for potential hackers. "I can now hack into that remote user, I can hack the wireless transmission wire, I can hack the backup data center, [there are] so many points by which I can ingress myself into your system," Kellermann says.

Dr. Eric Haseltine worries about an opposite problem, that cybersecurity efforts to reduce the federal government's "attack surface"—the external face of the system through which an attacker can enter—will simplify the attacker's path into our systems. He believes we should confess our ignorance of the laws that govern the cyberworld, a new realm whose fundamental laws we do not yet understand. Wouldn't it make sense to understand how the cyberworld evolves before trying to shape that evolution?

Biological metaphors come naturally to Haseltine, who has an eclectic background for a cyber geek. By training, Haseltine is a neuroscientist who believes "we understand the natural world, we understand the Newtonian world, but we don't understand the laws that govern the cyberworld, even though we act like we do." If he had his way, Haseltine would stop spending billions to defend cybersystems we imperfectly understand and instead begin with a pure science effort at mastering the rules of this cyberworld we've created.

Just as bacteria will eventually become resistant to an antibiotic, so too might CNCI's quest for a unified federal approach to cybersecurity breed the cyber equivalent of a superbug. Instead of one software platform with a preferred antiviral vendor, the federal government might do better to emulate Heinz's 57 varieties.

Another fallacy Haseltine sees in the federal approach to cybersecurity is an unshakable faith in "airgapping" computers—the belief that a computer system that is not connected to any other computer or to the Internet is safe. If evolution teaches us anything, it is that intelligent systems like to network.

Of course no computer is going to extend its own cable and plug itself in. But a computer doesn't have to network itself, because every computer comes complete with a parasite called a human, a creature with an irrepressible desire to network.

Federal chief technology officers design such airgapped systems for as many as 100,000 users, acting as if it is reasonable to believe that each individual will always act as he is supposed to act. If just one human inserts a stick drive into one computer, however, the entire plan is instantly compromised. With large numbers of people, Haseltine asks, how reasonable is it to suppose that not one of them will insert that drive? Such plans, Haseltine says, are "very precise and have zero validity."

In comparing natural laws from biology and physics to try to unearth the hidden principles of the digital world, Haseltine says that we need to also consider "unnatural law" (meaning natural laws of the cyberworld we do not yet fully understand). Dr. Haseltine borrows a phrase that originated in social planning circles to call the challenge of cybersecurity a "wicked problem," one that is difficult to solve because of incomplete, contradictory, and changing boundaries that are hard to recognize. Afghanistan is a wicked problem, as are health care and global warming. Cybersecurity is a wicked problem par excellence. What can we do when we know enough to let go of the Jesus bar?

In lacking a clear definition of the laws that govern the cyberworld, we are obliged to begin to solve the problem in order to discover what the problem is.

The best way to do that? Haseltine says, "Go on the offense." Take the fight to the hackers. Disrupt their systems, find their assets, rock their world. It is only when we acquire the agility and exploitative capabilities of the world's legions of hackers—some sponsored by malevolent states, some by gangsters, some by Mom's cooking—that we will have a fighting chance.

Cyber theorists often borrow from their intellectual predecessors in the defense community, applying the well-worn theories of nuclear deterrence to this new world. This, Kellermann believes, is a mistake.

"This is not nuclear destruction, there is no endgame, there is no second or third strike," he says, taking issue with a famous prediction of former White House cyber chief Richard Clarke, who predicted that a digital "Pearl Harbor" could decimate the country in fifteen minutes.

"The enemy doesn't want to conduct a cyber Pearl Harbor," Kellermann says. "In his [Clarke's] evangelism of this issue in coining that term, he made everyone focus on denial of service and disruption of service as the number one dangerous thing that could happen. And it's not. Your enemy would rather take you over, essentially take over your nervous system and turn you into their puppet . . . The name of the game is colonization."

Kellermann sees us less like the U.S. Navy on the morning of December 7, 1941, and more like the Maya awaiting the conquistadors. "How are we actually going to create shared risk and elevate and create the level of discomfort not just technologically but through hard and soft power of those adversaries who seek to colonize us in cyberspace?" Kellermann says. "How do you incentivize the developing world, most of which doesn't see cybercrime as illegal, away from institutionalizing the problem of organized hacking?"

Kellermann envisions a public policy response with three legs.

Nation-states that institutionalize cyberattack and employ nonstate actors as proxies constitute one leg. Kellermann would directly tie foreign assistance through the World Bank, USAID, and IMF to incentivize state actors to change behavior.

Second, Kellermann would "increase the level of discomfort" for alternative payment channels that launder the funds. "The reality is that the money is not moving through the financial sector," he says. "It is moving through these alternative payment channels. I am not going to name them in this interview, because I don't want to be a dead man walking when you print this book. I will tell you that there are more than two hundred of these alternative payment channels out there."

He praises PayPal for having a standard of care and due diligence that sets a global standard. "If everyone were to act like PayPal, we wouldn't have this monstrosity of a trillion-dollar shadow economy," he says.

The third leg of his approach would be to address the larger hosting economy, the server farms, which lack standards of due diligence and regulation. "They are hosting the child porn, the hacker services, the malware, the stolen financial credentials, the stolen national secrets," he says. "And if you don't tackle these three legs through soft and hard power, then you don't stand a chance of dealing with this issue. You are never going to build a Fortress America in cyberspace unless you create a brand-new protocol."

He agrees with Haseltine that offensive measures are needed. "It is functionally important that we begin to appreciate that nation-state adversaries are in our systems to stay, and that being the case, if they are in your capital, then you need to build a better dungeon, and create better torture equipment in that dungeon."

Compare the science of cybersecurity today to the U.S. space program, and it is clear we are not yet even in the Project Mercury phase.

Takeaway—Basic Protection

Given the vulnerability of computers, you might be tempted to throw your hands in the air in helpless frustration. That is an understandable response, one that many adopt. But that is the wrong response.

It is possible, bordering on likely, that criminals will enlist the unused capacity of your computer to mount botnet attacks. This is creepy, but it need not shut you down. Every computer is wide open to hacking. But in every herd, there are some cagey animals that are less vulnerable than others.

Or think of it in terms of home security. For your home and family, you already do the logical things necessary to protect them. You might reinforce windows and doors. You might install sophisticated locks and burglar, fire, and smoke alarms. You might time lights to go on and off at different nights and different days. You might ask neighbors to watch or check your house when you are traveling. Some have a dog or an automated dog-barker so people approaching your home will take heed.

None of these measures could possibly keep a world-class cat burglar from getting into your house. But these measures work well enough to discourage the greater threat—that you will be targeted by the garden-variety house burglar. In a similar way, everyone should adopt the full measure of practices and systems available to discourage the likely attack.

- Defend your personal and small business computers with the latest version of three layers of defense—the best firewall, the best antivirus, and the best antispyware software products. Evaluate leaders like Symantec and McAfee. Microsoft Security Essentials is one of the best free antivirus softwares. If you are a more sophisticated user and a more likely target, however, you might use quality but lesser known security products, since "firewall killers" are most frequently built for the most popular programs.

- Set your software security settings to automatic update.

- Keep up with automatic updates to keep your software and web browsers current.

- If you have a wireless connection at home, reset the router password with your passcode, a robust series of numbers, letters, and ASCII code (the funky little symbols on your keyboard). Enable wireless encryption so you won't be an open store to your neighbors and anyone passing by on the street.

- You cannot secure a home wireless network. If this is intolerable, then go with a hardwire. But if you do use a router, guard it with that elaborate passcode to make it more secure.

A good way to set a passcode is to hark back to a favorite childhood memory, perhaps a beach vacation, that not even someone who knows you would necessarily think of—and certainly not something anyone who studies you from afar could discover. If, for example, you still relish the memory of the day your parents took you to, say, Rehoboth Beach, your passcode might be:

R#h@b@thB#@ch!

All you have to do is remember to capitalize the "R" and the second "B," replace the "o's" and "a" with an ampersand, and the "e's" with hash marks, and end it with an exclamation point, then add in numbers—but not your birthday or that of anyone in your family. Such a passcode is not unbreakable. But it would be enough work to discourage all but the most sophisticated hacker.

Once you've created your passcodes, share them only with your spouse—and then only if you are reasonably certain that you are not headed to divorce court.

- Configure your webmail account—Yahoo! Hotmail, Google—to use "https" (the "s" is for "secure") instead of "http." Shop on https websites, and look for the lock icon in your browser frame. You might consider the Electronic Frontier Foundation's "HTTPS Everywhere" plug-in. It forces websites wherever possible to use the https standard.

- If you use an e-mail client, configure the client to use "SSL" and "TLS," cryptographic protocols, according to the vendor recommendations.

- Study and select the most appropriate privacy settings when you use social networks services like Facebook. Be cautious. Don't be like the vast majority of people who automatically accept "friend" requests from beautiful strangers.

- Never click on an e-mail attachment or link without knowing or verifying the source.

- Sensitive business and credit card transactions must never be made on public computers or on a public Wi-Fi networks. Turn off your Wi-Fi when you are not using it. Bluetooth security is pretty strong, but to avoid getting "bluesnarfed," use your device's "hidden" mode instead of leaving it "discoverable."

- Never open an e-mail offering you a solution to a new "monster virus." That is likely the monster itself. Go straight to your preferred vendor.

- If you still use a desktop with a dedicated hardline, you might unplug the line to the Internet when not in use. If your house has Wi-Fi, you might want to that off when not in use.

- To stay current, go to the "Alerts and Security Tips" section of U.S.-CERT, the United States Computer Emergency Readiness Team.

Postscript: The Most Unpredictable Factor

In the last minutes of the twentieth century, a group of U.S. generals assembled deep in the headquarters in the Cheyenne Mountain Complex in Colorado Springs. They sipped coffee and nervously watched the second hand turn on the clock. An air of quiet tension rose until midnight. At the stroke of the new year, the generals anxiously sprang into action, contacting the commanders of the prime strategic systems of the United States.

One of the authors was briefed on this incident, in which the issue at hand was Y2K. There was a fear among the brass and military CIOs that software, computers, and information systems used in military operations, which like their civilian counterparts were not built to accommodate date changes to the twenty-first century, would go haywire.

Patches were installed, but it was far from certain how well they would work. Insiders say that the greatest source of worry was of course how the transition might affect strategic systems.

Even since the fall of the Soviet Union, Moscow and the United States had on several occasions been spooked by bad data from satellites, radars, and computer systems. The world had come close to nuclear war before because of computer misinterpretations of solar reflection, a Norwegian scientific rocket, and a "go-to-war" missile test tape that was inadvertently injected into the main operating systems.[55]

Could Y2K cause a glitch that would cause a strategic miscalculation by either power? Russia dispatched military and political leaders to sit next to their American counterparts inside the Cheyenne Mountain complex, a sure sign of how serious the issue was. When it was clear that nothing significant would happen, they joined their American colleagues in breathing a sigh of relief. Everyone relaxed as morning came.

Then came some Y2K surprises no one had envisioned. At the stroke of midnight, Russian President Boris Yeltsin stepped down, to be replaced by Vladimir Putin—a stark surprise for the generals. Not long after, U.S. spy satellites caught the unmistakable glint of rocket engines igniting in the Russian interior. Russia was launching missiles.

Was Y2K causing accidental launches? Or had Putin inaugurated his administration by launching World War III?

Once it was determined that the glints were from intermediate-range missiles, could they represent an attack on U.S. forward-deployed bases in the Middle East? A retired military officer one of the authors spoke to was there in the Cheyenne Mountain control room. He recalls, "We had done everything technically right. And still we had a moment of surprise."

Sensors determined that these missiles were actually tactical SCUDS, heading on a trajectory against Moscow's opponents in Chechnya and not against U.S. forces in the Middle East, Mediterranean, or Europe. The Russians present soon assured their American colleagues that these missiles were not launched because of any Y2K-related computer glitch.

"Still, for a few tense moments, we knew what it felt like to be on the brink," the retired officer says.

> The greatest surprises will always come from humans, not from technology.

10:// Swimming in the Silicon Sea

> We have to abandon the idea that schooling is
> something restricted to youth. How can it be, in a
> world where half the things a man knows at 20 are no
> longer true at 40—and half the things he knows at 40
> hadn't been discovered when he was 20?
>
> **—Arthur C. Clarke**

INFORMATION TECHNOLOGY AMPLIFIES and globally distributes every human want, answer, whim, and foible. As it changes in the near few years, how might technology change us? How might it reshape society? How will technology affect our concerns about security, reputation, and privacy? Above all, what fresh challenges will we be grappling with in a few years that will be as unexpected as those we are grappling with now?

We should first take a step back and assess the changing technology and media landscape. It is actually more of a combat space, one in which Facebook and Google struggle for dominance, cyber insecurity will grow, reputational wars will open up in the new space of combat marketing, and reformers will look more and more to the best practices of the commercial world for answers.

The Window and the Mirror

Google is our great window on the world. Facebook is the mirror in which humanity sees its reflection. These are two distinct models of the Internet, and like two robust plants in the same pot, they are slowly trying to strangle each other.

The insight of Google was revolutionary—the notion that a page's value is determined by how many inbound links there are to that page. In contrast, Facebook is working to deliver search results based on a different proxy for popularity, on what you and your friends have liked in the past. In 2011, the window and the mirror are starting to look a little more alike. Google Social Search lets you see what your friends "like." Googlet is a full rejoinder to Facebook, one that allows for more discrete seperation of friends by categories. Facebook Connect's aggressive promotion is a breach of the walled garden; and some social media watchers are predicting Facebook will open up more of its data to search indexes.

They still remain two fundamentally different ways of approaching the world.

Google is the great democratic leveler that incentivizes the breaking down of all walls so that everyone and everything can be found. This is a transformative technology, though it might be undone to a degree by the proliferation of apps that bypass traditional search to go straight to given transactions.

Facebook, meanwhile, chips away at Google's ideal of unlimited access, threatening to break up the Internet into archipelagos of social groups. Increasingly, we will be tempted to e-mail, exchange videos, buy and sell, make friends, and set up events on Facebook through the "social graph," or nodes of our friends, their recommendations, and shared experiences online without ever venturing out into the wider world.

"Facebook, Tumblr, Twitter give you kind of a sense of what it's going to be like," says Ned Desmond, who has devised strategies and built websites for some of the world's largest media companies. "It's going to be more like the world of Instant Messaging when it comes to connections between people than it is going to be like the world of conventional publishing.

"Google is an older model, which is more intuitive to most of us, at least for my generation, the notion that there is content out there, I can type in some keywords, and I can with that retrieve the content that I'm looking for," Desmond says. "Facebook is not content specific, though it can include content. It has to do more with finding things not through keywords but through frames of reference that are fundamentally about people." And about what they *like*.

How effectively will digital attacks work in the future? In a Google world, an anonymous digital assassin can post an assertion about an individual, product, or company. It seems to arise out of nowhere and hang in cyberspace without any context. In a Facebook world, "an attack on you arising out of nowhere that has no relevance to the established social graph and activity patterns would make it far more suspect," Desmond says. It is the difference between being attacked on the street or attacked in your home, surrounded by twenty of your best friends.

When it comes to search, however, if all searches are somehow suggested by our "social graph," we might stand to lose something valuable—the serendipitous adventure that random web surfing can be.

In a typical surf, for example, you might look for background on the 2010 movie *Inception,* and get caught up in one of its stars, Ellen Page. Where did this wisecracking bright-eyed wonder come from? Then you learn that her character, Ariadne, is named after the character in Greek myth who helped Theseus kill the Minotaur, which leads you to delve into ancient Cretan civilization, something you had always kind of known about, but not much. This of course leads you to thinking about Crete as a good vacation destination. Except that the blogs advise you that the Cyclades or even the Turkish coast may be better for what you're looking for. So you set out to learn more about the making of *Inception* and you wind up booking a summer beach vacation in Ephesus.

Google is like that. You start out looking for one thing and you wind up in a completely different universe of ideas and activities. The sheer randomness of it tends, if you are curious, to fill in gaps in your knowledge.

Before the Internet, such strolls through the informational universe occurred only in libraries and reading rooms, restrained by time and space. In the window world of Google, every fact is Kevin Bacon, ready to skip a few degrees of separation to any other fact.

In a Facebook world, we run the risk of being narrowed by the "likes" of our self-chosen friends.

Vivid, Mobile, Networked, and Smart

Like compound interest, which transforms pennies into fortunes, the exponential growth in computing power continues to create media that promise to be millions of times more powerful than anything we enjoy today. The most obvious shift will be the way in which technology becomes ever more vivid. The vibrant images on today's HDTV sink into the brain in a way that the ghostly shadows of the black-and-white images of the first Philcos or even the flat, pixilated color of conventional television never did. With 3-D without goggles and "telepresence" around the corner, we are fast approaching a time when the term "virtual reality" will no longer be an exaggeration.

While the media experience becomes richer and more tactile, many of the most disruptive technologies will sneak up on us. Take, for example, Bell Labs's Picturephone that dazzled millions at the 1964 World's Fair in New York but never took hold.

Then suddenly, when the idea of a videophone seemed like a relic of a World of the Future exhibit, Skype subversively infiltrated our laptops. Many new technologies will creep in like Skype, especially as television fully converges with the Internet.

Television itself, as with radio and cinema and much of the old media, will not disappear. It will just get subsumed. Those who want to watch a football game or to enjoy the big-screen experience of *Lawrence of Arabia* will turn to the large screen format of something that looks like TV. Those who want to watch *30 Rock* will go to the small screen of a mobile device. "Programming will flow to where it fits in terms of how people use it, and of course the size of the screen and the quality of the resolution they need to enjoy it," says Desmond. "It will be who you are, what stage of life you are at, what is the nature of the programming, just call it down and watch it on the relevant device."[1]

Whatever the device you are using, while you watch *30 Rock* you will be able to buy Tina Fey's scarf or Alec Baldwin's tie, or search for the bio of that squirrely character actor whose name you can't quite remember.

Mobile devices, of course, will be smaller, thinner, faster, and less expensive, with stronger batteries. Dumb appliances will be smarter and networked, and most content will be "device agnostic."

Some of our devices—and perhaps our house and car—will acquire simulated human voices. And these won't be the monotone of automatons like your GPS. Machines of the near future will cut through the ambiguity of human speech to converse with us in a way that will finally meet the requirements of the Turing test—that is to say, will be indistinguishable from a human being. The rub may be, as Jaron Lanier wrote in his master polemic, *You Are Not a Gadget,* that the Turing test may cut both ways. "You can't tell if a machine has gotten smarter or if you've just lowered your own standards of intelligence to such a degree that the machine seems smart."[2]

New, New Media

The Twitter mode of bite-sized chews is going to drive old media leaders like *The Wall Street Journal, Bloomberg Businessweek,* and many others toward punchier and shorter stories. Already the web-based sites of the major TV networks break up the nightly news and other programs into similarly bite-sized pieces, as shows formatted to the half-hour and hour slots are disaggregated into YouTube-like clips. Stories lose clear boundaries as they are expanded by multiple links to other sources, perspectives, and visual media. Our shorter attention span will be well served by media, although sites will be able to back up their reporting with unprecedented depth of written, video, and audio material that once would have been edited out and lost to posterity.

Another trend will be the blurring of media categories. If you look at nytimes.com or abcnews.com or your local TV, radio, and newspaper websites, you will see in each case a combination of video, downloads, slide shows, and text. As these media channels become more and more distant from their physical origins, the distinction between a newspaper, a radio show, and a television show—already blurred—will be more a matter of emphasis and legacy.

Social media will continue to erode the ability of columnists and critics to act as the gatekeepers of politics and culture. Already, celebrities and movie stars find more value in their Facebook and Twitter followings than in the obligatory and more dangerous round of interviews with journalists. There will always be a latent demand for quality and exclusiveness. So Rotten Tomatoes aggregates critics' judgments in its Tomatometer. But the critic Hollywood cares about most is the judgment of the crowd in Rotten Tomatoes' Audience meter.

Claire McCaskill, a Democrat from Missouri, is still a relative newcomer to the U.S. Senate. But she has built up a hugely influential following among the press and blogging community with her frequent, pithy tweets. Chris Christie, the iconoclastic Republican governor of New Jersey, has perfected the art of the verbal slapdown with what amounts to his YouTube channel. Barack Obama is the first politician to fully utilize the Internet to organize and fund-raise. Sarah Palin will be remembered as the first politician to brand her social media outlets as if she were a social media Oprah. And, of course, Representative

Anthony Weiner of New York will forever be remembered as an opposite example of a politician who let a Twitter controversy wreck his image and turn him into an object of ridicule.

While new media creates dedicated channels for people and movements, the traditional media—led by Rupert Murdoch's paywalled *Wall Street Journal* and iPad-enabled *The Daily*—will be in a slugfest against Google's drive to live out the dictum of Stewart Brand, of *Whole Earth Catalog* fame, that "information wants to be free."

Actually, Brand said at the first convention of hackers (meaning programmers) in the decidedly non-Orwellian year of 1984: "On the one hand information wants to be expensive, because it's so valuable. The right information in the right place just changes your life. On the other hand, information wants to be free, because the cost of getting it out is getting lower and lower all the time. So you have these two fighting against each other."[3]

Brand's formulation will define the polarities of the media wars of the second decade of the twenty-first century. And while the giants slug it out in this war, pygmies will conquer. Consider *The Cove,* which won Best Documentary Feature at the 2010 Academy Awards. It was an amateur effort led in part by Ric O'Barry, Flipper's trainer, to expose the slaughter of dolphins that turned an idyllic cove next to a Japanese village blood red. It was directed by a former *National Geographic* photographer, Louis Psihoyos. What is telling about *The Cove* is that the dolphin movement was a poor stepchild of the mainstream antiwhaling efforts of Greenpeace. It had little formal publicity and no celebrity endorsement or support.

The Cove was funded by a dotcom billionaire, a documentary filmmaker, and O'Barry, with help from experts once with Industrial Light and Magic to create rock sculptures to hide HD cameras that the crew seeded around the cove, *Mission: Impossible* style.[4] *The Cove* went viral when Facebook users started replacing their photo with the movie poster, with O'Barry giving Skype webinars from Japan. This happened without all the traditional celebrity-driven heft of the mainstream environmental movement.

"The Japanese didn't really know what hit them when this film came out and went viral," James Lee says. "Sure, they were used to American reporters coming over, the odd celebrity, the antiwhaling stuff, and the

Greenpeace guys. They were used to that. They weren't used to this international wave of people cutting, pasting, sharing, tagging, liking, and promoting this film."[5]

From Michael Moore to James O'Keefe's phony Muslim donor sting of NPR, documentaries and exposés from small, ideologically driven groups, marketed by social media, will increasingly edge out even edgy organizations such as Greenpeace, MoveOn.org, and the Tea Party. The edgiest of all, in the mode of the Yes Men and BPGlobalPR, will wrap their *Saturday Night Live*–style webisodes against corporate targets under the banner of political commentary and satire, bulletproofing themselves for now under the First Amendment. Imitators will proliferate.

Similar attacks could easily become viral political ads in corporate politics as "access to the proxy" campaigns heat up. Expect to also see a raft of "Lonely Girl"–style phony testimonials and mashed-up imagery to fill up the screens of 4G mobile devices.

As satirists and documentary filmmakers explore ways to mau-mau targeted institutions, trial lawyers will be working to erode Section 230 protections of interactive computer services providers. All they need is an opening. Internet companies and foundations may give it to them.

The leaders of Google acted decently but perhaps unwisely when they briefly moved against the offensive Michelle Obama image, citing malware concerns.[6] Online services are going to be increasingly challenged by other cases that cry out for correction. What will they do?

An act of favoritism or even compassion by Google or Wikipedia as well as Internet service providers could open a loophole through which a runaway jury could drive a Mack truck to treat these technology platforms as content providers.

We should at the least expect renewed assaults on Section 230 protections by lawsuits trying to piggyback off discrimination and copyright law.

The Coming Cyber Crisis

As we become more networked, the nodes and networks themselves will become ever more insecure. "At least in the short term—three years to five years—hacking is going to get easier," Yakutis says. "The number of organizations that have the funding to put in true intrusion detection systems and implement them at the level at they are intended to be used, with the correct monitoring, the correct auditing, the correct penetration testing, are very few."[7]

Identity theft will remain rampant. You can expect the steady boil of personal and business cyber insecurity to continue. Governments and large and small businesses will be assaulted by the wholesale theft and compromise of secrets by groups and their mirror sites that will be far more shadowy than WikiLeaks.

"The thing that I don't think the world has fully comprehended that it is not just the Citibanks that will be attacked," says Rich Daly, chief executive of the giant technology services firm Broadridge Financial. "It's going to be the guy selling gazebo parts by mail order, patients' records—you name it, that will be vulnerable."[8]

We may or may not see Richard Clarke's predicted full-scale cyber 9/11, but there will almost certainly be such attempts at mass mayhem. Some Stuxnet-like cyberattacks will go physical, with the attempt to inflict injury and death, either as a result of a cyberattack in tandem with a terrorist attack or the skillful hacking and sabotage of a critical part of our national infrastructure.

Cyberattacks, stolen data, and the seven swords of digital assassination will lead to ever more persistent cries for authentication—so that only the right people can access the right facility or data, and that those who make accusations on the Internet have to stand by them with their real identities. As the crisis deepens, many will turn to biometrics as the answer—retinal scans, voiceprints, thumbprints.

Biometrics, however, is probably at best a stopgap solution. Why? Biometrics ultimately reduces physical characteristics to algorithms. And such algorithms, once stored, can be reproduced infinitely at will. The first company that maintains a database of retinal scans for its customers is going to be a prime target for the world's best hackers.

How bad will cyber insecurity become? Having no history to turn to, we look to our imagination and science fiction for lessons for the future, where many of the consequences of cyberwars have already been explored. In the reimagined TV series *Battlestar Galactica,* the only humans who survived a combined physical and digital attack by cyborgs were stationed on a decommissioned starship that was being turned into a museum. The ship was the only one in the fleet to survive because its systems had never been integrated into the fleet's network.[9]

More and more real-world institutions are going to be tempted to become Battlestar Galacticas. Some are going to forgo the advantages of the digital age in order to be more secure. There will be more closed loops, more virtual private networks, more walled gardens.

In short, the digital city of the future will still have freeways, but with more guards and gated communities. A few eccentrics will try, as much as possible, to live off the grid altogether.

The Death of Privacy . . .

At the end of his life, the great science-fiction writer Arthur C. Clarke collaborated with author Stephen Baxter to write a novel, *The Light of Other Days*.[10] It was not a masterpiece. The characters are a bit thin and the plot is stuffed with filler scenes that don't amount to much. None of this keeps the book from being a great read, because the book's premise is startling.

In this futuristic novel, scientists develop an invisible microscopic "wormhole camera" that allows them to see anything happening anywhere on Earth. Over time, the technology becomes as cheap and commoditized as cell phones. Soon anyone can open a wormhole to learn what anyone else is doing.

The result is the WikiLeaks vision taken to the extreme, the utter and immediate loss of all privacy, the figurative dropping of all walls. There is no discussion inside the White House, CIA, or any other governmental or corporate entity in the world that cannot be seen and overheard by millions of people. There is no love affair, no payoff or bribe, no minor vice, that can be performed without instant discovery and public observation.

After a number of years, the loss of privacy begins to alter the essence of what it means to be human. Some people walk around in the nude and shamelessly perform every bodily function imaginable in public. Others who once had disgraceful secrets to protect carry on as they did before, only now without apology or shame. But many people conform to the standards of the society that is watching them, slavishly mugging for the cameras and making anodyne statements about virtue. In this novel, Robin Williams's Little Snitch finally makes the full transition to becoming Big Brother.

While a right to privacy is found nowhere explicitly in our Constitution, most Americans feel they have one. A famous 1890 *Harvard Law*

Review article by Louis Brandeis and Samuel D. Warren enunciated this right to privacy, which is now seen today as a modern necessity. Arthur C. Clarke and Baxter showed us that the expectation of privacy is essential to being human. Without it, we would all go a little bit nuts.

And, as we have seen throughout these pages, that is exactly what is beginning to happen.

. . . And the Ascension of Anonymity

The strange fact of the Internet, however, is that while it strips away privacy from victims, it readily bestows anonymity on the attackers. Facebook Connect provides a partial answer by encouraging us to log on to third-party websites, mobile devices, and gaming systems with our Facebook identity. If this is a trend, if everyone actually did go without a mask on the Internet, would that really be a good thing?

Think of the unanimous decision by the U.S. Supreme Court in 1958 to prevent the State of Alabama from forcing the NAACP from revealing its membership list. Had the NAACP been forced to do so, individual members would have been subjected to state retribution, and the NAACP itself subjected to fines as an out-of-state ("foreign") corporation.

The court found a constitutional principle, related to free association, that allowed the NAACP to keep its membership list private. But the same principle invoked to protect the membership of the NAACP was also invoked to defend the confidentiality of another organization prominent in Alabama at that time—the members of the Ku Klux Klan (though the courts later upheld state laws unmasking them).[11]

Identification makes people take responsibility for their assertions and actions. But it would also be a victory for conformity and for those who would persecute whistle-blowers and the outspoken.

One proposal often bandied about is to make pseudonymity a social standard. The idea is that if users were encouraged to have one consistent virtual identity, they would still be more open than their analog selves, but they would have enough reputational equity in that secondary identity so that they would be more careful about what they post, an incrementally better standard.

If we could know who everyone was—or if they had a consistent pseudonym—then the crowd could regulate the digital conversation. This self-regulation is already a long-held practice in the commercial space. Many commercial sites shine a spotlight on reviewers who use their real names. Amazon and eBay were among the first companies to start to regulate the conversation, with Yelp recently having taken steps in this direction. Broadridge Financial is doing the same in the shareholder arena. Commercial companies now routinely give more weight to commentators with a history, people who had engaged in commerce, who dealt honestly at both ends of the transaction, whose posted commentary was fair and accurate, and who generated more results and more of a following.

Commercial space lets crowds regulate themselves. When people are malicious or obstreperous or have no history and therefore no standing to make sweeping pronouncements, the crowd drowns them out.

But how do we keep track of who's who in the vast Venetian ball of the greater Internet? How do we manage the fine balance between the protections of anonymity and the need to know who is making an accusation?

There might be a way to automate the cleaning up of digital assassinations by search engines. Steven J. Horowitz, while still at the Harvard Law School in 2007, proposed an interesting approach to search. His proposal "would require search engines to remove a web page from their indexes when an individual notifies them that the page contains defamatory content, while allowing those who post the content to respond with counter notices or other legal action," he wrote in the Yale Law Journal Online.[12]

Horowitz's plan might create reciprocity—the poster could maintain his accusation on search results, but only if he pulls off his mask and steps forward. This would neatly defuse many Google bombs while allowing the current regime of unfettered, free, and anonymous expression to reign on the message boards of the world.

Cass Sunstein, a regulatory czar in the Obama administration and a faculty member at the Harvard Law School, suggests a right to "take down" notices of defamatory material modeled after the Digital Millennium Copyright Act. "It is true that this approach might be burdensome," he acknowledges.[13] In fact, if any such claim would have to be judged and adjudicated, it might require something that not even Google could afford—an army of lawyers the size of India.

Horowitz, while still a student, seems to have the better understanding of what can and cannot be done on the Internet. Unlike other, more chimerical schemes from hallowed legal scholars, Horowitz's proposal would not necessarily require millions of lawyers and millions more for lawyers. In fact, his scheme might be automated.

Social Media Upheaval

What happens to people and society in the next few years?

Some will begin to suffer from "digital depression" caused by "social comparison" when they see on Facebook where the Joneses went for vacation. More dangerous will be the addictive nature of digital activity—call it "virtual confusion"—when users decompress from the vivid, enhanced, exciting virtual worlds into the glum real world of jobs, taxes, and dateless weekends. Like the guide in Mombasa says in *Inception,* the elderly men go to a opium-den-like dream room not to sleep, but to be waked up. "The dream has become their reality."

The troll phenomenon—whether the funeral rants of the Westboro Baptist Church or the hipper precincts of Internet's trolldom—will continue to invade our screens. Jokes about the deaths of children and racist-misogynistic-homophobic rants will continue to be explained by troll apologists as Socratic ironies meant to point to deeper truths, though they never get around to expressing what these deeper truths truly are. One can only hope that the more extreme members of the troll community will one day see their reflections in the Westboro Baptist Church and realize they are at that segment of the ideological wheel where libertarianism touches anarchy and anarchy gives way to fascism.

In the midst of all these challenges, we must struggle to keep in mind that the positives of digital technology will continue to outweigh the negatives. We must never lose sight of the remarkable age of discovery before us.

Scholars of the humanities, for example, are finding ways to use digital technology to map collaborations across the history of jazz. Stanford and Oxford scholars are "Mapping the Republic of Letters" between Voltaire and other eighteenth-century figures to graph the flow of Enlightenment ideas.[14]

Reverend Carol Howard Merritt sees "genius constellations" of new media infused with the intellectual enthusiasm of Parisian cafés in the twenties and the artistic energy of the Harlem Renaissance. In her online chats with other progressive ministers, she says, "There is definitely a kind of electricity that is there that isn't there at regular mainline denominations."[15]

In the political sphere, the limits of social media to organize will be tested. Some have argued that social media breeds weak links—affinity groups centered around soccer or collectibles or some other fascination—but lacks the leadership and resources to effect significant social change. The Egyptian man who named his firstborn daughter Facebook—after the leaderless uprising that overthrew Hosni Mubarak—is a living rebuke to the weak-links argument.[16] It will remain to be seen, however, how effective social media will be in managing the aftermath and the myriad disappointments that will follow revolutionary euphoria.

For business, social media's scale and reach will continue to level the playing field between small and large enterprises, in which boots on the ground will not be nearly important as strategy and the ability to influence markets through new media.

The power of wikis to bring crowd wisdom to tasks will be more fully expressed by new technologies. In institutions of all kinds, chief information officers will become more deeply involved in netcentric management, encouraging workers at all levels of the hierarchy to create spontaneous teams by task.

Deloitte and Booz Allen Hamilton are pioneering social networks that help managers quickly find information inside the institutional human memory. The authors learned of at least one Marine Corps general who is finding that classified blogs are a more efficient way to get a quick answer to his queries than through the traditional military hierarchy.

Technology and the Internet will foment a renaissance of rural communities. High incomes can be accessed by the talented and the educated in less expensive and more wholesome environments. With so many retirees financially unprepared for retirement, many will live on their Social Security payments in scenic places like rural Colorado, or exotic and inexpensive locales like Panama and Thailand, while using vivid online connections to stay close to family and grandkids, perhaps by Skype HD 3D.

Digital Alienation, Conformity, and Conditional Truth

For Ned Desmond, the big question about the near future of social media is "what does it mean to be in real-time contact with so many more people?" He sees especially profound implications in the melding of mobility and constant contact through social media. For younger people born into this way of life, "they have their phones out all the time, and it's not even that they're text-messaging," Desmond says. "They're checking a lot of different things—they're checking posts, organizing to go do things as a group, and when doing things as a group they still have got their phones out, organizing as a group to do things later.

"It's quite impressive, this sort of organization on the fly, mobile computing linked up with Facebook," Desmond continues. "This combination of mobile and social in real time has got to be one of the most profound social developments in human history. I don't know what comes of it, but the behavior by itself is so objectively immense that it can't be innocuous."

Desmond worries that not all of the implications will be healthy. "When you are reporting on everything about yourself, pretty much in real time, and you're organizing for the next crowd in real time . . . there is a certain level of thought that appears to go completely missing," he says. Just as obsessively taking photos of your vacation can put you at a distance from your own vacation, can the full-time tracking, reporting, and comparing of real-time experience alienate you from your own life?

Desmond also worries about digital technology enforcing conformity. He once lived in Japan, where he noted that the ready adoption of mobile apps seems to make it easier for individuals to navigate in Japan's conformist culture. "I can see this same conformity being driven through my kids' lives, whether there's a group that wants to do something and you've got to go along with the group. Because you're either in the group or out of the group—and if you're out of the group, who knows what they might be saying about you?" he concludes.

The strikes of silent slashers, evil clones, and assassins and attackers will be softened by friends coming to one's defense. But will digital attacks present the human brain with a task we are not evolved to manage:

the dilemma of living with conditional truth about people, brands, and businesses?

Internet lies are global and lasting. Will the vividness of online media make lies sink in? And how easily will we be able to dismiss these images and statements when the images are utterly realistic and follow us room to room in full motion 3-D, with statements made to us in the calm, cultivated voice of our house computer?

Skepticism is one thing. To half believe something is another. Will a coming age of conditional truth force us to adopt a kind of Schröding-er's cat attitude toward everything and everyone?

Combat Marketing

"It's always easier to tear something down than to defend it," James Lee says. "But eventually, the defenders catch up." He likens the future of reputation management to the "virus wars" between garden-variety black hats and security companies like Symantec and McAfee. Over a long period of disruption, the security companies gained enough experience to counter ordinary viruses. The struggle soon settled into the equivalent of trench warfare, where defenders and hackers "just lob stuff at one another periodically, but there is no real movement. Everyone is stuck in the Argonne forest, nothing changes."

Now we are fighting the "reputation war," Lee says, and this war is less like the stalemate of World War I than like the early phase of World War II when the Germans blasted through Poland. And make no mistake, in Lee's metaphor, most of us are Poland.

The battle space is not completely without organized resistance. Reputation.com (Reputation Defender's new name) is a first generation company that counters bad information on the Internet. While reputation companies evolve, corporations will turn to marketing and consulting firms that promise not only to help their brand but to damage the other company's brand without fingerprints. It is easy to foresee the emergence of combat marketing companies, and a technological arms race between these combat marketers and a slew of reputation management firms that will attempt to do for reputation management what Symantec and McAfee do in security.

Lee imagines boutique firms that will surreptitiously make and post viral videos that put their clients' competitors in a very bad light. "In the digital reputation arena, you will see companies out there trashing products, trashing people, trashing candidates," he says. "You're going to see similar companies out there trying to set the record straight or erase those comments, or manage that process, or verify who is saying those things."

Much of the business of reputation defense today involves laborious keyword searching, quick evaluation of difficult context, and the penetrating of paywalls and other barriers to get at and counter all the trash on message boards with positive content. It is a complex process requiring contextual judgment that cannot yet be fully automated. "The company that comes up with a way to automate either destroying someone's reputation online or defending and resurrecting their reputation online is the one that is going to win that battle," Lee says. "The automation and the 24/7 ability to do it without human intervention is what separates a company's ability to be successful in this arena—just as it has in the virus wars."

The practices of consumer companies, which pay the highest dollar per user for content and cognitive data mining, are beginning to migrate to the less profitable areas of politics, public affairs, and ideological nonprofits. Witness the successful use of RapLeaf data in that recent California initiative campaign.

In reputational attacks, businesses will be the most frequent targets. "Companies can defend themselves in a court of law," Lee says. "They can't always defend themselves in the court of public opinion. The court of public opinion is more devastating to the brand than what happens litigationwise."

In the meantime, Lee believes that the 2012 election will stimulate "a really unholy year on social media sites," forcing corporations, institutions, and individuals to get realistic about fighting back in the reputation wars. "One of the biggest challenges is for law firms to figure out how to get ready for this next wave of product and brand assassination."

Staying Human

Put off for a few more decades the question of whether or not computers will achieve sentience and what that would mean for humanity. There are already profound philosophical questions emerging now about how digital technology is affecting human nature, from shorter attention spans to a loss of critical thinking skills.

The yeastiest of all debates now under way was sparked by Jaron Lanier, whose *You Are Not a Gadget* raised the humanist objection that we are degrading our culture and allowing ourselves to be treated as "digital peasants," peripheral to the network instead of the reason for the network. In the Web 2.0, the "combination of hive mind and advertising has resulted in a new kind of social contract. The basic idea of this contract is that authors, journalists, musicians, and artists are encouraged to treat the fruits of their intellects and imaginations as fragments to be given without pay to the hive mind. . . . Culture is to become precisely nothing but advertising."[17] When everyone can publish an e-book or offer a song for free, the web pries "culture away from capitalism while the rest of life is still capitalistic," turning culture into a slum.[18]

And in Facebook, Lanier sees us straining to live within trite boxes devised for us by a Harvard sophomore. In the world of the mirror, connections matter more than the content. The result, he says, is the trivialization of culture.

Novelist Zadie Smith, in a tart *New York Review of Books* essay on Lanier's ideas and the movie *The Social Network,* worries about the cultural impact of Facebook. "When a human being becomes a set of data on a website like Facebook, he or she is reduced," Smith writes. "Everything shrinks. Individual character. Friendships. Language. Sensibility. In a way it's a transcendent experience: we lose our bodies, our messy feelings, our desires, our fears. It reminds me that those of us who turn in disgust from what we consider an overinflated liberal-bourgeois sense of self should be careful what we wish for: our denuded networked selves don't look more free, they just look more owned."[19]

Writer Alexis Madrigal pushed back in *The Atlantic*: "But we will never live on the Internet in the way we lived those other places. Let's not reify our online meanderings. The angst of a body slowly dying doesn't go away no matter how many times you type something into a box and then hit return. And that is a good thing. Smith wants to say, 'You are who you appear to be on Facebook.' But who believes that of themselves or anyone else? She makes the drastic overstatement only to serve as her grounds for outright rejection of the service."[20] Madrigal ends the piece with a digital snapshot of cute farm animals sent to him by his girlfriend. The snapshot made him think of *her*—the hands that took the picture, the woman behind the camera.

Our own take is that Facebook and the wider Internet so far seem to move us in both directions. We confess to exchanging platitudes on web-based platforms that, if spoken, would mortify a used-car salesman, as well as clicking on our share of videos of singing dogs and laughing babies.

But we have also heard some of the best poetry, seen environmental images of rare and unearthly beauty, and profited from video posts of some of the most thought-provoking material we have ever encountered shared with us by e-mail and by Facebook friends.

Another debate will be about how the Internet defines deviancy down. How many of the 75 million monthly visitors to porn sites would have ventured into an adult bookstore a generation before? Or how many of the millions who access adult dating sites would have so readily sought sex with strangers?[21]

And with file sharing, one doesn't have to be a hacker to break the eighth commandment (this is stealing, in case you've forgotten). In the days before broadband, consumers turned to file-sharing services that allowed them to get faster downloads, depending on how much music they themselves shared with the network. Given this incentive to stuff the database, many people—who would never dream of lifting a CD from an old-fashioned record store—sought to increase their download speeds by stuffing the system with pirated music.

Finally, how many of us would have so readily, on a daily basis, compromised our privacy twenty years ago as easily and as often as we do now with virtually every free service and platform that we use?

The trade-offs are real, the outcomes unclear. The debates will rage on.

Outsourcing Our Thinking

The average American is flooded by 100,000 words a day from all media—heard on television and radio, and encountered in print and the Internet.

In less than five days, the average American encounters more words than are in *War and Peace*.[22] Over a year, American households consume 3.6 zettabytes of information in all forms, from words to pixels (a zettabyte is equal to 100 billion copies of all the books in the Library of Congress).[23]

But more than information is coming our way. In very real sense, the computer now functions as a part of our brain, serving as our memory and even performing some of our thought processes for us. More than once, we have started to commit a fact, a timeline, a joke, a quote, or a riff to memory—only to stop and realize that it is no longer necessary. The Internet will remember it for us.*

Wiki research on any given topic also allows us to get to the core of a selected issue much faster than we could by ourselves. It is a kind of a SparkNotes for everything. By getting us to the essence of any issue quicker than we could on our own, the crowd is doing much of our thinking for us.

As a peripheral to human intelligence and a companion to our imagination, the computer is undoubtedly a boon. And just as we are tempted to celebrate this fact, we read a quote from Eric Schmidt, who with his gift for Orwellian statements, predicted that Google would one day know so much about us that it will be able to help us plan our lives. "I actually think most people don't want Google to answer their questions," Schmidt said. "They want Google to tell them what they should be doing next."[24]

If that statement fills you with "an intense and crushing feeling of religious terror," as Wally Weaver says in *Watchmen,* "don't be alarmed. That indicates only that you are still sane."[25]

The Final Takeaway—In a Machine World Be More Human

The greatest danger is that what now serves as a useful tool will become a crutch, and the crutch will atrophy those skills that make us most human.

Perhaps the most important response will be to properly educate the first generation of humans to use this technology from infancy. There is immense promise in more deeply integrating technology into teaching. Digital technology lets anyone climb the Ivy wall by downloading Yale's Open Courses lectures, whether it be historian Donald Kagan's descriptions of the Peloponnesian War or philosopher Shelly Kagan's meditations on death.

Software has the infinite patience to expose a student to every conceivable permutation of a math problem, to diagnose the cognitive roadblock, and then to lead that student to the best way to solve it.

---

* No sooner were these words written than researchers reported in *Science* that online databases do, in fact, affect the way people remember information—"the Google Effect."

Technology will be critical to restoring mastery of the subjects of science, technology, engineering, and mathematics that must be recaptured in the United States and other developed countries, who are failing to graduate sufficient numbers of engineers and scientists. But education must also include the emotional intelligence and social skills that arise from team sports and from team-based, team-building intellectual projects. Every student should be engaged in activities that teach them etiquette and respect for the knowledge of others. We don't want to raise a generation of social outcasts, painfully shy and morbidly obsessed, whose most developed aspects are their thumbs. Education must also include world history and literature to provide perspective for the seemingly new dilemmas of the technological age.

In short, we need the sort of education that will prepare people to function well in the spontaneously forming teams that netcentric organizations will require. They will need to be steeped in Postel's law for both the digital and analog worlds—to be conservative in what they do, liberal in what they accept from others.

In a technological world, the killer apps will belong to the well rounded, to the trustworthy, to those who can communicate well with customers or write a deft response on Yelp. The future will belong to the high touch.

Above all, people who understand human behavior, based on the age-old motives of money, sex, power, and envy, will still have the best grasp on things to come. This insight is needed as never before when our computers will have us relate to them by a familiar name. It will be a world of robots, androids, and intelligent homes and cars.

Will technology degrade our culture or liberate it? Will it devalue individuals or magnify us?

Will it foster so much mixed truth that we will lose our bearings? Or will it be the most powerful instrument in history for separating truth from untruth?

And when the day comes that the unseen computer behind our walls whispers a lie, will we have the presence of mind to keep our own counsel?

11 :// The Seven Shields of Digital Assassination

> If you don't know where you are going, you'll wind up somewhere else.
>
> **—Yogi Berra**

THE SEVEN SHIELDS of digital assassination are, the means to prepare against the seven swords of digital assassination. The seventh shield culminates in a game plan on pages 235–36 that must be adapted and personalized.

Even if you are Internet savvy, the first half of this chapter, "Managing Reputation," imparts broad strategic guidance from the seven shields on how to build and maintain a defense. If you are not Internet savvy, the second section of this chapter, "Managing Digital Platforms," provides basic explanations for maintaining a positive image on Facebook, Yelp, Twitter, Wikipedia, and other technology platforms.

Social media is changing all the time. Best practices are always evolving. Visit our website, www.DigitalAssassinationBook.com, to stay current.

Managing Reputation

Think strategically about your defense. But first, what do we mean by "you"? You can be your business, your product, your brand, your celebrity. Even when you just means you, things are not quite so simple.

Appreciate the interaction between your two selves, the self that you know or think you know, and your online self, the public profile that you can shape but never fully own.

This distinction became clear when Yogi Berra sat next to one of the authors at a private dinner a few years ago. When asked about the body of oxymoronic sayings attributed to him, Yogi said with a world-weary sigh, "I'm not sure I said all of those things."

Yogi is a smart, engaging man, an accessible icon whose grit and maneuvers as a catcher, outfielder, and manager are baseball legend. Like all public figures, he has two personas. One is the character—in the ordinary sense of the word—of his private life, the Lawrence Peter "Yogi" Berra who strikes at the truth with a unique and colorful style of expression. The other is the public image of Yogi, which is sometimes that of a goofball whose obtuse sayings have a Zenlike quality.

Like Yogi, each of us has two personas. One is our actual self. The other is our public self, with varying degrees of agreement between the two.

In Yogi's case, his greatness established, he is free to regard the goofier part of his public profile with sardonic humor. For most of us, our digital self is our significant public profile—and how that profile is perceived becomes our personal brand. Perceptions about brand can determine the fate of careers, reputations, products, or businesses. That's why digital profiles are so important.

The difficult truth is that we will never own our digital profile—the Internet owns it. However, this profile is within our power to shape and manage.

Here is where Yogi's advice is again pertinent: If you don't know where you are going, you will wind up somewhere else. And it usually is someplace you really don't want to go.

For that reason, we tell clients that it is absolutely necessary to take control of how you are perceived.[1]

Whether you are a corporate executive or mid-level manager, entrepreneur, restaurateur, doctor, lawyer, accountant, consultant, a singular sensation or a team leader, celebrity, model or fashion designer, parent or grandparent, you must manage your reputation or others will do it for you.

The First Shield of Digital Assassination:
Back to School

If you are Internet savvy, you keep up with changes in cyberspace by reading online sources like Mashable, Ars Technica, Chris Brogan's advice on digital media marketing, Gawker Media's Gizmodo, Boing Boing for amusement, and Wired for the take of the digital establishment. *If you surf these sites without giving them a second thought, proceed to the second shield.* If not, please read on.

If these websites sound like Martian names to you, there are many other places to visit and easily, painlessly expand your knowledge about social media.

Learning social media is like learning to play the piano. To be proficient at it, you need hands-on education, learning through the actual keystrokes. It is easy to find such instruction in public libraries or civic groups, business associations, colleges, and continuing education programs. There are myriad one- or two-day boot camps on the Internet and social media, many offered as webinars, video on demand, or podcasts. SlideShare.net has many slide decks from such presentations. Similar classes are offered by associations in many professions.

Local chambers of commerce, clubs, and business or professional associations organize regular and ongoing lectures about new media. Also, you might seek help from younger office colleagues or relatives, those who are born swimmers in this digital age. Keep in mind, however, that youth may be far behind you in thinking carefully about privacy or exercising good judgment on the Internet.

Read everything possible about platforms or services. Use search engines to find explanations for any information you do not understand. Study question-and-answer sections or discussion areas of search engines, major blogs, and free services. Clear answers in everyday language are at your fingertips.

Don't stop until you understand—*with your fingertips*—how search engines really work, how to start a blog and maintain it with an easy free software like Word-Press; how to access the popular social networking services like Facebook, Tumblr, or Jaiku; how a search term can be optimized; how to use Google AdSense.

Whether you take classes, learn online, or explore with your fingertips, you are not equipped to manage your reputation until you can comfortably navigate and post and actively participate on the Internet.

The Second Shield of Digital Assassination:
I Am, Therefore Who Do I Think I Am?

After you have developed an understanding of the power and reach of the Internet, now undertake a brutally honest assessment of the first of your two selves—your actual self.

To do this well, act as your own father confessor. It might be necessary to write down everything—*just not on your computer.* Be brutally honest with yourself about your sins, shortcomings, and bad raps.

So how do you begin? Do a brain dump—not a brain freeze—by asking a series of probing questions about your subject.

Who are you—really?

Who are your detractors, and why are they detractors?

Who are your enemies, and how did they become your enemies?

Who wants to get back at you for something you did in high school or college or during your career?

Do your detractors, enemies, and revenge seekers have a point? Would you feel the same way they do if they had treated you the same way?

Why were you once fired? What were the worst customer-relations or product disasters you managed? How did they happen? Have you addressed the problem that led to these failures?

What about that nasty breakup? What is your ex saying about you?

You assessment of yourself should not be a quest for fairness or justification. One digital expert we know is an acknowledged technology leader who was discreetly cashed out of a corporate Fortune 500 job after having his decisions second-guessed by his wayward board. Now a nationally recognized entrepreneur, he is still haunted on Google by a blog from a former colleague that offers excruciating detail on his departure from that old job.

What failing do you have buried in your background, no matter how well papered over, that could be pumped up into stark words in primary colors by a blogger?

Most of all, what have you done in your private life that someone somehow could find out about you? What might people learn about you that you currently believe no one could possibly know?

Consider a female executive who is married, politically well connected, a community leader. A few years ago, she went in for a medical procedure that required anesthesia. Like many patients in the twilight state of moderate sedation, she became disinhibited and recounted a graphic sexual experience. Like others who have done this, she likely has no memory that she said anything.

A few months after her procedure, one of the nurses who was in the operating room committed a gross violation of medical ethics. She related the woman's story to a friend over a glass of wine. This should not have happened, but it did.

Now that friend, whenever she sees this executive, can't help but marvel that he has access to a secret from her unconscious mind that she surely could never suspect he knows.

What secrets do you have that could conceivably come to light?

Be brutal. Be hard on yourself. Think of yourself as the target you aim to destroy and you will have completed this task.

Place yourself on the scale of risk.

Are you like most people, a sometime target?

Are you at moderate risk, a person with some visibility and enemies?

Or are you at high risk, a person with a public presence? Are you an individual—a celebrity, ultrarich, a politically active person—who is very high risk?

Once you've defined vulnerabilities, review the seven swords and imagine all the ways you could be attacked. Write them all down on paper and put them to the side.

The Third Shield of Digital Assassination: Peekaboo, I See Me

You've made a brutally honest personal assessment of your life. Now turn from your actual self to your perceived self, the profile or personal brand as it is perceived on the Internet.

What do people seem to believe about you? What do they likely believe that they might not tell you? What does that biggest brain of all—the web—know about you, and say about you, true or false?

It is easy to stand inside your home or business and look out. Today everyone must stand outside and look in to see what friends, employers, clients, customers, fans, investors, and others see about you.

Look at yourself from the point of view of a digital assassin. What is out there that would make a lethal weapon?

To do this, look beyond the surface search results and into the databases of the "deep web"—sources of personal information not indexed on the major search engines. Before beginning, turn off personalized accounts, like Gmail and other services that could otherwise skew the search results.

- Check out your online profile on iSearch, Pipl, ZabaSearch, and similar "people search" sites that pull data from public sources like from Wikipedia, Facebook, Flickr, Twitter, and government data centers. Check out OpenSecrets.org to see if it reports your campaign donations and political activity.
- If it is a complicated history, consider spending up to about $40 on a background source like Intelius or BackgroundChecks .com to see what pops up.
- Check county or city databases to see if speeding tickets or any other civil or criminal information pops up. The formats differ among jurisdictions, but you can pull up liens, violations, court appearances, and tax issues online. Even if you have never been arrested, check to see if someone with a similar name has. This is very important to know and understand if malefactors are out there with the same name as yours.
- In the United States, check your credit score on AnnualCre ditReport.com, a free credit report you can access once a year.
- Check out how your home or office looks from Google Maps and Street View. Check out your real estate evaluation on sites like Zillow.com.
- If you have a business, you might want to spend a little bit more and do a D&B on it—the Dun & Bradstreet website with access to deep web material on your small business.

The greatest tool at your disposal is the most accessible—Google's exquisitely precise advanced search function, which allows refined searches and eliminates irrelevant results. Search for your name, subject, or key phrases—in as many likely variations as you can think of—to access a 360-degree review.

If you were divorced, arrested, fired from a job, put in every conceivable search term that might pull up a negative thread about that.

Review as many search engine results pages as necessary until the relevance to you completely thins out.

If you have a rare name—Xavier Stoneberry, for example—check for any conflation of your identity with that of a namesake—there could be another among the world's 7 billion people. This could unfortunately lead searchers to conclude that negative information about that other Xavier Stoneberry is about you.

On the other hand, if you have a common name, you will find it is relatively easy to hide among the trees.

While conducting the search, keep in mind that comments posted on message boards or behind paywalls may not show up. Still, you can uncover a lot of data about yourself with free sources.

Here are some key resources to flesh out the self-search.

- *Identity:* KnowEm is a site that can check to see if an evil clone is using your name, or forms of online identity, or if a brandjacker has hijacked your business on social media.
- *Message Boards:* BoardTracker, Boardreader, and Omgili are free services that catch a lot of what might be said about you or your subject on message boards and discussion threads.
- *Social Media:* Google Blog Search is a good place to start to take in what blogs are saying about your area. Social Mention can track what is being said on social networks like Facebook and blogs. IceRocket is another good blog search engine. Technorati indexes blogs, breaks them into helpful categories, and performs searches. BlogPulse tracks blogging trends that might affect you. Addict-o-matic, whose motto is "inhale the web," can collate a load of material from across the social media universe.*
- *Business:* Yelp is the essential self-search for small or consumer business. Search sites specific to sector, such as Revinate, which tracks online reviews of hotels. Use Radian6 and Alterian SM2 to monitor social media conversations about your brand or product.

---

* Keep in mind that the openness of various social media platforms is not uniform. Even for major sites like Twitter and Facebook, how searchable they are continues to change. How data points from social networking sites are indexed is an ongoing negotiation between data owners and search engines.

- *News:* The Internet is rich with free searches from news organizations. If mentioned or quoted in a story, searches tend to be time sensitive. So be sure to use the correct time parameters if you are searching about news about yourself. To do a robust search, access Factiva or Nexis, or search local news outlets, many of which require payment.
- *Images:* Google, Bing, and Yahoo! image searches are a critical, often overlooked part of any search. Keep in mind that TinEye can perform a reverse search on an image, telling others who you are from an online photo.

Are there any photos, images, or cartoons of you that are accessible on obscure sites? Check out the photo indexes on your friend's Facebook sites. Keep in mind that someone may have posted a college photo of you and that seven-foot bong that you had long forgotten about.

If an image exists, it can go viral. And if it goes viral, your identity can be tracked down, just like the photo that forced a Republican congressman to resign after he posted that shirtless photo of himself as a Craigslist's personal.

Keep in mind that the goal is just to see how the search appears online. Now take look at all this online information—information that is true, not true, or suggestive—and ask:

How could a silent slasher use it?

Could someone use available information to create an evil clone?

Is there anything that could be distorted to ignite public indignation and make you the target of the human flesh search engine?

And the hardest question of all: Is there a bad fact about you that might be remixed to make it look far worse?

Truth remix is the difficult problem. It forces contingency planning, deciding in advance that if push comes to shove, whether to admit to some imperfection, what to disclose, how to explain, and where to explain.

Finally, after all the facts have been inventoried from your brain dump to the web, then inventory the information inside your computer and how it might be used by an assassin practicing clandestine combat.

If you were digitally assassinated, like Steve in chapter 5, do you have pictures, letters, or documents in your computer that would be deeply embarrassing or items that could falsely incriminate you? If you do, either you need great confidence in your security or you need to store it somewhere else—like a cheap, airgapped laptop.

Compare your inventory of real-world vulnerabilities from the second shield against your online profile. What is revealed? What is distorted? What is made up?

In short, match your online profile with your offline life, that other you. What did you find? Then, regularly monitor the online profile of your brand, product, or celebrity for anything new that changes instantaneously on the web.

The Fourth Shield of Digital Assassination: The New and Improved You

The fourth shield protects by creating a new and improved image of you on the web. It involves a set of affirmative, positive actions to build what we call a "reputational cushion"[2] to absorb blows against your public persona.

This concept becomes clear when we compare the fates of two California politicians. The first was a little-known executive who ran for office. Just as he was getting his campaign off the ground, an embarrassing incident surfaced in the media. This man was an avid jogger who had been changing in his office for a run when a female colleague opened the door and caught a glimpse of him naked.

The story spread, making it a staple of drive-time humor.

No matter what the candidate did after that—no matter how qualified he might have been—he was forever more just the "naked guy." His campaign was soon swept away.

Now compare him to Arnold Schwarzenegger, running for governor of California when he was attacked by a *Los Angeles Times* series of stories of sexual excess and even harassment of women in his youth—charges far more serious than inadvertently being spotted naked.

Some of the charges Schwarzenegger laughed off as the folly of his youth. The more serious charges he denied.

An unknown candidate would have been dead then and there. Schwarzenegger survived because after years at the top of the box office, we felt as if we knew him personally. And because his wife, Maria Shriver, unequivocally supported him. Schwarzenegger had a baseline of respect, that cushion, that allowed him to take a reputational beating without folding. Schwarzenegger's reputational armor was only destroyed—and his return to the movies delayed—when substantive proof, in the form of a "love child" caused his wife to walk away from him.

You don't have to be a movie star to build such a cushion. What is needed is a solid, compelling, and attractive online persona that comes to the fore in any search—so that any static, like someone accidentally catching a peek at you naked, is swept into a proper context.

To immunize yourself as much as possible, several pages of positive or neutral hits on search engine results pages are necessary. To create these hits and protect your brand, link your name and business to as much positive content as possible.

Social media engagement is therefore a must to maximize reputation.

First, have a storefront on the web. This site is your controlling digital anchor from which all other efforts radiate and to which they link back. It can be a personal website or blog, your page on your company, business, or product site, or a blog about your celebrity or hobby.

Fill out a Google Profile. It influences search results, and consider opening a Twitter account to tweet to friends or to create a following on a topic in which you have a deep interest or expertise. Namechk.com is a good place to establish a user name or vanity URL across all social media.

Naturally, be careful in choices of images, words, or style. Your posts speak before all audiences: employees and coworkers, family and friends, investors and analysts, clients, customers, the media, and all other constituents. Give a brief autobiographical description of yourself on your website—keep it professional but light.

In this effort, we can learn a lot from how big corporations deepen their relationship with customers through detailed product-related blogs.

- Dialogue is central. The iconic corporate example is Dell's IdeaStorm, which lets customers suggest ideas that Dell engineers evaluate and a community of fans vote up or down on. If you have a small business, having a moderated "suggestion box" that you act on might be one way of enticing customers into a deeper relationship.

- Tone is also vital. Southwest Airlines hosts Nuts About Southwest, a popular corporate blog. It opens a dialogue with customers in the casual, slightly flippant tone that is a hallmark of that airline's culture. For many small firms, such a friendly, open tone is just right.

Whether you are cultivating a brand or business, use this same spirit of openness, responsiveness, and above all, dialogue, to present a positive public profile and image.

Consistent and valuable blogging on areas of expertise will draw a crowd that keeps coming back. If you are passionate about a hobby, offer hints about growing decorative winter cabbage, adopting a shelter dog, or lifting free weights.

Establish a dialogue with other bloggers and link to a host of positive material on sites concerning your subject. But stick to your area of expertise and meet the expectations of visitors by offering consistent information in this area.

If you write a letter to the editor to your local paper, cohost a charity ball, or speak at a PTA meeting, these are all items and images that can be posted and linked to other groups that come up high in search results.

If you own a small business—a bakery, say—you might offer regular advice on cooking, recipes, and seasonal treats. If you are an accountant, you might blog about common tax and payroll pitfalls or common mistakes of recordkeeping.

Post less frequently but with quality advice that has great "nutrient density." Or go in another direction and offer a steady diet of low density, high frequency posts that will raise the prominence of positive material in searches. Visitors are always eager for helpful tips, from cooking to pet grooming.

Another technique is to "pack the database"[3] with plain vanilla information. This means linking to descriptive data—the roster of your high school or college class, professional associations, faith community. Simple vanilla data can be useful in pushing down unwanted results on a search page.

Optimizing Reputation

In posting positive and neutral data, understand the three steps that companies use to maximize search engine optimization (SEO). These steps boost your profile in a search, according to Laszlo Horvath, founder of ActiveMedia, a website optimization company.

- The first SEO step is what Horvath calls "mind reading," the analysis of popular keywords that—without theory or intuition—*tell* you what people are thinking. As in the third shield, think of yourself as a brand and try every permutation of every conceivable keyword about yourself—light, dark, and humorous. Use Google Analytics to see the keywords that brought visitors to your website. Like a compass, this analysis will point to what people are thinking about you, your brand, and business.

- The second SEO step is to make sure that your website has the right architecture—the keywords that link you to your subject ("baking," "tax time," "intellectual property expert") that will help the search engine's spider index your website where you want it. But keep these keywords in context. Overuse them and Google's algorithms might think you are trying to game the search and kick you down the rankings.

- The third SEO step is to link all your websites and social media sites together and to legitimately encourage as many links from others as you can.

This is central. Today links are the currency of the web. The boost in visibility that occurs when one website links to another is called "link juice."

Links are the insertions of hypertext that, when clicked, take the visitor from one site to another. Making such links does not require a deep knowledge of coding. It can easily be found in the "help" part of your toolbar, in free software like WordPress, or in the encoded software of many social media sites.

There are illegitimate ways to generate link juice, which happens when black hats create the equivalent of spam links. Link farms are shady businesses that increase links with content that is high in volume, but with little or no meaning or value. Google adjusts its algorithms daily to catch billions of spamblogs created to game the rankings.

Take the opposite approach by making organic links to valid communities of interest. This includes every club, association, and civic or faith organization in your life. Colleges and universities, for example, are especially highly ranked sites, so any connections of your sites to a higher education site provide some link juice.

Positive content created by individuals is increasingly taking multimedia forms. Now that digital cameras are cheap and it's easy to upload video on free platforms like YouTube, anyone can create his or her own digital "channel" with video blogs, or vlogs, inexpensively and instantly. Your vlog might be a brief talk about a business issue, an interview with a guru in your sector, or a view of a rare aurora borealis from your backyard.

If you are politically minded, and don't mind being open about your views, blog about a hot political topic and link to sites with high search rankings, like the Huffington Post or National Review Online.

Once you have completed this, link all your sites to each other and link as many of them as you can to friends. You might do a friendly "hat tip" to an insight on a popular blogger's post, giving him a reason to link back to you.

A risky but potentially successful strategy arises out of a tendency of human nature: a fight tends to attract a crowd. Taking issue with the position of another blogger—as long as he or she is rational and not prone to personal attacks or derogatory hate speech—can drive both of your rankings.

Whether a major blogger or site wants to pick a bone with you or steer consumers to you for advice, either is link gold. In short, the more positive, neutral, and interesting items you post and link, the more reputational cushion you create on your search engine results against the blows of digital assassins.

The Fifth Shield of Digital Assassination: Regulating the Ether

"The Internet is an odd thing," an analyst for Shore Communications writes. "In some ways it is a medium that acts in essence like radio, but with a nearly infinite number of broadcast channels. Sometimes this 'ether,' as radio was termed in its early days, is used for one-to-many communications, as in websites and feeds; sometimes it's used for one-to-one communications, as in email, instant messaging, and IP telephony."[4]

How do we regulate something as amorphous as the ether?

On the broadcast side—Facebook and the other social media platforms—find one or two, but not three or four, specific themes to promote about yourself and stick to them. Few bloggers are so interesting or so well positioned by television or celebrity that visitors will keep coming back to hear their views on everything. If you are a butcher known with a huge following among foodies for maintaining a deep, informative blog about quality meats, your visitors will be put off if they come to your landing page and see that you've written about the crisis in Syria.

If you think about it, the most famous people are essentially known for one or two things. You will attract a following by offering deep information on a handful of areas of expertise germane to your profession, business, or personal passion. A simple but deep profile is a manageable profile likely to attract a community of followers.

This is true as well for business. One of the authors saw a Fortune 500 client lose the impact of months of communications planning for the company's CEO succession. The goal was to regulate the ether in the announcement of the new CEO, using his wide name recognition and sterling credentials, by keeping him at the top of the headlines for several days after the announcement.

The announcement was released at 7:00 A.M. EST, well before the market opened in New York. It was to be followed by transatlantic news conferences and key employee and constituent calls. The whole company was told by the general counsel's office not to release anything. At just after 11:00 A.M. on that very day, a division of that same company released a four-page product news release on the wires. An hour later, another division announced a new midlevel manager.

The story about the new CEO sank out of sight.

Businesses of all sorts should take note when they "broadcast" across the ether. Good news, special sales, and new products should be released in a disciplined, staggered way, even if you operate a neighborhood bakery. We all know people who compulsively post the most anodyne material about themselves—like that ancient Pompeian in chapter 4 who "posted" the graffito, "On April 19th, I made bread." What was true in the days of the Caesars is true today. It is for people like this that Facebook created a "hide" function that lets you eliminate chatty friends from your news feed.

In narrowing one-to-one communications, you can be as chatty or as intimate as you like. Remember that any message you send to any one person can be resent by malice or by accident with a single click and posted for the world to see.

We all write things we don't want the world to see. *Never* ever write anything that would actually make a bad news story, would get you in trouble with regulators or law enforcement, or would mean you lose the respect of your profession, employer, future employer, or family.

Be careful even about what you say, how you say it, and where you say it in the offline world in this age of Little Snitch. A friend of one of the authors was mortified to learn how close he came to being surreptitiously video-recorded while making an irreverent joke at a public hearing by a man slowly panning the room with his PDA.

Strategic Advice for Businesses, Corporations, and Celebrities

Almost all corporations, brands, or high-profile people are not ready to handle the instantaneous blow of digital assassins. Few would look to such an attack as an opportunity. But never lose sight of the profound effects a digital attack will have on you, your brand, or your business.

Over the past few years, one of the authors developed a strategy manual, some secret sauce, for his corporate clients to use when they are digitally attacked. Here is a distillation of the topline points from this manual, elements of which can be adapted to small businesses and even individuals.

Before a Digital Attack Occurs

Have at the ready response plans that include a fairly elaborate decision tree, a set of "if this . . . then that" set of responses. Playing out realistic scenarios based on likely events is also useful. War-gaming and role-playing offer the visceral learning people need to be ready to launch into instant action.

While future steps should not be cast in concrete, you should have some sense of whether your response to a given attack will be to defend, to counterattack . . . or both. Ask ahead: What is the strategy? What are the messages?

What tactics should be employed? Think through these questions, and make key decisions in advance. Planning will help you to remember: ready, aim, fire. Not: ready, fire, aim.

Once attacked, an organization should take the following action steps:

- Create a war room and a war room environment. Who is in that war room? Different points of view are needed: operations, legal, communications, sales, marketing, and human resources. Are business line heads included so you have realistic assessments of what can and cannot be done?

- CEOs should not run the war room or the crisis team. One corporate head has to have ownership of the war room—usually PR, marketing, or the general counsel. But no one discipline should dominate. The CEO needs to hear all points of view—legal, sales, investor relations, communications, etc.

- Legal and logistical considerations may delay the actual (as opposed to the promised) response. But the real issue is, *could* you react in a digital day if you had to? Could you post a YouTube response within two to four hours? Could you get a statement through legal, PR, and the C-suite in an hour? Remember, a digital day is at most eight hours long.

- More important than having the camera and technology in place for a YouTube upload, does top management understand the need to have such a capability? Is management willing to rearrange sacrosanct schedules?

Responding to an Attack

As soon as an assassin attacks, continually monitor and analyze blogs and video posts. Where is the chatter spreading from? What keywords are driving it?

- Define, if you can, who is attacking and why. Is it a disgruntled customer or employee? A competitor? Uninformed investors panicked by a rumor? A special interest, activist, or extremist group? Or just someone, to again quote *The Dark Knight*'s Alfred Pennyworth, who just wants to watch the world burn?

- List constituencies affected by the attack. Immediately set up short-term and long-term responses to address each constituency's concerns.

- Understand that attacks do not just go away—never, ever. If you ignore them, they get worse very quickly.

- A digital attack often cannot be handled internally. Staff is often constrained by corporate culture, turf, and personalities. Professional outside objective counsel is often necessary, though its advice is sometimes difficult to digest.

- For a variety of legal, logistical, and regulatory reasons, an instant business response—a rebate, a recall, the setting up of a call center—may be the worst thing to do when the facts are unclear or the organizational response will take time. *But at the very least some kind of responsive message must be issued, one that shows a willingness to listen, to be in dialogue, not monologue.*

- With an eight-hour digital day, a response forty-eight hours later is five digital days late. Aim to respond within a two- to four-hour window. Your initial response can always be enriched and sharpened as you move along. Remember: In today's digital world, if you are silent or even just late, you are guilty.

- Identify which media platforms are being used to promote the attack. Can you use the same platforms to defend yourself . . . and perhaps punch back? Can you activate friends who have an organic interest in backing up your response?

- When the values of a company or product are called into question, a personal response on YouTube is often called for. Don't forget the immense usefulness of the posting and targeted distribution of a news release. Once wastepaper sent scattershot to a thousand uninterested reporters, the humble news release is now an indexable response that can be searched by all interested constituencies instantly, globally, without filters on a twenty-four hour basis. This is for media and digital pundits, all constituents—customers, employees, vendors, investors, government officials, and other stakeholders.

- The tone of the statement should be appropriate to the facts. Have you been smeared? Show outrage. Has someone made too much of a legitimate mistake? Show some contrition, while setting out the facts. Define in simple language what happened, perhaps why it happened, and most important, what you are doing about it. This will be repeated many times to many constituencies in the days ahead. Don't get caught up with who is at fault or legal issues at this time unless this is necessary. Show how you are solving the problem and address those issues later.

- Deploy your spokesperson. Media interviews must be planned to reach strategic opinion gatekeepers. Work all media to tell your story and get your messages in the public arena.

- Top executives must demonstrate leadership first, then management. These are not the same. Leadership creates a vision to inspire people to rise to challenges they could not normally meet. Management is the deployment of the resources of finance, operations, and people.

- Be visible, communicative, and responsive.

- The CEO and top executives must make wise judgments that can be communicated in simple language, that creates a balance with those immediately affected by the attack as well as the company's stakeholders.

- Never lie. Never fib. Admit what you don't yet know, and promise to get back with an answer. Correct any factual inaccuracies immediately. Understand that a difference of opinion is not a factual inaccuracy.

Human Resources (HR) officers report a particularly nasty crisis arising in social media—the tendency of a few employees or ex-employees to run down the reputation of their company, its products, or its leaders. Even some large companies do not have a solid policy governing employee social media communications. Many seem unaware that their employees are putting up such posts in real time from the office through their mobile devices on Facebook, LinkedIn, Twitter, and other platforms.

This is a multidisciplinary problem that involves HR, legal, sales, and communications. Companies need to formulate policies, make those policies clear in their hiring, constantly monitor what is being said about them, and have consultants at the ready to counter an inside or outside job by a digital assassin.

On the other hand, companies need to distinguish legitimate—if harsh—criticism from digital assassins. When the neck of musician Dave Carroll's $3,500 Taylor guitar was broken by baggage handlers while Carroll and his band were connecting from one United flight to another and the airline refused to reimburse him, Carroll retaliated by posting a catchy song on YouTube, "United Breaks Guitars," that received more than 10 million hits in less than two years. Taylor Guitars stepped in and offered Carroll guitars for his next YouTube song. United's embarrassment was Taylor Guitars' opportunity, though United later apologized, belatedly offered Carroll compensation, and asked to use his video in its employee training.[5]

On the other hand, if you are being attacked unfairly, can you distinguish whether the charge is being intentionally driven or if it is organic? Is the story naturally snowballing or does it appear that someone is purposefully accelerating it? If you see the same charged words being repetitively echoed across multiple blog sites, from detractors who link to each other, then you can surmise that the attack is deliberate.

An attack can come at you without warning, on holidays, weekends, in the middle of the night. And it can happen to anyone. Ask Domino's, Dow Chemical, or Apple. You can't control how a story breaks, but you can manage how a story spins.

The Sixth Shield of Digital Assassination: Lean on Me

In the future, which is now, we will all have our fifteen minutes of shame. The Internet can be a cold, black, indefinite place. When the moment comes, there will be no authority to which you can appeal for fairness. This does not mean that you are completely powerless, but it does mean that the Internet is not like most other social situations. In the digital era, the buck stops . . . nowhere.

In order to level the playing field you cannot depend on appeals to justice or fairness to ultimately vindicate yourself. But you can call on friends, both real and virtual, to help. Being actively connected to a community of friends is the greatest resource in the face of a digital assassin. They can also alert you when you are making a digital mistake.

An old Italian proverb holds that, loosely translated, only your real friends will tell you that your face is dirty. Friends are not only helpful when you need to be warned about your dirty face. They can defend when you, your business, or your brand come under attack, with a credible counter.

Some trolls, flamers, or just angry individuals are best ignored. But if you choose to respond, quickly provide as much relevant data as you can to get your digital friends' support. Their support may be strictly internal, within the discussion board of an organization. They may just let everyone they know on their Facebook pages that you are the victim of an unjust attack.

Or they might, as the friends of Reverend Merritt's church did, add stars to a rating or come to your defense on blogs indexed by the search engines.

What people actually do with what you tell them will be beyond your control. Your part is to send them an accurate, dispassionate brief that lets the facts drive their response. If the facts are outrageous enough, those facts will inspire campaigns that grow organically.

And if there is an element of ideology to your case, more "friends" will appear than you know you had.

- On the left, this happened when USDA official Shirley Sherrod was forced to resign after conservative blogger Andrew Breitbart released an excerpt of her speech that made her sound like a racist. When the full import of her speech was made public—Sherrod was describing how she overcame her own racial biases—the NAACP reversed its statement that it was "appalled" by her remarks and launched a fierce and successful social media campaign to vindicate her with a complete video of her whole speech.[6]
- On the right, a social media campaign was waged to reinstate two prolife Claremont McKenna College students, banned by the neighboring and affiliated Pomona College, for videotaping tough questions put to a Planned Parenthood representative. Conservative students, outraged at what they saw as an

abuse of the discipline process to shut down speech, mounted a Facebook campaign that recruited CMC students, faculty, and alumni to reverse the ban.[7]

In both cases, the perception of injustice against an individual drove the crowd. Whenever an affinity group believes that it has its very own Dreyfus affair, the resulting campaign will go viral—with increasing rates of "infection."

If the digital attack is not quite so hot-button, requiring only deflection, an effective way to enlist friends is to adopt an emotional stance that is the opposite of outrage. A good example occurred during the 2008 U.S. presidential campaign, after John McCain ridiculed Barack Obama in an ad as a vapid, Paris Hilton–like celebrity. Paris Hilton sent out a response to "the white-haired dude," a funny YouTube video that ended with her rattling off the elements of a plausible energy strategy that sounded more succinct and grounded than anything the two candidates were saying.

Who won? Paris Hilton won.

Google really won.

But it was the "friends" of Paris Hilton who helped her make her riposte go viral.

If you have a strong, supportive community of followers and trusted fans, they will automatically come to your defense when you are attacked. "Remember, George," the angel Clarence inscribed in the classic Frank Capra film *It's a Wonderful Life*, "no man is a failure who has friends."

The Seventh Shield of Digital Assassination: Virtual Silver Bullets or Olive Branches?

In this final shield, we work out a game plan for responding to a digital attack. A chart of action steps is on pages 235–36 to help master the elements of defense.

The first question that must be answered in the aftermath of an assassin's attack is whether or not to respond at all. Like encapsulated cancers or asbestos lining old buildings, sometimes it is best to leave an ugly post alone.

The reason, of course, is the Streisand Effect—the way in which an effort to repress something online winds up propagating it. Don't make matters worse by chatting online about or causing others to link to the offending site(s), which will only raise its prominence.

This is what happened to one property management company. It sued a woman for $50,000 in damages over a tweet about "moldy apartments." This lawsuit took a story that fewer than twenty-two people had seen and made the company's name a global search result for mold.

Or consider Liskula Cohen. She may have won a similar pyrrhic victory when she used legal means to force Google to unmask the blogger who called her the biggest "skank" in New York City. The upside? Cohen was allowed to proceed with her lawsuit to out the blogger, one Rosemary Port. The downside? Glenn Reynolds, a law professor, wrote on Instapundit, "I never would have heard the words, 'Liskula Cohen' and 'skank' together if it hadn't been for her blogger-outing litigation efforts."[8]

The first and biggest question is whether to ignore, appease, or counterattack a digital assassin.

- In deciding whether or not to act, ask yourself if the offending material is likely to have real-world negative consequences. Will it cost you that next job, a client, or a promotion?
- Second, who has seen it? Use Alexa.com or Quantcast to check the traffic of the offending site. Profile the site and its readership. Are these your constituents or crowd? Is something negative here likely to be seen by your cohorts? If the answer to these questions is no, then decide the safer play: To keep a close eye on the attack or to try to nip it in the bud?

When a digital attack occurs, first understand who is attacking you. Can you identify the attacker, or can you correlate his user name with a website or blog?

Does the attack appear organic, going viral over community anger over your perceived misdeeds, or cruel humor at your expense? Or do you see the repetition of keywords and text that indicates that you may be the victim of deliberate keyword stuffing?

Is there an organization behind this attack? If so, can donors be identified? Leaders of the organization give a clue to a possible hidden enemy who is subsidizing the attack.

Once these questions are answered, take the following steps:

- If the offending material is on a third-party website, go to the contact page of that website containing the offensive material and e-mail the web host. Send them a polite request to please remove the material. Explain why this information is inaccurate or harmful.
- Don't let anger seep into the conversation. Don't make accusations or threaten the webmaster.
- This same approach of sweet reason and appeal to fairness even extends to the actual attacker, if they can be identified. A threat might egg them on. Some vicious people delight in your entreaties, as a predator might enjoy the squeals of his prey. If it seems, however, as if the attack is based on a misunderstanding, politely set the attacker straight.
- If the webmaster or actual attacker agrees to remove the post—and they have not posted it on a major review site—ask them to use Google's public URL Removal Tool to eventually wash it out as a cache copy or snippet in Google's search results.
- Why are they attacking you? If this is a case of someone using mixed truth against you—and not a troll or a dedicated assassin—try to entice the person who made the post into an offline conversation. Let him know how hurtful his remark has been, without expressing legitimate anger. But while you are being reasonable, collect as much information as possible. For example, be sure and capture their IP address from any e-mails. In many cases, however, a reasoned, civil approach can do the job.
- Celebrities pay top dollar to separate fact from fiction and respond to rumors and lies on ICorrect. Find your equivalent. Don't post a response on a site where the message board can make you the equivalent of the clown in the dunking booth. In clarifying mixed truth, you may be forced to own up to facts you would rather not mention. Fully understand that a digital confession is forever. Will you make it worse by responding? If you have to explain some personal shortcoming to put it in context, at least make your statement on a site where you have some control.
- In running down a rumor, follow the example of McDonald's, which rebutted the ground-worm rumor by talking about the

quality of its beef. In an online world, it is best not to repeat the graphic terms of the charge; otherwise the offending keywords are boosted as search terms.

If these appeals fail, face the Streisand Effect head-on. Will responding make it worse? Is there enough truth to what is being said or shown that you will damage yourself by reacting at all?

If response is the plan, there are concrete steps you can take to blunt the attack.

- If the offensive material continues to rise in search engine rankings, hire a search engine optimization firm to try to bury it in the rankings.
- If the attacker must be unmasked, consider filing a Doe subpoena. If the IP address can be found, take the next step and subpoena the internet service provider to divulge the identity of the attacker. If the IP address represents a network, or if the Internet service provider has undertaken a routine change of addresses, or if the attacker has taken steps to cloak his identity, then you've hit a dead end. Understand that a lawsuit can cost thousands of dollars. It will enrage an attacker and his friends, possibly activating mirror sites. And it may require follow-through on the lawsuit, which will likely result in no real compensation. Still, some assassins are so egregious that you might feel their attacks merit nothing less than a lawsuit.
- Consider a ToS—or terms of service—response. At the bottom of most websites, next to a link to its privacy policy, is a link to its terms of service. For example, Popeater, the celebrity gossip site owned by AOL, states AOL's policy requiring you not to post anything "that contains explicit or graphic descriptions or accounts of sexual acts or is threatening, abusive, harassing, defamatory, libelous, deceptive, fraudulent, invasive of another's privacy . . ." This, by the way, includes a site dedicated to tracking the words and deeds of the likes of Charlie Sheen and Lindsay Lohan. Taken seriously, most ToS statements would exclude perhaps the lion's share of the Internet. Unless the post is pornographic or threatens violence, the likely response from most webmasters will be to yawn. Still, it

may be worth citing ToS language to appeal to a webmaster's sense of fairness. If the site would appear deeply offensive to an objective observer, a litigious response would be to threaten legal action against the hosting site for a violation of its own ToS for failure to remove the offending post if it clearly violates its own stated terms. Use litigation—and threats of litigation—sparingly, if at all.

■ Another approach, if the site itself is defamatory to an extreme, send a snail mail letter to the legal department of the web hosting company that serves the website. Go to a WHOIS search site and enter the domain name of the offending site to reveal the web hosting company. Go to their main page and look up their ToS or acceptable use policy. Hosting companies have boilerplate ToS language. The web hosting service Go Daddy, for example, forbids users from posting anything that "promotes, encourages or engages in defamatory, harassing, abusive or otherwise objectionable behavior."

■ If you are the target not of defamation that feels violent to you, but of actual threats of physical violence, the digital assassin has crossed into an area in which the law is fully on your side. Companies will respond to such ToS violations with alacrity, especially if you come armed with a court order.

■ If your child or grandchild is the victim of a cyberbully, keep records of the attack, make a screen shot of it, print it out, and record identifying details about the attacker. Teach your children to try not to respond to such attacks. Any knee-jerk response could muddy the waters and make it less clear who is the victim and who is the attacker.

■ If a cyberbully attack is irritating, take the matter up with the attackers' parents. If it is disturbing, consider taking it up with the school principal, depending on the policy of your school district. If violence is threatened, take it to the police immediately. For a tutorial, check out wikihow.com/Deal-With-Cyber-Bullying-As-a-Child-or-Teen, or check out the latest advice from Norton's Internet Safety Advocate, Marian Merritt, on cyberbullying.

Game Plan for Digital Defense

Here are the elements of a digital defense, boiled down to their essentials into a ready game plan.

Getting Prepared
Go back to school on social media.

- Understand how search engines work, how to create a blog and maintain it, use social networking sites and optimize search terms.

Understand yourself, the facts about your life and career that are discoverable through investigation, coincidence, or hacking.

- Know your digital profile from aggregators like Pipl, background sources, public databases, credit checks, Google searches, and free searches.
  - Identity checks: KnowEm
  - Message boards: BoardTracker, Boardreader, Omgili
  - Social media: Google Blog Search, Social Mention, IceRocket
  - Business: Yelp, Kosmix, sector specific trackers
  - News: Yahoo!, Google, "news" searches
  - Images: Google/Bing/Yahoo!, Google Maps and Street View, TinEye

- Boost your profile.
  - Create a "storefront" website.
  - Fill out Google Profile.
  - Open accounts on Facebook, LinkedIn, Twitter, Yelp, etc.
  - Link to plain vanilla data—professional associations, alumni groups, etc.
  - Sprinkle keywords in your network of sites that will help index positive and neutral material about you.
  - Link websites and social networking sites.

- Manage your profile.
  - Regulate your news and announcements.
  - Keep online conversations clean.

- If you are in a large business, develop a "war room" and a plan.
- Develop a list of real and virtual friends to call on if attacked.

In the Face of an Attack

- Approach the webmaster or digital assassin with a calm plea for relief.

  Upside

  Might clear up a misunderstanding

  Downside

  Might encourage more attacks.

- If the answer to your plea is yes, ask them to use Google's URL removal tool.

- File a Doe subpoena.

  Upside

  Might unmask your attacker for legal accountability

  Downsides

  Costs money

  Court will make you attest that harm merits subpoena

  Recovery unlikely

  Might enrage friends of assassin, create mirror sites

- A terms of service appeal to the webmaster or web hosting company.

  Upsides

  Possible near-term gratification

  If one site bans material for a ToS violation, you can use that precedent to argue to others that they should as well

  Downsides

  A bank shot

  Might enrage assassin, escalate attacks on other sites

- Obtain a court order, if the post contains a threat of violence.

  Upsides

  Stops attack

  Creates legal record of a threat

  Downside

  Might enrage an unbalanced person

One or none of these options may work. Even if they do, do not expect your digital profile to change overnight. The only strategy that always works in your favor 100 percent of the time is the positive approach of creating a reputational cushion.

The only way to obtain at least some protection is to create as much positive and descriptive information about yourself, link all your sites together, and then make as many organic links as you can to others.

- If driving the offensive material off your first search page is successful, that's a major victory.
- If only positive or neutral content is on your first three pages of search, that's a complete victory—for now. But keep in mind that anything negative in deep search can always move up in ranking.

Throughout, keep Postel's law of tolerance in mind if you should manage to get the upper hand. It reflects what John Seigenthaler did when he used legal proceedings to track down his digital assassin. "I called him on the phone, and told him I was pissed off and [asked] why did he do it," Seigenthaler says. "He teared up. It was just before Christmas and my wife was listening as I came into the house, and I was talking to him. She heard me react with surprise when she heard that they asked him to resign and she told me, 'It's just before Christmas, you can't let him lose his job.' I said, 'Pardon me, but can you tell me whose side you're on here?'"

The next day Seigenthaler called his assassin's boss and asked if the firm would take him back. The man was rehired.

As a result of Seigenthaler's classy way of handling the issue, his reputation online and offline has only been enhanced.

Managing Digital Platforms

Now we come to the actual keystrokes you need to undertake a tactical defense. The rest of the chapter deals with the means to grow and manage reputations on the most popular platforms: Facebook, Twitter, Yelp, Wikipedia. And it imparts the basics of good image management through the elements of search engine optimization.

Facebook

The section concerning the Fourth Shield, "The New and Improved You," explains the importance of developing an online presence. Have as many online sources of positive and truthful information about yourself established as possible. Doing so will provide greater leverage in the event that you are the victim of cyber character assassination.

One tool in that toolbox is a Facebook profile (for individuals) or page (categories: Local Business or Place; Company, Organization, or Institution; Brand or Product; Artist, Band, or Public Figure; Entertainment; Cause or Community). A critical question to answer when building out a Facebook profile is whether to use it primarily for business or personal use or perhaps for a combination of both.

Whatever purpose you choose, be sure to carefully manage what kind of information is disseminated on Facebook. Determine how much is shared (i.e., interests, photos, status updates, and so forth) down to individual friends. However, it is helpful to post only things that you ultimately could live with being available to the entire public.

Facebook has long faced criticism for its highly fluid approach to privacy controls. Google's Matt McKeon has a helpful chart that details these changes over time: http://mattmckeon.com/facebook-privacy.

Facebook substantially changed their privacy controls three times just between November 2009 and April 2010. The lesson here is to be vigilant. Monitor the Facebook Blog (http://blog.facebook.com) for changes and be sure to make adjustments accordingly.

To manage privacy controls, log into Facebook. In the upper right-hand corner is a tab "Account" with a drop-down menu. Select "privacy settings." As of this writing (summer 2011) there are five options to control who can see what information you share. We recommend using the "custom" level in order to fully understand what bits of data may be shared and to choose whatever makes you comfortable.

One final note on Facebook is the Facebook Connect platform. You may have seen other websites that offer the option to log into them via Facebook Connect (examples: www.WashingtonPost.com and www.Pandora.com). You may inadvertently log into one of these websites using Facebook, and then whatever you do on that website might be broadcast quite publicly. Actions like "liking" a piece of content (for example, an article or video) or making a comment would then be visible on that website and then reported back into Facebook, broadcast to your friends, and depending on your privacy settings, to the entire Internet.

Despite such risks, establishing a Facebook profile is an important way that you can claim a brand identity online as well as create communications that you control. If you haven't done so already, be sure to establish your vanity (or unique) Facebook URL by going to http://www.facebook.com/username. This will allow you to claim the URL www.facebook.com/yournamehere.

Facebook can easily enable evil clones, because anybody can create a profile with any name and any picture. Those attacking from a Facebook page may not be who they say they are.

Likewise, someone can spoof a profile that pretends to be you. The latter is even more reason to claim your own piece of digital real estate in order to bolster credibility should you need to deny the validity of an imposter.

Twitter

Twitter is another potential source of consternation for online victims. Many popular personalities and companies have been spoofed on Twitter. One way that Twitter has responded to this is to establish a "Verified" account. For example, if you look at President Barack Obama's Twitter page, http://twitter.com/BarackObama, the blue symbol indicates that his page legitimately represents the person it says it does.

Signing up for Twitter takes less than five minutes, but building influence to reach people in the case of a crisis takes patient and consistent effort (do it here: https://twitter.com/signup). Keep in mind that Twitter, like tennis, requires constant attention. Verbal volleys you send out will come back at you. Unless you are a mega-star, then, Twitter is not a broadcasting tool. It is a conversational media. For this reason, Twitter requires a commitment of time and resources that is not appropriate for everyone. If your Twitter account is not interacting and creating dialogue, it will not have long-term growth or any real traction.

Twitter messages can be up to 140 characters and may include links.

Build up a follower base—slowly and organically. Faster methods do exist but they tend to rely on less-than-aboveboard tactics.

First, publicize your Twitter account on other platforms, such as

Facebook, your blog, an e-mail to your contacts. Let people know what they can expect to get from following your Twitter updates.

Are you announcing company news? Giving your quick reaction to the day's news? Sharing the best must-read article?

Next, you can follow people that you are interested in and hope that they reciprocate. When seeking to build such a network, you must do more than just click "follow." You need to interact and engage. Respond to questions that others may pose or share your feedback to the content they are broadcasting. Twitter is more than a repeating station—it is social media, after all.

You have three primary means of communication on Twitter:

- The basic tweet
- An "@" reply
- The direct message

A basic tweet is typed into the box titled "What's happening?" (or into the tweet update section of your third-party application—more on that later). This is broadcast to all who have chosen to follow you and is placed in their "Timeline." The Timeline is displayed in reverse chronological order. Keep in mind that anyone following more than a few people will see a constant churn of new tweets.

The basic tweet is also publicly available, unless you choose to make your tweets private, and will be discoverable by anyone on the Internet. Technically, tweets may be deleted after being sent, *but like all content that is originally public on the Internet it can be cached and it is likely that someone can find it even after it is removed.*

The second way to publish a tweet is via an @reply, which is just a normal tweet that mentions another Twitter user. For example, the Washington Nationals, the Major League Baseball team, using their official Twitter account @nationals, tweeted: "Special #FF: RHP Stephen Strasburg @stras37 has joined the Nats Twitter Family. Give him a follow!"

Stephen Strasburg is a rising star pitcher who has just launched his own Twitter account, which is @stras37. So the Nationals' status mentioned Strasburg's account.

This means that the Nationals' tweet would show up under Strasburg's "@mentions," which is a search option on the home page of every

Twitter account. Any Twitter user can easily check to see if they have been mentioned in a tweet by clicking the @mention link.

The third method of communicating on Twitter is via direct message. Unlike the first two methods that are entirely public, this is private. It is the Twitter equivalent of an e-mail. It is as secure and private as your e-mail password.

In order to send a direct message your intended recipient must be following you. To send a direct message begin your tweet with the letter "d" and the name of the Twitter user you are messaging. For example: "d nationals hey there!"

In addition to directing tweets to specific individuals, you can also append your messages with hashtags. In the National's message mentioned above, they included "#FF" in their tweet. Anyone can create a hashtag by simply including the "#" sign before a word or phase (with no spaces). #FF refers to "Follow Friday," which is a Twitter cultural phenomenon where Twitter users recommend other interesting people to their own follows. Using those hashtags allows people to quickly search all of Twitter for any tweet that relates. It is just a shorthand indexing or labeling system.

The true power of Twitter comes alive in its integration with a myriad of third-party applications. These applications can help you search for keywords mentioning yourself or your company, organize your followers into manageable groups, schedule tweets so that you can maintain a digital activity during times in which you aren't literally in front of your Twitter-enabled device.

We recommend checking out two services: TweetDeck (http://www.tweetdeck.com) and Hoot Suite (http://hootsuite.com). There are many alternatives to these, but going to their sites and understanding how they work provide a good primer.

Yelp

The primary problems that people run into on sites like Yelp fall into two categories: spurious complaints and legitimate complaints.

Every business owner knows that there are those occasions where the company policy wasn't executed as it was intended. If you are receiving honest complaints about your business on a review site like

Yelp, then you have an opportunity to turn that negative review into a compelling positive story.

If you do not respond to these complaints—or worse, if you respond poorly—then you can further mire yourself in negativity. For a cautionary tale, a small bakery in Arizona was criticized by a first-time customer who posted a detailed negative review conveying why he felt the bakery wasn't up to snuff—poor service, reheated food, high prices, and so forth. The owner responded, and in the first sentence of her lengthy angst-filled response begins using ALL CAPS and name-calling.

Does Yelp Make Things Worse?

Some business owners might feel like the existence of websites like Yelp is at best an exhausting annoyance and at worse a serious liability. As we discussed in truth remix, some have even accused Yelp of extorting ad dollars in order to "help" business owners overcome negative reviews. The truth is that overall, Yelp's existence really is a net plus for business owners.

After all, consider what the world would look like if Yelp didn't exist. We live in a world where social networks allow everyone to be an instantly published critic and where colorful commentary can easily go viral. In a world without Yelp, local business owners would still face the problem of negative online reviews—only without an effective platform on which to respond.

Without Yelp, potential customers would still search for information on the Internet and would instead have to learn to muddle a hodgepodge of individual postings on various websites.

If anything, Yelp empowers business owners by organizing the way that customers share and discover reviews. Putting these reviews into an organized fashion makes it easier to keep track of what people are saying, while also allowing business owners the chance to respond directly—either privately or publicly—to anyone's comments.

Yelp has in fact developed algorithms that punish reviewers who appear only to have written into Yelp to grind their axes. These reviews are given a low quality score and are pushed to the bottom of a business's page and are hidden by default.

Responding to Yelp Negative Reviews

The primary thing to keep in mind when responding to negative reviews is to remain unemotional and businesslike to avoid escalating the situation. In the case of the small bakery, her over-the-top response only brought her further negative publicity. Threatening people or arguing with reviewers is very ill advised.

To begin, read Yelp's own guidelines on how to respond to reviews. These are thorough and include tips like keeping the following in mind as you consider responding:

1. Your reviewers are your paying customers.
2. Your reviewers are human beings with (sometimes unpredictable) feelings and sensitivities.
3. Your reviewers are vocal and opinionated (otherwise they would not be writing reviews!).[9]

They also give a host of examples of bad and good reviews for you to consider. The focus is—as when you are responding to anyone's negative emotions—listen first, then empathize, then focus on how things can be different next time.

Yelp stresses that you should avoid coming across as highly impersonal or corporate. Limit the public promise of coupons or freebies. Offering something complimentary by private message can in some cases be appropriate if it is accompanied by a sincere acknowledgment of the reviewer's concerns.

With the rise of social media, however, customers increasingly expect to have a conversation with the businesses with which they interact. The gold standard example that Yelp offers is when you can assure a customer that his feedback has contributed to shaping actual changes within your business. You will need a Yelp Business account (it's free) in order to interact with your reviewers. You can set that up here: https:// biz.yelp.com.

As with Facebook and Twitter, claim your piece of the Yelp community before you run into problems. Establishing an active presence on Yelp in advance of any negativity will help generate goodwill that you can draw on when a crisis arises.

Wikipedia

Wikipedia entries are usually near the top of most search results. It is a radical experiment in human knowledge and crowd-sourcing that has largely been successful. We have shown, however, that it is subject to abuse. Though Wikipedia's standards for Biographies of Living Persons (BLPs) have been tightened up since the attack on John Seigenthaler, it pays to know how to correct abuses when they occur.

Creating BLP Entries

You must have a BLP before you can worry about inaccuracies in your BLP. There are various criteria, the most important of which is that a person must be "notable." Wikipedia says, "A person is presumed to be notable if he or she has been the subject of multiple published secondary sources which are reliable, intellectually independent of each other, and independent of the subject."[10]

You should never try to write your own BLP, an act of vanity looked down upon by the Wikipedia community. However, there is nothing to stop a friendly person from creating one if there are in fact legitimate published secondary sources about you that meet Wikipedia's criteria. Just keep in mind that once a BLP is created, *anyone* can edit it. There are many people with Wikipedia BLPs who wish they didn't have one.

If you are thinking about writing a BLP for someone else, then be sure to:

1. Read the BLP main article (http://bit.ly/BLPinfo).
2. Read the Wikipedia Manual of Style on BLPs (http://bit.ly/BLPstyle).
3. Follow formatting guidelines.

Formatting guidelines can vary depending on the level of public detail about the subject of a BLP.

Take Stephen J. Dubner, the coauthor of *Freakonomics* as an example. If you look at his Wikipedia entry, http://en.wikipedia.org/wiki/Stephen_Dubner, you will find it to be relatively brief with a short background and a few categorized lists of other information (books, affiliations, etc.). Now look at the "Edit" version of the Dubner's page: http://bit.ly/BLPexample. If you scroll down through the code, then you will see those same categories demarcated by double equal signs (e.g., "==Books==").

Unless you are writing a very short BLP, then you will want to organize the information into the most natural categories. Review other

BLP entries for help in choosing the most appropriate categories for the page you are creating.

Editing Existing Entries and Responding to Inaccuracies

Editing Wikipedia entries is a tricky business, a task to be approached with caution. Do not assume that it will be a quick or painless process.

The first step is to create a Wikipedia account. This can be done by clicking the link in the upper right-hand corner of any page on Wikipedia entitled "Log in / create account." Choose a user name and know that your IP address will be associated with any edits you make. While you don't have to give your real name, don't make any edits that would be embarrassing should your real identity be connected with them.

To make a change to a Wikipedia entry, either adding something that is missing or correcting an error, you need to have the details of whatever you are looking to have included be verifiable—details publicly available from a reliable published source. For more on verifiability, see this: http://en.wikipedia.org/wiki/Wikipedia:Verifiability. Self-published sources or nonpublic mediums are not acceptable.

If your information exists in a verifiable source, then the next step is to post it in Talk (the page title), Discussion (tab). Technically speaking, you can just hit the edit button and make the change you want immediately. But doing so decreases the odds of your edit will actually remain in place.

The Discussion or Talk page lets you raise a good faith concern with the community of editors of any particular page. The ideal scenario is that when the community of editors is presented with a verifiable source of information they will permit an edit to go forward. Especially for contentious edits, try to win over the support of the community in advance of making any changes.

See the Talk page on the "Coal" entry for examples of how users raise issues of concern to them before moving forward with their own edits (http://en.wikipedia.org/wiki/Talk:Coal).

On this page, one Wikipedia user, Bridgetttttte, says, "In certain parts of the world, pro-coal or anti-coal statements can get a person elected to a government office. I have a POV on this issue: Many of these people could not pass freshman chemistry! So, as an encyclopedia, how do we describe the political aspects of coal without bias?" Raising an issue this way will help generate some goodwill, deference, and trust from the user community as you make your case.

Whether you are making edits directly or engaging in dialogue on the Talk Page, you should never create multiple Wikipedia accounts to inflate the apparent support for your efforts. Attempts at this sock puppetry can be easily uncovered, causing a vicious boomerang (or at least an accusation of it, as a post alleged against Bridgettttttte).

The similar tactic of enlisting a friendly person to create accounts and weigh in on your behalf on Talk Pages, called meat puppetry, has its reputational risks (don't ask your sister to do it). But it is technically permissible and can lend critical momentum.

Again this strategy, like every action within Wikipedia, is not a foolproof solution; you might find yourself unable to ultimately get exactly what you want. Nevertheless, patience and calm persistence is critical to building support and credibility—the ultimate currency in the Wiki economy.

Search Engine Optimization (SEO)

When you search for a name or a company's name, Google or Bing uses a complicated algorithm to determine what links to display and in what order. You and potential character assassins can manipulate this algorithm for good or ill.

Keywords

One of the ways the search engine algorithms can be used in a forthright way for higher search results is by frequent but appropriate use of keywords in the copy on a website. One example is the blog Fuel Lines written by Michael Gass, which is dedicated to helping small to medium-sized ad agencies develop new business. Gass publishes a new post every few days and typically finds a way to incorporate the phrases "ad agency" and "new business" in every post title.

For example, Gass wrote three blog posts in a five-day period with the following titles:

- "Survey: Economy Improving, New Business Is Up for Small to Midsize Ad Agencies"

- "Study: 50% of Ad Agencies Generate New Business Through Networks and Referrals"
- "The History and Evolution of Social Media for Ad Agency New Business"

Note that the two key phrases aren't always immediately next to each other, but he finds a way to work them in. Doing this consistently enables Gass to completely dominate the rankings for the search term "ad agency new business."

There is an entire industry devoted to playing the keyword ranking game. To learn more about that check out tools like Raven (http://raventools.com) or SEOmoz (http://www.seomoz.org/tools).

For the purposes of this book, be aware that keywords can be specifically leveraged by repeatedly using them in copy on websites. Have influence over what content appears at the top of a search results page for any given keyword that is important to your name, product, company, or brand.

One way you can build up insurance against attacks is to consistently publish positive information with your name. This is where establishing social media profiles on Facebook, Twitter, and LinkedIn can help tremendously, as they often can easily rise to the top of a search for someone's name. It is also why establishing a website or blog where you regularly post under your name builds up the number of search results that you have influence over.

The more laissez-faire your approach to establishing positive keyword references, the easier it is for potential assailants to hijack the search results page for your name or brand.

Link Juice and Authority

Keywords are just the beginning of the search engine rankings game. Another way that search engines determine what to place at the top of rankings is whether many people on the Internet associate a particular link with a particular keyword. This intentional associating between URLs and keywords can be called anchoring or using anchor text.

Search engines pay attention to the text phrases in which website links are embedded. For example, if I run a blog about personal finance, then I will want other websites to link back to my website and embed that link with inside terms like "getting out of debt" or "investing basics."

However, not all websites are created equal in the eyes of the search engines. As we've seen before, the more links pointing to a given website, the more authoritative that website becomes. So an anchor text link from a website like CNN or *The New York Times* carries greater influence on the search engine results page than MyObscureBlog.com.

Google Bombing and Bowling

This sort of anchoring strategy can be used for satire or for malice. Like the "French military victories" link, detractors can embed anchor text that links your name with a scandalous website. This intentional deceptive manipulation is sometimes referred to as Google bombing.

Google is constantly refining its search algorithms. Over the years, search engines have taken steps to mitigate the influence of this kind of anchor text manipulation—whether intended for good or bad—by punishing especially greedy anchor text generators. This punishment usually takes the form of being pushed down toward the bottom of a search engine results page.

Google bowling occurs when attackers go about manipulating anchor text (or other SEO strategies like link building) in a way that appears to be benefiting you or your company. As a result, Google will punish your website, burying your company or product at the bottom of the search results.

Monitoring Online Activity

Earlier we discussed ways to assess your existing online profile. That of course is just a first step. You must protect yourself online by actively monitoring the Internet for potential threats. Fortune 500 companies can spend tens of thousands of dollars per month for robust online monitoring reports. However there are easy-to-use and free solutions for individuals and small business to establish a basic ability to keep tabs on the constant churn of the Internet.

Google Alerts

Head over to http://www.google.com/alerts and you can enter your name—or any keyword of interest—and select a frequency by which you will be notified of new (or updated) websites that contain that keyword. This tool is a good way to easily stay up-to-date on what is being said about you or your company.

Social Mention

Like Google Alerts, Social Mention offers a similar service, but it tracks social networks and blogs. You can also sign up with them to receive alerts based on keywords of your choosing at http://socialmention.com/alerts.

Google Reader

In addition to Google and Social Mention Alerts, you can also create search tools from a variety of forums and other websites. For example, head to Twitter Search (http://search.twitter.com) and enter a keyword (e.g., "Chuck Norris"). The results page will show you the most recent tweets mentioning that keyword.

In the upper right-hand corner is a link "Feed for this query." Clicking on that will enable you to import an automatically updated feed of the latest tweets mentioning whatever keyword you are interested in following. Google and Social Mention Alerts can also be delivered via RSS feed.

RSS stands for really simple syndication because it works like an automated newswire. Whenever a new piece of content—be it a blog post, a tweet, or whatever—is published on a website that offers an RSS feed, then a copy of that same content is also sent to its RSS subscribers. One of the benefits of using RSS is that you can easily organize the content of many websites (or search engines) into one place.

When it comes to online monitoring, RSS feeds are useful because they can keep the barrage of updates separate from your e-mail inbox. To do this you need an RSS reader. RSS readers are like special inboxes that have "unread" and "read" items. You can put RSS content into file folders or flag it for later follow-up.

One easy-to-use and free reader is Google Reader (http://www.google.com/reader).

Domain Defense

Your domain is your base identity inside your website's URL, or uniform resource locator. All domain names are registered with a name and contact information of the owner, the administrative contact, and the technical contact. This information is publicly available for every website on the Internet and can be easily searched for free. You can do so by going to http://www.whois.net.

The Whois Database

Take the New Deals coupon website as an example. Go to www.whois .net and enter www.dealnews.com. While the owner is listed as dealnews .com, Inc., two human contacts are also listed. In addition to an e-mail address, there is a physical address and a phone number listed.

If a website is publishing negative and false information, then checking the Whois database is a good place to start. In some cases the website may not provide any means of communicating with them, so the Whois database can help you contact the owner. Also, it is possible that the owner of a website is unaware that there is negative information on their website about you. Smaller websites that may have been long since abandoned by their original owner are often easily hacked and malicious content can be uploaded onto their domain.

But beyond responding to attacks, it is important to check to see what shows up in the Whois database for your personal and company website. We have had clients who had a personal blog domain that listed their family's home address and phone number. Scammers can easily collect all publicly available information from Whois databases that can lead to identity theft. Moreover, if someone is trying to seek you out personally, then having that information available may be a security issue.

Private Domain Registration

Keep your domain registration private. But how? To own a domain, you are required to include contact information, which is then publicly available. By using a service like Domains by Proxy, you can keep your domain registration private. For an annual fee, they will publish their own information, but forward any e-mails or letters to you.

The obvious downside of a service like this is that if you are trying to identify the owner of a website, they may have private registration as well. You will still be able to send them information, but their identity won't be revealed unless they contact you.

Domain Poaching

Another piece of information that is publicly available in the Whois database is when any domain was registered, when it was last renewed, and when it will expire. This data makes it easy for scammers to monitor when domains are about to expire and they can swoop in and purchase your domain out from under you.

The critical steps that you need to prevent this from happening are twofold: make sure that you have your domain registrar account set to auto renew, and make sure that your credit card or other payment information is up-to-date. Even if you have your domain set to auto renew, if on the day the registrar attempts to charge your credit card only to have it bounce back that the card is expired, then domain poachers can capitalize on your mistake.

Domain Theft

While domain poaching can be frustrating and is a borderline legal gray area, outright domain theft is also common (despite being obviously illegal). The most common method of domain theft occurs when a thief initiates a domain transfer.

Honest domain owners may want to transfer their domain from one registrar to another for a myriad of reasons: cost savings, different features, better customer service. In order to conduct a domain transfer, the owner generates a transfer code from the current registrar. This code is then sent to the e-mail address associated with the domain name. Once you have that transfer code you can enter it into a new registrar and the controls are moved.

Therefore, all a crook needs to do is to gain access to the e-mail address associated with any domain that they want to transfer. E-mail addresses can often be hacked with ease because most passwords aren't complex enough.

The first line of defense against domain theft is to create a secure passcode of the sort we discussed earlier for your e-mail account. The second is purchasing a "domain lock" service from your registrar. This kind of service typically carries an annual fee for which the registrar will prevent any transfer codes from being generated unless you go through a laborious unlocking process.

Laws of the Land—A Refresher

Again, on the Internet, the buck stops nowhere. Any legal recourse available to those who have endured wrongful behavior is through a patchwork of state, federal, and international law. The most famous and most often used online legal statute is the Digital Millennium Copyright Act or DMCA.

This law protects copyright owners from having their material unlawfully used online. The most common way that copyright owners attempt to deal with infringement is by sending a "cease and desist" or "take down" letter to the website hosting the illegal content. You can read a summary of the DMCA here: www.copyright.gov/legislation/dmca.pdf.

It should be noted that there are major exceptions to the law. The Safe Harbor provision, also known as DMCA 512, limits the liability of websites who may find themselves accidentally hosting copyrighted materials. The advocacy group Chilling Effects helpfully documents the requirements for a website to be granted the Safe Harbor exception:

A service provider who hosts content must:

- have no knowledge of, or financial benefit from, infringing activity on its network
- have a copyright policy and provide proper notification of that policy to its subscribers
- list an agent to deal with copyright complaints[11]

The Communications Decency Act of 1996

The most relevant section of the Communications Decency Act for those facing online attacks to their reputation is Section 230. This law rarely provides any satisfactory means of recourse, as there are broad protections for website owners. Website owners are not obligated to remove any content created by visitors to their sites. This user-generated content exception means that an anonymous person can post libelous or other harmful content on a website and the liability for that act remains with that person alone.

As with any human activity, it is easy to get discouraged by the catalog of horrors that is the Internet. And yet for all its misuses, digital media is a liberating technology that brings people together as never before and allows them to transform vast mountains of data into useful knowledge.

The web contains all wisdom, all faith, and all science, not just the darker precincts of the human psyche. It is no better or worse than the people who create it every day.

To comment, share your stories or solutions, and to stay current, join us at DigitalAssassinationBook.com.

Notes

1. The Digital Mosh Pit

1. John Seigenthaler, "A False Wikipedia Entry," Editorial/Opinion, *USA Today,* November 29, 2005, http://www.usatoday.com/news/opinion/editorials/2005-11-29-wikipe dia-edit-x.htm.
2. Linsey Davis and Emily Friedman, "New Jersey Governor Wonders How Rutgers 'Spies' Can Sleep at Night After Tyler Clementi's Suicide," ABC News, September 30, 2010.
3. Tamara Linse, "A Senator's Suicide," *Casper* (WY) *Star-Tribune,* November 1, 2004.
4. CNET news.com, October 23, 2008; Jim Goldman, "Steve Jobs Talks New iPods, Health: My One on One," TechCheck, CNBC.com, September 9, 2008, http://www .cnbc.com/id/26628547/Steve_Jobs_Talks_New_ iPods_Health_My_One_on_One.
5. Tom Krazit, "Engadget Sends Apple Stock Plunging on iPhone Rumor," CNET Asia, May 16, 2007, http://asia.cnet.com/reviews/mobilephones/0,39050603,62013674,00 .htm.
6. Howard Kurtz, "Clinton Hoax Retracted," *Washington Post,* January 22, 1999.
7. Patrick Byrne, "Roddy Boyd Sucks It Like He's Paying the Rent (Fortune Magazine)," DeepCapture.com, October 10, 2008, http://www.deepcapture.com/roddy-boyd-sucks-it-like-hes-paying-the-rent/; Patrick Byrne, "Today's Yawn: Scoffers of Law Rocker-Gradient Ignore Court Order & Roddy Boyd Shills, Exhibit Z," DeepCapture.com, January 14, 2010, http://www.deepcapture.com/rocker-gradient -scoff-at-law-and-roddy-boyd-shills/.
8. Roddy Boyd, "America's Nastiest CEO," The Big Money, January 19, 2010, http:// www.thebigmoney.com/articles/judgments/2010/01/19/americas-nastiest-ceo.
9. Bethany McLean, "Phantom Menace," *Fortune,* November 14, 2005.
10. "About Deep Capture," http://www.deepcapture.com/about-deep-capture.
11. McLean, "Phantom Menace"; Joe Nocera, "Overstock's Campaign of Menace," *New York Times,* February 25, 2006; Susan Antilla, "Overstock Blames with Creepy Strategy," Bloomberg.com, February 21, 2007, http://www.bloomberg.com/apps/

news?pid=newsarchive&sid=aLDKLcXDf9PU; "Copper River Partners Settles Lawsuit with Overstock.com, Inc.," PR Newswire, December 8, 2009, http://www .prnewswire.com/news-releases/copper-river-partners-settles-lawsuit-with-over stockcom-inc-78832152.html.

12. Tom O'Neil, "How Far Have Oscars' Campaign Budgets Dropped?," Gold Derby (blog), Los Angeles Times, February 12, 2009, http://goldderby.latimes.com/awards _goldderby/2009/02/oscars-campaign.html#more.

13. Claire Atkinson, "Friending Oscar," New York Post, January 10, 2011.

14. Nikki Finke, "Much Ado About Oscar," New York, March 15, 1999.

15. "John Nash's Beautiful Mind," interview with Mike Wallace, 60 Minutes, CBS News, March 17, 2002, http://www.cbsnews.com/stories/2002/03/14/60minutes/ main503731.shtml; David Kohn, "Nash: Film No Whitewash," 60 Minutes, CBS News, March 17, 2002; Matt Drudge, "Universal Rips Drudge After Nash Bash," March 8, 2002; Tom Tugend, "An Anti-Semitic Mind?" The Jewish Journal, March 14, 2002.

16. Rick Lyman, "A Beautiful Mind Meets Ugly Oscar Tactics," New York Times, March 16, 2002.

17. Ibid.

2. America's First Bloggers

1. Socialnomics09, "Social Media Revolution 2," accessed February 16, 2011, You-Tube, http://www.youtube.com/watch?v=lFZ0z5Fm-Ng&feature=related.

2. "Memorable Quotes for Thirteen Days (2000)," Internet Movie Database, accessed February 17, 2011, http://www.imdb.com/title/tt0146309/quotes.

3. The First Sword: New Media Mayhem

1. Interview with Leo Yakutis by Mark Davis, October 8, 2010.

2. Interview with James Lee by Mark Davis, November 1, 2010.

3. Andy Greenberg, "The Streisand Effect," Forbes.com, May 11, 2007, http://www .forbes.com/2007/05/10/streisand-digg-web-tech-cx_ag_0511streisand.html.

4. Steve Lohr, "Library of Congress Will Save Tweets," New York Times, April 14, 2010.

5. Interview with Bill Livingstone by Mark Davis, October 10, 2010.

6. Perezhilton.com, January 27, 2010.

7. Generation M2: Media in the Lives of 8- to 18-Year-Olds, Kaiser Family Foundation, January 20, 2010, http://www.kff.org/entmedia/mh012010pkg.cfm.

8. Verizon Business RISK Team, 2009 Data Breach Investigations Report, http://www .verizonbusiness.com/resources/security/reports/2009_databreach_rp.pdf.

9. "Report: Most Companies Unprepared for Quick Response to Attack," DarkReading .com, October 5, 2009, http://www.darkreading.com/security/vulnerabilities/220 301057/index.html.

10. Bill Gertz, Washington Times, February 17, 2000. Central Intelligence Agency In-spector General, Improper Handling of Classified Information by John M. Deutch, Report of Investigation (unclassified), February 18, 2000.

11. Frank Wolf, "Wolf Reveals House Computers Compromised by Outside Source," press release, June 11, 2008; "Rep. Wolf: China Hacked Congressional Computers," FoxNews.com, June 11, 2008, http://www.foxnews.com/story/0,2933,365635,00 .html.

12. "Pentagon Source Says China Hacked Defense Department Computers," FoxNews .com, September 4, 2007, http://www.foxnews.com/story/0,2933,295640,00.html.

13. Andrew LaVallee, "AT&T Counters Verizon Ads with Luke Wilson's Help," Digits (blog), *Wall Street Journal,* November 20, 2009, http://blogs.wsj.com/digits/2009/ 11/20/att-counters-verizon-ads-with-luke-wilsons-help/.

14. Andy Soltis, "It's 'Starve Wars,'" *New York Post,* January 20, 2010.

15. Kathy Kristof, "Diet Smackdown," CBS MoneyWatch.com, January 20, 2010.

16. Jack Neff, "Burt's Puts Bees in Bonnet of Skin-Care Marketers," *Advertising Age,* January 31, 2008; mcmilker, "Attack the Ingredient Not the Brand—Is Burt's Bees' New Campaign on the Right Track?," Ecopreneurist.com, February 12, 2008, http://ecopreneurist.com/2008/02/12/attack-the-ingredient-not-the-brand-is-burts -bees-new-campaign-on-the-right-track.

17. *Advertising Age,* February 1, 2008.

18. L. Gordon Crovitz, "Facebook's Anti-Google Fiasco," *Wall Street Journal,* May 15, 2011; Sam Gustin, "Boom! Goes the Dynamite Under Facebook's Google Smear Campaign," *Wired,* May 12, 2011.

19. *Trial Lawyers, Inc.: A Report on the Lawsuit Industry in America, 2003,* Manhattan Institute for Policy Research.

20. "About Us," Huffington Post Investigative Fund, beta version accessed February 13, 2011, Huffpostfund.org./about-us.

21. "About," Franklin Center for Government and Public Integrity, http://www .franklincenterhq.org/about/.

22. Mike Hess, "Talking Poop, Nudity and Twitter with Robin Williams and Bobcat Goldthwait," PopEater.com, August 20, 2009, http://www.popeater.com/2009/08/ 20/talking-poop-nudity-and-twitter-with-robin-williams-and-bobcat/.

23. Mary Foster, "James O'Keefe, Accomplices Plead Guilty in Landrieu Break-in, Get Probation, Community Service, Light Fines," Huffington Post, May 26, 2010, http://www.huffingtonpost.com/2010/05/26/james-okeefe-pleads-guilty-sentenced _n_590559.html.

24. "Congressman Conyers Reads Playboy on Plane to DC," YouTube.com, November 25, 2010, http://www.youtube.com/watch?v=l9yhHiRc4-4.

25. "KFC Sink Trio Finger Lickin' Fired," Sky News, December 12, 2008, http://news .sky.com/skynews/Home/World-News/KFC-Bath-Prank-Three-Girls-Fired-From -California-KFC-After-Bathing-In-Restaurant-Sinks/Article/200812215178233.

26. Patrick Vogt, "Brands Under Attack: Marketers Can Learn from Domino's Video Disaster," *Forbes,* April 24, 2009.

27. Ibid.

28. A. J. Daulerio, "Duke 'Fuck List' Author Gets Potential Book, Movie Deals," Deadspin.com, October 1, 2010, http://deadspin.com/#!5653266/duke-fuck-list -author-gets-potential-book-movie-deals.

29. AOL Legal Department, Decisions & Litigation, *Zeran v. AOL* Opinion in the United States District Court for the Eastern District of Virginia, Alexandria Division, http://legal.web.aol.com/decisions/dldefam/zeranopi.html.

30. *Zeran v. America Online Inc.,* 129 F.3d 327 (4th Cir. 1997).

31. "Quotes for Alfred Pennyworth (Character)," Internet Movie Database, accessed February 15, 2011, http://www.imdb.com/character/ch0000204/quotes.

4. The Second Sword: Silent Slashers

1. Glaukôpis, "HBO's Rome ep 5," Glaukôpidos (blog), September 27, 2005, http://glaukopidos.blogspot.com/2005/09/hbos-rome-ep-5.html.
2. Suetonius, *The Twelve Caesars,* trans. Robert Graves (New York: Penguin, 1957), 231–32.
3. Ibid.
4. Portrait of Nero, from Paavo Castrén and Henrik Lilius, *Graffiti del Palatino,* ii, *Domus Tiberiana (Acta Instituti Romani Finlandiae,* IV) (Helsinki: Akateeminen Kirjakauppa, 1970), http://commons.wikimedia.org/wiki/File:Nero-graffito.jpg.
5. Mary Beard, *The Fires of Vesuvius: Pompeii Lost and Found* (Cambridge, Mass.: Belknap Press of Harvard University Press, 2010), 59.
6. Ibid., 202.
7. "The Writing on the Wall: Graffiti," quoting from the *Corpus Inscriptionum Latinarum,* vol. 4, *Destruction and Re-discovery,* accessed February 20, 2011, http://sites.google.com/site/ad79eruption/the-writing-on-the-wall.
8. Ibid.
9. Ibid.
10. Jamie Schram and Lukas I. Alpert, "Bar Goon's Slash and Smash Past," *New York Post,* July 31, 2008.
11. George Rush, "Outed Blogger Rosemary Port Blames Model Liskula Cohen for 'Skank' Stink," *New York Daily News,* August 23, 2009.
12. Owen Thomas, "Model Sues Google over 'Skank' Blog Post," Gawker, January 6, 2009, http://gawker.com/#!5124621/model-sues-google-over-skank-blog-post.
13. Jose Martinez, "Model Liskula Cohen Sues Google Over Blogger's 'Skank' Comment," *New York Daily News,* January 6, 2009.
14. David Margolick, "Slimed Online," Portfolio.com, February 11, 2009, http://www.portfolio.com/news-markets/national-news/portfolio/2009/02/11/Two-Lawyers-Fight-Cyber-Bullying.
15. Ibid.
16. Ellen Nakashima, "Harsh Words Die Hard on the Web," *Washington Post,* March 7, 2007.
17. Amir Efrati, "Students File Suit," Law Blog (blog), WSJ.com, June 12, 2007, http://blogs.wsj.com/law/2007/06/12/students-file-suit-against-autoadmit-director-others/.
18. Christopher Andrew and Vasili Mitrokhin, *The Sword and the Shield: The Mitrokhin Archive and the Secret History of the KGB* (New York: Basic Books, 1999), 245.
19. Interview with Sir Martin Gilbert, Pave the Way Foundation, http://www.barhama.com/PAVETHEWAY/gilbert.html.
20. Ibid.
21. Ion Mihai Pacepa, "Moscow's Assault on the Vatican," *National Review,* January 25, 2007, http://www.nationalreview.com/articles/219739/moscows-assault-vatican/ion-mihai-pacepa.
22. Andrew Ferguson, "You Don't Say?," *Forbes Life,* November 8, 2010.
23. Susan Stellin, "Hoteliers Look to Shield Themselves from Dishonest Online Reviews," Itineraries, *New York Times,* October 26, 2010.
24. Peter Martin, "Boyfriend Uses Netflix to Exact Revenge on Cheating Girlfriend," Cinematical: News (blog), moviefone.com, December 2, 2010, http://blog.moviefone.com/2010/12/02/boyfriend-netflix-girlfriend-cheating/.

59. (No byline), CNBC.com, "GE Rebuffs Tax Refund Report as 'Hoax,'" April 13, 2011, http://www.cnbc.com/id/42570045.

60. Evan Buxbaum, "New York Post Not Laughing at Climate Change Spoof," CNN .com, September 22, 2009, http://articles.cnn.com/2009-09-22/us/new.york.fake .newspaper_1_climate-change-climate-meeting-new-yorkers?_s=PM:US.

61. "The Yes Men—Exxon Hoax: Vivoleum," YouTube video, 9:59, from a broadcast on bnetTV, posted by bnetTV, June 19, 2007, http://www.youtube.com/watch?v= WkLzK13rI-Y.

62. Stuart Elliott, "Prankster Lampoon Chevron Ad Campaign," Media Decoder (blog), *New York Times,* October 18, 2010, http://mediadecoder.blogs.nytimes.com/2010/ 10/18/pranksters-lampoon-chevron-ad-campaign.

63. The Yes Men, "Help Us Keep Chevron's Campaign on the Skids!," TheYesMen.org, accessed February 25, 2011, http://theyesmen.org/blog/help-us-keep-chevrons -campaign-on-the-skids.

64. Interview with "Steve" by Mark Davis, November 27, 2010. All names and identifying details of the story of "Steve" and "Linda" have been changed.

65. http://www.senatorsimitian.com/images/uploads/SB_1411_Fact_Sheet.pdf.

66. Aaron Kelly, "Consequences of Filing a False DMCA Takedown Request," Aaron Kelly Intellectual Property Law Blog (blog), Lawyers.com, December 8, 2010, http://intellectual-property.lawyers.com/blogs/archives/10363-Consequences-of -filing-a-false-DMCA-Takedown-Request.html.

6. The Fourth Sword: Human Flesh Search Engines

1. Mary Kay Magistad, "China Web Attacks Get Personal," phonetic transcript of a radio broadcast, *PRI's The World,* 1/15/10, http://www.theworld.org/2010/01/china -web-attacks-get-personal/; Venkatesan Vembu, "The Meow Murderess Brought to Heel," DNAIndia, March 18, 2006, http://www.dnaindia.com/world/report_the -meow-murderess-brought-to-heel_1018584.

2. Jonathan Krim, "Subway Fracas Escalates into Test of the Internet's Power to Shame," *Washington Post,* July 7, 2005.

3. Isaiah Wilner, "The Number-One Girl," *New York,* May 7, 2007.

4. Magistad, "China Web Attacks Get Personal."

5. Mattathias Schwartz, "The Trolls Among Us," *New York Times Magazine,* August 3, 2008.

6. "Jail for Lab Boss Attacker," BBC News, August 6, 2001, http://news.bbc.co.uk/2/ hi/uk_news/1494924.stm; Andrew Alderson, "The Men Who Stood Up to an Animal Rights' Militant," Telegraph.co.uk, January 17, 2009, http://www.telegraph.co .uk/news/uknews/law-and-order/4276376/The-men-who-stood-up-to-animal -rights-militants.html.

7. "A Controversial Laboratory," BBC News, January 18, 2001, http://news.bbc.co.uk/ 2/hi/uk_news/1123837.stm.

8. Marco Evers, "Britain's Other War on Terror: Resisting the Animal Avengers," Spiegel Online, November 19, 2007, http://www.spiegel.de/international/europe/0,1518, 517875,00.html.

9. "A Controversial Laboratory," BBC News.

10. Zoe Broughton, "Seeing Is Believing—Cruelty to Dogs at Huntingdon Life Sciences," *Ecologist,* March 2001, http://findarticles.com/p/articles/mi_m2465/is_2 _31/ai_71634854/?tag=content;col1.

11. Ibid.

12. David Harrison and Daniel Foggo, "Terrorists Target Lab's Shareholders," Telegraph .Co.Uk, December 3, 2000, http://www.telegraph.co.uk/news/uknews/1376731/Terrorists-target-labs-shareholders.html.

13. Evers, "Britain's Other War on Terror."

14. Harrison and Foggo, "Terrorists Target Lab's Shareholders."

15. "Animal Rights or Wrongs," The Money Programme, BBC News World Edition, October 23, 2001, http://news.bbc.co.uk/2/hi/programmes/the_money_programme/archive/1602541.stm; "Pressure Builds on Animal Tests Lab," BBC News, January 16, 2001, http://news.bbc.co.uk/2/hi/uk_news/1120259.stm.

16. Jo-Ann Goodwin, "The Animals of Hatred," *Daily Mail* (London), October 15, 2003, transcribed at DawnWatch.com, http://lists.envirolink.org/pipermail/ar-news/Week-of-Mon-20031013/008215.html.

17. Harrison and Foggo, "Terrorists Target Lab's Shareholders."

18. Goodwin, "The Animals of Hatred."

19. Ibid.

20. Megan Murphy, "Activists in Live Testing Trial Deny Blackmail," FT.com, October 6, 2008.

21. Evers, "Britain's Other War on Terror"; "A Controversial Laboratory," BBC News.

22. Confidential interview with security consultant by Mark Davis, November 2010.

23. Heather Tomlinson, "Huntingdon Delays Listing After Attacks," Guardian.co.uk, September 8, 2005, http://www.guardian.co.uk/business/2005/sep/08/research.animalrights.

24. Goodwin, "The Animals of Hatred."

25. Fran Yeoman, "Extremists Face Long Jail Sentences After Blackmail Conviction," *Sunday Times* (London), December 24, 2008, http://www.timesonline.co.uk/tol/news/uk/crime/article5391798.ece.

26. Confidential interview with security expert by Mark Davis, November 2010.

27. Anonymous, "I Had a One-Night Stand with Christine O'Donnell," Gawker, October 28, 2010, http://gawker.com/#!5674353/i-had-a-one+night-stand-with-christine-odonnell.

28. Andrew Sullivan, "Defending Christine O'Donnell," Daily Dish (blog), *Atlantic,* October 29, 2010, http://andrewsullivan.theatlantic.com/the_daily_dish/2010/10/smearing-christine-odonnell.html.

29. Interview with Carol Howard Merritt, by Mark Davis, December 16, 2010.

30. Carol Howard Merritt, "Why Evangelicalism Is Failing a New Generation," Huffington Post, May 1, 2010, http://www.huffingtonpost.com/carol-howard-merritt/why-evangelicalism-is-fai_b_503971.html.

31. Leslie Katz, "Calif. Court Drops Charges Against Dunn," CNET News, March 14, 2007, http://news.cnet.com/Calif.-court-drops-charges-against-Dunn/2100-1014_3-6167187.html.

32. Interview with Tom Kellermann, by Mark Davis, November 18, 2010.

33. Amanda Hess, "Web Site Attempts to Convince Gay Priests to Stop Being Hypocrites," *Washington City Paper,* November 19, 2009, http://www.washingtoncitypaper.com/blogs/sexist/2009/11/19/web-site-attempts-to-convince-gay-priests-to-stop-being-hypocrites/.

34. Stephanie Condon, "Wiki Site Wants Help Finding Dirt on Meg Whitman," Political Hotsheet, CBS News.com, March 9, 2010, http://www.cbsnews.com/8301-503544_162-20000195-503544.html.

35. Ginger Adams Otis, "Taliban's Chilling Hunt and Slaughter: Pak-Trained Killers 'Used Facebook' to Track Aid Group," *New York Post,* August 15, 2010.

36. Michael Bristow, "China's Internet 'Spin Doctors,'" BBC Mobile News, December 16, 2008, http://news.bbc.co.uk/2/hi/7783640.stm.

37. Ibid.

38. Matt Richtel, "In Web World of 24/7 Stress, Writers Blog Till They Drop," *New York Times,* April 6, 2008.

39. Damian Grammaticas, "Chinese Woman Jailed over Twitter Post," BBC News Asia-Pacific, November 18, 2010, http://www.bbc.co.uk/news/world-asia-pacific-11784603.

40. "PayPal Says It Stopped Wikileaks Payments on US Letter," BBC Mobile News Business, December 8, 2010, http://www.bbc.co.uk/news/business-11945875.

41. Schwartz, "The Trolls Among Us"; numerous troll sites.

42. Elinor Mills, "Hacker in AT&T-iPad Security Case Arrested on Drug Charges," CNET News, June 15, 2010, http://news.cnet.com/8301-27080_3-20007827-245.html.

43. "User Talk:Donations," Encyclopedia Dramatica, accessed February 26, 2011, http://encyclopediadramatica.com/User_talk:Donations.

44. David Margolick, "Slimed Online," Portfolio.com, February 11, 2009, http://www.portfolio.com/news-markets/national-news/portfolio/2009/02/11/Two-Lawyers-Fight-Cyber-Bullying.

45. "Pressure Builds on Animal Tests Lab," BBC News; "Jail for Lab Boss Attacker," BBC News.

46. The Torrenzano Group trademark.

7. The Fifth Sword: Jihad by Proxy

1. Brian Williams, "Questions Over Business Links: Greenie in Carton War," *Courier-Mail* (Brisbane, Australia), February 10, 1995; Bob Burton, "Sometimes Truth Leaks Out: Failed PR Stunts 'Down Under,'" PRwatch.org, 4th quarter 1996, http://www.prwatch.org/prwissues/1997Q4/badpr.html.

2. Williams, "Questions Over Business Links"; Jim Pollard, *Herald Sun,* February 9, 2007.

3. Interview with digital expert by Mark Davis, November 12, 2010.

4. Jo-Ann Goodwin, "The Animals of Hatred," *Daily Mail* (London), October 15, 2003, transcribed at DawnWatch.com, http://lists.envirolink.org/pipermail/ar-news/Week-of-Mon-20031013/008215.html.

5. Marco Evers, "Britain's Other War on Terror: Resisting the Animal Avengers," Spiegel Online, November 19, 2007, http://www.spiegel.de/international/europe/0,1518,517875,00.html.

6. Goodwin, "The Animals of Hatred."

7. Ryan Sager, "Keep Off the Astroturf," op-ed, *New York Times,* August 19, 2009.

8. Ben Smith, "The Summer of Astroturf," Politico.com, August 21, 2009, http://www.politico.com/news/stories/0809/26312.html.

9. Jim VandeHei and Paul Fahri, "POWs Shown in Film Join Swift Boat Group's Anti-Kerry Efforts," *Washington Post,* October 14, 2004.

10. Jim Kuhnhenn, "Chamber Emerges as Formidable Political Force," Associated Press, August 21, 2010, http://www.msnbc.msn.com/id/38797920/ns/politics-decision_2010/.

11. Michael Luo, "Left's Big Donors Gather to Plot Strategy," *New York Times,* November 15, 2010.

12. Interview with a political consultant by Mark Davis, December 15, 2010.
13. R. Jeffrey Smith, "The DeLay-Abramoff Money Trail," *Washington Post,* December 31, 2005.
14. Ibid.
15. Susan Schmidt, "Ex-Lobbyist Is Focus of Widening Investigations," *Washington Post,* July 16, 2004.
16. Dana Milbank, "One Committee's Three Hours of Inquiry, in Surreal Time," *Washington Post,* June 23, 2005; Alex Gibney, "The Deceptions of Ralph Reed," Atlantic.com, September 26, 2010, http://www.theatlantic.com/politics/archive/2010/09/ralph-reed-is-a-liar/63568/.
17. "About TVC," Traditional Values Coalition, accessed March 2, 2011, http://www.traditionalvalues.org/about.php.
18. Susan Schmidt and James V. Grimaldi, "How a Lobbyist Stacked the Deck," *Washington Post,* October 16, 2005.
19. Ibid.
20. James V. Grimaldi and Susan Schmidt, "Lawmaker's Abramoff Ties Investigated," *Washington Post,* October 18, 2005; R. Jeffrey Smith, "Foundation's Funds Diverted from Mission," September 28, 2004.
21. Susan Schmidt, "Casino Bid Prompted High-Stakes Lobbying," *Washington Post,* March 13, 2005.
22. Eric Reguly, "How Far to Go for Gold?," *Globe and Mail* (Toronto), last updated November 23, 2010, http://www.theglobeandmail.com/report-on-business/rob-magazine/how-far-to-go-for-gold/article1775540/.
23. "Environmental Benefits," QwikReport, Gabriel Resources, accessed March 2, 2011, http://www.gabrielresources.com/s/QwikReport.asp?IsPopup=Y&printVersion=now&XB0W=133378,128087.
24. Reguly, "How Far to Go for Gold?"
25. "Actual Situation in Rosia Montana," ProRosia Montana, accessed March 2, 2011, http://prorosiamontana.ro/voices-of-rosia-montana-actual-situation-in-rosia-montana/actual-situation-in-rosia-montana/.
26. Alan R. Hill, "The Facts of the Matter: Who Is Behind the Opposition to the Rosia Montana Project—And Why It Matters to All Romanians" (speech, Bucharest, Romania, September 5, 2007), http://www.gabrielresources.com/i/pdf/Alansspeech FINAL.pdf.
27. Reguly, "How Far to Go for Gold?"; "In Partnership: For the Economy," Gabriel Resources, accessed March 2, 2011, http://www.gabrielresources.com/benefits-econ.htm.
28. Cultural Benefits Report, Gabriel Resources, accessed March 2, 2011, http://www.gabrielresources.com/s/CulturalBenefits.asp?ReportID=128090.
29. "Cyanide Spill Reaches Danube," BBC News, February 13, 2000, http://news.bbc.co.uk/2/hi/europe/641566.stm; Reguly, "How Far to Go for Gold?"
30. Reguly, "How Far to Go for Gold?"
31. Ceremony Remarks, "Stephanie Danielle Roth: Romania Oil & Mining," Goldman Environmental Prize 2005 video 4:22, http://www.goldmanprize.org/node/158.
32. "Stephanie Danielle Roth: Romania Oil & Mining," Goldman Environmental Prize, http://www.goldmanprize.org/node/158.
33. Hill, The "Facts of the Matter."
34. Mary Katharine Ham, "The Forgotten Mammal," Townhall.com, January 26, 2007,

http://townhall.com/columnists/marykatharineham/2007/01/26/the_forgotten_mammal.

35. "Redgrave in Romanian Mine Rumpus," BBC News, last updated June 23, 2006, http://news.bbc.co.uk/2/hi/5110784.stm.

36. Reguly, "How Far to Go for Gold?"

37. Hill, "The Facts of the Matter."

38. Ibid.

39. Ibid.

40. Dorothy Kosich, "Soros Fund Holdings Favor Aluminum Corp of China, CVRD, Gold Stocks," Mineweb, August 15, 2007, http://www.mineweb.com/mineweb/view/mineweb/en/page60?oid=25124&sn=Detail.

41. Hill, "The Facts of the Matter."

42. Ibid.

43. Jesse Westbrook, "SEC Delays Proxy-Access Rules Amid Legal Challenge," *Bloomberg Businessweek,* October 4, 2010, http://www.businessweek.com/news/2010-10-04/sec-delays-proxy-access-rules-amid-legal-challenge.html.

44. "Help: How to Research Front Groups," SourceWatch, accessed March 2, 2011, http://www.sourcewatch.org/index.php?title=Help:How_to_research_front_groups.

45. Hill, "The Facts of the Matter."

46. Phelim McAleer and Ann McElhinney, "Green Lies and an Inconvenient Truth," *Irish Mail on Sunday,* February 18, 2007.

8. The Sixth Sword: Truth Remix

1. Murray Wardrop, "Young Will Have to Change Names to Escape 'Cyber Past' Warns Google's Eric Schmidt," Telegraph.Co.UK, August 18, 2010, http://www.telegraph.co.uk/technology/google/7951269/Young-will-have-to-change-names-to-escape-cyber-past-warns-Googles-Eric-Schmidt.html.

2. David Margolick, "Slimed Online," Portfolio.com, February 11, 2009, http://www.portfolio.com/news-markets/national-news/portfolio/2009/02/11/Two-Lawyers-Fight-Cyber-Bullying.

3. "About Us," Yelp, accessed March 4, 2011, http://www.yelp.com/about.

4. Ibid.

5. Interview with Washington, D.C., dentist by Mark Davis, November 21, 2010.

6. "About Us," Yelp.

7. Robin Wauters, "Yelp Hit with Class Action Lawsuit for Running an 'Extortion' Scheme," TechCrunch, February 24, 2010, http://techcrunch.com/2010/02/24/yelp-class-action-lawsuit/.

8. Leena Rao, "Complaints Against Yelp's 'Extortion' Practices Grow Louder," TechCrunch, March 17, 2010, http://techcrunch.com/2010/03/17/complaints-against-yelps-extortion-practices-grow-louder/.

9. "Yelp Elite Squad," Yelp, accessed March 4, 2011, http://www.yelp.com/elite.

10. Claire Cain Miller, "Yelp Will Let Businesses Respond to Web Reviews," *New York Times,* April 10, 2009.

11. Kirstin Downey Grimsley and Jay Mathews, "Executives' Privilege? In Boardroom, Sex Seldom Leads to Censure," *Washington Post,* September 16, 1998.

12. Adam Lashinsky, "Mark Hurd's Moment," *Fortune* online, CNNMoney.com, last updated March 3, 2009, http://money.cnn.com/2009/02/27/news/companies/lashinsky_hurd.fortune/index.htm.

13. Lashinsky, "Mark Hurd's Moment"; Connie Guglielmo, Ian King, and Aaron Ricadela, "HP's Mark Hurd Resigns After Sexual Harassment Probe," *Bloomberg Businessweek,* August 7, 2010, http://www.businessweek.com/news/2010-08-07/hp-chief-executive -hurd-resigns-after-sexual-harassment-probe.html.

14. Ben Worthen and Joann S. Lublin, "Woman in Hurd Case Regrets Dismissal," *Wall Street Journal,* August 9, 2010.

15. Ibid.

16. Ashlee Vance, "Boss's Stumble May Also Trip Hewlett-Packard," Technology, *New York Times,* August 8, 2010; Guglielmo, King, and Ricadela, "HP's Mark Hurd Resigns."

17. Ashlee Vance, "Oracle Chief Faults H.P. Board for Forcing Hurd's Resignation," Technology, *New York Times,* August 9, 2010.

18. Ashlee Vance and Matt Richtel, "H.P. Followed a P.R. Specialist's Advice in the Hurd Case," Technology, *New York Times,* August 9, 2010.

19. Ibid.

20. Jordan Robertson, "HP, Hurd Reach Settlement over Oracle Gig," *USA Today,* September 21, 2010.

21. Jesus Diaz, "How Apple Lost the Next iPhone," Gizmodo, April 19, 2010, http:// gizmodo.com/#!5520438/how-apple-lost-the-next-iphone.

22. Peter Kafka, "Mobile Blogger 'Boy Genius' Unmasked, Acquired," MediaMemo, All Things Digital, *Wall Street Journal,* April 26, 2010, http://mediamemo.allth ingsd.com/20100426/mobile-blogger-boy-genius-unmasked-acquired/; Jacob Schul-man, "BlackBerry Storm 2 Dropping SurePress Screen?," Engadget, May 15, 2009, http://www.engadget.com/2009/05/15/blackberry-storm-2-dropping-surepress -screen/.

23. Engadget, July 27, 2009.

24. Wardrop, "Young Will Have to Change Names."

25. Seth Freeman, "Me and My Algorithm," op-ed, *New York Times,* January 17, 2011.

26. Jessica Bennett, "What the Internet Knows About You," *Newsweek,* October 22, 2010, http://www.newsweek.com/2010/10/22/forget-privacy-what-the-internet-knows -about-you.html.

27. Jeffrey Rosen, "The Web Means the End of Forgetting," *New York Times Magazine,* July 25, 2010.

28. Rosen, "The Web Means the End of Forgetting"; Brian Krebs, "Court Rules Against Teacher in MySpace 'Drunken Pirate' Case," Security Fix (blog), *Washington Post,* December 3, 2008, http://voices.washingtonpost.com/securityfix/2008/12/court_ rules_against_teacher_in.html.

29. Wardrop, "Young Will Have to Change Names."

30. Ibid.

31. Noirin Shirley, "A Hell of a Time," NerdChic (blog), November 5, 2010, http://blog .nerdchic.net/archives/418/.

32. Comment by lucisferre, December 2010, on Noirin Shirley, "A Hell of a Time: Sexual Assault at Tech Conferences," on Reddit, accessed March 5, 2011, http:// www.reddit.com/r/programming/comments/e20ct/a_hell_of_a_time_sexual_ assault_at_tech/c14nozg.

33. "Killed in Stevenson Home, Girl Shot Accidentally by Former Vice President's Grandson," *New York Times,* December 31, 1912.

34. Joseph Cummins, *Anything for a Vote: Dirty Tricks, Cheap Shots, and October Sur-prises in U.S. Presidential Campaigns* (Philadelphia: Quirk Books, 2007), 210.

35. John McArdle, "Florida, 'Taliban Dan' TV Ad Backfires on Grayson," *Roll Call*, September 30, 2010, http://www.rollcall.com/issues/56_33/atr/50384-1.html.

36. Kyle Western, *Men's Health*, 12/2010; Tom Espiner, "Private Browsing Tools Still Leave Data Trail," ZDNet Asian Edition, August 10, 2010, http://www.zdnetasia .com/private-browsing-tools-still-leave-data-trail-62201970.htm.

37. Samuel D. Warren and Louis D. Brandeis, "The Right to Privacy," *Harvard Law Review* 4 (December 15, 1890).

38. "Celebs Beware! New Pandora's Box of 'Personal' Drones That Could Stalk Anyone from Brangelina to Your Own Child," dailymail.co.uk, November 8, 2010, http:// www.dailymail.co.uk/sciencetech/article-1327343/Personal-recreation-drones -developed.html.

39. "Man Pleads in Apparent Sextortion Case," Myfoxla.com, July 19, 2010, http:// www.myfoxla.com/dpp/news/local/man-pleads-in-apparent-sextortion-case -20100719.

40. Anjeanette Damon and David McGrath Schwartz, "Sharron Angle Offers Juice to Tea Party of Nevada Opponent," *Las Vegas Sun*, October 5, 2010.

41. HKLawposterous.com; Dan Hicks, "Online Attacks Are Very Real Crises," Communicating Through a Crisis (blog), Institute for Crisis Management, March 10, 2009, crisisexperts.blogspot.com/2009/03/online-attacks-are-very-real-crises.html.

42. Cummins, *Anything for a Vote*, 120.

43. Ibid., 126.

44. Ibid., 52.

45. Richard H. Davis, "The Anatomy of a Smear Campaign," *Boston Globe*, March 21, 2004.

46. Suetonius, *The Twelve Caesars*, trans. Robert Graves (New York: Penguin, 1957).

47. Marcus Tullius Cicero, *Secondary Orations Against Verres*, Book 1, www.Uah.edu/ student_life/organizations/sal/texts/latin/classical/cicero/inverrems1e.html.

48. Ibid.

49. H. Paul Jeffers, *An Honest President: The Life and Presidencies of Grover Cleveland* (New York: William Morrow, 2000), 106–107.

50. Ibid., 108.

51. Allan Nevins, *Grover Cleveland: A Study in Courage* (New York: Dodd, Mead, 1933); Jeffers, *An Honest President*.

52. Interview with Leo Yakutis, by Mark Davis, October 8, 2010.

53. Nevins, *Grover Cleveland*, 169.

9. The Seventh Sword—Clandestine War

1. "Estonia Hit by 'Moscow Cyber War,'" BBC News, May 17, 2007, http://news.bbc .co.uk/2/hi/europe/6665145.stm.

2. Interview with Leo Yakutis by Mark Davis, October 10, 2010.

3. Ashley Fantz, "Assange's 'Poison Pill' File Impossible to Stop, Expert Says," CNN U.S., December 8, 2010, http://articles.cnn.com/2010-12-08/us/wikileaks.poison .pill_1_julian-assange-wikileaks-key-encryption?_s=PM:US.

4. Tim Weber, "Cybercrime Threat Rising Sharply," BBC Mobile News, January 31, 2009, http://news.bbc.co.uk/2/hi/business/davos/7862549.stm.

5. "Ponemon Study Shows the Cost of a Data Breach Continues to Increase," Ponemon Institute, January 25, 2011, http://www.ponemon.org/news-2/23.

6. Bill Brenner, "Heartland CEO on Data Breach: QSAs Let Us Down," Q&A, CSO,

August 12, 2009, http://www.csoonline.com/article/499527/heartland-ceo-on-data
-breach-qsas-let-us-down; "Alleged International Hacker Indicted for Massive Attack
on U.S. Retail and Banking Networks," news release, U.S. Department of Justice,
August 17, 2009, http://www.justice.gov/opa/pr/2009/August/09-crm-810.html; *Privacy in the Cloud Computing Era,* Trustworthy Computing: Policymakers, Microsoft,
November 2009, http://www.microsoft.com/about/twc/en/us/Policymakers.aspx.

7. Network World, "Spear Phishers Hunting PR Firms and Lawyers, Says FBI," PC-
World, November 18, 2009, http://www.pcworld.com/article/182536/spear_phishers
_hunting_pr_firms_and_lawyers_says_fbi.html.

8. Julia Angwin and Jennifer Valentino-DeVries, "Apple, Google Collect User Data,"
Wall Street, Journal, April 22, 2011.

9. Julia Angwin and Jennifer Valentino-DeVries, "Race Is On to 'Fingerprint' Phones,
PCs," *Wall Street Journal,* December 1, 2010.

10. Emily Steel and Geoffrey A. Fowler, "Facebook in Privacy Breach," *Wall Street Journal,* October 18, 2010.

11. Emily Steel, "Web Pioneer Profiles Users by Name," *Wall Street Journal,* October
25, 2010.

12. Ibid.

13. Steel and Fowler, "Facebook in Privacy Breach."

14. Julia Angwin, "The Web's New Gold Mine: Your Secrets," *Wall Street Journal,* July
30, 2010.

15. Ibid.

16. Niall Firth, "Facebook 'Accidentally Outing Gay Users' to Outside Firms Through
Targeted Ads," *Daily Mail* (UK), October 22, 2010, http://www.dailymail.co.uk/
sciencetech/article-1322916/Facebook-accidentally-outing-gay-users-advertisers.
html#ixzz13OvImASl.

17. Angwin, "The Web's New Gold Mine."

18. "Privacy Fears as Eight in 10 Kids Have Photos Online," Breitbart.com, October 8,
2010, http://www.breitbart.com/article.php?id=CNG.c81a656973793fe072f583c5
20733516.841.

19. Cecilia Kang, "FCC Probes Google over Street View Program's Collection of Personal Data," *Washington Post,* November 10, 2010; Vanessa Allen, "Google Finally
Admits That Its Street View Cars DID Take Emails and Passwords from Computers," Mail Online (UK), last updated October 28, 2010, http://www.dailymail.co
.uk/sciencetech/article-1323310/Google-admits-Street-View-cars-DID-emails-pass
words-computers.html.

20. Kim Zetter, "Hacker Spoofs Cell Phone Tower to Intercept Calls," Threat Level
(blog), Wired.com, July 31, 2010, http://www.wired.com/threatlevel/2010/07/inter
cepting-cell-phone-calls/.

21. Luke Salkeld, "Scariest Speed Camera of All . . . It Checks Your Insurance, Tax and
Even Whether You Are Tailgating or Not Wearing a Seatbelt," Mail Online (UK),
November 3, 2010, http://www.dailymail.co.uk/sciencetech/article-1326035/Speed
-camera-checks-insurance-tax-wearing-seatbelt.html.

22. Clark Boyd, "Cyber-War a Growing Threat Warn Experts," BBC News, June 17,
2010, http://www.bbc.co.uk/news/10339543.

23. "Partial List of Celebs Targeted by Hackers," TMZ.com, March 17, 2011.

24. Marian Merritt, "Alicia Keys MySpace Hack," Norton.com, November 15, 2007.

25. Marian Merritt, "Bots and Botnets: A Growing Threat," Norton.com, February 19,
2008, http://us.norton.com/familyresources/resources.jsp?title=bots_and_botnets.

26. Rik Ferguson, "Japanese Porn Extortion," CounterMeasures (blog), Trend Micro, April 14, 2010, http://countermeasures.trendmicro.eu/Japanese-porn-extortion.

27. Donald L. Evans, speech, Forum on International Property Rights Protection, January 13, 2005, http://www.america.gov/st/washfile.

28. "GM Daewoo-Chery Copyright Suit Settled," Asia Times Online, November 22, 2005, http://www.atimes.com/atimes/China_Business/GK22Cb04.html.

29. John Leyden, "Couple Charged over Hybrid Car Industrial Espionage Plot," *Register* (UK), July 23, 2010, http://www.theregister.co.uk/2010/07/23/hybrid_car_espionage _scam/.

30. Christopher Drew, "New Spy Game: Firms' Secrets Sold Overseas," *New York Times,* October 17, 2010.

31. Interview with security expert by Mark Davis, December 12, 2010.

32. Ryan Tate, "Apple's Worst Security Breach: 114,000 iPad Owners Exposed," Gawker, June 9, 2010, http://gawker.com/#!5559346/apples-worst-security-breach -114000-ipad-owners-exposed.

33. Thomas Claburn, "Cold Boot Attack Defeats Encryption Software," *Information-Week,* February 21, 2008, http://www.informationweek.com/news/personal-tech/ showArticle.jhtml?articleID=206801184&queryText=thomas%20claburn.

34. Interview with security expert by Mark Davis, November 4, 2010.

35. Interview with Bill Livingstone, by Mark Davis, October 5, 2010.

36. Interview with Tom Kellermann by Mark Davis, November 11, 2010.

37. Interview with security expert by Mark Davis, December 1, 2010.

38. "Political Hacktivists Turn to Web Attacks," BBC News, February 10, 2010, http:// news.bbc.co.uk/2/hi/8506698.stm.

39. *Privacy in the Cloud Computing Era,* Trustworthy Computing: Policymakers, Microsoft, November 2009, 2, http://www.microsoft.com/about/twc/en/us/Policymakers .aspx.

40. Chuck Bennett, "Terror Target Breach," *New York Post,* December 6, 2010.

41. "Cyber Wars: US Is Stepping Up Defense Against Digital Attacks," Reuters, October 5, 2010, http://m.cnbc.com/us_news/39518423/1. Jim Wolf, "The Pentagon's New Cyber Warriors," special report, Reuters, October 5, 2010, http://www.reuters .com/article/2010/10/05/us-usa-cyberwar-idUSTRE69433120101005.

42. Fahmid Y. Rashid, "Cyber-Attacks Targeting Power, Gas Utilities on the Rise: Survey," IT Security & Network Security News, April 04, 2011.

43. Marshall Abrams and Joe Weiss, *Malicious Control System Cyber Security Attack Case Study—Maroochy Water Services, Australia,* Computer Security Resource Center, National Institute of Standards and Technology, July 23, 2008, http://csrc.nist.gov/ groups/SMA/fisma/ics/documents/Maroochy-Water-Services-Case-Study_report.pdf.

44. "Staged Cyber Attack Reveals Vulnerability in Power Grid," YouTube video, 1:05, from a Department of Homeland Security video televised by CNN, posted by "fpzzuuulzgaxd," September 27, 2007, http://www.youtube.com/watch?v=fJyWng Dco3g; "Cyber War: Sabotaging the System," *60 Minutes,* CBS News, first broadcast November 8, 2009, updated June 10, 2010, posted June 13, 2010, http://www .cbsnews.com/stories/2010/06/10/60minutes/main6568387_page5.shtml.

45. "Cyber Wars: US Is Stepping Up Defense," Reuters, October 5, 2010; Jim Wolf, "Pentagon's New Cyber Warriors," Reuters, October 5, 2010.

46. Ibid.

47. Mike DeBonis, "Hacker Infiltration Ends D.C. Online Voting Trial," *Washington Post,* October 4, 2010.

48. Michael R. Crittenden and Shayndi Raice, "Chinese Firm 'Hijacked' Data," *Wall Street Journal,* November 17, 2010; "Report: Massive Hack Targeted Government, Military," CBS News, November 17, 2010, http://www.cbsnews.com/stories/2010/11/17/world/main7062928.shtml.

49. Ellen Nakashima, "Chinese Leaders Ordered Google Hack, U.S. Cable Quotes Source as Saying," *Washington Post,* December 4, 2010.

50. "China Leadership 'Orchestrated Google Hacking,'" BBC News Asia-Pacific, December 4, 2010, http://www.bbc.co.uk/news/world-asia-pacific-11920616.

51. David Leigh, "How 250,000 U.S. Embassy Cables Were Leaked," *Guardian* (UK), November 28, 2010, http://www.guardian.co.uk/world/2010/nov/28/how-us-embassy-cables-leaked.

52. Javier Salido and Patrick Voon, "The Case for Data Governance," part 1 of *A Guide to Data Governance for Privacy, Confidentiality, and Compliance,* 4, Trustworthy Computing, Microsoft, January 2010, http://www.microsoft.com/privacy/datagovernance.aspx.

53. Open Security Foundation, "Data Loss Database—2009 Yearly Report," updated March 7, 2011, http://datalossdb.org/yearly_reports/dataloss-2009.pdf.

54. Shaun Waterman, "Gaps in Authority Hamper Military Against Cyber-Attacks," *Washington Times,* September 23, 2010.

55. Geoffrey Forden, "Russia's Nuclear Warriors: False Alarms on the Nuclear Front," NOVA Online, PBS, updated October 2001, http://www.pbs.org/wgbh/nova/missileers/falsealarms.html; Jonathan Schell, "The Forgotten Threat: 'Countdown to Zero' on Nuclear Weapons," *Nation,* July 27, 2010.

10. Swimming in the Silicon Sea

1. Interview with Ned Desmond, by Mark Davis, November 22, 2010.

2. Jaron Lanier, *You Are Not a Gadget: A Manifesto* (New York: Knopf, 2010), 32.

3. Stewart Brand, quoted in "Information Wants to Be Free . . . ," Roger Clarke's Web-Site (blog), amended August 28, 2001, http://www.rogerclarke.com/II/IWtbF.html.

4. Brian McRee, "The Cove (2009)—Dolphin Safe," Film Consumer (blog), July 12, 2010, http://www.thefilmconsumer.com/2010/07/cove-2009-dolphin-safe.html.

5. Interview with James Lee, by Mark Davis, November 1, 2010.

6. Matt McGee, "Google Removes Offensive Obama Image; Was It Justified?," Search Engine Land, November 19, 2009, http://searchengineland.com/google-removes-offensive-obama-image-was-it-justified-30165.

7. Interview with Leo Yakutis, by Mark Davis, October 8, 2010.

8. Interview with Rich Daly by Richard Torrenzano, January 19, 2011.

9. "Miniseries, Night 1," Battlestar Galactica Wiki, last modified November 22, 2009, http://en.battlestarwiki.org/wiki/Miniseries.

10. Arthur C. Clarke and Stephen Baxter, *The Light of Other Days* (New York: Tor Books, 2000).

11. Anita L. Allen, "*NAACP v. Alabama,* Privacy and Data Protection," EPIC Alert 15.13, last modified June 27, 2008, http://naacpvalabamaat50.org/.

12. Steven J. Horowitz, "Defusing a Google Bomb," Yale Law Journal Online 117, Pocket Part 36 (September 7, 2007), http://www.yalelawjournal.org/the-yale-law-journal-pocket-part/intellectual-property/defusing-a-google-bomb/.

13. Cass R. Sunstein, *On Rumors: How Falsehoods Spread, Why We Believe Them, What Can Be Done* (New York: Farrar, Straus and Giroux, 2009), 79.

14. Patricia Cohen, "Digitally Mapping the Republic of Letters," ArtsBeat (blog), *New*

York Times, November 16, 2010, http://artsbeat.blogs.nytimes.com/2010/11/16/digitally-mapping-the-republic-of-letters/.

15. Interview with Carol Howard Merritt, by Mark Davis, December 16, 2010.
16. Alexia Tsotsis, "To Celebrate the #Jan25 Revolution, Egyptian Names His First-born 'Facebook,'" TechCrunch, February 19, 2011, http://techcrunch.com/2011/02/19/facebook-egypt-newborn/.
17. Lanier, *You Are Not a Gadget,* 83.
18. Ibid., 87.
19. Zadie Smith, "Generation Why?," review of *The Social Network,* a film directed by David Fincher, with a screenplay by Aaron Sorkin, and *You Are Not a Gadget: A Manifesto* by Jaron Lanier, *New York Review of Books,* November 25, 2010.
20. Alexis Madrigal, "Literary Writers and Social Media: A Response to Zadie Smith," TheAtlantic.com, November 8, 2010, http://www.theatlantic.com/technology/archive/2010/11/literary-writers-and-social-media-a-response-to-zadie-smith/66257/.
21. "Pornography Statistics," Family Safe Media, accessed March 21, 2011, http://www.familysafemedia.com/pornography_statistics.html.
22. Nick Bilton, "Part of the Daily American Diet, 34 Gigabytes of Data," *New York Times,* December 9, 2009.
23. Roger E. Bohn and James E. Short, "How Much Information? 2009 Report on American Consumers," Global Information Industry Center, University of California, San Diego, updated January 2010, http://hmi.ucsd.edu/pdf/HMI_2009_ConsumerReport_Dec9_2009.pdf.
24. Murray Wardrop, "Young Will Have to Change Names to Escape 'Cyber Past' Warns Google's Eric Schmidt," Telegraph.Co.UK, August 18, 2010, http://www.telegraph.co.uk/technology/google/7951269/Young-will-have-to-change-names-to-escape-cyber-past-warns-Googles-Eric-Schmidt.html.
25. "Memorable Quotes for *Watchmen* (2009)," Internet Movie Database, accessed March 21, 2011, http://www.imdb.com/title/tt0409459/quotes.

11. The Seven Shields of Digital Assassination

1. The Torrenzano Group, LLC, trademark philosophy of doing business, 1996.
2. Ibid.
3. Ibid.
4. John Blossom, "Regulating the Ether: The FCC Confronts the Limits of Net Neutrality," ContentBlogger (blog), Shore Communications Inc., April 7, 2010, http://www.shore.com/commentary/weblogs/2010/04/regulating-ether-fcc-confronts-limits.html.
5. "Dave Carroll's Songwriting Revenge," News, Taylor Guitars, July 10, 2009, http://www.taylorguitars.com/news/NewsDetail.aspx?id=102; Mark Tran, "Singer Gets His Revenge on United Airlines and Soars to Fame," News Blog (blog), Guardian.co.uk, July 23, 2009, http://www.guardian.co.uk/news/blog/2009/jul/23/youtube-united-breaks-guitars-video.
6. Karen Tumulty and Ed O'Keefe, "Fired USDA Official Receives Apologies from White House, Vilsack," *Washington Post,* July 22, 2010.
7. "Political Retribution," *California Catholic Daily,* March 13, 2009, http://www.calcatholic.com/news/newsArticle.aspx?id=df9e1f03-ef76-49d3-bba0-ada8239b419c; interview with recent Claremont McKenna College students by Mark Davis, March 11, 2011.

8. Glenn Reynolds, "I Never Would Have Heard the Words 'Liskula Cohen' and 'Skank' Together," August 24, 2009, http://pajamasmedia.com/instapundit/83934/.
9. "Responding to Reviews," Support Center, Yelp for Business Owners, Yelp, accessed May 1, 2011, https://biz.yelp.com/support/responding_to_reviews.
10. "Wikipedia: Notability (people)," Wikipedia, accessed January 31, 2011, http://en .wikipedia.org/wiki/Wikipedia:Notability_(people).
11. "DMCA Safe Harbor," Chilling Effects, accessed February 5, 2011, http://www .chillingeffects.org/dmca512.

Index

WORLD
CHANGERS

WORLD
CHANGERS

25 Entrepreneurs

Who Changed Business

as We Knew It

JOHN A. BYRNE

PORTFOLIO / PENGUIN

PORTFOLIO / PENGUIN
Published by the Penguin Group
Penguin Group (USA) Inc., 375 Hudson Street, New York, New York 10014, U.S.A.
Penguin Group (Canada), 90 Eglinton Avenue East, Suite 700, Toronto, Ontario, Canada M4P 2Y3
(a division of Pearson Penguin Canada Inc.)
Penguin Books Ltd, 80 Strand, London WC2R 0RL, England
Penguin Ireland, 25 St. Stephen's Green, Dublin 2, Ireland (a division of Penguin Books Ltd)
Penguin Books Australia Ltd, 250 Camberwell Road, Camberwell, Victoria 3124, Australia
(a division of Pearson Australia Group Pty Ltd)
Penguin Books India Pvt Ltd, 11 Community Centre, Panchsheel Park, New Delhi—110 017, India
Penguin Group (NZ), 67 Apollo Drive, Rosedale, Auckland 0632, New Zealand
(a division of Pearson New Zealand Ltd)
Penguin Books (South Africa) (Pty) Ltd, 24 Sturdee Avenue, Rosebank, Johannesburg 2196, South Africa

Penguin Books Ltd, Registered Offices: 80 Strand, London WC2R 0RL, England

First published in 2011 by Portfolio / Penguin, a member of Penguin Group (USA) Inc.

1   3   5   7   9   10   8   6   4   2

Illustration credits appear on pages 269–70

LIBRARY OF CONGRESS CATALOGING-IN-PUBLICATION DATA
Byrne, John A.
World changers : twenty-five entrepreneurs who changed business as we knew it / John A. Byrne.
p. cm.
Includes bibliographical references and index.
ISBN 978-1-59184-450-1   4864 7654 6/12
1. Businesspeople—Biography. 2. Entrepreneurship. 3. Success in business. I. Title.
HC29.B97 2011
338.092'2—dc23
2011036087

Printed in the United States of America

ALWAYS LEARNING   PEARSON

To Kate

for her love and support through everything

CONTENTS

PREFACE

What if you could sit down to dinner with some of the world's most accomplished entrepreneurs and have a great conversation with them?

That simple notion is the genesis of the book in your hands. Within a short period of time in 2009, I had the pleasure of interviewing onstage both Howard Schultz of Starbucks at Ernst & Young's annual Strategic Growth Forum in Palm Springs, California, and Reed Hastings of Netflix before magazine editors and publishers in New York. After an hour or so of deep conversation, I walked off those stages so thoroughly jazzed by those experiences that I ultimately decided to start my own company. But I also wondered how I could recreate those inspiring and motivational experiences for others.

Imagine having the chance to listen and learn from a Steve Jobs, a John Mackey, or a Fred Smith on the most important things they've learned from their experiences in creating Apple, Whole Foods Market, and Federal Express. Imagine being able to engage in a meaningful conversation with Bernie Marcus and Arthur Blank on how they came up with the idea of The Home Depot and got it off the ground. Or having the benefit of the self-reflection of a Howard Schultz, who, like Jobs and Michael Dell before him, had to come back to the company he originally created to reinvent it and himself?

Of course, it was not possible to deliver any one of these rock star entrepreneurs to your dinner table—no matter who was doing the cooking or what you were serving. The next best thing? I could be your ambassador. I could attempt to interview twenty-five of the world's greatest living entrepreneurs, people who have truly changed the way we live and think, the way we work and play, the way we now see the world itself. That's exactly what I attempted to do.

How were these twenty-five extraordinary people chosen? Largely on the basis of their impact. How original was their idea? How influential had it become? Did it transform our personal lives in any significant way? Did it alter our professional lives to allow us to become more productive, more thoughtful, and better able to accomplish things to make our own mark in this world? Admittedly, the answers to these questions are entirely subjective. So, too, are the choices of the entrepreneurs in this book. All of them are world changers whose products and services have found their way—big and small—into our lives.

We may now call home to speak to our children on a phone that became the dream of a famous Silicon Valley entrepreneur. We may eat healthier foods because of the realized dream of a man who believed that natural and organic foods were better for you long before most people knew what organic food was. We may fly more cheaply in the skies because of a person who thought the existing airline architecture was poorly built by a bunch of corporate stiffs who forgot they had customers to satisfy.

No less important are the organizations these entrepreneurs have crafted. Unlike many of the places where people work, these are not companies that insulate decision makers from realities. These are not organizations headed by leaders who surround themselves with people who never contradict them. And these are not companies without a clear and overriding purpose that reaches far beyond the bottom line. As important as the products and services these entrepreneurs have brought to market are, they also have deserved reputations for creating places of work that encourage creativity, innovation, and meaning.

Some cynics might accuse me of a little hero worship. No matter. All my life, the people who create great organizations and great products have fascinated me. Over the course of my own career as a journalist, author, and editor, I have been fortunate to interview thousands of people, including some of the most celebrated entrepreneurs and executives of our time. I've been lucky enough to have Steve Jobs personally demonstrate the very first iPhone weeks before the product first came to market. I've been flattered to have had General Electric CEO Jack Welch, an intrapreneur if ever there was one, ask me to work closely with him on his memoir—a collaboration that resulted in my spending more than a thousand hours with him. And now I am extremely grateful for the time many of these entrepreneurs have made to let me into their formidable minds and biggest adventures.

I want this book to be both a meditation on entrepreneurship and an inspiration for those who want to create something meaningful on their own. It was not always possible to arrange an interview. Most of the entrepreneurs featured in this book are incredibly busy people, often consumed with their business and booked over a year in advance. Yet many rearranged their schedules to allow me the opportunity to engage them. Whether it was through a personal interview or a deep dive into everything ever written and uttered by one of these great entrepreneurs, the goal was to bring that person's experience and wisdom to these pages for the benefit of others— to inspire, to motivate, to learn, to achieve.

PROLOGUE

For a quarter of a century, some of the world's greatest entrepreneurs have been celebrated like Academy Award–winning actors and actresses. In a ceremony that has all the flash and glitz of the Oscars, the winners' names are called out on a brightly lit stage. Then the entrepreneurs proudly march past on a red carpet to the applause of their peers.

Many of the stars of this show—Ernst & Young's World Entrepreneur Of The Year program—are among the entrepreneurs in this book. People like Jeff Bezos of Amazon.com and Herb Kohler of Kohler Co. and Bernie Marcus and Arthur Blank of The Home Depot. Many more are less well known but as accomplished and worthy of recognition.

That is why E&Y began to celebrate the most extraordinary entrepreneurs twenty-five years ago at an event in Milwaukee. It was the firm's partners there who first realized that the companies having the most impact on their community were those founded by entrepreneurs. "They weren't getting the ink to celebrate their contributions," says Jim Turley, global chairman and CEO of E&Y. "We wanted to recognize and reward them. Our people love doing it. The celebration of these extraordinary people has value to our brand, and it helps us in what is arguably the most important space in the future."

Year by year, the celebration has expanded, reaching into all the corners of the world to be truly global. Argentina, Mexico, and Jordan are among the latest of some fifty-five countries where Ernst & Young annually searches for the best entrepreneurs.

It certainly made sense to treat entrepreneurs as economic heroes. It's now well established that virtually all new jobs created in the United States from the late 1970s through the Great Recession to the present—some 40 million net jobs—were due to new and young firms, those less than five years old. E&Y has played a crucial role in the success of many of these companies.

The firm had made early bets on Silicon Valley, the world's epicenter of entrepreneurship and innovation. "You can go back to the early waves of innovation," explains Turley. "Many start-ups were our clients. We invested our time and best talent in them many years ago. And with each successive wave of change in Silicon Valley, we've stayed with the many companies founded by highly passionate, incredibly creative people."

Entrepreneurship, of course, has become a global phenomenon, says Turley. "As societies realized more free market capitalism, the animal spirits of entrepreneurship were unleashed. Speaking to the entrepreneurs in these markets shows that there is much more similarity than difference in how they think. They all start not thinking about themselves. They start thinking externally. All the successful entrepreneurs see needs that exist out there. They don't think about creating wealth. They have a vision to evolve a product or service or idea to meet the needs they see. They've got this incredible courage to take risks, to chase these dreams, and the persistence to realize them."

Dan Lufkin, who in the 1960s cofounded the pioneering Wall Street firm Donaldson, Lufkin & Jenrette, has as good and as succinct a definition of entrepreneurship as any. "*Entrepreneur*," he says, "is a grand word for someone who works hard. I think an entrepreneur has two ingredients. The first is self-confidence, and the second is high energy level."

Notice that having a great idea is not a necessary ingredient. It's assumed that if you're extremely confident, work hard, and have the energy to bring passion and intensity to something, you're likely to succeed.

Motivations come in all different sizes and forms. Bernie Marcus and Arthur Blank founded Home Depot out of sheer desperation. They were both fired from their jobs and had nowhere else to go. It was a $40 late fee on a video rental that so thoroughly embarrassed Reed Hastings that led to his founding of Netflix. John Mackey had a simple idea when he and his then girlfriend opened a small grocery store in a Victorian home in Austin, Texas. The cofounder of Whole Foods Market wanted to make natural and healthy foods more available. Howard Schultz wanted to create a comfortable and welcoming place where people could go for a cup of great coffee away from home and work.

Yet, while entrepreneurs may all start from different places, they also share a set of common behaviors and attributes. Ernst & Young's own research has identified what it calls the essence of an entrepreneur. It is, if you will, the shared DNA of people who are using their life's work as an expression of self.

There are three core attributes every entrepreneur shares:

An Opportunistic Mind-set

Where others see disruption and chaos, entrepreneurs see opportunity. It is a simple, even romantic, notion of entrepreneurship, perhaps. Still, many great businesses have been created by people who were able to clearly spot opportunity in the chaos of a crowded marketplace. Organizing the vast amount of information in the world was seen as a great intellectual challenge but also an amazing opportunity by Larry Page and Sergey Brin, even though they had no idea how search could be monetized at the time.

It was the amazing growth rates of the Internet that caused Jeff Bezos to quit a job in New York, move across the country to Seattle, and start Amazon.com in a garage. He immediately grasped the opportunity to use the technology of the Internet to offer customers a vast selection of products at the lowest possible prices.

Acceptance of Risk and Potential Failure

Entrepreneurs are willing to embrace far greater risk than most corporate types, but that doesn't mean they are reckless or naïve about the possibility of failure. More commonly, in fact, most entrepreneurs take very calculated risks. They use great care to ensure that they evaluate opportunities carefully and assess the risks that their venture will face.

Consider Reed Hastings, the cofounder of Netflix. Even when he saw the Internet as a disruptive technology that could be leveraged to challenge incumbent player Blockbuster in the video rental business, he knew that the model he was about to create would soon be supplanted by yet another disruptive technology—the widespread availability of broadband reception. So from day one, Hastings was thinking and investing in the technology to stream videos over the Web, even as he was starting his DVD-by-mail business model. It's why he called his company Netflix—and not DVD-by-Mail. He had carefully assessed the risks his venture would face long before they were apparent to anyone else.

And while entrepreneurs are far more willing to assume the necessary risks that come with creating something new, they are just as willing to allow for the possibility that they could be wrong. Dead wrong, at times. So they are willing to discount, to some extent, the decisions they make, to not so heavily invest in them that they're not open to course correction or complete reversal.

Southwest Airlines founder Herb Kelleher, for example, notes that you can never obtain perfect knowledge to make a decision. "That means when I make a judgment, I'm taking a risk by definition," he says. "But you have to be prepared to take those risks. You have to be prepared to make those judgments. And you have to be prepared to move ahead. And you have to be prepared to correct quickly any mistakes that you might make— quickly—not have mistakes that you're so egotistical about that you say, 'Oh my Lord, I can't do anything about this because it'll admit I was wrong.'"

Being wrong, of course, sometimes results in failure, even catastrophic failure that can lead to the collapse of a new enterprise. But one of the profound differences between entrepreneurship in the United States and in much of the rest of the world is our tolerance of failure. Among venture capitalists, in fact, failure is viewed as something of a badge of honor. They consider the learning that comes from early business failures vital experience for future success. So do the entrepreneurs as well.

As Amazon's Jeff Bezos puts it: "What's dangerous is not to evolve, not improve, not invent, not improve the customer experience. If you're going to invent in green fields, you have to have a willingness to repeatedly fail. Failure is an essential component of innovation and invention. If you know it's going to work, then it's not an experiment. Amazon.com was nothing if not a grand experiment."

Independence and Control

Almost everyone wants to have a sense of independence and control over his or her life. But with entrepreneurs, having independence and control is as much a need as it is a want. People who create businesses have the drive and fortitude to act on this need in ways that others do not. What's more, they do it consistently and with a sense of urgency over a sustained period of time.

Make no mistake about it: The need for control is fundamental to an entrepreneur, whether it is conscious or not, and control in an entrepreneurial sense requires what some believe is an internal focus. Manfred Kets de Vries, a professor of entrepreneurship at INSEAD, maintains that individuals with an external focus of control typically believe that events happen as a result of circumstances that are beyond their control. By contrast, people who possess what he calls an internal "locus of control" believe that the events in their life result directly from their own actions or behavior. Entrepreneurs, says de Vries, habitually have a strong internal locus of control.

This notion is also supported by the E&Y research. The firm has found that an internal locus of control tends to appear more frequently in market-based economies that celebrate business success, such as the United States. Those with a single-minded focus on individual achievement, such as Japan, China, or Korea, are also likely to give risk to businesses run by entrepreneurial leaders with a strong internal focus of control.

To these three core strands, entrepreneurs bring drive, tenacity, and persistence. They live what they believe, building success on the basis of a strong culture and values. They seek out niches and market gaps. They are the architects of their own passionate and focused vision. While being non-conformist, they also are team players. And they are voracious networkers, building an ecosystem of finance, people, and know-how.

An often common though little noticed trait among many of the most successful entrepreneurs is personal tragedy. Carlos Nuzman, the Olympian volleyball player who helped bring the Olympics to his home country of Brazil, lost his mother at the age of ten. Oprah Winfrey was sexually abused from the age of nine to thirteen. Ted Turner's father crawled into his bathtub and shot himself dead when Turner was twenty-four years of age. Steve Jobs was unwanted by his parents and given up for adoption at birth. Arthur Blank and Bernie Marcus were unceremoniously fired.

It is as if their singular pursuit of achievement was a refuge from the pain of some tragic loss. "They have often faced adversity and have shown an ability to survive and thrive," says Maria Pinelli, global vice chair of strategic growth markets at Ernst & Young. "There's this desire to overcome every obstacle. It comes from their belief in themselves, but so many of these entrepreneurs have in common this fundamental adversity. If there is turmoil in their lives, there seems to be a vision to move far beyond it."

And finally for every entrepreneur there are a series of Gail Sheehy-like passages, challenging phases through which every successful organization must pass. In the early days, it's typically access to capital, mentors, and networks. In the growth phase, the number one challenge is balancing the entrepreneurial spirit against the need to build process and controls into the organization. "That is a difficult hurdle," says Pinelli, who oversees E&Y's Entrepreneur of the Year competition. "This is where most entrepreneurs have the potential to lose outstanding talent. The finance and legal teams can become the sales prevention people. The sales and technical teams argue over what the customers really want. If you don't have a very good leader at the top of the house, it can spiral out of control."

All of those traits and challenges are highly evident in the following conversations with some of the world's greatest entrepreneurs. These exceptional institution builders offer a treasure chest of insights: how to seize new opportunities, build important and lasting companies, lead people, think more creatively, and overcome obstacles. All of them know how to win. All of them are winners.

JOHN MACKEY

WHOLE FOODS MARKET

When John Mackey and his then girlfriend Renee Law-son opened their first vegetarian food store in 1978, their ambition was to make a simple living, have fun, and help people live healthy lives by eating better. A bearded, shaggy-haired college dropout, Mackey had just turned twenty-five years of age and thought profit was a "necessary evil."

Yet in an old Victorian home in Austin, Texas, he and his girlfriend began selling bulk foods and produce and slept on a futon in the third-floor office above the store. They called their little grocery Safer Way, a cheeky play off the behemoth chain Safeway. Even though they didn't take any salary, the pair managed to lose half their capital in the first year—$23,000 out of $45,000. In year two, they turned a $5,000 profit but realized the store was too small to compete over the long haul. "I wanted to do a bigger store and I pitched the original investors who had already lost half their money," recalls Mackey. "Of course, they didn't think it was a very good idea."

They told Mackey to stay in his current location and prove that his concept could be successful. "I think if we stay here we'll probably fail over the long term," Mackey retorted. "I learned enough by then to know we needed to be in a bigger location. They said, 'If you can find somebody else to put in more money—another $25,000 to $50,000—we'll look at it.' Their basic strategy was to hope that I wouldn't be able to find someone dumb enough to invest any more money in this thing."

His investors underestimated Mackey's persuasive abilities. The entrepreneur convinced a person with whom he played pickup basketball to toss in the extra money. With the cash in hand, Mackey merged his business with a competing natural foods store, Clarksville Natural Grocery, and in 1980 they opened the first Whole Foods Market in a former Austin nightclub. It was a ten-thousand-square-foot store at a time when there were fewer than half a dozen natural foods supermarkets in the United States.

It was an immediate success. "We were profitable by three in the afternoon on the first day," says Mackey, "which was a good thing because we were broke by the time we got that store opened. We ran out of money and couldn't make payroll. We had to open the store in order to sell some food to pay our employees. We didn't have a meat department. We didn't have any beer and wine. We just sort of filled the store with what we had and it was a hit."

Within a couple of years, Mackey says the supermarket was racking up the highest volume of any natural food store in the United States. But as any entrepreneur knows, there were endless setbacks and hurdles to overcome. After Whole Foods had been in business eight months, Austin suffered its worst flood in one hundred years. Eight feet of water flooded the store, nearly wiping Mackey and his partners out of business. But the flood had a positive impact as well. Customers came back to the store to help clean it up and get it reopened, and it convinced Mackey that he couldn't have all his eggs in one basket. He would have to expand.

Today, Whole Foods Market has more than three hundred supermarkets in North America and the United Kingdom. It employs 61,000 team members, and its revenues will top $10 billion in 2011. More important, however, cofounder and co–chief executive Mackey has helped to change the daily diets of millions of consumers and has transformed the way Americans produce, buy, and consume food.

Whole Foods's remarkable success also has had a transformative impact on the industry's mainstream competitors. It's now impossible to walk the aisles of any supermarket and not find natural foods on the shelves. Even Mackey is astonished at the changes that have worked their way through the entire food system. "If you told me twenty years ago that Walmart would be one of the leading sellers of organic foods in the world, I would have thought that was ridiculous," he says. "But I've seen big changes occur."

Not only has his company evolved to a spectacular success; so has Mackey. As one writer so elegantly put it, "The evolution of the corporation has often traced his own as a man; it has been an incarnation of his dreams and quirks, his contradictions and trespasses, and whatever he happened to be reading and eating, or not eating."

Once a person with, in his own words, "socialistic leanings," Mackey is now an unabashed evangelist for capitalism, an avid admirer of Ayn Rand, Milton Friedman, and Ronald Reagan. One of his life's passions has become what he calls "conscious capitalism"—the attempt to make more people conscious of the fact that business creates great value for everyone— employees, customers, suppliers, and communities. Central to this belief is the requirement that every business pursue a higher purpose than the goal to maximize profits or share price.

It is a good place to start.

Purpose is a big and important word for you. How has the purpose of Whole Foods Market evolved over time?

It has evolved a lot over time and it is an important thing because the two most common questions I get from journalists are "Gosh, did you ever think you would get this big when you started it?" And the answer to that is, of course not. And the second most frequently asked question is, "Did you have this purpose when you started?" And of course the answer is no. A business evolves over time and purpose evolves over time.

The original purpose when we created the company was a simple one: we wanted to sell healthy food that we thought was going to be good for people and better for the environment and we could earn a living doing it. As the company has grown and evolved, that purpose has gone through several phases. I just did a keynote talk at our tribal gathering—which we do every three years—on the higher purpose of Whole Foods. The original purpose I just articulated lasted until about 1985.

We had a crisis at that point. We had gotten up to six stores and a couple of the new stores were losing money. In fact, the company lost money for the first time. That really upset one of the cofounders and he ended up leaving the company. Before he left, the company split into camps. To sort of heal that division, we went through what we called a vision clarification process. We brought an outside consultant in and we went through our purpose and mission. The company was pretty small back then. We ended up going through that process and came up with our mission statement called the declaration of independence. That was the first time we articulated our ideas to stakeholders: customers, team members, suppliers, investors, communities, and the environment.

In our declaration, we made a very strong statement that we were trying to create value for all of them.

The next evolution occurred because we realized that the declaration was long and we wanted to distill that down and so we came out with our five core values that we used as a shortcut for the purpose of the business: selling the highest quality natural and organic foods, satisfying and delighting our customers, striving for team member happiness and excellence, creating wealth through profits and growth, and being good citizens in our communities and environment. Those are our five core values. With that in place, the company raised venture capital money. We went public. We began to do some acquisitions. We rapidly increased our growth. That carried us for ten to fifteen years and then the purpose began to evolve again as we added two new core values in the past few years. Our suppliers felt like we didn't single them out, so we committed ourselves to a core value to create win-win partnerships with our suppliers, and then we came out with our healthy eating education program. So we also said we are dedicated to healthy eating education for all of our stakeholders.

In my keynote speech I identified four higher purposes. The highest purpose is a heroic one. I came up with that in the highest ideals humans can strive for: the good, the truth, the beautiful. I added "heroic" a few years ago. Our team members are pretty clear that the heroic purpose most resonates with our team member base: to have the courage to change and improve the world. What we're doing there is to help evolve our agricultural system to one that is more sustainable yet has a high degree of creativity to it. We are trying to help people have a healthy lifestyle and we are really ratcheting that up because of the deep problems we see in America with the lifestyles Americans have with heart disease, cancer, diabetes. We are doing many things but we are going to do a lot more to help people change their diets to avoid these diseases and try to help them achieve their optimum health.

The third purpose is through our Whole Planet Foundation. We are now in twenty-nine countries. We will be in fifty-six countries in a couple of years. We have helped literally hundreds of thousands of people lift themselves out of poverty working with Muhammad Yunus and the Grameen Bank.

And the fourth higher purpose is helping people reconceptualize what business and capitalism is. We think both are misunderstood by the critics and the defenders. We are attempting to rebrand, remarket, and reconceptualize business and capitalism. Those are the four higher purposes we have identified. They are all big hairy audacious goals. Heroic is not a bad category for us to identify with.

Why is purpose important to a business?

It's very important. One way to think about business is that it is not any different than any other human community in the sense that humans seek to be fulfilled within their communities. The ideals that motivate humans in their daily lives are the same ideals that can motivate people when they go to work for a corporation. To be fully human, to represent the aspirations of people, it's important for businesses to have purpose. It's not very inspiring for most people to be told that the purpose of business is to maximize profits and shareholder value. Maybe that's highly motivating for people who work on Wall Street. For most people that just doesn't cut it. Most people want more transcendent values. They want to believe and understand how their work is contributing to helping other people and making the world a better place.

Purpose inspires people. Purpose releases creativity. When people are really enthusiastic about the purpose of the business, they're going to bring a greater depth of commitment and a greater level of creativity to their work. That is good for the business and obviously good for all the stakeholders who trade with our business. It is the first principle of conscious capitalism.

Many businesses struggle with attempts to define their purpose, particularly in terms that are naturally motivating. How did you reach consensus on what the purpose of Whole Foods is all about?

When we came up with our original core values and our original declaration of independence, we went into retreat mode. We were a much smaller company then but we had sixty team members—roughly 10 percent of the company in 1985—volunteering to help us come up with our mission statement and create our core values. The purpose evolves not just by the team members' interacting with it but by all the stakeholders, the customers, the suppliers, the investors. They all interact with the business. They all have aspirations for the business as well. They all have desires and needs. So the business is interacting with that. Whole Foods has a very participatory and inclusive type of culture.

I sometimes think that my job is to help interpret that. Let me give you an example. When I came up with those four higher purposes and put it under the category of heroic, I didn't think Whole Foods was heroic. I had us in the category of good. We were a retailer, fundamentally a service business trying to take care of its customers. And to do that, you have to be a good place to work. We were primarily focused on hiring the best team members we could find and making sure they were well trained and well motivated to really care for the customers. I really saw us in the service business or, in that sense, the pursuit of the good. And yet as I would go around and talk to team members and customers, they had bigger aspirations for Whole Foods than I did. They would consistently tell me that I had it wrong. That Whole Foods actually had higher purposes than I was giving it credit for and I needed to get with it. So I do think that the stakeholders of a living organization coevolve it and they do that through their passion, their interactions with the business. Obviously, the leadership has to evolve along with it.

These decisions get made through the dialogue. A business is always talking to its stakeholders. Someone may put out an idea. I might grab on to it and then articulate it to the larger group. And you see how people react to it. Does it resonate with them? Is it something they agree with? Or do they disagree with it? When I was articulating my belief that my deepest purpose was about service and the pursuit of the good, the team members pushed back. They said, "No, we think it's more than that. We think it's about changing and improving the world. You're selling us short."

How does purpose become actionable? It sounds good, feels good, but how does it become real?

I articulate it. I put it out there. And then everybody else makes it real. Whole Foods is different from many other companies. It's not this top-down organization where the CEO develops the mission statement and then issues a bunch of directives. A month ago, at our tribal gathering, when I did my higher purpose talk, there were eight hundred leaders in the company that heard it. That has now rippled out and inspired a lot of people. They are going out and making it happen in their own unique and creative ways. Innovation flourishes at Whole Foods because we aren't this top-down, command-and-control organization. In terms of making it happen, I am giving permission for it to happen. I am encouraging it to happen. But it has to resonate with people so that they sign up for it and believe in it because they have to make it happen.

If it doesn't resonate I can give all the speeches I want, but nothing is going to happen. In Whole Foods' case, people get jazzed up and then they go out and do things. We've got sixty thousand people working for us and I'm not saying that every team member who works for us is passionately on fire about everything we're doing. But a pretty large percentage are, and they are out there living the core values every single day, talking it up with our customers and our vendors. That's how things happen at Whole Foods. You turn on the team member base and they interact with the other stakeholders and stuff happens.

Going back to the early days, was the original concept of Whole Foods Market disruptive?

I don't think about it in those terms. That is almost like a consultant's way to speak. If you want to think in those terms, I do think Whole Foods has a disruptive business model. But we don't think about it in those ways. We are not a bunch of business school graduates who are trying to come up with a disruptive business model. We are a purpose-driven business, which is attempting to fulfill its mission. It just so happens that a lot of what we're doing is disruptive, but that is accidental rather than deliberate. We are not attempting to come up with a disruptive business model. We are just attempting to fulfill our mission and that is disruptive because it's so different from how other food retailers are doing.

Over the years, you've faced growing competition from even mainstream retailers. There have been long-expressed worries that when Walmart started stocking natural foods, it would impact Whole Foods. It hasn't really happened. Why?

I think there are a lot of reasons. Again, even though it's not intentional, the fact is we do have a disruptive business model. We do things very differently from conventional supermarkets, from our purpose to our stakeholder principles to the way we organize, our decentralization, our empowerment, our entire business strategy is very different than any other food retailer. These more traditional food retailers are attempting to be one-stop shopping. They are attempting to be all things to all people. When they look at what Whole Foods is doing, they say, "Hmm . . . these guys are stealing our market share. We need to sell some organic foods." They come in, look at the products we're selling and try as much as possible to knock those products off. And that's their strategy. But they are not focused on it. They don't have the same kind of depth of product mix dedicated to what we're doing so they just skim off a selected number of the products they think are the bestsellers.

Meanwhile, our company is not sitting still. We are coming up with new products and new services all the time, including private label brands that they aren't able to knock off and copy, even if they wanted to. At the same time, as people begin to make changes in their dietary patterns and lifestyles, they tend to want to come to Whole Foods Market because in a sense we're dedicated to it. We're authentic. Even though you can find some of our products at Walmart or Safeway, you can't get the same selection. So that is one way that makes it difficult to compete. We have a depth in our products, a different atmosphere and service environment to what we think our customers want. Walmart and the supermarkets are mass merchants. They're attempting to please everyone. We're not.

We're attempting to fulfill our mission with a customer base that resonates with that mission. Admittedly, it's a small percentage of the total population, but a big enough percentage that we will do $10 billion in sales this year and keep growing at a very rapid rate. But still that only ends up being 1 percent of the total market share of food retailing in the United States.

Our stores look different. They feel different. They have a much bigger selection of prepared foods. They've got a different kind of atmosphere. Our service levels by our team members are extraordinarily high. We have high levels of customer service. We don't appeal to everyone. But we do appeal to a sizable sector of the population. And year by year, it is getting larger and larger. People thought that when Walmart said it was going to sell organic Whole Foods would be in trouble. They weren't understanding that most of our customers don't want to shop at Walmart. They don't resonate with Walmart's values or with Walmart as a company. So Walmart isn't a threat to Whole Foods. In fact, you could argue the opposite might be true. As Walmart and these other supermarkets legitimize a lot of these natural products, they are helping to speed people to make lifestyle shifts. When those lifestyle shifts occur, they are more likely to want to shop at Whole Foods Market. Here is the key fact: we are not losing market share to those guys. We are gaining market share, and that has been the case for thirty years. We're taking it away from them.

I'm a little bit of a Civil War buff, and the officers who reported to General Grant would say, "What are we going to do about what Lee is doing? We have to adjust to account for that." And Grant said, "You don't understand. Lee has to adjust to what we're doing. We're the aggressor." And Whole Foods is the aggressor in this category. We're the innovator.

We're now really putting a commitment into our healthy eating programs. First with our team members with healthy incentive discount cards. We are going to create wellness clubs. This is a whole other way that our company is going to create disruptive technologies with our emphasis on healthy eating. We are very early in this process. But I think it is a totally disruptive idea. I think it will change health care in America. I really do. Because most of what is killing us is lifestyle diseases: heart disease, diabetes, obesity, life cell diseases, and cancer. Whole Foods is going to lead the way on that.

Where did that idea come from? Did it bubble up from your team members?

That has always been in the DNA of the company from the very beginning. What's different now is the science. We knew intuitively when we got started that you ought to eat a whole foods diet—mostly plants, fruits, and vegetables. But now the science is really coming through to show the relationships between what people eat and the diseases they get. If you make lifestyle alterations, you can in many cases prevent or reverse these diseases. So the science is lining up with what we intuitively knew a long time ago.

Let me give you an example of how it is transforming Whole Foods. A year and a half ago, we began to do what we now call Total Health Immersions. What that means is we take our most sick team members, those who are obese, those who have diabetes, heart disease, or those who are at high risk because they have high blood pressure or high cholesterol and are on a lot of medications. They have to apply for this, but then we allow them to go to one of these Total Health Immersions. We do three in the spring and three in the fall. We've taken 1,200 team members through it in a year and a half. It has been unbelievable.

They go off on these retreats for about a week and have intensive education about healthy eating and they eat a really healthy diet for about a week. We teach them how to cook and raise their consciousness about food and lifestyle. And it's simply been phenomenal. We have literally had dozens and dozens of team members lose over one hundred pounds in less than a year. We've had many people reverse type-two diabetes, which is supposed to be a noncurable disease.

Yet we found if you make radical shifts in your diet and lifestyle, you can get off your insulin and return to a normal life. The way we treat heart disease in America is through bypass surgery. We give people drugs to lower their blood pressure and their cholesterol. And yet we found that through making dietary and lifestyle shifts you can get people off their cholesterol medicine. It can plummet to very low levels very quickly. You can get off your high blood pressure medicines. We're seeing these amazing shifts in the health of our team members. We think this has huge implications for our society and for health care.

Our company spent $200 million on health care for our team members in 2010, and yet most of that is spent on a relatively small percentage of the team members. And a lot of it is these lifestyle diseases. We believe that we can radically reduce our costs in health care and this is something other corporations will be able to do as well. This is how purpose evolves. We do this and find out, "Oh my God, I had no idea people could heal this quickly." It was a total wake-up call for me.

One of our regional presidents who is obese went to an Immersion a month ago. He was skeptical. He really didn't want to go. He felt it would be a waste of time and money, but he had heard so many good things that he decided to go. I saw him because I stopped in at that Immersion and spent a couple of days there. The first thing you do when you go in is you do your blood and they check your weight and you get your blood pressure checked. And you do the same thing after a week. I saw him right after he had gotten his blood work done the second time. In that week, he had already lost ten pounds, his blood pressure dropped thirty points, and his cholesterol dropped forty points and he loved the food. "This is going to change my life," he said. He has already sent me two thank-you e-mails and he has already dropped thirty pounds in the first month. And he is the president of one of our twelve regions. This is what purpose is about and it is also how purpose evolves. He is going to enlist other leaders in his region. You can force this, but when people see the good effects people are having, more people are going to want to sign up.

The next step for us is what we call these Wellness Clubs. We need to take this to our customer base. Why should this be restricted just to our team members? So we are going to be creating these Wellness Clubs and we're basically going to have customers join this for a monthly fee and they will have unrestricted access to cooking classes, healthy eating classes, and they will also get 10 percent off on all the healthiest whole foods we sell. We're doing a prototype store. We're going to work out the business model. That is a disruptive business model. Time will tell. The first one opens in September (2011). Then five will open within eight weeks of each other: Boston, Oakland, New York, Chicago, and Princeton. Five different regions and once we work the bugs out, we're going to roll that out throughout the country.

We've recruited three of the doctors who were on our medical advisory board. So it's outsourced, but they are doing our programs. And now we hired two doctors who have become full-time team members to put our Wellness Clubs together. So we are beginning to hire doctors. We may outsource it or may end up bringing more doctors in-house. Beginning in 2012, we are going to take the Immersion concept to our customer base. We are going to make it public. It's very important to understand that, because we're taking high-risk people with diseases for which they receive intensive medical care. This is a medical program. There is all this education, but when people are on all these medications, you need a doctor who can help you with it. It's not something that Whole Foods could do by itself. You need experts to do this.

How do you keep innovations like this coming at a time when the company is getting bigger and bigger and more complicated, too?

There is a sort of premise in that question. Your premise is that as you get larger it must get harder to innovate. I think it's the opposite. With our culture, it's easier to innovate because we have more creative people working for us. Because we are a decentralized, empowered organization, we have more people generating good ideas. We are innovating more rapidly today than we were innovating five years ago or ten years ago. Our innovations are accelerating.

How do you measure your progress on innovation?

Why would we want to? I can see the innovations because I tour our stores. And I see more creative ideas springing up every place I go than we used to have five years ago. I don't need to measure because I'm certain that innovation is accelerating at Whole Foods. The Total Health Immersions and the Wellness Clubs are big innovations, but in fact most of the innovations are occurring at the store level and they are occurring every day because the team members are encouraged and allowed to be innovative and creative.

Again, this is one of our competitive advantages because in most other food retailing companies the innovations are done at corporate. At Whole Foods, we're allowing them to occur at the store level. We have a lot more people involved in innovation and unleashing their creative instincts. Most of the innovations are incremental type improvements. They occur in teams that run our produce, grocery, and meat departments. They are organized into self-managing work teams that have a team leader and the team underneath them is empowered. They are running a little business. They have the ability to spend capital within certain constraints. They are allowed to evolve and change their departments. So the innovations occur in a lot of bubble-up stuff.

Let me give you an example. We actually own a coffee company called Allegro. And the team in our New York store asked, "Why should we buy all these beans from Allegro and have them roast it and then transport it here? That means the beans aren't as fresh. What if we started roasting the beans in our store? We would be doing something that no one else is doing and we would have a fresher product." So we did that in one store and it was hugely successful. It was cool. It created theater. You could see the beans being roasted. And pretty soon that began to spread. Nobody made it spread. It did naturally all over the company. We found out that for this to pay, a store has to have a certain sales volume in coffee. Otherwise, it's not turning the inventory fast enough to justify the labor cost of those doing the roasting. That is a bubble-up innovation that occurred at one store and spread and then got altered by other stores. Where they did the roasting and when they did it created incremental innovations along the way, much like the Japanese philosophy of Kaizen, of continuous improvement. We now have hundreds of these coffee roasters in our stores.

John, you've become an advocate for what you call "conscious capitalism"—the effort to make the general public more aware of value created by business. Why is conscious capitalism important?

I have become a total radical for capitalism. I'm a student of history, and the human lot for most of history has been pretty miserable. Just two hundred years ago, 85 percent of the people alive on the planet earth lived on less than one dollar a day. That percentage has now dropped, due to capitalism, down to 20 percent. Still, that's over one billion people, but that's a lot better than having 85 percent of the people on the earth in that situation. If you look at the trend lines, we will end poverty at the end of the twenty-first century, if we don't destroy ourselves.

Capitalism is the engine for almost all the progress that is occurring in the world. It doesn't get credit for it, but it is, in fact, what is radically different about humanity today than what it was any time prior to the birth of capitalism.

Capitalism spreads prosperity and allows more and more humans to live the good life and that is a good thing in my opinion. But capitalism is misunderstood. It's attacked. It's criticized. Inequality is blamed on capitalism when in fact humanity has always had inequality and it has always been dirt poor. What capitalism has been doing is unleashing the minds of billions of people, allowing them to aspire to a better life and a higher living standard. Just look at India and China as they have embraced market reforms. Hundreds of millions of people in those two countries alone have escaped poverty because they have moved away from socialism toward capitalism. So I think the critics and the defenders misunderstand capitalism. They don't understand how much value capitalism creates, and what conscious capitalism does is it helps people understand that. It helps them understand that business is not just about maximizing profits and share-holder value.

I've known hundreds of entrepreneurs in my time and very few have told me they started their business to get as rich as possible. They want to make money. There's nothing wrong with making money. But they started the business to actualize a dream. This is true in most of the other profes-sions. If you ask a doctor why he devoted his life to medicine, he doesn't say "I wanted to make as much money as possible and I try to maximize rev-enues as a doctor." A doctor will tell you he wants to make a good living, but he wants to cure sick people. A teacher wants to educate people. Archi-tects design buildings. Even lawyers are taught in law school to promote justice. It's only in business that the critics have come out and said business is primarily about making money and therefore business becomes suscep-tible to all the attacks of selfishness and greed and exploitation.

Business is a value creator because capitalism is based on a voluntary exchange in the marketplace. No one is forced to trade at Whole Foods Market. Our customers have alternative places to shop. Our employees have alternative places to work. Our suppliers have alternatives to where they can sell. Investors have alternative places to invest their capital. Our communi-ties have alternatives as to which businesses they will allow in their com-munities. So you've got a voluntary exchange at the core of business and capitalism. And because that is there, the value that is being created by busi-ness is being created for all of these stakeholders trading with the business.

I've watched hundreds of our suppliers become prosperous over the years, partially as a result of trading with our company. When we started in 1980 we were worth nothing. Today our market cap is about $11 billion. Capital-ism is about creating value for people—not just for a few, but for the many. Conscious capitalism is trying to make people more conscious of the pur-pose of the business and the value that it creates for other people. It is a value-creating machine. It's awesome. That's what people don't understand.

When you deliver that message, do you run into quite a few skeptics who see excessive pay to many chief executives and complain about compa-nies that lay off their employees in search of the cheapest labor in the world?

Of course. Business is seen as greedy, selfish, exploitative, and evil. Peo-ple think business has to redeem itself through good works. Because people don't understand that business is creating value. Business is already on the defensive and somehow or another has to atone. That's how the critics see it. I see that business is fine if it is socially responsible and if it is focused on the community stakeholder. But even if it didn't, business is naturally socially responsible because it is creating value for customers, employees, suppliers, investors, taxes for the government, donations to nonprofits. That is all highly desirable. That's good.

When you founded Whole Foods were you as conscious of the benefits of capitalism as you are today?

It is all part of my own evolution. I am probably less conscious today than I will be in five years. I'm a human being, like anybody else. I'm learning. I'm growing. I'm evolving just as our company is. I know a lot more today than I knew thirty years ago. In fact, when I started the company, I would have categorized myself as a progressive. I would have considered myself as someone with socialistic leanings. I came from the point of view that business was not such a good thing and that government was good. But having to meet a payroll and then seeing that we were creating value for customers and employees, I realized that business has been misunderstood. So I have become an evangelist to see the good and the beauty that is inherent in business and capitalism.

Sometimes when I'm making these arguments people will say, "Well, yeah, that's true for Whole Foods but it's not true for most other businesses." I really disagree with that. I think it's true for most businesses. You can always find some exceptions for businesses that are not creating as much value but they are the exceptions to the rule. Sometimes some businesses or individuals can act unethically but that doesn't make all businesses bad. Business is often judged by the Enrons or Bernie Madoffs. The whole of business has been tarnished by the actions of a few bad people. And that is unfair. Most businesses are creating great value for the people who trade with them. Business should not be judged and condemned for the actions of a few.

You want to have a higher purpose and think in terms of all your stakeholders. Oftentimes when people criticize the stakeholder model, they say "Well, that all sounds good, but there are all these inevitable trade-offs." They still have a zero-sum mentality where if you are doing good for one stakeholder you are cheating another stakeholder. They see these stakeholders in conflict with each other. If we pay our employees better, that must mean we are going to have less profit for investors, not understanding the synergies and harmonies that exist in business. It's not that there are never any trade-offs, but when you are managing the business in a conscious way to create value for all your stakeholders you usually find innovative solutions that allow you to avoid the trade-offs. That is not always easy and it can be a challenge but that is what business should strive for.

You've said in the past that you feel as if you've been in the jungle, hacking out a path for organic foods, conscious capitalism, and animal welfare. What do you mean by that and how far do you think you've been able to cut through the jungle?

I've watched organic foods go from nowhere to getting a 3 percent share. And I've watched Whole Foods now go from nothing to a $10 billion business. And yet the critics will say, "Well, you should have done more. Couldn't you have gone further?" You know what? It's easy to be a critic. It's a lot harder to create anything. I have been out in the wilderness hacking away trying to create a path on these different things I care about and am passionate about. Why don't you get out of your car and take a machete and hack along with me? Why don't you create something?

My advice to them: Don't just be a critic. Go out and use your own creative energies to make a difference in the world. We need more innovation and creativity. Humanity has serious problems. So when I talk to young people, I usually put that challenge out there because oftentimes I get these questions that somehow put responsibility on me. I say when I was born the world was totally screwed up. I found it screwed up just like you. And I have given my life energy to try and be creative and come up with some solutions. I think we've done a pretty good job. Now this is a challenge I put to you: You're young. You're idealistic. Don't just tell me what is wrong with the world. Get out there and make a difference. Start a company. Start a not-for-profit. Use your creative energies to try to make the world a better place.

ARTHUR BLANK and BERNIE MARCUS

THE HOME DEPOT

"You're fired!"

Those are not exactly two words anyone wants to hear, but they are the words that kicked a pair of executives in the rear to pursue an entrepreneurial dream that literally changed the world of retailing.

It was on April 14, 1978, when the self-proclaimed "Ming the Merciless" had summoned to his office Bernie Marcus, then chief executive of Handy Dan Home Improvement Centers, and Arthur Blank, then Handy Dan's vice president of finance. "Ming" was actually "Sandy" Sigoloff, who had taken his nickname from the villain in the old Flash Gordon movie serials of the 1930s.

Sigoloff was the boss from hell: a mean-spirited, money-grubbing man who ruled by fear and fancied himself a turnaround ace. Sigoloff once told Marcus that when employees left him, "it was very important that he affect them economically, emotionally, and physically, so that people think twice before they ever turn on him." It was the great misfortune—or lucky break—of their lives to find themselves in his employ.

They were called into Sigoloff's offices in West Los Angeles for what was supposed to be a corporate planning meeting at Daylin, Inc., which owned 80 percent of the company they worked for. Instead, it was an execution. Sigoloff first fired Marcus, then Blank, and yet another executive on their team, falsely accusing them of trumped-up violations of National Labor Relations Board rules involving a decertification battle with a labor union.

It probably was the best thing that ever happened to them. Soon enough, the pair began meeting regularly at a coffee shop in the City of Commerce, putting a business plan together for what would become The Home Depot. They took everything they had learned but couldn't implement under Sigoloff to create one of the most successful retail concepts in history.

Unlike existing home improvement stores, they envisioned immense warehouse stores of up to seventy-five thousand square feet (the largest Handy Dan store was less than half that size), with merchandise stacked to the ceilings. They'd buy direct from manufacturers, eliminating the middlemen, and only put highly trained people on the selling floor who could help customers through any home repair or improvement. The goal: to build the first nationwide chain of home improvement stores based on low prices, massive selection, and high customer service.

Ken Langone, who had made a good sum investing in Handy Dan, put together an investment group that coughed up $2 million in seed capital in exchange for 55 percent of the company. After many turndowns, Marcus and Blank persuaded a bank to extend a $5 million line of credit. And on June 22, 1979, the first two Home Depot stores opened in Atlanta with their children and wives handing out five hundred one-dollar bills to lure customers inside. The stores were cavernous, sixty-thousand-square-foot warehouses that dwarfed the competition and stocked twenty-five thousand different SKUs. Hundreds of empty boxes and thousands of empty paint cans were piled on the top racks of the store to give the impression that the place was stocked to the gills with merchandise.

It took months for customers to discover The Home Depot, but when they did they loved the place. Within six months, Marcus and Blank had three stores, two hundred associates, $7 million in sales, and losses of nearly $1 million. By 1980, however, the company was in the black by $856,000, and it went public in 1981 with almost double the profit, using the proceeds from the sale to begin its march across the country to become the nation-wide retailer Marcus and Blank had envisioned.

The founders viewed the structure of the company as an inverted pyramid, with stores and customers at the top and senior management on the bottom. Blank demanded that associates take risks to succeed, saying, "It is your business, your division, your market, your store, your aisle, and your customer."

From the start, associates were able to offer the best customer service in the industry, guiding customers through projects such as laying tile, changing a fill valve, or handling a power tool. Not only did store associates undergo rigorous product knowledge training, but they also began offering clinics so customers could learn how to do it themselves. The Home Depot revolutionized the home improvement industry by bringing the know-how and the tools to the consumer while saving them money.

Over the next two decades, the pair turned the original no-frills stores in Atlanta into a phenomenon: nearly 1,200 outlets in North and South America, $46 billion in annual sales, a great brand, and the instantly recognizable "orange apron," which came to symbolize great customer service. By the time they would both leave their operating roles in the late 1990s, more than one thousand of the company's associates had become millionaires.

Years later, Marcus and Blank are still close friends. They met me at their golf club in Atlanta for a long breakfast just before going off to play a game together with Ken Langone, Home Depot's original investor.

I guess the best thing that ever happened to you was you were fired.

Bernie: We didn't believe that at the time, but in retrospect it was really fate for both of us. Many people who have success in their lives, it doesn't happen because it's planned. They are basically thrown into that chasm. In our case, being fired was probably the worst time I ever had outside the death of my parents. I had always been very successful at what I did. I had made money for a lot of people I worked for.

Sigoloff really was a monster. He called himself "Ming the Merciless" and he was proud of it. He loved the fact that he could destroy people. He loved firing people. He was one of these people who was called in to reorganize companies and he took great joy in being able to look people in the face and say, "I'm taking away your livelihood and not only that, I'm going to destroy you financially, mentally, physically, and emotionally." And he did. I remember having breakfast with him one morning in Beverly Hills and I asked him, "How do you do that?" He said, "Because I really like it." I remember going home that night and telling my wife Billi, "I just met a monster."

He hated me because I always questioned him. At the time, our company was the only one he owned that made money. The company was very successful. He was jealous of it. He didn't like the fact that we were independent. He didn't like the fact that his board of directors was very engrossed with our management team. For Sandy Sigoloff, that was a no-no. In fact, I remember being in a board meeting when succession came up. He told the board he was going to start working on it. And one of the directors in the room said, "Why do you have to do that? Don't knock yourself out. You've got the successor sitting in the room."

And that was the end of my life. A year later, I was fired. Arthur was out of this but he was my guy. He was at the hip with me and being at the hip was at that time not a good place to be. It was like carrying a tumor on your side. So Arthur got sacked along with me.

Were you thinking about doing something on your own while you were still working for Sigoloff?

About three years before, I happened to be with Ken Langone (a New York investor who was a major shareholder in Handy Dan). And I was telling him about a concept I had in mind that was going to put our store out of business. What we have to do now, I said, is build a new fence. It was really the concept of The Home Depot. It was going to be bigger than our store, carry a lot of merchandise. I wasn't going to tell him or anyone else the details about the idea because anybody who heard about it might have tried it. Three years later, when we were fired, both Arthur and I didn't have a clue about what we would do. Kenny (Langone) brought it up again. He said, "You've been hit in the ass by a golden horseshoe." And so we began to talk about the idea. We put the concept on paper. Arthur put the budget together. From Sigoloff, what I personally learned was how never to deal with people in my whole life. Right, Arthur?

Arthur: I can just sit back and enjoy. I've heard these stories hundreds of times. I'm his greatest audience—thirty years' worth of laughing at the same jokes, but I like it.

Bernie: No, I actually have new ones.

Arthur: Sprinkle them in but the old ones are good, too.

Bernie: Arthur and I used to have lunch every day and we used to talk about this maniac and how he dealt with people. No matter what we did, we learned a lesson: how *not* to deal with people, how not to treat people, how not to be offensive to people, how not to get the most out of people. We wanted people to respect us, not fear us. This whole culture concept really started with our mentor, Sandy Sigoloff.

He really hated us because we ran Handy Dan the same way. We respected our employees. We dealt well with our vendors and our banks. He hated everybody.

And the plan for the business was really hatched in a coffee shop in L.A.?

Bernie: Yeah. We went to this coffee shop, depressed most times.

Arthur: Most of our meetings were face to face. But after doing our original five-year plan, I remember calling Bernie on the phone and saying, "Listen, the numbers don't work. They don't add up. The expenses are too high and the volume is too low."

And he said, "Well, just change the volume."

"What do you mean?" I said.

"Well, nobody knows how much volume these stores are going to do anyway. We have no history. So just change the volume."

"I'm going to have trouble doing this, Bernie," I said. But it was true there was no history, no way of knowing for sure what our sales per square foot would be. It was conjecture based on the success of the forty-thousand-square-foot stores we had at Handy Dan. So I changed the volumes.

By how much?

Bernie: Not enough.

Arthur: But they were changed enough to get the positive attention of all of our initial investors. We were always forthright with our investors. We always worked on under-promising and over-delivering. That was our core philosophy from the very beginning. We told them this was a model. We think we could do it and ran through all the rationale.

How old were the two of you when you started the business?

Arthur: I was thirty-four.

Bernie: I was forty-eight.

Arthur: We are fourteen years apart.

Bernie: He's the baby.

What gave you the confidence at that age to go out and start a business from scratch, especially one that was so ambitious?

Bernie: The word *confidence* is wrong. It was desperation. We were out of work. Neither of us had a lot of money. My parents were broke altogether. I was basically supporting my mother. We didn't have any money to speak of and the question was what are we going to do with our lives? It was desperation time. I think that is a driving force. When you are desperate, you know you have to make it. We knew if we didn't make it, that was it. For me, at the age of forty-eight, it was all over. Arthur had his CPA and his career ahead of him. I had been a pharmacist, and at that point they had already taken my license away. I couldn't even go back to pharmacy.

It was desperation time and nobody had done this concept before: a big store, low prices, one-stop shopping, with qualified people on the floor. But we had to buy direct from manufacturers to get the prices that low. There were a lot of ingredients in this. Whether we could pull it off, we didn't know for sure. Arthur was right in questioning me because the margin in the plan was the smallest in our industry. Many people, in fact, said, "You can't do it."

They thought we were going to fall on our face. We were going to operate at a margin that nobody could afford and make it up on volume.

Arthur: We were fortunate because in the first two years we were private. We lost half our start-up money in the first nine months we were in business. Over that two-year period, all the competitors would come and visit, hearing about the big stores. But nobody knew what the volumes were. So everybody who came in said, "These poor bastards are going to go broke. They have too much inventory, too many people, the prices are too low, the service is too good." They thought we would be out of business. There was no fear in our industry, "Oh, here comes The Home Depot."

When we went public in the fall of 1981 and our numbers obviously were available to everybody, people really began to pay attention and got quite nervous. Even then, we controlled our expansion plans very carefully and everyone thought it would take us two hundred years before we expanded to Chicago and the rest of the country. Here's what was really amazing to me at the time. Wherever we opened, every competitor felt their customers would be loyal to them because they were in business for ten, twenty, or thirty years. They were all convinced, regardless of how many towns we had successfully run through, that if they just continued to run their business, their customers would stand by them.

When we got to each city and the customers saw what we did, their loyalty shifted very quickly.

It seems to be that there were two very big contrarian ideas that you brought to the table: 1) Selling goods at low prices with high levels of service. If people paid less, they generally expected not to get much service. That was the cost of getting something for a bargain. 2) If you have low margins, you generally have to carry less inventory because you often lack the cash to put that much stuff on the shelves.

Bernie: That ignores the magic of the numbers. Take low prices and service. Our theory was if you had service, you could sell the customers products they might not feel they needed. The whole thing boils down to the quality of the people on the floor. We paid the highest price in retailing for our partners at that time and even today. We hired professional people: plumbers and electricians. We wanted to start something that had never been done before—the do-it-yourself business. We really invented the do-it-yourself business in the U.S.

If you were a homeowner before and your toilet went out, you would have to call a plumber. People didn't put new lights in. They didn't do it because you couldn't buy the products. You had to go to a wholesale house. Everything was locked in. The magic of Home Depot was we invented and then had to sell the DIY concept. We spent a lot of time in every advertisement saying you could do it yourself. We'll teach you. When people would come into the stores with a faucet looking for a replacement, our people would say, "You don't need a new faucet. Why don't you just put a new washer in?" We'd take their faucet apart on the floor and fix it for $2. That happened thousands of times.

Another example? Arthur started the ceiling fan business in the United States. Imagine people putting up a ceiling fan? It was unbelievable. The magic of the story is that guys would work for five hours putting a ceiling fan up. They would press the button and the thing would work and it was like a miracle. They could call their kids, their aunts, their uncles to show them the ceiling fan. The beginning of the DIY movement started at Home Depot.

Did you know when you began the business that you would really have to educate the public? If so, that was an incredibly ambitious goal.

Arthur: We did know that. There was some DIY in the United States, but the level of service that Bernie is describing was not there. The difference was that in most cases in retailing, the emphasis is on how to spend as little as you can on your employees. You control your payroll by controlling the dollars you are spending. Our notion was that payroll was not an expense. It was an investment and it belongs more on the balance sheet than on the operating statement. We hired the best people and thought of it as a capital investment in the business. We knew that if we hired the most experienced people in lumber, gardening, plumbing, and electrical supplies, they would produce for us the maximum amount of sales over time.

Most retailers thought if they could hire two people for $5 an hour, that was better than one person at $10 an hour. And we basically believed you're better off hiring one at $10 an hour because not only is that person going to sell more, he or she is better trained and will set a better pace for the whole store. They would help you develop a trust relationship with the customer. Once that trust relationship is established, you can build on that. So customers really began to feel that when they came to Home Depot it was not about a transaction: how much they can get from me. Rather, it was about how can they solve my problem for the least amount of money? So when it came time to redo my bathroom or my kitchen or add a new room on the house, they would come back because the last time Bernie saved them some money on the faucet. Not only did the associates wear orange aprons, which meant that they bled orange, they wanted our customers to wear the orange inside of them. We had earned their loyalty. The customers felt this was "my store. I'm going to be treated well here. I trust the people here."

Bernie: If somebody came in and saw a reciprocal saw that sold for $350, our people would say, "What do you do for a living?"

"Well, I'm a salesman."

"How often are you going to use that?"

And they would say, "Infrequently." And the sales guy would tell him, "You don't need that. We have one for $250."

This never, ever happens in a retail business. Think about this for a second. You come in and want to buy the Cadillac and the guy is selling you the Ford? On the contrary, you would be told, "The cheaper one is going to break. It's not good enough. You need the better one." This goes back to the bond we had with the customer. Because of it, you couldn't take our customers away.

Arthur: It also had an impact on our associates. They understood that an important part of our culture was to walk in the shoes of our customers.

They had a tremendous amount of personal pride in the company they were working for. They saw the company had great values. They knew we were not trying to take advantage of a customer by overselling him. That made them feel good about their jobs and who they worked for. They believed this company had a higher purpose than just selling.

Your idea didn't take off right away, though. Even when you had your wives and children outside the store in Atlanta handing out dollar bills to get people to come inside, it didn't quite work.

Arthur: We had young children so we took them out of school in the morning. The store closed that night and they were still standing outside with dollar bills—and there was a limited number of dollars to give. Bernie and I were in one store and Pat Farrah (another member of the founding team) was in the other. We agreed to meet at Wendy's for lunch. All three of us walked in at noon and sat down. And I remember we just stared at each other. No one said anything. I still can remember who finally said the first word.

Bernie: I did. I said, "Who's going to pay for this meal?"

Arthur: This was not going as we expected. We didn't have a lot of traffic in our stores.

Bernie: We had more salespeople on the floor than customers.

Arthur: Over the next nine months, we really didn't find our way by locking ourselves in a room. What we really did was spend an inordinate amount of time on the floor of the stores asking questions of our customers. "What do you like? What don't you like?" We constantly changed and refined the model during that period of time. Bernie, myself, Pat, and others were fairly self-confident as human beings, but when it came to this, we thought we had the right concept but we really subordinated our feelings to those of the customer. We had a real sense of humility about that. We spent a lot of time listening to customers, changing the mix of merchandise, changing prices, changing vendors, changing service levels. And that began to pay off.

One of the important innovations became the regularly held DIY clinics to help your customers do their home projects. Did that come out of your conversations with customers?

Arthur: We were trying to expand the industry. This was not just an attempt to grab market share. The DIY industry even then was growing.

But how to accelerate that and put it on steroids that were approved was through these clinics. In many cases, customers walked in. They had the money and the desire. They just didn't know how to do something. If they agreed we had the merchandise and the price was right but they felt no confidence in taking on the project, they weren't going to do it. So we began to impart the product knowledge through formal clinics in the front or back of the stores and in one-on-one clinics that took place in the aisles. That was the difference.

How did you solve the inventory hurdle of carrying so much merchandise when your margins were so low and you didn't yet have the volume to offset those slimmer margins?

Bernie: When we opened up, I would say that we talked about buying direct from the manufacturer in order to cut the price. The truth is, that never happened. We were buying through distributors. We did not have the ability to buy direct. Most manufacturers would not sell to us. It was a locked-in deal. And so we would go to someone like GAF or Georgia-Pacific and they wouldn't sell to us. Breaking that down probably took seven to eight years. We literally had to teach the vendors how to sell to us.

Let me tell you a great story. We would take these vendors out to dinner and at the end of the night they would say, "You know, you're great guys. We really enjoyed this, but we can't sell to you." Then, we would come back three months later and then months after that. We would be drinking tequila to get them to sell to us. Most of them still turned us down.

You once said you had to be psychologists, lovers, romancers, and con artists to get vendors to sell directly to you.

Bernie: All of them. If you couldn't get the product at the direct price, our model wouldn't work. Plus, people would come to our stores and not see that product. There were many vendors who didn't allow their products to be in our stores, even buying through distributors. About 80 percent of the vendors refused to sell to us when we started. Ten years later, there were maybe three vendors who hadn't sold to us.

I remember I was on a bus traveling to Chicago and we had worked on one vendor for three years and he finally agreed to sell to us. I remember sitting on a bus with the vice president in charge of sales. We had just closed the deal and he said to me, "Well, Bernie, you finally got it."

And I asked, "When is your delivery going to be?"

And he said, "Probably in two months or so."

"What are you talking about?" I asked.

"Well, we're in a backup now. We have a seven-week backup on our orders. We're doing great."

"What do you mean you're doing great with a seven-week backup?"

"Oh yes," he said, "our business is based on how big the backup is."

"So if I put an order in today, when will I get the product?"

He said, "When we have it—maybe in a month or two."

I said, "Shove it up your ass. I'm not interested in even having the product. You guys don't even understand volume."

Pat and I had to actually go out and teach the vendors how to produce product. We had to explain to them that if they produce more, their business would get better. Everybody found out he could sell twice as many toilets if we had them in stock. So we had to teach them how to supply our stores. It was like pulling teeth to get them to understand that. But then, all of a sudden, when they started to pile up stuff in our stores, it would disappear. They had never seen that before. They were used to dealing with hardware stores where they sold two or three. We would put stuff in and sell thousands.

The really smart ones would focus their business on getting product into our stores. We had the customers on one end. We had our associates on the other. And then we had the manufacturers who we had to teach how to deal with this business. We created many multimillionaires who were total schmucks when they started with us.

Arthur: One guy who never learned was Jack Welch [of General Electric].

Bernie: He never did. In fact, we threw his light bulbs out of the store for that reason. I had a place in Florida and when you went down there in October and November, you sell a lot of bulbs due to the switch to daylight savings time. And GE was making our bulbs then. I went into the stores in Florida and found out we didn't have a single sixty-watt bulb in stock.

I remember calling Jack up and saying, "Jack, this is insanity. We don't have bulbs."

"We'll have to check into it," he said.

It was total bullshit. He sent the head of GE lighting down to see us and he said, "There won't be a problem next year. We'll definitely take care of you. You just have to give us the orders ahead of time."

We did that and when October and November came it was the same goddamn thing. There were no bulbs in the stores. And I found out the reason for it is because their year-end bonus was based on how much inventory they had at the end of the year. The following year, I flew to the Netherlands, met with the Philips people, and I came back and told Jack, "No more problems. We're throwing you out."

And we threw GE out. Philips built factories to supply us with bulbs in the United States.

How did Jack Welch respond?

Bernie: "Why would you do that to us? We're friends," he said.

Arthur: On the positive side, Jack understood that their system was so geared to efficiency—their return on capital and their incentive plans—that they only knew one way. Our customers didn't know or care when a vendor's year-end is. They just want product. To his credit, Jack recognized that as being a deficiency in the company. That whole company was built on Black Belt efficiency. He understood they had taken this thing too far. He knew we were a customer-driven, customer-service business.

Bernie: He was full of crap. His thing was bottom-line oriented and ours was customer oriented and it just didn't match. It didn't work. We bought a few things from him, including refrigerators. But he never got the bulb business back. He didn't deserve to get it back. And we helped to build Philips into a powerhouse in the United States. That was true of American Standard as well because Kohler refused to supply us for many years.

A lot of the strategy we learned as we went along. We weren't that brilliant. What we did was listen very carefully to our associates and our customers. They knew more than we ever did. And so the arrogance wasn't there. We knew our lives depended on these people.

Arthur: I remember one of the most critical times for our company, when we were approaching a billion dollars in volume. I was having lunch with Joe Ellis of Goldman Sachs, who was Goldman's retail analyst at the time. He was considered a retail guru on Wall Street. I remember Joe saying to me, "You know, when you guys reach a billion in volume, this unique culture is going to change. You will not be able to run this company the same way. You won't be able to maintain it."

Bernie and I had been involved in hands-on training and would constantly visit stores. I remember being sobered by Joe's comments. I went to see Bernie and told him what Joe said. Coming from Joe, this was not like some drunk in the street or some guy wandering out of Harvard Business School. This was a seasoned Wall Street veteran.

From that point forward, we realized we couldn't really touch every associate moving forward. We did these breakfasts with Bernie and Arthur. We did a lot of video stuff, and we traveled the stores a great deal. We did everything we could, but at some point the numbers got so humongous—opening two hundred stores a year—that it became physically impossible to visit all the stores.

But when we promoted people, we realized that either they got the culture or they didn't. They had to understand it. They had to understand what we were about. That became the ticket to get into the game. If you didn't understand that, you never got promoted. We only promoted people who understood the culture, lived it, and would become the ambassadors for that culture.

Bernie: Arthur and I actually loved the customers. When I would go into stores, I would hug and kiss customers because I recognized that everything I had in my life came from them. That is the difference between me and Jack Welch. With Jack, the bottom line was the most important thing. With us, we said if we treat the customer right, we eventually would have the bottom line. Remember most customers are on loan. But if the customer is loyal to you, your company will be good, no matter what else happens. The customer comes first. Number two was the associate. We knew that the associate was critical. We loved our associates. We would walk into stores and hug them. And they knew we loved them. The feeling was there and it was mutual.

Listen, I can't tell you how many people we had who got buried in orange aprons. That loyalty went so deep. That's why we had ESOPs, stock options, and bonuses. Our associates were paid the highest amount in the retail industry, bar none. And we weren't unionized. We did it because it was the right thing to do and they deserved to be treated that well.

Another factor was we always bought quality merchandise. Have it there for the customer and have it in the amounts that they need and a price that is reasonable and fair and as low as you can possibly sell it. That was the culture of The Home Depot, but it started with the customer.

As the company got bigger, the associates had to become the teachers. A district manager who had one hundred people working for him had to become Arthur and Bernie. He had to become us.

Arthur: When a couple of consultants at McKinsey & Company were writing a book called *The War for Talent,* they went across the United States and Canada and interviewed many of our store managers and associates, including cashiers. I was the last to be interviewed, and the gentleman who came in was out of Chicago and he said, "I've been doing this for a lot of years. I've never seen a company where everyone could articulate the policies that Bernie and you express. And I spoke to about a hundred people. I don't know how you've done it, but you have. It's absolutely unbelievable."

Bernie: Arthur, it happened because we believed it and lived our lives that way. We behaved that way. We demonstrated who we were. To say great words and not do it doesn't work.

Arthur: The other thing we didn't do was change the message every year. That was a big deal. So it wasn't like, this year our top ten commandments are these. And a year from then say, "Okay, they're stale. Let's change them and put in another ten." I was there twenty-three years saying the same stuff a thousand times over. There was never any confusion about what the company was about. It didn't change while we were there. This was our culture.

Our business changed. Our store sizes changed. Our merchandise assortment changed. But the culture and the essence of what we were talking about never changed. They changed after we left the company, but those had been the core values of our company.

Bernie: Arthur and I were very consistent throughout the years we were together. We never confused anybody. If Arthur and I came to a different conclusion on an issue, no matter what it was, we would both eventually agree on a decision. From that point on, we never deviated. In typical partnerships and businesses, you always have somebody working against you. At Home Depot, our team could never work both sides of the street. You know the way a kid has a mother and a father and the father turns the kid down and then he goes right to the mother? They couldn't do that in our company. We had disagreements. We would talk it over and say this is the policy.

And from that point on, it was unified. Everything fell in favor of the customer, the customer, the customer. We would say to people that everything we have in our lives and everything you have in your life depends on that customer. Your life and your career, whether you will be able to pay your mortgage or put your kid through college, everything depends on that guy who comes through the door every single day. We said it so frequently that they began to believe it.

REED HASTINGS

NETFLIX

t was a personal embarrassment that led to the creation of one of the most ingenious companies of the past century.

In 1997, Reed Hastings had rented the movie *Apollo 13*, misplaced it, and forgotten to return the VHS by its due date. Six weeks later, when he finally brought the videocassette back to the rental store, he owed a late fee of $40. "It was no one's fault except my own," he recalls.

Hastings paid the fine but was so embarrassed by it that he didn't want to tell his wife. "And I thought, 'Oh great, now I am going to compromise the integrity of my marriage over this late fee.'"

When he got back home, he quickly fessed up—and then he began thinking about the Internet, a new emerging technology—DVD—about to replace bulky VHS tapes, and how a business might be able to work without those damn late fees.

The idea became an obsession. On his way to work out one day, it occurred to Hastings that his gym had a much better business model than his video rental store: you pay $30 to $40 a month and exercise as little or as much as you want.

Suddenly, all the thoughts began crashing together. Would it be possible to create a movie-rental business by mail, abolish all late fees, and ask customers to pay monthly subscription fees as if they were members of a fitness club?

Within days, Hastings ran out to Tower Records in Santa Cruz, bought a few audio CDs, stashed them into envelopes, and then mailed the pieces of plastic to himself. "It was a long twenty-four hours until the mail arrived back at my house," Hastings recalls. "I ripped them open and they were all in great shape. That was the big excitement point."

The person who had conducted this little experiment had already founded and sold one company for $750 million—in the same year he paid the $40 in late fees. He had also sold vacuum cleaners door-to-door, had trained as a Marine officer, and had taught algebra and geometry in northwest Swaziland, where he lived in a thatched hut and slept on a cot as a member of the Peace Corps. "Once you have hitchhiked across Africa with ten bucks in your pocket, starting a business doesn't seem too intimidating," he says.

It was while he was in the Peace Corps in 1985 that Hastings decided to get a graduate degree in computer science. He had majored in math at Bowdoin College, finding the abstractions "beautiful and engaging." Originally from Boston, he wanted to go to MIT. But the school turned him down. Instead, Hastings got an invite from Stanford University. "I had never been to California and arrived in late summer," he remembers. "Driving up to the campus I saw palm trees. It was dry and brown. I asked myself, 'Where's the ivy?' But within a week, I had fallen in love with California."

His first job out of Stanford was at Adaptive Technology, where he invented a tool for debugging software, but Hastings left in 1991 after three years to found Pure Software, a company that produced products to troubleshoot software. For a thirty-one-year-old engineer with no management experience, he found himself ill equipped to deal with the challenges that make their way into a CEO's office.

"As the company grew from 10 to 40 to 120 to 320 to 640 employees, I found I was definitely underwater and over my head," Hastings says. "I was doing white-water kayaking at the time, and in kayaking if you stare and focus on the problem you are much more likely to hit danger. I focused on the safe water and what I wanted to happen. I didn't listen to the skeptics." Twice, after losing confidence, he tried to fire himself as the CEO. But the board wouldn't let him go. Revenues were doubling every year, and Hastings learned how to become a true entrepreneur. By 1995, he had taken the company public. Two years later, he sold it to Rational Software for $750 million.

So when Hastings got the idea for his new movie-rental business, he also had the means to fund it. Good thing. Netflix lost money for four straight years before breaking into a profit in 2002, the year the company eventually went public. Hopes to do an IPO earlier were dashed by the dot-com bust, which Hastings failed to foresee. "It's hard to know when you're inside a bubble," he says. It was a difficult period, a time when Hastings had to tell his employees, "Tomorrow when you come to work, if what you do isn't making the customer happy, moving the business forward, and saving us money, don't do it. Everything we do has to meet these three criteria."

But the company has experienced one of those hockey stick trajectories that end up in business plans but rarely come true. In year one, Hastings signed up 239,000 subscribers. Today, Netflix has more than 24 million subscribers who pay at least $8.99 a month for access to its movie and TV show library. The company will surpass $3 billion in revenue in 2011 and likely have operating income in excess of half a billion dollars.

Hastings has changed how the entertainment business reaches its audience and how that audience is able to access content. His disruptive business model has survived a challenge from Walmart and also has vanquished Blockbuster, which was forced into bankruptcy reorganization in 2010 and sold at auction in April of 2011. It's also successfully made the early transition from the U.S. Postal Service to streaming video into the home via computers, iPads, TVs, and game consoles. Shipments of DVDs are now declining as more users stream. And *Time* magazine named Hastings one of the one hundred most influential people this year of 2011.

"Being an entrepreneur," he says, "is about patience and persistence, not the quick buck, and everything great is hard and takes a long time."

How in the world could you ever have gotten that $40 late fee—and aren't you lucky you did?

Sometimes there are little things in life that have unintended consequences.

I just forgot about it. The point is I remember it so clearly because I didn't want to tell my wife about it. "My God," I thought, "I'm thinking about lying to my wife." That was one of the big influences. As the Internet grew, I thought there was a market for doing online movie rentals.

At first we looked at the business as VHS by mail. And the problem is a VHS tape cost about four bucks to mail, four bucks to mail back, and four bucks to rent. There was a pretty small market for $12 video rental. And then a friend told me about DVDs. "They're just like CDs," he said, "and DVDs are coming out next year," but you couldn't buy any yet. So we ran down to Tower Records and thought, "Wow, if you could mail them would they get destroyed? Or not?"

We bought a bunch of CDs, ran down to the post office, and mailed them to ourselves. Then we had to wait a day to see if our great idea would work or would we get all these broken shards. The next day the postman came and we opened them all up, and all the CDs were in perfect shape. And you could mail them for 36 cents then.

Did you have trouble selling the idea? You had a big monster called Block-buster out there that essentially had the market for rental video all to itself. And in the dot-com era, mailing DVDs via the post office wasn't exactly sexy.

The challenge in raising venture financing for Netflix is we were doing it in the bubble of '96, '97, '98, and '99. At that point, everything was changing so fast that people said, "How is this going to work? We are going to be beaming movies to your watch in 2000?" This ridiculous stuff was getting funded, and it took us a long time to get funded because the idea was so practical. We did get some venture capitalists, and then the company grew and we eventually got profitable and went public in 2002.

Ultimately, your secret sauce is customer service: the fast turnaround, the vast selection, and the notion of taking advantage of the long tail due to your deep selection of independent and foreign films.

Is the secret sauce customer service? That's a little simplistic. Everyone tries for great customer service. Depending on what you do, it can be too expensive and unprofitable. There are edges that you have to figure out. You have to decide which customers make the most sense to best serve.

As an example, when we started with DVDs only, it was extremely expensive to have every new movie in stock during the first two months because there is a lot of demand for them. Three months later, it's easy to have the movies in stock because there is not much demand. So we are always trying to manage to our costs versus the satisfaction of our customers. I don't think it's fair to just say all we do is salute the flag of customer service. We try to figure out where we can efficiently serve some sector of customers who are a little bit tolerant on new releases and love the vast catalog of a hundred thousand titles with overnight delivery. If there is a secret sauce, it is that we think very carefully and strategically about which set of customers to serve well. For those customers we are a blessed experience, but it's more focused.

Everybody can't have a blessed experience, especially when you have so many millions of customers. So what have you learned about retaining your customer base?

The relationship that people had with Netflix, especially in the early days, was that people turn it on for three months and then off and come back. Every fall we have huge numbers of signups and nobody leaves. And in the spring the churn rate is astronomical because people want to be outdoors. We get the reverse phenomenon in the hottest parts of the country. In winter, they're more outside and people cancel.

So we have evolved to a place where churn is not a deathly thing that we work hard to prevent. In fact, in some way it's a natural part of the rhythm of people. At one point, we had the typical AOL kind of exit. By that I mean, you click on the screen and up would pop a window that said, "No, you don't really want to do that." And then you would have to go through nineteen screens until it said, "Now call this number." And then you call and it's busy and you're put on hold. It was an awful experience. We had that in '02 and '03. Then we decided to get rid of it and allow customers to leave with just a single click and the message: "Okay, thank you. We hope you come back again." Because it's so easy to exit and people have so much tension around that, they are much more likely to come back. So we have shifted to go with their flow as opposed to helping our subscription methods. We win them back with great service and selection. But that was a great lesson for us: making it as easy to cancel as it is to sign up.

Reed, you're essentially a disrupter. You looked at the existing business model of movie rentals, figured out that users were frustrated by it, and then tapped into new technologies—the Internet and the switch from VHS tapes to DVDs—to invent a new model to upend a powerful incumbent player, Blockbuster. A lot of businesses are getting disrupted today. The obvious question, though, is why didn't Blockbuster react as quickly as one would have thought to protect its business model?

Everyone wants to know when you miss a big thing coming. The facts are we launched our service in 1999, we went public in 2002, and Blockbuster didn't enter against us until mid-2004, about five years after we started. The question is, did they wait too long? The answer is clearly yes.

But it's actually much harder than it appears. It turned out that our threat turned into a big threat. But the game of business is like the game of chess. A master chess player doesn't explore every possibility in brute force twenty moves out. He is constantly pruning and trying to figure out where the threats are. You follow a few potential sequences down to great depth. If you miss one and you prune a branch you shouldn't have, you can get checkmated. So master chess players get very good at pruning which things could amount to real problems and which ones are not likely to. They're not going to spend the time thinking about all the possibilities on the limited clock they have.

All the time, threats come up. People come to me and say, "Look at this new mobile device that goes off a satellite. It is going to transform the business." I don't think so. Most of business is about focus. We are good pruners. We prune the tree of possibilities down to some manageable set and then try to have our people execute on our core beliefs.

By and large, Blockbuster had actually done a fantastic job of pruning. When the bubble was there in '99 and 2000, and things started going crazy, their big competitor Hollywood Video wasted $400 million trying to sell VHS online. Blockbuster was much more disciplined. They did a great job. They actually were systematically good pruners.

They weren't sitting down in Dallas smoking cigars saying, "Nah, Netflix didn't matter." They were very careful market researchers. They spent a lot of time interviewing our customers. They guessed at that point that we could get to maybe a million subscribers and then the market would saturate. Therefore, it was not worth their putting a lot of effort into it.

They turned out to be wrong. They just pruned the tree wrong. We got to a million, to four million, and we kept going. By the time we got to a million, they said, "We were wrong. We have to run after them." It was just a slight error in judgment as opposed to being asleep at the switch. All of us in management are trying to figure out what to focus on and that is one of the core executive tasks. I think they just made one error on that.

What's interesting is that they came after you with full firepower. They spent $500 million and they still couldn't put a dent in your business model. Why?

They did put a dent on us. Our stock dropped from $39 to $9. That felt denty. The challenge that they had is, if you attack a company like ours, we had enough cash so we were unlikely to go bankrupt. We had nowhere to run. We had infinite exit costs. If you attack an area with infinite exit costs, it's very expensive. They could hurt us, but all we would do is cut prices to survive. It ends up in mutual destruction, and that's in fact what happened for a while. What they should have done is started a new model: the $1 kiosks in supermarkets and other stores that became Redbox's business. That would have been an enormous new market opportunity.

So what they should have done is an end run around us. Instead of wasting money doing exactly what we did, they should have taken their $500 million of capital and invented a new market. Blockbuster would have been hugely successful. The lesson there is that if you duplicate someone who is already successful, your chance of profit is pretty low.

Of course, you built a model that you knew would eventually be disrupted itself. That's why you called it Netflix and not "DVD by Mail." So have you worried about someone else coming along to disrupt Netflix just as you did to Blockbuster?

The Internet is the disrupter. I've just been a stamp licker. Most of our volume and all of our profits came from mailing things to people. We were as afraid of the future as anyone else. We thought that the Internet broadband would allow streaming video that would eventually upend our business model. But we knew it was coming when we started. We've grown up with this thing as opposed to a scenario where we had a great profit stream and then something new comes along to disrupt that. But predicting the

Internet and what will happen is impossible. No one I know would have predicted Facebook a few years ago.

Clearly, this connectivity that the Internet brings is a force that is as fundamental as the domestication of the horse, the advent of shipping, the railroads, and the automobile. Only it's in a really compressed time frame. So it will happen over thirty years and everyone is going to have one hundred megabits, full streaming, high definition, two-way conversations over the Internet. When we get to full video interactivity that is immersive with avatars, the stuff that we faced over the last ten years will seem relatively trivial.

Typically, you might have two strategies if you are caught between a new technology that will render your product obsolete: you either milk the cow you own until it goes dry or you double down on a bet for the future. How do you come to that decision?

The most important thing is that you know if you are in double-down or in milk mode and all your constituencies agree that you're in one or the other. The awful stuff happens when you go back and forth. You don't want to be in a milk-the-cow mode because that sounds bad, but we're not really prepared to invest. That is certainly not going to result in any good. In milk mode, you've got ten or fifteen years of steady profits and you organize the company for that. In double-down mode, you are essentially saying there is not much equity value left in your business model. We are going to take all the profit and be like a start-up and try to figure out the new world. If you get the backing to do that, it can be really fun. What's not fun is half the company thinks you should double down and half the company is in milk mode. I will be lucky to figure it out in movies.

You're predicting that your core business is going to decline and now video streaming is growing very fast. So how do you manage the tension between what you should milk and what you should invest in?

For a long time, our DVD shipments continued to grow as more video stores closed. That drove a lot of business online. We got to grow with that and then there is the streaming business where we offer all of our customers the ability to watch movies instantly on their laptop or on their TV. I think it's tremendously exciting because it is fundamentally lowering our mailing costs.

That doesn't generate incremental profit at this point [Netflix has since moved to a new pricing plan that requires customers to pay for streaming]. It is a way to evolve people forward. What we have tensions on internally is there are all the people who work on the DVD business. They work really hard to make it a better and better service, and they feel somewhat devalued. And then we have all the people on the streaming side who are working really hard but they can't believe that they have to go along with this DVD thing. So we do have those tensions.

Internally, we've had to clarify our strategy and tell people it's necessary to improve the service by strengthening streaming and trimming DVD. And we had to explicitly give our internal groups permission to treat the DVD side as more in cash cow mode and that wasn't anti to customer or anti to company because the overall service was improving, especially if you view the overall service as a combination of streaming and DVD. But that is a shift. A few years ago, we were in a pattern of maintaining (the DVD business) and doing something, and now we are in trim and do a lot. Overall, that creates a better customer experience, but it doesn't create a better customer experience for every single customer.

Plus, the competition in streaming will be far greater, right?

Well, it's more ambiguous for sure. The long-term competition in streaming is unclear. It's not clear if it is Apple, Google, Hulu, or Amazon. It is a very small market and it will have a lot of competition. Whereas on the DVD side, it's pretty clear the competition is Blockbuster and Redbox. So it's a known set and it feels less scary. On the streaming side over the next ten years, it is going to be wildly competitive.

How do you see this playing out over the long term?

What is coming is a titanic battle between the forces of freedom and the forces of control. The forces of freedom want you to be able to select whatever content you want when you want. It's the pure on-demand world driven by the Internet. The forces of control want to pick the programming that you see. You have so many channels. You have remote control. It's two hundred to five hundred channels and they say, "You pick it." Often when people look at this they say, "Well, this is biased. You're calling it the forces of freedom and isn't that always the natural winner?" But that's not always true in business. Often the forces of control win because they can deliver a higher-quality experience. Every time you pick up your remote control and change a channel it always works.

So the powerful part of the control paradigm is that the supplier gets great control and is able to deliver a high-quality experience. On the other hand, the forces of freedom can give you chaos. It's the Internet. You get error pages. You're forced to your PC. But the benefit you get is rapid innovation. It's chaotic, and there are errors but huge innovation. Think about blogs. No one ever heard of a blog five years ago. Now it's more than a third of all words written on the Internet. It's incredibly powerful. It's an enormous amount of content getting created.

The rate of new media creation and innovation on the side of the forces of freedom is tremendous. I think the long term looks like, the Web is television and the remote control is the keyboard. And you are browsing the Web for all of your content. And you've got three channels going at once. That's what it will look like in ten or twenty years. The market is growing so fast that there will be a lot of winners: the primary winners are those who deliver large Internet bandwidth: the telephone companies and cable companies who deliver high-speed Internet. Content creators will get more ways to get to customers.

I think the forces of freedom will outcompete the forces of control. It's really moving to an on-demand world. Our belief is that Netflix will be one of the movie channels in that forces-of-freedom world.

No doubt, you've made plenty of mistakes in the thirteen years since the beginning of Netflix. Your foray into social networking, for example, didn't seem to work. What did you learn from that?

Well, we mostly failed at it. We put a lot of effort in over five years. At one point, we started something called "Netflix friends," and if you and a friend were both Netflix members you could give each other permission to see your movie ratings and what you're watching. The good news is we saw early that there was a potential for something great. What we didn't appreciate is that if you were sharing with a friend, you didn't just want to share only your movies. You wanted to share your movies, your music, your ideas, your concepts. Social belonged to Facebook, not Netflix. We are an application on top of a social operating system. And we put all this work into being the system. So now we flipped to just making an easy connection through Facebook.

Any final advice for would-be entrepreneurs?

Target a specific niche. When there's an ache, you want to be like aspirin, not vitamins. Aspirin solves a very particular problem someone has, whereas vitamins are a general "nice to have" market. Netflix was certainly aspirin.

You should stay flexible. We named the company Netflix, not DVDs by Mail, because we knew that eventually we would deliver movies directly over the Internet. DVDs will be around a long time, but for years we've been building for the day when they're not.

Don't underestimate the competition. We erroneously concluded that Blockbuster probably wasn't going to launch a competitive effort when they hadn't by 2003. Then, in 2004, they did. We thought, well, they won't put much money behind it. Within four years, they invested more than $500 million against us.

And there are no shortcuts. Occasionally great wealth is created in a short amount of time, but it's through a lot of luck in those situations. You just have to think of building an organization as a lot of work. It may or may not turn into great wealth. But it will be an exciting and fulfilling adventure.

HOWARD SCHULTZ

STARBUCKS

n December of 2007, Howard Schultz was vacationing with his family in Hawaii when he ran into Michael Dell. Less than a year earlier, the founder of what had become the world's largest computer company had returned to Dell as chief executive, replacing his handpicked successor. Now Schultz, who had given up his job as CEO of Starbucks seven years earlier, was thinking of returning as well.

The once high-flying companies they founded were both struggling and in crisis, just as Apple Computer was when Steve Jobs made his return to the company he had cofounded with Steve Wozniak. Schultz found their parallel circumstances a bit uncanny, even though their respective businesses, coffee and computers, could not have been more different.

During a three-hour bike ride along the Kona coast, Schultz confided to Dell that he had become increasingly distressed over Starbucks' deteriorating position. For the first time in its history, the company was consistently reporting negative daily comps—falling sales from existing stores—in the double digits. Every day, fewer people were coming into Starbucks' stores and those who did were spending less money than they had in the past.

"The numbers were so bad I felt paralyzed," Schultz would later say. "I simply did not know what to do with myself. I couldn't eat breakfast. I couldn't enjoy my family. I could barely move. It was as if everything I feared was coming true."

Two of the world's most famous entrepreneurs were now meeting regularly while still on their family vacations. Dell was advising Schultz on how to manage Wall Street if he decided to go back into the job and how to maintain morale in a company that was clearly losing its mojo. One day the pair rode back to Dell's house where he walked Schultz through a narrative of what he had done since his return, pulling out memos and documents of detailed plans to turn Dell around.

By the time Schultz left Hawaii for Seattle, he knew he was going to fire then Starbucks CEO Jim Donald, who had been recruited for the job from Walmart, and assume the leadership of the company he had once made great. But could Schultz do what Steve Jobs had already done? Could he really return in the top job to a much larger yet troubled company and bring back the magic he had originally created? After all, the Starbucks he knew had been almost a fairy-tale story of entrepreneurship and Schultz was as much a part of the fairy tale as anyone.

He had grown up poor in the projects of Brooklyn, New York, paid his way through college, and moved to Seattle to take a job as head of marketing for a small company called Starbucks. In September of 1982, Schultz began work in the first Starbucks store in Pike Place Market, scooping fresh beans for customers and sealing them in small bags.

On a business trip to Italy, he fell in love with the small espresso bars in Milan and Verona, marveling at their ability to connect people and create community over a simple cup of coffee. When he returned to the States, Schultz was determined to bring the romance of Italian espresso bars back with him. He left Starbucks to strike out on his own, opening a pair of espresso bars called Il Giornale.

In 1987, Schultz found himself in a position to buy his former employer Starbucks out. With the support of a few investors, he merged his stores with the six Starbucks outlets and kept their name. By the end of the first year, he had eleven stores, one hundred employees, and a dream to create a national brand.

By the time he left the job as CEO in charge of day-to-day operations in 2000 to assume the role of chairman, Schultz had built Starbucks into a company with annual revenue of nearly $2 billion. Since 1992, Starbucks had achieved a compounded annual growth rate of 49 percent. More important, though, it had dramatically changed the consumer's relationship with coffee, re-creating with a lot of American marketing pizzazz the espresso bar experience that had inspired Schultz in Italy years earlier. It also had become a model for what a good business could be: Schultz had made Starbucks the first U.S. company to offer comprehensive health-care coverage as well as stock options to part-time employees who worked at least twenty hours a week. The company had become an American icon.

But when Schultz went on his bike rides with Dell in Hawaii, the recession was beginning to take its toll—and so was the company's rapid growth rate, which led to an overexpansion and unprofitable stores. The company that Schultz would return to as CEO was a $10 billion company, five times larger than the one he left, with more than seven thousand stores in North America alone. But it also was a company in a deepening crisis as sales continued to plummet along with profits—and the company's stock price.

Among the many things that Schultz would do to turn Starbucks around, the most agonizing and painful decision came six months after his return: he would shutter some 600 underperforming stores—8 percent of its U.S. company–owned and –operated outlets—and eliminate 12,000 positions. Starbucks would have to take a $340 million charge to shut down the stores. Shockingly, seven out of ten stores he was closing had been opened in the past three years, when Starbucks expanded to an additional 2,300 locations.

Within a week of the announcement in early July of 2008, the company's stock fell to a fifty-two-week low. Wall Street and much of the media had written off Starbucks as dead, a victim of a deep recession that had changed consumer habits forever. But Schultz couldn't and wouldn't believe it.

The lowest point would actually come in December of that same year, on the evening before he had to face Wall Street analysts in New York to give them still more bad news. Schultz confessed to a friend that he thought the stock could drop to just $5 a share, making the company vulnerable to a takeover. The thought occurred to him that he could easily lose the company to someone else. That scenario never played out. Instead, the game plan he put in place not only would turn the iconic chain around, it would restore the company's lost values and culture as well.

Howard, at the very height of the company's troubles in 2008, less than four months after closing hundreds of stores and losing thousands of employees, you did something that many thought was pretty strange. You spent more than $30 million on, of all things, a company retreat. Why?

We certainly were in a crisis mode. Despite the external pressures to do things that were not consistent with the values and culture of the company, I felt we had to go back to the core purpose of what we stood for. We have always been a people-based business. Unlike almost any company, we have no secret sauce, no secret technology. Anyone can open up a coffee store. The essence of our company has always been the guiding values and principles.

From the very beginning we always believed that the only way we could exceed the expectations of our customers was to exceed the expectations of our people. So given the external pressures, the cataclysmic financial crisis, it was time to return to the intimacy of communicating directly with our people, galvanizing our organization against a core purpose, and asking our people to understand what was at stake.

We needed their personal commitment. If we got it, I believed very strongly that the equity of our brand and the loyalty of our customers would return. But without their understanding of the issues and a reinvestment in them, we could not do this. Candidly, I came under significant pressure from institutional shareholders who began to hear about this conference. This was an extremely expensive event to organize.

But you did it anyway. You brought your people to New Orleans, which was still struggling to recover from Hurricane Katrina, which had devastated the city three years earlier.

Every municipality in the country wanted this event because tourism was over. People were not traveling. We went to New Orleans because it was so fitting for us to go back there and demonstrate to ourselves and to that community the essence of Starbucks' original business plan: to make a profit and to balance that, though it is hard at times, with a social conscience.

While we were there, we donated fifty thousand hours of community service. There wasn't a press release. It was not marketing. It was really authentic. It began to build the foundation for the comeback of the company. We would not be here without having demonstrated our recommitment to our people.

Let's go back to ten months before the event when you came back as CEO in January of 2008. You are, along with Steve Jobs and Michael Dell, three of the greatest entrepreneurs of our generation. All of you were drawn back to your companies because each of you profoundly believed that what you created could completely disappear. But the big question was, could you actually bring it back? How did you know you could really make a difference?

I'll introduce a word that is not commonly used in business but it's so truthful to me: it's love. When you build something from the ground up and you have so much at stake—the legacy, the respect, and the responsibility of 200,000 people and their families—it's very hard to watch it drift. I knew it needed a new level of nurturing.

I came back because I felt very strongly that the company required not a set of business principles, but it needed love and nurturing. We also had to remind people why Starbucks was great. In many ways, the growth of this company had been fantastic—fifteen consecutive years of positive comp store sales, almost 6,000 percent growth in terms of the stock price. It was the darling of Wall Street. We could do nothing wrong.

And all of a sudden, not only did we hit the wall, but there was a death march from the media and the financial analysts who said Starbucks' best days are over. I just could not under any circumstance allow that to happen. Not that I am some healer, but I felt I had an unusual understanding of the issues and the circumstances that created the problems, and that I could bring back a group of people to solve those problems. And I felt that literally we would be a better, stronger company for having gone through it. Because we had to admit to ourselves that mistakes were made, and some of them were self-induced. And we did develop a new muscle, a new discipline in the company that would be permanent.

Your succession didn't go so well. How come?

The fact that I came back is not an editorial about Jim Donald. At the end of the day, the weakness that occurred was not his fault. It was ours. We did not do a very good job of having a successor ready from inside the company. It presents a very steep challenge for someone outside when things start going awry. The commitment I've now made is that I want to see this through and I am here for the long term.

Jim Collins has said a lot of companies go through five stages of decline. The first is hubris born of success. The second stage is the undisciplined pursuit of more. The third stage is denial of risk and peril. The fourth stage is grasping for salvation, and the fifth stage is capitulation to irrelevance or death. Starbucks certainly went through several of these stages. What stage did you think the company was in?

I have a lot of respect for Jim Collins, but I would rather put this in my own words. We were simultaneously dealing with five different theaters—not stages. The first theater was we had to admit to ourselves and our people that there were self-induced mistakes, whether they were real estate mistakes or issues around growth. And we had to own them. We had made some very critical decisions that were not correct. We had to admit it. Fix them and cleanse ourselves of those issues.

Two, at the exact same time when we were going through these errors of judgment and decision making, there was a cataclysmic financial crisis. And Starbucks, unbeknownst to lots of people, was a leading indicator of the downturn and recession. We started feeling it very early and in many ways we had to make decisions without perfect information. We were navigating through a financial storm that we did not understand. No one did.

The third thing was we had competition. We had never had competitive pressures before. All of a sudden, McDonald's was announcing that they were going to spend a billion dollars in capital to build McCafés and put $100 million in advertising behind them. And the world decided that McDonald's was going to kill Starbucks.

The fourth theater might surprise you. For whatever reason, the Web and the bloggers started using Starbucks as the poster child for excess in the economy, and the Web became a method in which consumer confidence and confidence in our own people weakened and damaged the equity of the brand.

And the fifth issue was, how do you preserve the integrity of the most valuable asset in our company: the values and culture of our people at a time when we had unbelievable pressures and had to make tough decisions?

Any one of these issues could have done serious damage to the company. In the end, each one of them was dealt with and we really overcame them. The Web is a great example. Starbucks is now the number one consumer brand on Facebook. It's the number one consumer brand on Twitter. We've turned the Web into an advantage in which the social media of the company has become an art form.

And McDonald's made us better. The more they advertised, the better we got because people saw there was a big difference. And it also brought up a little bit of fear and courage in us. Competition is not a bad thing. The turnaround occurred because of our belief in the values of our company, the core experience that we've created, the quality of our coffee, and what we stand for.

The worst thing we could have done is thrown some Hail Mary pass that other people were suggesting: whether it was to license and franchise the system, break up the company, or end health-care coverage for our part-time employees. We are spending $300 million on health care a year to cover the health insurance of every single employee. We were the first company in America to provide comprehensive health insurance to part-time workers. We got enormous pressure for at least two years from people on the outside saying, "Howard, this is a fantastic time. You have all the cover in the world to cut that benefit." I wouldn't do it. The investment that we make in our people has to be consistent and actually has to be more in the future than it has been in the past.

That is just another counterintuitive decision you made. First, you spend millions to bring thousands of people to New Orleans for a company retreat when the company is in total crisis. You refuse to cut health insurance to your part-timers when many analysts believe you didn't have the money to continue to pay for it. And then you close all your stores for an afternoon at great cost to retrain your baristas. Why did you do that?

Let me go back to the first theater: an admission of guilt. I couldn't face myself or our people and ignore the fact that I believed we were not doing as good a job as we once did in making a perfect cup of coffee. I felt the growth of the company in many ways had covered up that issue. I wanted to go back to the earliest days. We literally closed every single store in an afternoon at great cost—lost sales and unbelievable labor costs. The media and the financial analysts again said, "This guy is out of his mind. The board has got to act. It's got to get him out of there."

But I felt we had to go back to the roots. I stood up in front of all of our people and said, "We've been operating at too lofty a place. The success of the company has been great, but have we earned it? Are we as good as we think we are?" I didn't think we were. I wanted to get back in the mud. I wanted to get dirty. I wanted us to get back to the roots of our business, closer to the customer. And every time there is an issue I want to deal with it. I no longer wanted us to ignore any of the signs that caused our problems. I started traveling the world and having listening tours with customers. We started closing stores at night and had open forums with customers behind closed doors. I asked, "Tell us what we need to do that we're not doing."

What did you learn?

What I learned, first off, is that our customers really wanted us to win. They had such respect for the company. There is a large reservoir of trust around the values of the company. Our customers know we provide health care to our people. They know what we're doing with Product Red and how much we're giving back to Africa. They also know, though, that there are lots of people selling good coffee across the street. And if we don't measure up, they might go somewhere else.

I also learned that despite the growth and ubiquity of the company, it was critical for us to be locally relevant. We were once great at that. We now needed to create a new level of decision making and flexibility on a local and regional level where our stores can really be community based and we're not seen as this large company—but rather a company that is large, doing great work in the local community.

One of the things you've had to do on this journey back is to do something you had never done: to close stores and lay people off. How hard was that for you personally and for the company?

The one thing I started doing early on when I came back was to communicate at multiple levels in all different ways with great transparency. Whether it was physical meetings, visiting stores, e-mails, voice mails, writing memos to our people, I was constantly trying to put them in a place where they really knew how much I cared and what were the issues and challenges we had as a company. I set the stage for the fact that we were beginning to have to face the issues that we had with underperforming stores. One of the tragedies of self-admission is that we had open stores that needed to be closed but the majority of the stores had been open less than two years.

In fact, 70 percent of the stores you closed were only in existence for three years or less.

When I first realized that, I was sick. How could we open stores and within twenty-four or thirty-six months have to close them? But the truth is, we had stretched the brand beyond its demography. Once the financial crisis occurred, those stores were no longer relevant. Closing those stores meant that we had to lay off people. Fortunately, lots of those people were able to find jobs in existing stores. But we also had to lay off a significant amount of our workforce in our support center, where we employ four thousand people.

The day of the layoffs we had a companywide meeting. I didn't do this behind closed doors. I stood naked in front of every single partner in the company, and I truthfully said this is the hardest day for me in the history of our company. But in order to secure the future of our company, we have to make these decisions. I promised people we would do this with compassion, respect, and dignity, and they could hold me accountable to that, but these decisions had to be made. It was a very, very tough day. At the core of the equity of the Starbucks brand has always been a large reservoir of trust from our people, and in many ways that trust has transferred to our customers. The only way we could make these decisions, as tough as they were, was for everyone to understand the unequivocal, unvarnished truth. Though they were upset and concerned, the one thing they had to say was that Howard is telling us the unvarnished truth.

How did you keep them in the fold?

I don't have a great answer for that other than to tell you that the people of Starbucks rose to the challenge. New Orleans served as a great foundation of bringing people together and working toward a common goal. Michael Dell helped me with this early on because it is something he had done. We created a blueprint called the Transformational Agenda. This wasn't something that was held by ten people or fifty leaders in the company. We handed that blueprint out to everyone at Starbucks so they could understand the strategic objectives and how they related to each person's role. It gave people a blueprint for success.

You have to provide people with hope and aspiration. Against all odds, the resurrection or the transformation of Starbucks was also linked to a tremendous amount of innovation. That innovation has gotten our people so excited again. It reminded them of what the early days of Starbucks were like. What I said to our people is, "We have to remember what it was like when we opened one store and were fighting for survival. What it was like when we couldn't make payroll. What it was like when we had vendors who we couldn't pay and asked them to hang with us."

We grew up in an environment where the Bank of Starbucks was thought to be so big, we could do everything. Well, life isn't like that. We had to go back to the early days.

Well, yes and no. Because you also had to do a lot of things differently, right?

True. It wasn't enough to embrace the status quo of the old days. We had to link the heritage and tradition of Starbucks with a new day, a new level of innovation, and a new way of thinking.

All of this has also meant that you had to reinvent yourself. You had to change from being a highly creative growth guy in the go-go years to someone more nuanced, who now had to manage a fairly large company in trouble.

I haven't changed. I am the same guy, the same entrepreneur, pushing for self-renewal and reinvention. However, the reality of the situation demanded a new level of personal discipline. The rules of engagement had so significantly changed that we had to refine our strategy. We also had to understand that the old way of doing things had to be challenged. There had to be creative tension in the room. We needed a level of conversation about how we were going to market and how we were going to take costs out.

We took out $580 million of costs in 2008. Some 90 percent of it has been permanent. None of it is consumer facing. That was there for many years. Why did it take a crisis to allow us to have the courage to do that? So I wouldn't say I changed. The environment created a new playing field. You had to adjust your style and decision making in order to survive and succeed.

I was going to be damned if I was going to allow any coffee maker on the planet to take away what we created. Every single day in my office what I thought of was the 200,000 people who worked for the company and their families. They were relying on their leaders to preserve and enhance the company.

You've also taken cost control and applied innovation to that. One of the most surprising stories involves how Starbucks was losing tens of millions of dollars by pouring steamed milk down the drain. Someone

thought of an ingenious way to end that practice and save the company a lot of money. Explain how that happened.

You wouldn't think a steaming pitcher could be sexy. But it became very sexy at Starbucks. We don't want to re-steam milk because it doesn't create a good-tasting beverage for our customers. So invariably, for the past forty years, we would pour out the remaining milk after we made someone's latte or cappuccino. It was just common practice.

Someone starting to do the math on this said when we looked at every line item of cost control and cost containment, we have to go after dairy. It's almost impossible to hedge against dairy, so we started looking under the hood and we discovered this problem. An ingenious idea was to create a serrated internal ring inside the pitcher that would guide how much milk to put in for one or two cups of coffee. We stopped pouring out milk as a result of that little idea, which turned into a major opportunity to save money.

That kind of focus on efficiency eluded Starbucks in the growth years.

There was no efficiency at Starbucks. We were flying high without instruments. I say that with a smile but we shouldn't be proud of that. But growth and success cover up a lot of mistakes. It's hard to look in the rearview mirror when you are looking forward all the time. We were opening so many stores in so many markets, and everything we did for fifteen consecutive years worked. So no one ever said anything about these kinds of issues.

You know, it's never one thing that creates success. It's never one thing that causes a problem. But it does take a laser focus on what's important. The strategy now is to push for new levels of innovation and maintain the discipline and financial muscle of not allowing creep into the company's cost side.

Another good example of innovation is Via, the instant coffee you launched in 2009. There's a great story about the person who walked into one of your stores one day with a powder that he asked your store manager to try out. It was his formula for instant coffee that tasted like Starbucks. How and why did you decide to launch an instant coffee in the middle of the company's crisis?

His name was Don Valencia and he was an immunologist. He lived in Sacramento, California, and every time he went on vacation, he would go into his lab and try to crack the code on making an instant version of Starbucks. Twenty years ago, he walked into our store in Seattle, gave it to a store manager to taste, and she was blown away.

A few days later, they brought him to my office. They didn't tell me I would be served an instant cup of coffee. We sat down and the coffee was served.

And he said, "What do you think of that?"

I said, "It's great. Why?"

"It's instant."

I said, "Bullshit."

A few months later we hired Don Valencia to head up R&D at Starbucks. I should tell you that twenty years ago no one at Starbucks knew what the letters R&D meant. He created R&D at Starbucks, but was never able to commercialize the product for the scale of the company. It always broke down. He was able to do a number of other great things, including creating the core ingredient in bottled Frappuccino and blended Frappuccino. Don retired eleven years after being with the company, devoted his life to the church and Habitat for Humanity, and unfortunately was diagnosed with cancer and passed away.

When I returned as CEO I asked the now large R&D group to resurrect Don's work. Six months later, they literally brought me a patent pending process that replicated the taste, body, and acidity of a Starbucks cup of coffee. Again, the media jumped all over us and all over me. It was billed as "Another desperate move by Howard Schultz to save Starbucks. The board has got to take this guy out!"

But this is a $21 billion global category within our core business. There was no innovation to speak of for over fifty years. It was a category dominated by one company. And we thought we could crack the code on not only the taste and profile of a cup of Starbucks coffee, but also successfully bringing it to market. It's been a big success. It's turned into a new growth platform for the company.

Just like Don tried it on you, you tried it on your wife and friends on the sly.

I make morning coffee for my wife before I leave, and I would always say, "How's the coffee?" I served it at dinner parties as well. But I would never tell anyone. People loved the coffee and my wife could never tell.

How do you launch a new product like that? You're very conscious of brand equity. How did this jibe with the Starbucks experience, which is essentially in the store?

The conventional wisdom of launching an instant coffee product would have been to take it to where it is sold: the grocery channel. If this product is going to have any chance of succeeding, it has to be embraced by our people first. The first opportunity we had was to convince everyone in our stores that this was good coffee. We didn't try to sell them, but we did have rallies all over the country to introduce the coffee, tell them the story, and make sure they believed it performed in the cup.

We had many products over the years and they only failed when and if our partners didn't accept them. When they reject something, it fails. When they accept it, we win. They not only became ambassadors for it. They became zealots about the opportunity. Then, we came up with the idea of not having a taste test against a competitor. Let's taste it against our number one brewed coffee and create a national event over a four-day period where we invite everyone to come into our stores nationwide to taste it.

That's totally counterintuitive as well.

We didn't want them to view this as Starbucks' instant coffee. This is Starbucks coffee in an instant. As a result of the taste challenge, the largest majority of people couldn't tell the difference and 67 percent of the people who tasted it bought it.

The innovation went against the grain of cost cutting as well. How hard was it to do both—cutting costs and yet spending money to launch new products—at the same time?

All of this is about reinvention. You are not going to save your way or cost your way to prosperity. We have to create new exciting opportunities for our people and our customers. We have to create new levels of innovation, and we have to invest in the future of the company. The question is what to invest in? Take big bets. Make sure you've done your homework, and make sure the marketplace is ready. Despite how big Starbucks had become, we had to bring back that entrepreneurial courage and creativity and balance that with the right process and discipline. What I'm really proud of right now is that the entrepreneurial spirit is back at Starbucks and it reminds me of our early days.

During the crisis, I tried to reach out to almost anyone who would take my call. When I sat down with Jim Sinegal from Costco, he had some real solid advice that we did use. His advice was that the most important customer base in this environment is your core customer. And the cost of losing those core customers and having to spend money to get them back would be significantly higher than retaining them. So the battle plan was to maintain and retain our core customers at all costs. That was very sound advice. The Starbucks Rewards program (which rewards customers for repeat visits with free drinks and other perks) turned out to be the right strategy.

During the lowest points, where did you get the inspiration? All around you—in the media and on Wall Street—was a constant barrage of doubts. So many people were writing an obituary for Starbucks. What do you draw upon to keep you optimistic?

In many ways, this is the hardest thing I've ever had to do, coupled with the most gratifying. My kids, who are in their twenties, say, "Dad, I have never seen you have so much fun in many years." I think that's true. When you do love something, when you care as much as I do, and when you feel the responsibility, you find another gear.

It is lonely, though. There's not a lot of people to talk to. And when you have fear of failure as a motivator, it's a strong motivator. I have had fear of failure my whole life. I came from a poor family in Brooklyn. I grew up on the other side of the tracks. I also felt a sense of, "Am I good enough to do this? Am I good enough to be in that room?" It has brought out the best in me. The hardest part of the last few years was not embracing a strategy that I knew in my heart might solve a problem for a quarter or two, but in the end we would be so sorry for.

I believed the company could endure. The short answer is, fighting for survival, fighting for respect and getting up every day believing in what you're doing means a lot. I know it sounds so trite. But you are willing to do almost anything to defend what you love.

JEFF BEZOS

AMAZON

Perhaps no entrepreneur has been written off more often than Amazon.com's Jeff Bezos. Eager to be the first to write an obituary for his e-commerce business, one analyst and journalist after another has predicted the company's demise.

Back in 1997, when Barnes & Noble finally launched its rival Web site, Forrester Research chief George Colony famously claimed that Bezos's little venture would soon be "Amazon.toast." At the time, Amazon had 150 employees to Barnes & Noble's 30,000.

When the dot-com bust forced thousands of e-commerce Internet players out of business, Amazon's stock crashed, wiping out billions of dollars of market cap. And the critics emerged yet again. Some Wall Street analysts were even calling Bezos something of a fraud and urging shareholders to dump the stock. The entrepreneur just shrugged it all off.

In 2001, he showed up at PC Forum, a conference packed with leading figures in the tech business, and put up a pair of stunning slides. First, he pulled out a stock chart that showed Amazon shares falling from their $100 peak to just $6. If you look at things this way, he said, you're a pessimist. His next slide showed another stock chart. This time it charted the company's cumulative wealth creation from the day it went public for $1.50 a share until the day of the presentation when it was nearly $12. I prefer to look at it this way, Bezos told the crowd, and that's why I'm an optimist.

"If you go back in time," Bezos says, laughing, "we have been called 'Amazon.toast,' 'Amazon.con,' and 'Amazon.bomb.' And this was all in the first three years of our existence. When we were Amazon.toast, somebody wrote that we had a great two-year run, but now the big boys have shown up and they are going to steamroll us. We had an all-hands meeting with our 150 employees. Every employee had read the Amazon.toast article. In fact, every mother of every employee had read it and called to ask, 'Are you okay?'

"I said, 'Look, you should wake up worried and terrified every morning. But don't be worried about our competitors because they are never going to send us any money. Let's be worried about our customers and stay heads-down focused.' "

And that's exactly what Bezos did. In his self-professed desire to build "an important and lasting company," he put his head down and worked like mad to fulfill Amazon's mission to be "the earth's most customer-centric company." It took Amazon more than six years to report its first quarterly profit at the end of 2001. But it now is the world's largest e-commerce company, with revenues of more than $34.2 billion in 2010 and more than a billion in net profit. All this, for a company whose business plan was drafted by Bezos during a cross-country drive from New York to Seattle.

The Bezos story would be a familiar one to many entrepreneurs. His cleverness was apparent from the start when as a toddler he tried to dismantle his crib with a screwdriver. He was born in Texas, where he spent much time on his maternal grandparents' ranch doing odd jobs and helping them take care of the cattle. At home with his parents, Bezos demonstrated an intense and broad interest in a number of scientific areas, so much so that he converted the family's garage into a science laboratory, like many budding inventors. He built a cooking contraption out of an umbrella—and important for a teenager with young siblings—an alarm system from a Radio Shack electronics kit to maintain his privacy.

He went on to Princeton University with the plan to study physics, but changed his major to electrical engineering and computer sciences, graduating summa cum laude. Bezos then moved to New York to work for a high-tech start-up, where he built a computer network for financial trading. Bezos quickly moved to Bankers Trust where he became the youngest vice president, before taking off for D. E. Shaw & Co., an investment management firm, where he met the woman who would become his wife, MacKenzie. At Shaw, Bezos described his role as "sort of an entrepreneurial odd-jobs kind of a person," looking for business opportunities in the insurance, software, and Internet sectors. He excelled in the role, becoming senior vice president in 1992. It was here that the idea for Amazon came to him.

He was drawn to Seattle due to the city's large population of software engineers. It helped that Washington didn't have a state tax and that Seattle also was less than four hundred miles away from Roseburg, Oregon, home to the largest book distribution warehouse in the country, Ingram. In the garage of his rented home, Bezos and his first three employees set up computers and began writing software for the new business. He originally planned to call the company Cadabra. Fortunately, his friends convinced him that, while the name might have magic connotations, it sounded very similar to "cadaver." So Bezos opted for Amazon, after the world's largest river. The company launched in July of 1995 with a mission to use the Internet to transform book buying.

His company has done much more than that. As the world's largest retailer on the Internet, Amazon has revolutionized e-commerce and changed the very nature of the book business. Bezos helped to create the Kindle, the best selling e-book reader of all time. The incredible success of that product allowed Amazon to begin selling more digital books than those in either hardcover or paperback in 2011.

On how he came up with the idea for Amazon:

I came across the fact that Web usage was growing at 2,300 percent per year. I'd never seen or heard of anything that grew that fast, and the idea of building an online bookstore with millions of titles—something that simply couldn't exist in the physical world—was very exciting to me. I had just turned thirty years old, and I'd been married for a year. I told my wife MacKenzie that I wanted to quit my job and go do this crazy thing that probably wouldn't work since most start-ups don't, and I wasn't sure what would happen after that. MacKenzie told me I should go for it.

As a young boy, I'd been a garage inventor. I'd invented an automatic gate closer out of cement-filled tires, a solar cooker that didn't work very well out of an umbrella and tinfoil, baking-pan alarms to entrap my siblings. I'd always wanted to be an inventor, and she wanted me to follow my passion.

I was working at a financial firm in New York City with a bunch of very smart people, and I had a brilliant boss that I much admired. I went to my boss and told him I wanted to start a company selling books on the Internet. He took me on a long walk in Central Park, listened carefully to me, and finally said, "That sounds like a really good idea, but it would be an even better idea for someone who didn't already have a good job." That logic made some sense to me, and he convinced me to think about it for forty-eight hours before making a final decision.

Seen in that light, it really was a difficult choice, but ultimately, I decided I had to give it a shot. I didn't think I'd regret trying and failing. And I suspected I would always be haunted by a decision to not try at all. After much consideration, I took the less safe path to follow my passion, and I'm proud of that choice.

On Amazon's mission:

Our mission is to be earth's most customer-centric company. Right after World War II, Masaru Ibuka, the guy who founded Sony, set as the mission for Sony that they were going to make Japan known for quality. You have to remember that this was a time when Japan was known for cheap copycat products. And Masaru didn't say he was going to make Sony known for quality. He said he was going to make Japan known for quality. He chose a mission for Sony that was bigger than Sony. And when we talk about being the earth's most customer-centric company, we have a similar idea in mind. We want other companies to look at Amazon and see us as a standard bearer for an obsessive focus on the customer as opposed to an obsessive focus on the competitor.

There are three things we know are critical for a customer: low prices, vast selection, and fast, convenient, reliable delivery.

In a typical company, if you have a meeting, no matter how important it is there is always one important party who is not represented: the customer. So it's very easy inside a company to forget about the customer. Hopefully, if you were to walk around Amazon.com and ask people why do you do something this way, a lot of times I would hope you would hear because it's better for the customer.

We can customize and personalize the store for individual customers. This is something you can't do in the physical world. In the physical world, the store has to be laid out for the mythic average customer. That needn't be the case for an online store, and it shouldn't be the case. A great online merchant is going to get to know their customer the same way a small-town merchant did fifty years ago. When you come in, they are going to greet you by name and help you find the things they know you want quickly and efficiently.

On strategy:

Again, we have always had the mentality that we are going to be obsessed over our customers and not obsessed with our competitors. There are many advantages to being a competitor-focused company. You can pursue a close-following strategy. You don't have to go down a bunch of blind alleys when you are inventing. You can just follow the leader. Let them spend all the investment resources to go down the blind alleys and when they do something that works you can follow them quickly. That can be an effective business strategy but that is not what we do.

If you base your business strategy on things that are going to change, then you have to constantly change your strategy. But if you formulate your strategy around customer needs, those tend to be stable in time.

The impact of the Internet on selling:

The balance of power online moves away from the merchant and toward the consumer. This is because customers have better information online. Comparison shopping is just a click away. In the physical world, nobody is going to drive to two different stores to save a dollar. There may be a few such people but they need some help. But in the online world, that's easy. You just click and go to a store.

So customers have great information and they have a powerful megaphone—the Internet itself—to express their displeasure if someone lets them down. If we make a customer unhappy they don't tell a few friends as they would in the old world. They tell five thousand friends. The good news is if you understand this you can also work very hard on customer experience and turn customers into evangelists. Then they can use that megaphone to actually promote your service. Word of mouth is such a good amplifier.

On the Internet, word of mouth is more powerful than it has ever been before. On the Internet, everybody buys ink by the barrel. Everybody has opinions and they share them—on blogs, on social networking sites, by e-mail, text messages, and so on. This is a very powerful and positive phenomenon for society.

In the old world you wanted to take 30 percent of your energy, time, and dollars and focus that on customer experience and put 70 percent on marketing. In the new online world you flip that around. You want to spend 70 percent of your time on customer experience and 30 percent shouting about it. You still have to do both but the emphasis changes.

On why it's not enough to merely listen to your customers:

It is not enough to only listen to your customers, but you also need to invent on your customer's behalf. It's not the customer's job to invent on his or her own behalf. There are two ways to extend. One is to take an inventory of your skills and what you're good at and then extend from your skills. The second is to look at customers and determine what they need, even if it requires you to get new skills. Kindle is a great example of working backward from the customer need, because what we really saw was that there were a few different technologies that were converging and becoming mature enough so that we could meld them together and create a whole end-to-end service that became the Kindle and the underlying store that all works together.

I had been selling e-books for a long time. No one was buying them. And then, after three years of work, we came out with the Kindle. What we realized at the time is that there were a few technologies that were converging. If we could combine them together in the right recipe, it would be transformative in the world of electronic reading. For me, one of the most interesting questions was why hadn't books been digitized earlier. The physical book is highly evolved and so elegantly suited to its purpose that it is hard to improve on. It isn't like some other artifact or object. It is something that is very, very emotional and personal for people.

But the book has a feature, which I think is hard to notice but it is the book's most important feature: it disappears. When you're reading, you don't notice the paper, the ink, the glue and the stitching. They enter a mental flow-state. All of that dissolves and what remains is the author's world. The ability for a book to disappear became our top design objective for Kindle. We knew that if we couldn't replicate that aspect of a book, nobody would use this device.

We also knew we had to go beyond the book (with features that include looking up definitions of words, searching the text, and bookmarking pages) but one thing you couldn't do is out-book the book. By that I mean we have to look for things that we can do that you could never do with a paper book. We would always get asked in the early days, How are you going to do virtual book signings? Well, we never figured that out. Instead, we've done things that physical bookstores could never do like customer reviews. You have to play to your strengths, like customers who bought this also bought that. That is another thing that a physical bookstore can't do.

Any physical retailer who isn't focused on creating an extremely compelling experience using the physical medium will be in trouble. Physical retailers will not be able to compete with online retailers with respect to price. If you look at the economics, it just doesn't work. That doesn't mean that physical retailing isn't going to continue and flourish. In fact, what is going to happen is that online retailers are going to make physical retailers become better. The stores are going to be cleaner; the sales associates will be friendlier. The decor will be more entertaining. You'll see a big transformation here over the next twenty years.

The physical world is the best medium ever created. This is why Disney World is so successful. Real space is the best and people evolved in that medium. That's where we grew up as a species. Technology has to get way better before that changes. The people who predicted that the movie theaters were going to go out of business when the television came along were dead wrong. Then they said that when the VCR came out, well this time for sure. I hear it again now for DVDs and home theater systems. The people who predict that don't understand human nature. We are a gregarious species. We like to get together.

On taking time away from the job to think:

After the end of every quarter, I usually go away for a few days. I try to isolate myself from everything. It's just because with a little bit of isolation I find I start to get more creative. I do spend a lot of time Web surfing during those two or three days and just looking at what hobbyists and hackers are doing. What are the sorts of things that are on the cutting edge, and then I will usually write two- or three-page documents, just memos. Sometimes they are just memos to myself. For me, that's a very valuable time. Doing it once a quarter is the right kind of metronome. I just lock myself away. There are no distractions from the office. No phones ringing.

I have certainly come up with principles, themes, big directions, even certain tactical inventions during these days. The important thing is I bring them back to the office and socialize those things with the broader executive team. What I find is by the time that process is done, I'm never really sure if I invented anything or not because it starts here and ends up there. That's what you want if you have a bunch of smart people. Somebody says, "Well, that will never work because you forgot *x*, *y*, and *z*." And then you step back and recognize that's true and then it morphs and builds.

One of the things we're doing right now came out of one of these retreats. It's called Fulfillment by Amazon. We let our third-party sellers take their inventory and send it to us. We stow it in our fulfillment centers and we do the fulfillment for them. They still own the inventory but stow it in our fulfillment center. The great thing about it is that it provides better customer service. If you order two things, they will come in one box. It saves on transportation costs. This is a service that is great for the sellers because if you are a small seller, they can't take a vacation because if they do it's unpaid. There is no one there to ship the products.

On Amazon's disappointments:

We have had many failures. If you want to be inventive, you have to be willing to fail because you have to be willing to do experiments. And it's not an experiment if you know in advance it's going to work. For example, we licensed Web search from Google and launched a different user interface called A9.com and tried that for three years and nobody came and a couple of years ago we shut it down. I couldn't even get my mom to use it. You try these things. They don't always work.

Go back in time further than that and we launched Amazon auctions. We could never get auctions to work. Now the good news was that auctions led ultimately to our third-party sales business with fixed prices. We have done it in our own way and one of the things I've noticed on the Internet is that me-too companies tend not to do very well. If somebody has a different way of doing something that can be successful. But if you just try to do it as a me-too offering and customers are already doing something with someone else, why would they do it with you?

On dealing with Wall Street as a public company:

With respect to investors, there's a great Warren Buffettism. You can hold a rock concert and that can be successful, and you can hold a ballet and that can be successful, but don't hold a rock concert and advertise it as a ballet. If you're very clear to the outside world that you're taking a long-term approach, then people can self-select in. You get shareholders who want you to relentlessly lower prices. As Buffett says, you get the shareholders you deserve.

On international markets:

We have discovered that every time we enter a new country, on the big things people are the same everywhere. People want low prices. You never go to a new country and hear, "Oh, I love Amazon. I wish the prices were high."

They all want vast selection, and they all want accurate, fast, convenient delivery. There are always small things that are different. Our starting point is, "Let's just assume that people are very similar all over the world." When we entered Japan, we were told customer reviews would never work. People in Japan just won't write customer reviews. I said, "Well, let's just try it." And of course they wrote customer reviews, just like people everywhere in the world. You have to be very careful.

Companies have tendencies to over-exaggerate the differences in different geographies. There are things that are different. For example, in China, a lot of our payment is done by cash on delivery instead of with credit cards because credit card penetration is not very high in China. We have to have a network of regional fulfillment centers. We employ our own bicycle couriers in China. We have to adapt to local business conditions. But what customers want is the same.

On being in the trenches:

I've not seen an effective manager or leader who can't spend some fraction of time down in the trenches. If they don't do that, they get out of touch with reality, and their whole thought and management process becomes abstract and disconnected.

On the difference between a gift and a choice:

As a kid, I spent my summers with my grandparents on their ranch in Texas. I helped fix windmills, vaccinate cattle, and do other chores. We also watched soap operas every afternoon, especially *Days of Our Lives*. My grandparents belonged to a Caravan Club, a group of Airstream trailer owners who travel together around the United States and Canada. And every few summers, we'd join the caravan. We'd hitch up the Airstream trailer to my grandfather's car, and off we'd go, in a line with three hundred other Airstream adventurers. I loved and worshipped my grandparents and I really looked forward to these trips. On one particular trip, I was about ten years old. I was rolling around in the big bench seat in the back of the car. My grandfather was driving. And my grandmother had the passenger seat. She smoked throughout these trips, and I hated the smell.

At that age, I'd take any excuse to make estimates and do minor arithmetic. I'd calculate our gas mileage—figure out useless statistics on things like grocery spending. I'd been hearing an ad campaign about smoking. I can't remember the details, but basically the ad said, every puff of a cigarette takes some number of minutes off of your life: I think it might have been two minutes per puff. At any rate, I decided to do the math for my grandmother. I estimated the number of cigarettes per day, estimated the number of puffs per cigarette, and so on. When I was satisfied that I'd come up with a reasonable number, I poked my head into the front of the car, tapped my grandmother on the shoulder, and proudly proclaimed, "At two minutes per puff, you've taken nine years off your life!"

I have a vivid memory of what happened, and it was not what I expected. I expected to be applauded for my cleverness and arithmetic skills. "Jeff, you're so smart. You had to have made some tricky estimates, figure out the number of minutes in a year, and do some division." That's not what happened. Instead, my grandmother burst into tears. I sat in the backseat and did not know what to do. While my grandmother sat crying, my grandfather, who had been driving in silence, pulled over onto the shoulder of the highway. He got out of the car and came around and opened my door and waited for me to follow. Was I in trouble? My grandfather was a highly intelligent, quiet man. He had never said a harsh word to me, and maybe this was to be the first time? Or maybe he would ask that I get back in the car and apologize to my grandmother. I had no experience in this realm with my grandparents and no way to gauge what the consequences might be. We stopped beside the trailer. My grandfather looked at me, and after a bit of silence, he gently and calmly said, "Jeff, one day you'll understand that it's harder to be kind than clever."

Cleverness is a gift. Kindness is a choice. Gifts are easy—they're given after all. Choices can be hard. You can seduce yourself with your gifts if you're not careful, and if you do, it'll probably be to the detriment of your choices.

HERB KELLEHER

SOUTHWEST AIRLINES

I f you were writing the script for a movie on entrepreneurship, you might be tempted to open the first scene with a shot of two friends huddled together at a bar sketching out their ideas for a new business on a cocktail napkin. The business that would come from it would then be one of the most successful enterprises ever created, generating more wealth for investors than any other company for more than twenty years.

Trouble is, no one would believe it.

Yet that's exactly what happened when attorney Herb Kelleher and Rollin King got together in 1966 at the bar of the St. Anthony's Club in San Antonio. The napkin scrawls outlined a plan to create a low-fare airline in Texas. When King initially suggested the idea, Kelleher's immediate reply was none too promising: "Well, that sounds kind of nutty to me."

In those days, the airline industry was heavily regulated, and all the entrenched carriers would do everything and anything to keep newcomers out. But there was a loophole in the law, allowing for the creation of an airline that would fly only intrastate routes.

So Kelleher put in $10,000 of his own money to get Southwest Airlines started and then spent the first ten years of the company's life defending Southwest against lawsuits from existing competitors Braniff Airways and Texas International. "It was like all of the hounds of the Baskervilles were simultaneously ripping and nipping at us," he remembers. "One of the papers at the time said, 'Don't bother spending your money on a movie or going to see a play or attending a concert. Just come over and watch Herb Kelleher and the lawyers for Braniff and Texas International cut each other into little bits and pieces.'"

Three years into the battle, Southwest ran out of money. "The board of directors said, 'Let's just shut this down.' And I said, 'I'll pay all the costs out of my own pocket and work for nothing to see if we can get this thing going.' And fortunately, it did go."

"Go" is one of the most understated ways to describe what next occurred. Though it took five long years from the meeting in the bar to the first flight in June of 1971, Southwest turned out to be one of the greatest entrepreneurial stories ever written. In an industry plagued by fare wars, recessions, and skyrocketing fuel costs that have led to vast amounts of red ink, Southwest marked its thirty-eighth consecutive year of profitability in 2010, a feat unmatched in U.S. aviation history. Now the largest U.S. domestic airline, Southwest totes up more than $12 billion in annual revenues, boasts thirty-five thousand employees, and flies to seventy-two cities. No less important, one analyst noted that the airline has been responsible for 90 percent of all of the low-fare competition that exists in America.

Kelleher, now retired from the airline, long set the pace for what had become known as one of the most enjoyable places to work in America. He was the embodiment of the company's fun culture, known to dress up as Elvis for corporate events, help with baggage handling during the holidays, and hand out Wild Turkey bourbon during flights.

For such an outsized, fun-loving person, you would never have guessed that tragedy found Kelleher early. His father, general manager of a Campbell Soup plant in New Jersey, died when he was all of twelve years of age. One of Kelleher's brothers was killed in World War II. His sister went to work in New York, leaving Kelleher and his mom at home. It was not unusual, he recalls, for his mother to stay up until four in the morning engaged in deep conversations with him. "She talked a lot about how you should treat people with respect," recalls Kelleher. "She said that positions and titles signify absolutely nothing. They're just adornments; they don't represent the substance of anybody. I was kind of her disciple. She taught me that every person and every job is worth as much as any other person and any other job."

When he took an aptitude test at Wesleyan University, where he was majoring in English, Kelleher discovered that there were three things he was best suited for: being a journalist, an editor, or a lawyer. He chose law, going to New York University Law School, and found it "exceedingly valuable training. Find out what the facts are, not gossip. Identify what the issue is, then find a resolution. That's helpful in anything you do in life."

It certainly prepared him, especially for all those years of litigation to get Southwest off the ground. Even after the company was flying its first routes, the cofounder continued to practice law, becoming chairman of Southwest in 1978. But it wasn't until early 1982 that Kelleher moved over full-time as chief executive. By the time he left the top job in 2001, the company's market capitalization was larger than American's, United's, and Continental's combined—and Kelleher had become an entrepreneurial legend.

On culture:

The business of business is people. In a lot of companies you have to surrender your personality when you show up for work. People think you're not really being serious and diligent and applying yourself the way you should unless you look like an automaton. We never felt that way. We always felt that if you allow people to be themselves at work, they will enjoy what they are doing. They'll be more productive as a consequence of enjoying it. Another thing we've done is we don't think you should just be interested in people for their work persona. We take a great interest in their personal lives as well. There is no one at Southwest Airlines who has any significant event in his life, be it good or bad, a birth or a death, who doesn't hear from us.

We've always tried to be sensitive to the needs of our people and recognize the things that are important to them in their personal lives.

At Southwest Airlines, you can't have a baby without being recognized— getting communication from the general office. You can't have a death in your family without hearing from us. If you're out with a serious illness, we're in touch with you once every two weeks to see how you're doing. We have people who have been retired for ten years, and we keep in touch with them. We want them to know that we value them as individuals, not just as workers. So that's part of the esprit de corps.

And then, we put in the first profit-sharing plan in the airline industry. Our people were very cognizant that they were owners. And there are two stories that I just love. Western Airlines asked to borrow a stapler in Los Angeles, and our customer-service agent went over with the stapler to their counter, and the Western ticket agent said, "Why are you waiting?" He said, "Because I want the stapler back. That affects our profit sharing."

Another classic was down in San Antonio, when one of our customers was railing at one of our customer-service agents and said, "Don't you know I'm a shareholder of Southwest Airlines?" And the customer-service agent looked at her and said: "Lady, we all are."

That was powerful. [Yet] we've never thought that compensation was the primary motivator. If somebody was working just to be compensated, we probably didn't want them at Southwest Airlines. We wanted them working in order to do something in an excellent way. And to serve people.

So we said to employees: "This is a cause, this is a crusade. This isn't just an ordinary corporation, and you're doing a lot of good for everybody. We're proud of you, and we want you to have psychic satisfaction when you come to work." We get people who take a 25 percent cut in pay because they say: We just want to enjoy what we're doing.

They've done pretty well with their 401(k) and stock options. But those are variable. People are willing to take that risk and take lower pay because they want to feel fulfilled in the workplace.

A ramp agent from Oklahoma wrote me one time and said: "Herb, I'm on to what you're doing." He said: "You're making work fun—and home work."

On managing and leading:

We tell people if you want a suggestion box you have identified yourself as a failure as a manager because really if you were talking to your people the way you should you don't need a box. A box is a way of establishing distance between people, not bringing them together. We've always operated on the thesis that a company can have a personality and people can be themselves.

Years ago the business schools used to pose it as a conundrum. They would say, "Well, who comes first? Your employees, your shareholders, or your customers?" But it's not a conundrum. Your customers come first. And if you treat your employees right, guess what? Your customers come back and that makes your shareholders happy. Start with the employees and the rest follows from that. And of course you have to find the right people with wonderful attitudes. We did a lot of digging (for the right people).

I was talking at the Yale Graduate School of Business some years ago. In the Q&A session, one of the students stood up and said, "It seems to me you're talking more about a religion than a business." And I said, "If you feel that way about your business, I think that's good. That's a plus."

The word *power* really aggravates me. The word *power* should only be used in connection with weight lifting and speedboats. Forget about power. Think about nurturing and growing people and giving them the opportunity to do a lot of different things. It's amazing how many businesses slot people. And once you're in a slot, that's it. It's like the post office. The letter goes into that slot and that's where it remains. But people have greater potential and far greater capabilities than you'll ever realize unless you give them the freedom to go into areas and to experiment with different things. We had some people come to us one day and they met with three of our folks on a very complex systems issue. After they left they called me and said, "Herb, we were tremendously impressed with the people who represented Southwest during this meeting." I said, "Well, it may interest you to know that not one of them has a college degree." Collegiality and fluidity is how Southwest works.

On hiring the right people:

We are probably more religious about hiring than many priesthoods. Hiring well is a religion at Southwest. We have a People Department. Not human resources, which sounds as if it's mining coal or steel. So one day somebody in our People Department comes to me and says, "Herb, I'm getting a little embarrassed because I've interviewed 34 people for a ramp-agent position in Amarillo." You know what my response was? "If you have to interview 134 people to find the appropriate person to be a ramp agent in

Amarillo, do it." Because the most important thing is to get the right people, and if you get the wrong ones, they start poisoning everybody else.

If someone is not comfortable with our culture it's probably best to part ways. Then we try to assist people in any way that we can.

We have a good many MBAs, but we look at them for attitude as well [as business smarts]. We will hire someone with less experience, less education, and less expertise than someone who has more of those things and has a rotten attitude. Because we can train people. We can teach people how to lead. We can teach people how to provide customer service. But we can't change their DNA.

You might say that we tend to hire humble MBAs—people who think they're just starting out on their career and have a lot to learn. Like any lawyer will tell you, it takes at least five years to become a really good practitioner. And that's why we look for humble MBAs. They understand they have to get to know the operations of the company, to get to know how we treat people. They have to know how to handle customers. And once they've done all that, then they're ready to start doing planning and all those other things.

On why Southwest has been so successful:

First of all, low costs are very important, but if you don't have a lot of capital, you can't fight a war of attrition. And we're the strongest airline in the industry financially. So if somebody wants to charge the same fares as we do with higher costs and lose money, that's fine. If they want to fight a war, we're ready to go two years or five years or ten years—whatever it takes—in order to be successful.

But it's not just the low fares. We have the best customer-satisfaction record, based on Transportation Department statistics, of any airline in America, the fewest complaints filed per 100,000 passengers carried. So you're not just getting low fares, you're also getting wonderful customer service. One thing I tell our people is that the intangibles are much more important than the tangibles because anybody can buy the tangibles, but nobody can replicate the intangibles very easily. And I'm talking about the joie de vivre—the spirit of our people.

When deregulation took place, our fabulous Austin advertising agency, GSD&M—otherwise known as Greed, Sex, Drugs, and Money, for what reasons, I have no idea—said to me: "Herb, now we have deregulation.

Anybody can fly anyplace they want to. They can charge anything they want to. What's special about Southwest Airlines?"

I said: "Our people." And that was the origin of the "Spirit of Southwest Airlines" campaign. Now, that's a big risk because you know what you're doing in the newspapers? In the magazines? On television, on radio? You're telling all your prospective customers: Our people are the best. They're warm. They're hospitable. They're happy to see you. They want to help you.

If you're wrong, you slit your own throat. We've gotten one complaint in five years that said: Southwest Airlines employees aren't that way. But here's the kind of letter that we got: "Herb, I went through El Paso the other day, and I was sold a ticket by a customer-service agent who just isn't like Southwest Airlines. There is something wrong with this agent."

You see the distinction? Not that Southwest Airlines is a bad apple, but this person is a bad apple, and I don't understand how you can allow that person to continue to work for you. And so, it was proven in the field through that kind of exposure that our people are special.

A guy calls our Dallas reservation center from St. Louis, and he tells the reservation agent that TWA has canceled its flight out of DFW [Dallas–Fort Worth airport] to St. Louis on which his eighty-five-year-old mother was supposed to fly, and that he's very concerned about her coming over to Love Field after having to make an intermediate connection in Tulsa. So the reservation agent says: "I'm going to be off in five minutes. I'll pick her up at DFW, drive her to Love Field, and fly with her to St. Louis to make sure that she gets there okay."

That's the kind of devotion I'm talking about.

A guy has a heart attack at Love Field. He goes to the hospital. Our ticket agent stays there all night, calling his wife to let her know how he's doing. I got a letter from a passenger on another airline who said, "Herb, I couldn't believe it. I had gotten off the airline, went to the parking lot, and I had a flat tire. And one of your people came along and changed the tire for me, and I said, 'You know I didn't fly Southwest Airlines.' He said: "I don't care.'" That has nothing to do with whether you fly Southwest Airlines. That's the kind of folks that we want.

We say everybody is a leader, no matter what your job is. We want you to focus on customer service—and not just to the outside world—[we want] customer service to the inside world. If [employees] pollute our other people internally and they in turn savage the people who are doing the work outside, the whole company has just rotted.

On giving employees equity:

All the employees at Southwest Airlines get stock options because we feel that everybody, no matter where they work or what they do, should have an ownership position in the company. And we have seven, I think— or maybe eight—collective-bargaining agreements with our unions.

We're the most heavily unionized airline in America that also has a stock-option base. [Employees] get options as part of their union contract, and they've done pretty well. I flew into San Antonio once, and Connie, who's been working there for a good many years—about fifteen, I guess— said, "Herb, can I talk to you alone?"

"Sure," I said.

And she said, "My stock is down to $1.2 million. Are you going to do something about that?"

I try. We had a pilot who just retired and took with him $8 million in profit sharing, not including his 401(k).

And when you look at the expense of an option, what is it? If the options are underwater, they have no cost because no one ever exercises them. If they do exceed the strike price, then all the other shareholders benefit enormously.

It used to be that stock options made people owners—aligned them with the goals of the corporation. And everybody worked harder and better together as a consequence.

Then all of a sudden, they fell into disfavor. I suspect because some companies, particularly in high tech, were handing them out 100 million at a time.

On layoffs:

The thing that would disturb me most to see is layoffs at Southwest. Nothing kills your company's culture like layoffs. Nobody has ever been furloughed here, and that is unprecedented in the airline industry. It's been a huge strength of ours. It's certainly helped us negotiate our union contracts. One of the union leaders—a Teamsters leader—came in to negotiate one time and he said, "We know we don't need to talk with you about job security."

We could have furloughed at various times and been more profitable, but I always thought that was shortsighted. You want to show your people that you value them and you're not going to hurt them just to get a little more money in the short term. Not furloughing people breeds loyalty. It breeds a sense of security. It breeds a sense of trust. So in bad times you take care of them, and in good times they're thinking, perhaps, "We've never lost our jobs. That's a pretty good reason to stick around."

On Wall Street:

It wasn't just the other airlines that were contemptuous of what we were doing. The New York financial community was as well. Every time I'd go up there, they'd give me a lecture, and they'd say, "Well, Herb, now that we're deregulated, you've got to be just like the other airlines." And I said, "No, I don't think so."

And after about maybe nine or ten years, [an analyst] with Credit Suisse First Boston got up at an investor seminar and said, "For ten years we've been telling Herb Kelleher how to run Southwest Airlines, and for ten years he's been telling us to bug off. Since they're the most profitable airline in America, how about if we all bug off?" But nobody believed that it would work, and the other carriers thought that we were just an annoyance, not something permanent.

There were only two carriers that supported deregulation—United, which was the biggest, and Southwest, which was the smallest.

I was so amused because people in Washington would say, "We understand why United is for this, but you, little bug, why do you support it?" And I said: "Well, I think we've demonstrated in Texas that we can compete pretty well against the other airlines, and we'd just like more latitude to do that." And then I got a letter from a Texas congressman who said, "Herb, I want to tell you something. You're going to ruin Southwest Airlines if you take it beyond the boundaries of Texas."

So I wrote back and said, "Congressman, I beg to remind you that man, not God, created the boundaries of Texas." And you know what his response was? "Dear Herb, Are you sure?"

On launching a company today:

I think it was easier to be an entrepreneur in the thirties than it was in the sixties and seventies, and I think it was easier in the 1890s than it was in the thirties. As society becomes more regulated, it becomes more difficult to launch entrepreneurial ventures.

Well, when I started practicing law, maybe 5 percent of a law firm's business was dealing with the government [and the rest with clients]. Today, it's only 50 percent or 60 percent on behalf of clients.

So I would say that it's harder today—but not impossible. You must be very patient, very persistent. The world isn't going to shower gold coins on you just because you have a good idea. You're going to have to work like crazy to bring that idea to the attention of people. They're not going to buy it unless they know about it.

You're going to have to have probably five times as much capital as you thought you would. Because if you're an entrepreneur, you're optimistic by nature. So you think, in six months, we're going to be sailing. But that optimism causes you to raise a lot less capital than you need in most cases, and it's very lonely.

Everybody in Texas would tell me that they thought I was nuts trying to start Southwest Airlines. There probably weren't ten people in the state who would have given a plug nickel for our chances of making a dollar. So sometimes, you need a little courage, too, just to buck popular opinion.

STEVE JOBS

APPLE

" I think you're bad for Apple and I think you're the wrong person to run this company. You really should leave this company. I'm more worried about Apple than I have ever been. I'm afraid of you. You don't know how to operate and never have."

The words came out of Steve Jobs's mouth slowly, almost quietly, in a tense but controlled voice. It was May 24, 1985, and the most celebrated entrepreneur of our time was addressing his handpicked CEO, John Sculley, in the company's boardroom at an executive staff meeting.

With the enthusiastic encouragement of the board of directors, Jobs had brought Sculley into Apple two years earlier from PepsiCo, where he had been president. But the partnership that had been heralded in the media as "The Dynamic Duo" had fallen apart.

"John," Jobs went on, getting more wound up, "you manage by monologue! You have no understanding of the product development process. You don't know how manufacturing works. You're not close to the computer.

The middle managers don't respect you. In the first year, you helped build the company, but in the second, you hurt the company."

For Jobs, it was the beginning of the end. His attempt to turn the company's executives and then the board against Sculley backfired. Instead, they backed the man who had become his adversary and supported the decision to remove Jobs from his day-to-day management role. Jobs would be relegated to the position of chairman, moved out of his office into a different building, to work on "new product innovations and strategies." Within four months, Jobs would resign.

What happened to Steve Jobs in the mid-1980s is every entrepreneur's worst nightmare. The company you pour your best sweat, blood, and tears into is stolen from you because the "professional manager" recruited to help build your organization wants you out—or perhaps the investors you counted on for vital capital in the early days believe the company has grown beyond your ability to manage it.

It has been said that it is easy to do anything in victory. It's only in defeat that a man reveals himself. Pushed aside in his own company, Jobs understandably showed himself to be a highly bitter person, but also a remarkably resilient one who threw himself into his work.

At the time, a devastated Jobs told an interviewer: "I hired the wrong guy. He destroyed everything I had spent ten years working for, starting with me, but that wasn't the saddest part. I would have gladly left Apple if Apple had turned out how I wanted it to. I feel like somebody punched me in the stomach and knocked all my wind out. I am only thirty years old and I want to have a chance to continue creating things."

From the sidelines, at other companies he formed from NeXT Computer to Pixar Animation, he watched as Apple fell apart. "What ruined Apple wasn't growth," Jobs said. "What ruined Apple was values. John Sculley ruined Apple, and he ruined it by bringing a set of values to the top of Apple which were corrupt and corrupted some of the top people who were there, drove out some of the ones who were not corruptible, and brought in more corrupt ones, and then collectively paid themselves tens of millions of dollars. [They] cared more about their own glory and wealth than they did about what built Apple in the first place—which was making great computers for people to use."

Yet Jobs's departure from Apple in 1985 set the stage for one of the most unlikely comebacks in the history of business. The arc of this narrative ranks with any story ever put to paper by Shakespeare. It is literally the stuff of dreams, an entrepreneurial journey that is as improbable as the sun setting in the east.

It would take eleven years before Jobs would return, years in which a long accumulation of bad decisions by a succession of chief executives would nearly bankrupt the company. It was only when Apple barely had a pulse left that Jobs was invited back as interim chief executive in 1996.

"It was on the rocks," recalls Jobs. "Apple was about ninety days from going bankrupt back then. It was much worse than I thought when I went back. I expected that all the good people would have left. But I found these miraculous people there, these great people. I tried to ask this as tactfully as I could: 'Why are you still here?' A lot of them had this little phrase. They said, 'Because I bleed in six colors.' Which was the old six-color Apple logo. That was code for 'I loved what this place stood for.' That just made all of us want to work that much harder to have it survive and bring it back."

The rest is, as they say, history—and very public history at that: the reemergence of the Mac in both desktop and laptop forms, the unprecedented successful launches of the Apple retail store, iPod, iTunes, iPhone, and iPad. Apple has gone from a floundering enterprise losing $1 billion a year to one of the most profitable, admired, and most valuable corporations in the world, with more than $100 billion in annual revenue.

Steve Jobs, meantime, has become the quintessential American entrepreneur, worshipped all over the world as a visionary, a genius, and a business savior. He had been worth over $1 million when he was twenty-three; over $10 million when he was twenty-four; and over $100 million when he was twenty-five and said it really didn't matter to him at all. Now Jobs, who works as chairman for only $1 a year at Apple, is worth more than $8 billion. In August of 2011, Jobs shocked the world when at the age of fifty-six he resigned his role as CEO after years of health problems. He had been diagnosed in 2004 with pancreatic cancer, which later spread to his liver and required a liver transplant. Though Jobs did not elaborate on his reasons for stepping down, many worried that his health had taken a turn for the worse. "I have always said if there ever came a day when I could no longer meet my duties and expectations as Apple's CEO, I would be the first to let you know," Jobs wrote in his resignation letter to the board of directors. "Unfortunately, that day has come."

For Jobs, it has been a long and endlessly fascinating journey. A child of the sixties, he vividly recalls spending restless nights, tossing and turning, in the midst of the Cuban Missile Crisis in 1962. "I was afraid that if I went to sleep I wouldn't wake up," he said. And he clearly remembers walking across the grass of his schoolyard in Mountain View, California, all of eight years old, when he heard someone shout that President John F. Kennedy had been shot and killed.

His father Paul, a machinist who never graduated from high school, sectioned off a portion of his workbench in the garage to allow his son to tinker with things. But it was a Hewlett-Packard engineer who lived just a few houses down the street who eventually turned Jobs on to electronics. Jobs would eventually work as a summer employee for Hewlett-Packard, where he would meet the geeky but tech-savvy Steve Wozniak, who would later become the cofounder of Apple. Jobs was just sixteen years old at the time; Wozniak was twenty-one.

In 1972, Jobs graduated from high school and enrolled at Reed College in Portland, Oregon, but quit after just one semester. He stayed a bit longer, however, auditing classes at Reed while sleeping on the floor in the apartments of friends, returning Coke bottles for food money, and going to the local Hare Krishna temple for free meals. In the fall of 1974, Jobs returned to California, landed a job as a technician at video games maker Atari, and began attending meetings of the Homebrew Computer Club with Wozniak.

It wasn't until 1976 that the pair founded Apple based on a crude personal computer mashed together by Wozniak. They previewed the hand-built machine at the Homebrew Club in May of that year and quickly landed an order for fifty of them from the owner of a local computer store who agreed to pay $500 for each machine.

A business was born and so was one of America's greatest entrepreneurs.

On connecting the dots:

I dropped out of Reed College after the first six months, but then stayed around as a drop-in for another eighteen months or so before I really quit. So why did I drop out?

It started before I was born. My biological mother was a young, unwed college graduate student, and she decided to put me up for adoption. She felt very strongly that I should be adopted by college graduates, so everything was all set for me to be adopted at birth by a lawyer and his wife. Except that when I popped out they decided at the last minute that they really wanted a girl. So my parents, who were on a waiting list, got a call in the middle of the night asking: "We have an unexpected baby boy; do you want him?" They said: "Of course." My biological mother later found out that my mother had never graduated from college and that my father had never graduated from high school. She refused to sign the final adoption papers. She only relented a few months later when my parents promised that I would someday go to college.

And seventeen years later I did go to college. But I naively chose a college that was almost as expensive as Stanford, and all of my working-class parents' savings were being spent on my college tuition. After six months, I couldn't see the value in it. I had no idea what I wanted to do with my life and no idea how college was going to help me figure it out. And here I was spending all of the money my parents had saved their entire life. So I decided to drop out and trust that it would all work out okay. It was pretty scary at the time, but looking back it was one of the best decisions I ever made. The minute I dropped out I could stop taking the required classes that didn't interest me, and begin dropping in on the ones that looked interesting.

It wasn't all romantic. I didn't have a dorm room, so I slept on the floor in friends' rooms, I returned Coke bottles for the five-cent deposits to buy food with, and I would walk the seven miles across town every Sunday night to get one good meal a week at the Hare Krishna temple. I loved it. And much of what I stumbled into by following my curiosity and intuition turned out to be priceless later on.

Let me give you one example: Reed College at that time offered perhaps the best calligraphy instruction in the country. Throughout the campus every poster, every label on every drawer, was beautifully hand calligraphed. Because I had dropped out and didn't have to take the normal classes, I decided to take a calligraphy class to learn how to do this. I learned about serif and sans serif typefaces, about varying the amount of space between different letter combinations, about what makes great typography great. It was beautiful, historical, artistically subtle in a way that science can't capture, and I found it fascinating.

None of this had even a hope of any practical application in my life. But ten years later, when we were designing the first Macintosh computer, it all came back to me. And we designed it all into the Mac. It was the first computer with beautiful typography. If I had never dropped in on that single course in college, the Mac would have never had multiple typefaces or proportionally spaced fonts. And since Windows just copied the Mac, it's likely that no personal computer would have them. If I had never dropped out, I would have never dropped in on this calligraphy class, and personal computers might not have the wonderful typography that they do. Of course it was impossible to connect the dots looking forward when I was in college. But it was very, very clear looking backward ten years later.

Again, you can't connect the dots looking forward; you can only connect them looking backward. So you have to trust that the dots will somehow connect in your future. You have to trust in something—your gut, destiny, life, karma, whatever. This approach has never let me down, and it has made all the difference in my life.

On innovation:

It comes down to trying to expose yourself to the best things that humans have done and then trying to bring those things into what you're doing. Picasso had a saying: "Good artists copy, great artists steal." We have always been shameless about stealing great ideas. Part of what made the Macintosh great was the people who were working on it were musicians, poets, artists, historians, zoologists, who also happened to be the best computer scientists in the world.

On business models:

My model for business is the Beatles: They were four guys that kept each other's negative tendencies in check; they balanced each other. And the total was greater than the sum of the parts. Great things in business are not done by one person; they are done by a team of people.

On new possibilities:

One might sometimes say in despair no, but I think yes. And the reason is because human minds settle into fixed ways of looking at the world and that's always been true and it's probably always going to be true. I've always felt that death is the greatest invention of life. I'm sure that life evolved without death at first and found that without death, life didn't work very well because it didn't make room for the young. It didn't know how the world was fifty years ago. It didn't know how the world was twenty years ago. It saw it as it is today, without any preconceptions, and dreamed how it could be based on that. We're not satisfied based on the accomplishment of the last thirty years. We're dissatisfied because the current state didn't live up to their ideals. Without death there would be very little progress.

One of the things that happens in organizations as well as with people is that they settle into ways of looking at the world and become satisfied with things and the world changes and keeps evolving and new potential arises but these people who are settled in don't see it. That's what gives start-up companies their greatest advantage. The sedentary point of view is that of most large companies. In addition to that, large companies do not usually have efficient communication paths from the people closest to some of these changes at the bottom of the company to the top of the company which are the people making the big decisions.

There may be people at lower levels of the company that see these changes coming, but by the time the word ripples up to the highest levels where they can do something about it, it sometimes takes ten years. Even in the case where part of the company does the right thing at the lower levels, usually the upper levels screw it up somehow. I mean IBM and the personal computer business is a good example of that. I think as long as humans don't solve this human nature trait of sort of settling into a world-view, after a while there will always be opportunity for young companies (and) young people to innovate. As it should be.

On entrepreneurship:

A lot of people come to me and say "I want to be an entrepreneur." And I go, "Oh, that's great, what's your idea?" And they say, "I don't have one yet." And I say, "I think you should go get a job as a busboy or something until you find something you're really passionate about because it's a lot of work." I'm convinced that about half of what separates the successful entrepreneurs from the nonsuccessful ones is pure perseverance.

It is so hard. You put so much of your life into this thing. There are such rough moments in time that I think most people give up. I don't blame them. It's really tough and it consumes your life. If you've got a family and you're in the early days of a company, I can't imagine how one could do it. I'm sure it's been done but it's rough. It's pretty much an eighteen-hour day job, seven days a week for a while. Unless you have a lot of passion about this, you're not going to survive. You're going to give it up. So you've got to have an idea, or a problem or a wrong that you want to right that you're passionate about. Otherwise you're not going to have the perseverance to stick it through. I think that's half the battle right there.

On his ultimate goal:

Our goal is to make the best personal computers in the world and to make products we are proud to sell and would recommend to our family and friends. And we want to do that at the lowest prices we can. But I have to tell you that there is some stuff in our industry that we wouldn't be proud to ship, that we wouldn't be proud to recommend to our family and friends. And we can't do it. We just can't ship junk. So there are thresholds that we can't cross because of who we are. But we want to make the best personal computers in the industry. And there is a very significant slice of the industry that wants that too. What you'll find is that our products are not premium priced. Go out and price our competitors' products and add the products you have to add to make them useful and you'll find in some cases they are more expensive than our products. The difference is we don't offer stripped-down lousy products.

On market research and consultants:

We do no market research. We don't hire consultants. The only consultants I've ever hired in my ten years is one firm to analyze Gateway's retail strategy so I would not make some of the same mistakes they made [when launching Apple's retail stores]. But we never hire consultants per se. We just want to make great products.

When we created the iTunes Music Store, we did that because we thought it would be great to be able to buy music electronically, not because we had plans to redefine the music industry. I mean, it just seemed like writing on the wall, that eventually all music would be distributed electronically. That seemed obvious because why have the cost? The music industry has huge returns. Why have all this [overhead] when you can just send electrons around easily?

On recruiting people to Apple:

When I hire somebody really senior, competence is the ante. They have to be really smart. But the real issue for me is, Are they going to fall in love with Apple? Because if they fall in love with Apple, everything else will take care of itself. They'll want to do what's best for Apple, not what's best for them, what's best for Steve, or anybody else.

Recruiting is hard. It's just finding the needles in the haystack. We do it ourselves and we spend a lot of time at it. I've participated in the hiring of maybe five thousand-plus people in my life. So I take it very seriously. You can't know enough in a one-hour interview. So in the end, it's ultimately based on your gut. How do I feel about this person? What are they like when they're challenged? Why are they here? I ask everybody that: 'Why are you here?' The answers themselves are not what you're looking for. It's the metadata.

On love and loss:

I was lucky—I found what I loved to do early in life. Woz and I started Apple in my parents' garage when I was twenty. We worked hard, and in ten years Apple had grown from just the two of us in a garage into a $2 billion company with over four thousand employees. We had just released our finest creation—the Macintosh—a year earlier, and I had just turned thirty. And then I got fired. How can you get fired from a company you started? Well, as Apple grew we hired someone who I thought was very talented to run the company with me, and for the first year or so things went well. But then our visions of the future began to diverge and eventually we had a falling out. When we did, our board of directors sided with him. So at thirty I was out. And very publicly out. What had been the focus of my entire adult life was gone, and it was devastating.

I really didn't know what to do for a few months. I felt that I had let the previous generation of entrepreneurs down—that I had dropped the baton as it was being passed to me. I met with David Packard and Bob Noyce and tried to apologize for screwing up so badly. I was a very public failure, and I even thought about running away from the valley. But something slowly began to dawn on me—I still loved what I did. The turn of events at Apple had not changed that one bit. I had been rejected, but I was still in love. And so I decided to start over.

I didn't see it then, but it turned out that getting fired from Apple was the best thing that could have ever happened to me. The heaviness of being successful was replaced by the lightness of being a beginner again, less sure about everything. It freed me to enter one of the most creative periods of my life.

During the next five years, I started a company named NeXT, another company named Pixar, and fell in love with an amazing woman who would become my wife. Pixar went on to create the world's first computer-animated feature film, *Toy Story*, and is now the most successful animation studio in the world. In a remarkable turn of events, Apple bought NeXT, I returned to Apple, and the technology we developed at NeXT is at the heart of Apple's current renaissance. And Laurene and I have a wonderful family together.

I'm pretty sure none of this would have happened if I hadn't been fired from Apple. It was awful tasting medicine, but I guess the patient needed it. Sometimes life hits you in the head with a brick. Don't lose faith. I'm convinced that the only thing that kept me going was that I loved what I did. You've got to find what you love. And that is as true for your work as it is for your lovers. Your work is going to fill a large part of your life, and the only way to be truly satisfied is to do what you believe is great work. And the only way to do great work is to love what you do. If you haven't found it yet, keep looking. Don't settle. As with all matters of the heart, you'll know when you find it. And, like any great relationship, it just gets better and better as the years roll on. So keep looking until you find it. Don't settle.

On death:

When I was seventeen, I read a quote that went something like: "If you live each day as if it was your last, someday you'll most certainly be right." It made an impression on me, and since then, for the past thirty-three years, I have looked in the mirror every morning and asked myself: "If today were the last day of my life, would I want to do what I am about to do today?" And whenever the answer has been "No" for too many days in a row, I know I need to change something.

Remembering that I'll be dead soon is the most important tool I've ever encountered to help me make the big choices in life. Because almost everything—all external expectations, all pride, all fear of embarrassment or failure—these things just fall away in the face of death, leaving only what is truly important. Remembering that you are going to die is the best way I know to avoid the trap of thinking you have something to lose. You are already naked. There is no reason not to follow your heart.

[In 2004] I was diagnosed with cancer. I had a scan at seven thirty in the morning, and it clearly showed a tumor on my pancreas. I didn't even know what a pancreas was. The doctors told me this was almost certainly a type of cancer that is incurable, and that I should expect to live no longer than three to six months. My doctor advised me to go home and get my affairs in order, which is doctor's code for prepare to die. It means to try to tell your kids everything you thought you'd have the next ten years to tell them in just a few months. It means to make sure everything is buttoned up so that it will be as easy as possible for your family. It means to say your good-byes.

I lived with that diagnosis all day. Later that evening I had a biopsy, where they stuck an endoscope down my throat, through my stomach and into my intestines, put a needle into my pancreas and got a few cells from the tumor. I was sedated, but my wife, who was there, told me that when they viewed the cells under a microscope the doctors started crying because it turned out to be a very rare form of pancreatic cancer that is curable with surgery. I had the surgery and I'm fine now.

This was the closest I've been to facing death, and I hope it's the closest I get for a few more decades. Having lived through it, I can now say this to you with a bit more certainty than when death was a useful but purely intellectual concept:

No one wants to die. Even people who want to go to heaven don't want to die to get there. And yet death is the destination we all share. No one has ever escaped it. And that is as it should be, because Death is very likely the single best invention of Life. It is Life's change agent. It clears out the old to make way for the new. Right now the new is you, but someday not too long from now, you will gradually become the old and be cleared away. Sorry to be so dramatic, but it is quite true.

Your time is limited, so don't waste it living someone else's life. Don't be trapped by dogma—which is living with the results of other people's thinking. Don't let the noise of others' opinions drown out your own inner voice. And most important, have the courage to follow your heart and intuition. They somehow already know what you truly want to become. Everything else is secondary.

HERB KOHLER JR.

KOHLER CO.

When Herb Kohler Jr. walked away from his family's business, there was no reason to expect him back. It was, after all, the 1960s, and Kohler was in his late teens and in full rebellion. He grew his hair long, stopped communicating with his father, and even joined the circus at the age of seventeen, where he learned how to walk a high wire sixty feet above ground and how to be a catcher on the flying trapeze.

He became a poet, dropping out of Yale University after a distracted year, only to enroll as a theater major at Knox College in Illinois, a liberal arts school founded by social reformers. In the ultimate act of rebellion for the offspring of a father who ran the country's most famous maker of sinks, faucets, and bathtubs, Kohler even developed an aversion to washing. One of his friends dubbed him "the first of the great unwashed."

In short, he did everything he could to separate himself from his father and the family business back in Sheboygan, Wisconsin. "My father and I were not close at that time at all because I was in a period of rebellion against everything he stood for," recalls Kohler. "He had prescribed an educational path for me and one that led directly into the company, and I decided I had to discover what this person Herb Kohler Jr. was all about. His path was a little too suffocating, so I went off and did a lot of crazy things."

His father was a formidable man. He had been on the Yale wrestling team and had also been an officer in the U.S. Cavalry during the First World War. When he gulped back a glass of beer or wine with friends, his customary toast was a loud and firm "Mud in your eye, soldier." "He was very competitive," remembers Kohler. "He was strong. But underneath a number of layers, he was a very sweet man. He was two generations ahead of me so it was not easy for us to have a close relationship."

Nonetheless, the road back began unexpectedly when Kohler tried out for the part of the samurai in the Japanese play *Rashomon*. "When I looked at the casting list, I found out I was chosen to play the notorious bandit who kills the samurai and rapes his wife," remembers Kohler. "I was the rogue and the renegade. I asked the director why and she said: 'Herb, for heaven sakes, it's typecasting.'"

By the time the play closed, Kohler had fallen in love with his director, and married her in 1961. "Then, I realized I better sober up. I reapplied to Yale and in I went to major in business administration. It was a total about-face." But the rift with his father remained unresolved. "I didn't go out of my way to let him know where I was or to visit him or see him or anything of the sort."

It wasn't until six months after Kohler picked up his Yale diploma that he received a phone call from his father, who asked him to come back and work in the family business. Junior insisted that if he did, he would have to be treated like any other employee. A promise was made (and kept), and the young Kohler finally went back to Sheboygan to work for the family business founded by his grandfather in 1873. "It was the last thing [my father] expected, but he must have been thrilled," says Kohler.

He started as a research and development technician, then a schedule coordinator, a supervisor of packing and shipping in the warehouse, until finally becoming manager of factory systems. It was while he was still in this job that the company, then doing some $150 million in sales, fell into a major leadership crisis in July of 1968. The nonfamily president died of a heart attack at the age of fifty-six. One week later, Kohler's father passed away at the age of seventy-six from a heart attack as well.

"In a matter of one week, the company was left without its two senior executives," recalls Kohler. "For a small privately owned company, it was a severe blow." His father had run the company from 1937 to 1968. Two weeks after the funeral, three remaining executives sat down with the younger Kohler for an emergency meeting to decide what to do. When the session broke up, the company's vice president of labor relations was named CEO and chairman, while the company's treasurer was named president. Kohler became vice president of operations. "On that day, the man to whom I reported in the morning reported to me in the afternoon."

Kohler was twenty-nine years old. "Obviously, I made a lot of mistakes, but it was the greatest learning experience of my entire life. I absolutely loved it." Within a year and a half, he was made executive vice president over manufacturing, engineering, and sales. In 1972, Kohler was elected chairman and chief executive. Today, Kohler is one of the largest privately held companies in the United States, with annual revenues of more than $5 billion.

The dominant player in things like commodes, sinks, showers, and tubs, Kohler also makes furniture under the brand name Baker and McGuire, plumbing, kitchens, engines, and generators. All told, there are more than twenty companies on four other continents. The grandson has built ten plants alone in China, where 90 percent of the output stays in China and where Kohler is recognized by the government as one of only five companies to be called "a famous brand." "If someone copies us in China today," Kohler says with a laugh, "we take out our certificate, show it to the magistrate, and you would be amazed at how many copy cases we can get resolved real quick."

Though Kohler Junior is obviously not the founder, he has so completely put his own stamp on the company that it is synonymous with him. Under his leadership, the company has nurtured an entrepreneurial culture that has made it an innovation champion. And at the age of seventy-two, he's still in charge as chairman and chief executive. His only son, David, is president and chief operating officer. His two daughters, Laura and Rachel, are both company executives. We spoke just two weeks after he took his entire family on a five-day white-water rafting trip on the Salmon River in Idaho.

Herb, you were a hippie who has been called the "reluctant prince of porcelain." I can only imagine how happy your father was to have you return home and work in the company he loved. But I wonder, how did

your rebellious behavior inform your later business judgments and the way you led the company over all these years?

It gave me much more confidence in understanding who I was. When I came back I felt that I could reach far in anything I explored. And I had a strong curiosity for many things. My period of rebellion really helped me to develop a sense of confidence and this ability to reach and discover new things.

You're one of only two entrepreneurs in this book who actually wasn't the founder of the company. But you're clearly one of the world's great entrepreneurs, given how you've led the family business over all these years. Do you actually consider yourself a "professional manager" or an "entrepreneur"?

It's really a mix. I consider myself a professional in the sense that we maintain the disciplines of a publicly held company, but I think of myself as an entrepreneur because we have maintained the freedoms of a privately owned company. We really emphasize entrepreneurial pursuits. Our first guiding principle is to live on the leading edge of design and technology in product and process all the time. With thirty thousand people that becomes a little more difficult, but it is possible and to a large extent we are able to get it done.

But I see this mix. We never talk about quarters at Kohler. We don't even have quarterly reports. We have bimonthly board meetings. And we take probably a little more time investigating projects than some publicly held competitors, but when we are ready to go on a project we do it very thoroughly. And when we invest it's for the long term.

You've never even considered bringing the company public to raise capital?

Never. Never. Never. Never. In my lifetime, we never will. And I don't think in my kids' lifetimes, they will. Privacy is an amazing benefit. Not because you are concealing anything. Internally we are very transparent. Concealment is not the issue. It's a whole different set of rules. As a private company, you can sustain a project in periods of adversity that our competitors would quit. We keep going most of the time. Our thinking in managing and operations is at least for a year, not the quarter.

At the top, we're thinking as long as five to ten years out. And 50 percent of my life is very different because we're not public. I can think more creatively instead of trying to appease twenty-two-year-old graduates on Wall Street.

And you've never needed the capital?

We have five guiding principles. I mentioned the first one. The second is to invest an average of 90 percent of our earnings each year back into the business. Only 10 percent or less goes to the shareholders. That's the juice that has allowed us to invest at a proper rate. Accordingly, we have a record during my tenure as CEO of 10.7 percent average compound growth in book value a year. The S&P average over that same time is 7.5 percent. That difference I attribute to the fundamental differences between managing a public versus a private company.

What are the other guiding principles?

Another is to maintain a single level of quality in all product categories regardless of price point. Along with the principle to be at the leading edge of design and process, if you practice these two in particular it has an enormous impact on your reputation. Maintaining a single level of quality is really important. We have price points in most of our product and service categories that go from the lower end of the mid-market to the higher end of the mass market. So that's a very broad range of prices. Our prices differ because of differences in function, material, and design detail. But we try to never let it vary in quality. The quality is always impeccable. Our ability to maintain that and at the same time stay on the leading edge and never copy is what really does the job.

And we have two other guiding principles that are very important. The next one is to provide a consistently quick delivery to the end user. That ability across a variety of product lines becomes more and more important. The last one is to employ service-minded people who enjoy solving problems, are passionate about their work and the business, who take ownership and are accountable. We put these five principles together and they have really enabled us to make progress on a continuing basis on our mission to contribute to a higher level of gracious living for those touched by our products and services.

So what would you say it takes to build a successful business?

Sell more than something costs. For us, it's those guiding principles. That's what we know. That's what we live. And that is what has produced an extraordinary record of growth over a long period of time.

You also have a measurement tool of sorts called the "vitality index" to ensure that the company is innovating a significant portion of its product mix every year. Can you explain how that works?

Absolutely. Vitality plays no small part in our success. We take the sales volume of all new products developed and sold in the last three years and divide by the total sales of any business you are trying to measure. For any manufacturing business in a fashion-oriented industry, we really drive to maintain a long-term average of not less than 20 percent per year. If you do that, you should be very successful. If you don't, you're looking around for reasons why you're not doing it. Lo and behold, it's because you haven't developed enough new product.

Every successful year makes it harder the next year. But if you can consistently deliver on the vitality index or come reasonably close and then combine it with that business of living on the leading edge, now you've got a real powerful combination in establishing a reputation—and that's what has made Kohler tick. That's the secret sauce. Then, when you reinvest 90 percent of your profits back into the company, that really keeps the energy going.

So how do you motivate people to hit the vitality index number?

We measure it for each business and that's one of the few things people have to report out on. In addition to the vitality index, I'm also a gatekeeper. I review many of the new product endeavors before they go to market and that causes a lively interchange about why we're doing something or why we're not pursuing something else. Interestingly, though, I am a person who doesn't believe in vision.

Why not?

Obviously, I have some strong ideas about what I want to get done, but if I were to prescribe a vision for each of our major businesses I feel I would restrict how they develop. So we strongly encourage development in product processes within the confines of the business. I don't want to narrow it or alter it. I don't want to wipe out significant alternatives. We have a pretty thriving development community as a result.

Do you link incentive pay with the vitality index?

No. Fundamentally, people are measured on their overall management of the operation, and bonuses are paid on the basis of stakeholder return on investment. That stakeholder return is heavily influenced by their success on the vitality index.

You always have some nonbelievers who try and contain their costs by not investing in the R&D as they should, and you always have to be on the alert for that. But the people who are investing and producing for five or six years in a row find that their stars just continually rise. They separate themselves from the pack. Their competitors simply can't keep up. When you employ those first two guiding principles and have a strong vitality index, competitors don't have a prayer.

Name a key inflection point for the company under your leadership.

One of the very first was one of the most exciting things for me. I made a decision and I guess it was because of my background in factory systems. I wanted to pull the company out of the arcane world of manual processes in making cast iron. If we were going to drive this material long into the future, I had to find some automated processes that would enable this and produce a much more consistent level of quality. I hunted around and finally found this little firm in Herman, Pennsylvania, and together we designed the largest molding system ever created in the world. It could produce more tonnage per hour than anything currently available, and we built this thing for bathtubs, kitchen sinks, and lavatories on this machine.

Just after I had made the decision to invest we went out for a public debenture which had a greater than 10 percent interest rate on it (this was in late 1972). At the time, the executive vice president of American Standard, which was number one in the industry, gave a speech in which he said cast iron is an obsolete material. It's too heavy. It's made with manual processes. It's time that it be totally replaced with synthetics.

And here I am having put the company on the line as the new CEO. I am right on the edge of my seat. Talk about betting the store. That was it. Damn, if it wasn't that decision and our persistence in pursuing it—it took five years to get it to work properly—but by the time we did in 1978 it was the primary factor that allowed Kohler to surpass American Standard in the industry. It was an amazing experience.

Another key decision was to dramatically expand your footprint in the world, right?

When you take your first steps, you are always a little bit anxious. We had quite a history of exporting around the world. We were selling into China in the 1930s before the revolution. It was absolutely amazing. One day in the seventies, I had an amazing experience of taking my family to an interior city of China. We visited a building that was used as the Communist headquarters. It was a house designed by a French Vietnamese architect in the thirties and this house had Kohler plumbing from top to bottom.

In the early nineties, we made our first investments in China. We have ten plants today and are building a plant a year. We have a compound growth rate of over 28 percent for the past ten years, and this year we'll run at 32 percent.

Many entrepreneurs are often faced with the decision to have family members involved in the business. In your case, all three of your own children work for the company in very prominent roles. Your son, David, became president and COO in 2009. Your oldest daughter, Laura, is vice president of human resources, and your youngest daughter, Rachel, is president of the company's furniture business as well as a boutique plumbing business. Has it been a difficult transition to bring your children into the business?

My father said that any Kohler could work in the company, but to get a promotion you had to prove yourself about twice as much as anyone else. That weeded out a lot of Kohlers. I never talked to my children about the company as they were growing up, unless they inquired. I didn't want them to go through the same rebellion as I did.

Did any of them rebel?

None, because we never talked about the business. They could pick schools of their own choosing and do their own thing. Two went to Duke; one went to Princeton. One went for a master's in fine arts at Catholic

University in Washington; one got an MBA at the University of Chicago and the other got an MBA at Kellogg. The first developed her own theater company. The second one became a consultant for Booz Allen and a very good one. And the third one became a manager at Dayton Hudson in Minneapolis. He was the boy.

When I happened to have a job that might fit their interests and skills I would call them up out of the blue and tell them about the job and the pay level. One by one, each came into the business.

The family knows that whenever there is a conflict between the interests of the family and the company, the interests of the company come first. All three of them are quite different, but all three are clear leaders in their fields. And yet for some reason or another a couple of years ago, the girls independently decided that the boy was to be their candidate as my successor. I sort of balked at that initially, but finally accepted their judgment. He has been on a pretty good learning curve.

What advice will you give him when you turn it over?

I'll tell him to live our core competencies and follow our guiding principles. We have four competencies in this company and we ask everyone in management down to the foreman level and on up to become somewhat expert in them. The first is to build trust. The second is to set a high standard of performance for yourself personally and for your team—and especially before someone else comes along and tries to do it for you. The third core competency is continuous improvement, and we do mean continuous. We say thank you very much for what you did yesterday, but today is a new day. And the fourth one is to always focus on the end customer, his or her needs and requirements. Yes, your immediate customer, the trade, is important, but you really have to deliver and improve the quality of life for the end customer.

DAN LUFKIN

DONALDSON, LUFKIN & JENRETTE

t was May of 1969 when Dan Lufkin went to his very first meeting as a newly elected governor of the New York Stock Exchange. The investment banking firm he cofounded with two partners, Donaldson, Lufkin & Jenrette, had just filed a prospectus to take their company public.

At the time, it was an incredibly audacious move because Wall Street was dominated by private partnerships and there was no public ownership of the firms that effectively ran the markets. Yet the leadership of the Exchange was resistant to change even when it was becoming increasingly obvious that the status quo could not survive. As trading volume soared higher and the market demanded heavy investments in computers and professional management, many of these partnerships were starved for capital. Virtually all the cash they could raise came from either general or limited partners in their own firms and every investing partner had to be approved by the Exchange.

Just as constraining, a firm's net capital had to match its trading volume every day. If not, a firm would be in violation of the Exchange's rules and face a shutdown. By the late 1960s, Wall Street was in a severe crisis as a result. In 1969 and 1970, more than one hundred NYSE member firms, nearly one sixth of the country's brokerage firms, would disappear. They either merged with other firms or simply went out of business. Thousands working in the securities business lost their jobs and careers.

Without broader access to more capital, Wall Street was facing collapse. Still, the old guard was reluctant to embrace change. They strongly believed that the rules brought personal accountability to the Exchange and were vital to the public's trust in the markers. To take Donaldson, Lufkin & Jenrette (DLJ) public and gain access to public capital, Dan Lufkin and his partners would have to persuade the Exchange to alter its rules so that an investment bank could have public shareholders.

So when Lufkin walked into the august chambers of the Exchange for his first meeting, he carried with him a pair of brown Bloomingdale's shopping bags overflowing with the company's offering documents for the twenty or so governors who ruled the New York Stock Exchange. Lufkin went straight to Robert Haack, a governor who also held the position of president.

"Mr. Haack," he said, "I thought you should be the first to see this. You may want to distribute it to the other governors."

Recalls Lufkin: "His face went pale and he looked at me as if I had lost my mind. He took the bags I handed him and he literally ran to the podium where Bunny (Bernard) Lasker, the chairman of the Exchange, was conducting the meeting and said, 'Mr. Chairman, I think you'll want to see this.'"

For the next several minutes, after the documents were passed around the table, all one could hear was the shuffling of paper. Suddenly, breaking the silence in the room, Felix Rohatyn, then a partner at Lazard, stood up, holding the prospectus like a torch over his head.

"Judas Iscariot," he shouted. "You forced us and you denied us thrice before the cock crow."

Since the start of the Exchange, it had been a private club where tradition, ritual, and ego ruled. By attempting to go public, DLJ was breaking down the doors of that club to allow the public to get a piece of the action. To everyone in the room, that was heresy.

"To use the word that Felix used, I was a traitor. They had a traitor in their midst," Lufkin recalls, laughing.

It would take nearly a year of intense debate, but ultimately the Exchange altered its rules and DLJ became the first of the private partnerships on Wall Street to go public, paving the way for other firms to tap the public markets for capital. In the process, DLJ became a huge success, one of Wall Street's top brand names, a firm involved in everything from securities underwriting and sales and trading to investment banking, venture capital, and asset management. When the company was sold in August 2000, Credit Suisse paid $11.5 billion for it.

At first, it would seem that Lufkin was an unlikely entrepreneur. When he went to Harvard Business School for his MBA degree in 1955, he had no idea of what he was going to do. Then, in his second year, Lufkin became fascinated by finance. Armed with his MBA, he went to work for a private investor, Jeremiah Milbank. It was there that the idea for DLJ was born. With William Donaldson and Richard Jenrette, Lufkin founded the firm just two years later in 1959.

Dan, how did DLJ come about?

Commissions on stock trades were fixed at that time, which was the late 1950s, so at Jeremiah Milbank we paid a lot of commissions supposedly for research that wasn't very good. We did our own research and concluded we should invest in smaller companies where the returns were greater. We would go visit companies, spend time with competitors and suppliers, and conduct other kinds of research to do our own basic background work on industries and companies.

In good measure, the thrust of a small company is the long shadow of a single person. As the company grows, you get further and further away from that. We were interested in, and defined the market for, servicing institutions, and we did this by focusing on small, high-growth firms.

By and large, large member firms did not pay attention to smaller companies because there were no shares outstanding to speak of. The way large member firms made money was through the commission process, buying and selling large volumes of stock. If you were a small company, there wasn't any stock or there was very little of it. It didn't cover the overhead. It didn't pay you to do any work on those companies. What we discovered was that the people we called on were so pleased to have someone take an interest in them that when they wanted to sell stock they would come to us.

Paul Williams, the president of O.M. Scott, the lawn care company, came to me and said, "You know I have some shares I want to sell." It was a very thinly traded stock. And I called one potential investor and said, "I am going to offer you thirty thousand shares of O.M. Scott & Sons. I'm buying it from the president for $30 a share and I'm charging you $31.50."

He said, "What?"

I said, "That's what I'm doing. I think that's fair."

"Oh my God," he said, "that's a five percent commission."

"Well," I said, "we don't sell this every day. We don't have this every day. I think it's really worth it. Look at it on the basis of the value you're buying, not on the basis of five percent one way or another."

And he said, "Well, I'm not interested."

"You're wrong," I said. "You should be interested, and I called you first, but there will be plenty of people I'll call second."

It hadn't been five minutes when the investor called me back.

"You're right," he said. "I want to apologize. I believe your valuation of the company. I'll buy the whole thing."

That was something that was very beneficial to Paul, and as his company grew and they needed capital for a new plant or to enter a new market, they came to us. He said, "You know my company. You understand my company. You understand what we're doing." And then as the company grew and the principals began to build estates, they would come to us and ask, "What do we do with our money?" Well, we said, "We're setting up an investment management capability and we would love to manage your money." They knew us. We knew them. They trusted us. We did a lot of work for them. That was a logical extension of our services. That's how that grew.

So you were learning the perspective of the customer, then, which led to the insight that you could create a firm based on research.

We also were learning another lesson, and this was the basis of DLJ and it was until it was sold. The integrity of the job and the character of the people are absolutely first and foremost. If you were going to provide these services, the sine qua non is that you are doing it with integrity, character, and in the customers' interest. It's obvious but not always in practice on Wall Street. A wise old professor at Harvard Business School once said,

"Integrity is a function of the strain put upon it." We made sure there was no strain put upon our integrity.

I would much rather be in the second-best business with the best people than in the very best business with the second-best people. If you're defining the best people, it's a given, assuming you've checked the person out, that he has management skills and knows the business that he's involved with. Ultimately, however, the success of the business is going to depend on the character of the people running the company, and that's what we looked for in our research.

The character of the people manifests itself in so many different ways. It is manifested in the loyalty of employees, the way the company treats its suppliers, and how the company articulates its responsibility to its employees and customers. These things ultimately spell success in a company. I don't care what the company is selling or what kind of services it provides. Without that character, the company may get along for a while, but when the going gets tough, without that underpinning of strength and integrity, the company is not going to stay together.

When you got together with Donaldson and Jenrette to create the firm, what was the reaction on Wall Street?

When we started DLJ, I called on more than ten industry leaders on Wall Street.

Not a one said DLJ was a good idea. Sidney Weinberg came close to it when he said, "I won't say it's a stupid thing, but I don't see how you can compete on the issues and in the areas you're describing compared with the strength Goldman Sachs has, which shares your objectives but on a worldwide scale. And how will you compete with a Lehman Brothers, who has a hundred odd years of experience and a history of relationships? Relationships are enormously important." He said, "I won't say don't do it, because you never know, but I wouldn't say it's an odds-on favorite." That was the closest it came to "Maybe," and everyone else said, "Are you crazy? Are you nuts?"

We didn't rock or shake anything on Wall Street. One fellow at Lehman Brothers, who has since turned into a good friend, said, "We're going to squash you like a fly on the wall."

We had no business going into business. We had no source of income when we started. In fact, we didn't have a business plan. We didn't have any idea how long it was going to take. We raised around $240,000, mostly from our friends, because nobody else would give us a shot. Most of the people who put in money were our age, and included our classmates and friends.

I love the story about the reception you got when the governors at the New York Stock Exchange discovered you were going to go public. But what would have happened if the Exchange didn't go along?

Well, in that prospectus there were risk factors associated with the offering. One of them was that if the New York Stock Exchange did not change its rules, we would have lost 70 percent of our revenues and would have been well into the red. Anyone buying these securities had to recognize they were at the whim and will of the New York Stock Exchange. And if it didn't change the rules—and there was no indication they intended to—our volume would be cut by 70 percent and we would be making no money. Those are tough bananas. Had they not made that rule change, we would have tried to go public but I don't think there would have been a guy in the world who would have bought the stock.

Help someone who didn't grow up in that era more completely understand what the New York Stock Exchange was like in those days.

The Stock Exchange was about as undemocratic an organization as you could imagine. It was just a money machine until fixed commissions were eliminated in the middle of the seventies. And they were very interested in maintaining the status quo. There was no reason for any change nor was there any reason to do something differently. Everything was working just fine. If it was not broken, don't fix it. Their fiefdom was intact.

The night after that meeting where I brought the prospectus I went to an Exchange dinner. It was the changing of the guard. The old governors were going out and the new governors were coming in. I go there and I'm by myself. I go to talk to someone and he turns away. I am standing by myself in the corner. I'm having a beer and no one will talk to me. So I just drank my beer and finally Gus Levy, the former chairman of the Exchange and a partner at Goldman Sachs, came over to me and said, "Well, I don't agree with what you've done today, and I certainly don't agree with the way you've done it. I don't like it and I don't like it one bit. But I will say one thing: I admire your courage to come to this dinner tonight."

And I burst out laughing and said, "Well, it did take a little courage. You're absolutely right."

So why in the world would you have had any confidence that the New York Stock Exchange would change the rules?

Confidence may be too strong a word. But we really felt this was the right thing to be doing. The underpinning of equity capital in Wall Street was very much in danger. Not only was it modest in numbers, it was dangerous. When partners retired they had the right to withdraw their capital, and there were some provisions that allowed a retiring partner to space those withdrawals out. So not only was the number small, but the permanent capital, which was even more devastating, was transient.

It not only made common sense but it was almost a necessity that there be permanent capital. And the only form of permanent capital was shareholdings, which is why you could sell the shares and not impact the capital of the corporation. It just changed who owned it. I had worked with the chairman of the Exchange to try to energize a commission the Exchange had formed five years earlier called the Rockefeller commission. It never did a damn thing. I don't even know if they had meetings. There was nothing coming out of it. I tried to talk to Pat Rockefeller and he had no interest in the subject. That wasn't going anyplace. We figured we had to look at another tack.

Couldn't you have raised more capital under the existing rules?

You could always raise more capital if you had people willing to put it in. But remember, there was always a time frame attached to it. The net capital rule was a complicated thing, but the bottom line was that you needed a certain amount of capital to do a certain volume of business. And you report your net capital every day, every single day. So by 3 P.M., the operations manager had a form he filled out and it reflected the volume of business you were doing on the Exchange and reflected the net capital. And that was a calculation made of your ability to do business at a certain volume. It was very strictly controlled and regulated and very strictly adhered to.

So yes, you could raise more capital but it was not easy. It was locked-in capital. It was private and there was no market. So it was not easy at all. The amount of capital you needed and what you had to give for that if you could get it was growing exponentially. When the capital was needed most was when the market was in stress. There were a number of violations of the net capital rule in the late sixties and early seventies due to merger mania. Many firms were driven into forced marriages to get capital to support the growing volume they were handling. Not only was there impermanence of capital through the partnership structure, but the nature of the beast was that there were failures, dislocations, and back-office screwups. To raise permanent capital in that environment was doable but certainly not easy.

Had the rule ever been challenged before?

No. It never had. The rule was that you could have anyone you wanted but they had to be approved individually by the board of governors of the New York Stock Exchange. If you're selling shares to the public and the offering goes effective in the morning, and six thousand people buy shares, they are illegal until they are approved by the New York Stock Exchange. You can imagine how unworkable that was. You had to get rid of the fact that each shareholder had to be approved by the governors. That's what we were challenging.

Ultimately, your filing changed the face of Wall Street by allowing all the firms to raise public capital.

It happened almost immediately. All of the people who were yelling traitor and Judas suddenly looked around and said, "You know something. This solves our problem. This works for us." I'll never forget a man we knew and had done some business with. Tom Staley was his name. He was a very fine gentleman and banker.

I got a letter from Staley a year later saying, "I just want you to know I was against what you did. I didn't think it was correct or appropriate for the Exchange. But I was wrong, totally wrong. And had you not done what you did our firm wouldn't exist today. So I thank you from the bottom of my heart."

You've attributed your greatest success in life to having the right people around you and your greatest failure to having the wrong people.

That's true. We were looking at the character involved, and especially when someone had to make difficult decisions when he or she was in the minority—to travel unwaveringly down a difficult road. I think back on the Exchange and the decision to go public. It did take a bit of courage. And we had to stay the course. There were times when we wondered what were we doing here. Those were tough times. That is true in any great business. You have to have the courage to stay the course. And there are times when you don't even know if it will work, but you have to stay the course. That goes to the technical skills of the people involved, the product quality, the sales organization, the service organization, all those things play into it.

A lot has been said about the risks entrepreneurs often take. Certainly, you were taking a big risk in assuming that the Exchange would change its rules to allow you to go public. What's the greatest risk an entrepreneur can take?

I think the greatest risk of an entrepreneurial career is not to embark on a venture. I think you can't lose in an entrepreneurial career. You gain enormous experience.

Whether you fail or win, it is time very well spent. You learn a lot about yourself. You gain great self-confidence. And most other people don't have it. Wasn't it Teddy Roosevelt who said that the real crime is not to try? That's what I've learned more than anything else.

People associate entrepreneurship with risk. Entrepreneurs don't think about it that way. They think, "I can get this done." The only risk an entrepreneur can take that is untenable or stupid is to go ahead without having enough capital or time to really see their venture work or not work, whatever the case may be. It's one of the reasons our plan for DLJ only encompassed one thing.

We didn't have a business plan, but we had an idea. We didn't have any way of knowing how it was going to play out, but we said we wanted to give it a chance. So we figured out how to finance three years of business without ever earning a dollar. We could have built nothing in the first three years and still been in business. Most entrepreneurs underestimate the amount of money or time it's going to cost to get the job done—and time is another form of money. As a result, entrepreneurs underfinance. When they do this, unless they have the good luck of being able to go back to investors again and again, entrepreneurs will not have the opportunity to see an idea through to the end, right or wrong. I think that is when a risk is unnecessary and foolish to take.

When you look back at having opened the door for the private partnership on Wall Street to go public, do you have any regrets? Because there are some who believe that public ownership allowed firms to gamble with other people's money and to become reckless.

The truth is there would be no Wall Street, and we would not have the greatest capital market in the world. And we would not have had the growth that was engineered in the sixties, the seventies, the eighties, and the nineties without significant expansion in the capital base of Wall Street. It just would not have been. You wouldn't have had anything. That's someone trying to be smart.

If you were to launch a business today, what would it be?

If I had the smarts, I would be right in the Web. I would be doing apps for Apple. That's what I would be doing. They used to say, if you don't have any money, you do one of two things: You go into real estate where you borrow the moon, or you go into the creative world where your talent is your money. Today you can go and develop apps for Apple and Google.

Dan, you've said that everyone looks for a return on investment and very few people look for a return on life. What did you mean by that?

I think that as you get older, as you move through life's stages, you begin to look for different kinds of return. There's a return on life, which is happiness, and we all forget the ultimate measure of success, which is good health.

One of the things I often refer to is *The Little Prince*. There is a quote in there that I have written down: "A rock pile ceases to be a rock pile the moment a single man contemplates it, bearing within him the image of a cathedral." I think if you try to put one thing down about what makes an entrepreneur, he looks at the rock pile and sees a cathedral.

My mother-in-law asked me one day, when my children were quite young, "If you could leave one thing to your children what would it be?"

I said, "You mean an inheritance?"

And she said, "No, no. One characteristic."

I thought about it and told her I would leave self-confidence. In all of the things we discussed, whether it's integrity and character, the way you run your business, seeing a cathedral in the rock pile, going public when people are calling me a traitor, you need an underpinning of self-confidence to make it work.

MICHAEL DELL

DELL INC.

When he was twelve years old, Michael Dell netted $2,000 in his first business venture selling stamps.

At sixteen, he earned $18,000 in his first year selling newspaper subscriptions to *The Houston Post*.

At nineteen, he was making up to $80,000 a month upgrading personal computers from his college dorm room.

And at twenty-seven, he became the youngest CEO ever to lead a Fortune 500 company.

Those early successes in the life of Michael Dell helped to make him one of the most celebrated entrepreneurs of the twenty-first century. But if his parents had their way, their son might have been a doctor. They had hoped he would pursue medicine as a student at the University of Texas. Instead, he dropped out of college and with $1,000, he started a small business customizing personal computers with more memory and disk drives.

The big idea that allowed Dell to become the world's largest maker of personal computers was a simple one superbly executed. Dell realized he could significantly lower the price of a computer and provide far higher levels of service by selling directly to customers of all sizes.

That was the simple idea on which Dell built his revolutionary business model. He then transformed supply-chain logistics, creating a highly efficient way to build computers to customer specs within hours of getting an order. And he did it by linking the supply chain of parts makers with his own manufacturing operation, driving down costs and virtually eliminating excess inventory. Together, the original idea and the business model that supported it made Dell number one of the top IT companies in the world.

After a twenty-year stint as chief executive, Michael Dell decided in 2004 to give the CEO job to Kevin B. Rollins, a former consultant at Bain and Company who had served as Dell's top lieutenant for eight years. Sales had just surpassed the $40 billion mark, and Michael Dell was all of thirty-nine years old.

Within a year, however, Dell's revenue growth slowed. Soon, Hewlett-Packard had recaptured the title of the world's largest personal computer maker. Michael Dell reengaged as CEO in 2007, noting that "it feels like 1984 and I am starting over again. Only this time I have a little more capital."

Dell has since led a major transformation of the company from a personal computer maker to a broad-based information technology company selling services, servers, storage, and data center solutions.

The Dell success story has been well told. From your dorm room in 1984, you created a phenomenally successful company in the personal computer business—and you did it with a remarkably disruptive business model focused on logistics and execution. What was it like to shift that model and move into what you call "the core of information technology, into the data center"?

Like most companies of our size, we've made significant changes to our strategy—especially over the past couple years as we've evolved to become a broader IT solutions partner to our millions of customers worldwide.

Today, we are in the business of providing end-to-end technology solutions designed to meet the needs of just about any IT user on earth. That includes mobility devices like PCs and smartphones, data center infrastructure from servers to storage to networking gear, as well as the IT services and applications that enable cloud computing.

We also work in an industry where rapid change is the only constant. What may be deemed "disruptive" one day can be considered mainstream the next. But change for the sake of change isn't what matters—it's making sure that the foundation of your business is grounded in your customers' needs. That's been an important guiding factor for Dell since we first opened our doors.

As a matter of fact, the first big shift in our business strategy was inspired by a customer visit to our office in 1985. Dell didn't start out as a PC company. We were in the storage business, formatting hard drive upgrade kits for early IBM PCs. Back then, PCs were sold with very little memory and no hard disk, so customers came to us for these kits that enabled them to boost their computing performance and storage capacity.

One day we got a call from one of our big corporate customers. They wanted to buy 150 of these hard drive upgrade kits, which we were selling at the time for roughly $500 each. It was a huge order for us, and I remember a moment of panic across our small team when the customer asked if they could come tour our factory. It wasn't much of a factory and looked more like a dorm room than a high-tech office environment.

The tour was going well. Then the customer noticed some computers off to the side that we were using to format these hard drive upgrade kits. IBM PCs were very expensive at that time, so we'd made our own for the sole purpose of formatting the drives. He pointed over at our PCs and asked if we sold those. We had never offered our PCs for sale, but in that moment, it sure seemed like a good idea to me! Within three months our entire business had shifted, and we began designing and selling build-to-order PCs. That pivotal, strategic shift came out of listening to a customer, and it's a lesson that I have never forgotten.

Listening carefully to the very people who purchase and use our IT solutions is one of our core values at Dell. That discipline has guided us in the right direction time after time and has formed the basis for much of the evolution you've seen in Dell's business model in the past couple years.

Was there a lot of internal debate over the changes you've been undergoing in recent years?

I've found that there is always healthy debate over a shift in strategy, and I think that lack of debate within a strong leadership team should be a red flag for just about any business. The very nature of our industry fuels healthy discussion at Dell. The molecular ingredients—semiconductors, software, processors, network fabrics, devices—these are all constantly evolving and transitioning, making possible in the next generation of IT what was impossible the generation before.

As a result, our customers' IT requirements are constantly changing, and what I like to call "combinatorial inventions" come together to create new and exciting opportunities for how we use technology.

The companies that remain competitive and win in our industry are those that understand ways to bridge the gap to help technology users do more—innovate, connect, solve problems, whatever it is they want to do and love to do—with IT.

So flash back a few years ago. Our industry was at an inflection point. We were starting to see the potential and promise of a time along the continuum of IT defined by the rise of virtualization, a shift in mobility and the early days of cloud computing.

So, to answer the question, the debate was never about if we should change our strategy, but how we would do so.

We developed a solid, customer-focused strategy and leveraged the strengths of our leaders and team to execute it.

I think that's an important lesson for anyone starting or growing a business. Surround yourself with really smart people and encourage idea sharing, collaboration, and healthy debate. And of course, know your customers and your industry like the back of your hand. Innovative, game-changing ideas will likely follow.

Has the transition been more difficult because Dell was so large and expansive a company?

Yes and no. Obviously, it's easier to make major strategy adjustments when you are a smaller organization. Today we have a global team of more than 100,000 professionals, and a large percentage directly interact with our customers every day—to the tune of several billion interactions per year. It's imperative that we each embrace and understand the business strategy and can convey the benefits to our customers. Sometimes that can be a challenge, but we also know it's a huge advantage for us when managed the right way.

We've been able to aggressively grow our skills and capabilities, both organically and inorganically, through strategic acquisitions of key intellectual property and the talent and expertise of the people behind those companies.

While we are certainly a large corporation today, I still consider us very much a start-up at heart. We approach new problems and opportunities in a very entrepreneurial way. Our leaders are constantly encouraging their teams to embrace breakthrough thinking and thoughtful risk taking. These are some of the same qualities that launched our business more than twenty-five years ago and continue to help guide us today.

In leading now, how have you had to alter your style and approach?

Let's face it, the world has gotten a lot smaller. Geography is no longer an obstacle, whether you're looking for a job, sharing ideas with a colleague, or connecting as friends.

Additionally, a new generation of workers has entered the scene: a generation that expects 24/7, anytime, anywhere access to their information and applications. I would say that those of us who work in technology are among the most demanding IT users I know, so every day at Dell we are constantly living and breathing the changes we're seeing all around us.

These dynamics have certainly required some adjustments, not just for me and our team but for anyone managing people or building a successful business.

The concept is not new, but the means to truly collaborate, exchange ideas, and activate the collective potential of every bright mind has exponentially moved forward. And I believe it will forever change the way we work, live, and interact with each other.

Companies that are starting out in this age of unencumbered collaboration and connectivity have tremendous advantages. But this also requires a new flavor of leadership, one that is more connected, more engaged, and more responsive to real-time needs of customers, team members, and stakeholders.

When I was a teenager, I used what we then called an electronic bulletin board system to connect with other early technology adopters. We shared code, posted messages, exchanged news, and connected through this bulletin board. The ability to connect with people I'd never met through the computer in my room at home changed the way I viewed technology and the power of collaboration. It also became a catalyst for why I started Dell a few years later.

Bulletin board aside, today I'm a very active user of social media—both internally and externally—to keep in touch with our customers and our global team. I can think of no better way to connect and listen to what influencers and customers are saying 24/7 about our brand.

You have something in common with two other great entrepreneurs of all time: Steve Jobs and Howard Schultz. You gave up the position of chief executive officer and then, three years later, were asked by the board to return. What was that experience like? What was it like to come back as the returning founder?

The reality is that I never really left Dell. I was chairman of the board and very involved in the company's business during that time. I had the same office and the same hours. So the experience of resuming the role of CEO was a natural choice.

But as I mentioned earlier, it was also a unique time in our industry. Not only was technology changing at lightning speed, but customers' IT needs and expectations were rapidly changing, too. We were at a turning point as an industry and as a company. I knew we had to evolve our strategy to continue to deliver on our promise to customers.

Being the founder of a company brings with it an interesting dynamic. Founders are often given special permission to make the kinds of sweeping changes a company needs to grow. So for Dell, it was the right time for me to reengage as CEO and guide our leadership team through some tough but necessary decisions about our business strategy.

We are making great progress toward our goals. And while some people will attribute our performance to one or just a couple of individuals, the reality is that we have an incredibly strong team that directs the path and evolution of Dell.

On a personal note, it's been very rewarding and exciting to lead through this particular era in our history. I'm privileged to work in what I believe to be the most exciting industry in the world. Technology is enabling human potential and solving problems once thought unsolvable. Who wouldn't want to be an integral part of that? Every day I wake up with a curiosity and passion about what will come next.

I remember as a child being fascinated with my father's adding machine. You could type in an equation, it made some really cool noises, and out came your answer with minimal effort or time. The machine did the tactical work while I dreamed up more complex equations to input.

On a much greater scale, that's what's happening today. Computing power combined with the limitless capabilities of the human brain to create, innovate, and imagine is unlocking the mysteries of the world.

Think about all the big opportunities and challenges that exist around energy, health care, education, government, and science. More often than not, you'll find a computational problem at the heart of it. Today's IT, just like my dad's adding machine those many years ago, is all about solving those computational problems. As technology evolves, you'll see more and more answers found to the global questions surrounding us.

It's exciting to have a seat at the table and to lead a company that is delivering the solutions and devices facilitating those discoveries.

In a recent interview with Schultz, he recalled the day the two of you were in Hawaii on a bike ride in late December 2007. Howard confided in you, saying he thought he would have to go back into the CEO job at Starbucks. He remembered going to your house where you spoke to him about your "Transformation Agenda." Can you describe what that was and how it guided your view of what next had to be done at Dell?

Howard is a great friend and a great leader. I've been very fortunate over the years to build lasting relationships with other CEO entrepreneurs like Howard. Being able to bounce ideas off each other in those types of very thoughtful conversations is something I think we all appreciate and enjoy.

What I shared with Howard that day was a framework for how we were looking at Dell's strengths, where we wanted to take the business, and the kind of evolution that would be required to get there. The strategic change we're undergoing today to expand the breadth and depth of our IT offerings is an outcome of that planning and thinking.

What's the most difficult transition you've had to make as an entrepreneur/ leader? Was it this one or something else?

Without a doubt, the most challenging times were in the first couple years of the company's existence. Every day posed a "transition" of some kind. Like all start-ups, we were in a constant state of change and, on more than one occasion, I wasn't entirely sure our business would be alive the next day.

The lessons we learned over the years have certainly prepared us for the journey we're on right now. What has made this most recent strategy shift unique is that it has required us to look very carefully outside our company for the new intellectual property, skills, and capabilities we know we need to accomplish our goals. This has meant making changes in leadership, in our talent strategy, and getting serious about acquisitions.

This is fundamentally different from how we grew and managed our business for the first twenty-seven years. But we knew we had to adapt to the rapidly evolving needs of our customers and our industry, so we did.

As part of our strategy shift, we've completed a series of acquisitions, and the results have been pretty astounding. For example, early in 2011 we added a highly successful, cutting-edge storage company to the Dell family. This was a very strategic move for us, given the data explosion under way and the growing importance of information management and security to our millions of customers.

Not only did this new team bring best-in-class products and services to the table, they gave us instant credibility and brought tremendous talent and expertise to Dell in an area that is paramount to our solutions strategy. In turn, we gave them the resources they needed to grow and innovate. In a matter of months, we were able to double revenues for that solution alone.

It's a slam dunk by any standard. However, where I think we have really gotten it right is the way we've integrated these new teams into the Dell "mother ship," as the founders of our acquired companies sometimes jokingly call it.

It's easy to acquire companies, but all the value is created in successful integration. Remember, the founders of these companies are very successful entrepreneurs in their own right. We understand that and make it a priority for Dell to be a good place for them to continue to innovate, challenge and grow their teams, take risks and succeed—both personally and professionally. By joining Dell, we give them a much bigger stage to play on.

I have to think our own entrepreneurial roots really influence the way in which we engage our acquired companies.

What advice would you give entrepreneurs?

Experiment, and learn from those experiences. Don't wait for the perfect plan. Look for opportunities where you can truly bring a better offering forward to the customers and market you serve.

Following someone else's lead is usually not the answer. Be unique for your customers and seize the opportunity to create value for them in a way that your competitors either don't want to or cannot.

The greatest business successes of our time have always been about giving customers something they truly loved. This requires evolution, transformation, and sometimes even radical change to stay relevant and ahead of your customers' changing needs. That's entrepreneurialism at its best.

REID HOFFMAN

LINKEDIN

I n the fall of 2002, Reid Hoffman had begun a sabbatical in Australia that was to last a full twelve months. It was a long-deserved respite, designed to clear his head. For the past five years, Hoffman had been working flat out, first on his own start-up called Socialnet, a social site that predated Facebook by more than six years, and then on PayPal, the online payments company, where he had been a member of the founding team.

Within weeks of hanging out with a friend in eastern Australia, Hoffman was getting antsy. He had been toying around with three different ideas for another start-up. Suddenly, not much more than two weeks into his vacation, Hoffman came to the conclusion that he couldn't afford to take any more time off. If he wanted to create a new consumer Internet company, he felt the timing was ideal.

The dot-com bust had forced the venture capital money out of the space, along with a lot of entrepreneurs with business plans that weren't going to get funded. "Generally speaking," he says, "it's easier to get money when the capital markets are bullish. But it's actually much easier to build a great company when the capital markets are down because your real competition isn't Google and Microsoft. It's all the other start-ups and everyone trying to find the rocket ship. So when lots and lots of companies are being financed, it's just a brutal battle."

He rushed back to Silicon Valley, gathered up a coterie of people he had largely worked with before, and then subleased an office from a friend whose start-up had folded. Before the year was out, Hoffman and his buddies brought their laptops, cell phones, and brains to the space. LinkedIn, the networking site for business professionals, was in business. Less than six months later, on May 5, 2003, the Web site was launched.

Some 4,500 people signed up to become members the first month. Today, it is the world's largest professional network on the Internet, with more than 100 million members in over two hundred countries. Roughly one million new members join LinkedIn weekly. Hoffman was the founding CEO for the first four years before becoming chairman and president in 2007. He is now executive chairman of LinkedIn.

When LinkedIn went public in May 2011, it was the biggest Internet IPO since Google Inc.'s debut seven years earlier. By the time the market closed on the first day of trading, the stock had soared 109 percent to $94.25 a share, giving the company a market value of $8.9 billion.

More important, though, LinkedIn has transformed the world of professional employment and job mobility. Almost all job searches start and end with the networking site, and thousands of companies now use LinkedIn to find business talent.

Hoffman, one of Silicon Valley's most prominent angel investors, never imagined he would one day become a serial entrepreneur. The son of a successful San Francisco lawyer he had entertained the notion of becoming a professor or intellectual. After graduating from Stanford University in 1990 with a degree in cognitive science, Hoffman went to Oxford University to earn a master's in philosophy.

Ultimately, he says, "I realized academics write books that fifty to sixty people read and I wanted more impact." When he returned to California, he landed a job with Apple Computer and then Fujitsu before cofounding the social site Socialnet. Hoffman has since invested in more than one hundred tech start-ups, including Facebook, Flickr, Groupon, and Zynga, both on his own and as a partner in the well-known venture capital firm Greylock Partners.

You launched LinkedIn not long after the dot-com bust when everyone thought Internet businesses were dead in the water. How come?

A lot of the people who founded companies in the tech space in '93 and '94, many of them with substandard ideas, all made some good returns. And some of the great big companies came out of that period, including Yahoo! and eBay. I thought 2002 was like the same period. All of the venture capitalists were saying the consumer Internet is over. But I believed the consumer Internet was just beginning. Everyone had been predicting it would transform our lives. It just didn't happen at the speed everyone expected.

Despite the crash, the Internet had the capacity to cause lots of disruptive change. And if you're about to start on a new venture, you need to ask yourself: What is becoming possible or necessary that wasn't possible before? Is a new product or service able to take over an existing market or create a new market? With LinkedIn, I looked at all the opportunities created by the Internet and thought that eventually everyone would need a professional profile online. The disruption was that people were able to directly reach the best candidates rather than hoping for responses from a listing in the paper or an ad on a Web site.

So when I was in Australia, I said to myself, "Oh no, now is the right time to go in." I should triple down on the consumer Internet.

You had several ideas, though, and some of your friends were skeptical about LinkedIn. What made them think it couldn't work?

Well, one of the things that serial entrepreneurs do is that when they are not in the middle of an idea, they are basically constantly toying with ideas. I had basically three ideas and thought LinkedIn was the best of them. One of the things about ideas and starting companies is you want to be contrarian and right. Contrarian and right is where you've got something that not a lot of other people are doing or thought of and you can make happen. LinkedIn was partially contrarian because it would take a fairly large number of people in the network before anyone realized any value from it. I believed I could get enough people to experiment with it and try it out.

But it would take the first million people to give it a real value proposition. If someone was looking for an expert on open source software, they could probably find one then. Or if you were looking for a smart marketing person to join your company, you could find one. Once you have a million people, you begin to get results on those searches.

The reason why my friends didn't like LinkedIn as much is because they didn't think I could get to the million. I was talking to a bunch of them to get their feedback. It's one of the things you do as an entrepreneur. You talk to everyone who is intelligent who could potentially give you good feedback. It is very easy for creative innovators to get caught up in their own story rather than learning where they should be headed. If people don't think the idea is valuable, you hold on to it or you move it forward differently than you otherwise would. So you can pivot or change your idea even before you start raising money, hiring people and start coding. Many times, you end up with a lot of pivots. So I was testing two or three ideas and the principal objection that was coming up was: Can you get the first million people in?

I said, "I think I can and that will be problem number one." And actually in fact, because I made some money off PayPal, I didn't have to raise money to get it going. I just put my own money in because persuading other people that I could get to the first million people without a live product would have been much harder.

What made you so confident that you could quickly get to critical mass on something that was so new and different?

It was a couple of things. As I said, all the VCs were heading out of the consumer Internet. To them, the Internet was boring. There wasn't that much going on, and yet people still had an appetite for it. They were asking, How can I use this and what would be good for me? Part of it was the rise of Friendster (another social network Web site launched in 2002 which had three million users within the first few months). Here was this nifty but simple service that people were playing with. Some people thought of it as a dating site and some people thought of it as two or three degrees away from a Hell's Angel or a person walking around nude at Burning Man. Just that was interesting enough to cause this massive rise in Friendster.

So if people thought the Internet was now boring, I asked myself how it could be made interesting enough for people to poke around it and discover who they know. I thought we could get enough people so we would actually grow to the one million. That was essentially the bet. I understand virality well. I understand the invitation process. As part of the process of getting LinkedIn to its critical mass, I invented some of the tools that have now been copied by other people, such as expiring invitations and uploading your address book to get more members. Those were the kinds of things I created to get to that first million people.

Clearly, one million was the magic number to get the networking effect. How long did you think it would actually take you to hit that mark?

You don't really know. You can't really know, so you have a range. One part of the range was no one invites anybody. Another part was we have a trickle of inviting, but it's not compounding. And then the other one is it is compounding and going at super-linear rates. We hoped it would go super-linear from day one. Getting a million could be six months or nine months. We all hoped it would be within a year, but preferably within six months. We launched with 112 invites that 13 employees sent out. By month one or two we were in the linear trickle. We were growing, but it wasn't compounding. If we continued to grow at this rate, we knew we were basically dead. And so what we did was ask what most people would want when they arrived on the site. Mostly they want to know who else is here. So we built a feature called the address book and that shifted us from linear growth to super-linear.

I'm assuming here that you learned quite a bit from both SocialNet and PayPal and you put those lessons to work on LinkedIn, right?

There was a stack of things that came out of SocialNet. One of them was that financing strategy is the most fundamental, then product distribution strategy, and then finally product strategy. Most people tend to think, "Oh, I have an idea for a product, so product strategy is the most fundamental." But actually, it's not, because if you build a great product without great distribution, the product dies. So you have to know how you will get your product in the hands of millions of people. It's a fatal point. What's more, if you can't raise money it doesn't matter if you have a great product.

With only two exceptions, our founding team was a combination of people I had worked with at SocialNet and PayPal. The exceptions were Eric Ly, who I knew since we were both undergraduates at Stanford, and Konstantin Guericke, who I knew back in 1996 because he was the head of marketing and I was the head of product for competing virtual world companies. So those two guys I knew for a long time and everyone else I had worked with before. One of the things we were pushing on was a maxim that your time to market is critically important.

The way I usually express that is, if you are not embarrassed by your 1.0 product release, you've released too late. With my first start-up, Social Net.com, it took us nine months to launch the first product. That was a disastrous mistake. We wanted to have all the detailed functionality right away, including social controls so people could decide to connect or not with the people in their networks. We wanted everyone to "Ooh" and "Aaah" about how terrific the product was. We wasted a bunch of time and it put us months behind on more important problems that needed to be solved, such as how to get our product in the hands of millions of people.

As it turned out, with LinkedIn we needed to do more work to get the viral distribution working. In April of 2003, my four cofounders, were Eric, Konstantin, Jean-Luc Vaillant, and Allen Blue, said, "No, we're not ready to launch. We need to put in this feature to allow users to broadcast their network. We don't think people will know how to use the site unless that feature is there."

I said, "Okay, look, will the site function without that feature? Can you sign up, invite people, can you do a profile, search for people, and communicate through referral to people on the site?" They said, "Yes," and I said, "We're launching that. If it so happens that the very first feature that we need to do afterward is contact finder, we'll do it then." As it turned out, we had some bugs in the site we didn't know about so we fixed those. And the second was that virality wasn't what we were hoping or expecting it to be. So we had to work on that.

The top question people had when they signed up was, "Who else do I know is here?" And we figured out that if we could get them to upload their address book, we'd be able to show you exactly who you know is here. If enough people did that, it would make it really easy to send out other invitations. Creating those two things was important to our success. And we had to work on those right away.

I also learned the importance of bringing in high-powered generalists because they help you do all kinds of things. In an early stage start-up, there are all these different tasks you have to do and all different ways you can die. You need to get office space. You need to set up a medical plan. You need to work on a marketing plan. Amex calls you and wants to do a business development deal. It takes a while for you to be a fully staffed company, so having generalists is really key. At SocialNet, I tended to hire people with just the expertise for the job. What I realized since then is that hiring people who can adapt very fast and do a wide variety of things is really critical to navigating all the land mines in an early stage start-up.

How did your early plans match up with how the business actually played out?

About a year ago, we won the Harvard Business School Entrepreneurial Company of the Year Award and Mark Kvamme, who was the Sequoia partner who invested in us in 2003, really wanted to do the introduction. As it turned out, he did this great introduction. I had forgotten that when we did the Series A investment with Sequoia Capital, we had presented a plan to break even but I decided that it wasn't a good idea. I said, "I think we should totally focus on growth, so we are going to put off our business plan by a year." Mark thought that made sense so we did it. At the HBS dinner what he said is that our plan—what our business would be, how our business model would work, how we would make money, and what the aggregate sums per year would be—were basically on target within 10 percent three years out.

It surprised me because when you are living it, you're just running through the minefield. You're solving this problem, moving on to the next problem. And you're not really thinking, "Oh yeah, what financial model did I give my investors?" You never go back and ask yourself that question because all you're trying to do is build up the business as soon as you can. And the model you gave them wasn't a proof. It was, "Look, I think we could do this." But we pretty much hit our numbers. We had premium subscriptions and an advertising and job listings business model. We didn't have the corporate side yet. We ended up building that earlier than expected because we had much more demand from corporations to use our services than we expected. Lots of pieces of the business were conceptualized in the very beginning.

Reid, I'm sure it wasn't smooth sailing. No start-up ever is. So what were some of the major hurdles you had to overcome?

The first crisis was not unexpected but real. Our growth rate was not what it was expected to be and if we keep on this growth rate we are going to die. So we immediately focused on what was keeping people from signing up and what do people want when they are here. And we found that they weren't signing up because they thought they could do it later and what they were most interested in doing was knowing who else is there. Those things called for a virality fix.

The other thing was we went through the whole Series A without a dime of revenue, just focusing on growth. It took us 464 days to get to one million members. It's now more than 100 million. Despite the fact that we thought we had launched a pretty unique idea, there also were a number of different professional networks. There was Spoke.com, Zero Degrees Network, Visible Path, and some other ones, too. They were all doing the professional network idea. So to get it to one million members and breaking through that was really key. We had a bit of a crisis when we discovered that Spoke was also trying to do a public and private network in the professional space. But none of them got nearly the traction we got.

And you have to attribute that to what you learned earlier: getting the product out as quickly as possible and racing to get to one million members, right?

Yep. Doing the things that got people engaged with sending invitations, accepting invitations.

The rules for success in the consumer Internet space are very different than they might be in other entrepreneurial areas. Give us a sense for some of the key differences.

There is high-impact business and there is a successful business. For the latter it's simple: You find the market where you can provide a competitive product. For a high-impact business in the consumer Internet space, it's different. With extraordinarily rare exception, you need to think about massive scale when you get to the consumer Internet. One of the errors in the Internet boom and bubble was that some people thought the value of an online banking customer has the same value as a regular Wells Fargo customer. That's not true. So you really have to get to scale in order for it to work. And the second thing is unless it is a SAS business or an e-commerce business, you need to essentially have a strong user acquisition model that is not paid. There's no other way to get to millions of members. If you have to buy your members, it's just death.

How has LinkedIn changed the way people look for jobs or companies recruit employees?

Hopefully we're just at the beginning of all this. There's now a wide swath of people who believe it's useful for them to have a professional identity online. So you can be found by a long-lost colleague or someone looking for a candidate for a great job opportunity or a start-up entrepreneur who is looking for someone for their advisory board or someone who wants you for consulting. And now there is a centralized place to be found. And what's more, it doesn't look like I'm out there shilling for my services because I'm there with my colleagues and my network.

That's one major trend that LinkedIn has caused naturally to happen. If someone Googles you, what do you want them to find? You want them to find your professional identity first. And then what we have been learning the last couple of years is how do you stay up-to-date? How do you stay connected with what's going on with your company, your industry, and your professional space? And that is part of what we're doing with the Twitter and LinkedIn mashup as part of LinkedIn Today, where we show members the most shared articles relevant to them.

You seem to have timed your public offering exceptionally well. Was there a strategy to that?

At some point, you've got to go public for both employees and investors in venture-backed companies or get purchased. So it became a question of when was the best point for the company to maximize the value in going public. About a year ago, CEO Jeff Weiner and I were talking about it and we thought next year—2011—would be the year when lots of companies would line up and go out. We thought it would be better for us to be at the beginning of that pack and not in the middle of that pack. When you are at the beginning, you get a lot of attention from investors. And you can tell your story more clearly—that you're investing money back into the company to grow. We got out early and now lots and lots of people are going out. We were able to tell our story more coherently to the investment bankers because we started the trend.

Reid, you're a prolific angel investor in Silicon Valley. You see a lot of business plans and a lot of ideas. What would you say are the most common mistakes entrepreneurs make in pitching you?

Some of this is obvious. You better present a good plan. You need to explain why the market you're going after is big. Why do you actually have a good competitive edge on that market? How can a small player do it? How is the team you assembled an asset to getting your plan achieved? A lot of presentations just fail on those. Let's say you have all that. Then, what are the things you need? Well, one of the things I exhort entrepreneurs to do is to clearly describe the risks. For any sort of venture, there are risks. If you don't describe them, you are either lying to your prospective investors or you are dumb because you think it's completely risk free. That is not a great way to establish a partnership. Investing should be considered sort of a financial cofounding. So you want to have a robust, honest, transparent interaction with your partner.

When you are doing a start-up, you are necessarily going into a difficult, stressful period. Every start-up has a valley of the shadow moment. It's when everybody—investors and founders—are saying, "Why did we think this was a good idea?" You want someone who will be a good partner with you in those times. So you really need to make sure you select your partners well. Entrepreneurs frequently maximize price or minimize dilution as a function of that. And actually what you are really trying to do is maximize success. If you choose a partner on the basis of maximizing price or reducing dilution you can put a heavy risk factor on the business.

In fact, in each of the four rounds of financing I did at LinkedIn I could have gotten a higher price. But I was trying to maximize value by building a coherent, effective team. Your board is as important a part of your team as your executive staff. Let me give you one good example. When our team was coming up with features to generate revenue for the site, they thought up a pretty cool product. It was LinkedIn Answers (which allows users to pose questions and get them answered by other members with expertise in the question asked). We later launched it as a free product.

They said, "This is what we think we should charge people for: getting business intelligence from the network. We think we can get money for that." So we presented it at our board meeting and David Sze, our board member from Greylock Partners, asked the really basic question: "So you are both launching a new feature that you are hoping to get engagement from and you are hoping people will pay for? You have a 2X problem there. It's a feature they haven't yet been using and they are going to have to pay for it. It's a pretty big risk. If this doesn't work, you are going to be scrambling to get revenue."

We went back to the drawing board and decided not to do that product next. That is an instance where the board helped us avoid a mistake. We hadn't started coding it yet. So I asked, "What are people using the network for?" And they were using it for people search. So the question became, "What is the people search product that would be acceptable to our network that you can have as paid?" At that time, the only way you could communicate with people was through referral. So if you could search everybody and be able to communicate with everybody that is a product people will pay for. So we built that and it was pretty clear that would get us to profitability.

Reid, you have a book coming out in February 2012 entitled *The Start-up of You* in which you argue that professionals need a new mind-set and skills to compete. What's the core message here?

You need to be the entrepreneur of your own life. The idea for this came after I was asked to do the commencement address at my old high school last year, the Putney School in Vermont. The old paradigm of climbing up a stable career ladder is dead and gone. No career is a sure thing anymore. The uncertain, rapidly changing conditions in which entrepreneurs start companies are what it's now like for all of us fashioning a career. Therefore you should approach career strategy the same way an entrepreneur approaches starting a business.

You can't just say, "I have a college degree, I have a right to a job, now someone else should figure out how to hire and train me." You have to know which industries are hot and what is happening inside them and then find a way to add value in a way no one else can. For entrepreneurs it's differentiate or die—that now goes for all of us.

I basically told the students they have to act like their own entrepreneurs, and there are four principles to follow.

The first principle of entrepreneurship is you don't just accept the world as you find it. You figure out how you want the world to be, and then figure out if you can do something to make it so. Entrepreneurs do exactly that—by inventing a product or service that they feel needs to exist.

For me, I realized that I wanted to create Internet services that helped people navigate their lives better. So I first learned the basic skills that I needed through working at Apple and Fujitsu, and then started a company as soon as I could. So I made myself into the person who could start Internet companies.

The second principle of entrepreneurship is to take intelligent risks. There's a useful aphorism—"nothing risked, nothing gained." By living, you take risks. So take them proactively. You can only achieve something of note if you take a risk. What I learned as an entrepreneur is to distinguish between "mortal" and "painful" risks. Mortal risks are those, when you lose the roll of the dice, you cannot play again. Avoid taking those risks except when you absolutely need to. "Painful" risks are risks where when you lose the roll of the dice, it is painful to correct. Taking intelligent risk is not avoiding risk, but choosing the right painful risks for achieving what you want.

Life is full of taking the right painful risks to achieve wonderful results. It ranges from asking an interesting person out on a date, to the decision on which college, what to major in, or what work to experiment with. Learn to relish these jumps and transitions that are part of life; the jumps of risk are how you get somewhere interesting. For me, I learned this principle by stepping out of the sequence of moving from high school at Putney to college at Stanford to graduate school at Oxford by finishing Oxford with no exact plans. At the time, it felt like all of my friends were moving on with their lives—law school, entering the workforce, and all with concrete plans. I felt that I was moving too slowly and my friends were leaving me behind. It took that transition, that risk of spending a while without any concrete plans, to realize that I should start trying to do things that I wanted to do rather than the academic path in front of me.

This leads to the third principle of entrepreneurship: taking the road less traveled. Normally, when people quote this Robert Frost poem, they mean self-discovery. And self-discovery is good. But here, I mean how you accomplish something interesting with your life. When you take the road more traveled, you simply wear the path down that many other people have walked. When you take the side paths, or make your own path, you have a much greater likelihood of discovering or making something very interesting. Entrepreneurs do this by jumping into the abyss and trying to create a new product or service, where they leave the security of a job with a steady paycheck for creating something new.

And the fourth principle of entrepreneurship is to plan for luck—both good and bad. It may seem paradoxical. How can you plan for the unknown? Actually, it's rather simple. In terms of planning for good luck, you stay alert to opportunities that you find in your travels—and jump on them. And by the way, you are far more likely to find lucky opportunities on the road less traveled—which is an important part of the reason to choose the side or new path.

BILL GATES

MICROSOFT

On the morning of June 27, 2008, Bill Gates went to his office at Microsoft Corp. and worked his last full day at the company he had famously cofounded. Over the course of those thirty-three years when his focus was nothing but Microsoft, Gates had achieved unfathomable success as one of the world's most influential and powerful entrepreneurs. The day after June 27, he began devoting himself full-time to philanthropy, using his extraordinary wealth to become the world's most famous social entrepreneur.

In a sense, Gates began trying to change the world twice. After helping to usher in the personal computer revolution that changed the way people worked and lived across the world, he now threw himself into the stubborn challenges of global health, public education, and low-income communities. As cochair of the Bill and Melinda Gates Foundation, the largest philanthropic foundation in history, he pledged to eradicate polio from the world and to mount an effort to fight malaria as well.

One of the great business stories of all time began on a day in 1975 when Gates and his friend Paul Allen were walking through Harvard Square and spotted a magazine on a newsstand that made both of them do a double take. Inside the January issue of *Popular Electronics* was a story on a new microcomputer called the Altair 8800.

The two had met at Lakeside, a private school in Seattle, and had discovered a mutual passion for computers. Gates began programming in his spare time when he was in the eighth grade. Gates was a student at Harvard, while Allen had gotten a job as a computer programmer in Boston with Honeywell. But now, fearful they were missing a crucial turning point in the development of the computer, they sprang into action.

"We'd thought about what kind of software could be done for it, and it was happening without us," remembers Gates. "And for all we knew maybe they had some software people; they were just going to go charge off and do this thing."

The pair drafted a quick letter to the maker of the computer in Albuquerque, New Mexico, offering to do software programming for the machine. "We didn't know how long it would take us," adds Gates. "And it was kind of funny because we were sort of acting like we had it already. We went to work day and night."

In fact, they didn't have an Altair and had not written any code for it. But now they had to muscle together the code for a version of BASIC computer language that worked on the new machine. The night before Allen was to fly out to demonstrate their handiwork, Gates stayed up all night to make sure none of the instructions were miscoded. When Allen came back, he not only had a deal to sell their software to the company—Micro Instrumentation and Telemetry Systems—he also would be hired into the firm as its vice president of software. Gates dropped out of Harvard, taking an official leave of absence, to work with him in Albuquerque in November 1975.

They named their partnership "Micro-Soft," dropping the hyphen within a year. And then in 1979, the pair moved the company to Seattle. Their big break would come in 1980 when IBM would commit one of the biggest blunders in the history of business. Thinking that most of the value of its soon-to-launch personal computers lay in the hardware, IBM turned to Microsoft to develop the operating system for its new product. The modern PC era was here, and Gates and Allen had secured one of the most valuable contracts ever drafted. As part of the deal with IBM, the pair negotiated a clause restricting IBM's ability to compete with Microsoft in licensing the MS-DOS operating system to other computer makers.

"We wanted to make sure only we could license it," recalls Gates. "We did the deal with them at a fairly low price, hoping that would help popularize it. Then we could make our move because we insisted that all other business stay with us. We knew that good IBM products are usually cloned, so it didn't take a rocket scientist to figure out that eventually we could license DOS to others. We knew that if we were ever going to make a lot of money on DOS it was going to come from the compatible guys, not from IBM."

It was a brilliant stroke, one that outmaneuvered IBM and laid the foundation of the company's massive success. And IBM's mistake allowed Gates to grow what had been a backroom start-up into the world's largest software company worth, at its peak, $400 billion. Among all of the company's vast achievements is the fact that two of its core products—the Windows operating system and the Office application software—became the only two products in the world with more than a billion users.

With his great wealth that at one point made Gates the richest man in the world, the entrepreneur began to study the work of Andrew Carnegie and John D. Rockefeller, and in 1994 sold some of his stock in the company to create a foundation. It put him on the path to create one of the greatest second acts in history.

On Microsoft's secret sauce:

The key for us, number one, has always been hiring very smart people. There is no way of getting around that, in terms of IQ, you've got to be very elitist in picking the people who deserve to write software. Ninety-five percent of the people shouldn't write complex software. And using small teams helps a lot.

You've got to give great tools to those small teams. So pick good people, use small teams, give them excellent tools; vast compilation, debugging, lots of machines, profiling technology, so that they are very productive in terms of what they are doing. Make it very clear what they can do to change the spec. Make them feel like they are very much in control of it.

Have lots of people read the code so that you don't end up with one person who is kind of hiding the fact that they can't solve a problem.

Design speed in from the beginning. A lot of things have helped us, even as the project teams have become larger, and the company has become a lot larger than it was. It is not some methodology where there is a lot of funny documentation. Source code itself is where you should put all your thoughts, not in any other thing. So our source codes, although there are a few exceptions, tend to be very well commented on in a very structured way.

On change:

With technology we've always got that people tend to overestimate what can change in a year or two, and they underestimate the cumulative effect of change that can take place in a ten- or fifteen-year period. We're also subject to cycles of overoptimism and pessimism. Certainly the late nineties were kind of an insane period, where every start-up was going to replace your bank and your retail store, and people forgot that there are some benefits to experiences working those other ways, and the economic proposition that's brought there. And in any medium where the barrier to entry is very low, the ability to build up an asset is all the more difficult. So only a few of those companies managed to get to the critical mass and do something interesting.

That was a fantastic thing, there was some crazy investment. It was like the gold rush. Some people did lose money, but that's what capitalism is good at, taking lots of wild ideas and continuing to back the ones that work. So it was a period of, in the final analysis, quite a bit of innovation.

Then when that bubble burst some people went to the other extreme thinking that these changes were not really valid, that it had all been overhyped. But it was only overhyped in the sense of the time frame. Some of the things were not thought through. Some of the technical foundations were not there yet.

On entrepreneurship:

If you're going to start a company, it takes so much energy that you'd better overcome your feeling of risk. Also, I don't think that you should necessarily start a company at the beginning of your career. There's a lot to be said for working for a company and learning how they do things first. In our case, Paul Allen and I were afraid somebody else might get there before us. It turned out we probably could've waited another year, in fact, because things were a little slow to start out, but being on the ground floor seemed very important to us.

If you're young, it's hard to go lease premises. You couldn't rent a car when you were under twenty-five, so I was always taking taxis to go see customers. When people would ask me to go have discussions in the bar, well, I couldn't go to the bar.

That's fun, because when people are first skeptical, they say, "Oh, this kid doesn't know anything." But when you show them you've really got a good product and you know something, they actually tend to go over-board. So at least in this country, our youth was a huge asset for us once we reached a certain threshold.

On competing in the technology business:

The technology business has a lot of twists and turns. Probably the rea-son it's such a fun business is that no company gets to rest on its laurels. IBM was more dominant than any company will ever be in technology, and yet they missed a few turns in the road. That makes you wake up every day thinking, "Hmm, let's try to make sure today's not the day we miss the turn in the road. Let's find out what's going on in speech recognition, or in arti-ficial intelligence. Let's make sure we're hiring the kinds of people who can pull those things together, and let's make sure we don't get surprised."

Sometimes we do get taken by surprise. For example, when the Internet came along, we had it as a fifth or sixth priority. It wasn't like somebody told me about it and I said, "I don't know how to spell that." I said, "Yeah, I've got that on my list, so I'm okay." But there came a point when we real-ized it was happening faster and was a much deeper phenomenon than had been recognized in our strategy. So as an act of leadership I had to create a sense of crisis, and we spent a couple of months throwing ideas and e-mail around, and we went on some retreats. Eventually a new strategy coalesced, and we said, "Okay, here's what we're going to do; here's how we're going to measure ourselves internally; and here's what the world should think about what we're going to do."

That kind of crisis is going to come up every three or four years. You have to listen carefully to all the smart people in the company. That's why a company like ours has to attract a lot of people who think in different ways, it has to allow a lot of dissent, and then it has to recognize the right ideas and put some real energy behind them.

On his best business decisions:

I'd have to say my best business decisions have had to do with picking people. Deciding to go into business with Paul Allen is probably at the top of the list, and subsequently, hiring a friend—Steve Ballmer—who has been my primary business partner ever since. It's important to have someone who you totally trust, who is totally committed, who shares your vision, and yet who has a little bit different set of skills and who also acts as something of a check on you. Some of the ideas you run by him, you know he's going to say, "Hey, wait a minute, have you thought about this and that?" The benefit of sparking off somebody who's got that kind of brilliance is that it not only makes business more fun, but it really leads to a lot of success.

On making mistakes:

When you do a product a little bit later than you wanted to it can be a mistake. We should have gotten serious about Internet search four years earlier than we did. It is a business where if you are early that's okay. Internet TV we were early. Tablet computers we were early. But we could just keep improving it and wait until all the trends came together to create a new huge phenomenon. If you are late, then everything coalesces around who's doing that. You have to look for a paradigm shift, something dramatic, to contribute there. We missed one or two things. You could say those are our biggest mistakes, but the list of mistakes has a large taxonomy.

There were a lot of missteps in the early days, but because we got in early we got to make more mistakes than other people. I had customers who went bankrupt and didn't pay us. Customers who we spent a lot of time with who never built microcomputer-based machines.

In retail marketing, we made a number of mistakes that were important for us to learn from. We had, in a few countries, agents. And you really don't want to use agents. You want to have your own people. If you are going to be a serious company, take a long-term approach. You should hire people in all the countries you are going to be in and make sure they are there cementing long-term relationships—not just generating short-term commissions. I think we learned that one pretty quickly.

We did hire in some very sharp business people, and got them to share their experience so it wasn't just us technical guys and the other people. We were very young. I mean, Steve Ballmer and I were kind of driving the business and Paul Allen and I were driving the technology. We were optimistic in thinking we could get things done sometimes faster than what we did. The project of the moment always seemed very exciting. And some of them never generated much in the way of royalties. But all correctable stuff as long as we sort of wake up and see what the results were.

On creating a corporate campus:

Well, I was always thinking that the environment we did product development in should be a fun environment, a lot like a college campus. And this idea of using small teams means you want to give them all the tools, all the computers, an individual office, whatever it takes so that they feel like they can concentrate on their jobs and be very creative. And in the Northwest, having a lot of trees around, you know, one-, two-, and three-story buildings where offices are very good sized. That made sense to me. And we had been looking ever since we moved up to Seattle for a piece of land that wasn't too far away and yet that would let us grow as a company. And in 1986 we actually got to move into our corporate campus.

Initially, there were four buildings clustered around a lake, and each of the main development groups got their own building. And that meant that we really had the best of all worlds. People felt that it was a fun environment, but yet we were really close to each other as far as working together. Things like people joggling or riding unicycles around, having barbecues outside, having company meetings where everybody would stand around.

On going public:

Microsoft had started giving out stock options to people as early as 1981. So we were sharing in the success we thought we'd have. As we did that, the options had about a five-year vesting period. And so as some people were starting to vest on quite a bit of their stock, there was the question of how would they get liquidity. Now you could just let it be traded privately, but then the price would fluctuate a lot because the supply would be so short. And I was quite reluctant to go public because of the overhead. We had been able to track our stock price internally up in a very linear way. And with the market sort of maybe over-anticipating the future, or getting paranoid—you know the stock would be very volatile.

But I was convinced that it made sense. And as long as we were going to do it, it was an opportunity to really expose the company broadly. Talk about our vision where we had done well, where we were taking the industry. And it did become something that was covered very, very broadly by a lot of people. And it was extremely successful. The stock took off after this offering at $21 and it just zoomed up from there for many, many years.

Going public is not without its complexities in terms of dealing with analysts and all the reports. It is a little convoluted about when can you keep things secret versus having to go out and talk about those things. So it is not totally simple. But the benefit of having the stock be very liquid for everyone was very positive. We didn't use any of the money that we raised. We just put that money in the bank and it sat there with all of the money that we had earned, because we were very profitable and had plenty of cash by this time. So our reason for going public was very different than any other company that was going public.

On being a technologist:

Of my mental cycles, I devoted maybe 10 percent to business thinking. Business isn't that complicated. I wouldn't want to put it on my business card. Scientist is better, unless I've been fooling myself. When I read about great scientists like, say, Crick and Watson and how they discovered DNA, I get a lot of pleasure. Stories of business success don't interest me in the same way. Part of my skill is understanding technology and business. So let's just say I'm a technologist. Business is not the hard part. Let me put it this way: Say you added two years to my life and let me go to business school. I don't think I would have done a better job at Microsoft.

On his management style:

I do know that if people say things that are wrong, others shouldn't just sit there silently. They should speak. Great organizations demand a high level of commitment by the people involved. That's true in any endeavor. I've never criticized a person. I have criticized ideas. If I think something's a waste of time or inappropriate I don't wait to point it out. I say it right away. It's real time. So you might hear me say, "That's the dumbest idea I have ever heard" many times during a meeting.

On being called a geek:

Hey, if being a geek means you're willing to take a four-hundred-page book on vaccines and where they work and where they don't, and you go

MOREHOUSE, GENNEVIEVE O

Unclaim : 11/8/2017

Held date   : 11/1/2017
Pickup location : Hillsboro Brookwood Library

Title   : World changers : 25 entreprene
urs who changed business as we knew it
Call number   : 338.04 BYRNE 2011
Item barcode   : 33614048647654
Assigned branch : Hillsboro Brookwood Library

Notes:

off and study that and you use that to challenge people to learn more, then absolutely. I'm a geek. I plead guilty. Gladly.

On philanthropy:

In the same way that during my Microsoft career I talked about the magic of software, I now spend my time talking about the magic of vaccines. Vaccines have taken us to the threshold of eradicating polio. They are the most effective and cost-effective health tool ever invented. I like to say vaccines are a miracle. Just a few doses of vaccine can protect a child from debilitating and deadly diseases for a lifetime. And most vaccines are extremely inexpensive. For example, the polio vaccine costs 13 cents a dose.

This year 1.4 million children will die from diseases for which there are already vaccines—diseases like measles, pneumonia, and tetanus. Those lives can be saved if we can reduce the costs of vaccines and raise enough money to buy and distribute them. If we simply scale up existing vaccines in the five countries with the highest number of child deaths, we could save 3 million lives (and more than $2.9 billion in treatment costs alone) over the next decade. In addition, researchers are inventing new vaccines for malaria, AIDS, and tuberculosis, and these would save millions more lives. But generous aid is required to realize the true lifesaving potential of vaccines. The most direct way of saying this is that every $2,000 cut in the most effective aid spending causes a child to die.

On his legacy:

Legacy is a stupid thing! I don't want a legacy. If people look and see that childhood deaths dropped from nine million a year to four million because of our investment, then wow! I liken what I'm doing now to my old job. I worked with a lot of smart people; *some* things went well, some didn't go so well. But when you see how what we *did* ended up empowering people, it's a very cool thing.

I want a malaria vaccine. If we get one then we'll have to find *the* money to give it to everyone, but the impact would be so huge we would *find* a way. Understanding science and pushing the boundaries of science is what makes me immensely satisfied. What I'm doing now involves understanding math, risk taking. The first half of my life was good preparation for the second half.

SIR RICHARD BRANSON

VIRGIN GROUP

When Sir Richard Branson, Britain's most famous entrepreneur, launched Virgin Mobile USA, he did it in typical Branson style. Hoping to differentiate the new product from existing competition, he wanted to reinforce the brand message "nothing to hide" because there would be no hidden charges for the service. So Sir Richard rose above New York's Times Square on a crane, then stripped down to a "nude" bodysuit, his loins covered with a Virgin cell phone. The cast of Broadway's *The Full Monty* surrounded him, all in the same pose.

The flamboyant stunt earned him the publicity he sought—and yet another brand was launched in the sprawling entrepreneurial empire that is Virgin. With hundreds of companies all over the globe and roughly $10 billion in annual revenue, Virgin is—more than anything else—a reflection of Branson's own interests, passions, and whims. Throughout the company's history, many of Virgin's most auspicious ideas—air and rail travel, cell phones, finance, Internet, hotels, and travel packages—have sprung from Branson's wants and needs as a customer himself. "The reason I went into business originally," he says, "was not because I thought that I could make a lot of money, but because the experiences I had personally with businesses were dire and I wanted to create an experience that I and my friends could enjoy."

No one would ever have guessed that Branson could have pulled it off. He quit school at the age of fifteen to start his first business—a *Rolling Stone*–like magazine where he could voice his personal objections to the Vietnam War. At the time, in 1966, he had no interest in running a business. Though he had dyslexia, Branson most wanted to be an editor. He turned out to be a far better salesman, selling some $8,000 in advertising for the first issue. With all his costs covered by ad sales, he didn't even have to charge for the magazine on the newsstand.

Suddenly, Richard Branson, the teenager, was an entrepreneur. His initial fortune would ultimately be built in the music business. He bought crates of "cut-out" records from a discounter, selling them out of the trunk of his car until opening a successful mail order business in 1970. His strategy: simply undercut Britain's stodgy retailers. Record albums were then sold under restrictive marketing contracts that limited price cutting. He later opened his first music store in London's Oxford Street. Branson picked the name "Virgin" after it was suggested by one of his early employees because they were all new to business.

By 1972, Branson formed the Virgin Records music label, becoming successful by signing artists that no other record label would touch. When punk music emerged, for example, he signed the Sex Pistols. Later came contracts with Genesis, Peter Gabriel, and the Rolling Stones, making Virgin and Branson major players in the international music business. He eventually sold off the music business in 1992 to keep his airline company afloat.

Branson's more daring ways can be traced to his mother, Eve, a former showgirl who relished adventure. She was one of the first flight attendants to fly over the Andes, when passengers had to don oxygen masks because the cabins were unpressurized. She also snuck into a male-only glider pilot training program by pretending she was a boy. Although his father, Ted, was a lawyer, he, too, encouraged his son's risk taking—from crossing oceans in a hot air balloon to his latest efforts to create commercial space travel under the brand name Virgin Galactic. In July 2011, Branson announced that the company had taken over 440 deposits from future astronauts totaling $58 million.

I feel best in surroundings where other people are smarter than I am because I feel like I can always learn something from it. One of the other big lessons that I've learned, particularly in business, is that you have a responsibility to yourself to learn as much about your business as you can. I sign every check. Although it is now tedious because the bills that come in from running and maintaining a studio—everything from Federal Express to Xerox, to every tape that needs to be repaired, and so forth—it gets to be a lot.

I have stacks and piles of checks to do, and I know that there are a lot of successful people who don't do that. I still have a tenement mentality. I've been very poor in my life, and so the idea of having money and not being responsible and knowing how much money you have and keeping control of it is not something that I personally can accept. I know that there are other people who can, but it's just not a possibility for me. I need to know where it is. There are times when I think I want to go to the bank and say, "Show it to me." Because just seeing it on a piece of paper—anybody can print out a piece of paper. So I watch it very carefully and try to maintain responsibility for it.

When I first started being a "business woman," I worried about "How do you do this?" And I realized that you do this the same way as you do anything else. You be fair. You try to be honest with other people, and be fair.

On her company's mission:

I've already done the work of creating a team of people who understand not to propose a show idea to me unless there is an intention behind the idea. Tell me what the intention is first so that we know that the intention is in line with [Harpo's] mission. It's a broad mission, to transform the way people see themselves, to uplift, to enlighten, to encourage, to entertain. So you get a really broad canvas in which to do that, but whatever show idea you're bringing me has to fit into that category.

On failings:

Nobody's journey is seamless or smooth. We all stumble. We all have setbacks. If things go wrong, you hit a dead end—as you will—it's just life's way of saying "time to change course." So ask every failure—this is what I do with every failure, every crisis, every difficult time—I say, what is this here to teach me? And as soon as you get the lesson, you get to move on. If you really get the lesson, you pass and you don't have to repeat the class. If you don't get the lesson, it shows up wearing another pair of pants—or skirt—to give you some remedial work.

And what I've found is that difficulties come when you don't pay attention to life's whisper, because life always whispers to you first. And if you ignore the whisper, sooner or later you'll get a scream. Whatever you resist persists. But if you ask the right question—not why is this happening, but what is this here to teach me?—it puts you in the place and space to get the lesson you need.

My friend Eckhart Tolle, who's written this wonderful book called *A New Earth* that's all about letting the awareness of who you are stimulate everything that you do, he puts it like this: He says, don't react against a bad situation; merge with that situation instead. And the solution will arise from the challenge. Because surrendering yourself doesn't mean giving up; it means acting with responsibility.

On managing by intuition:

Learning to trust your instincts, using your intuitive sense of what's best for you, is paramount for any lasting success. I've trusted the still, small voice of intuition my entire life. And the only time I've made mistakes is when I didn't listen.

It's really more of a feeling than a voice—a whispery sensation that pulsates just beneath the surface of our being. All animals have it. We're the only creatures that deny and ignore it.

How many times have you gone against your gut, only to find yourself at odds with the natural flow of things? We all get caught up in the business of doing, and sometimes lose our place in the flow. But the more we can tune in to our intuition, the better off we are. I believe it's how God speaks to us.

Of all the major moves in my life—to Baltimore, to Chicago, to own my show, and to end it—I've trusted my instincts. I listen to proposals, ideas, and advice. Then I go with my gut, what my heart feels most strongly.

On motivation:

There is the voice that everybody hears that is your parents' voice, your professor's [voice], it's the world's voice saying to you, "You should do this, you should be this, you ought to, you got to." And then there is the still small voice—for some people it's not so small—inside of every human being that calls you to something that is greater than yourself.

If you only desire to make money, you can do that. But what I will tell you—and I know this for sure too—is that the money only lasts for a while in terms of making you feel great about yourself. In the beginning, the money is to get nice things. And once you've gotten those nice things, I think some of the most unhappy people I know are the people who've acquired all the things and now they feel like, What else is there? What else is there? What else is there? And that feeling of "what else is there" is the calling—is the calling trying to say to you [that] there is more than this. There is more than this.

On doing the right things:

How do you know when you're doing something right? How do you know that? It feels so. What I know now is that feelings are really your GPS system for life. When you're supposed to do something or not supposed to do something, your emotional guidance system lets you know. The trick is to learn to check your ego at the door and start checking your gut instead. Every right decision I've made—every right decision I've ever made—has come from my gut. And every wrong decision I've ever made was a result of me not listening to the greater voice of myself.

If it doesn't feel right, don't do it. That's the lesson. And that lesson alone will save you, my friends, a lot of grief. Even doubt means don't. This is what I've learned. There are many times when you don't know what to do. When you don't know what to do, get still, get very still, until you do know what to do.

And when you do get still and let your internal motivation be the driver, not only will your personal life improve, but you will gain a competitive edge in the working world as well. Because, as Daniel Pink writes in his bestseller, *A Whole New Mind*, we're entering a whole new age. And he calls it the Conceptual Age, where traits that set people apart today are going to come from our hearts—right brain—as well as our heads. It's no longer just the logical, linear, rules-based thinking that matters, he says. It's also empathy and joyfulness and purpose, inner traits that have transcendent worth.

These qualities bloom when we're doing what we love, when we're involving the wholeness of ourselves in our work, both our expertise and our emotion.

TED TURNER

TURNER BROADCASTING

Ted Turner was all of twenty-four years old when his father crawled into the bathtub of his home in South Carolina and shot himself dead. His father had been a volatile and increasingly unpredictable man, taking heavy doses of prescription drugs to ease a depression that had gripped him. He lost his battle with those inner demons in March of 1963.

For Turner, it was an unspeakable tragedy that would ultimately change the course of his life. Though his alcoholic father had sent him to boarding school at the age of four and beaten him with a wire hanger as a child, Turner felt as if he had lost his best friend. His father had been his best man at his first wedding. And his father had taught him the fundamentals of business.

"It was a terrible loss and I tried not to dwell on it," Turner recalled years later. "When he passed away, I went to work even harder and worked eighteen hours a day so I wouldn't have to think about it. If I sat down in a chair in a room and thought about it, it might have killed me. It was so painful."

When he died, his father had a net worth of some $2 million. After estate taxes and some $500,000 that had been left to Turner's stepmother, the rest of the estate—worth slightly under $1 million and largely composed of his father's billboard company, Turner Advertising Co.—had been left to Turner.

As the family's only living child, Turner took the company over and poured every ounce of himself into his work as chairman and president. It was a business he knew well because at the age of twelve, he was already laboring forty-two-hour weeks during the summer for his father, posting signs and cutting down weeds in front of the billboards along the highways. And when he was suspended from Brown University for having a girl in his dorm room, Turner left school to join his father's business.

He used the billboard company's cash flow to buy several radio stations and then a UHF TV station in Atlanta that would ultimately set the stage for his biggest accomplishment: as founder of the cable news network CNN, the first dedicated twenty-four-hour cable news channel. It would revolutionize the coverage of news around the world and make Turner a billionaire many times over. He also founded WTBS, the first superstation in cable television.

After merging his business with Time Warner in 1996, he was soon worth $10 billion. But shortly after the deal and a disastrous merger between Time Warner and Internet player AOL, Turner was pushed aside by Time Warner brass, even though he was vice chairman and the company's largest individual stockholder. Then the Internet bubble burst and AOL Time Warner stock went into a free fall. Turner lost nearly $10 million a day for two and a half years. "I sat there loyally and went down the drain with everybody else," he says.

When it was all over, he had lost $7 billion of his $10 billion fortune. Still, he pledged to give away $1 billion of what was left to the United Nations. Turner has also devoted his assets to environmental causes. He was the largest private landowner in the United States until surpassed by cable mogul John C. Malone in 2011. On his ranches, Turner has amassed the largest herd of bison in the world and is the cofounder of Ted's Montana Grill restaurant chain, which has now grown to forty-six restaurants in sixteen states.

On what his father taught him about business:

My dad had some unusual ideas but he was a very clever businessman. He was also as ethical and honest as the day is long. Before he got into billboards he owned a little car business and he called it "Honest Ed's Used Cars." There were many days when he'd drive me to and from work and the entire ride he'd only talk to me about business. We'd cover everything from detailed accounting principles like depreciation to broader concepts like motivation techniques and the importance of luring and motivating good people.

As a boy I saw firsthand the value of hard work and customer relations. It was almost as though he gave me the business degree I didn't get in college. Oftentimes he'd punctuate his lessons with funny stories or memorable expressions. Once, to drive home a point about the difficulties of attracting good, loyal employees, he told me, "Heck, Jesus only had to pick twelve disciples and even one of those didn't turn out well." One of his favorite mottos was one I've used myself ever since: "Early to bed, early to rise, work like hell and advertise!"

On creating something from scratch:

You have to have a lot of courage, and you have to have a lot of imagination. You can do a lot of things from scratch that aren't going to work out. I can tell you how I did it. I spent a lot of time thinking. I had done a lot of reading, and when I had spare time, a lot of times I would just think and not waste my time watching TV. I watched very little television growing up, hardly any at all. Your mind is just like any other muscle in your body. If you want to have a sharp mind, you need to use it. Just like if you want to have strong muscles, you better work out a lot, so I worked my mind out all the time, and then when I needed it, I would put it to use. Like developing CNN, for instance.

The mistake I made was losing control of the company. But I didn't plan for that, just everything went wrong. But in a way, that was good, too, because I had had so much success for so long, and I didn't get the big head, but I did perhaps overestimate just how much strength that I would have with the Time Warner merger. As long as it was just Time Warner, I had 7 or 8 percent of the company when I merged with Time Warner, but when we merged with AOL, I went down to 3 percent, and that is when they phased me out. I got laid off in a restructuring, but that's okay.

On creating a twenty-four-hour news channel:

I thought it was a no-brainer. It was something you could afford to do. It really doesn't cost that much more to do twenty-four hours of news than it does two-and-a-half hours of news. You've got to have the news gathering organization. You have to have basically the same stories, but you need more stories and more different kinds of programs if you're going to do twenty-four-hour news, unless you're going to do something like Headline News, which is basically a half-hour rolling format that you tune in and out of, and you don't expect somebody to stay with it more than a half an hour. But if you want people to have an opportunity to watch for extended periods of time, you need programs like *Larry King Live* and debate programs like what used to be *Crossfire*. You need financial reporting. You need extended sports reporting, if you're going to do a good job. Basically, there's a number of cable news networks now, but we were the only one in the beginning. I didn't think it was hard to figure out how it should be formatted and what it should do. The main thing it was going to provide is news availability when people had a chance to watch it, rather than when the networks wanted people to watch it.

When I made the decision to do it, about a year before it went on the air, there was no question in my mind. Now the only question was: Would I run out of resources before it turned the corner? There was no way I could know about that until I went ahead and did it, because I didn't have enough capital to see it through. But in my study of history, Erwin Rommel in the desert never had enough petrol for his offensives against the British to finish them. He had to depend on capturing fuel supplies from the British by attacking so quickly and catching them off guard that they would retreat and leave some petrol for him to finish. It was dicey, and it didn't always work, but I knew that was what I was going to have to do. I was going to have to hit hard and move incredibly fast. And that's what we did: moved so fast that the networks wouldn't have time to respond, because they should have done this, not me, but they didn't have any imagination, or didn't have adequate imagination.

On the first Gulf War:

It was one of the most exciting moments of my life. I knew what was coming. We knew that the attack was coming imminently because we had been warned by the State Department. Even the president called the president of the network and strongly recommended that we get our people out of Baghdad, but I made the decision that—as long as they would volunteer to stay—that they could stay. We were freedom of the press, we were going to get the story. I was in Jane Fonda's room. She was working, and I had the afternoon off. And it was about 5 or 6 P.M. East Coast time and 2 P.M. West Coast, and I was watching CNN and the war started. I flipped over to KCBS and Dan Rather was in the studio talking. And I flipped to NBC and Tom Brokaw was in the studio talking, and I flipped over to ABC and Peter Jennings was in the studio talking, and I flipped over to CNN, and the tracer bullets were going and the rockets were getting down, and I said "Yippie! This is the greatest scoop in the history of journalism!" And one network had the start of the war from behind enemy lines.

On efficiency:

There probably are some ways that I work and live that might be a little different from other people you come across. For one thing, I go to great lengths to be efficient with my time and try to make the most of every minute of every day. When I run meetings, they start on time. A lot of that came from my father. For much of my career, I didn't even waste time getting to and from work. There were long stretches when I spent most of my weeknights sleeping in my office, and later, when I could afford to, I built an apartment on the top floor of CNN. So when millions of Atlanta drivers were wasting their time sitting in traffic, my commute was nothing more than walking up a flight of stairs, and I had that much more productive time to work every day.

Another way I save time is by managing information efficiently. A lot of people become inundated with paper and e-mails, but I make a point to keep a clean desk. I never let things pile up. I couldn't do this without a great executive assistant, and for the last twenty years, it's been Debbie Masterson. She is invaluable, and in addition to keeping me on track and on schedule, I've always counted on her to screen out correspondence that I don't need to see. The volume of mail I receive is tremendous—from business reports, solicitations, and so forth—but over 90 percent never makes it to my desk. For most requests, Debbie knows how to respond. The 10 percent that makes it to my desk still amounts to a lot and I try to answer it all that day so that I don't get bogged down with unanswered messages.

On delegation:

Basically, I ran my company the same way I ran my boat. I found the best people I could to run our businesses while I stepped back to keep an eye on our overall strategy and what our next move should be. A lot of entrepreneurs and company founders have trouble leading as their company grows. Part of the problem is that they become so used to having their hands in everything when the company is small that they find it difficult to delegate successfully once the business gets big. I stayed on top of key issues relating to our individual businesses, but I let my managers manage. This gave me time to focus on the big picture.

On advice to young people:

Well, if you want to be an entrepreneur, you better get out there and hustle, because it's tough out there. There's a lot of other people trying to get to the top, too. So if you're going to be an entrepreneur, and if you want to be a success in life, you better be prepared to work hard and be smart and think a lot, at least I think so. Unless you're just a genius or you just are tremendously lucky. Every now and then, somebody wins the lottery with a two-dollar ticket, worth $20 million with a two-dollar ticket. You can do that. You can play the lottery, but I wouldn't recommend it.

On inspiration:

I was inspired by the Rotary Club. My father was a Rotarian and I as a very young man in Macon, Georgia, was a Rotarian. The Rotary's motto was, "He profits most who serves the best." That was my motto through my life and it still is. I believe that. It worked for me. Just by being honest and having a lot of integrity saves you a lot of trouble. A lot of these business-men who cut corners end up in jail, embarrassed and disgraced. I didn't want that.

On giving away a billion dollars:

I was going to be honored as the man who made the greatest contribu-tions to the UN that year in the United States, and I wanted to have some-thing to say, and I figured that on my way to New York—I was waiting for the last minute to work on my speech. I said, "What are you going to say, Turner?" I said, "Well . . ." because the United States was about a billion dollars in arrears. We hadn't paid our debt for two years, and it was about a billion dollars. I said, "Well, why don't you just give a billion dollars to the UN," and I'll just make up for what the United States didn't pay. You know, step forward, like if your uncle doesn't pay his bills down at the grocery store, you pay them for him. So that's what I decided to do. I was worth three billion at the time, and I gave away over half of what I had, because I gave another half a billion to other causes, too.

On losing control over CNN:

It's hard, very hard. But when I merged with Time Warner, I didn't think there was any way they could squeeze me out but when they merged with AOL I was diluted down to where they could and they did. I took a chance and I lost. Hardly anybody wins all the time. I've won more than most, so I'm not going to complain about it. I've pretty much gotten over it, but it still hurts. I'm trying to be a good sport about it. I'm not crying. I'm out at the UN working and helping and I started a new restaurant business with a partner and I'm really proud of that.

The television business was relatively easy. There are no barriers to entry in the restaurant business so everybody with $200,000 and a kitchen can be a restaurateur. I mean it's tough. But I wanted to do something tough, and I want to be a success in the restaurant business because the television business was relatively easy because the barriers to entry were very high. At the time I came into it there were only three people in it: CBS, NBC, and ABC. So there was an unmet need for competition. I used to say I spent a lot of time trying to kick the networks and what did I have to show for it after ten years: broken toes.

FRED SMITH

FEDERAL EXPRESS CORPORATION

His grandfather was the captain of a paddleboat on the Mississippi River. His father was the founder of both a restaurant chain and a motor coach company that ultimately became a key part of Greyhound Lines.

So perhaps there is little wonder that Federal Express founder Fred Smith would find himself in the transportation business as well. Smith, who earned his pilot's license when he was fifteen years old and used it to fly crop dusters, had ambition and desire in his blood. Building from scratch a massive global transportation company was the process of connecting all the dots in his life.

Like so many entrepreneurs, he experienced tragedy early in life. Smith lost his father at the age of four and was raised by his mother and uncles. Four years later, he contracted a little-known disease called Legg-Calvé-Perthes that put him on crutches for more than two years.

At his mother's urging, he went to Yale University in the fall of 1962, and the experience would change his life. Smith, who hung a Confederate flag on his dormitory wall, went out for football, joined the exclusive Skull and Bones society, spun records as a disc jockey at the campus radio station, and joined the student platoon leader training program of the U.S. Marine Corps Reserve.

Though Smith now says it is more apocryphal than real, it was his junior-year term paper in Economics 43A that would plant the seed for what eventually would become Federal Express. The paper—not much more than fifteen typed pages—captured Smith's belief that every aspect of life would become far more automated as a result of major advances in technology.

When he graduated from Yale in 1966, his entrepreneurial wanderlust would have to wait. Instead, Smith enlisted in the Marines. His father and three of his uncles had served in the military, and Smith had trained in the summers while in the Marine reserve. From 1967 through 1969, he would serve two tours of duty in Vietnam, first as a rifle platoon leader and later as a company commander and a forward air controller. He once recalled that an enemy bullet severed the chin strap of his helmet without so much as giving him a scratch, though he earned a pair of Purple Hearts. By the time he returned to civilian life, Smith had flown on more than two hundred combat missions at the tumultuous height of the war.

It was a profoundly formative experience. For one thing, Smith got to see up close the remarkable logistics efforts of the military, effectively mobilizing more than half a million troops and millions of tons of supplies. For another, the discipline, training, and leadership experience absorbed as a Marine captain would stick with him for the rest of his life. "When people ask me what principles have guided me since I started the FedEx Corp. years ago," he says, "my answer often startles them: it's the leadership tenets that I learned in the U.S. Marine Corps during my service in Vietnam."

When Smith returned home, he initially bought a controlling interest in an aircraft maintenance company, Ark Aviation Sales, and a year later in June 1971 Smith founded Federal Express with his $4 million inheritance. It took nearly two full years before FedEx began operations with 14 small planes, delivering 186 packages to 25 U.S. cities on April 17, 1973. The early days were tough: FedEx lost $27 million in its first two years and the company was on the verge of bankruptcy.

Smith, however, was able to renegotiate his bank loans and keep the company afloat. In 1978, FedEx went public. From a tiny start-up with a few planes, FedEx is one of the biggest entrepreneurial success stories ever. Smith built a global transportation company that racks up more than $38 billion a year in revenue, employs nearly 300,000 people, and delivers millions of shipments a day in 220 countries.

Fred, much has been made of your term paper at Yale. Legend has it that as a junior you pretty much laid the groundwork for Federal Express in your economics class. But it seems to me that your experience in the Marines was even more critical to the founding of the company. If you had started your company straight out of Yale would it have been as successful?

The answer to that question is no, for a couple of reasons. First and foremost, the story about the term paper is a bit apocryphal, as a lot of things in life are. The paper I wrote was not about Federal Express. It was about the automation of society and how an entirely different type of logistics system was going to have to be developed to support this automated world.

Circa '65 and '66 in New Haven, Connecticut, I was flying around on charter flights and one of the things we did was to pick up critical parts from IBM, Xerox, Burroughs, and Sperry UNIVAC and fly them around for these computers they were putting in place. It struck me that as things automated, the efficacy of a manufacturer's business depended on getting fast replenishment of parts and pieces to keep the machines running. The problem was that the transportation systems were not built around these new types of automated technology-based systems.

What you had then were mostly supply push systems. Think of a lumber yard: you cut trees down, you mill them, you put two-by-fours and six-by-eights in the lumber yard, and then the builders come and take them away to build a house. Or think of groceries that depend on distribution centers filled with Heinz ketchup and mustard and cereal. They are pushed out to the stores from inventories based on what's selling and what's not.

The customer was in essence giving up his ability to compensate for variability or any type of outage of the equipment because it was automated. When Chase Manhattan Bank was right down the road from IBM where they were making 360 computers, IBM could keep those bank computers working all the time. When IBM tried to sell computers to the Bank of San Angelo in Texas, that was irrelevant. Yet the Bank of San Angelo was being asked to get rid of all of their clerks who did the debits and the credits and instead use this IBM 360 computer. It was quantumly more efficient and infinitely more accurate than the manual systems that it replaced. But both the manufacturer and the potential customers would have to rely on a completely different supply chain. IBM could tell you in those days with great certainty how many parts and pieces they would need within an installed universe. The problem is they couldn't begin to tell you which one was going to need a particular part. So even a mighty company like IBM couldn't follow all the parts and pieces that they needed to keep their universe of computers operating.

The same thing was true in those days for Boeing, McDonnell Douglas, and Lockheed. They were automating the cockpits in the airplanes and the airports were automating. All of that was really beginning with a tremendous amount of momentum by the middle part of the 1960s. That is what the paper was about.

And I suppose your experience in Vietnam helped to confirm all this as well?

Yes. I saw a massive supply push logistics system in operation. The Navy would bring in these huge ships of sea rations and ammunition and six-by-six trucks and they would echelon them forward. The problems always came when you had any type of high-tech equipment that required support. My roommate from college was an F-4J pilot and he was always mortified because the F-4J was a sophisticated phantom fighter that should never have been given to the Marine Corps. They could never keep them operating. It was a perfect example of the phenomenon. This is the difference between beans, bandages, and bullets and sophisticated electronics. I go in the Marine Corps and come back and resurrect this idea. In the six years I was in the Marines, society had dramatically moved forward toward a high-technology-based infrastructure.

So I resurrected the idea and at the same time I started looking at the Federal Reserve System. The reason is because it was a microcosm of all the commerce in the United States. In those days there were very few bank wire transactions. The vast majority of people used checks and cash. There were thirty-six branches and district banks in the Federal Reserve System and every one of them transferred checks with each other every day. So the formula for that is thirty-six times thirty-five. It's N times N minus one. Something like ten thousand separate traffic lanes connected those banks every day.

The Bank of New York and the Bank of Boston would transfer twenty thousand pounds of checks every night because there was a huge amount of commerce going between those two locations. So they would have a truck going from New York to Boston every night. The Bank of Montana also exchanged checks with New York and Boston and each of the other thirty-three banks around the country, but they might have eight pounds of checks going to New York and six pounds going to Boston. So it was a model of the commercial flows of the United States.

The story goes that you went to the Federal Reserve and tried to convince them to use the air cargo network you were putting together but they said no way.

That's true, and that's where the name Federal Express came from. The problem was that if they had to move a check from California to New York it would take three days. People were making a living on bank float. And what caused float was the inability of the transportation system to move those checks over those ten thousand discrete lanes.

So I went to the Federal Reserve and said, "Look, this system you have is crazy. Here is an unsolicited bid to put in a system that would allow you to move the checks from the Bank of Montana to a small Federal Reserve Bank across the country in the same exact time frame that you could move the twenty thousand pounds of checks from Boston to New York. You could eliminate float."

This was just completely revolutionary to them. The higher-ups loved the idea because it solved one of the biggest problems the Federal Reserve had at this time: how to get rid of this float. And the only way to do it was this hub-and-spoke system where you sent everything to a single point and then every point was connected to another point on a nondiscriminatory basis. So it was absolutely, positively overnight from all points to all points.

Rather than having ten thousand separate connections with all of the sorting on the origin and the collection on the end, you had one spoke from each bank. So there were thirty-six versus ten thousand. If you took the Federal Reserve and Detroit, the transaction between it and Chicago looked a little bizarre because you would go from Detroit to Memphis before you went to Chicago. But it wasn't any more absurd than any other mathematical formula that had been used by the telecommunications companies. Otherwise, the entire country would have been buried under two feet of copper wire with every phone having to be connected to every other phone directly.

And where did the Marine Corps experience come into play?

The only other thing I did was to use my experience from the Marine Corps that it was not heretical to have ground and air groups together. I had served in both. And that has always been a strong point for the Marines. When you come ashore in landing boats, you don't have any artillery so the Marine Corps is the branch of the service that actually invented close air support, dropping ordnance close to you. So I made Federal Express an integrated air-ground system. It had its own pickup and delivery operation on the ground that was integral to the hub-and-spoke air operation. I tried to sell it to the Federal Reserve but I couldn't.

You got a better reception, though, from companies that were making high-value parts and needed a way to overnight stuff to customers to fix sophisticated equipment that would otherwise be idle.

The people who were supplying all this automated, high-tech equipment said, "Eureka. That is a solution. I can get the part to the bank in San Angelo, Texas, as fast as I can get it to the Chase Manhattan branch down the street. So sign me up." That's how it happened.

It was such an incredibly ambitious idea to build a network that had to essentially cover the entire country from scratch. I wonder where you got the confidence to do it?

A business proposition was not daunting to me. I was very confident the thing would work. The only problem was that to have a product, the network had to exist. You couldn't go to people and say, "Gee, I have a wonderful service for you for a third of the United States." It just doesn't work. So you had to have at least the top markets in the network from day one. We did three separate independent marketing studies and it showed that the requirement was absolutely there.

The only real problem we had in retrospect was the first oil embargo in 1974. If that hadn't taken place, we would have been profitable from the minute the network was turned on. It was just made more difficult because the price of fuel went up by a factor of three and you had to go to the government to get an allocation for fuel. If you didn't have a previous record of using fuel, it was very difficult.

That's why I am so involved to this day in trying to get the United States to come up with an energy policy and why I serve on this Energy Security Leadership Council. We are headed toward a major confrontation with Iran and other people if we don't do something differently. I've been living with this ever since I had gone into business.

Your first move out of the military was interesting because you didn't simply go with your idea. Instead, you bought an aircraft maintenance firm. Was that because you didn't quite have the full idea in your head or you wanted a corporate shell from which to build your company?

It was some of both. The main thing was to convert the airplanes and the small freighters and that company had the capability to do that.

What business is Federal Express really in? Aviation? Logistics? Information?

We are in the information business and that was the second, and in retrospect, maybe the most important of the intellectual insights. Once we started operating, it immediately became apparent that when people were using transportation to substitute for inventory, there was little room for error. Most of the management systems in those days were by anecdote or audit. People would describe quality as "Gee, I had a nice stay at the Holiday Inn." It was very amorphous or it was by after-the-fact audit. You would go in and take a survey of customers and ask, "How many of you people found the restaurant to be acceptable?"

The problem with that is as you go forward and get bigger and bigger, percentages are no longer acceptable because a 98 percent or 99 percent completion rate sounds wonderful, but you would not be very happy if your bank statement was 99 percent correct. It's completely unacceptable. So what was very obvious to me was that we could not manage Federal Express by anecdote or after-the-fact audit. We had to have a real-time control system that measured each shipment from the time we picked it up until the time we delivered it, a system that would allow us to intermediate any untoward event in between or, at the very least, be able to tell the customer what had happened.

We began a big process of staffing up an IT unit and I had the very good luck to buy the IT department of Cook Industries in Memphis, which was headed by a former IBM salesman named Jim Barksdale. Jim was originally our chief information officer and later our chief operating officer. He went on to help invent the modern telepathy business as the CEO of Netscape. Under Jim's leadership, we developed this online real-time tracking system. We had to invent a completely new industry to do it. Nobody had ever printed sequential multiform labels. They had printed universal product codes on grocery items that said "I am a Campbell Soup can," but nobody ever printed a multipart form with five copies and said "I am shipping one, two, three, four, seven." We had to take that information in its bar-coded form and get it back in our computers.

We first started out with a little handheld device that was the size of a breadbox and finally it got down to the size of a candy bar when it started making sense. At one time, we were the largest user of radio frequencies in the country. We installed a radio device in all our vehicles so the information could be transmitted from the location into our mainframes. Every day, we could measure with great precision every shipment and whether it was delivered on time. That led in turn to the recognition that information was very useful to our customers and we began to migrate it into our customers' shipping orders. And at one time, we were the largest purchasers of PCs in the country. We gave our customers these little PCs that allowed them to track these shipments themselves. When you think about it, a warehouse is nothing more than a place to put something so you know you got it. It has no utility other than that.

So for the first time in human history you could monitor inventory, whether it was at rest in a warehouse or in motion with us. It completely revolutionized the world of logistics. Today, nobody would even think about shipping something of any kind of importance if you couldn't track it and trace it and couldn't get the date of delivery online. It all came from that observation that the information about the package is as important as the package itself.

And then finally we used that information to develop a very extensive quality management system based on the doctrines of the quality experts W. Edwards Deming and Joseph Juran. We used our tracking and tracing system to help us improve service and costs instead of trying to manage through anecdote and audit. That put us so far ahead in the express business that we never looked back from there.

All of this required massive amounts of capital to pull off—the planes and equipment, the people, the technology and IT systems. Was that ever a hurdle?

We had plenty of capital other than the Arab oil embargo. We got the capital in place to do what we needed to do and then we went public and we never had to raise money otherwise. We went through a period of time when we were growing very rapidly, and after United Parcel Service came in the business we did a lot of leasing of airplanes. But that is the only capital we raised.

Fred, I also noticed that in the company's operating manual there is a tremendous amount of detail that suggests you run a very tight ship. In the corporate operating manual, weekly reports have to be delivered before 8:30 A.M. every Friday to the head of each core company and all business meetings must produce a summary with conclusions and follow-up assignments. Where did all this come from?

Some came out of the military. It governs each of the four major segments of the company today. In the main, we operate these highly choreographed networks. And they do require a significant amount of precision, industrial engineering, operations research, and detailed execution. Our hub here in Memphis is the biggest industrial activity in the world. We take 160 wide-bodied airplanes and bring them in here from 10 P.M. to 1 P.M. and then relaunch them from 2:30 to 5:30. There is no question that I got a lot of my orientation out of the military, and a lot of my management and leadership concepts come straight out of the military.

I've read that you are still deeply involved in the company's operations.

I'm not all that hands-on. I'm very much a believer in delegation and holding people accountable. If by hands-on you mean I'm shouting orders from the bridge, the answer is no. If you mean I spend a lot of my time trying to get the right people to be my teammates and to work with me, yes I am hands-on in that respect. But certainly I am not involved in the day-to-day operations of FedEx at all. And even in the earliest days, I always believed that because of my military experience I had a certain role. If you are a battalion commander you better be a battalion commander. You can't be a platoon leader.

What have you borrowed from the Marine Corps?

My leadership philosophy is a synthesis of the principles taught by the Marines and every organization for the past two hundred years. When people walk in the door, they want to know: What do you expect out of me? What's in this deal for me? What do I have to do to get ahead? Where do I go in this organization to get justice if I'm not treated appropriately? They want to know how they're doing. They want some feedback. And they want to know that what they are doing is important. If you take the basic principles of leadership and answer those questions over and over again, you can be successful dealing with people.

We tell our executives that the key to their success is to rely on their first-level managers (FedEx's counterparts of NCOs); to set an example themselves; and to praise in public when someone has done a good job. All these are standard operating procedure in the Marines.

In the Navy, a ship's captain flies Bravo and Zulu signal flags when his crew has done a good job. Our FedEx managers affix a sticker with *BZ* pennants on it to reports from subordinates that are particularly good. Workers who excel get to wear a *BZ* lapel pin, adorned with Bravo and Zulu flags. When an employee goes out of his way for a customer, he gets a "BZ check" of $150 to $200. Except for the bonuses, these practices come straight out of the Marine Corps leadership manual. And although I'm chairman of the corporation, I can't get myself to cut into the line in the company cafeteria. Somewhere, a voice reminds me that a good officer lets his troops eat first.

What do you look for in the right people?

First of all, you have to have technical expertise in what you're doing. We have many, many technical fields that have to work together in concert, so you have to have people who are technically competent. And in general management you have to understand Henri Fayol and Peter Drucker and all of the great students of management if you are going to be an effective general manager.

The second thing you have to do is have somebody who can be very objective. At the end of the day, if you can't be objective about things, particularly the facts as they are presented to you, and that includes objectivity about one's own strengths and weaknesses, it's impossible to be an effective manager at any substantial level. I always found that the willingness to seek the truth and to be objective about things to be very, very essential.

In our particular area, you have to be team oriented because it takes so many disciplines to do what we do. You can't be a hot dog. You have to play well on a team. You have to be very results oriented. You have to be tough. I have often said it's better to ask forgiveness than permission. It requires everybody out there making decisions at whatever level. Our people have to be action oriented and willing to take responsibility for their piece of the pie. You have to be articulate and have a sense of truthfulness.

And the last thing is, I can't imagine anybody working for me who doesn't have a sense of humor. There are not many epaulets around FedEx.

What are some of the mistakes you've made?

Oh gosh. You are going to have some setbacks in life and you are going to make some errors in judgment. You're going to drill some dry holes or whatever analogy you want. The whole secret of life is trying to turn adversity into advantage and to learn from mistakes. A good example of that is we expanded too early in Europe, thinking that the European Union was going to become a more integrated market. So we had to retreat and write off a couple of smaller acquisitions we made that weren't really thought out. From that, we developed a very disciplined and improved corporate development capability and we changed our strategy in Europe. And for the first time, we're able to offer overnight service from Europe to the United States. That is an example of taking a setback and turning it into an advantage.

The secret is to be bold and take risks, and if you take risks, you are going to have some failures but the decisions that pay off will dwarf them.

Fred, one of the biggest problems successful entrepreneurs have is keeping their organizations nimble and innovative when their companies get really big. FedEx is really big and global, so how have you done that?

We drill into everybody's head that not to change is to atrophy, not to innovate is to be surpassed by someone who does. You have to embrace change and innovation. And if there is one thing we push constantly it is, how do we differentiate? All businesses, and I don't care how different they are, have to be built around a differentiated product or service. You can be protected by a patent; you could find a great location; you could create a great product; but commerce being what it is, somebody is going to find a way to turn your advantage into a weakness. They are going to figure out how to segment your market or differentiate what they do versus you and peel off part of your market. So you have to constantly differentiate.

We do all kinds of things to keep people motivated. We have broad participation in incentive compensation programs. We have a very disciplined annual and five-year planning process integrated with our Management by Objectives system. We do all of those things that I think are required of world-class companies: our broad use of technology, our quality-driven management system, and so forth. The other thing you need to do is you just have to work like hell to make sure you don't get bureaucratic and fat with a lot of managerial levels that are unnecessary. That is easier to do today with the managerial technology and control systems out there than used to be the case. A lot of middle management used to be nothing more than transmitting information downstream. That's not required at all.

Barack Obama could actually have been in command of the Seal Team Six that had gotten Bin Laden. He could communicate and possibly see what those youngsters were seeing through their helmets. Think about that in terms of command-and-control systems in terms of what George Marshall and Eisenhower had just fifty or sixty years ago. So a lot of the people that military organizations had were there for no other reason than command and control. In the corporate world, the same thing is true. You have to make sure that you don't add a lot of staff and managerial people that don't add value to the enterprise.

Fred, what's your advice to a young person who may want to start his or her own company today?

One, make sure you have a viable and sustainable business proposition. Make sure you are fulfilling some need that has been unmet and make sure it's differentiated from everything else out there and that it is defensible. If the idea doesn't meet that first criterion, at best you may be able to make a living out of it. But you won't have any sort of financial return that leads to wealth accumulation.

You've got to have an idea that makes sense. Usually I get youngsters who then say, "Well, give me an example?" And I tell them to go in your pants pocket and tell me if you have a car key in there.

And they say, "Yeah," and I say, "Well, take it out. Did you know that twenty-five years ago nobody at all would have thought you needed an electronic key that locks your car, turns on the lights, and opens up the trunk. It never would have occurred to anyone. Someone synthesized in their mind that the miniaturization of batteries, RFID [Radio Frequency Identification], and the small electric motor could be put together to make a useful product. Today you wouldn't even remotely think about buying a car without it.

That is an example of an innovative idea that nobody had been thinking about and that you could put into the marketplace. The second thing I would say is you need to have good verification of your idea and a detailed plan in terms of execution. And finally, if you need other people to help you carry it out you've got to get teammates and not people who are waiting for you to bark orders out.

The point about the key in the pants pocket is that you have to have a vision for what is likely to change in the future and how you can take advantage of that change. It's what Wayne Gretzky said about hockey: "A good hockey player plays where the puck is. A great hockey player plays where the puck is going to be."

No question about it. On any kind of industrial product and service, generally you are seeing a need before someone else sees that need. Clearly, the little door opener was created because people didn't want to leave their car unlocked and they wanted to turn on their lights at night before they got to the car for convenience and safety. It is an example of a now ubiquitous product that nobody saw the need for until someone realized it would make a useful product.

Is it easier or harder today to come up with a differentiated idea?

If you have a differentiated idea, it's easier to get it funded to get it out there. I think it's quantumly harder to be in business than it used to be. Those are two different things. If you have a good idea today, you can get the money. There is such a huge swash of money out there in the venture capital area today compared to what there was forty years ago. But business as a whole is much more difficult and much more treacherous. If you are starting a company today and somebody doesn't work out, it's a potential lawsuit. Those didn't even exist thirty years ago. Today jobs have been interpreted as property rights. You have to be careful that you're not doing damage to the environment even though an activity can be quite modest.

That's really one of the biggest reasons we're having such a problem these days. As an entrepreneur, you are distracted so much these days from focusing on the customer and value creation. Instead, you're trying to meet regulatory requirements, avoiding litigation, and being risk averse, covering your ass or anything you want to call it. That is so much more a part of business today than it used to be.

NARAYANA MURTHY

INFOSYS

I t took an unjustified arrest and mistreatment by Bulgarian police to convert Narayana Murthy from a confused leftist to one of India's greatest entrepreneurs.

It was 1974, fifteen years before the Berlin Wall would fall, and Murthy was hitchhiking from Paris to his hometown of Mysore in India. An engineer by training, he had been working in France and decided to return home. A driver who had picked up Murthy dropped him off at the railway station in Nis, a border town between the former Yugoslavia, now Serbia, and Bulgaria. It was 9:00 P.M. on a Saturday night and the restaurant was already closed. So was the bank.

Murthy, then twenty-eight, slept on the railway platform until 8:30 A.M., when the Sofia Express pulled into the station. He boarded the train and found himself in a compartment with two other passengers, a girl and a boy. "I struck up a conversation in French with the young girl," recalls Murthy. "She talked about the travails of living in an Iron Curtain country, until we were roughly interrupted by some policemen who, I later gathered, were summoned by the young man, who thought we were criticizing the Communist government of Bulgaria."

After the police led the girl away, Murthy's backpack and sleeping bag were confiscated. "I was dragged along the platform into a small eight-by-eight-foot room with a cold stone floor and a hole in one corner by way of toilet facilities," Murthy remembers. "I was held in that bitterly cold room without food or water for over seventy-two hours. I had lost all hope of ever seeing the outside world again, when the door opened. I was again dragged out unceremoniously, locked up in the guard's compartment on a departing freight train and told that I would be released twenty hours later upon reaching Istanbul. The guard's final words still ring in my ears—'You are from a friendly country called India and that is why we are letting you go!'

"The journey to Istanbul was lonely, and I was starving," says Murthy. "This long, lonely, cold journey forced me to deeply rethink my convictions about communism. Early on a dark Thursday morning, after being hungry for 108 hours, I was purged of any last vestiges of affinity for the Left. I concluded that entrepreneurship, resulting in large-scale job creation, was the only viable mechanism for eradicating poverty in societies."

Ultimately, the event would lead to the founding of one of the most successful entrepreneurial ventures in India. Murthy and six colleagues founded Infosys, the software development company and IT consulting firm, with just $250 in cash in 1981. Today, Infosys is a global technology powerhouse with more than $6 billion in sales and more than 130,000 employees.

More than any other entrepreneur, Murthy prevailed against unbelievable obstacles in building Infosys in an environment that was hostile to business start-ups. In the end, he proved that India could compete with the world by taking on work that had been the province of the West. As the company's CEO for twenty-one years, he helped to spark the outsourcing revolution that has brought billions into the Indian economy and transformed the country into the world's back office.

Murthy, known as a humble and self-effacing leader, turned over the CEO job to cofounder Nandan Nilekani in 2002. Though he retired from his executive position four years later, he remains chairman emeritus of the company he founded.

What trends were apparent to you in the early 1980s when you decided to try to start your own firm?

It was 1980 when three trends became very clear. The first was the unbundling of software from hardware. This was thanks to a ruling in a U.S. court that it should be possible for third-party software to be run on hardware sold by the hardware manufacturers. Until then, the hardware manufacturers were the ones that actually sold software, too.

The second trend we saw was the emergence of super minicomputers, which were much less expensive than the mainframes but had tremendous power and flexibility. Data General Corp. and Digital Equipment Corp. brought these to market. And finally we noticed that India was producing a large number of engineers who hardly had any job opportunities. These super minicomputers made the total cost of owning powerful computers much lower. We realized that more and more corporations would be installing such computers and therefore there would be greater opportunity for software to be developed for large corporations.

We said, look, we believe that the opportunity for software development would explode in the West, particularly in the United States, and here we are in India with a large number of available engineers who could develop software for customers abroad. That's how I got together a set of youngsters and said, "Look, why don't we think of starting a company, which will develop customized software applications for corporations in the West." That was the rationale for starting Infosys.

The story of how you came to become an entrepreneur is fascinating. Were you really a leftist who only reluctantly turned after being treated so badly by the Communists?

I was a leftist when I was a student because it was so easy to be a leftist in India. We all came under the influence of Jawaharlal Nehru, who had embraced socialism. He was much closer to the Soviet Union. Therefore it was very easy. Also in any postcolonial society, socialism is what generally appeals to people much more than capitalism.

When I was incarcerated, I spent seventy-six hours without food or water. That in some sense was the last nail in the coffin of my sympathy for the Left. I said, if this is how a Communist society treats friends, I don't want to be part of that. I don't want to go anywhere near that. It was on the train journey back to India where I said to myself, "I will go back to conduct an experiment in creating wealth, legally and ethically." That is how I got myself transformed from being a confused leftist to a gentleman capitalist. That was the first inflection point in my life.

But you didn't immediately create a company, right?

Along with one of my professors, I founded a think tank, which was using mathematics, systems theory, and computer science to solve the problems of large-scale public systems. I still had a lot of interest in public systems. But pretty quickly I realized that all the reports we produced were just gathering dust on the shelves of government offices. Therefore I said I'm not going to waste any more time. I must join the private sector.

I wanted to understand how corporations work, how they get customers and how they attract employees. And I joined a private sector firm in Mumbai as the head of corporate development. That was in '77 or so. In 1981 I decided to start Infosys because I wanted to conduct an experiment in creating wealth and jobs, legally and ethically. That's how I attracted these youngsters to work with me and that is how we founded Infosys.

India was not an especially welcoming place for business start-ups in the early 1980s. I understand there were unusual hardships and obstacles placed in your way. Can you give us some sense of what you were up against?

At that time friction to business in India was extremely high. Before the economic reforms of 1991, the friction was so high that most people were scared of doing any business in India. It took me about forty to fifty visits to Delhi and an elapsed time of three years to get a license to import a computer worth about $300,000. It would take us about fifteen days to get permission from the central bank to obtain foreign exchange to travel abroad for a day. It took us about two to three years to get a telephone connection.

There used to be a joke in India: half the people were said to be waiting for a telephone and the other half are waiting for a dial tone. So the context was completely stacked against us. However, I realized there was going to be an exploding opportunity for software development in the West, particularly in the United States. We started the company on the seventh of July 1981, and in the first nine years our progress was very slow because of all these reasons I talked about.

The whole thing changed in 1991 when we had economic reform. In 1990 we had come to approximately half a million of revenue per year and were reasonably profitable, and there was an offer to buy us out for one million dollars by one of the industrialists in India. Some of my colleagues got excited. They said a million dollars is a lot of money, and we had never seen that much money and we should sell. We had a four-hour discussion and debate on a Sunday morning in Bangalore. When it was my time to give my opinion, I said, "We have walked this path for nine years now, and somehow I believe we will soon see the light at the end of the tunnel. Therefore, I don't want to sell, and if you do I can buy your shares."

They were all surprised because they didn't think I had that much money. They asked me to explain my confidence. I started to explain how things are changing in this country and how the politicians and bureaucrats are getting frustrated as well. "Sooner or later," I said, "and I would think sooner, we will get all these bottlenecks to our business removed. Therefore, I don't want to leave this."

Within an hour or so, they all agreed not to sell their shares. Today, we have a market cap of $36 billion. In other words, one dollar at that point of time is now worth $36,000. Now they all tell me I was a genius. It was that I somehow was so attached to the company and the initiatives that I was hoping against hope that things would clear out.

What gave you the confidence not to sell out?

Out of the seven people I was the one who had made a few sacrifices. I was in a very senior position and I left that. By then, I had two children and my wife had left her job. I realized that I had to succeed because going back was not easy, because my position was a pretty senior one. For the rest of my colleagues, they were in very junior positions so the employment opportunities were very high for them. Second, by nature I am an optimistic person. The more I work hard, the more I face difficulties, I generally come out stronger. I said, "Look, we have run this marathon for nine years."

There were a couple of things that happened that gave us the confidence things would change. Sometime in '85 or '86 the government made the process of importing somewhat easier. And second, they also gave us some special facilities because we were exporting software. You can import software from the United States equal to the net foreign exchange that you generate for the company and sell it in India and make decent profits. So there were a few indications that things would improve, not huge indications but a few. And as an optimistic person, I believed that things would get better. And more importantly I was enjoying what we were doing and our needs were pretty small. My children and my wife lived a very simple lifestyle. In fact, none of us had any cars at all for the first ten years. But we were okay with that.

I came from a family of teachers. We were not businesspeople. This is the first time that anybody from the family entered business. For us, ignorance was bliss. For us, there was nothing to lose. We did not know how difficult it would be, so therefore I jumped into it pretty happily.

What other difficulties did you encounter?

Well, in 1991, the country had run into a very precarious situation in its foreign exchange reserves. We had foreign exchange just for fifteen days of imports. The government of India took all the gold it had and pledged it with the Bank of England to borrow money. That is the time the government realized the folly of its policies and liberalized our economy considerably. For example, in my industry they removed licensing completely. Then they abolished the office of the controller of capital issues, who was an officer of the government of India who had no idea how capital markets worked but he was the one who decided at what price any new company had its shares valued. He rarely gave any premium over the par value of the shares.

So the entrepreneurs were not keen on IPOs because they would give away most of their shares and could raise very little money. The entrepreneur and investment banker would decide on the pricing and have full control over the IPO process.

Finally, the government allowed any business to get whatever foreign exchange it wanted for its professionals to travel abroad, to open offices abroad.

So in 1991 the reforms totally transformed companies like Infosys because it was easy for us to travel abroad, open offices, and get ourselves consultants to improve our quality processes and brand equity. And the growth of Infosys came from 1992 onward.

We had to do some innovation here if we wanted to be attractive to our customers abroad. In 1981 when we went to a customer in the United States they would give us a cup of tea and be very nice but they would say, "Don't call us. We'll call you if we need you." And we came back and said, "Look, now that friction to business has been removed in India, we have to inno-vate how we develop software so we become attractive to customers."

That is when we invented the concept of the Global Delivery Model. Basically what it does is it splits a large-scale software development project into two classes of activities. The first has very high interaction with the customer and therefore has to be delivered on the customer's site or near the customer's site. And the second one has to have very little interaction and therefore it can be delivered from remote development centers in countries like India.

In the first two or three months, when we are in a phase of the project called rapid reaction warranty, we will station our employees at our cus-tomer's site because problems that come up have to be solved quickly. On the other hand, activities like architecture, functional design, technical design, database design, programming, testing, performance engineering, documentation, and long-term warranty can be delivered remotely from these scalable, talent-rich development centers in countries like India.

In a typical project, anywhere between 20 and 30 percent of effort belongs to the first part of activities that have to be delivered at the cus-tomer's site. The rest can be delivered remotely. The customer gets better quality software on time and within budgeted cost. Just to give you an idea, as late as 1990, only 45 to 50 percent of software projects were completed on time and within budget. A large percentage of them, in fact, were aban-doned midway. At Infosys today, 92 percent of our projects with clients are delivered on time and within budget.

That happens because we have spent a lot of money in training our employees. We have the world's largest training center in Mysore. We can train fifteen thousand engineers on any given day. Second, we invested heavily in quality processes and systems. Just as Deming was rejected by the United States and embraced by the Japanese, Indian companies took quickly to the capability and maturity model of the Software Engineering Institute at Carnegie Mellon. So we embraced ISO 9001; we embraced the Carnegie Mellon ideas and we embraced the principles of Malcolm Bald-rige. So we improved our quality. And we invested a lot in technology and tools so our productivity increased. In Bangalore today we have a place where twenty thousand software professionals work. In Pune, we have built infrastructure for twenty-five thousand software professionals. In fact, we have eleven centers in India. We have centers in China, Melbourne, Tokyo, and the Czech Republic. When you get good talent and train them well and provide them with good technology and good processes then they are bound to improve the probability of success of projects.

At one point, you also decided to list the company on the NASDAQ in the United States. How come?

In '96, we said if we want to enhance the confidence of our customers, it will be a good idea to be listed on an American stock exchange because then every day they would see our stock being traded. We would be accountable to the SEC and they would say, "these guys are in business to stay and they can be trusted." So starting in '96 we voluntarily started recasting our financial statements according to the generally accepted accounting principles of the United States. On March 11, 1999, we got listed on NASDAQ and as I was sitting on the high stool at the NASDAQ headquarters I was asked about the significance of Infosys being listed on NASDAQ. I borrowed the words of Neil Armstrong, which he used when he landed on the moon. I said, "It is a small step for NASDAQ but it was a giant leap for Infosys and the Indian software industry."

What about capital? How did you get the money to grow the company?

I realized pretty early that finance was not our strength. We put together only 10,000 rupees, and at today's exchange rate, it is $250,000. I knew that it wouldn't take us anywhere. So I negotiated with our first client. I said, "Look you have to give us a certain advance and pay us every month on the last day." We managed the company that way. Because at that point it took us three years to get the license to import a computer, my colleagues went to New York and developed the software there. I stayed back in India because I wanted to get the license to get a computer and it took me two and one half years to get the license, and I arranged capital to import this computer from the state financial and industrial development corporation. So we got at that point a loan of something like $350,000 to $400,000. But all of our working capital was given to us by our clients.

In the United States, with open access to venture capital, a great university system, it seems so much easier for entrepreneurs.

Most days no bank would give us any loans because banks wanted collateral to give any capital loan. It meant that when you import a computer they would give the loan against the computer and they would say if you don't pay the loan we will seize the computer. Or they would give you a loan for buying a machine or building a factory. But in the case of software they had nothing as collateral because they did not understand the value of software. Therefore it was impossible for us to get any loans from a bank. There were no loans being given to software entrepreneurs. That is how we went and convinced the state government that they should look at software in a different way and loan us money.

We had no data communications facilities. You won't believe this, but we used to send software by faxes to our customers. We sent source code by faxes to our customers. After that, we used to send software by magnetic tape, but the process of sending the tape to the customer and getting those tapes passed through the Indian customs was quite torturous. It could take a week or ten days to get the tapes cleared by customs for our customers. In 1983, one of our customers said, "Look, you guys are reasonably smart, therefore we trust you. I will loan you a secondhand computer, a mainframe, and you can develop software from Bangalore. However, I want you to report your progress once a day by telephone. We could not get a telephone connection for two years and therefore we could not start the project in Bangalore.

And when you don't get working capital from banks or capital loans and don't have big office space, it's not easy to attract good quality employees. So we went through all those things, but there was one thing unique about this group: everybody was a crack designer or crack programmer, and when we went to educational institutions we used to ask the students to give us some puzzles in computer science. And we would solve these puzzles in front of them because we had to somehow create a differentiation in front of the best minds. And when they saw these seven fellows solving those puzzles so quickly they all must have thought, "These guys are pretty bright, and I think they will do something to make sure our future is not bad." That's how we attracted smart talent, because we had no big fancy office, no facilities, we did not have much bank balance. We had nothing.

So you did overcome these obstacles. What would you say have been the most important lessons you learned in both creating and growing Infosys?

There are many lessons. The first one is if you want to become a successful entrepreneur you must have an idea whose business value to the market must be expressible as a simple sentence. Not a complex sentence. In other words, it should be very easy to pitch your uniqueness to the customer.

Second, the market must be ready to accept your idea. If the market is not ready, it won't succeed. In the early seventies, Philips came out with a wonderful minicomputer. By then HP, Digital Equipment Corp., and Data General had produced minicomputers in the United States, and they were sold and pretty successful. Philips produced a pretty good computer but [it] didn't succeed because the world somehow didn't think that buying a Philips computer would be a good idea. So the market must be ready to accept and buy your idea.

Third, you need a team of people who have a common and enduring value system because entrepreneurship is all about deferred gratification. It is all about sacrifice today, fulfillment tomorrow. It is all about sacrifice, hard work, lots of frustrations, being away from family, in the hope that someday you will get adequate returns from that. You need a good value system because at the end of the day it is all about being willing to pay a certain price or cost for your convictions.

Let me give you a simple example: Let's say we are going on a road and we see a $100 bill. And you say, "Some poor guy has dropped it. Let me pick it up and go and give it to the police station so that the fellow who lost it might be able to get it back." And I would tell you, "No, no, no. Nobody else has seen this, only the two of us. Why don't we split it, fifty bucks to you and fifty bucks to me?" So your value system is clearly better than mine because you are willing to forgo the $100 because you are an honest man. You want to sympathize with the fellow who lost the $100. So value systems translate to a certain cost that you are willing to incur for your convictions.

Entrepreneurship is all about that journey because you believe that you will transform the world at some time. And because you believe that transformation will make you better. It may bring you laurels and money and power, whatever it is. You are willing to make a lot of sacrifices today and willing to pay a huge cost. So therefore the team has to have an enduring value system.

Finally, it is ideal if you can bring complementary strengths amongst the founders of the corporation. For example, when Paul Allen and Bill Gates founded Microsoft, Paul Allen looked after the development of software, and Bill Gates looked after selling that stuff, by and large. So their strengths were complementary. If both of them focused only on developing software, I don't think they would have been successful. And if both of them focused only on selling, there would be nothing to sell. Therefore I believe you have to bring a team of people who have mutually exclusive but collectively exhaustive sets of skills, expertise, and experience. These four points are the essential attributes for success as an entrepreneur.

At the end of the day there is only one entity that puts food on the table for all of us and that is the customer. Therefore every day before having my dinner I say amen to the customer. Because it is thanks to the customer I am able to eat my dinner. So we have to have an unflinching focus on adding value to the customer and we have to obtain the trust of the customer. That trust comes from our competence, our character, and our relationships.

The next lesson that we have learned is that investors understand that every business will have ups and downs, but what they want you to do is to level with them at all points of time. They want you to bring the bad news early and proactively. At Infosys we say two things: one, "When in doubt disclose," and second, we say, "Let the good news take the stairs, but the bad news must always take the elevator."

Ours is a people-based industry. It is really the power of the mind that creates differentiation. Therefore if we want quality people to join us we have to foster an environment of openness, a meritocracy, discussion, debate, and pluralism. We have to treat every professional with the required courtesy, dignity, and respect. Every transaction would have to be started on a zero base without bringing in the biases from prior transactions. Every transaction must be discussed in an environment of harmony and decent behavior. That is why we say you can disagree with me as long as you are not disagreeable. That is extremely important because if we create such an environment, then youngsters will come up with new ideas. They will say, "Okay, last time my idea was shot down because it was not good enough, but this time I have a higher chance of success."

The other thing that we have always done is made sure that every transaction is decided on data and facts, because that is how you come to merit-based decisions. And your value system must be communicated to your people by using very simple but powerful adages. One of our adages is, "In God we trust, but everybody else brings data and facts to the table."

Of course, change is often hard for organizations because it's hard for people. How did you cope with change as the company became larger and larger?

The biggest bottleneck to progress all of us have is our own mind. All the problems are there in our mind. If we can work on the problems in our mind then we can work on the problems in the exterior. Most of us fight a constant battle between our mind, which is the engine that makes the progress, and our mind-set. Our mind-set is the collective set of our experiences and our assumptions. Only those of us who are able to defeat the mind-set in favor of the mind are the ones who will make progress.

In Infosys, most of the problems were simply because we could not think outside the problem because they were really the problems in our mind. I also realized that leaders have to lead by example. Leadership is all about transformation, big-ticket change. The primary job of a leader is to raise the aspirations of his people, to make them feel more confident, to make them think of doing the plausibly impossible stuff. As Robert Kennedy once said, "Most people see things as they are and wonder why. I dream of things that never were and then say why not?" I think this defines the role of the leader very well. The role of the leader is to think of things that others have not thought about and then to say why not?

Achieving anything worthwhile requires a lot of hard work, a lot of sacrifice and commitment. If you want your people to put in all of this dedication and hard work they must have implicit faith in you, like people had faith in Moses. That faith comes from trust.

If you want your people to trust you, then you have to lead by example. When a leader demonstrates leadership by example what he or she is saying is, "I believe in what I am preaching. I practice what I am preaching. Therefore, what is good for me is good for you and what is good for you is good for me."

Until five years ago, I used to be in the office by 6:20 A.M. Then, automatically my colleagues realized I was coming early to the office and they would come too. But on the other hand, if I asked them to come to the office early and I went late, they would say this guy doesn't walk the talk. He doesn't practice the precept. Therefore we have no confidence in what he says. What he says is probably good for him and not good for us.

In today's world it is best that you obsolete your own inventions proactively rather than your competitors obsolete your ideas and inventions, because when you do it yourself you are in control of that obsolescence. If your competitor releases a product, which obsoletes your product without you knowing, then you are in serious trouble. So at Infosys we always tell our people to do continuous innovation and obsolete their own innovations proactively and as early as possible.

We have also realized that it is best that we think of competition on a global level. In today's world, you don't know where the competition will come from. Once upon a time, companies in America believed competition would come primarily from the United States or Europe. But today that's not true. It could come from China, India, Brazil, or any other country. Therefore it is best that we benchmark ourselves on a global level in every aspect of our operations.

You have often used the term "compassionate capitalist" to describe your version of entrepreneurialism. How would you define that term?

I believe a compassionate capitalist is one who is a capitalist in the mind and a socialist at heart. His mind will work harder and harder to create greater wealth, to make his corporation bigger and bigger. At the same time his heart will tell him, "Friend, you have to play an ethical and fair game. You cannot do illegal stuff. You have to give back to society. You have to realize that society contributes customers, employees, and investors. Creating goodwill with a society is very important."

A compassionate capitalist will always have a part of his brain which says, "I need to become the largest and the most successful in the world." But the other part is influenced by the heart, which says, "I have to do it legally and ethically. I have to do it in a manner that brings respect from society."

It's really interesting, when we founded the company in 1981 seven of us sat down in my small apartment in Mumbai to decide on the objectives of the company. One of my Indian friends said, "Why don't we want to become the software company with the highest revenue in India?" Another colleague said, "We must be the most profitable software company in India."

And finally when my turn came I said, "Look, friends, why don't we say we want to be the most respected company in India, not just in software, but in every field. If you seek respect then you will do everything right. If you seek respect from customers, you will not shortchange them. If you seek respect from your fellow employees, you will treat them with respect and dignity. You would be fair with them. If you want respect from your investors, you will follow the finest principles of corporate governance. If you want respect from government, you will not violate any of the laws of the land. If you do all this, revenues will automatically come with profits and market capitalization."

In some sense a compassionate capitalist is one who seeks respect from every stakeholder while maximizing the shareholder value.

What advice would you give an entrepreneur today who is just starting a new business?

I would say the opportunities are enormous, but I would tell them the four attributes for successful entrepreneurship that I mentioned earlier: You must have an idea whose value to the market can be expressed in a single sentence; the market must be ready for the idea. Therefore they must do some test marketing before they go further. They must put together a team with an enduring value system because entrepreneurship is all about deferred gratification; and finally they have to build a team with complementary strengths.

LARRY PAGE and SERGEY BRIN

GOOGLE

For years people kept mixing the two of them up.

Which one is Larry Page again? Is Sergey Brin the one with the accent?

It was understandable because they both are roughly the same height, mild-mannered, and lean toward the introverted yet passionate personalities that fit the stereotypical "computer geek."

And for years they both have sported ear-to-ear grins thanks to starring in the ultimate Revenge of the Nerds story—not only did they both "get the girls," they practically own the world. The world of information, that is, which had been their goal from the start.

When the two initially met at Stanford University in March 1995, Page, then twenty-two, was visiting Stanford to decide whether to attend. Brin, already a gifted grad student and twenty-one, was assigned to show him around campus. Legend had it that they disagreed about almost everything during their first meeting. Regardless, soon after Page enrolled in the PhD program, the pair began collaborating on a search engine called BackRub.

Page wanted to download the entire contents of the Web onto a computer as part of his research for his dissertation. He confidently told his professor at the time that it would take him only a week. This gross miscalculation (by the end of the year he had only a small portion downloaded) spurred him on to create what would become one of the most innovative and disruptive companies in the world—Google. At the same time, Sergey Brin was making his name by creating a software program for a formatting markup language.

A self-proclaimed "university brat," Page was raised on college campuses. His father, Carl, was a Michigan State computer science professor. Both his parents shared an early fascination with technology and computers, with his father moving on to obtain three degrees from the University of Michigan in the subject. So it was no accident that the son came of age in a world where computers were ever present. As he recalls, "We had computers laying all over the place and I was the first kid in my class to turn in a paper that had been typed on a word processor."

Literally halfway around the world, meantime, Sergey Brin was beginning his own adventures in computing. Born in Moscow to Jewish parents, Sergey's father, Michael, had long dreamed of becoming an astronomer, but had been denied entry to the best universities due to anti-Semitism. Instead, he earned his degree in mathematics at Moscow State University. They lived in a three-room, 350-square-foot apartment shared with his paternal grandmother until the family emigrated to the United States when Brin was six years old. When they applied for their exit visas, both parents lost their jobs.

In 1979, the family settled in Maryland, where Michael Brin eventually became a professor in the mathematics department of the University of Maryland. Like Page's father, Brin's father was able to actively raise his son, encouraging his love of mathematics. Brin was a strong student and graduated with honors from the University of Maryland. As his interest in computer science grew, he set his sights on moving west to California, where the majority of computer development was taking place.

After the two met at Stanford, they became fast friends. Page's project "to organize the world's information and make it universally accessible and useful" quickly gained the attention of the computer department. Brin joined his friend's effort and by the fall of 1997 they called the initial search product BackRub. The name obviously wouldn't stick. After several days of brainstorming different ideas they came up with Google, after the numerical term *googol*, referring to 1 with one hundred zeros after it. With its new name, Google was made internally accessible to those at Stanford University and history was in the making. The following year they moved the budding company to a friend's garage, following in the footsteps of two other well-known Stanford entrepreneurs, Bill Hewlett and Dave Packard.

Page and Brin were classic bootstrappers. Maxing out three credit cards and gathering some spare cash from friends and faculty, they bought three servers off the back of a truck. They were then able to capture the attention of a cofounder of Sun Microsystems, who wrote them a check for $100,000. There were at least five prominent search engines available at the time. But what differentiated Google and allowed it to quickly return more accurate searches was its approach: Page and Brin developed algorithms to process the link structure of the Web based on the theory that the more others linked to a piece of information the more important it ultimately was.

From 1998 to 2001, Page served as chief executive until Eric Schmidt, the former chief technology officer of Sun Microsystems and a former CEO of Novell, was recruited to the job. Schmidt helped to bring Google public in 2004 and helped to lead its massive growth. In his last year as CEO, Google revenues exceeded $29 billion and its net profits were $8.5 billion. With more than 28,000 employees, Google became one of the biggest entrepreneurial success stories ever. Page took back the CEO's job in early 2011, while Brin retained his focus on product development.

On the early beginnings:

Page: We didn't start out to do a search engine at all. In late 1995, I started collecting the links on the Web, because my adviser and I decided that would be a good thing to do. We didn't know exactly what I was going to do with it, but it seemed like no one was really looking at the links on the Web—which pages link to which pages. So it is a huge graph. I figured I could get a dissertation and do something fun and perhaps practical at the same time, which is really what motivates me.

I started off by reversing the links, and then I wanted to find basically, say, who links to the Stanford home page, and there's ten thousand people who link to Stanford. Then the question is, which ones do you show? So you can only show ten, and we ended up with this way of ranking links, based on the links. Then we were like, "Wow, this is really good. It ranks things in the order you would expect to see them." Stanford would be first. You can take universities and just rank them, and they come out in the order you'd expect. So we thought, "This is really interesting. This thing really works. We should use it for search." So I started building a search engine. Sergey also came on very early, probably in late '95 or early '96, and was really interested in the data mining part. Basically, we thought, "Oh, we should be able to make a better search engine this way."

On dealing with the management of a company at a young age:

Page: I think the age is a real issue. It's certainly a handicap in the sense of being able to manage people and to hire people and all these kinds of things, maybe more so than it should be. Certainly, I think, the things that I'm missing are more things that you acquire with time. If you manage people for twenty years, or something like that, you pick up things. So I certainly lack experience there, and that's an issue. But I sort of make up for that, I think, in terms of understanding where things are going to go, having a vision about the future, and really understanding the industry I am in, and what the company does, and also sort of the unique position of starting a company and working on it for three years before starting the company. Then working on it pretty hard, whatever, twenty-four hours a day. So I understand a lot of the aspects pretty well. I guess that compensates a little bit for lack of skills in other areas.

On dreaming your entrepreneurial idea:

Page: You know what it's like to wake up in the middle of the night with a vivid dream? And you know how, if you don't have a pencil and pad by the bed to write it down, it will be completely gone the next morning? Well, I had one of those dreams when I was twenty-three. When I suddenly woke up, I was thinking: what if we could download the whole Web, and just keep the links and . . . I grabbed a pen and started writing! Sometimes it is important to wake up and stop dreaming. I spent the middle of that night scribbling out the details and convincing myself it would work.

Soon after, I told my adviser, Terry Winograd, it would take a couple of weeks to download the Web—he nodded knowingly, fully aware it would take much longer but wise enough to not tell me. The optimism of youth is often underrated! Amazingly, I had no thought of building a search engine. The idea wasn't even on the radar. But much later we happened upon a better way of ranking Web pages to make a really great search engine, and Google was born. When a really great dream shows up, grab it!

On advice to would-be entrepreneurs:

Page: Don't settle. It's very, very important if you are starting a company to have the right people involved. I can't stress that enough. I have been enormously happy with people we have involved at Google with my cofounder and with Eric. We took a long time to find these people. It took over a year to hire Eric. Having great people involved who you really like and who are compatible with you is tremendously important. You are never going to question the equity you gave up or any of the other things if you have that.

The other thing I think we really benefited from was being real experts. We worked on Google together for many years at Stanford before we started the company. That was a pretty nice position to be in. We understood all aspects of search. We talked to all the search companies. We really knew a lot about what was going on. You can do that pretty cheaply. It's just your labor. You can invest a year or two and you can learn something really well before you start having hundreds of people working on the problem.

I went to a leadership seminar once in Michigan, where I came from, and they have a great slogan, which was "Have a healthy disregard for the impossible." What this means is that you should set stretch goals that you are not sure you can achieve but are sort of reasonable. You don't want completely outlandish goals. One thing I didn't realize when I was starting Google is that it's often easier to have aggressive goals. A lot of times people pick very specific things they want to do because they think it's easier to attain. If you are being more specific, you also get less resources. So the question isn't how much resources you can get. It's can you make a case for what you're doing and does it make sense and do you have a real advantage?

On this theme, it's okay to solve a hard problem. That's why you get paid if you're a company. It's for doing something that other people can't do easily. A lot of times it's important to do the whole problem. So don't be afraid of the hard problems. That's where you get the big leverage.

Finally, don't pay any attention to the VC bandwagon. A lot of companies still get started because some space is hot. And honestly, I don't think that's a very good reason to start a company. In fact, we see hundreds or thousands of people who come to us who want us to commercialize something or who want us to collaborate with their business. We actually look at these, and I look at quite a few of them. And my guess is there may be one a year we are interested in. The trick is to have the one that somebody is going to be interested in because it's a good idea and not be one of the thousands that come through all the time. If you're the one good deal or you have a good idea and you really understand the area you're in, the funding environment doesn't matter. It doesn't matter if it's a hot area. I guarantee you'll be able to get people to help you out.

On staying innovative when getting bigger:

Brin: The way I like to think about it is not to maintain our culture but to improve it and increase it. Scale presents challenges but also opportunities. For example, if you look at the infrastructure we have in computational facilities. Now when we want to run an experiment we can get it done in a few hours' time. This really opens new possibilities. At the same time, you have to make sure that scale doesn't slow you down in terms of doing innovative things. The way we have historically come at it is we try to divide our company into chunks. It's the 70-20-10 rule. About 70 percent try to work on the core efforts of the company, 20 percent goes to adjacent areas and expansion, and for the 10 percent anything goes. As we have expanded our breadth of offerings, it's actually harder and harder to find the 10 percent out there. But I think that's important to let people be really creative and think outside the box. The real challenge in scale has been offering a coherent set of services to our end users, because there is a limit to my ability and to everyone's ability to choose among fifty different things. So we've been trying to change the paradigm from products to features to enhance the capability of all our existing offerings across the board rather than creating a new silo out there.

On disagreements among key players:

Brin: We have relatively few disagreements, actually. And most of the time you usually don't care so much or all three of us don't care so much. Honestly, we try to go for two out of three. It's good to have an odd number. When people feel really strongly about something, you have to take the time to talk it through. The most controversial thing I recently did was to reduce the amount of snacks we have available. It took a long time to persuade Larry and Eric, but even after having accomplished that, then the rest of the staff was resistant. No matter what we said, food kept arriving in vast quantities in the snack bins. After a couple of years I prevailed and they reduced the amount of food.

Page: They recently reversed that call.

Brin: I know. You need to watch those things.

On mega-ambitious dreams:

Page: I think it is often easier to make progress on mega-ambitious dreams. I know that sounds completely nuts. But since no one else is crazy enough to do it, you have little competition. There are so few people this crazy that I feel like I know them all by first name. They all travel as if they are pack dogs and stick to each other like glue. The best people want to work the big challenges. That is what happened with Google. Our mission is to organize the world's information and make it universally accessible and useful. How can that not get you excited? But we almost didn't start Google, because my cofounder Sergey and I were too worried about dropping out of our PhD program. You are probably on the right track if you feel like a sidewalk worm during a rainstorm! That is about how we felt after we maxed out three credit cards buying hard disks off the back of a truck. That was the first hardware for Google. What is the one-sentence summary of how you change the world? Always work hard on something uncomfortably exciting!

On balance:

Brin: To be productive means working hard, but it doesn't mean working crazy. It means having a life outside of work. If you have blinders on and [you're] sitting in front of a computer for hours and hours, that makes you shut down.

Page: I think it definitely helps to be really focused on what you are doing. You can only work so many hours, and I try to have some balance in my life and so on. I think a lot of people go through this in school. They work really hard. You can do that for part of your life, but you can't do that indefinitely. At some point, you want to have a family. You want to have more time to do other things. I would say that it is an advantage being young. You don't have as many other responsibilities.

On legacy:

Brin: In terms of being remembered, I think I want to make the world a better place. That's a pretty generic answer, but I mean it in several ways. One is through Google, the company, in terms of giving people access to information. I'm sure I will do other endeavors in terms of technologies and businesses. The second is just through philanthropy. I don't have a significant amount of wealth beyond that on paper right now, but I hope that I have the opportunity to direct resources to the right places. I think that is the most important thing to me. I don't think my quality of life is really going to improve that much with more money.

On ten core principles that guide their actions:

Page and Brin: Focus on the user and all else will follow.

Since the beginning, we've focused on providing the best user experience possible. Whether we're designing a new Internet browser or a new tweak to the look of the home page, we take great care to ensure that they will ultimately serve you, rather than our own internal goal or bottom line. Our home page interface is clear and simple, and pages load instantly. Placement in search results is never sold to anyone, and advertising is not only clearly marked as such, it offers relevant content and is not distracting. And when we build new tools and applications, we believe they should work so well you don't have to consider how they might have been designed differently.

It's best to do one thing really, really well.

We do search. With one of the world's largest research groups focused exclusively on solving search problems, we know what we do well, and how we could do it better. Through continued iteration on difficult problems, we've been able to solve complex issues and provide continuous improvements to a service that already makes finding information a fast and seamless experience for millions of people. Our dedication to improving search helps us apply what we've learned to new products, like Gmail and Google Maps. Our hope is to bring the power of search to previously unexplored areas, and to help people access and use even more of the ever-expanding information in their lives.

Fast is better than slow.

We know your time is valuable, so when you're seeking an answer on the Web you want it right away—and we aim to please. We may be the only people in the world who can say our goal is to have people leave our home page as quickly as possible. By shaving excess bits and bytes from our pages and increasing the efficiency of our serving environment, we've broken our own speed records many times over, so that the average response time on a search result is a fraction of a second. We keep speed in mind with each new product we release, whether it's a mobile application or Google Chrome, a browser designed to be fast enough for the modern Web. And we continue to work on making it all go even faster.

Democracy on the Web works.

Google search works because it relies on the millions of individuals posting links on Web sites to help determine which other sites offer content of value. We assess the importance of every Web page using more than two hundred signals and a variety of techniques, including our patented Page-Rank algorithm, which analyzes which sites have been "voted" to be the best sources of information by other pages across the Web. As the Web gets bigger, this approach actually improves, as each new site is another point of information and another vote to be counted. In the same vein, we are active in open source software development, where innovation takes place through the collective effort of many programmers.

You don't need to be at your desk to need an answer.

The world is increasingly mobile: people want access to information wherever they are, whenever they need it. We're pioneering new technologies and offering new solutions for mobile services that help people all over the globe to do any number of tasks on their phone, from checking e-mail and calendar events to watching videos, not to mention the several different ways to access Google search on a phone. In addition, we're hoping to fuel greater innovation for mobile users everywhere with Android, a free, open source mobile platform. Android brings the openness that shaped the Internet to the mobile world. Not only does Android benefit consumers, who have more choice and innovative new mobile experiences, but it opens up revenue opportunities for carriers, manufacturers, and developers.

You can make money without doing evil.

Google is a business. The revenue we generate is derived from offering search technology to companies and from the sale of advertising displayed on our site and on other sites across the Web. Hundreds of thousands of advertisers worldwide use AdWords to promote their products; hundreds of thousands of publishers take advantage of our AdSense program to deliver ads relevant to their site content. To ensure that we're ultimately serving all our users (whether they are advertisers or not), we have a set of guiding principles for our advertising programs and practices:

We don't allow ads to be displayed on our results pages unless they are relevant where they are shown. And we firmly believe that ads can provide useful information if, and only if, they are relevant to what you wish to find—so it's possible that certain searches won't lead to any ads at all.

We believe that advertising can be effective without being flashy. We don't accept pop-up advertising, which interferes with your ability to see the content you've requested. We've found that text ads that are relevant to the person reading them draw much higher click-through rates than ads appearing randomly. Any advertiser, whether small or large, can take advantage of this highly targeted medium.

Advertising on Google is always clearly identified as a "Sponsored Link," so it does not compromise the integrity of our search results. We never manipulate rankings to put our partners higher in our search results, and no one can buy better PageRank. Our users trust our objectivity, and no short-term gain could ever justify breaching that trust.

There's always more information out there.

Once we'd indexed more of the HTML pages on the Internet than any other search service, our engineers turned their attention to information that was not as readily accessible. Sometimes it was just a matter of integrating new databases into search, such as adding a phone number and address lookup and a business directory. Other efforts required a bit more creativity, like adding the ability to search news archives, patents, academic journals, billions of images and millions of books. And our researchers continue looking into ways to bring all the world's information to people seeking answers.

The need for information crosses all borders.

Our company was founded in California, but our mission is to facilitate access to information for the entire world, and in every language. To that end, we have offices in more than 60 countries, maintain more than 180 Internet domains, and serve more than half of our results to people living outside the United States. We offer Google's search interface in more than 130 languages, offer people the ability to restrict results to content written in their own language, and aim to provide the rest of our applications and products in as many languages and accessible formats as possible. Using our translation tools, people can discover content written on the other side of the world in languages they don't speak. With these tools and the help of volunteer translators, we have been able to greatly improve both the variety and quality of services we can offer in even the most far-flung corners of the globe.

You can be serious without a suit.

We built Google around the idea that work should be challenging, and the challenge should be fun. We believe that great, creative things are more likely to happen with the right company culture—and that doesn't just mean lava lamps and rubber balls. There is an emphasis on team achievements and pride in individual accomplishments that contribute to our overall success. We put great stock in our employees—energetic, passionate people from diverse backgrounds with creative approaches to work, play, and life. Our atmosphere may be casual, but as new ideas emerge in a café line, at a team meeting, or at the gym, they are traded, tested, and put into practice with dizzying speed—and they may be the launchpad for a new project destined for worldwide use.

Great just isn't good enough.

We see being great at something as a starting point, not an endpoint. We set ourselves goals we know we can't reach yet, because we know that by stretching to meet them we can get further than we expected. Through innovation and iteration, we aim to take things that work well and improve upon them in unexpected ways. For example, when one of our engineers saw that search worked well for properly spelled words, he wondered about how it handled typos. That led him to create an intuitive and more helpful spell checker.

Even if you don't know exactly what you're looking for, finding an answer on the Web is our problem, not yours. We try to anticipate needs not yet articulated by our global audience, and meet them with products and services that set new standards. When we launched Gmail, it had more storage space than any e-mail service available. In retrospect offering that seems obvious—but that's because now we have new standards for e-mail storage. Those are the kinds of changes we seek to make, and we're always looking for new places where we can make a difference. Ultimately, our constant dissatisfaction with the way things are becomes the driving force behind everything we do.

CHARLES SCHWAB

THE CHARLES SCHWAB CORPORATION

I f ever there was a natural born entrepreneur, someone who had the desire to create and build a successful enterprise in his blood, it would have to be Charles Schwab. As an eight-year-old, the person who would invent the discount brokerage business in the United States made his entrepreneurial debut by picking and selling walnuts in California, packing them into hundred-pound sacks that he sold for $5 each.

"Some other kids thought I was a little crazy, spending my free time rooting through the twigs and leaves," he recalls. But Schwab absorbed some early lessons from his entrepreneurial instincts. "Although plenty of people didn't want to buy, I quickly learned that if I kept at it and plowed right through the rejections, I would eventually get someone to buy my wares. If I wanted to accumulate extra spending money, I had to pick up extra walnuts. If I wasted my effort on the cheaper but more plentiful [black] walnuts, I'd earn that much less."

He can remember at the age of ten going to high school football games gathering Coca-Cola bottles so he could turn them in for a nickel a piece. And by the time he was thirteen, he gathered up about twenty-five chickens and turned them into a money-making machine. Years later, when Schwab went to Stanford University for his MBA degree, he would quip that before he could shave, he owned a vertically integrated business that leveraged every aspect of farming chickens. "I sold the eggs," he says. "I learned to kill and pluck fryers for market; and I developed a list of clients for my own chicken fertilizer."

Those early entrepreneurial instincts would serve him exceptionally well, especially because he also suffered from a lifelong handicap with the written word. Unbeknownst to him until much later in life, Schwab struggled with dyslexia, the disability that makes it unusually difficult for someone to read, write, and sound out letters. He recalls reading the classics but in comic book form, the only way he could plod through school reading assignments. As a Stanford University freshman in 1955, Schwab was "completely buried," flunking both French and freshman English before finding safety and comfort in economics. He got through Stanford by reading summaries of books and borrowing the lecture notes from fellow classmates.

There was little surprise when, after college, he launched an investment newsletter with two other partners. After all, besides his entrepreneurial bent, at the age of thirteen, he had begun reading the stock market tables in the *Santa Barbara News-Press* with his father, finding himself amazed that the prices of shares would change each day.

Though at its peak it reached a subscriber base of three thousand users, the newsletter barely survived. But in 1973, with a $100,000 loan from his uncle, Schwab made his big move, waging a war against the Wall Street giants. His aim was to exploit fixed-rate commissions, which ended in 1975, when the government mandated negotiated commission rates. While many brokerages took the opportunity to raise commissions, Schwab seized the chance to create the first discount brokerage, opening his first branch in Sacramento, California.

Charles Schwab & Co. was a huge success, helping to slash more traditional broker revenues and driving dozens of old line firms out of business. Schwab was the first brokerage firm to extend service hours to customers, the first to use an automated transaction and record-keeping system to bring down the cost of trades, and the first to offer a twenty-four-hour, seven-day-a-week order entry and quotation service.

There were ups and downs through different market cycles. At one point, in 1983, Schwab sold his company to Bank of America, only to buy it back four years later. After completely giving up the CEO's job to his handpicked successor, David Pottruck, Schwab came back just fourteen months later to replace him in 2004 when the firm hit difficult times. But the story of Chuck Schwab is really the story of a financial revolution that has attracted tens of millions of Americans as investors.

Today, Chuck Schwab remains chairman of a company to which investors have entrusted $1.66 trillion. With more than thirteen thousand employees, The Charles Schwab Corporation is one of the largest brokerage firms in the world.

On getting through Stanford with dyslexia:

Man, I struggled through Stanford. It was just hard work all the time. In fact, I got in on a golf scholarship and thank God I had this athletic capability. It wasn't my academics that got me in. I had no trouble with numbers or conceptual ideas. It was the inability of decoding words into meaning in a rapid way. It's not only reading. It's writing, too. It's very difficult in college when you are taking notes from a lecture. I always had people I went to and borrowed their notes.

I didn't discover I had dyslexia until my youngest son had a difficult time in first and second grade and we went to have him tested. I was in my early forties. That's when I discovered that what I had was what he had. In some sense I'm glad I didn't know, because I just struggled as hard as I could.

On being an entrepreneur:

I have been an entrepreneur all my life—having come from a time when things were pretty tough. My dad was a small-town lawyer, and our family conversations were about how limited resources were.

I did as much as I could: raising chickens, pushing an ice cream cart, bagging walnuts, driving a tractor on a beet farm, working on the railroad. I think this eclectic career helped me a lot in life. I really encourage kids to get those kinds of jobs.

On naming the company after himself:

In '73, I changed the name from what it was, First Commander, to Charles Schwab and Company. To establish the name, you have to go to the state, and they had other Schwab companies. There was a Schwab drugstore, a Schwab this, a Schwab that. Finally I said to the lawyer, How about Charles Schwab? They can't take my name away from me, for goodness' sakes!

On his company's mission:

Our mission statement was to be the most ethical and most useful financial services company in the world. We really emphasize the word *ethics*. We work on it. We thrive for it. It is critically important to us. Any kind of conflicts we have or might have we talk about. We let our customers know about them on our Web site.

On selling his firm by selling himself:

Way back when, we had an advertising executive here who said, "Chuck, let's take that picture of you and put it in the ad." I had all the reticence you could imagine: what kind of an egomaniac would do that?

But what happened was the results were five- or six-fold what they were without some kind of figurehead talking about something that is quite passionate to him—what we could do for clients. The results were just tremendously better than not having a real spokesman, or having some actor do this stuff.

Then we got into a phase where we were using lots of celebrities. Coming back to the "Talk to Chuck" thing was brilliant. It distinguished our company over the years that there really is somebody there who cares and takes responsibility for what we do, every day.

On the importance of customers and keeping costs low:

Every company, a mature company, can look at their costs and redundancies. It's natural for every company that's successful to build up infrastructures that are inefficient. We're all human. We all do that. And you want to take whatever savings you can out of that and figure out how to get it back to your loyal clients. They will reward you with additional business, even if you mess things up.

The most important part is that your clients have to sense that they are valuable. Because at the end of every day, having a clientele that speaks well of you, that's the largest source of business.

I don't care what kind of business you're in: clients who refer us to their friends or relatives is so much more powerful than any advertising we could ever do. We talk about that a lot around here: "What do our clients say about us?" The ultimate question to ask a client is, "Would you recommend us to a friend or relative of yours?" That's the ultimate test. If they say, "Well, I don't know," that's not a good outcome.

So our organization just has to outfox our larger competitors by really emphasizing our value proposition, which is really outstanding compared to them. We have to make sure our clients feel that there is personal service here, there is indeed someone at Schwab who cares about them, whom they can talk to and get the kind of help they want. Some people want a lot of help. Others just need a tiny bit of help, such as "How can I navigate on Schwab.com better than I do today?"

On advice he would give a young entrepreneur:

You've got to start with your gut, with something you are really passionate about, for a good reason. You won't get there by sitting in a closet and thinking, "Boy, I know the world must want this." You have to get some real-world experience that tells you what people want. Luck helps every successful entrepreneur. But it doesn't come [without] a lot of preparation and hard work.

On surviving bear markets as a financial firm:

You've got to understand that markets go both ways, up and down. Over longer periods, stocks generally have always gone up. But any specific stock may never come back. Buy an index fund, and you're going to have long-term growth almost to a certainty. Buy an individual stock, and you never know. You could go to zero.

And there's a whole other area, which is how you react. We get very emotional and do dumb things. Look back at October 2002 [when the Dow sank below 7300]. Everything was going wrong, and you were feeling pretty horrible. But that was the most opportune time to invest! What kind of a thing is that?

On buying back his firm from Bank of America:

In our case, we were a small company at the time, about $50 or $60 million in revenue, and this humongous company bought us. It never really got around to the appropriate level of synergy that should have come about. There was resistance within the big corporation to allow the little child to flourish. So we were battling old bureaucracies within the old enterprise.

After several years of that I just got sick and tired of it. Eventually, they had fallen on bad times and wanted to sell several of their assets because of their bad loans to foreign governments. I said, "Why don't you sell us, too?" And they did. The story was we stole the company back. We didn't.

This is the definition of a crazy entrepreneur. I paid the bank five times what they paid us for the firm just four years before. So they made a bundle off of us. I was so happy to get out of there. Freedom was something else. As a young man, I started with not too much. They dangled a whole bunch of money in front of me at a certain age. And I thought, "Gosh, I could become really respectable and go on their board and do all these things and it would be pretty neat." Little did I know what I was getting into. It was a stage in my career and something I never want to go back to.

On taking back his full-time job as CEO in 2004:

When I came back—not that I'd completely left, I was still chairman of the board—it was time for me to make some really bold decisions. Only a founding father could really do these things, because they were pretty scary for anyone else to do and because they were potentially risky. What we had to do was dramatically reduce our cost, but the benefit of the reduced cost was going to be a dramatic reduction in our prices. So the benefit of all that went directly to our clients in the form of lower prices.

We had allowed ourselves over a period of time to get disconnected with our clients. We got somewhat arrogant, all caught up in the dot-com arena, all that wonderful explosion of new accounts, transactions, valuations. From 1998 to 2002 there was an unbelievable circus of things that went on. Some people like to say it was an unbelievable party at the end of the millennium, and then we all suffered the consequences in the aftermath of it in 2002.

Anyway, I had to reduce costs dramatically. We ended up using an outside firm that helped us organize our thinking, Bain & Company, to help us review every cost center that we had here and take out $600 million in costs. That was painful. Usually the costs end up being not just space, but people. We had to reduce our head count, and it is extremely painful. We did not have expertise in that, since we had been growing the company consistently since 1973. Each year was going to be a better year than the prior year.

The other thing I had to do was to de-layer the company. We'd built up our overhead and our bureaucracies, and our business activities were sort of far flung. We had international activities, capital markets activities, a lot of different things that needed to be assessed. The conclusion was [that] we needed to really refocus the company on our core, which was serving individual investors and helping them do a better job with respect to their investing. So we ended up selling our capital markets, all of our international activities, anything that deviated really from our focus on our core business, which is the individual investor.

I sensed what had to happen. Most of us use consultants to confirm things we already know we need to do. It's not a mystery when they come and say, "Look, you have excess costs, redundancies here, inefficiencies here, loss of market share there." Those are things that generally speaking I sensed, but I had to have a reconfirmation of just how bad it was. In some respect, the company had grown and matured and thought it could do everything. And it wasn't the case. We had a core capacity, a core culture, and we needed to get back to the basics. It took my management group a good year and a half to see that we could really do it.

MUHAMMAD YUNUS

GRAMEEN BANK

t is a customary courtesy for the Nobel Foundation to call new winners of its prestigious Nobel Peace Prize to let them know they have
won the award. But there's another purpose for the phone call as well:
it's to capture for posterity the winner's spontaneous reaction to the
news in a one-minute recorded interview.

On an otherwise typical October day in 2006, the Nobel Foundation
in Stockholm placed its call to Muhammad Yunus, the banker to the poor
and the world's most acclaimed social entrepreneur. Yunus's life-changing
idea was stunningly simple: loan minuscule amounts of money to the poor
so they could fund their own entrepreneurial ventures and lift themselves
out of poverty.

At the time, the mid-1970s, his home country of Bangladesh was in the
grip of a devastating famine. The university professor saw misery and sickness everywhere. "People were dying of hunger, and I felt very helpless,"

Yunus recalls. "As an economist, I had no tool in my tool box to fix that kind of situation."

When he came upon his idea for microlending, the mainstream bankers said it wouldn't work. The poor were not creditworthy, he was told. They wrote him off as an incredibly naïve though well-intentioned egghead. They laughed him out of their offices. And when, after several months of failure, he offered to become the guarantor of the loans to the poor, the bankers warned him that he would end up paying off the debt himself.

Undaunted, Yunus began handing out small amounts of money to destitute basket weavers in a Bangladesh village. The results were startling. For people living on pennies a day, just a few dollars could transform their lives—and in many cases it did. Much to even his surprise, they paid off their loans—on time. Yunus moved from one village to the next, finding all sorts of projects to fund.

In 1983, he founded and became managing director of the Grameen Bank, the entrepreneurial institution that helped Yunus pioneer and spread the concept of microcredit.

By the time the Nobel Foundation made its phone call, the Grameen Bank had outstanding loans to nearly seven million poor people, some 97 percent of whom were women, in 73,000 villages in Bangladesh. The repayment rate on those loans was a stunning 99 percent.

No less profound, Yunus created a global movement toward eliminating poverty in the world through microlending. If imitation is the sincerest form of flattery, Yunus was flattered beyond belief. Replicas of the Grameen model spread to more than one hundred countries worldwide, affecting the lives of tens of millions of people.

At first, the Nobel caller reached Yunus's brother. Then, after a few minutes, Yunus came on the phone.

"Is there any particular message you would like to use this opportunity to get across?" asked the Nobel representative.

"The one message that we are trying to promote all the time: that poverty in the world is an artificial creation. It doesn't belong to human civilization, and we can change that. We can make people come out of poverty. So the only thing we have to do is to redesign our institutions and policies, and there will be no people suffering from poverty. So I would hope that this award will make this message heard many times, and in a kind of forceful way, so that people start believing that we can create a poverty-free world. That's what I would like to do."

"Does your work with the Grameen Bank over the last three decades make you more hopeful that this is possible?"

"Oh yes, very much. We see the demonstration of it every day. People come out of poverty every day. So it's right in front of us and it can be done globally, it can be done more forcefully. This is not a theoretical issue, it's a very real issue. People can change their own lives, provided they have the right kind of institutional support. They're not asking for charity. Charity is no solution to poverty. We didn't do anything special. All we did was lend money to poor people. That did the trick, that makes change."

Born in 1940 in the seaport city of Chittagong, Professor Yunus studied at Dhaka University in Bangladesh, then received a Fulbright scholarship to study economics at Vanderbilt University. He received his PhD in economics from Vanderbilt in 1969 and the following year became an assistant professor of economics at Middle Tennessee State University. Returning to Bangladesh, Yunus headed the economics department at Chittagong University.

Luckily, for poor people all over the world, he didn't stay there all that long.

On how he came up with the idea of microcredit:

I became involved in the poverty issue not as a policy maker or a researcher. I became involved because poverty was all around me, and I could not turn away from it. In 1974, I found it difficult to teach elegant theories of economics in the university classroom, in the backdrop of a terrible famine in Bangladesh.

Suddenly, I felt the emptiness of those theories in the face of crushing hunger and poverty. I wanted to do something immediate to help people around me, even if it was just one human being, to get through another day with a little more ease. That brought me face to face with poor people's struggle to find the tiniest amounts of money to support their efforts to eke out a living. I was shocked to discover a woman in the village, borrowing less than a dollar from the moneylender, on the condition that he would have the exclusive right to buy all she produces at the price he decides. This, to me, was a way of recruiting slave labor.

I decided to make a list of the victims of this moneylending "business" in the village next door to our campus. When my list was done, it had the names of forty-two victims who borrowed a total amount of $27. I offered $27 from my own pocket to get these victims out of the clutches of those moneylenders. The excitement that was created among the people by this small action got me further involved in it. If I could make so many people so happy with such a tiny amount of money, why not do more of it?

On how microfinancing has changed his country:

All of Bangladesh has changed if you look from the bottom up. In general, you see Bangladesh is still a poor country and so on. But empowerment has come to the women of Bangladesh—even the poorest women in Bangladesh. It's tremendous. It's a dramatic change that has taken place. Women have access to money. They can now plan. They can now dream. Their children are in school. Many of them are going into higher education through Grameen Bank financing. New communities are emerging.

A new generation is emerging. New technology has been brought in—information technology, mobile phones, and so on—in a country where 70 percent of the people have no access to electricity. We brought solar energy—self-contained electricity—and connected it to the mobile phones. Housing has been brought in, and new infrastructure. The economy as a whole has changed. People are creating their own jobs. They are not waiting for anybody else to hire them.

On creating self-confidence among unlikely entrepreneurs:

The microcredit we give to the women is a tool to explore one's self, how much capacity that is stored up inside: "I never knew that I had the capacity. That creativity. That ingenuity. To make money to express myself. So that money gives, for the first time, an occasion for me to find out how much I can do."

When you were successful in the first round, when you took tiny amounts—$30, $35—and went into business and paid back the loan, you are now much more equipped to do better. Bigger. So you ask for a $50 loan, a $60 loan, because you think you can do bigger business and more challenging business than when you first took out an easy loan.

If you go through ten rounds and fifteen rounds you are ready for a much bigger challenge than you thought. We introduced information technology into the system. We created a cell phone company called Grameenphone and brought the phone into the villages of Bangladesh. We gave loans to the borrowers to buy a cell phone and start selling phone service. It became a growing business. Now that they are already confident businesswomen, they can very easily come into a business which they never heard of before. They never saw a telephone in their life but they accepted it as a business idea, and there are now more than 100,000 telephone ladies all over Bangladesh doing good business and connecting Bangladesh with the rest of the world.

It's a business itself. If I have a phone, since nobody else has a phone, they have to come to me to use it. They make a call and pay. It's like a public telephone call office. The owner of the phone becomes a one-person public phone office.

On how he would redefine what an entrepreneur is:

By defining "entrepreneur" in a broader way we can change the character of capitalism radically, and solve many of the unresolved social and economic problems within the scope of the free market. Let us suppose an entrepreneur, instead of having a single source of motivation (such as maximizing profit), now has two sources of motivation, which are mutually exclusive, but equally compelling: a) maximization of profit, and b) doing good to people and the world.

Each type of motivation will lead to a separate kind of business. Let us call the first type of business a profit-maximizing business, and the second type of business a social business.

Social business will be a new kind of business introduced in the marketplace with the objective of making a difference in the world. Investors in the social business could get back their investment, but will not take any dividend from the company. Profit would be plowed back into the company to expand its outreach and improve the quality of its product or service. A social business will be a nonloss, nondividend company.

Once social business is recognized in law, many existing companies will come forward to create social businesses in addition to their foundation activities. Many activists from the nonprofit sector will also find this an attractive option. Unlike the nonprofit sector where one needs to collect donations to keep activities going, a social business will be self-sustaining and create surplus for expansion since it is a nonloss enterprise.

Social business will go into a new type of capital market of its own, to raise capital.

Young people all around the world, particularly in rich countries, will find the concept of social business very appealing since it will give them a challenge to make a difference by using their creative talent. Many young people today feel frustrated because they cannot see any worthy challenge, which excites them, within the present capitalist world. Socialism gave them a dream to fight for. Young people dream about creating a perfect world of their own.

Almost all social and economic problems of the world will be addressed through social businesses. The challenge is to innovate business models and apply them to produce desired social results cost-effectively and efficiently. Health care for the poor, financial services for the poor, information technology for the poor, education and training for the poor, marketing for the poor, renewable energy—these are all exciting areas for social businesses. Social business is important because it addresses very vital concerns of mankind. It can change the lives of the bottom 60 percent of world population and help them to get out of poverty.

On creating a stock market for social businesses:

To connect investors with social businesses, we need to create a social stock market where only the shares of social businesses will be traded. An investor will come to this stock exchange with a clear intention of finding a social business, which has a mission of his liking. Anyone who wants to make money will go to the existing stock market.

To enable a social stock exchange to perform properly, we will need to create rating agencies, standardization of terminology, definitions, impact measurement tools, reporting formats, and new financial publications, such as *The Social Wall Street Journal*. Business schools will offer courses and business management degrees on social businesses to train young managers how to manage social business enterprises in the most efficient manner and, most of all, to inspire them to become social business entrepreneurs themselves.

On changing the mind-sets of people:

My greatest challenge has been to change the mind-set of people. Mind-sets play strange tricks on us. We see things the way our minds have instructed our eyes to see. We think the way our minds have instructed our minds to think. We are familiar with one way of thinking. Most of it comes during our academic years, during our student years. The teachers we had, the books we read—they made up our mind-set, and ever since we are stuck with that. We cannot break through this.

If you are a successful student in a university, actually you become the "mini" of the professor whom you liked and admired most. So that's what mind-set does. When you bring in a new thought, you are in conflict with those old thoughts. You struggle, but the old thoughts still prevail because the mind-set is so strong. It would be good if we could have an educational system, a learning process, where we could retain our originality and at the same time accumulate insight and never become a mini professor, but remain ourselves and still absorb different views. Yet institutions have their own mind-sets, and it's very difficult to penetrate and change them. So changing has to be done faster. It's a faster world—particularly in the twenty-first century—but human minds, our academic system, make change slow. So this has been the hardest challenge that I have faced along the way.

On bonsai trees and poor people:

To me poor people are like bonsai trees. When you plant the best seed of the tallest tree in a flower pot, you get a replica of the tallest tree, only inches tall. There is nothing wrong with the seed you planted, only the soil base that is too inadequate. Poor people are bonsai people. There is nothing wrong in their seeds. Simply, society never gave them the base to grow on. All it needs to get the poor people out of poverty is for us to create an enabling environment for them. Once the poor can unleash their energy and creativity, poverty will disappear very quickly.

RATAN TATA

TATA GROUP

When Ratan Tata was just a boy, his grandmother used to send what he recalls as a "huge and antiquated" Rolls-Royce to pick him and his brother up at school. The car would bring them to Tata Palace, a white Baroque Revival–style building in the center of Mumbai tended to by a retinue of fifty servants. "Both of us used to be so ashamed of that car that we used to walk back home," says Tata now, laughing.

If anything, the memory is a reminder of his aristocratic lineage. It was his great grandfather, Jamsetji Tata, who is thought of as the patron saint of Indian business and one of the early builders of India's economy. He and his family built the country's first steelworks, its first hydroelectric plant, its first airline, and its first luxury hotel, the world famous Taj Mahal Palace hotel in Mumbai.

So Ratan Tata, whose father had risen to deputy chairman of Tata

Group, has long been an essential part of India's business aristocracy. And yet he is also one of the country's great entrepreneurs, a man who came of age just as India itself became a global economic powerhouse. He reshaped the formidable enterprise and led it to become India's most valuable public company.

If his early schooling was any indication, few would have thought that Tata would surface as a business icon so closely aligned with the country's own emergence on the world stage. Though he enjoyed French and English literature, Tata notes that "whether you liked it or not, most of us were forced to go to school. It seemed terrible when you were there, questionable when you got out of it, and cherishable in the latter years of your life."

For his university education, Tata was sent to the United States, where he studied architecture and structural engineering at Cornell University. After his graduation with a bachelor's degree in 1962, he returned to India. On the advice of his uncle, J.R.D. Tata, who was then in control of the family company, he turned down a job with IBM. Instead, he was dispatched to the shop floor at Tata Steel, where he shoveled limestone and helped to feed a raging blast furnace, along with the factory's other blue-collar workers.

His uncle cast him in the role of a turnaround expert, putting Tata in charge of one troubled company after another in fields as varied as consumer electronics and textiles. When J.R.D. Tata finally relinquished his job as chairman of Tata Industries in 1981, he became his uncle's successor. Ten years later, as the newly named group chairman of the Tata Group, Ratan inherited a sprawling, and loosely controlled, group of more than eighty companies in every possible business. "My goal at that time was to restructure so that we had a much more cohesive, smaller number of companies, and the rest we would try to divest," says Tata.

The effort was not without controversy. When he sold the company's soap business to Lever Brothers, the response was blistering. "The reaction I had from our employees, from the media, from the shareholders, was unbelievable," he recalls. "I didn't have a friend—yet I had actually made a lot of money for the shareholders, and I negotiated a no-layoffs deal with Lever. I thought I did a very honorable thing for everyone, but I got so battered publicly that I have to admit I lost my courage, and the great restructuring plans that I had for the rest of the group sort of took a backseat."

Still, over time, he prevailed, bringing sorely needed discipline and coherence to the enterprise, transforming Tata Group from an Indian-centric conglomerate to a true global company with annual revenues of $60 billion a year. He acquired Tetley, Jaguar, Land Rover, and Corus. Against the advice of friends and colleagues, he pushed the development of India's first indigenously made car, the Indica, in 1998, and then the cheapest car in the world, the Nano, in 2009. And he has emerged as a humble yet effective statesman for Indian business the world over.

Was it predestined that you would join the company and assume its leadership?

No, I don't think so. I graduated from college in the United States and one thing I didn't take to was the cold weather in Ithaca, New York. I just could never get used to it. So I headed for a warm part of the U.S., Los Angeles, and was working very happily in an architect's office and had no intention of returning to India. At that age, there was no way to come back to India, let alone work for the firm. But a year and one half in that job, my grandmother fell ill and asked for me. She had really brought me up because my father and mother divorced when I was very young. So I went back temporarily to be with her.

In fact, the first job I had, which was short-lived, about fifteen days, was with IBM World Trade because I had met [IBM CEO] Mr. [Tom] Watson in the States and he said if you're going back you've got to see our people and wrote a letter, which became my first job when I got back to India. I never had really gotten into the job because my uncle contacted me more out of an issue of shame. He said, "You can't work somewhere else. You have to work with us." In those days, electric typewriters were very scarce. But I remember sitting in the IBM office and writing my first résumé, which I gave to my uncle because he and I were not very close. We hardly even knew each other. Then they said I was to go to our truck company for a training program, which I accepted and did. And that was where it started.

Because your last name was Tata were you immediately viewed as a likely star in the company?

Not really. The first seven or eight years I was very frustrated, and I almost went back to the States two or three times. My grandmother had passed away. I think it was only six or seven years before [my uncle] actually stepped down that I became one of the possible contenders for his job. He had been there for fifty years. When he stepped down, he was ninety. I know it sounds ridiculous but we had all come to believe he was immortal. The day he decided to hand the company over to me was a bit of a shock. By then we had become very close, more on a personal basis than on a work basis.

Did your uncle mentor you for the role of chief executive?

I looked at it as if he was really being hard on me, but in hindsight, he probably consciously or unconsciously was giving me tough assignments one after another. I couldn't understand what he was doing. Any company that was either going bankrupt or failing I got assigned to. We were in the textiles business and it was really doing badly. I got assigned to that. There was no interest on my side to be involved in textiles. There was a small electronics company that was going under before that. I was put there, and I turned that around.

But I didn't know where I was going. I was sent off to Australia to set up a joint venture company, which I did. I was bobbing all over the place and thinking to myself, I'm not going anywhere. I went to him and said, "Can I just have an assignment where I would have a chance to prove myself and to get job satisfaction?" He said, "Yeah, yeah. That's going to happen." And it just went that way.

The day he actually told me I would succeed him, I remember walking into his office in the morning and he had a pat phrase he used like, "Hi. What's new?" And I said, "There's nothing new. I met with you on Friday."

And he said, "Well, I have something new. I'm going to hand over the company to you."

I said "What? How are you going to handle all the other people who want this job?"

And he said, "You leave that to me."

And he went and did it. So the first four or five years, I had a fair amount of opposition from the contenders. I spent the first four or five years dealing with them. They were all people of great stature who in fact felt they should have that job, and there was quite a lot of backstabbing and negative moves in the media and everything else. It was not a smooth transition. I don't think that there was a long-term plan by my uncle or a long-term aspiration on my side.

And when you assumed leadership over the company you had to clean house. That could not have been very easy to do in an environment of backstabbing.

With humility, I have to say that I didn't succeed very much in what I set out to do. We were in forty different businesses in eighty companies and I had wanted to bring this down to a much lower number of companies by merging them in synergistic businesses. The first thing I did was to sell our soap company, which was sitting in the middle of steel and automobiles and software. I sold it to Lever's [Lever Brothers] and they had become a life-long enemy of every employee in this company. Many of the employees were second-generation employees of our group.

I thought we did a very dignified sellout that hurt nobody. Shareholders got Lever shares, and Lever signed an agreement that they wouldn't lay off anyone for three years. The vendors and suppliers had a lock-in situation for a period of time. But the media just attacked me and within the company people just went for me. I was cast as a guy who was throwing tradition to the wind. They asked, "What will happen to our core businesses?"

I got cold feet. So we did very little after that. We did reposition the ownership of companies so when we had businesses akin to steel, we put these companies under our steel company. But we did very little to sell off or divest ourselves of the companies that I had on my initial list. If you looked at the group, we had fewer companies because they were folded into fewer businesses. Some of them closed down over a period of time or just got absorbed into the larger company. But it wasn't in the way that I had undertaken to do.

What did you learn from that experience?

I learned a very intangible thing: that people in this part of the world were much more important than the business. Everybody went for you if you did things to people. You had to be sensitive to what you were trying to do. After that, in the steel company, we were a company of seventy-eight thousand people producing two million tons of steel because it was legacy, man-powered, old systems. As we modernized, we could never be truly competitive or contemporary. I devised a scheme whereby people retired voluntarily because you can't lay off anybody in India. We would pay them their current wages for the rest of their working life. If somebody retired at forty, for the next twenty years we would pay him his current wages so his family wouldn't be concerned where money would come from. We have brought that seventy-eight thousand down to around forty-five thousand, which is an unheard of thing in India, and still every year we go through a process of this for three thousand or four thousand people. So I learned that there is another way to deal with this other than the straight divestiture or closure.

You and your company very much came of age as India did economically. In the early days, given the lack of infrastructure and the deep involvement of the government, how difficult was it to be entrepreneurial?

This was before I was involved in the running of the group. But prior to the reforms, being entrepreneurial depended on getting a license and those licenses were very constrictive. Let's say you made automobiles. You would get a license for 20,000 automobiles and you couldn't produce 20,001. You were criminally liable if you did. Everything was based on the government's planning commission deciding that India would make 40,000 autos and produce 200,000 minicomputers. And then the capacity was divided up among the people given licenses to do that. It was getting more and more destructive as we went into systems because the way the system worked was, you had to get a license for censors, processors, and something else. Putting all these things together, you couldn't say how many systems you were going to deliver and what the component parts of those systems were.

So the whole system was coming under a certain degree of overload. My uncle was always shouting for reform and taking away the protection. And when they did, we just zoomed forward because we had been crying for that all along. Many of the other businesses unfortunately spent their time trying to hang on to their protected environments, blocking new entrants. We did not. So we moved ahead much faster because we didn't spend our energy trying to regain the protection that was lost. We just marched on ahead in this new free environment. It really made a difference.

Did you have a vision for what you wanted to accomplish with the Tata Group?

Not immediately. I sat down and tried to draw a vision, which I then enunciated and understandably everybody thought we could never do that because it involved doubling the revenues in three years. I had a plan to do it, but they didn't think it was possible. It did become possible and we actually achieved that in four years. After that I think the group has been tremendously responsive to the goals we have set. We also restructured ourselves into seven core business areas and regrouped our company into those. By that time, we were moving with a certain momentum. We added two other facets: acquisitions, which we had never done before, and the other was looking outside the country for growth. We had been very inward looking as a group before that.

Given India's explosive growth in recent years, what caused you to look outside the country for opportunity? I would have thought there was plenty of opportunity to exploit inside the country.

In the commercial vehicle business, we already had a 70 percent market share. As the barriers came down, other people started entering the business. Some of our competitors spent all of their energy trying to block people coming in, so they would try to create difficulty for a Mercedes-Benz or a Navistar to do business in India. We decided to fight ferociously for our market share but we would also look at how we could grow outside India. It wasn't in the United States, but in Asia and Africa. So we started to look for exports or assembly in a very discreet manner in the sense that we would study South Africa or Zambia and go into those countries with products they wanted.

In some cases, we looked at growth outside India where policy would still be a problem. For example, we had been waiting six or seven years for permission to build a new steel plant in India. So where would our steel company grow? So we went and in 2006 acquired Corus (an Anglo-Dutch steel company), which gave us twenty million tons of extra capacity overnight. In the case of acquiring Jaguar and Land Rover it was more of an opportunistic thing that would give us new brands that we would never hope to replicate from India and give us a base in the Western world. So it's been more on the basis of filling strategic gaps in our portfolio or business model in each of our companies. Contrary to what people might think, we have been investing more in India in other areas such as hotels and software.

What have been some of the important learning points for you through these changes?

We have never looked outside India to become bigger. It's always been a careful look strategically as to whether country A or B provided an opportunity. The learning has been not to go on an acquisition spree to become bigger but rather to strategically fill a gap. We also learned in acquiring companies in other countries that wherever we can we try to leave that company alone. When we bought Tetley Tea, we tried to leave that company with its own identity, very discreetly connecting it with our source of tea. With Jaguar and Land Rover, there was a lot of apprehension that we would try to move their manufacturing to India. Their products are not mixed with ours. I think we have probably done a little more sensitive job on that than Ford did for many years, which moved all the decision making to Detroit. Ours is in Birmingham [Michigan] and I go there once every month. But the management is the management of that company.

One might criticize us because we don't have a unified culture. You go to Tetley and it's different from Jaguar and Land Rover. But they all tie in to a code of conduct and a value system, which we impose and we then try to operate the business through those managements that we put in place. But we don't have a transition group that goes in on Monday morning and takes over the company after we acquire it. We have to be sensitive to the fact that there can be a lot of resistance to an Indian company trying to take over a company in the U.K. or the United States. It's been a good policy, a little more difficult to integrate.

You made what many considered to be a very risky decision: to build cars in India. How come?

At first, all my friends in the auto industry and elsewhere said, "Don't do that. It is foolish to do this. No one has done this without going through a licensing agreement. You just can't produce a car. It's not like producing bakery products." I felt it could be done and we did, in fact, produce a car. We really fired up a bunch of young engineers to work on something that hadn't been done before. We produced this car and we had problems with it. When the car came out even my friends in India started to distance themselves from me because to be too closely connected to failure was not a good thing.

On the test of public scrutiny:

Business, as I have seen it, places one great demand on you: It needs you to self-impose a framework of ethics, values, fairness, and objectivity on yourself at all times. It is easy not to do this; you cannot impose it on yourself forcibly because it has to become an integral part of you.

What has to go through your mind at the time of every decision, or most decisions, is: Does this stand the test of public scrutiny in terms of what I said earlier? As you think the decision through, you have to automatically feel that this is wrong, incorrect, or unfair. You have to think of the advantages or disadvantages to the segments involved, be it employees or stakeholders.

What do you think will ultimately be the impact on the United States of what is shaping up as the Asian century?

I've often felt that this part of the world—India, China, and Asia— would play an important role in the dynamics of the world economy. Both India and China will have very high rates of growth. China has invested enormous amounts of money in its infrastructure. India has the opportunity to do the same. We are far behind what you would expect in this century. That is an opportunity. Also, as far as India is concerned, by the year 2030, we are supposed to have the largest working age population in the world.

What it means for the United States is there's a tremendous business opportunity in this part of the world in terms of market access, goods and services, and above all technology. But the United States will have to take a view that they will work more together with these countries to take advantage of the skill base, the low cost base, and the large market and have a virtual integration in terms of ties with China and India.

What advice would you give to a young entrepreneur in India today?

In India, a lot of young people tend to be entrepreneurial. We have almost a culture of shopkeepers. An entrepreneur is quite happy to set up a small business that may be substandard. All I would say is there could be a tendency among young entrepreneurs in India to cut corners in terms of ethics and values to get what he rightfully thinks he should have. I say to young people, Don't give up your value system for the business. Stay with it and work within the law rather than cutting corners where there is a tendency to do that because of high taxes.

What do you hope your legacy is?

I do not know how history will judge me, but let me say that I've spent a lot of time and energy trying to transform the Tatas from a patriarchal concern to an institutional enterprise. It would, therefore, be a mark of failure on my part if it was perceived that Ratan Tata epitomizes the group's success. What I have done is establish growth mechanisms, play down individuals, and play up the team that has made the companies what they are. I, for one, am not the kind who loves dwelling on the "I." If history remembers me at all, I hope it will be for this transformation.

PHIL KNIGHT

NIKE

These days, business schools toss seed money to MBA students who pitch new business ideas in competition with one another. Ultimately, the schools churn out thousands of entrepreneurs with well-formed business plans every year. But back in 1962, precious few graduates left school with an MBA diploma in one hand and a business plan in the other. Phil Knight was one of them.

While at Stanford Graduate School of Business in the early 1960s, Knight found himself in a small business class that would ultimately change his life. He had been known as an indifferent student during his undergraduate years at the University of Oregon, where he majored in journalism. But after a stint in the U.S. Army, he applied to Stanford and got in.

It was during Knight's second year that he took an elective course taught by Professor Frank Shallenberger. Known at Stanford as "the father of small business," Shallenberger devoted a significant part of his scholarly focus to the problems of start-ups and small companies at a time when almost all professors were far more interested in large-scale corporations. It was there in the professor's class that Knight brought his imaginative mind to bear on an idea that would some day become one of the most successful companies ever, Nike.

Shallenberger's assignment to his class was as standard as the task to write an obituary is in a basic journalism class: invent a new business, describe its purpose, and create a marketing plan for it. But Knight's resulting paper did more than merely toss out a new business idea. It asked a simple though compelling question: "Can Japanese Sports Shoes Do to German Sports Shoes What Japanese Cameras Did to German Cameras?" The paper went on to describe a plan to produce superior athletic shoes in Japan, where labor costs were substantially lower than in Germany or the United States. In other words, Knight foresaw the possibility that a different business model for making shoes could potentially disrupt the existing marketplace.

"That class was an 'aha!' moment," Knight recalled years later. "First, Shallenberger defined the type of person who was an entrepreneur—and I realized he was talking to me. I remember after writing that paper, saying to myself: 'This is really what I would like to do.'"

Knight's father, a lawyer and newspaper publisher in Portland, Oregon, had other ideas. He wanted his son to land a "real" job with an accounting firm. Knight acquiesced, but before starting his position as an accountant, he followed up on the curiosity expressed in his term paper. He flew to Japan, where he became captivated by Japanese business practices and culture. During that trip, in November 1962, Knight stopped in Kobe, where he discovered Tiger brand running shoes made in Kobe by the Onitsuka Tiger Co. They were knockoffs of more expensive shoes made by Adidas.

But Knight was so impressed with the quality and low cost of the shoes that he talked his way into a meeting with the company owner, Mr. Onitsuka. Before he left, Knight had gotten the Japanese entrepreneur to allow him to sell Tiger's shoes in the United States. The first samples from Onitsuka arrived in January 1964, and Knight immediately mailed two pairs to his old track coach Bill Bowerman at the University of Oregon in Eugene. Bowerman was something of a legend at the school. He had been an Olympian himself, an Olympic coach, and an inspirational mentor to many. He had been handcrafting shoes for his runners since the 1960s to give them an edge in racing. Knight, who had been a middle distance runner for Bowerman, was merely hoping to get an endorsement from his old coach to help him sell the imported shoes.

Instead, Bowerman wanted to become a partner with Knight, offering to provide some design ideas for better running shoes. They each threw in $500, shook hands, and created Blue Ribbon Sports in January 1964. For Knight, this was little more than a side business while he did his accounting work. But the first shipment of three hundred pairs arrived three months later and sold out in three weeks. In the first year, the company produced profits of $3,240.

In the very beginning, Knight would drive his green Plymouth Valiant to local and regional track meets across the Pacific Northwest, selling Tiger running shoes from the back trunk. Other times, he would sell them out of his father's basement. But by 1969, Blue Ribbon's sales reached $1 million, and Knight quit his job teaching accounting at Portland State University and never looked back. In 1972 Bowerman and Knight began manufacturing their own shoes. Bowerman used his wife's waffle iron to create a shoe with greater traction than those currently on the market. "The idea was that we can make shoes that runners want," Knight says.

Blue Ribbon was an okay name for a running shoe importer, but it lacked sex appeal as a brand name for a running shoe. So Knight thought up the name "Dimension Six." It went nowhere. Instead, it was a friend, fellow runner and first employee Jeff Johnson, who proposed a name that came to him in a dream: Nike, for the Greek winged goddess of victory.

"Now that we had a name, we had to have a trademark for the side of the shoe," says Knight. "It was 1971, and Ford had spent two million dollars getting a trademark. We didn't have two million dollars, so I went by the graphic arts department at Portland State, and there was a woman there saying, 'I don't know how I'm going to get enough money for the dress for this prom.' And I said, 'I have a job for you.' I paid her two dollars an hour, and she spent seventeen and a half hours. So thirty-five dollars and she came up with what is now the swoosh."

Ending its relationship as an importer of shoes in 1972, Knight began manufacturing running shoes in Mexico, designed by Bowerman, under the brand name Nike. The company took off. It sold $3.2 million of shoes in 1972, and the next year, Knight signed his first professional athlete, Romanian tennis star Ilie Nastase, to an endorsement contract. Profits doubled each of the next ten years. When Nike went public in 1980, it passed Adidas to become the industry leader. And when Knight convinced a young basketball player named Michael Jordan in 1984 to endorse a sneaker, Nike became a true marketing phenomenon. "He was a great player, he was handsome, he was articulate, he was educated, and he was perfect," Knight says. "He was sent from central casting, and we jumped on it right away."

But he also admits a little luck helped out. "It wasn't planning," concedes Knight. "We could see that he was a charismatic guy who jumps over the moon and is very competitive, but nobody could have predicted what he would become to our culture."

Or, for that matter, to Nike. The success of that celebrity endorsement would pave the way for a strategy that would revolutionize the business. Today, Nike has annual revenues of some $19 billion and employs more than 36,000 employees around the world, including 7,000 people at its headquarters in Beaverton, Oregon. Knight remains chairman of the company.

On how he ran track and met his cofounder:

Up until the time I was fourteen years old, I was sure that I was going to be a big-league baseball player. But that dream came to a rude awakening when I got cut from my high school baseball team. I switched to track in college. I was very aware of shoes when I was running track. The American shoes were offshoots of tire companies. Shoes cost $5, and you would come back from a five-mile run with your feet bleeding. Then the German companies came in with $30 shoes, which were more comfortable. But [Bill] Bowerman still wasn't satisfied. He believed that shaving an ounce off a pair of shoes for a guy running a mile could make a big difference. So Bowerman began making shoes himself, and since I wasn't the best guy on the team, I was the logical one to test the shoes.

He was a great leader and great man, and being able to be associated with him is a big part of the dream. He was about teaching you how to respond competitively to different challenges. Obviously, they were on the track, and they were about getting prepared to compete and competing well and competing better than you thought you could do, and accepting victory and defeat.

On scraping by as an early entrepreneur:

We had no master plan. It was totally seat-of-the-pants. At first, we couldn't be establishment, because we didn't have any money. We were guerrilla marketers, and we still are, a little bit. But as we became number one in our industry, we've had to modify our culture and become a bit more planned.

On being in the sports business:

We're not in the fashion business, as *The Wall Street Journal* wrote the other day. We're in the sports business, and there's a big difference. Sports is like rock and roll. Both are dominant cultural forces, both speak an international language, and both are all about emotions.

On sticking with golfer Tiger Woods after the controversy:

We think that athletes are human beings and have foibles just like human beings do. We've known [Tiger] for eighteen years and worked with him for fifteen, and he had a three-year span in there where he kind of went off the reservation a little bit in some of the things he was doing, which he apologized [for] to the company and everybody involved. We think the essence of Tiger Woods is basically very, very good, and over the long run, people will see that.

On staying ahead of the curve:

Sometimes I look out there and I get goose bumps. But you better not spend much time doing that, because every six months is a new lifetime, and you've got to worry about what's coming up to stay ahead of the curve. If you want to spend time saying this is cool, you're going to get your ass kicked.

On the importance of marketing:

For years, we thought of ourselves as a production-oriented company, meaning we put all our emphasis on designing and manufacturing the product. But [we came to] understand that the most important thing we do is market the product. We've come around to saying that Nike is a marketing-oriented company, and the product is our most important marketing tool. What I mean is that marketing knits the whole organization together. The design elements and functional characteristics of the product itself are just part of the overall marketing process.

We used to think that everything started in the lab. Now we realize that everything spins off the consumer. And while technology is still important, the consumer has to lead innovation. We have to innovate for a specific reason, and that reason comes from the market. Otherwise, we'll end up making museum pieces.

On understanding the customer:

In the early days, when we were just a running shoe company and almost all our employees were runners, we understood the consumer very well. There is no shoe school, so where do you recruit people for a company that develops and markets running shoes? The running track. It made sense, and it worked. We and the consumer were one and the same. When we started making shoes for basketball, tennis, and football, we did essentially the same thing we had done in running. We got to know the players at the top of the game and did everything we could to understand what they needed, both from a technological and a design perspective. Our engineers and designers spent a lot of time talking to the athletes about what they needed both functionally and aesthetically.

It was effective—to a point. But we were missing something. Despite great products and great ad campaigns, sales just stayed flat.

We were missing an immense group. We understood our "core consumers," the athletes who were performing at the highest level of the sport. We saw them as being at the top of a pyramid, with weekend jocks in the middle of the pyramid, and everybody else who wore athletic shoes at the bottom. Even though about 60 percent of our product is bought by people who don't use it for the actual sport, everything we did was aimed at the top. We said, if we get the people at the top, we'll get the others because they'll know that the shoe can perform.

But that was an oversimplification. Sure, it's important to get the top of the pyramid, but you've also got to speak to the people all the way down. Just take something simple like the color of the shoe. We used to say we don't care what the color is. If a top player like Michael Jordan liked some kind of yellow and orange jobbie, that's what we made—even if nobody else really wanted yellow and orange. One of our great racing shoes, the

Sock Racer, failed for exactly that reason: we made it bright bumblebee yellow, and it turned everybody off.

Whether you're talking about the core consumer or the person on the street, the principle is the same: you have to come up with what the consumer wants, and you need a vehicle to understand it. To understand the rest of the pyramid, we do a lot of work at the grassroots level. We go to amateur sports events and spend time at gyms and tennis courts talking to people.

We make sure that the product is the same functionally, whether it's for Michael Jordan or Joe American Public. We don't just say Michael Jordan is going to wear it so therefore Joe American Public is going to wear it.

On success:

We knew the industry would get bigger. We had no idea . . . we would compete as successfully as we have. It was all a labor of love in the early days and really to this day. It's a fabulous industry, and the people who work out there, they love being in it. I mean, it's sports, it's fitness, it's international.

On outsourcing:

Our business practices are no different than those of our competitors. But we are bigger, and thus more visible, so we get more flak. Basically what drives me is not money. I'm not in this for money anymore. I've got enough. What I want to do before I go to the great shoe factory in the sky is make this as good a company as I can make it. I simply have a basic belief that Americans don't want to make shoes. That is not their ambition. They don't want to make shoes. They don't want those jobs.

CARLOS NUZMAN

RIO DE JANEIRO ORGANIZING COMMITTEE
FOR THE OLYMPIC GAMES

At precisely 6:30 P.M. on October 2, 2009, Carlos Arthur Nuzman heard the news that would make the day one of the happiest in his life. It was the day Rio de Janeiro was named host city for the 2016 Olympic Games. In Copenhagen, where the final presentations were made, Nuzman's bid team celebrated their triumph by hugging, dancing, crying, and waving Brazilian flags.

The group, dressed in uniform navy and moss green blazers, had overcome many hurdles to win the victory, including a personal appeal to the International Olympic Committee by President Barack Obama in favor of a rival Chicago bid. The president flew to Copenhagen, along with his wife, Michelle, television talk show celebrity Oprah Winfrey, and Chicago mayor Richard Daley, in support of the city's attempt to get the games. But Chicago was eliminated in the first of three rounds of voting.

In that first round, Brazil trailed Madrid by two votes, 28–26. It pulled ahead in the second round when Tokyo was eliminated, and in the final third round beat Madrid by a decisive 66–32 vote—the largest margin in Olympic history. When the vote was announced, Nuzman, who headed up Brazil's National Olympic Committee and the Rio 2016 Bid Committee, jumped into the air, yelling, "We did it! We did it!"

Winning the right to put on the biggest sporting event in the world is a quintessential entrepreneurial venture. It requires the raising of substantial capital, the crafting of a smart business plan and strategy, and the recruitment of a crack team that can work closely together to compete against formidable rivals who want this sporting prize as much as you do.

For Nuzman, a former Brazilian volleyball star turned lawyer and entrepreneur, the Copenhagen victory was the culmination of a ten-year effort. But it also helped lay to rest a horrific tragedy that had befallen him at the tender age of ten. It was a Sunday in 1952 when his mother, Esther, decided to take a bath. She lit a match to ignite the water heater in the room and it exploded. The resulting fire engulfed her.

Young Nuzman heard the screams and saw his mother in flames. His father, Izaac, rushed to her aid, wrapped her in a blanket, and carried her out of the house and straight to the hospital. Eight days later, she died. "My father came and sat with me and my sister and told us that the moment had arrived and my mother had died," recalls Nuzman. "I would never see her again. So the image I have of her is as a torch."

Ultimately, Nuzman sought refuge in a sport that he came to love and was very good at: volleyball. It was his father and his grandmother, Anita, who brought him to a volleyball club, where Nuzman learned the finer points of a hotly competitive game. At the age of seventeen, he made the state team of Rio de Janeiro. Three years later, he became a key player on Brazil's national team and went to the former Soviet Union to play in the world championships. When the sport was included in the Olympics for the first time in 1964, Nuzman played on Brazil's team in Tokyo and again in the world championships two years later in Czechoslovakia.

The sport changed Nuzman, giving him the self-confidence to move beyond the tragedy and to find purpose in life. "I finally took leadership of my own life," says Nuzman. "All the fears that I had since I lost my mother had disappeared. My attitudes and feelings had changed. I became a lawyer. I was in the army as a soldier for a year. It was very important to my life."

Though he finished his athletic career in 1972, he remained passionate about the sport and stayed active in it, first as president of the Rio de Janeiro Volleyball Federation and then, in 1975, as president of the Brazilian federation. On the day he took office, Nuzman announced a goal that many thought could never be achieved: to help Brazil take home the Olympic gold medal in volleyball.

At the time, the men's team from Brazil was ranked thirteenth in the world. Borrowing ideas from Japan, then the current Olympic champion, he drilled the team relentlessly. They trained eight hours a day, seven days a week. They were told that the goal of winning was more important than any other objective in their lives. In 1976, Brazil would finish seventh in the Olympic games in Montreal; then fifth in the 1980 games in Moscow. In 1984, Brazil won the silver in the Los Angeles games, and then in 1992, it brought home the gold from Barcelona and in 2004 from Athens.

More than just winning the gold for the Brazilian team, however, Nuzman became a highly effective advocate for the sport. Over a period of years he successfully lobbied the country's primary television network to air key volleyball games. By staging an exhibition tournament in Rio in 1993, he helped to convince the International Olympic Committee and the Atlanta Olympics Organizing Committee to include beach volleyball as a sport, which they did in 1996. And he helped to elevate the popularity of volleyball in Brazil so that it is today the second most popular sport in the country, behind only soccer.

In his efforts to win the Olympic games for his home country, Nuzman traveled 500,000 miles, racked up some 1,000 flying hours, and led the team that assembled a 568-page dossier supporting its bid. Over this period he counted on the relentless support of his wife, Marcia Peltier, whom he married in 1998 but says he has met in past lives, such is the extent of change she brought to his life.

During this presentation in Copenhagen, he smartly displayed a map of the world that showed all the countries that had been Olympic hosts since 1896. All of South America was glaringly absent.

"Europe has staged the games thirty times," Nuzman told the IOC members. "North America, twelve times, including eight in the United States; Asia, five times; and Oceania, twice. It is time now for South America to have our chance.

"When you push your voting button today, you can inspire a new continent. Vote Rio, and we offer a gateway to 180 million passionate young people in South America. We are ready. We are ready to serve and we are ready to deliver history."

Nuzman is now in charge of making sure the games get off without a hitch. He is managing an organization with a $2.8 billion budget. Brazil's government will spend some $11.6 billion more on venue and infrastructure projects to get the city ready for the Olympics. And the economic impact of the games on the country's economy is huge. It is estimated that the 2016 Olympics will bring the nation $51.1 billion, including the creation of 120,000 jobs a year until 2016 and then 130,000 jobs a year until 2027.

What does it take to win an Olympic bid?

We worked on this for exactly ten years, starting in December of 1999.

The Brazilian Olympic Committee decided not to run for the 2008 Olympic Games, but to go for the Pan American Games to show the world that we could organize the event. The second largest multiple-sport event in the world is the Pan American games. We defeated San Antonio, Texas, to put them on in Brazil. We knew this would be an important stepping-stone for us to win the Olympics. We showed we worked together in an extremely competent way. We had full alignment with three levels of government—federal, state, and city—to pull it off. In the end, the president of the Pan American Sports Organization and the international media concluded we organized the best games ever.

We worked every day, day and night, concentrating on the Olympic campaign. We first bid for the 2012 games during 2004, but we didn't have the right conditions to win. We were not included in the short list, but at that time I announced to the IOC our intention to bid for the 2016 games and told them we planned to win.

I told our team what I told our athletes: that we need to have the adrenaline of an athlete when he is on top of the world. You needed to be modest, but have the courage and respect and the interior feelings that you can win. You never can think you are less than any other athlete or team in the world. You needed to have the philosophy of the winner and needed to believe that you will become the winner.

We didn't have any holidays. Together with the team and the three levels of government (federal, state, and city), we had five hundred people working on the bid book. I told my team that I didn't want to have lobbyists and that we needed to be recognized as having the best presentation of any country wanting the event. And in 2008 we were included on the short list. The first host city was Tokyo, then Madrid. Third was Chicago, and Rio was fourth. Everybody said, "You have no chance. You are the last of the group."

But I told my team this is the best possible outcome we could ever have hoped for. We traveled all around the world and worked to present our case to all the IOC members, and we had strong arguments. Brazil was the eighth largest economy in the world, and South America had never received the games.

There were two very important moments. In March of 2009 in Denver, Colorado, we had the Sport Accord meeting with all the international federations, a lot of the IOC members, and the international media. We were in Boulder to rehearse our speeches, and one day I woke up with the idea to have an Olympic map. This map became the most important weapon in our campaign. It showed how all the continents had the games with the exception of South America and Africa. Yet in South America alone there are 180 million young people under the age of eighteen, and 65 million of them are in Brazil. It represents a third of the population of the country. The Olympics would be especially inspiring to those young people. By showing this on a graphic map, I felt this was our weapon to make the point that it was time to give South America a chance.

The second most important event was when the IOC decided to have a technical presentation on the merits of the bid to its members. We did this in June of 2009 in Lausanne. All the members said that if the election were held then, Rio would become the winner. We kept this momentum. We continued to work and travel and have beside us the president of Brazil, the governor of the state, and the mayor of Rio. All of them were united with us.

I met all the IOC members at least five times to explain our games project and the reasons we wanted to host the Olympics. We prepared our estimate of the way the votes would go, and one week before the actual vote in Copenhagen, we wrote that Rio would win with sixty-seven votes against Madrid with thirty-three. The final result was Rio sixty-six versus Madrid with thirty-two.

How were you able to predict the outcome that well?

We knew that when you start a political campaign for election, you start with a base of votes. In our case, it meant a group of countries that would be most likely to vote for us. We started with this, focusing first on the Latin and African votes. We thought Chicago would have the Anglo-Saxon votes, Madrid would have some European votes, and Tokyo, the Asian votes. I talked with a lot of the IOC members and some said, "Yes, I will vote for Rio." From those conversations, we understood that Chicago and Tokyo had less support.

While it may not be obvious to many that it takes a great entrepreneur to organize and win an Olympic bid, that is exactly what you did. Can you talk a little about what you learned in the process?

One is to work well together. You need to work together with the three different levels of government (federal, state, and city). They need to be your partners and your friends through something like this. You need to bring the spirit of the country together. You had to be open and honest. You needed to respect everybody and show you are on the same level. You cannot think you are better than anyone else. It doesn't matter what kind of city in what country. You needed to be very clear and open all the time to present a strong project because you cannot win only through politics.

I think that life prepares you for this moment. I had a chance in my life that people gave me and I grew step by step. There was no gift. In the 1970s and 1980s in Brazil, we didn't have schools or teachers who could teach you drive as a sports official. But I tried to take note of everything then. I copied the good things from everyone who could inspire me. After losing my mother, I had the support of my family. But I needed to have a lot of confidence in myself. So I observed in others how they worked and how they prepared. As a sports official and organizer, I never had anyone to teach me what was right or wrong. I needed to observe it and learn it.

All the time, I had to show my capacity for being professional. You have to have the desire and the skill to get things done. I am always endeavoring to take things to a new height. I love challenges, and this was one of the great challenges of my own life.

When you won how did you feel?

I felt that I was completely alive. This was the first feeling. I was alive because I arrived at the end of the race with the gold medal. It was the most important victory of my whole life. We were very focused not to allow emotions to take control of us. But it was a moving experience, a dream come true. Everybody was crying. I couldn't cry because I was so focused on this for so long. I cry easily, but not at that moment. I was thinking that the youth of Brazil will have a chance to be inspired by this event and that it would help us develop the human capital of our people.

Of course, now you have the monumental task of making all this happen. Do you worry much about Brazil's ability to pull off a very successful Olympics?

I have great confidence that I have the capacity to lead the human capital I need to organize the games. In August of 2011, we had 170 people in our organizing committee. By the end of this year [2011], we'll have 260. And by 2016, we'll have 4,000 people, along with a task force with another 35,000 and around 90,000 volunteers. I'm ready. We feel good about the preparations so far. I have no doubt we'll organize wonderful and spectacular games for Rio and for the country.

What does it take to build an effective team?

You've got to make sure you accommodate various skills, backgrounds, and views within the team. Hierarchy is paramount, but managers need to be inspiring and lead by example. Team selection must ensure staff and organization share a common set of objectives and are fully behind the project. Dedication and hard work should be mandatory requirements.

Good internal communication and intermediate goal-achieving rewards are effective ways of sustaining motivation. There must be a sense of pride for one another's achievements and a feeling of ownership for the organization's results. It's also crucial that self-improvement among staff is fostered by the offer and encouragement of training opportunities.

I would think that if there is one thing you wished you could have, it would be to have your mother see this accomplishment. Yes?

Ever since her death, I have prayed every night for her and she is with me. I lost my father in 1988 and my sister in 1993. My grandmother became my second mother and she passed away in 1999 at the age of ninety-five. I've had a lot of difficulties in my life. I think that the sport of volleyball came into my life as a kind of activity that made me strong enough to go ahead. My life prepared me to be strong and to face many challenges.

MARK ZUCKERBERG

FACEBOOK

f there is a single entrepreneur today who is inspiring millions of young people to consider following their own entrepreneurial dreams, it has got to be Mark Zuckerberg. The dropout who famously founded the social networking site Facebook already has been the subject of a blockbuster Hollywood movie, a *60 Minutes* profile, an Oprah Winfrey TV show, and *Time*'s Man of the Year.

Though Facebook was only launched by Zuckerberg and his friends in February 2004, the site now has more than 750 million active users who spend over 700 billion minutes per month on the Web site. During the summer of 2011, when rumors began spreading that Facebook was planning a public offering, some observers believed the company could be valued at anywhere between $40 billion and $100 billion.

Yet Zuckerberg never really thought about creating a business when he and cofounders Dustin Moskovitz, Chris Hughes, and Eduardo Saverin launched Facebook from his Harvard University dorm room. In fact,

Zuckerberg claims that was the last thing on his mind. Instead, he and his pals had been deeply immersed in conversations about what kind of control people might have over the increasing volume of information in the world made accessible by the Internet.

Those animated discussions led Zuckerberg, then just nineteen years old, to build an application to allow Harvard's six thousand students to stay connected with their friends and family. Amazingly, it took him just "a couple of weeks" to knock out the code to do it.

"I actually explicitly did not want to build a company," he says. "And that is why, early on, when most people would probably launch it at schools that they thought would have the highest chance of working, I launched it at the schools that I thought it would have the lowest chance of working. So those were schools that already have some kind of school community. And the reason why I did that was because I wanted to know, early on, if this was something that was just worth spending a lot of time on as a project."

Clearly, it was. So in March 2004, only a month after the app hit Harvard, Facebook expanded to Stanford, Columbia, and Yale. Zuckerberg and his friends moved to Palo Alto, California, in June, expecting to stay through the summer and then return to Harvard. But the excitement of building the company in Silicon Valley took hold and they stayed. By the end of that first year, Facebook had nearly one million active users. After getting $12.7 million in funding from Accel Partners in May of 2005, Facebook expanded to more than eight hundred colleges.

Zuckerberg was able to make progress so quickly because he was a crack programmer himself. He began using computers and writing software in middle school. His father, Edward, a dentist, taught him Atari BASIC programming in the 1990s, and also hired a software developer to privately tutor Zuckerberg. The kid took to it easily, becoming something of a prodigy, developing communications tools, games, and even a music player. Zuckerberg's Synapse Media Player used artificial intelligence to learn a user's listening habits and earned the attention of both Microsoft and AOL, which tried to buy it and recruit Zuckerberg straight out of Phillips Exeter Academy. Instead, he chose to go to Harvard.

It was a smart move. In his sophomore year, Zuckerberg wrote the code for a software program called CourseMatch that allowed students to select classes based on the choices of other students. It also helped students form study groups. Then he created a program he first called Facemash, in which students could vote on the best-looking or "hotter" person from a selection of photographs. The site went up over a weekend, but became so popular it overwhelmed Harvard's server and the school shut it down. From there came Facebook. And the rest, as they say, is history—though history in the making.

On how the idea became a business:

From those conversions that I had with my friends in college, we had this very broad idea of where we thought the world should go and kind of guide Facebook's development to this date. But a lot of it was also just good technical decisions, getting really smart people in to work on it. Some of the smartest people that I've known were a lot of the original people involved in Facebook, and a lot of them are still here. I mean, people who were my teachers in school, people who were my classmates.

It occurred to me that building a company was the best way to align a group of people toward building something great. If they're building something that's good, you can work with partners and reward them if the product that you're developing works well. I built the first version of Facebook in a couple of weeks. It was pretty quick, especially for the scale that it eventually was offering. I rented a server for $85 a month. And on that, we were basically doing millions of page views a day. Because at some point like 10 or 20 percent of all Harvard students were logged in at the same time. This was just in the first week.

I just got more and more smart people around me to join. Eventually we moved out to California. Originally when we went out, we weren't expecting to move out there. We wanted to go for the summer because we had this feeling like, "Okay, all these great companies come from Silicon Valley. Wouldn't it be cool to spend the summer out there and get that experience."

But we expected to go back to Harvard in the fall. But Harvard has this great policy that lets you take as much time off as you want. So we decided, "Okay let's go ahead and take one semester off and continue just building things out." And more people joined our team, and at that point, we formally incorporated the company and got our investment from our first investor, Peter Thiel. And then things were just growing and we got up to a million users on our first year of running the site.

And then we decided, "Okay, let's take a second term off from Harvard." And then, you know, just things kept on growing and we got up to about 5 million users and we were like, "Okay, let's take a whole year off." And then like, "All right, I guess we're not really going back." But I mean it was never this big decision where it's like, "Okay, at this point, I am going to drop out of school and start a company." It just happened very gradually and at each step, we were just doing what made sense to do next.

On Internet start-ups:

One of the great things about the Internet is these markets are very efficient. With more traditional businesses, it would take often years of investment before you hit some kind of curve where you knew whether your thing was going to work. Now it's possible to build something in a weekend or, you know, two weeks as the first version of Facebook took. And just launch something and see if it addresses the market or [is something] that anyone will really use. From there you can get real-time feedback and adjust what you're doing very quickly.

On Facebook's hacker culture:

I looked around at Valley companies. I really wanted to build a technology company. Some call themselves technical companies. But they're not. We were always really committed to just kind of maintaining technical folks and entrepreneurs running the company. Even in nontechnical roles, one of our marketing roles is someone who has a technical background.

As we've grown it's become more apparent to us how we're different from other companies. Google is a technology I admire. They have a really strong academic culture. They do a lot of research and have a lot of PhDs. What we pride ourselves on is having a lot of impact, having a strong hacker culture, giving people a chance to grow—those are things that we work on. We have more than 300 million users and less than three hundred engineers. The ratio of users to engineers is far more than any other company.

One of the things we're committed to is having a smaller team. We have frequent pushes for code. We encourage people to build a lot of their own stuff. We have a technology company that's really a hacker company.

Our goal isn't necessarily to keep people forever. There are companies that train people really well. A lot of Harvard people went on to McKinsey.

A lot of people went to IBM because that was the best place to learn sales. A lot of people go to USC to learn how to play football. One of the things at Facebook is [to] have a place where it's one of the best places to learn how to build stuff. If you want to learn how to build really good products and practices and have a large impact, I would argue there's no better place to do that than at Facebook.

If people want to come here for one, two, or three years. Steve Chen, who founded YouTube, was working on Facebook before. I'm not encouraging people [who] work at Facebook to leave. But I think you learn valuable skills. We're not pretending we're building a company that hackers are going to want to work at forever. I want to be a part of building some institutions to be a great hacker institution in the long term.

On having focus and moving fast:

You need to focus on a few things you care about. Moving fast. You need to give up some things you need to do that. I think that is a really big part of a CEO's job. You hire the team that's going to go build everything. You set up the direction. What really comes off is what trade-offs you're going to make.

We think eventually you get judged not by how you look but by what you build. I think there's a lot of pressures inside of companies where people want to optimize for a launch to go smoothly. But really you want to be the best over time. Take more risks. If we do those, we have a good shot at succeeding.

On taking risks:

The biggest risk you can take is to take no risk. In a world that's moving quickly, you know that if you don't change you'll lose. Not taking risk is the riskiest thing you can do. You have to do things that are kind of bold even if they're not obvious.

We made this change yesterday that lets you see the most recent stuff or the most interesting updates. Regardless of what we do, if it changes the site, change is really disruptive for people. Especially if you're providing a Web service that people aren't opting into directly.

Values are worthless unless they're controversial. We want to move quickly. We're willing to give up a huge amount of stuff in order to move quickly.

On being in Silicon Valley:

I think it was really valuable because I was nineteen when I started this. There was just so much that I didn't know. There still is, and Silicon Valley is just a great place to meet a lot of great engineers. There's a lot of infrastructure built up to help get companies off the ground. Whether it's the investment community or the legal community, or just all these different areas. Undoubtedly that helped us. Although I think it can work both ways.

Why he has kept the title of CEO:

It's just my view of thinking through the technology industry and its history. I think the companies that have done the best have often been led by their founders. And I think that's because those people have the better sense of why the company was created and have a lot of credibility within the company to make the decisions that need to be made. The world changes so quickly, so being able to guide the company efficiently, I think, is an extremely important part of that. Someone showed me an interesting stat once that out of public companies, the ones that were still run by their founders outperformed others.

On having a strong sense of purpose:

We have a strong sense of purpose as a company. You know we didn't start Facebook to build a Web site or even start Facebook to build a company. We started this because we wanted to make the world more open and connected. Building a site is the first step toward that. I think that the platform that we're developing is what I'm most excited about. We have almost a million developers right now building things, ranging from groups of people building things in college, getting started like I did, to small and large businesses that have hundreds of millions of dollars in revenue. They've primarily built on top of the Facebook platform. That's really exciting.

On making mistakes:

There are so many things that I would have done differently. I mean, in general, it's just that you make a lot of mistakes and those are valuable mistakes. We're better off for having made most of those, but I also think that we've done a good job of staying true to who the company is and what we started off to do. And we've also made a lot of very good technical and product decisions along the way and good cultural decisions to make sure that we can make it so the best people can come and work here. And have a very big impact very quickly. I think that those are the most important things. And if you get those right then you can actually make a lot of mistakes.

Actually one of the core values of Facebook is "Move fast." And we used to write this down by saying, "Move fast and break things." And the idea was, unless you are breaking some stuff you are not moving fast enough. I think that's still basically true. I mean, right now, we've optimized so much of our culture around just making it so that people can come and build things quickly.

Whether it's everything from having the right tools in the right development environment to build things quickly, to nightly code pushes, hiring the best people who have a bias toward just pushing things very quickly—the whole culture is tuned around that. And I think there's probably something in that for other entrepreneurs to learn, which is that making mistakes is okay.

At the end of the day, the goal of building something is to build something, not to not make mistakes. In order to get any reasonable conclusion, you're going to make missteps along the way. And as long as you learn from them and those become valuable in getting to where you want to go, then I think that's fine.

EIKE BATISTA

EBX GROUP

No one ever accused Brazilian energy entrepreneur Eike Batista of failing to think big. Already the wealthiest man in his own country, with a net worth estimated at $30 billion, he has made clear his intention to become the richest man in the world. His competitive instincts, honed for years as a top-class speedboat racer, have led him to openly warn Mexico's Carlos Slim that he will soon speed by him. Considering his track record of high-class entrepreneurship in the past thirty years, achieving this goal won't be a total surprise.

"Once you compete you never get it out of the blood," explains Batista. "So I have to compete with Mr. Slim. I don't know if I am going to pass him on the right side or the left side. All I know is I'm going to pass him."

The good-natured bragging by Batista is understandable. Son of the country's revered former mining minster, Batista is a self-made billionaire who best personifies his own country's transformation from an economic basket case to one of the world's economic superpowers. His most innovative projects in natural resources and infrastructure sectors are helping Brazil to generate wealth and infrastructure improvements for its population.

As Batista puts it, for years Brazilians hid their success. He wants to inspire a new generation of entrepreneurs to follow his example and embrace their country's promise. So he keeps a Mercedes-Benz SLR McLaren sports car in his parlor as a decoration and puts the letter *X* in the name of all his companies as a symbol of wealth multiplication.

"I've made it a mission to help a new generation of Brazilian entrepreneurs be successful in a more transparent way," he says. "They should be proud of what they are creating."

Batista surely is. A college dropout, he got his start by following the gold rush into the Amazon, buying a gold mine at the age of twenty-four. His mining operations led to some Indiana Jones–style adventures deep in the jungle. Today his EBX Group fortune spans shipping, mining, power plants, logistics, and—above all—vast oil and gas holdings.

A huge boost in his wealth occurred after he made a bold $1 billion gamble in 2007 to buy the licenses to explore for oil off Rio's coastline. Batista discovered a bonanza, a massive oil find. He believes it will cost him no more than $18 a barrel to extract the oil, allowing for outsized profits from the resource for many years. That's what led to his decision to take his oil exploration firm OGX public in June of 2008. At the time, the IPO was Brazil's biggest ever, raising $4.1 billion.

Wheeling and dealing with wildcat gold diggers, he started an independent gold mining and trading company in 1980. Batista learned the business from the ground up. "In mining," he explains, "you go to some crazy place, you set up a camp. You start looking for water and energy and this way you can build anything. That's the mind-set. That's my life. That's how I started from zero."

As chairman and CEO of EBX Group, he runs his vast interests out of Rio de Janeiro. "I see myself as an entrepreneur," he says. "Somehow I have a pact with Mother Nature. I drill and I find things. Somehow you have to have luck."

Indeed.

Like many entrepreneurs, you dropped out of college. Were your parents unhappy with your decision at the time?

Parents always are disappointed, but after two and a half years at Aachen University in Germany I realized that I already had a grasp on the engineering part of the world, so I wanted to make money. Since I was very young I always had a great interest in engineering for the sake of making things better. I always loved cars. I liked mechanics, and I liked reading *Popular Mechanics* and *Scientific American* and research documents from universities in material sciences.

When we lived in Brussels for four years, and I was sixteen, I owned a motorbike that went 90 to 100 kilometers an hour. I spent hours trying to make it faster. I polished the spark plugs, changed the chain, and calibrated the tires. I was always trying to get some extra performance. In 1989, when I decided to race powerboats in Brazil, I became the Brazilian, the American, and the world champion because of two things: understanding how to build a team and smart engineering. It's a very dangerous sport and a five-cent piece could make you lose the race or even die.

What kind of influence did your parents have on you?

From the 1960s to the 1980s, my father was very busy building the international offices of Vale, the Brazilian steel giant. We moved from Switzerland to Dusseldorf in Germany to Brussels in Belgium and then I went to university in Germany. So I basically stayed in Europe from my twelfth birthday until my twenty-first. What my father taught me, what I learned from him, is to think big, because he built—there's a movie in Brazil called *Brazil's Engineer,* and it's about him, because he built part of Brazil's macro-infrastructure—railways, super ports for shipment of iron ore to Asia, back then to Japan. And so I learned to think.

But I was educated by my mother. I'm one of seven children, the second. And so my mother taught me discipline—she was German, from Hamburg—and so she taught me discipline and care, caring for others, which is very much what I got from her, which forged me in many ways.

When you dropped out of college, your first job was selling insurance, right?

I began selling insurance because my parents moved back to Brazil when I was eighteen and just going to university. My oldest brother was already at Aachen University studying medicine. When they left us there, they basically gave us an allowance that lasted not much more than fifteen days. We were brought up to be ashamed for asking for more money, so I decided after talking to friends that I could do a blitz course and sell insurance policies. This taught me how to talk to people. Some doors open and some do not.

It was a mixture of stress and a brutal desire to be financially independent. It was a very important stress period for me. I was never angry with

my parents. I just took it for granted. I tell young people, especially middle-
and upper-class youngsters, that parents should not make it too easy for
them. We pamper them too much. The other thing that happened to me
was when I was eleven or twelve I had asthma. My mother said I think you
could cure this through swimming. And she kept throwing me into a
swimming pool to the point that I solved my asthma problem. That was
added stress in my life, and it makes you tougher.

How good were you at selling insurance?

Within a month, I made more than double what I needed by selling
insurance. I bought an old Mercedes, so when I drove up to the doors I
could show off. I sold insurance in Germany and Belgium because my
father kept an apartment in Brussels. During the holidays when I went to
Brazil to see my friends, we talked about financial independence. The idea
came up about selling diamonds, basically being an intermediary between
the buyers in Antwerp in Belgium and the Brazilian pick-and-shovel miners from an office I rented. I made commissions out of it.

After two and one half years in Germany and Belgium, I went to visit
the Amazon in the northern part of Brazil, where lots of pick-and-shovel
miners were producing lots of gold. It was like the old Wild West. I organized a visit there over ten days and my father had the army chase me there
because he didn't know where I was. What I realized was that a lot of gold
was being produced and so my idea was to become a trader, to buy and sell
the gold. I didn't want to initially participate in the gold production because
local owners who had planes and controlled the landing strips to move the
gold out controlled it. The mules of the jungle were Cessna 186 planes.

I went to two jewelers in Rio and asked them to lend me some money.
I said I would bring the gold to Rio and São Paulo from the Amazon.
Somehow, they liked what I said and obviously it was gold, you know. I
don't think they would have given me any money if I asked them to buy
chocolate. They charged me a 20 percent interest rate on the money and
also wanted some of the product. So they wanted a double interest. But in
eighteen months, I managed to buy $60 million in gold and, after discount-
ing everything, I was left with a net of 10 percent. So I made $6 million
when I was twenty-two years of age. What happened was that during that
time other traders started to come into the area and I saw very clearly that
my 10 percent margin was going to go sharply down to perhaps 2 percent

or 3 percent. I said, "Well, it's time to think about something else." So looking at these pick-and-shovel miners producing gold very inefficiently, I decided I am going to buy one of these sites from an owner and mechanize the production of gold. So I bought a mine for $2 million and the first thing I did was I hired a Canadian drilling company that specialized in drilling alluvial deposits.

They came and measured the amount of gold I had there and put it in production. I was down to my last $300,000 because I had obviously underestimated logistics, diseases, and mechanical problems. I had to airlift the gold out. The closest road was 100 kilometers from the mine, so I had to make an air bridge over 100 kilometers long. At the mine site, I had to build my own camps. I needed clean water and food for the personnel. I needed oil and power. There was almost a military concept of logistics where you depend almost 100 percent on yourself. But I was going to produce a product that I had to ship out by plane.

It was very stressful, I must tell you. The thing started to run because the mine was so rich it was totally idiot-proof. It survived all my mistakes. In the group we have to this day a strong embedded culture of building only idiot-proof assets. When the mine started to produce, I was making a million dollars a month. The mine was so rich that I needed only 10 percent of the gold to pay for all the operations. I almost died in this process by flying around. I did it with my own hands. I know deeply the construction of these mines, and I ended up building nine mines around the world from scratch—five in Brazil, one in Chile, and three in Canada.

I always looked for rich mines, and I keep this culture up today. I arbitrage gigantic inefficiencies. We are building super ports to overcome Brazil's lack of efficient ports. In the resource arena, somehow I have a pact with nature. Everywhere I drill I find oil, coal, or gold.

Of course, early success breeds self-confidence and that is an important ingredient to success.

Yes, but it also brings arrogance because you can come to think that you can fly. It's very dangerous. I went into a very interesting diversification phase in the 1990s when I started a Jeep factory in Brazil. As you know, every single man would like to build his own car. So there I was trying to build my own Jeep. That was a failure that taught me a lot. It taught me that it's important to shut down your company when it's not going well and close it down properly. So you pay all the bills and indemnify your workers. It was a humbling exercise. Failures only make you grow. It makes you stress even further.

Why did your Jeep venture fail?

In my Jeep story I failed to pay attention to networks. After people bought the car they had maintenance problems because the network wasn't so large. You can't have a success if your dealership network isn't big enough to provide good service. If we had stayed at it longer, it's possible that it could have been a success because I consider myself one of the fathers of the small sport utility vehicles. My Jeep in 1990 was a small sport utility. I was probably ahead of my time with one missing link, which was the network. I lost more than $100 million.

I learned in all these years to read people and one of my best qualities today is to get the best out of incredibly qualified engineers and geologists. I have the best of the best. This is probably my biggest strength today. That is why I consider myself today as a massive arbitrager of inefficiencies using state-of-the-art concepts and equipment.

Why did you expand out of mining? You have essentially created a conglomerate in Brazil, which is unusual for most entrepreneurs.

I wanted to do other things, although I am on overload now. I'm spending $40 billion in ten years in natural resources and infrastructure sectors in Brazil, so there is a limit. If you look at the world through the eyes of an engineer, there are a lot of opportunities. America and Brazil have allowed the financial people to make money through money. We have forgotten to make things more efficient. In America, you should be driving electric cars today. So it's coming at least ten years too late. If things had started twenty years ago, people would have looked for efficiencies. It's incomprehensible that America doesn't have high-speed rail between major cities. The European car fleet has twice the energy efficiency than America.

One of the biggest bets you have made in recent years was to buy for $1 billion the exploration rights to drill for oil off the coast of Rio. What gave you the confidence that those rights were worth so much money?

I know how to read geology. I have on my team many geologists from Petrobras [the Brazilian energy giant] and they have more than forty years of experience in these fields. I built these things so many times so when I read a document on results, I read it differently than other people. I know how to get the best talent around me and let them do their thing. You know our hit ratio is in fifty-eight wells we hit oil in fifty-three, and this story is still to be told. It is in excess of 90 percent. And then we are going to break a record because we are going to start producing oil by the last quarter of 2011. From the first well drilled into production, it will be a world record.

We are making a revolution in the speed that you can develop these things. Oil companies, especially the big ones, are normally state controlled. They go through so many procedures. Yes, some of them are justified for security and safety reasons, but some are totally wrong. They don't use the maximum of efficiencies that you can get. These bureaucracies insist they had all this specific data and lack operational flexibility.

Still, you were bidding against all the giants of the oil industry and you prevailed.

Yes, it was an international auction. All the big boys were there. Petrobras or Exxon could have outbid me. I paid the biggest price and it came right out of my pocket. You only win if you pay the biggest price and I paid $1 billion. Everybody laughed at me back then. They said, "Eike Batista is crazy." I never worried I was overpaying because I felt strongly that it was worth it. I must admit that I didn't know it was going to be so big. I knew I would have a very nice return on my money. Of course, you only know after you drill, but like I said before somehow I have a pact with nature and it keeps giving back to me. It will cost me $16 a barrel to extract this oil. We have ten billion barrels in our area today. It's like a trillion dollars in the ground. It will cost me $160 billion to take out.

As an entrepreneur, you have surfed the wave of Brazilian prosperity. As Brazil came of age as an economic power, you have also prospered.

I was prepared by my father to think of a Brazil that would eventually work. Four of my brothers used to live in the U.S. and two now have come back to work for me. We had a military regime in the 1960s and 1970s, and in the 1980s we became a democracy. And we had incredible financial problems until the nineties. President Lulu says that he loves the animal spirits of the entrepreneur. Since then, Brazil has undergone a period of economic stability and growth, first during the administrations of Fernando Henrique Cardoso and Lula and now with Dilma. That is why Brazil opened up these auctions in the oil arena. The oil sector was denationalized from Petrobras in 1997. I was the first guy to hire talent from Petrobras and put $1 billion into this. With a few exceptions, the foreign oil companies were not successful in Brazil. Petrobras had an incredible pool of talent. So Brazil has allowed me to break the Petrobras monopoly.

Given the immensity of your operations can you still be deeply involved in running the company?

Yes, I can. I have great management and technical people in every single company. We have frequent meetings to explore synergies, which are massive. I have fifty executive directors in eight companies. If I want to talk to a director, I walk into his office, sit in front of him, and let him tell me his story. Normally, I have eight CEOs who report constantly to me, but I see monthly reports from every director. Several times a week, I have a lunch with them and they push everything out. Transparency and openness are a big part of this culture.

Eike, what advice would you give to young entrepreneurs in Brazil today?

First, obviously, you need to have this drive toward financial independence. This was a driver for me, a big one. I simply didn't want to get money from my parents anymore. This was very powerful. Then I would advise young people to leave their comfort zone. Go somewhere and don't say to yourself, "I live in Rio de Janeiro and so that is where I need to find a job or start a business." This country is big. The fact that I went out to the Amazon gave me a new dimension, a new way to look at opportunity.

Stress or pressure is important. Stress can destroy some people, but in certain dosages I think it's extremely welcome. It tests you, and it prepares you for meeting bigger challenges.

Entrepreneurs also need to take a long-term view. Projects that have quality take three to five years to be built. In my business, you can't think in the short term because this is a tropical mentality. This country's abundance has not helped investors or entrepreneurs to think longer term. I think of Brazil fifty to one hundred years forward. My advice to young people is start small and think long term.

What do you want to be your legacy?

I have a mandate to make Brazil very efficient and to instill a sense of community among Brazilians. I'm cleaning up a lake here in the middle of Rio and trying to preserve several natural parks. I want to leave a legacy of sharing.

We will now host the Olympics. Our economy is booming. It's creating a lot of new jobs. And we're proving that we are not only a country of soccer and samba. The entrepreneurial class in Brazil also has world-class leaders. If Brazilians are proud of having the best soccer player in the world or the most beautiful model, why not also be proud of having the best leaders in business?

The essence is making society as a whole think in terms of community and sharing.

CREDITS

153   Illustration based on photo by Alan Light, used under Creative Commons Attribution 2.0 Generic license, http://commons.wikimedia.org/wiki/File:Oprah_closeup.jpg.

161   Illustration based on photo by Luke Ford/lukeford.net, used under Creative Commons Attribution-Share Alike 2.5 Generic license, http://commons.wikimedia.org/wiki/File:Ted_Turner_LF.jpg.

169   Illustration based on photo courtesy of FedEx.

183   Illustration based on photo courtesy of Infosys.

197   Illustration of Larry Page (left) based on photo by Andreas Weigend, used under Creative Commons Attribution-Share Alike 2.0 Generic license, http://commons.wikimedia.org/wiki/File:Larry_Page_laughs.jpg.

197   Illustration of Sergey Brin (right) based on photo by Allen Lew, used under Creative Commons Attribution-Share Alike 2.0 Generic license, http://commons.wikimedia.org/wiki/File:Sergey_Brin.jpg.

209   Illustration based on photo by Larry D. Moore, used under Creative Commons Attribution-Share Alike 3.0 Unported license, http://commons.wikimedia.org/wiki/File:Charles_schwab_2007.jpg.

217   Illustration based on photo by Tanveer Islam, used under Creative Commons Attribution 3.0 Unported license, http://en.wikipedia.org/wiki/File:Muhammad_Yunus_2.jpg.

225   Illustration based on photo by U.S. Embassy New Delhi (public domain), http://commons.wikimedia.org/wiki/File:Ratan_Tata_photo.jpg.

235   Illustration based on photo by AP Photo/Rick Bowmer.

243   Illustration based on photo by Wilson Dias/ABr, used under Creative Commons License Attribution 2.5 Brazil, http://commons.wikimedia.org/wiki/File:Carlos_Arthur_Nuzman.jpg.

251   Illustration based on photo by Guillaume Paumier, used under Creative Commons Attributions 3.0 Unported license, http://commons.wikimedia.org/wiki/File:Mark_Zuckerberg_at_the_37th_G8_Summit_in_Deauville_037.jpg.

259   Illustration based on photo by Wilson Dias/ABr, used under Creative Commons License Attribution 2.5 Brazil, http://commons.wikimedia.org/wiki/File:Eike_Batista.jpg.

NOTES

John Mackey: Interview with author, April 4, 2011.

Arthur Blank and Bernie Marcus: Interview with author, June 1, 2011.

Reed Hastings: Interview with author, October 4, 2009.

Howard Schultz: Interviews with author, May 18, 2011, and November 12, 2009.

Jeff Bezos: Interviews with Charlie Rose, July 28, 2010; February 26, 2009; November 19, 2007; January 27, 2001; June 28, 2000; May 26, 1999; and April 2, 1999; with Peter Burrows, "Bezos on Innovation," *BusinessWeek*, April 17, 2008; Academy of Achievement, May 4, 2001. Additional background information includes Bezos's Commencement Address at Princeton University, June 22, 2010.

Herb Kelleher: Interviews with Chuck Lucier, "The Thought Leader Interview," *strategy+business*, date unknown; with Mark Morrison, "Herb Kelleher on the Record," *BusinessWeek*, December 22, 2003; with Charlie Rose, June 8, 2001; with Katrina Brooker, "The Chairman of the Board Looks Back," *Fortune*, May 28, 2001.

Steve Jobs: Interviews with Walt Mossberg and Kara Swisher, All Things Digital 8 (allthingsd .com), June 2010; with Betsy Morris, "Steve Jobs Speaks Out," *Fortune*, March 7, 2008; with Walt Mossberg and Kara Swisher, All Things Digital 5, May 2007; with Daniel Morrow for the Smithsonian Institution Oral History project, April 20, 1995; with *Playboy*, February 1985. Additional background information includes Steve Jobs's Commencement Address at Stanford University, June 14, 2005; John Sculley with John A. Byrne, *Odyssey: Pepsi to Apple: A Journey of Adventure, Ideas and the Future* (HarperCollins, 1987).

Herb Kohler Jr.: Interview with author, July 2011.

Dan Lufkin: Interview with author, July 20, 2011. Additional background information from Harvard Business School Entrepreneurs interview with Amy Blitz, April 2002.

Michael Dell: Interview with author, July 22, 2011.

Reid Hoffman: Interviews with author, July 28, 2011, and July 31, 2011.

Bill Gates: Interviews with Caroline Graham, "A Rare and Remarkable Interview with the World's Second Richest Man," *Daily Mail* (London), June 11, 2011; with Academy of Achievement, May 17, 2010; with David Allison, National Museum of American History, date unknown; with Charlie Rose, December 22, 2008; with Walt Mossberg and Kara Swisher, All Things Digital 5 (allthingsd.com), May 2007.

Sir Richard Branson: Interviews with Charlie Rose, February 12, 2008; with Chris Anderson, "Life at 30,000 Feet," http://www.youtube.com/watch?v=DudfBIxw6do, October 13, 2007; with David Price, *CBS: The Early Show*, February 19, 2009; with Jane Martinson,

"Thoroughly PostModern Billionaire," *The Guardian*, April 28, 2006; with Jane Pauley, Jackie Gleason Theater in Miami Beach, Fla., October 18, 2005.

Oprah Winfrey: Interviews with *Piers Morgan Tonight*, CNN, January 17, 2011; Academy of Achievement, February 21, 1991; Additional background includes Martha Lagace, "Oprah: A Case Study Comes Alive," Harvard Business School, Working Knowledge (http://hbswk.hbs.edu/item/5214.html), February 20, 2006; Brian Stelter, "Talk Show Ends, and Oprah Moves On," *The New York Times*, May 22, 2011; Janet Lowe, *Oprah Winfrey Speaks* (Wiley, 2001).

Ted Turner: Interviews with Charlie Rose, April 1, 2008; with Morley Safer for *60 Minutes*, February 11, 2009; with Academy of Achievement, October 20, 2007. Additional background information includes Ted Turner, with Bill Burke, *Call Me Ted* (Grand Central Publishing, 2008).

Fred Smith: Interview with author, July 21, 2011.

Narayana Murthy: Interview with author, August 5, 2011.

Larry Page and Sergey Brin: Interviews with Israeli TV, March 28, 2009; Jim Fallows, Zeitgeist '07 (www.youtube.com/watch?v=7e3AR2kofoM), October 16, 2007; with Adi Ignatius, "Meet the Google Guys," *Time*, February 12, 2006; with Charlie Rose, July 26, 2001; Academy of Achievement, October 28, 2000; with David Sheff, "Google Guys," *Playboy*, September 2004. Additional background information includes Larry Page's Commencement Address at the University of Michigan, May 5, 2009.

Charles Schwab: Interviews with Mark Warren, "What I've Learned," *Esquire*, February 22, 2010; with Jason Zweig, "We Talked to Chuck," *Money*, July 6, 2007; with Ilana DeBare, "Interview with CEO of the Year," *San Francisco Chronicle*, April 9, 2007; with Steve Shepard, C-Span Video Library, January 16, 2003. Additional background information includes Charles Schwab, *Charles Schwab's Guide to Financial Independence* (Three Rivers Press, 1998), and John Kador, *Charles Schwab: How One Company Beat Wall Street and Reinvented the Brokerage Industry* (Wiley, 2002).

Muhammad Yunus: Interviews with Adam Smith for Nobel Foundation, October 13, 2006; CNN, November 5, 2007; with Charlie Rose, June 4, 2004. Additional background information from Yunus's Nobel Foundation Award speech, December 10, 2006, and other sources.

Ratan Tata: Interviews with Charlie Rose, March 2, 2006; with Shekhar Gupta, Tie Entrepreneurship Summit, December 2009; with Paul Sagoo, The Asian Awards 2010, October 27, 2010. Additional background information includes Dominic O'Connell, "Interview: Ratan Tata, India's Humble Business King," *The Sunday Times*, May 10, 2009, and various interviews from Tata Group.

Phil Knight: Interviews with Oprah Winfrey on *The Oprah Winfrey Show*, April 26, 2011; with Jackie Krentzman, "The Force Behind the Nike Empire," *Stanford Magazine*, January–February 1997; with Geraldine E. Willigan, "High Performance Marketing," *Harvard Business Review*, July 1, 1992; and with Michael Moore from the movie *The Big One*, April 10, 1998.

Carlos Arthur Nuzman: Interviews with author, August 12 and August 15, 2011. Additional background information includes Juliet Macur, "Rio de Janeiro Is Awarded 2016 Olympics," *The New York Times*, October 2, 2009.

Mark Zuckerberg: Interviews with Jessica Livingston at Y Combinator Startup School 2010 at Stanford University, October 16, 2010; with Henry Blodget on Business Insider: Innovation (businessinsider.com), October 1, 2009; with Diane Sawyer on *ABC World News*, July 21, 2010; with Walt Mossberg and Kara Swisher at All Things Digital 8 (allthingsd.com), June 2, 2010. Additional background information includes David Kirkpatrick, *The Facebook Effect: The Inside Story of the Company* (Simon & Schuster, 2010).

Eike Batista: Interviews with Charlie Rose, February 8, 2010; Michael Milken, May 2, 2011, at Mike Milken Global Institute; and May 2, 2011, lunch panel at Mike Milken Global Institute. Additional background information from Bloomberg and Reuters.

INDEX